D1317686

First-Year Writing: Perspectives on Argument

Third Custom Edition for
The University of Texas at Arlington

Taken from:
Perspectives on Argument, Seventh Edition
by Nancy V. Wood

The Craft of Argument, Third Edition
by Joseph M. Williams and Gregory G. Colomb

Having Your Say: Reading and Writing Public Arguments
by Davida H. Charney and Christine M. Neuwirth with David S. Kaufer
and Cheryl Geisler

Cover art: Courtesy of the University of Texas at Arlington. Images Courtesy of Brian Carroll, Photographer.

Taken from:

Perspectives on Argument, Seventh Edition
by Nancy V. Wood
Copyright © 2012, 2009, 2007, 2004 by Pearson Education, Inc.
Published by Prentice Hall
Upper Saddle River, New Jersey 07458

The Craft of Argument, Third Edition
by Joseph M. Williams and Gregory G. Colomb
Copyright © 2007 by Pearson Education, Inc.
Published by Longman
New York, New York 10019

Having Your Say: Reading and Writing Public Arguments
by Davida H. Charney and Christine M. Neuwirth with David S. Kaufer and Cheryl Geisler
Copyright © 2006 by Pearson Education, Inc.

This special edition published in cooperation with Pearson Learning Solutions.

All trademarks, service marks, registered trademarks, and registered service marks are the property of their respective owners and are used herein for identification purposes only.

Pearson Learning Solutions, 501 Boylston Street, Suite 900, Boston, MA 02116
A Pearson Education Company
www.pearsoned.com

Printed in the United States of America

9 10 11 12 13 VOUD 18 17 16 15 14

000200010271659073

SB

ISBN 10: 1-256-74450-6
ISBN 13: 978-1-256-74450-4

Contents

Welcome to First Year English Letter   P12

Letter from Dean Wright   P13

Frequently Asked Questions (FAQs) P14

The Rhetorical Situation P17

First-Year English Evaluation P21

English 1301 Course Description, Learning Outcomes, and Audience Information   P24

ENGL 1301 Essay Assignments   P26

Sample Discourse Community Analysis   P30

Sample Rhetorical Analysis   P37

Sample Synthesis Essay   P43

English 1302 Course Description, Learning Outcomes, and Audience Information   P48

ENGL 1302 Essay Assignments P51

Sample Issue Proposal P55

Sample Mapping the Issue   P63

Sample Researched Position Paper P70

1▶ A PERSPECTIVE ON ARGUMENT   2

What Is Your Current Perspective on Argument?   4

A Definition of Argument 5

Recognizing Traditional and Consensual Argument   6

Recognizing Visual Argument   8

Under What Conditions Does Argument Work Best? 11

Under What Conditions Does Argument Fail?   14

Recognizing Argument in the 21st Century   16

Engaging with Issues   18

How Should You Engage with Issues?   26

Review Questions   28

Exercises and Activities   29

Essays for Analysis

    FELIX CARROLL / *"No Escape from "Helicopter Parents'"*   30

    ABBY ELLIN / *The Laptop Ate My Attention Span*   32

Images for Analysis
Image 1. *Blessed Art Thou*   34
Image 2. *The Tide Is High*   34

2 ▶ THE RHETORICAL SITUATION: UNDERSTANDING AUDIENCE AND CONTENT   38

Analyze the Rhetorical Situation When You Read an Argument   39

Analyze the Rhetorical Situation When You View a Visual Argument   44

Analyze the Rhetorical Situation When You Encounter an Argument Online   46

Use the Rhetorical Situation When You Write an Argument   48

Conducting an Audience Analysis   51

Review Questions   55

Exercises and Activities   56

Essays for Analysis
CHRIS PIPER / *"A" Is for "Absent"*   42
WILL HARREL / *"A Defense of Grade Deflation"*   56
THE LIBRARY OF CONGRESS / *The Civil Rights Era*   60

Images for Analysis
Image 1: *Rosa Parks Rides in the Front of the Bus*   59
Image 2: *Auschwitz Victims of Medical Experiments*   61
Image 3: *Camp Officials at Leisure*   61

3 ▶ READING, THINKING, AND WRITING ABOUT ISSUES   64

Getting Started on a Writing Assignment   65

Read to Develop Arguments for Your Paper   69

Take Notes and Avoid Plagiarism   79

Write Your Paper, Read It, Think about It, and Revise It   82

Practice Your Process by Writing These Papers   89

Expressing Multiple Perspectives through Visual Argument   92

Review Questions   94

Exercises and Activities   94

Essays for Analysis
JERRY ADLER / *The Race for Survival*   77
GINA KOLATA / *PSST! Ask for Donor 1913**   95
RANDY COHEN / *When Texting Is Wrong*   99
CONGRESSIONAL RESEARCH SERVICE / *Flag Protection: A Brief History of Recent Supreme Court Decisions*   101

P4

Images for Analysis
  Image 1: *The Chinese Perspective*   93
  Image 2: *The German Perspective*   93
  Image 3: *The Israeli Perspective*   93
  Image 4: *The Iraqi Perspective*   93

4 ▶ THE CORE OF YOUR ARGUMENT: FINDING AND STATING A CLAIM   104

Exploring Claims Without Rushing to Judgment   105
What Kind of Claim Does Your Problem Require?   106
What Counts as a Claim Worth Considering?   109
What Does a Thoughtful Claim Look Like?   111
Writing Process: Finding and Stating Claims   115
Inquiries   117
Reflections   117
Tasks   118
Projects   118
Focus on Writing   119
In a Nutshell   121
Essays for Analysis
  Richard Berman / *Turkey Police, Beware*   119

5 ▶ SUPPORTING CLAIMS: APPEALING TO LOGOS, ETHOS, AND PATHOS   124

Appeals to Logos   125
Appeals to Ethos   131
Appeals to Pathos   133
Exercises   138

6 ▶ THE CORE OF YOUR ARGUMENT: REASONS AND EVIDENCE   142

Supporting Claims   142
Reasons and Evidence as Forms of Support   143
Distinguishing Reasons and Evidence   145
Distinguishing Evidence and Reports of It   146
Multiple Reasons   149
Using Reasons to Help Readers Understand Evidence   151
Writing Process: Reasons and Evidence   154

P5

Ordering Multiple Reasons   154
Integrating Quotations into Your Sentences   158
Avoiding Inadvertent Plagiarism   159
Inquiries   160
Reflections   160
Tasks   161
Project   162
Focus on Writing   162
In a Nutshell   174
Essays for Analysis
    Guns in America   172

7 ◗ THE CORE OF YOUR ARGUMENT: REPORTING EVIDENCE   176

Weigh Your Burden of Evidence   176
Make a Plan to Find Evidence   178
The Four Maxims of Quality   178
Trustworthy Reports of Evidence   180
Radical Skepticism   185
In the Readings. . .   186
Writing Process: Reporting Evidence   187
Inquiries   191
Reflections   191
Task   192
Projects   192
Focus on Writing   194
In a Nutshell   197

8 ◗ YOUR READER'S ROLE IN YOUR ARGUMENT: ACKNOWLEDGMENTS AND RESPONSES   198

The Importance of Other Viewpoints   199
Questions About Your Problem and Its Solution   200
Questions About Your Support   201
Questions About Your Consistency   202
Responding with Subordinate Arguments   204
Writing Process: Acknowledgment and Responses   205

Inquiries   211

Reflections   211

Tasks   212

Projects   212

Research Project   212

In a Nutshell   213

9 ▶ THE LOGIC OF YOUR ARGUMENT: WARRANTING CLAIMS AND REASONS   214

The Reasoning Behind Reasons   216

What Warrants Look Like   217

How Warrants Work   218

Knowing When to Use Warrants in a Written Argument   220

How to Test a Warrant   224

Distinguishing Reasons and Warrants   228

Review: A Test Case   229

Warranting Evidence   232

Arguing by Evidence Versus Arguing by Warrants   234

Writing Process: Warrants   234

Inquiries   237

Reflections   237

Tasks   239

Project   239

Focus on Writing   240

In a Nutshell   241

10 ▶ VISUAL ARGUMENT   244

Recognizing Visual Argument   245

Why Visual Argument Is Convincing: Eight Special Features   245

Using Argument Theory to Critique Visual Argument   254

Bias in Visual Argument   254

Sample Analysis of a Visual Argument   256

Add Visual Argument to Support Written Argument   258

Create Visual Arguments That Stand Alone   261

Review Questions   264

Exercises and Activities   264

Images for Analysis
 Image 1. *West Bank Barrier* 265
 Image 2. *Crossing Over* 266
 Image 3. *Coming Home to a Destroyed Neighborhood* 267
 Image 4. *LeBron James* 267
 Image 5. *At Home Outdoors* 268
 Image 1. *Adam and God* 269
 Image 2. *Play Ball* 269
 Image 3. *Robot with a Grappler* 270
Visual Arguments Created by Students
 Student Visual Argument 1. *Untitled* 274
 Student Visual Argument 2. *Never Again* 274
  Analytical Essay on Never Again 275
 Student Visual Argument 3. *Farm Town News* 276
  Analytical Essay on Farm Town News 278

11 ▶ ROGERIAN ARGUMENT AND COMMON GROUND 280

Achieving Common Ground in Rogerian Argument 282
Rogerian Argument as Strategy 283
Writing Rogerian Argument 286
Rogerian Argument in Academic Writing 287
Review Questions 288
Exercises and Activities 289
Essays for Analysis
 EDWARD O. WILSON / *The Future of Life* 289
 ANGELA A. BOATWRIGHT / *Human Cloning: Is It a Viable Option?* 293
 ERIC HARTMAN / *Let Those Who Ride Decide!* 297
 ELIZABETH NABHAN / *Dear Boss* 299
Images for Analysis
 Image 1. *Hands Across the World* 291
 Image 2. *Bridging the Gap* 291
 Image 3. *Bipartisanship and What It Can Achieve* 291

12 ▶ REVIEW AND SYNTHESIS OF THE STRATEGIES FOR READING, WRITING, AND VIEWING ARGUMENT 304

Reading for the Argument Analysis Paper 305
Writing the Argument Analysis Paper 305
Rhetorical Situation for "A Call to Unity: A Letter from Eight White Clergymen" and "Letter from Birmingham Jail" 307

Focus Topics to Help You Analyze the Letters   308

Essays for Analysis

WHITE CLERGYMEN / *A Call for Unity: Letter from Eight White Clergymen*   310

MARTIN LUTHER KING JR. / *Letter from Birmingham Jail*   311

Review Questions   325

Exercises and Activities   325

13 ▶ THE RESEARCH PAPER: PLANNING, RESEARCH, AND INVENTION   326

Understanding the Assignment and Getting Started   327

Writing a Claim and Clarifying Your Purpose   327

Some Preliminary Questions to Help You Narrow and Develop Your Claim   328

Developing a Research Plan   330

Understanding the Audience   331

Analyzing Your Class as Your Audience   333

Constructing an Unfamiliar Audience   334

Using Information about Your Audience   334

Get Organized for Research   336

Locating Sources for Research   337

Evaluating Sources   340

Create a Bibliography   343

Taking and Organizing Your Notes   345

Two Invention Strategies to Help You Think Creatively about Your Research and Expand Your Own Ideas   346

Review Questions   348

Exercises and Activities   348

Images for Analysis

Image 1: *The Result of a Careful Audience Analysis*   335

Image 1: *Welcome Clones of 2012!*   351

14 ▶ THE RESEARCH PAPER: USING SOURCES, WRITING, AND REVISING   356

How to Match Patterns and Support to Claims   356

Outline Your Paper and Cross-Reference Your Notes   358

Incorporating Research into Your First Draft   361

Make Revisions and Prepare the Final Copy   362

Present Your Paper Orally to the Class   363

Review Questions   365

Exercises and Activities   365

APPENDIX 1: HOW TO DOCUMENT SOURCES USING MLA   369

MLA: How to Cite Sources in the Body of the Text   372

MLA: How to Cite Sources in the Works Cited Page   377

MLA: Student Paper in MLA Style   386

Prisna Virasin / *The Big Barbie Controversy*   386

APPENDIX 2: COGNITIVE BIASES AND FALLACIES   397

Cognitive Biases   399

Fallacies   401

APPENDIX 3: CHARTS   409

Credits   422

Index   426

Please note that Chapters 1–3, 10–14, and Appendix 1 and 3 are taken from *Perspectives on Argument*, Seventh Edition, by Nancy V. Wood. Chapters 4, 6–9, and Appendix 2 are taken from *The Craft of Argument*, Third Edition, by Joseph M. Williams and Gregory G. Colomb; and Chapter 5 is taken from *Having Your Say: Reading and Writing Public Arguments*, by Davida H. Charney and Christine M. Neuwirth with David S. Kaufer and Cheryl Geisler.

P10

First-Year Writing
The University of Texas at Arlington

Welcome to First Year English

Dear Students,

Welcome to First-Year English at UT Arlington. Our two-semester sequence of courses, ENGL 1301 and ENGL 1302, provide an introduction to what we like to call an "arc of argumentation." Our course goals are meant to prepare you for the intensive writing and research you will encounter in your respective majors, anticipate the type of writing required in graduate programs, and prepare you to take on the writing challenges you will encounter after graduation and in your careers.

Whether you are pursuing a degree in Engineering, Nursing, Business, Science, History, Political Science, Education, or one of the other Bachelor's Degrees offered here at UT Arlington, the rhetorical knowledge you gain in First-Year English will assist your progress as a scholar.

Being able to think critically about what you read, hear, and see in media reports and interactions with other people makes you a better student, citizen, and future professional. A recent study led by New York University sociologist Richard Arum found that many students "didn't learn the critical thinking, complex reasoning and written communication skills that are widely assumed to be at the core of a college education." However, the report also noted that those students who completed college courses where they were assigned heavy reading and writing "showed higher rates of learning" (Mataconis). As part of the UT Arlington Core Curriculum, the First-Year Writing sequence focuses on foundational reading, writing, and critical thinking skills. Ultimately, you will be prepared to present your own ideas as well-considered and carefully researched arguments to a variety of audiences.

The members of the First-Year English faculty at UT Arlington are highly trained scholars and teachers who understand how important the courses they teach are to your success as a student. They are committed to their profession and to you, their students. They are here to guide you as you make the transition to UT Arlington and to college life. If you are a student who has been away from college life for a while, your FYE courses will assist you as you reclaim your knowledge and skills from earlier educational experiences. Whatever journey brought you here, First-Year English faculty members are eager to help you navigate the world of academic discourse and to help you find ways to add your own voices to the scholarly community.

Sincerely,
The Faculty and Staff of the UT Arlington English Department

Mataconis, Doug. "College Students Lack Critical Thinking Skills, But Who's To Blame?" *Outside the Beltway an Online Journal of Politics and Foreign Affairs Analysis.*18 Jan. 2011. Web. 10 Feb. 2012.

Letter from Dean Wright

Welcome to a wonderful challenge and adventure—one which will never end.

Many people enroll in core curriculum classes without being able to define why they are 'core'—of central importance. English Composition is one such 'core' subject: it is at the heart of every other subject. The activities in which you will be engaged in these classes—reading, writing, forming persuasive arguments—will do more than prepare you for all of your experiences in your college education. They will prepare you for your life.

How do I justify such a statement? I'll begin with a quotation which defines what writing can be:

> The good writer, the great writer, has what I have called the three S's: the power to see, to sense, and to say. That is, he is perceptive, he is feeling, and he has the power to express in language what he observes and reacts to.
> Lawrence Clark Powell (1906-2001 American librarian, writer, critic)

I do my best every day to become such a person: a writer who is perceptive, emotionally engaged, and eloquent. I do this when I reflect on what I am writing, when I rewrite a draft, when I incorporate feedback from a colleague.

I often meet UT Arlington alumni who tell me wonderful things: how their education made wonderful careers possible for them, how they've put what they learned to use, how every day they are grateful that they can draw upon the knowledge they gained by working with the exceptional faculty at UT Arlington. Whether it happened months ago or years ago, they remember their experiences in learning how to write. As one alumnus (a judge) told me: learning how to write transformed his life. I wish you such experiences, both now and in the years to come.

Beth S. Wright
Professor of Art History and
Dean
College of Liberal Arts

Frequently Asked Questions (FAQs):

Why are students required to purchase the *First-Year Writing* custom textbook?

Our custom textbook provides First-Year English students with a solid introduction to Rhetoric and Composition. In addition to select chapters from three outstanding writing textbooks, our custom book also includes introductory material that is specific to our UTA writing program. We have provided an overview of the courses, the assignment prompts, and some essays written by UTA students. Your one-time textbook purchase will carry you through two semesters of FYE since you will use it for ENGL 1301 and ENGL 1302.

What are sample essays and sample assignments, and how should I use them?

After each essay assignment prompt, you will find a sample essay. These samples are not perfect essays, but solid attempts at following the essay prompts. As you read over them, you may find places where the writer misses the mark or leaves something out. You may also note style issues or writing conventions that you don't particularly like. When reading a sample, it is a good strategy to use it as a way to help you understand the actual essay assignment. Additionally, you test your own acumen as a writer when you are able to find places for revision in the sample essay. Use sample essays as a way to improve your own writing and your expertise as a peer reviewer. Find the strengths and weaknesses in the sample essays and apply that knowledge to your own writing.

How are English classes at UTA different from high school classes?

First of all, UTA students come from many varied secondary school experiences. Some of you have had rigorous and demanding Advanced Placement or IB English classes. Others of you may have breezed through your high school English classes because you did what the teacher asked and turned in all of your assignments. One big difference between high school and college writing classes is the emphasis on student effort. Trying really hard to do your best work or spending a lot of time on assignments is important, but it won't be the determining factor in your grade. These practices are just expected of college students. At UTA, your grade will be based on how well you have actually written the assignment. In college you will have to motivate yourself to complete your class assignments, even though there will be many distractions. Managing your time and prioritizing your studies will be challenging tasks as you make the transition to college life. At the university, no one is telling you when to eat, sleep, or study. You have to manage all this on your own. Another big difference between high school English classes and your FYE classes at UTA is the way we approach a written text and analyze the communication between writer and reader. You will read more about this approach, which we call the Rhetorical Situation, in some of the following pages.

If my job or other commitments prevent me from attending class or turning in assignments, will my grade suffer?

All First-Year English classes have attendance requirements clearly stated in the course syllabus. Students are expected to follow the guidelines for attendance and to arrive at class on time. There really is no substitute for class attendance, and students who come to class regularly are more successful. You might lose points for tardies and absences, so be sure to read and follow the policies in your class syllabus. Assignments are to be turned in on time, and depending on your instructor's policy, you may not be able to turn in work after the due date, or you might have substantial points deducted. Once again, read and follow the syllabus policies. Students cannot earn a passing course grade in FYE if they do not turn in all major assignments.

How can I get more information or help from my instructor?

Every instructor in the First-Year English program keeps regularly scheduled office hours. These times are set aside for students to speak with their instructors about class issues. Writing conferences help point you in the right direction on your essay assignments by giving you the chance to discuss your work with your professor. Take the opportunity to draw upon your instructor's expertise and guidance. If you can't stop by during regular office hours, contact your instructor by email.

Where can I go for extra help with writing processes?

The UT-Arlington Writing Center, located on the fourth floor of the Central Library, offers a welcoming and supportive environment for students who seek assistance on a wide variety of writing assignments and needs. The Writing Center is here to encourage and to motivate student writers of all levels and to provide clients with the highest quality assistance available. Its first objective is to help student writers elevate the writing project in hand, but always with the goal of improving the general quality of their written work. Writing consultants are professionally trained and can assist undergraduate and graduate students with writing assignments in multiple subject areas.

The Writing Center does the following:

- Offers a positive and supportive environment.
- Assists students across the spectrum of writing achievement.
- Helps clients develop their ability to critically evaluate their own writing and ideas.
- Offers students focused, extended, and personalized consultations.

Please look through the website to learn more about the Writing Center at UT-Arlington: http://www.uta.edu/owl/

Where will I find assistance with research, writing, and MLA citations?

The UTA Library offers numerous resources for students. General reference librarians are located at the Reference Help Desk on the second floor of the Central Library. Additionally, library assistance if offered online and by video tutorials. Visit the UTA Library website to read about services offered for students: http://www.uta.edu/library/help/pddi.php

Does UTA have any place where I can talk to someone about academic or personal issues?

University College, located in Ransom Hall, offers an array of programs and services for students. While University College focuses on assisting freshman students as they transition to college, the programs and services serve all students who seek academic support during their career at UT Arlington. Below is a list of general services. More information is available at the website: http://www.uta.edu/universitycollege/index.php

- Counseling Services offers personal and group counseling as well as academic workshops.
- McNair Scholars program provides research and mentoring opportunities to eligible undergraduate students to prepare them for graduate study.

- University Tutorial offers no-cost and low-cost tutoring options to help students achieve higher grades and a better understanding of course material.
- University Advising Center advises all incoming freshman students (up to 30 credit hours) as well as undeclared and conditionally admitted transfer students. Academic advisors also guide students in the majors exploration process.

What are some steps I can follow to be successful in college writing?
Follow these Top Five Best Practices for College Writing

1. Know your audience.
All public writing is intended for an audience with specific expectations. You need to know as much about those expectations as possible. Of course in some sense your instructor is always your audience, but many instructors expect you to target an audience that is bigger than—and perhaps different from—themselves. Instructors find it annoying when students ask, "What do you want for this paper?" They will respond more favorably to the question, "Who is the audience for this paper?" If you are at all unsure about your intended audience, ask your instructor for more specifics!

2. An assignment sheet is a reference guide, not a jumping-off point.
Never read a paper assignment just once, assume you get the gist of it, and then never return to it. Continue to consult the assignment sheet throughout your writing process. Once you believe you've finished a paper, consult the assignment sheet a final time to make sure you've addressed every element of it. Here's a good rule of thumb: you should be able to read through an assignment sheet and point to the specific places in your paper where you've satisfied every requirement. If anything about the assignment is unclear, ask your instructor for more specifics!

3. Time is an essential component of your writing materials.
You probably already know this, but it bears repeating: you can't possibly do your best on college writing assignments if you complete them in one sitting (especially if that one sitting occurs the night before the paper is due). One of the best ways to improve a piece of writing is to get away from it for a while; you'll return to it with a new set of eyes, and it will be much clearer what needs to be changed/added/expanded. Of course this means you must begin a paper well in advance of its due date, allow yourself time away, and leave yourself time to make changes.

4. Understand that revising is not editing.
Revision does not mean "fixing" or "correcting" your paper; rather, it involves shaping a work in progress. You may get new ideas and shift the focus of the paper entirely; you may cut, expand, and reorganize. Only after a paper is essentially finished should you worry about editing, e.g. correcting typos; replacing individual words or phrases; and correcting errors in grammar, punctuation, spelling, and mechanics.

5. Have something to say.
You might think of good writing as saying something well. In college, it's much more important to say something significant. Your papers should contribute something new to an academic conversation. They should contain a thesis that is arguable, specific, and detailed, and that thesis should be supported by good reasons and evidence. Most instructors care more about the content of what you say than about whether you say it in beautiful, error-free prose.

The Rhetorical Situation

To this point in your education, you may have been taught to think of texts as "autonomous." According to this view, the meaning of texts is equivalent to what they say—meaning is conveyed fully and explicitly by the words on the page. Writers are charged with representing meaning as explicitly as possible, and readers are expected to logically analyze the words on the page. In order to demonstrate how autonomous text theories work, read the passage below and try to determine the situation being depicted:

> "I worry that our most valuable pitchers could crack in this heat," said the manager in one of his discouraged moods. I wanted to help, but all I did was hit a fly. "If only we had more fans," he continued, "we would all feel better, I'm sure. I wish our best man would come home. That certainly would improve everyone's morale, especially mine. Oh well, I know a walk would perk me up."

Chances are you can make an educated guess about the situation depicted in this passage because you have learned to interpret texts by analyzing the words on the page.

Alternatives to autonomous text theories are "rhetorical" theories, which take into account textual and contextual clues to determine the **rhetorical situation:** the writer or speaker and her/his purpose, the broad topic of the text, and the reader or listener. In Classical rhetoric, our impressions of the writer/speaker fall under the category of **ethos appeals,** the facts and logic of a topic are categorized as **logos appeals,** and the responses of readers/listeners are categorized as **pathos appeals.** The rhetorical situation of texts is often represented by a triangle:

facts and logic (logos)

writing/talking
about

to

text/speech

writer/speaker (ethos)   reader/listener (pathos)

Consider how the passage above is clarified when framed by its rhetorical situation:

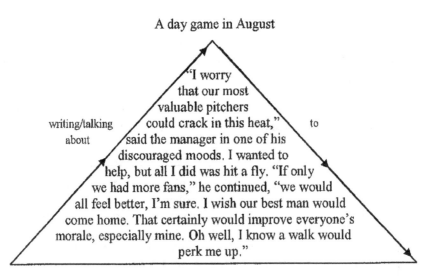

The words in the passage remain exactly the same, but we understand them more deeply due to our knowledge of the rhetorical situation. Still not convinced? Read the passage one more time, taking note of how the rhetorical situation has changed:

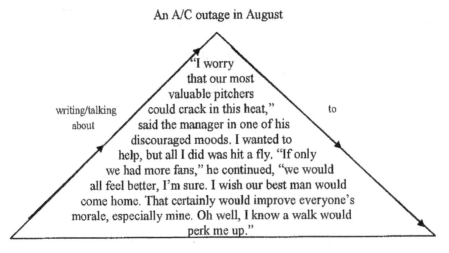

As you can see, the passage remains exactly the same, but now it "means" something entirely different because the rhetorical situation has changed. This exercise demonstrates the limitations of autonomous text theories and the importance of understanding the rhetorical situation of texts.

How do the assumptions that inform autonomous text theories differ from those informing rhetorical approaches?

Perhaps the best way to illustrate the differences between autonomous and rhetorical text theories is to compare assessments conceived from the perspective of each. For example, let's compare the TAKS Test and the AP English Language Exam to the reading you will do and the papers you will write in ENGL 1301 and 1302.

READING

On the TAKS and AP exams, students are presented with passages absent any information about the author, his/her purpose, or his/her audience, and students are not expected to possess any prior knowledge of the topic on which the passage is written. In ENGL 1301 and 1302, however, you'll be given ample time to reread texts and analyze them in detail; you'll learn and take into account information about the author, his/her purpose, and his/her intended audience; and you'll learn something about the broader topic/conversation in which the text is participating. We can chart the contrasting assumptions that inform these reading tasks as follows:

TAKS and AP	ENGL 1301 and 1302
1. Texts can be understood with little to no knowledge of their authors.	1. Texts must be understood as the actions of human beings writing from particular perspectives and for specific purposes.
2. Texts can be understood without prior knowledge of their topics.	2. Texts must be understood as moves in ongoing conversations about—and be informed by—specific topics.
3. Texts can be understood independent of their intended audience.	3. Texts must be understood in terms of whom they're written for.
4. Texts mean what they say; meaning exists in the words on the page.	4. Meaning varies from reader to reader and from reading to reading; it always depends on a combination of text and context.

WRITING

Although the TAKS and AP exams require very different types of writing (personal reflection and rhetorical analysis/argument, respectively), in each case the student's purpose and topic are predetermined, no prior knowledge of the topic is required, and students are not asked to write for a specific audience. In ENGL 1301 and 1302, on the other hand, you'll discover your own purpose for writing, all your papers will require activation of extensive prior knowledge, and you'll write for highly specific audiences. Once again, we can chart the very different assumptions that inform these two types of writing tasks:

TAKS and AP	ENGL 1301 and 1302
1. You write because you are told to and because your writing skills must be assessed.	1. You write because you have something to contribute to an ongoing conversation. You write because you want something to change.
2. You can write well about a topic you know almost nothing about.	2. Since you are joining a conversation, you must know something about the topic and what has already been said about it.
3. Your goal is to produce an ideal object or artifact, the textual equivalent of a "right" answer.	3. Your goal is to move a specific audience in ways you intend. You will never be right or wrong, but you will always be more or less effective.

SOME FINAL WORDS ON READING AND WRITING RHETORICALLY

Some of the advantages of reading and writing rhetorically should be clear to you by now. Here are some further reasons why you should ALWAYS consider the rhetorical situation of the texts you read and write:

1. **Rhetorical thinking accords with what we know about how language works.** We all know that even when an entire class reads the same text, not everyone comprehends, interprets, or recalls that text in exactly the same way. The rhetorical situation accounts for this variation because it changes every time the reader/listener changes.

2. **Rhetorical thinking increases reading comprehension.** Studies show that we comprehend texts more deeply when we know something about the person writing, know something about the topic of the text, and read with the expectation of responding in writing.

3. **Expert readers and writers think rhetorically.** Studies show that experts read as if they are in conversation with a friend: they activate everything they know about the topic, they activate everything they know about the writer, and, rather than trying to memorize the text, they think critically about it and respond to it by marking the text, writing notes in the margins, and speaking aloud to the text. When experts write, they do so because they feel the need to say something. They also investigate, and think long and hard about, the topic on which they're writing. Finally, expert writers give a lot of thought to the audience for whom they're writing.

4. **Rhetorical thinking is empowering.** If you've been taught to think that meaning exists in the words on the page, or that there's only one way to write effectively, then you might think that your struggles with reading and writing are a reflection of your intelligence. They're not. Your struggles may simply be an effect of being a newcomer to academic conversations. Rhetorical thinking can show you what is needed: to sit in and listen for a while until what you hear begins to make sense and you discover something to contribute.

First-Year English Evaluation Rubric

	Excellent	Above Average	Average	Below Average
EXIGENCE: Establishment of a significant question/ problem/gap within a rhetorical context	The essay clearly lays out the unanswered question/unsolved problem/unfilled gap to be addressed through appropriate content and phrasing. The essay argues effectively about the significance and impact of the question/problem/gap and explains what is at stake in the issue.	The essay lays out the unanswered question/unsolved problem/unfilled gap to be addressed relatively clearly. This move may seem a bit formulaic or overdone. The significance and impact of the question/problem/gap may not be fully explicated.	The essay attempts to lay out the question/problem/gap to be addressed, but relies too much on the reader to fill in the missing pieces. The significance and impact of the question/problem/gap may not be addressed, thus relying on the reader to supply it.	The essay does not immediately and may never elucidate a question/problem/gap to be addressed, and/or never indicates why the issue is significant.
THESIS: Effectiveness and feasibility of the answer/solution	The essay provides an easy-to-spot thesis that provides a clear answer/solution to the question/problem that has been introduced. The thesis is arguable, specific, and detailed.	The essay provides a thesis that might take a bit of searching to locate. The answer/solution addresses the question/problem relatively clearly, though there might be a slight mismatch between the two. The thesis might not be sufficiently arguable, specific, and detailed.	The essay provides a thesis that might be difficult to spot. The answer/solution inadequately addresses the question/problem, is overly vague, and/or is highly unrealistic. The thesis is not adequately arguable, specific, and detailed.	The essay may provide no apparent thesis, or may provide an answer/solution that does not appear to address the question/problem at hand.
PROOFS: Use of reasons and evidence	Claims are generously supported with varied and effective appeals; evidence comes from varied types of up-to-date sources, including published materials, personal experience, and reasoning; the available sources appear to have been thoroughly and creatively explored.	Most claims are supported with some solid evidence and effective appeals, but the variety of sources used may be fairly limited, leaving an array of other reference possibilities unexplored. There is a tendency to over-rely on a single source.	The essay attempts to support its claims with evidence, but this evidence may be outdated, not quite relevant, or merely anecdotal.	The essay offers little or no evidence to support its claims.
REBUTTAL: Acknowledgment and consideration of alternative positions	The essay indicates an understanding of other positions on the issue and explicates them fairly and accurately. Conceding certain points and/or sympathizing with alternative perspectives, the text offers a direct and thoughtful explanation about why it nonetheless retains its stated position, demonstrating an ability to determine and respond to subtle disagreements within broader arguments.	The essay acknowledges other positions on the issue, but doesn't necessarily characterize those other positions without bias. The text may concede certain points, but only in a limited or formulaic way as the writer rushes to offer a rebuttal. The rebuttal itself may not respond directly to opposing viewpoints or offer compelling reasons for continued disagreement.	The essay may acknowledge other positions but not introduce them adequately or represent them fairly. The text fails to make concessions, moving immediately to rebuttal. In general, opposing viewpoints seem to have been introduced for the sole purpose of knocking them down.	The essay does not acknowledge other positions and/or it does not anticipate objections to its own position(s).

First-Year English Evaluation Rubric

	4	3	2	1
STRUCTURE: Effectiveness of essay structure	The format and structure are seamless and coherent. The text arranges points according to a discernable and persuasive plan or pattern. Paragraphs are unified in support of the major claim.	The text's structure is, for the most part, solid and effective. It may, however, include tangents and/or elements that do not quite adhere to the defined structure. The text follows a clear pattern of organization, but that pattern may not be the most strategically effective one for the persuasive intent.	A generally consistent and loosely followed structure and format may be discernable. Or, parts of the text may be well structured enough to evidence an intended pattern of organization, but as a whole the text lacks a coherent structure.	There may be elements of an introduction and a conclusion, as well as some moments of coherent internal structuring, but as a whole the text evidences no discernable pattern of organization, no progress toward the development of a major claim.
CLARITY: Sentence-level clarity and precision	The style and voice are lively and engaging. The sentence flow is smooth; sentence structures are varied. Word choice is precise, descriptive, and non-repetitive. There are almost no errors in grammar, punctuation, and usage.	Some complex sentence structures are used, and though the sentence construction may become convoluted at times, meaning can be discerned easily enough through context. There may be some ineffectively choppy structuring and some repetitive or imprecise word choice along with a handful of grammar and punctuation errors, but these errors do not significantly interfere with the coherence of the argument.	Sentence style may be a bit monotonous, relying on only a few simple sentence constructions. The flow may be choppy and/or occasionally so convoluted that meaning becomes difficult to discern, and word choice may be repetitive and/or overly vague with a fair number of unspecified referents. One can hardly get through a paragraph without encountering grammar and punctuation errors (misplaced modifiers, fragments, run-ons, comma splices, etc.).	Most sentences can be understood, but the prose is so peppered with grammar and punctuation errors that it becomes a major distraction. A handful of sentences are so incoherent that they can't be parsed.
CITATION: Citation, documentation, and use of source material	The essay uses sources effectively and integrates them smoothly, para-phrasing and occasionally directly quoting authorities to help substantiate or support its own point(s). The text offers proper attribution to each source cited via in-text paren-thetical citation and a correctly formatted Works Cited page.	The essay uses sources somewhat effectively but may occasionally cite authorities in lieu of actually making a point and offering reasons. The text may demonstrate a tendency to over-quote, to take the reader away from its own voice and argu-ment; it may not adequately introduce or attribute a few quotations. A few sources may not be accurately documented, but in general the in-text cita-tion and the Works Cited page are constructed properly.	Several sources may be improperly documented; several quotations may be inadequately introduced. There is little attempt to integrate the sources, as many quotations are inserted into the essay with no transi-tions to tie them into the argument at hand (i.e., no "quotation sandwich"). There may be numerous errors in the Works Cited page and in the in-text parenthetical citations.	Source material may not be used at all or may be so poorly integrated and attributed that the text indicates little or no understanding of the process of using and documenting source material. For example, essay may include "hit-and-run" quotations with no introduction or explanation. The focus here is not on academic dishonesty.

English 1301
Course Information and Assignments

English 1301 Course Description, Learning Outcomes, and Audience Information

English 1301 RHETORIC AND COMPOSITION I: Introduction to college reading and writing. Emphasizes recursive writing processes, rhetorical analysis, synthesis of sources, and argument.

ENGL 1301 EXPECTED LEARNING OUTCOMES

By the end of ENGL 1301, students should be able to:

Rhetorical Knowledge

- Use knowledge of the rhetorical situation—author, audience, exigence, constraints—to analyze and construct texts
- Compose texts in a variety of genres, expanding their repertoire beyond predictable forms
- Adjust voice, tone, diction, syntax, level of formality, and structure to meet the demands of different rhetorical situations

Critical Reading, Thinking, and Writing

- Use writing, reading, and discussion for inquiry, learning, communicating, and examining assumptions
- Employ critical reading strategies to identify an author's position, main ideas, genre conventions, and rhetorical strategies
- Summarize, analyze, and respond to texts
- Find, evaluate, and synthesize appropriate sources to inform, support, and situate their own claims
- Produce texts with a focus, thesis, and controlling idea, and identify these elements in others' texts

Processes

- Practice flexible strategies for generating, revising, and editing texts
- Practice writing as a recursive process that can lead to substantive changes in ideas, structure, and supporting evidence through multiple revisions
- Use the collaborative and social aspects of writing to critique their own and others' texts

Conventions

▶ Apply knowledge of genre conventions ranging from structure and paragraphing to tone and mechanics

▶ Summarize, paraphrase, and quote from sources using appropriate documentation style

▶ Control such surface features as syntax, grammar, punctuation, and spelling

▶ Employ technologies to format texts according to appropriate stylistic conventions

A Word about Audiences in ENGL 1301 Essays

Composition scholars sometimes categorize audiences as simple (a single person or a group of like-minded people) or complex (a group of people who may have differing perspectives and be reading for different purposes). Audiences can also be familiar to us (we know them personally and understand their values) or unfamiliar (we do not know them personally and may be unsure of their values). Research shows that writing tasks become more difficult as audiences become more complex and unfamiliar. In ENGL 1301 and ENGL 1302, students practice moving from relatively simple and familiar audiences to more complex and unfamiliar audiences. The three major essays in ENGL 1301 offer students the opportunity to prepare their work for three different audiences

In the **Discourse Community Analysis,** students apply their knowledge of the rhetorical situation for the first time, so they write for a relatively simple and familiar audience: their instructor and classmates. Students must convince their instructor and classmates that they successfully joined a discourse community by mastering its rhetorical appeals.

Once students reach the **Rhetorical Analysis** assignment, they should feel more comfortable applying rhetorical concepts and be ready for a more challenging audience. In writing to a Shorthorn editor, students must convince a simple but largely unfamiliar audience that an article should (or should not) be published based on its appeal to the UTA community.

Finally, when students write the **Synthesis Essay,** they are ready for a complex and mostly unfamiliar audience. Students take a position on an issue addressed in their topic cluster and attempt to convince readers of a university-wide publication that their position is valid. Given the diversity of the UTA community and the controversial nature of the topic clusters, students must consider that many readers will disagree with their position.

ENGL 1301 ESSAY ASSIGNMENTS

Paper 1 – Discourse Community Analysis
English 1301: Rhetoric and Composition I

THE RHETORICAL SITUATION

One of the most difficult challenges you'll face in college is learning to join various academic discourse communities. A "discourse community" is a group of people who share knowledge of a particular topic, similar backgrounds and experiences, values, and common ways of communicating. Examples of academic discourse communities at UTA include those comprising mathematicians, engineers, biologists, sociologists, historians, etc.

Discourse communities seem particularly mysterious and intimidating when you are an "outsider," but the good news is that we all have experience joining discourse communities. You successfully joined a discourse community any time you learned to participate and feel comfortable in a new school, a new church, a new circle of friends, or a new interest group (e.g., people interested in a certain sport or sports team, a band or type of music, a television show, gaming, cooking, yoga, dance, etc.)

The purpose of this paper—and a primary purpose of ENGL 1301—is to demonstrate for you that the process of joining an academic discourse community is not so different from the process by which you've joined other discourse communities.

Write a paper to me and your classmates about a time when you successfully joined a discourse community. Show us how you learned to make ethos appeals (i.e., establish and draw on your credibility), logos appeals (i.e., draw on factual knowledge and ways of reasoning), and pathos appeals (i.e., draw on the values and emotions of other members) that were *specific to the community.*

Invention (i.e., discovering what you're going to say in this paper)

1. Your audience for this paper (your classmates and I) will want to know the main point of your paper right off the bat, so, after deciding what discourse community you want to write about, come up with a **claim** (*FYW*, p. 4) that you were successful in joining that community.
2. It's not enough just to make a claim—your audience will expect you to prove it. Thus, you need to explain why your claim is valid by **supporting it with reasons** (*FYW*, p. 4). Your reasons should state that you mastered ethos, logos, and pathos appeals that were *specific* to this particular community.
3. Even after you've made a claim and supported it with reasons, your audience still won't be satisfied. Readers will expect you to provide **evidence** (*FYW*, p. 4) that you really did master ethos, logos, and pathos appeals specific to your discourse community.

Where will you find evidence for this paper? You won't find it in the library or on the internet because it must come from you! Reflect deeply on your own experiences. Come up with specific examples and significant anecdotes that will prove to your audience that, indeed, you learned to make successful ethos, logos, and pathos appeals to other members of the community.

4. What if readers remain skeptical? Imagine them saying: "I'm not sure your accomplishments really qualify you as a full-fledged member of this discourse community." Is there merit to that objection? How would you reply?

5. Think about how you're going to come across to me and your classmates as a person of good character, good sense, and good will. Here are some tips:

   - Know what you're talking about. Provide details that show you've reflected deeply on your experiences, and supply enough evidence to support your reasons.
   - Show regard for your readers. Try to come across as approachable and thoughtful, not arrogant or insensitive.
   - Treat skeptical readers with respect—don't ignore or demean their opinions just because they expect more proof.
   - Be careful and meticulous in your writing, not sloppy or disorganized.

6. Think about the values and emotions that your classmates and I share, and consider how you might appeal to us. Here are some tips:

   - Draw on the lessons of Ch. 9 in *They Say/I Say* in order to mix standard written English with "the kinds of expressions and turns of phrase that you use every day when conversing with family and friends" (115). No need to stick to stuffy academic prose in this paper, but you also don't want to be so informal that your classmates and I can't understand you.
   - Try to evoke emotions (sympathy, outrage, anger, delight, awe, horror, etc.) in your classmates and me that make your paper more moving.
   - Try to evoke sensations (seeing, hearing, touching, tasting, smelling) in your classmates and me that make your writing vivid and help us to experience things imaginatively.
   - Appeal to values (freedom, justice, tolerance, fairness, equality, etc.) that your classmates and I share.

Arrangement (i.e., organizing what you're going to say in this paper)

Ultimately, you want to organize your paper in the manner you think will prove most effective with your classmates and me, but here are some general guidelines:

   - Heed the lesson of Ch. 1 in *They Say/I Say:* "To give your writing the most important thing of all—namely, a point—a writer needs to indicate clearly not only his or her thesis, but also what larger conversation that thesis is responding to" (18). In this case, the conversations you're responding to are the ones we've had in class about rhetoric, the rhetorical situation, and rhetorical reading and writing. Indicate at the beginning of your paper—before you state your thesis—that you're writing in response to those conversations.
   - Also mind the lesson of Ch. 7 in *They Say/I Say:* "Regardless of how interesting a topic may be to you as a writer, readers always need to know what is at stake in a text and why they should care. . . . Rather than assume that audiences will know why their claims matter, all writers need to answer the 'so what?' and 'who cares?' questions up front" (88-89). As harsh as this may sound, don't assume that your classmates and I care about what you have to say—*make* us care by explaining what is at stake in your paper and why it should be important to us.

Style (i.e., choosing the appropriate language for your paper)

One reason I'm asking you to write to your classmates and me is to break you of the habit of writing all your papers to some vague, generalized audience and/or attempting to make all your papers approximate some objective ideal. If you approach this paper in that way, your style will be ineffective because it won't be tailored to your specific audience. When reading your paper, it should be obvious to your classmates and me that you're writing to us specifically.

As mentioned earlier, heed the lesson of Ch. 9 in *They Say/I Say* and mix standard written English with "the kinds of expressions and turns of phrase that you use every day when conversing with family and friends" (115). One of the purposes of this paper is for your classmates and me to get to know you better, so you should write in an informal style that is distinctly your own—just make sure you're communicating clearly.

All readers appreciate coherent, unified paragraphs, so your paragraphs should include a topic sentence that clearly states the main idea of the paragraph and supporting sentences that cluster around the main idea without detours.

Proofread carefully; avoid errors in grammar, spelling, punctuation, and mechanics. Use *The Scott, Foresman Writer* for questions you have regarding style.

Other Requirements

Your paper should be **at least four pages and no longer than five pages**—anything beyond that length will be considered a failure to adhere to one of the assignment's basic requirements. It should be double-spaced, typed in Times New Roman font, with 12-point character size and one-inch margins all the way around.

Your first submission is due at the beginning of class on _____, and you should think of it as a final draft—something that is ready for your classmates and me to read. If your first submission does not meet every requirement of this assignment sheet, I will return it to you and count it as late. Both your first and final submissions must be turned in on time—you will be docked a full letter grade for each day either is late.

Peer reviews are due _____.

Final drafts are due _____.

Evaluation Criteria

Final Draft:
- Includes a snappy title that catches the reader's attention and indicates the topic and argument.
- Identifies a particular discourse community appropriate to the assignment.
- Explains how the essay contributes to the class conversation about rhetoric and discourse communities.
- Includes a contestable, specific, detailed claim that the author successfully joined the selected discourse community.

- Provides at least three well-developed reasons that the author mastered ethos, pathos, and logos appeals specific to the selected community.
- Answers the "so what" and "who cares" questions by explaining why the argument is significant and to whom.
- Supports reasons with carefully selected, well-developed examples and anecdotes from her/his experience.
- Anticipates counterarguments, considers them carefully, and responds to them fairly, conceding where others are right.
- Comes across as a credible writer, and appeals to the values and emotions of the audience.
- Develops a seamless, coherent, and well-organized argument.
- Sentences are lively, engaging, and relatively error free.
- Essay is 4 to 5 pages in MLA style (no Works Cited necessary) in 12pt. Times New Roman font with 1-inch margins.

Writing Process:
- Submitted complete drafts on time. Drafting process shows evidence of revision of content and style.
- Provided adequate help to peers during peer review.

SAMPLE DISCOURSE COMMUNITY ANALYSIS

In the first few weeks ENGL 1301, we have discussed the importance of mastering rhetorical skills. By making ethos, logos, and pathos appeals, writers or speakers can move their audience in the ways they wish, whether that be in everyday life (e.g., convincing your children to do their chores) or at work (e.g., gaining your boss's trust). In order to be accepted into a community, a person must learn the typical ways people in that community communicate and argue. In this paper, I will prove that I entered the discourse community of high school band by acquiring content knowledge, establishing my credibility, and learning to sway other members of the community. This is an important exercise because mastering ethos, logos, and pathos appeals will be the key to me joining future discourse communities. Writing this paper gives me confidence because it shows that I already have experience joining a discourse community. It also gives you, my instructor, and you, my classmates, a chance to know more about me.

In any community, members share knowledge and ways of thinking, as well as particular ways of communicating about this knowledge and thinking. I knew that to be accepted as a member of the band I had to demonstrate my proficiency as a flute player, but I also had to draw on my knowledge and skills when communicating with other members of the community. In other words, I used logos appeals to convince my band director and upper classmen that I belonged.

For example, my bandmates and I often discussed the importance of the "pyramid of sound," in which the base of the pyramid that supports the band is the low brass (tubas and trombones) and the tip of the pyramid is the flutes and piccolos. As a flute player, I know I want to "listen down" to the tuba players; if I can't hear them, I know I'm playing too loud. I also know that I want to listen to my own section and make sure that I am matching pitch from note to note with my fellow players. Plus, I know the importance of listening to who has the melody, making sure I play "under" the melody so as not to hide it. I developed these skills through practice, as my ears grew more accustomed to listening for every detail to make the ensemble sound good as a whole, but I also relied on conversations with bandmates and my director to help train my ear. I learned how to read and count rhythms as well as my major scales and the chromatic scale. I also learned what my minor scales and arpeggios were and that not every instrument is read in concert key. Even if the music sheet is written in bass clef or in a key for a trumpet player, I'm still able to tell whether notes are whole or half; whether the notes should be tongued or slurred; and whether a note is flat, sharp, or natural. When I hear someone sing "one-la-li two-la-li," it signifies two triplets, and if they sing "one-te two-ta-te-ta," it means eighth notes follow by sixteenth notes. If a director continues to sing "one-la-li two-la-li"over and over again, the music is probably in six-eight time. As I developed this knowledge throughout my four years in high school band, I also learned how to explain it to younger members who were still learning.

People may argue that anyone can learn to read music, and just because I can also read music, that doesn't qualify me as a member of the band community. I would agree that simply learning to read music isn't enough. A flute player might be able to read any music placed in front of her perfectly, but when asked to play it, she might play a wrong note or play a rhythm too slow or too fast. Why did she not play the music as well as she read it? Because she hadn't developed the skills she needed to play the flute. She knew that the note was supposed to be f sharp, but she didn't know the fingering and instead played it as an f natural. She knew how fast the eighth notes were suppose to go, but she didn't know her c major scale, which a set of eighth notes in the music were derived from, so she couldn't play it in tempo and stumbled with the notes. In addition to being able to read music, it's important to have all major scales and the chromatic scale memorized, full range. Not only that, the player needs to be able to play their major arpeggios and inversions full range. Having these basic fundamentals down allows the musician to more accurately play the music and sight read better. Throughout high school, I developed these skills until it didn't take much thought for me to play my major scales up and down full range, then blast through my chromatic scale. I even practiced all forty-eight minor scales. It was the combination of learning to read music as well as performing it that allowed me to master the knowledge necessary to join the band community.

Acquiring knowledge does not matter if the speaker or writer does not come across as a person of good sense, good will, and good intentions to other members of the community. In my last year of band I was able to build enough credibility that the band director and fellow band members trusted my knowledge. In *Eagle Squadron March,* my band director, Mr. Sisco, trusted my ability to play a difficult part in the song along with three other players. He knew I was capable of doing it because of how well I played my scales, my ability to sight read, and my understanding of how rhythms work. When one of the flute players didn't know a fingering to a note or wasn't too sure how to play a rhythm, he or she would ask me for help. Because I was a senior in the section, they trusted my years of experience to know all the fingerings to notes or to be able to read the rhythms. Once, a fellow band member asked me to listen to her while she played her region music and tell her how she sounded. Although she was in fact a much better player than I am, she trusted my experience and knowledge enough to let her know when her dynamics weren't enough or if a section of the music or a note didn't sound good.

Finally, a member of a discourse community must learn to appeal to the emotions and values of other members of the community. Although everyone in band is taught the same thing, at times there are differences of opinion between members of the band. In one instance, I sat next to the sophomore flute player who also played the piccolo for the band for the first time that year. At times when she played the piccolo, she wouldn't be matching pitch with the flutes. I told her she needed to listen down to the flutes and match with us, but she thought that the flutes were supposed to listen to her and match with her. As a beginner at the piccolo, she couldn't control the pitch as well as she could on the flute, and she seemed defensive about her lack of virtuosity on the piccolo. I told her that if the flute players listened up to her then the whole section wouldn't blend in with the rest of the band, and she herself would blend in more and not stick out as much if she listened down to the flutes. Growing increasingly frustrated, she replied that she was in tune according to the tuner on her stand. From my years of experience listening to the band director, I knew that being in tune according to the tuner isn't the main concern, but I knew I also risked angering her if I simply told her she was wrong. Thus, I affirmed for her that she was in tune, but I also told her that it was easier for one piccolo player to adjust to nine flute players than it is for those nine flute players to adjust to one piccolo player. The director would rather have everyone matching and not be in tune than for one person to be in tune and stick out of the texture. Even if the band as a whole isn't perfectly in tune, if they at least are matching each other it makes for a better sound and is more pleasant for the audience members or the judges. By assuring the piccolo player that there was nothing technically wrong with her playing, I was able to get her to match the flutes, creating more unity in the band's sound.

Some people may argue that my seven years of experience in band don't qualify me as a member of the discourse community because I didn't continue band in college. However, those years of experience are what I would I have needed to get into college band. My years of experience being in an ensemble gave me a more mature sound compared to someone else who lacked those years. Once at a competition, Mr. Sisco commented that a particular school's second band played better than its top band because they had a more mature sound. When he looked at the faces of the students in the ensemble, he realized that they were all upperclassmen, while the top band consisted of mostly underclassmen. Since the upperclassmen had more experience playing in an ensemble, they developed a more mature sound because they knew what to listen for and when and how to use the correct amount of dynamics. Even though I may not be the most talented player, perhaps not even talented enough to play in college, I know how to blend into an ensemble in order to make the whole band better. Most important, I have the content knowledge and terminology to interact successfully with those in band, even if my skills are not sufficient to play with them.

By reflecting on my membership in the discourse community of band, I understand how important mastering ethos, logos, and pathos appeals will be in my future careers. It took years for me to become a full-fledged member of high school band, but once I learned how to communicate with other members and appeal to them rhetorically, I was accepted. I know I will use these tools in future discourse communities I want to join.

Paper 2 – Rhetorical Analysis
English 1301: Rhetoric and Composition I

THE RHETORICAL SITUATION

For your Discourse Community Analysis, you applied rhetorical concepts to your past experiences in order to explain how you joined a community by learning its distinctive ways of communication. Any time we attempt to join an established group, we usually begin just by listening; this helps us learn the backgrounds of the participants, the common topics of conversation, the values of the group, the distinctive lingo, etc. To put it another way, we must carefully attend what "they say" before we make our own contribution.

For this paper, you will apply critical reading skills as a way of "listening" to a writer engaged in a conversation you're not yet familiar with. Read the designated article from the topic cluster you've selected. Then imagine that you're a guest editor for *The Shorthorn* and the opinion editor has asked you to analyze the article and offer your recommendation for or against publication. The editor is looking for columns that UTA students will find interesting, columns that are nuanced and complex, well-argued, relevant, and controversial. You'll evaluate the article based on those criteria and make your recommendation for or against publication accordingly.

Invention (i.e., discovering what you're going to say in this paper)

1. Your editor will need to know the author's central claim. To identify it, ask yourself the following questions as you read:

   - What claim does the author most want readers to grant? If the author could only guarantee that readers would agree to one claim, what would it be?

2. Your editor also needs to know what reasons the author is providing to support his/her central claim. Imagine that you could ask the writer in person, "Why do you believe that [central claim]?" Based on the information in the article, how do you think the writer would answer? Would the writer reply with just one reason, or would there be many? If there would be many, what would they be?

3. Of course, your editor will want to know whether the author provides evidence for his/her reasons and whether that evidence will prove convincing to *Shorthorn* readers. This means you must combine *analysis* of the text with *evaluation* of its effectiveness. Ask yourself the following questions:

   - Will *Shorthorn* readers believe the author's reasons are true automatically? (If so, then there's no reason for the writer to provide evidence.) If not, does the writer provide evidence to support his/her reasons? If so, is this evidence sufficient to convince *Shorthorn* readers that the author's reasons are true?

4. Your editor will want to know whether the author addresses potential opponents. Ask yourself the following questions:

- Does the author anticipate objections to parts of his/her argument? If so, does the author represent opponents fairly or set up straw men? Does the author concede certain points to opponents? Does the author provide a convincing reply to opponents?

5. The questions listed above in steps 1-4 deal primarily with the author's logos appeals, but your editor will also want to know about the author's ethos appeals. Ask yourself the following questions:

- Do the author's credentials make his/her claims more credible? Does the author seem knowledgeable and well-informed on the topic? Does the author consider alternate viewpoints and treat opponents with respect? Does the author seem to have the audience's best interests at heart? Does the author draw on values he/she shares with the audience?

6. Your editor will be particularly interested in the author's pathos appeals, since the main point of your analysis is to determine how the article will be received by *Shorthorn* readers. Ask yourself the following questions:

- Does the author evoke emotions in UTA readers that are likely to help his/her case? Does the author evoke sensations in UTA readers that will make the writing seem vivid? Does the author draw on values possessed by the UTA community?

Other Inventional Tips

Even though the main purpose of this paper is to analyze *another's* argument, you still need to include a thesis in which you make a claim for or against publication and support that claim with reasons. Your reasons will come from your judgment about whether *Shorthorn* readers will find the article interesting and relevant.

Your editor is not overly concerned with whether *you* find the author's argument interesting or persuasive because you are only one of the thousands of people who read *The Shorthorn*. Your personal response may be relevant, but only to the extent that your response is representative of the UTA community.

One of UTA's greatest strengths is its diversity, but this diversity also means that no article will prove effective with every single member of the community. Thus, it's perfectly legitimate—sometimes preferable—to note that the same appeal will prove effective or ineffective depending on the reader.

Arrangement (i.e., organizing what you're going to say in this paper)

Ultimately, you want to organize your paper in the manner you think will prove most effective with your editor, but here are a couple tips:

- Heed the lesson of Ch. 1 in *They Say/I Say:* "To give your writing the most important thing of all—namely, a point—a writer needs to indicate clearly not only his or her thesis, but also what larger conversation that thesis is responding to" (18). In this case, the conversation you're responding to is simply the one initiated by your editor's request. Indicate at the beginning of your paper—before you state your thesis—that you're writing in response to that request.

- Also mind the lesson of Ch. 7 in *They Say/I Say:* "Regardless of how interesting a topic may be to you as a writer, readers always need to know what is at stake in a text and why they should care. . . . Rather than assume that audiences will know why their claims matter, all writers need to answer the 'so what?' and 'who cares?' questions up front" (88-89). Even though you're writing at your editor's request, you can still make your analysis more significant by explaining why it is important for *The Shorthorn* to publish—or not to publish—the article you're analyzing. Feel free to use the templates in Ch. 7 of *They Say/I Say.*

Style (i.e., choosing the appropriate language for your paper)

In writing to an editor, you'll continue to practice writing for a specific audience rather than to some vague, generalized audience. When reading your paper, it should be obvious that you're writing to your editor specifically.

Continue to heed the lesson of Ch. 9 in *They Say/I Say* and mix standard written English with "the kinds of expressions and turns of phrase that you use every day when conversing with family and friends" (115). The more important lesson of that chapter is "that your judgments about the appropriate language for the situation should always take into account your likely audience and your purpose in writing" (121). You should adopt a slightly more formal style than in your first paper because you're practicing a type of professional writing. At the same time, since you're not writing for publication, you need not adopt the highest level of formality.

All readers appreciate coherent, unified paragraphs, so your paragraphs should include a topic sentence that clearly states the main idea of the paragraph and supporting sentences that cluster around the main idea without detours.

Proofread carefully; avoid errors in grammar, spelling, punctuation, and mechanics. Use *The Scott, Foresman Writer* for questions you have regarding style.

Other Requirements

Your paper should be **four pages**—anything beyond that length will be considered a failure to adhere to one of the assignment's basic requirements. It should be double-spaced, typed in Times New Roman font, with 12-point character size and one-inch margins.

Your first submission is due at the beginning of class on _____, and you should think of it as a final draft—something that is ready to be read by your editor. If your first submission does not meet every requirement of this assignment sheet, I will return it to you and count it as late. Both your first and final submissions must be turned in on time—you will be docked a full letter grade for each day either is late.

Peer reviews are due _____.

Final drafts are due _____.

Evaluation Criteria

Final Draft:
- Includes a snappy title that catches the reader's attention and indicates the topic and argument.
- Indicates that the author writes in response to a request from *The Shorthorn*'s opinion editor.
- Includes a contestable, specific, detailed claim for or against publication in *The Shorthorn*.
- Provides reasons for the decision to publish/not to publish
- Answers the "so what" and "who cares" questions by explaining why the argument is significant and to whom.
- Identifies the article's central claim and supporting reasons.
- Evaluates how effectively the author supports her/his claims and reasons with ethos, pathos, and logos appeals.
- Evaluates how effectively the author anticipates and addresses counterarguments
- Evaluates whether or not the argument will appeal to UT Arlington readers.
- Integrates examples from the article smoothly, paraphrasing and occasionally directly quoting the article to help substantiate or support points.
- Offers proper attribution to the article via in-text parenthetical citation.
- Comes across as a credible writer, and appeals to the values and emotions of the audience.
- Develops a seamless, coherent, and well-organized argument.
- Sentences are lively, engaging, and relatively error free.
- Essay is 4 pages in MLA Style (no Works Cited necessary) in 12 point Times New Roman font with 1-inch margins.

Writing Process:
- Submitted complete drafts on time. Drafting process shows evidence of revision of content and style.
- Provided adequate help to peers during peer review.

SAMPLE RHETORICAL ANALYSIS

I am writing in response to your request that I analyze David Horowitz's "In Defense of Intellectual Diversity" and make a recommendation for or against publication in *The Shorthorn*. I have considered the rhetorical appeals of Horowitz's piece and determined it will be largely unpersuasive with readers of *The Shorthorn*. That said, readers are likely to find the piece interesting, as it addresses the topic of political advocacy in the classroom, which is an important issue for students and professors alike. Nearly all members of the UTA community would agree that students should not be forced to agree with the political beliefs of their professors, and it is important to be aware of arguments like Horowitz's, which accuse college professors of failing to maintain neutrality on political issues.

Horowitz's central claim is that colleges and universities should adopt and enforce his Academic Bill of Rights. He provides three supporting reasons for his central claim, which he mentions toward the beginning of the article: "The bill's purposes are to codify the AAUP's tradition of academic freedom; to emphasize the value of 'intellectual diversity'; and, most important, to enumerate the rights of students not to be indoctrinated or otherwise assaulted by political propagandists in the classroom or any educational setting." These reasons are all valid because they rest on the shared assumption that colleges and universities should take action if academic freedom is not being protected and students' rights are being violated. Horowitz's reasons all relate to maintaining academic integrity, which is likely important to the readers of the *The Shorthorn*.

Although Horowitz may provide valid reasons for his claim, he does not provide sufficient evidence to support these reasons. For his first reason, that it is necessary to codify the AAUP's tradition of academic freedom, Horowitz mentions a conversation with the president of the Colorado University system in which the president expresses satisfaction with current guidelines. He then briefly follows with an observation of how tough it is to find AAUP principles on CU's website. He has simply shown what readers of the *The Shorthorn* already know: that information about academic freedom, while perhaps a few clicks away, exists and is publicly available. Further, many readers of *The Shorthorn*, particularly those who are heavily involved with UTA, likely know exactly where to find the University's statement on academic freedom.

For his second reason, that it is necessary to emphasize the value of intellectual diversity, Horowitz provides a blanket statement that academic fields should foster "a plurality of methodologies and perspectives" because of "the uncertainty and unsettled character of all human knowledge." Readers of *The Shorthorn* would want specific answers as to what, exactly, this would mean, especially since it would impact them all. Would this translate into mandates that opposing viewpoints be brought in for sake of "balance"? Readers might well hear the phrase, "Fair and Balanced," the FOX News slogan. And they would probably conclude that is not an appropriate way to develop a college curriculum. Opposing positions should not be brought in just to be "fair" any more than "flat earth society" members should be given equal time in the astronomy schoolbooks to balance out "round earthers," or that members of NAMBLA should be provided a respectful response against those pursuing the prosecution of pedophiles. It's not a matter of being fair, *Shorthorn* readers would argue; it's a matter of being correct, and being able to back it up with solid, objective research.

Finally, for his third reason, that it is necessary to remove partisan politics from the classroom, he provides anecdotal evidence such as the following: "At Duke University this year, a history professor welcomed his class with the warning that he had strong 'liberal' opinions, and that Republican students should probably drop his course. One student did." Although

Shorthorn readers probably think that students should feel comfortable in an academic setting, Horowitz does not provide enough information to convince them that this is a widespread problem. He also cites the number of political cartoons "ridiculing Republicans" plastered in the hallway of the Political Science department at the University of Colorado at Denver. Readers of *The Shorthorn* likely believe that the presence of these cartoons encourages intellectual and passionate discourse, which, in turn, promotes intellectual diversity. In a third anecdote, Horowitz describes a book required of all incoming freshman at North Carolina, Barbara Ehrenreich's *Nickel and Dimed*, as a "socialist tract," which works to alienate *Shorthorn* readers who have read, and perhaps think highly of, the text.

Horowitz does make an attempt to address counterarguments. He states his bill explicitly "forbids political hiring or firing." This would be a nugget of good news to *Shorthorn* readers. He says the bill is essentially apolitical, that its point is to remove "partisan politics from the classroom." But readers would then question who would be the judge deciding what information was considered partisan and what was not.

Horowitz attempts to establish credibility by reassuring readers that although he himself is a "well-known conservative," the ABR's intent is to protect the right *and* left-leaning professors. To further placate readers, Horowitz specifically names liberal academics he called upon to search the bill for political bias, and even admits to removing entire portions based on their feedback. On the other hand, he seems to think that a conservative writer/pundit has earned a right to critique professors, yet his own words incriminate him when he warns non-history professors who discuss current events in class that "intrusion of such subject matter, in which the professor has no academic expertise, is a breach of professional responsibility." Horowitz, in fact, has committed a breach of professional responsibility, intruding where he has no academic expertise.

Finally, Horowitz appeals to the emotions of his *Shorthorn* readers in ways that both help and hinder his cause. Early in the article, Horowitz tries to show his readers that his bill actually defends everyone regardless of political affiliation: "The bill thus protects all faculty members—left-leaning critics of the war in Iraq as well as right-leaning proponents of it, for example—from being penalized for their political beliefs." This early attempt to appeal to his readers is effective until he negates this claim in the next paragraph, stating that faculty hires should be made "with a view toward fostering a plurality of methodologies and perspectives." After a discussion about protecting faculty members by forbidding "political hiring and firing," he goes on to promote a politically-based process for hiring! Further, by attacking many of the very readers he is writing to, Horowitz evokes anger in them. He first shows great disrespect for faculty by claiming that they "focus merely on their own partisan agendas and abandon their responsibilities as professional educator." While there may be some *Shorthorn* readers who agree with this statement, the majority of them would not agree that this is a widespread problem at UTA. For me, and likely for many other UTA students, Horowitz unintentionally evokes frustration. He pleads with the reader to remove one-sided politics from the classroom, yet it is obvious, when all of his examples are against liberals, that he cannot rid his own paper of the same prejudice that apparently plagues our universities.

Horowitz's argument is so thin, so anecdotal, and insubstantial it would be shredded by most *Shorthorn* readers. But shredding an argument can be fun! Especially when it's on a topic of great interest to readers. This is why I conclude that although most *Shorthorn* readers will disagree with Horowitz's argument, we should publish the piece because these same readers will read it eagerly.

Paper 3 – Synthesis Essay
English 1301: Rhetoric and Composition I

THE RHETORICAL SITUATION

For your Discourse Community Analysis, you applied rhetorical concepts to your past experiences in order to explain how you joined a community by learning its distinctive ways of communication. For your Rhetorical Analysis, you prepared to join a new conversation by reading carefully what "they say" about an important topic. Now you are ready to make your own contribution, to take part in the "I say" stage of the conversation.

For this paper, you will take a position on an issue addressed in your topic cluster and write an argument that synthesizes the articles in that cluster. (Synthesis simply means you make connections between multiple sources in order to make a new argument.) Your audience will be readers of a UTA student publication that offers analysis and commentary about politics, news, and culture. Use your knowledge of UTA students: they are educated, generally fair-minded, politically diverse, and less knowledgeable than you about the issue addressed in your topic cluster.

Invention (i.e., discovering what you're going to say in this paper)

1. Your audience of UTA students will want to know immediately both the conversation you're responding to and your own position. Furthermore, they will want to know that you are *advancing* the conversation, turning it in a new direction, rather than just repeating another writer's argument. Consult Ch. 4 in *They Say/I Say* for tips on how to formulate your claim as a response to what someone else has written.
2. Of course, UTA students will expect you to support your claim with good reasons, so you should attach at least three reasons to your claim. What makes for a "good" reason? Well, assuming you provide sufficient evidence to support your reasons, would your audience agree to your claim? If so, then you've probably selected good reasons. If not, then you may need to select reasons that appeal more effectively to your audience's values.
3. Speaking of evidence to support your reasons, where will you find it? Certainly your personal experiences, observations, and logical reasoning count as evidence, but you should also mine the articles in your topic cluster for evidence that you can use to support your position.
4. There's no point in writing an argument that everyone will agree with automatically, so if you've constructed a good thesis, some readers will object to some parts of it. Address at least one main counterargument by:

    - naming and describing your opponent(s).
    - describing your opponents' positions fairly and accurately.
    - making any necessary concessions, i.e., identifying areas of agreement between you and your opponent(s).
    - responding with a well-considered and reasonable rebuttal.

Pay special attention to Ch. 6 in *They Say/I Say* for instruction in how to deal effectively with counterarguments.

5. Think about how you're going to come across to UTA students as a person of good character, good sense, and good will. Here are some tips:

- Know what you're talking about. Read all the articles in your topic cluster as carefully as you read the article for your Rhetorical Analysis, make sure you understand the articles deeply and thoroughly, and use information from the articles to provide sufficient evidence for your reasons.
- Show regard for your readers. Try to come across as approachable and thoughtful, not arrogant or insensitive.
- Treat skeptical readers with respect—don't ignore or demean their opinions just because they expect more proof.
- Be careful and meticulous in your writing, not sloppy or disorganized.

6. Think about the values and emotions that you share with fellow UTA students and consider how you might appeal to them. Here are some tips:

- Draw on the lessons of Ch. 9 in *They Say/I Say* in order to mix standard written English with "the kinds of expressions and turns of phrase that you use every day when conversing with family and friends" (115). Unlike your first two papers, however, this paper will be written for publication and for readers you don't know. Thus, you should adopt a more formal style and tone than in your first two papers.
- Try to evoke emotions (sympathy, outrage, anger, delight, awe, horror, etc.) in your audience that make your paper more moving.
- Try to evoke sensations (seeing, hearing, touching, tasting, smelling) in your audience that make your writing vivid and help readers experience things imaginatively.
- Appeal to values (freedom, justice, tolerance, fairness, equality, etc.) that you share with your audience.

Arrangement (i.e., organizing what you're going to say in this paper)

Ultimately, you want to organize your paper in the manner you think will prove most effective with your audience, but here are a couple tips:

- Heed the lesson of Ch. 1 in *They Say/I Say:* "To give your writing the most important thing of all—namely, a point—a writer needs to indicate clearly not only his or her thesis, but also what larger conversation that thesis is responding to" (18). In this case, the conversation you're responding to is the one constituted by the articles in your topic cluster. Indicate at the beginning of your paper—before you state your thesis—that you're writing in response to that conversation.
- Also mind the lesson of Ch. 7 in *They Say/I Say:* "Regardless of how interesting a topic may be to you as a writer, readers always need to know what is at stake in a text and why they should care. . . . Rather than assume that audiences will know why their claims matter, all writers need to answer the 'so what?' and 'who cares?' questions up front" (88-89). Unlike your first two papers, this one is unsolicited, which means you must work harder to demonstrate the exigence for your argument and to attract readers. Providing compelling answers to the "so what?" and "who cares?" has never been more important.

Style (i.e., choosing the appropriate language for your paper)

Once again you'll be writing to a highly specific audience, so you must continue to avoid writing to some vague, generalized audience. When reading your paper, it should be obvious that you're writing to fellow UTA students.

As always, heed the lesson of Ch. 9 in *They Say/I Say* and mix standard written English with "the kinds of expressions and turns of phrase that you use every day when conversing with family and friends" (115). The more important lesson of that chapter is "that your judgments about the appropriate language for the situation should always take into account your likely audience and your purpose in writing" (121). As mentioned earlier, your style should be more formal than in your first two papers, but this does not mean you should write in a pretentious style that is not your own.

All readers appreciate coherent, unified paragraphs, so your paragraphs should include a topic sentence that clearly states the main idea of the paragraph and supporting sentences that cluster around the main idea without detours.

Document your sources properly according to MLA style. Consult *The Scott, Foresman Writer* for instructions on how to format in-text citations and Works Cited entries.

Proofread carefully; avoid errors in grammar, spelling, punctuation, and mechanics. Use *The Scott, Foresman Writer* for questions you have regarding style.

Other Requirements

Your paper should be **no longer than four pages**—anything beyond that length will be considered a failure to adhere to one of the assignment's basic requirements. It should be double-spaced, typed in Times New Roman font, with 12 point character size and one inch margins all the way around.

Your first submission is due at the beginning of class on _____, and you should think of it as a final draft—something that is ready for publication. If your first submission does not meet every requirement of this assignment sheet, I will return it to you and count it as late. Both your first and final submissions must be turned in on time—you will be docked a full letter grade for each day either is late.

Peer reviews are due _____.

Final drafts are due _____.

Evaluation Criteria

Final Draft:
- Includes a snappy title that catches the reader's attention and indicates the argument.
- Identifies an appropriate topic related to one of the assigned essay clusters.
- Indicates that the essay responds to the conversation in the essay cluster.

- Includes a contestable, specific, detailed claim about the topic that advances the conversation.
- Provides at least three well-developed reasons to support the claim.
- Answers the "so what" and "who cares" questions by explaining why the argument is significant and to whom.
- Supports reasons with carefully selected, well-developed examples from multiple sources, as well as from personal experiences and observations.
- Anticipates counterarguments, considers them carefully, and responds to them fairly, conceding where others are right.
- Uses sources effectively and integrates them smoothly, paraphrasing and occasionally directly quoting authorities to help substantiate or support points.
- Offers proper attribution to each source cited via in-text parenthetical citation and a correctly formatted Works Cited page.
- Comes across as a credible writer, and appeals to the values and emotions of the audience.
- Develops a seamless, coherent, and well-organized argument.
- Sentences are lively, engaging, and relatively error free.
- Essay is 4 pages in MLA Style with Works Cited in 12 point Times New Roman font with 1-inch margins.

Writing Process:
- Submitted complete drafts on time. Drafting process shows evidence of revision of content and style.
- Provided adequate help to peers during peer review.

Sample Synthesis Essay
Intellectual Diversity: A Means to a Destructive End

The value of higher education is unquestionable, but it is now in jeopardy. Due to the unbalanced ratio of liberal to conservative faculty members in higher education, David Horowitz, founder of the David Horowitz Freedom Center, has proposed an Academic Bill of Rights in part to "emphasize the value of 'intellectual diversity.'" Horowitz argues that the central purpose of the university is to pursue the truth and, due to what he calls "the unsettled character of all human knowledge," the only reasonable way to do so is by offering many different perspectives and maintaining a balance between liberal and conservative faculty members. Although this may appear valid at first glance, those who have a stake in higher education argue that intellectual diversity would greatly limit the quality of education that professors provide by promoting non-academic "values" in academia. For example, in response to Horowitz's attempts to integrate intellectual diversity into academics, Dean Stanley Fish of the University of Illinois at Chicago College of Liberal Arts and Sciences asserts that "the value (if it is one) of intellectual diversity should be rejected." I agree with Fish that intellectual diversity is not an academic value and should therefore be rejected, but I further argue that mandating such a principle would be incredibly detrimental to academics. Classes would be dull, professors would not be allowed to share their expertise with students, and students would not be encouraged to think critically about the opinions of their professors. Obviously these are effects that no UTA student wants.

As a student, I believe that requiring professors to present multiple viewpoints would devalue the curriculum by making it static and, in turn, boring. The most valuable lessons I have had in the classroom have involved biased political statements, particularly in the College of Liberal Arts. In my experience, when professors are passionate about something, their lessons reflect that passion, are more interesting, and students are able to learn from them. For example, in an undergraduate persuasion class, we examined advertisements, many of which were political in nature, to learn effective ways to integrate persuasive principles. Had my professor not chosen liberal advertisements, the lesson would have been less effective because she may not have been as familiar with conservative advertisements and could not as easily have pinpointed effective uses of persuasive techniques. Further, because she was so clearly interested in the lesson, the class as a whole paid more attention and put forth more effort.

Classes that present some form of bias are also more interesting as a result of controversy. Michael Ellis, a student at Dartmouth College, emphasizes that "professors have a duty to inject some degree of controversy into the classroom, if for no other reason than to stimulate a healthy intellectual debate." If the goal of a university is to pursue the truth, then I see no better way than to bring an intellectual debate into the classroom and invite students to participate (intentionally or unintentionally). Ellis argues that one of the primary duties of higher education is to challenge students by "mak[ing] them reconsider their long-held assumptions, and . . . creat[ing] stronger thinkers in the process." By involving themselves in the process of discovering truth, students become more connected with their education. This connection helps to establish and promote a dynamic and effective curriculum.

In the same vein, maintaining the freedom that professors have in their classrooms continues to establish them as "experts in their subject matter," as Ann Marie Bahr, philosophy and religion professor at South Dakota State University, puts it. By integrating multiple perspectives on what should be considered the truth, professors risk calling their authority and expertise into question. That is not to say that students should never question the viewpoints of their professors; it is to say, however, that students should see their professors as experts in their subject matter. Bahr saw the effects of Horowitz's ideas in her classroom: "For the first time in my life, I felt as if I had to leave my commitment to the truth (which is what scholarship is all about!) at the door of the classroom." This is just one case of Horowitz's value of intellectual diversity undermining faculty expertise if, as in Bahr's case, it is not what the students want to hear. The university community should have confidence that its professors are experts in their fields of study and, as such, are capable of conveying the truth to their students (or pursuing it with them) without having to present multiple viewpoints. Horowitz claims there are many fields of study that rely on the fact that "knowledge is uncertain and, at times, relative" and thus deserve to be challenged, but he fails to acknowledge that these subjects are few and far between. Most subject matters in academia are indeed settled and rely on concrete evidence and facts.

Horowitz argues that implementing this "value" of intellectual diversity works to benefit all faculty members, as it would "remove politics from the classroom . . . [and] explicitly [forbid] political hiring and firing." While I do agree that hiring and firing should not be based on political agendas, Horowitz's plan will ultimately resort to political means. Although his plan is apolitical in nature, it is only a matter of time before it becomes politically biased. Horowitz has no ground to support a supposedly apolitical attempt at political reform. Political reform, by definition, has no direction to go but a political one. As Fish declares, "It is just a matter of which party seizes [the value of intellectual diversity] and makes it its own." Should this ideology fall into the wrong hands, a drive to promote balance in academia may lead to a concentrated effort to hire faculty members on the basis of their politics, rather than their subject matter expertise. What could be more political than that?

In addition to devaluing faculty members in this way, implementing intellectual diversity in academia underestimates the role of students in their own education. The primary goal of a university or college is to enhance the knowledge of the students who attend. Knowledge is best attained when the material can be grappled with and interrogated by students themselves. Michael Ellis, a Dartmouth College student, asserts that the primary goal of a college or university "is to challenge its students intellectually, to make them reconsider their long-held assumptions, and to create stronger thinkers in the process." Students should be involved in their education. They should not simply be presented with a multitude of viewpoints on a certain topic; they should have the opportunity to question and to come up with their own viewpoints. By being involved in their education, students are more likely to learn the material and grow from the process of learning it. Requiring professors to present multiple viewpoints on a topic sends a signal to students that they do not need to involve themselves in their education, and they will suffer from this. If students are not required to do higher level thinking, their application of knowledge in the real world will suffer.

If the goal of intellectual diversity is to enhance the classroom experience by eliminating partisan politics, it should be rejected on the basis that it would wreak havoc on academia as we know it. Higher education should support the student's endeavor to pursue the truth; David Horowitz's notion of intellectual diversity does nothing but disadvantage the student. College level courses should be interesting, and students should be able to question and provide additional information on certain subject matters. Professors should maintain their roles as experts in their fields who are capable of bestowing that expertise on their students. Politics should not be brought into the hiring and firing process, even if the attempt were to be to remove a seemingly political bias. Students need to feel as though they are a part of their education and that their presence in the classroom matters. The "value" of intellectual diversity must be kept out of academia in order to preserve the quality of higher education.

Works Cited

Bahr, Ann Marie B. "The Right to Tell the Truth." *Chronicle of Higher Education* 51.35 (2005). Web.

Ellis, Michael J. "Once More unto the Breach." *The Dartmouth Review* 8 April 2005. Web.

Fish, Stanley. "'Intellectual Diversity': The Trojan Horse of a Dark Design." *Chronicle of Higher Education* 50.23 (2004). Web.

Horowitz, David. "In Defense of Intellectual Diversity." *Chronicle of Higher Education* 50.23 (2004). Web.

English 1302
Course Information and Assignments

English 1302 Course Description, Learning Outcomes, and Audience Information

ENGL 1302 RHETORIC AND COMPOSITION II: Continues ENGL 1301, but with an emphasis on advanced techniques of academic argument. Includes issue identification, independent library research, analysis and evaluation of sources, and synthesis of sources with students' own claims, reasons, and evidence. Prerequisite: Grade of C or better in ENGL 1301.

ENGL 1302 EXPECTED LEARNING OUTCOMES

In ENGL 1302, students build on the knowledge and information that they learned in ENGL 1301. By the end of ENGL 1302, students should be able to:

Rhetorical Knowledge

- ▶ Identify and analyze the components and complexities of a rhetorical situation
- ▶ Use knowledge of audience, exigence, constraints, genre, tone, diction, syntax, and structure to produce situation-appropriate argumentative texts, including texts that move beyond formulaic structures
- ▶ Know and use special terminology for analyzing and producing arguments
- ▶ Practice and analyze informal logic as used in argumentative texts

Critical Reading, Thinking, and Writing

- ▶ Understand the interactions among critical thinking, critical reading, and writing
- ▶ Integrate personal experiences, values, and beliefs into larger social conversations and contextss
- ▶ Find, evaluate, and analyze primary and secondary sources for appropriateness, timeliness, and validity
- ▶ Produce situation-appropriate argumentative texts that synthesize sources with their own ideas and advance the conversation on an important issue
- ▶ Provide valid, reliable, and appropriate support for claims, and analyze evidentiary support in others' texts

Processes

- ▶ Practice flexible strategies for generating, revising, and editing complex argumentative texts
- ▶ Engage in all stages of advanced, independent library research
- ▶ Practice writing as a recursive process that can lead to substantive changes in ideas, structure, and supporting evidence through multiple revisions

▷ Use the collaborative and social aspects of writing to critique their own and others' arguments

Conventions

▷ Apply and develop knowledge of genre conventions ranging from structure and paragraphing to tone and mechanics, and be aware of the field-specific nature of these conventions

▷ Summarize, paraphrase, and quote from sources using appropriate documentation style

▷ Revise for style and edit for features such as syntax, grammar, punctuation, and spelling

▷ Employ technologies to format texts according to appropriate stylistic conventions

A Word about Audiences in ENGL 1302 Essays

Composition scholars sometimes categorize audiences as simple (a single person or a group of like-minded people) or complex (a group of people who may have differing perspectives and be reading for different purposes). Audiences can also be familiar to us (we know them personally and understand their values) or unfamiliar (we do not know them personally and may be unsure of their values). Research shows that writing tasks become more difficult as audiences become more complex and unfamiliar. In ENGL 1301 and ENGL 1302, students practice moving from relatively simple and familiar audiences to more complex and unfamiliar audiences. The three major essays in ENGL 1302 offer students the opportunity to prepare their work for three different audiences.

- In the **Issue Proposal (IP),** the student has the challenge of convincing classmates and the instructor that the issue being proposed will be suitable for a semester long examination. If the student can't convince this first audience that the issue is appropriate for investigation, then it is evident that more work has to be done to find a suitable issue. In the IP, the student has to demonstrate some understanding of the larger conversation about the issue, an idea about possible stakeholders interested in and opponents to the issue, and why the student finds this issue compelling. All of this has to be "tried out" on this first audience: classmates and instructor.
- When the student prepares the **Mapping the Issue** essay, the audience for this exploration of the issue expands to UTA students in general. Here the student has an audience that is a bit broader than just his/her classmates and instructor. He/she will have to prepare a credible and informative overview of the issue in such a way that the general UTA student would, upon reading it, have a good understanding of the various controversies surrounding the issue. Student writers will draw upon research presented in an **Annotated Bibliography** as they clearly explain three to five views on the issue. The goal here is for the student writer to convey his/her fuller understanding of the issue in a fair and thorough examination.

- Finally, in the **Researched Position Paper,** the student writer will select a specific audience to read his/her essay. This audience may be one that was identified earlier in the **Issue Proposal.** The audience must be a group or person who would realistically want or need to hear the student's position on this issue. By making a specific argument to a specific audience the student will have demonstrated rhetorical skills he/she will call upon time and again when they write in their major s and in their careers.

ENGL 1302 ESSAY ASSIGNMENTS

Paper 1 – Issue Proposal
English 1302: Rhetoric and Composition II

THE RHETORICAL SITUATION

In order for argument to occur, there must first be an "issue," which simply means an unsettled question that matters to a community. This semester you'll be conducting research on an issue that you select, and since you'll be reading and writing extensively on this issue throughout the term, it's essential that you choose one that truly interests you. As you consider potential issues, you may want to do some background reading to ensure that you are truly interested in the issue and that you can find enough sources to support sustained research. **Please note:** all the major assignments in this course build on one another, so once you select an issue, you may not change it.

For this paper, you will take stock of what you already know about the issue you select, organize and develop your thoughts, and sketch a plan for your research. Your audience will be your classmates and me.

Invention (i.e., discovering what you're going to say in this paper)

1. You must first make sure the issue you've selected is arguable. Apply the "Twelve Tests of an Arguable Issue" on p. 37 of *First-Year Writing*. If you cannot answer "yes" to all twelve questions, change or modify your issue until you can.
2. Your classmates and I will want to know more about the issue and your relationship to it, so brainstorm/freewrite/draft answers to the following questions:

   - How would you introduce this issue to an audience who knows nothing about it?
   - What do you know about the issue already?
   - How did you acquire your knowledge about the issue?
   - Why do you find this issue compelling?

3. Your classmates and I will also be interested in what you *don't* know (or are at least unsure about) regarding the issue. Brainstorm/freewrite/draft answers to the following questions:

   - What are the main questions you want to pursue/answer over the course of the semester? (Obviously these questions may change as you learn/think more about the issue.)
   - How would you answer these questions right now and why? (Your answers may change significantly as you research the issue.)
   - What more do you need to learn about the issue, and where might you go to find more information?

4. Finally, your classmates and I will be curious to know what audiences you have in mind as you look ahead to future assignments. Brainstorm/freewrite/draft answers to the following questions:

- What audiences would be interested in your ideas on the issue?
- What types of scholars, stakeholders, decisions makers, and pundits are interested in/affected by the issue?
- What sorts of people are likely to be your opponents? Your allies?

Arrangement (i.e., organizing what you're going to say in this paper)

You'll want to organize your paper in the manner you think will prove most effective with your classmates and me, but here are some general guidelines:

- Heed the lesson of Ch. 1 in *They Say/I Say:* "To give your writing the most important thing of all—namely, a point—a writer needs to indicate clearly not only his or her thesis, but also what larger conversation that thesis is responding to" (18). In this case, the conversation you're responding to is the one surrounding the issue you've selected. Indicate at the beginning of your paper that you're writing in response to that conversation, then state a thesis that previews what you'll be discussing in your paper and why it is appropriate for a semester of sustained research.
- Also mind the lesson of Ch. 7 in *They Say/I Say:* "Regardless of how interesting a topic may be to you as a writer, readers always need to know what is at stake in a text and why they should care. . . . Rather than assume that audiences will know why their claims matter, all writers need to answer the 'so what?' and 'who cares?' questions up front" (88-89). Don't assume that your classmates and I will understand why your issue matters—make us understand by explaining why your issue is important and why we should care about it.
- However you arrange the body of your paper, make sure you answer fully and in detail all the questions in the Invention section of this prompt.

Style (i.e., choosing the appropriate language for your paper)

One reason I'm asking you to write to your classmates and me is to break you of the habit of writing all your papers to some vague, generalized audience and/or attempting to make all your papers approximate some objective ideal. If you approach this paper in that way, your style will be ineffective because it won't be tailored to your specific audience. When reading your paper, it should be obvious to your classmates and me that you're writing to us specifically.

Heed the lesson of Ch. 9 in *They Say/I Say* and mix standard written English with "the kinds of expressions and turns of phrase that you use every day when conversing with family and friends" (115). The more important lesson of that chapter is "that your judgments about the appropriate language for the situation should always take into account your likely audience and your purpose in writing" (121). Since you're writing to your classmates and me, you should write in an informal style that is distinctly your own, but do make sure you're communicating clearly.

All readers appreciate coherent, unified paragraphs, so your paragraphs should include a topic sentence that clearly states the main idea of the paragraph and supporting sentences that cluster around the main idea without detours.

Proofread carefully; avoid errors in grammar, spelling, punctuation, and mechanics. Use *The Scott, Foresman Writer* for questions you have regarding style.

Other Requirements

Your paper should be **3-5 pages**—anything shorter or longer will be considered a failure to adhere to one of the assignment's basic requirements. It should be double-spaced, typed in Times New Roman font, with 12-point character size and one-inch margins all the way around.

Your first submission is due at the beginning of class on _____, and you should think of it as a final draft—something that is ready for your classmates and me to read. If your first submission does not meet every requirement of this assignment sheet, I will return it to you and count it as late. Both your first and final submissions must be turned in on time—you will be docked a full letter grade for each day either is late.

Peer reviews are due _____.

Final drafts are due _____.

Evaluation Criteria

Final Draft:
- Includes a snappy title that catches the reader's attention and indicates the topic and argument.
- Identifies an arguable/contestable issue appropriate to the assignment.
- Indicates that the essay responds to the conversation about that issue.
- Includes a contestable, specific, detailed claim about why the issue is appropriate for a semester of sustained research.
- Provides well-developed reasons about your relationship to the issue (what you know, what you don't know, what audiences you are considering, and how you will find the information you need) that support the claim.
- Answers the "so what" and "who cares" question by explaining why the research topic is significant and to whom.
- Supports reasons with thoughtful, well-developed examples anecdotes, ideas, and questions.
- Comes across as a credible writer, and appeals to the values and emotions of the audience.
- Develops a seamless, coherent, and well-organized argument.
- Sentences are lively, engaging, and relatively error free.
- If outside sources are used, they are used effectively and integrated smoothly to help substantiate or support points.
- If outside sources are used, there is proper attribution to each source cited via in-text parenthetical citation and a correctly formatted Works Cited page.

- Essay is 3-5 pages in MLA Style (Works Cited necessary if outside sources are used) in 12 point Times New Roman font with 1-inch margins.

Writing Process:
- Submitted complete drafts on time. Drafting process shows evidence of revision of content and style.
- Provided adequate help to peers during peer review.

SAMPLE ISSUE PROPOSAL

Working Hard Is Hardly Working: Challenges
Facing Working Families in the U.S.

For as long as I can remember, I have felt frustrated by the lack of institutional support for working women and families. In my high school Government and Economics classes I would get furious when we talked about the gender wage gap that means that women still earn only 83 cents for every dollar a man earns; the lack of a federal law guaranteeing women paid maternity leave; and the lack of affordable quality daycare for working families. As an adult I have an even more personal stake in issues facing working families because I have a full-time job and two young sons, a combination that creates situations that are comical and heartbreaking: I comfort a crying mother at my sons' daycare as she drops off her ten-week old infant on her first day back to work; I arrive at my own job 15 minutes late covered in spit-up; I see my oldest son playing with his collection of Happy Meal toys and feel ashamed because they reveal how many meals I'm not cooking; I nurse my youngest son to sleep at night while answering work emails. Conversations with other daycare mothers reveal that we're all stretched thin financially and emotionally as we struggle to do our best by our children, partners, employers—and ourselves. And the conversation isn't limited to daycare moms—high profile feminists like Michelle Obama argue that working families need stronger support from government and businesses in order for families and businesses to thrive. This semester I plan to research the lack of institutional support provided to U.S. women and families and the resulting lack of work/life balance, financial security, and family stability. I also want to examine the negative impacts on businesses that result from employees' struggles. This topic justifies a semester of sustained research because I have a personal investment and a passionate interest in it; because there's an ongoing conversation about the issue in the U.S.; because there are a lot of interesting ways I could enter the conversation.

The issue of support for working families is one that I have always had an interest in; I have always wondered why women make the choices they do and how they manage to survive (and hopefully thrive) within the personal/professional/financial constraints they face. I will certainly draw on my own experience when developing my essays because it relates directly to the arguments I want to make. I have already read a fair amount about this issue, and there are a lot of articles/data I can draw on: I love Arlie Hochschild's *The Second Shift* about the particular burdens facing working mothers, and I can look in JSTOR for articles that cite her; there's a Harvard study comparing U.S. maternity/paternity leave benefits to those in other countries; there was a *New York Times Magazine* article a few years ago about highly educated women leaving their professions after having children; *Ms.* magazine always has articles about this topic; I can look at websites of organizations like NOW; I can see what Michelle Obama has said about this and related issues.

I obviously have a lot of strong ideas about the challenges facing working families, but there are also a lot of questions I have to answer before I'll be able to focus my topic. Here are a few: What minimum legal/financial support/safety nets do state and federal governments provide for working families (Family and Medical Leave Act, CHIP, etc.)? Where are the Catch-22s in the system (e.g., women on welfare lose money for groceries after they make a certain amount of money even though amount isn't enough to live on)? Which employers in the Metroplex/ Texas/US provide more than minimum assistance/protections for working families? What kinds of benefits are they providing (subsidized childcare, paid maternity/paternity leave)? What are the benefits to employers of providing those extra "perks"? Which elected officials/public figures argue for more support for working families? What kinds of arguments are they making? What protections/benefits do working families have in other industrialized countries? What kind of arguments can I make to create common ground and convince business people, legislators, etc. that better support of working families benefits everyone? Answering these questions will help me figure out what specific issue I want to tackle and within the overall umbrella of "lack of institutional support for women who work outside the home."

I know that lots of people feel very strongly about this issue: feminist scholars have written a lot about "the second shift" and lack of support for working women and families; Michelle Obama has taken up this issue; state and local lawmakers make decisions all the time that directly and indirectly affect working families, as do CEOs and other decision-makers in large and small businesses around the country. I think there are several possibilities in terms of audiences: if I want to propose changes in Texas law, my audience could be my legislators in the Texas House and Senate; if I want to organize moms or families to work for change, I could write to readers of local mommy blogs like the one sponsored by the *Fort Worth Star-Telegram;* I could also make arguments to my own employer for benefits that I don't currently receive, although that seems rhetorically very tricky. My allies are feminist lawmakers and businesspeople who understand and sympathize with the challenges faced by working families. It may also be that conservatives who believe in the importance of family values could be allies. I think most lawmakers and businesspeople will oppose this issue because it can be seen as expensive and as doing for others what they should be doing for themselves. The hardest question for me is how to appeal to business folks/legislators who make the short-term financial bottom line the most important aspect of their business models. My initial idea is that I would appeal to the idea that providing financial and legal safety nets for working families is an important part of "family values." I will also argue that support for working families may seem expensive but benefits employers' bottom line in the long term.

Since it can be hard to get people to sympathize with the idea of work/life/school balance and/or support for working families, I might start by describing poignant anecdotes about challenges faced by working parents. For example, I know of women who leave their small children asleep in the car outside their workplace late at night because they don't have childcare and are scared to leave their kids at home. It's a dramatic example that illustrates the struggles that working parents face. Depending on my audience, leading with such an emotional appeal might backfire. If I'm writing to businesspeople, it might be better to start with a logos appeal—maybe I can find data about how better support of working families benefits the bottom line.

I am excited about learning more about this topic and writing a sustained argument about it. I have felt passionately about the topic for a long time, which makes sense given that I'm living it every day and watching women around me—including the First Lady—struggle with the same issues I face. I think writing about this topic will help me make sense of the challenges I face in my own life while at the same time allowing me to argue publicly for change. You better believe that my Researched Position Paper is going to be "for real"!—I'm definitely going send it to my chosen audience.

Annotated Bibliography Assignment
English 1302: Rhetoric and Composition II

An annotated bibliography is a list of sources on a specific topic that includes a summary of each source. As you research your topic, develop an annotated bibliography of relevant sources. Your final annotated bibliography should include annotations for at least 10 sources that represent multiple perspectives on your issue.

The list should be compiled in alphabetical order using the appropriate citation style—in this case, Modern Language Association (MLA) style. Consult *The Scott, Foresman Writer* for directions on how to format entries.

Your annotation for each source should consist of two paragraphs. In the first, answer the following questions:

1. What kind of source is it, e.g., a book, journal article, magazine article, newspaper article, encyclopedia entry, database summary article, website?
2. What is the genre of the piece, e.g., a news report, an editorial, a report of scientific research, a summary of a number of sources? What is the purpose of the text?
3. Who is/are the author/authors? What are the author's credentials? How does the author establish his or her authority to speak on this subject? Also consider the credibility of the publication venue.
4. Who is the intended audience? Consider where the text is published, the degree of specialized knowledge needed to understand the text, how objective or argumentative the text is.
5. When was the text published? How does the publication date affect the relevance and usefulness of the source?

In your second paragraph, summarize the content of the piece in a way that demonstrates you have read the source and understood its content. **If the source is an argument, as opposed to a purely informational text, identify its main claim and supporting reasons.** In addition, explain how you plan to use the source in your Researched Position Paper (obviously this plan may change as you conduct further research and begin drafting). Will you use the source for background information, and if so, what information specifically do you plan to use? Does the source contain evidence that you plan to borrow, and if so, what evidence? If the source is an argument, will you position it as an ally or an opponent and why?

Sample Entry from an Annotated Bibliography

Estes, Todd. "The Connecticut Effect: The Great Compromise of 1787 and the History of Small State Impact on Electoral College Outcomes." *Historian* 73.2 (2011): 255-283. *Academic Search Complete.* Web. 7 Mar. 2012.

This journal article was written by Todd Estes, an Associate Professor of History at Oakland University, and published in June 2011 in *Historian*, an academic history journal. Estes is credible because he is widely published in the discipline of history and has published numerous articles on the electoral process. Because *Historian* is an established journal in the field of history, the audience for this article comprises academic historians. That said, the article is accessible to non-specialists who possess some prior knowledge of the electoral process and how it was formed. Because the article was published within the last year, one can assume it represents current thinking in the field of history.

The article addresses how the Connecticut Compromise, which gave smaller states disproportionate representation in the Electoral College, has affected presidential election outcomes throughout the years. My plan is to use much of the information presented here as background information in my Mapping the Issue paper and my Researched Position Paper. Specifically, I will borrow Estes's comparison of the ratio of Electoral College voters to population in smaller states versus larger states.

Paper 2 – Mapping the Issue
English 1302: Rhetoric and Composition II

The Rhetorical Situation

For your Issue Proposal, you organized your preexisting knowledge on your issue and sketched a plan for research. You then compiled several sources and summarized their contents for your Annotated Bibliography. For this paper, you will map the controversy surrounding your issue by describing its history and summarizing at least three different positions on the issue—all from a completely neutral point of view.

Before people can make an informed decision on a controversial issue, they must know the history of the controversy and the range of positions available. Publications often meet this need by providing a neutral, unbiased description of an issue's history and the main arguments made on all sides (e.g., *The New York Times's* "Times Topics" section or *Slate's* "Explainer" section). Imagine you are writing such an overview of your issue for a UTA student publication that offers analysis and commentary about politics, news, and culture.

Invention (i.e., discovering what you're going to say in this paper)

1. Your audience of UTA students will want to know some background information on your issue, so draft answers to the following questions:

   - What caused the issue?
   - What prompted past and present interest in it?
   - Who is interested in the issue and why?

2. Your audience will also want to know the current, major positions on the issue, so reflect on the titles in your Annotated Bibliography, draft descriptions of 3-5 different positions, and identify which articles in your bibliography advocate the positions you've described.

3. Now that you've drafted descriptions of the background and major positions on your issue, draft a more detailed description of one position:

   - What are the main claims of those who advocate this position?
   - What reasons do they provide for those claims?
   - What evidence do they use to support their reasons?
   - What assumptions underlie their arguments?

Support your description by summarizing and analyzing at least one source from your Annotated Bibliography that advocates this position.

4. Repeat step 3 with a second position, again supporting your description by summarizing and analyzing at least one source from your Annotated Bibliography. Additionally, you should highlight the relationship between the two positions you've described by answering the following questions:

   - What are the points of intersection and diversion?
   - On what points do advocates of these positions agree, and on what points do they disagree?
   - What are the reasons for disagreement?

5. Repeat step 3 with all the remaining positions you plan to describe, always including a summary and analysis of at least one source from your Annotated Bibliography. Also, for every new position you introduce, explain its relationship to the previous positions you've described. Highlight points of intersection and diversion, describe points of agreement and disagreement, and explain the reasons disagreements exist.

6. Think about how you're going to come across to UTA students as a person of good character, good sense, and good will. Here are some tips:

- Describe the most significant positions across the entire field of the controversy; don't simply describe those positions that cluster around the position you favor.
- Summarize sources fairly and analyze them carefully. Accurately identify their main claims, supporting reasons and evidence, and implicit assumptions.
- Maintain neutrality. The time will come for you to take a stand on the issue, but don't do it now. Advocates of the positions you describe should feel that you have represented their views and arguments fairly, and your readers should finish your paper without any idea of where you stand on the issue.

7. Think about the values and emotions that you share with fellow UTA students and consider how you might appeal to them. Here are some tips:

- Appeal to readers' desire for information by presenting clear, well-organized, well-supported summaries that show you've read widely and closely and have developed a deep understanding of positions ranging across the entire field of the controversy.
- Appeal to readers' sense of fairness by providing truly unbiased descriptions of all positions/arguments.
- Draw on the lessons of Chapter Nine in *They Say/I Say* by mixing standard written English with "the kinds of expressions and turns of phrase that you use every day when conversing with family and friends" (115). Because you're writing for publication and for readers you don't know, you should adopt a more formal style and tone than in your first paper. This does not mean, however, that you need to abandon your unique ways of expressing yourself.

Arrangement (i.e., organizing what you're going to say in this paper)

You'll want to organize your paper in the manner you think will prove most effective with your audience of UTA students, but here are some general guidelines:

- Heed the lesson of Ch. 1 in *They Say/I Say:* "To give your writing the most important thing of all—namely, a point—a writer needs to indicate clearly not only his or her thesis, but also what larger conversation that thesis is responding to" (18). As was the case with your first paper, the conversation you're responding to is the one surrounding the issue you've selected. Indicate at the beginning of your paper that you're writing in response to that conversation, and then state a thesis in which you promise to describe the most significant positions on your issue.
- Also mind the lesson of Ch. 7 in *They Say/I Say:* "Regardless of how interesting a topic may be to you as a writer, readers always need to know what is at stake in a text and why they should care. . . . Rather than assume that audiences will know why their claims matter, all writers need to answer the 'so what?' and 'who cares?' questions up front" (88-89). Unlike

your first paper, this one is unsolicited, which means you must work harder to demonstrate why your issue matters and to attract readers. Providing compelling answers to the "so what?" and "who cares?" questions is crucial.

- However you arrange the body of your paper, make sure you answer fully and in detail all the questions/requests in the Invention section of this prompt.

Style (i.e., choosing the appropriate language for your paper)

You're writing for a highly specific audience, so avoid writing to some vague, generalized audience. When reading your paper, it should be obvious that you're writing to fellow UTA students.

Heed the lesson of Ch. 9 in *They Say/I Say* and mix standard written English with "the kinds of expressions and turns of phrase that you use every day when conversing with family and friends" (115). The more important lesson of that chapter is "that your judgments about the appropriate language for the situation should always take into account your likely audience and your purpose in writing" (121). As mentioned earlier, your style should be more formal than in your first paper, but this does not mean you should write in a pretentious style that is not your own.

All readers appreciate coherent, unified paragraphs, so your paragraphs should include a topic sentence that clearly states the main idea of the paragraph and supporting sentences that cluster around the main idea without detours.

Document your sources properly according to MLA style. Consult *The Scott, Foresman Writer* for instructions on how to format in-text citations and Works Cited entries.

Proofread carefully; avoid errors in grammar, spelling, punctuation, and mechanics. Use *The Scott, Foresman Writer* for questions you have regarding style.

Other Requirements

Your paper should be no longer than five pages—anything beyond that length will be considered a failure to adhere to one of the assignment's basic requirements. It should be double-spaced, typed in Times New Roman font, with 12-point character size and one-inch margins all the way around.

Your first submission is due at the beginning of class on _____, and you should think of it as a final draft—something that is ready for publication. If your first submission does not meet every requirement of this assignment sheet, I will return it to you and count it as late. Both your first and final submissions must be turned in on time—you will be docked a full letter grade for each day either is late.

Peer reviews are due _____.

Final drafts are due _____.

Evaluation Criteria

Final Draft:
- Includes a snappy title that catches the reader's attention and indicates the topic and argument.
- Identifies an arguable/contestable issue appropriate to the assignment.
- Includes a specific, detailed thesis about the history of the issue and the available range of positions on the issue.
- Answers the "so what" and "who cares" questions by explaining why the argument is significant and to whom.
- Provides background about the issue that provides a context for understanding the range of positions on the issue.
- Identifies, summarizes, and analyzes at least three positions on the issue.
- Supports analysis with carefully selected, well-developed examples from multiple sources.
- Maintains neutrality by describing each position fairly.
- Uses sources effectively and integrates them smoothly, paraphrasing and occasionally directly quoting authorities to help substantiate or support points.
- Offers proper attribution to each source cited via in-text parenthetical citation and a correctly formatted Works Cited page.
- Comes across as a credible writer, and appeals to the values and emotions of the audience.
- Develops a seamless, coherent, and well-organized argument.
- Sentences are lively, engaging, and relatively error free.
- Essay is 5 pages in MLA Style with Works Cited in 12 point Times New Roman font with 1-inch margins.

Writing Process:
- Submitted complete drafts on time. Drafting process shows evidence of revision of content and style.
- Provided adequate help to peers during peer review.

SAMPLE MAPPING THE ISSUE

Being a published author or artist doesn't mean what it used to. One cannot simply say "I wrote that *book*" or "I made that *painting*." The explosion of technology now causes one to instead say, "I came up with that *text*" or "I manipulated that *graphic image*" or "I uploaded that clip to YouTube and downloaded a remixed song off of Limewire to go with it." The internet's widespread, user-friendly interface that allows mass participation in information sharing, creativity, and idea exchange has brought a significantly larger demographic into the conversation of intellectual property and what constitutes publication and ownership. The transition of tangible media, like magazines and DVDs, to internet sites has expanded the definition of what copyright means. As a result, personal blogs, clothing, online books, and even pornography have become new and crucial elements in the world of art and technology distribution. In this paper I will review three main positions on the issue of copyright in the internet age. First, there are those who find themselves tangled between the two extremes of strict, exclusive ownership and absolute free sharing. With the expansion of creative and web-based industries, this first group is becoming less concerned with exclusivity and more concerned with the rights of the public domain. Second, there are those who remain adamant about having strict ownership of their ideas and creations and are uneasy with technology's ability to manipulate creative works and potentially copy someone's ideas. These people appeal to the courts and stamp trademarks all over their work. Third are those who are adamant about not having any limits; they embrace technology as a means of creating a free-share environment where everyone can use published works as they please with no regards to ownership or profitability.

Since 2008, fashion has significantly permeated the conversation on legal protection because it is tied to design as well as retail, consumerism, and direct public involvement. Thus, restrictions on fashion often fall between the extremes of protecting and sharing intellectual property, as clothing merges intellectual creative design with material sale items. Johanna Blakeley recently published an article on *Design Observer* entitled "The Costs of Ownership: Why Copyright Protection Will Hurt the Fashion Industry" in response to a new bill, The Innovative Design Protection and Piracy Prevention Act, which places strict copyright on fashion. Blakely states that while the bill will stimulate creativity and provide protection to some extent, it will hurt the fashion industry artistically and economically, as well as prove difficult to implement. Because fashion is utilitarian, it is difficult to classify clothing designs as entirely unique and creative. Here, fashion is a perfect example of an industry that is unlikely to ever set copyright limitations, be they strict or relaxed, based on its wide scope. At the very least, the industry remains unsure of how to implement a clear policy on copyright and is as unsure of what needs to be protected as any beginner artist would be. Writers like Blakely sympathize with designers, who work in an industry constantly under pressure to innovate. Blakely herself tends to be in favor of the freedom to copy designs, but she (like the fashion industry) remains in limbo on what the exact limitations ought to be, siding with the vast majority of those unsure of where to settle on the intellectual copyright spectrum.

The fashion industry is becoming a major participant in the copyright conversation. At the same time, this industry that thrives on people wearing clothes has a lot in common with an industry that thrives on people removing their clothes. In *The New York Times*, writers Kal Raustiala and Chris Sprigman contributed a piece earlier this year to the *Freakonomics* section about copyrighting pornography. Their argument mirrors that of Blakely's in that they find it difficult to pinpoint the limits of copyright when the product is one of direct use: "Pornography is, in large part, a utilitarian product, and for most consumers, the purpose for which it is employed is served just as well by a five-minute porn-tube clip" (Raustiala 1). The main concern is that sites like YouTube and its sub-site YouPorn are hurting the industry because they allow people to view for free the same clips once only available for purchase. Since these clips still "get the job done," producers worry that DVD sales will decrease and paid-subscriptions websites will close; however, the clips can also serve as ads for high-quality porn that continue to generate revenue. Though they comfortably accept the likelihood of coexistence for paid websites no matter what, the limits of copyright, again, remain obscure, especially for the producers. The permeation of intellectual copyright into industries like fashion and porn, which were once minor issues for them, reinforces the difficulty of placing copyright within solid boundaries. These industries struggle with legally explaining their policies under the umbrella of technology, but have managed to keep a balanced outlook that attempts to equally serve the artist and the public.

Still, not everyone is comfortable with leaving the limits of copyright obscure and open for interpretation, nor is everyone interested in a balance between maker and user. These people believe in the letter of the law as a defender of copyright, limiting both access and distribution for creative works. Instead of considering consumers, attention is focused on the creator's exclusive ownership rights. Mark Helprin sides with this firmer stance in *The New York Times* in a 2007 opinion piece, "A Great Idea Lives Forever. Shouldn't Its Copyright?" He argues that copyright should be permanently passed on like an inheritance, even after the creator's death. Those who are pro-strict-copyright would side with Helprin because they are most concerned with attaching a name to a copyright, much like a legacy. Indeed, like money, Helprin believes copyright is an exclusive, tangible right that cannot be easily taken away or manipulated into "public property," much in the ways Blakely and Raustiala and Sprigman argue for public domain to override the need for extreme ownership. While these writers see and support the benefits that an average consumer would receive from utilitarian items not restricted by copyright, Helprin is more focused on declaring exclusivity and legal ownership principally more important than public access. All three authors recognize the importance of intellectual property, but the outlook here does not endorse the practical benefits of distribution and consumption.

Regardless of his views, Helprin could seemingly have a reasonable discussion and come to terms with someone like Johanna Blakely, as they sympathize with the effort an artist puts into his/her work and the recognition it deserves. However, Helprin would become exceedingly frustrated with someone like Cory Doctorow, who is notorious for blogging and speaking about technology in the public domain. Unlike Helprin's claim of copyright being a crucial element in creativity, Doctorow sides completely with the consumer and their right to access pretty much anything. Like other internet-savvy writers looking to get their work noticed rather than legally manufactured, Doctorow often makes his own works available through a Creative Commons license. Though there are different levels of Creative Commons licensing (depending to what limit people will allow others to use their work), the willingness to use one at all indicates the championing of free distribution. An audio file entitled "Giving it Away" features a reading from Cory Doctorow's *Forbes* article in 2006 where he talks about a book he "publishes" as an ebook as well as a downloadable audio file. This action basically turns his work into a public object, less tangible than a book and harder to pinpoint for copyright. Unlike the writers of the articles on fashion, porn, and books combined, Doctorow claims there is no empirical way to prove that stripping copyright hurts an artist financially: instead, because it costs nothing to put out a free text, only positive reinforcement is likely to remain (increased sales, a wider readership, and the ability to translate, etc.) Indeed, artists who are new to the industry and do not have the means to afford "professional" publishing often do not pay as much attention to copyright. Doctorow sides with Blakely and Raustiala and Sprigman with the concern of reaching an audience as a key reason to loosening the reins on copyright laws, yet he neglects to mention any importance in protecting original intellectual ideas. Certainly, this reading is quite the opposite of Helprin's *New York Times* piece in that Doctorow would never allow legal mediation to dictate how he distributes material. So whether the limits of copyright matter or not, even the disregard for copyright is an argument in itself. More and more artists challenge their boundaries, and the average internet user must question how they access, share, and reproduce everyday internet content.

Works Cited

Blakely, Johanna. "The Costs of Ownership: Why Copyright Protection Will Hurt the Fashion Industry." *Design Observer.* 19 Aug 2010. Web. 12 Oct 2010.

Doctorow, Cory. "Giving it Away." *Content: Selected Essays on Technology, Creativity, Copyright and the Future of the Future,* read by Jan Rubak. mp3 audio file: *Internet Archive.* Web. 2 Nov 2010.

Helprin, Mark. "A Great Idea Lives Forever. Shouldn't Its Copyright?" *The New York Times.* 20 May 2007. Web. 2 Nov 2010.

Raustiala, Kal and Sprigman, Chris. "Copyrighting Porn: A Guest Post." *The New York Times.* 5 May 2010. Web. 2 Nov 2010.

Paper 3 – Researched Position Paper
English 1302: Rhetoric and Composition II

THE RHETORICAL SITUATION

For your Issue Proposal, you organized your preexisting knowledge on your issue and sketched a plan for research. You then compiled several sources and summarized their contents for your Annotated Bibliography. In your Mapping the Issue paper, you traced the controversy surrounding your issue by describing its history and summarizing the major positions on it. Now—finally—it is time for you to have your say on the issue.

For this paper, you will advocate a position on your issue with a well-supported argument written for an audience that you select.

Invention (i.e., discovering what you're going to say in this paper)

1. Choose a *specific* audience (no "American people" or "people interested in my topic") for your paper. Your audience should be a person, group, organization, website, publication, etc. named by a proper noun (i.e., you have to capitalize it) and with an address (physical or electronic) to which you could send your paper.

Make sure you investigate the characteristics and values of your audience.

2. Your audience likely will want to know immediately both the conversation you're responding to and your own position. Furthermore, they will want to know that you are *advancing* the conversation, turning it in a new direction, rather than just repeating another writer's argument. Consult Ch. 4 in *They Say/I Say* for tips on how to formulate your claim as a response to what someone else has written.

3. Your audience certainly will expect you to support your claim with good reasons, so attach as many reasons as you think necessary. To determine whether your reasons are "good," draw out the implicit warrant in each claim+reason, and then consider whether your audience will consent to those warrants. If so, then you've probably selected good reasons. If not, then you may need to select reasons that appeal more effectively to your audience's values. Alternatively, you may try to persuade your audience to grant your warrants.

4. For each of your reasons, provide sufficient evidence that your reasons are true. Your personal experiences, observations, and reasoning count as evidence, but you should also draw extensively on outside sources for evidence to support your reasons.

5. Address at least one extended counterargument to some part of your argument. You may choose a hypothetical naysayer or a real opponent found in an outside source. Make sure you:

   - name and describe your opponent(s).
   - describe your opponent's position fairly and accurately.
   - make any necessary concessions, i.e., identify areas of agreement between you and your opponent.
   - respond with a well-considered and reasonable rebuttal.

Pay special attention to Ch. 6 in *They Say/I Say* for instruction in how to deal effectively with counterarguments.

6. Think about how you're going to come across to your audience as a person of good character, good sense, and good will. Here are some tips:

   • Know what you're talking about. Find ample outside sources, read extensively on your topic, and use information from sources to provide sufficient evidence for your reasons.
   • Show regard for your readers. Try to come across as approachable and thoughtful, not arrogant or insensitive.
   • Treat skeptical readers with respect—don't ignore or demean their opinions just because they expect more proof.
   • Be careful and meticulous in your writing, not sloppy or disorganized.

7. Think about the values and emotions that you share with your audience and consider how you might appeal to them. Here are some tips:

   • Remember the advice of Ch. 9 in *They Say/I Say:* "your judgments about the appropriate language for the situation should always take into account your likely audience and your purpose in writing" (121). Because you are choosing your audience, it's up to you to determine the most effective style for your paper.
   • Try to evoke emotions (sympathy, outrage, anger, delight, awe, horror, etc.) in your audience that make your paper more moving.
   • Try to evoke sensations (seeing, hearing, touching, tasting, smelling) in your audience that make your writing vivid and help readers experience things imaginatively.
   • Appeal to values (freedom, justice, tolerance, fairness, equality, etc.) that you share with your audience.

Arrangement (i.e., organizing what you're going to say in this paper)

You'll want to organize your paper in the manner you think will prove most effective with your audience, but here are some general guidelines:

   • Heed the lesson of Ch. 1 in *They Say/I Say:* "To give your writing the most important thing of all—namely, a point—a writer needs to indicate clearly not only his or her thesis, but also what larger conversation that thesis is responding to" (18). As has been the case with all your papers, the conversation you're responding to is the one surrounding the issue you've selected. Indicate at the beginning of your paper that you're writing in response to that conversation, and then state a thesis that includes your claim and reasons.
   • Also mind the lesson of Ch. 7 in *They Say/I Say:* "Regardless of how interesting a topic may be to you as a writer, readers always need to know what is at stake in a text and why they should care. . . . Rather than assume that audiences will know why their claims matter, all writers need to answer the 'so what?' and 'who cares?' questions up front" (88-89). Like your last paper, this piece is unsolicited, which means you must work hard to demonstrate why your issue matters and to attract readers. Providing compelling answers to the "so what?" and "who cares?" questions is crucial.
   • However you arrange the body of your paper, make sure you include all the information requested in the Invention section of this prompt.

Style (i.e., choosing the appropriate language for your paper)

You're writing for a highly specific audience, so avoid writing to some vague, generalized reader. When reading your paper, it should be obvious that you're writing to the audience you've identified.

All readers appreciate coherent, unified paragraphs, so your paragraphs should include a topic sentence that clearly states the main idea of the paragraph and supporting sentences that cluster around the main idea without detours.

Document your sources properly according to MLA style. Consult *The Scott, Foresman Writer* for instructions on how to format in-text citations and Works Cited entries.

Proofread carefully; avoid errors in grammar, spelling, punctuation, and mechanics. Use *The Scott, Foresman Writer* for questions you have regarding style.

Other Requirements

Your paper should be **5-10 pages**—anything shorter or longer will be considered a failure to adhere to one of the assignment's basic requirements. It should be double-spaced, typed in Times New Roman font, with 12-point character size and one-inch margins all the way around.

Your first submission is due at the beginning of class on _____, and you should think of it as a final draft—something that is ready to be read by your intended audience. If your first submission does not meet every requirement of this assignment sheet, I will return it to you and count it as late. Both your first and final submissions must be turned in on time—you will be docked a full letter grade for each day either is late.

Peer reviews are due _____.

Final drafts are due _____.

Evaluation Criteria

Final Draft:
- Includes a snappy title that catches the reader's attention and indicates the topic and argument.
- Identifies an arguable/contestable issue appropriate to the assignment.
- Addresses a specific audience.
- Includes a contestable, specific, detailed claim that advances the conversation about the topic.
- Provides well-developed reasons to support the claim.
- Answers the "so what" and "who cares" questions by explaining why the argument is significant and to whom.
- Supports reasons with carefully selected, well-developed examples from multiple sources.
- Anticipates counterarguments, considers them carefully, and responds to them fairly, conceding where others are right.

- Uses sources effectively and integrates them smoothly, paraphrasing and occasionally directly quoting authorities to help substantiate or support points.
- Offers proper attribution to each source cited via in-text parenthetical citation and a correctly formatted Works Cited page.
- Comes across as a credible writer, and appeals to the values and emotions of the audience.
- Develops a seamless, coherent, and well-organized argument.
- Sentences are lively, engaging, and relatively error free.
- Essay is 5-10 pages in MLA Style with Works Cited in 12pt. Times New Roman font with 1-inch margins.

Writing Process:
- Submitted complete drafts on time. Drafting process shows evidence of revision of content and style.
- Provided adequate help to peers during peer review.

SAMPLE RESEARCHED POSITION PAPER

The website *Jezebel* is bookmarked on my computer for a reason. There are few other websites that I can regularly rely on for coverage that is meaningful to me, delivered in the form of entertaining and intelligent commentary on everything from women's health issues to current events. As the website manifesto states, "we wanted to make the sort of women's magazine we'd want to read," and I would assert that while accomplishing that goal, the creators have also created a web-magazine that I, and many others like me, *love* to read. It is precisely my admiration for *Jezebel* that makes me concerned about the role it, along with the rest of mass media, may play in influencing young women.

Like many *Jezebel* readers, I have followed the site's coverage of the extensive use of photo manipulation in the regular series, "Photoshop of Horrors." The series' targets—popular women's magazines' celebrity covers and clothing retailers' fashion advertisements—are harrowing to say the least. In addition to following the disturbing examples of image manipulation, I also read contributors' commentary on the media's employment of photo manipulation, specifically Jenna Sauers' "Regulating Photoshop: A Hazy Proposition, Not a Solution" and Dodai Stewart's "Photoshop Legislation Won't Fix the Real Problem." I find their opinions to be well-considered, balanced, and enlightening. However, after carefully weighing the positions on whether Photoshop should be banned, permitted with restrictions, or unconditionally allowed, I must say I do not find the "real" problem to lie with the practice of image manipulation at all. Instead, I center the blame on a misplaced acceptance, not of the super-skinny body ideals that *Jezebel* writers claim are the source of the problem, but with young women's misplaced trust in mass media outlets, specifically women's magazines, that, knowingly or not, set these unattainable beauty standards while continually reinforcing a reliance on the opinions and standards that they create for wide consumption. As a loyal reader of *Jezebel*, I include it in this category. Rather than merely altering the media's content to either exclude Photoshopped images or include a wider variety of models, I posit that women's magazines should shift their content away from promotion of celebrity-obsession, product coveting, and belief in useless affirmations. These lady-mag staples promote low self-esteem in readers and are the true problem in the Photoshop debate.

Stewart writes in her article that "although extensive Photoshop is detrimental . . . the real issue is that what we consider 'attractive' has also become, for the most part, unattainable." Stewart's position, while effectively identifying what many would agree is the root of the problem behind the Photoshop controversy, does not plumb the subject deeply enough to expose the overarching role of media outlets in establishing body-image ideals. The "ideal woman" stereotype is not only promoted visually in magazines, but established again and again in articles such as "Your Breasts: An Intimate Q&A on What's Normal and What's Not" (*Glamour* July 2010), "Curb Your Cravings! Without Feeding Your Face" (*Cosmopolitan* March 2010), and "Forget the Face Lift! Remove Wrinkles Without the Knife" (*Elle* March 2010). Articles such as these encourage insecurities in readers, which are then merely reinforced with digitally enhanced images of women with no apparent excess body fat, wrinkles, and perfect proportions. If women's magazines shifted away from such inane content as this, the images, which are intended to support the articles' impact, are sure to follow.

It is easy to understand why an individual who is employed by a women's media outlet would not want to identify themselves as a possible culprit of the very practice that they are condemning. *Jezebel* attempts to distance itself from competing media outlets, such as *Glamour, Cosmopolitan*, or *Elle*, by stated in its mission statement that its goal is to "reverse the cycle . . .

perpetuated by the women's media." By including frank discussions on topics such as eating disorders, gay rights issues, and racial concerns, I would agree that *Jezebel* has broken the mold. However, for every step forward that *Jezebel* makes in releasing such progressive articles, two backward steps are made when regular features such as "Fashion GoodBadandUgly," "Celebrity DirtBag," "Celebrity SnapJudgement," and "This Week In Tabloids" are published. Famously decrying photo retouching may be in keeping with *Jezebel*'s overall mission, but I fail to see how the site's own articles do not reinforce many of the same image ideals and celebrity worship that leads to the demand for Photoshop in the first place. Writer Amanda Fortini clearly agrees when she notes what she believes is the reason *Jezebel* has made Photoshop demonization its signature platform against women's media in her article, "In Defense of Photoshop: Why Retouching Isn't As Evil As Everyone Thinks":

> Retouched images . . . spike page views, and not because of an attentive desire on the part   of readers to protect vulnerable teens. The endless cavalcade of before-and-after shots is   an outgrowth of the voyeurism, gossipmongering, and schadenfreude that fuel our   celebrity industrial complex.

Observations such as these support the idea that rather than "revers[ing] the cycle" *Jezebel* is perpetuating the cycle. The site's writers like Sauers and Stewart are correct that Photoshop should not be the scapegoat for a clear lack of appropriate body image ideals, but women's magazines should not overlook the negative role that they play in all of this by exercising the power to declare what an appropriate body image ideal is in the first place.

In fact, studies have proven that mass media plays a much larger role in perpetuating negative body images than the images themselves. Recently, the University of Missouri-Columbia released the results of a study that found viewing pictures in women's magazines for only three minutes affected all women negatively regardless of their "size, shape, height or age" (Bortz). Based on this data, it is logical to assume, then, that adverse affects were recorded in even the thinnest of the experimental group. Therefore, can simply demanding diversity in magazines when it comes to different shapes and sizes be considered a viable option to alleviate the underlying problem *Jezebel* claims is at the roots of the Photoshop debate? It is logical to assume that no matter the size or shape of the women in the magazine, they will still have professionally executed hair, makeup, wardrobe, lighting, and, yes, perhaps even Photoshop to improve their appearance; this will only result in a similar negative effect on viewers. Rather than undertaking the mammoth task of reversing every bit of conditioning that the mass media has pushed upon us by, as Stewart says, "train[ing] ourselves not to believe that thinner is better," it is more feasible to simply close the magazine and refuse to support an industry whose very survival depends on establishing viewer dependence on its hype. The University of Missouri-Columbia study came to a similar conclusion: "the majority of women would benefit from interventions aimed at decreasing the effects of the media, regardless of weight . . . reducing the acceptance of mass media images of women and trying to stop the social comparison process is important for helping all women." As we can see, it is not the images themselves that are negatively affecting the women of the world, but the fact that they rely on magazines to tell them what to think.

Recently, Jessica Coen argued in the article "Why You Must See Untouched Images, and Why You Must See Them Repeatedly" that *Jezebel's* continuing coverage of digitally manipulated photos is motivated by the need to defend impressionable minds: "[E]very day a young woman somewhere sees one of these overly polished pictures for the first time . . . and has no idea that they're not real . . . And maybe she doesn't have someone in her life to point out that this is complete and utter bullshit." Coen is absolutely right—in fact, we as Americans are bombarded by up to *40,000 images a day,* and without the proper education about "how our Jen Aniston sausage gets made," the public will continue to blindly absorb these images as photo reality (Bortz). However, I question how practical it is to assume that there remains a significant portion of the American population that has absolutely no inkling that images are retouched before put in magazines. In our tech-savvy culture, where children have access to the copious amounts of information that the internet brings into our households daily, I would be very interested in some actual studies being done on the effectiveness of *Jezebel's* anti-Photoshop campaign. Logically, one would look to the website's own readers for evidence. The comment that I find the most interesting is from reader *lostinalunchbox:* "I stopped hating on myself in my mid-twenties, when I stopped reading the ladies mags and I stopped watching TV. Coincidence? I think not." This commentator cites a link between a higher self-esteem and simply lowering the number of images she is exposed to daily, rather than obtaining any sort of knowledge about the widespread use of image manipulation. Granted, shutting oneself off from much of media's influence, as this reader has done, is an unreal expectation for the majority of women, but her post is evidence that avoidance of the female ideals perpetuated in magazine pages actually results in a higher self-esteem. Just imagine if these magazines used their widespread influence to promote healthy body image and self-acceptance as well as replacing the "Must-Haves" with more attainable and productive goals for women to aspire to than owning this season's Manolos.

In response to the pressure placed upon them by individuals and others who are of the same mindset as *Jezebel,* women's magazines have attempted to include a wider variety of body types and races. Anna Wintour, the editor-in-chief of American *Vogue,* has made statements assuring the public that her magazine does not make use of Photoshop to make their models look thinner, only to erase small imperfections, and that *Vogue's* editors have "made a commitment to feature a wider variety of body types" (Baldwin). To follow through, American *Vogue* released a "Shape Issue" featuring plus-size models, and *Vogue Italia* now features a website devoted to plus-size fashion and black models, *Vogue Curvy* and *Vogue Black* (Sulmers). Sure, this is a step in the direction that Photoshop detractors call for, but they seem to have been merely intended to quiet the critics rather than to address a real need for a variety of body image ideals. As plus-size model Whitney Thompson said, "I applaud *Vogue* for having a shape issue, but screw *Vogue* for not having shapes in every issue" (Sulmers). By not including these women in the mainstream editions of the magazines, but reserving space for them sandwiched between ads featuring the typical skinny, white models, *Vogue* practically acknowledges its own guilt. To make matters worse, these "special edition" magazines are used to attract publicity, an observation supported by *Jezebel's* Dodai Stewart in her article "*Italian Vogue's* All Black Issue: A Guided Tour," when she comments that efforts like these are "gimmick[s]" and "stunt[s]." Stewart's claim harks back to Fortini's own opinion that when *Jezebel* draws attention to the "Photoshop of Horrors" it is little more than a stunt itself. *Jezebel* got upwards of 10 million monthly views in 2007; now, three years later, imagine how many individuals have been introduced to the site based on the hype that its Photoshop coverage has received. To reiterate my earlier point, this cycle is seemingly perpetuating itself. It is in mass media's best interest to keep this debate raging in order to ensure the clicks on the laptop and the turning of the magazine pages. I suggest that to stop the madness, the public should demand that the media alter their message to promote readership and articles that encourage high self-esteem.

As I stated earlier, I am a fan of *Jezebel.* I am critical of it only because I am critical of every message I ingest. I do not doubt that this is precisely the sort of vigilance that the site would advocate. I care about this matter because I, as a young woman, am not excluded from the impact of this debate. However, it troubles me that with all of the knowledge that I have on the widespread use of image manipulation as well as the lack of diversity in magazines I am still negatively affected by the plethora of images that I see every day. I still do not think that I match up to the ideal that our culture advocates. I, like *lostinalunchbox*, gave up years ago on magazines that made me feel less-than every time I turned a page. However, I am more disappointed that *Jezebel*, which claims to be essentially the anti-women's magazine, resembles its foes more and more every day.

I hope that *Jezebel* will consider its original manifesto and whether it has steadfastly stuck to the original goals set forth. The site has a unique readership, one that could in fact influence the way this debate pans out, but in order for this to occur the finger-pointing needs to turn away from Photoshop or the lack of diversity in magazines and be aimed at the mirror.

Works Cited

Bortz, Fred. *ScienceBlog*. "Sexy Women Make Everyone Feel Bad." 6 Nov. 2008. Web. 29 Nov. 2010

Coen, Jessica. *Jezebel*. Gawker Media, 21 May 2007. Web. 30 Nov. 2010.

Fortini, Amanda. "In Defense of Photoshop: Why Retouching Isn't As Evil As Everyone Thinks." *The Cut: New York Fashion*, 29 Aug. 2010. Web. 2 Nov. 2010.

Moss, Hilary. "Anna Wintour: Vogue Doesn't Photoshop Girls To Make Them Look Thinner." *Huffington Post*. 25 Mar. 2010. Web. 30 Nov. 2010.

Sauers, Jenna. "Italian Vogue's 'All Black' Issue: A Guided Tour." *Jezebel*. 14 July 2008. Web. 15 Nov. 2010

Sauers, Jenna. "Regulating Photoshop: A Hazy Proposition, Not a Solution." *Jezebel*. 26 July 2010. Web. 2 Nov. 2010.

Stewart, Dodai. "Photoshop Legislation Won't Fix the Real Problem." *Jezebel*, 21 Sept. 2010. Web. 2 Nov. 2010.

Sulmers, Claire. "Vogue Italia launches Black and Plus-Size Sites." *Black Voices*. 25 February 2010. Web. 30 November 2010.

University of Missouri-Columbia. "Women Of All Sizes Feel Badly About Their Bodies After Seeing Models." *ScienceDaily* 27 March 2007. 30 November 2010. Web.

A Perspective on Argument

After studying this chapter, you will be able to:

LO1 Identify and explain your own perspective on argument. (p. 4)

LO2 Define the basic features of argument. (p. 5)

LO3 Describe the characteristics of traditional and consensual argument. (p. 6)

LO4 Identify visual arguments. (p. 8)

LO5 Describe the conditions of a successful argument and an unsuccessful argument. (pp. 11, 14)

LO6 Define what constitutes an arguable issue in the 21st century. (pp. 16, 18, 26)

Y ou are engaged in argument, whether you realize it or not, nearly every day. Argument deals with *issues*, ideas or topics that have not yet been settled, that invite two or more differing opinions, and that are consequently subject to question, debate, or negotiation. Pick up today's newspaper or a current newsmagazine and read the headlines to find current examples of societal issues such as these: What should be done to reduce global warming? Should the Internet be censored? To what extent should one government participate in solving the problems of other governments? How should youthful offenders be punished? Should public officials be held to higher ethical standards than everyone else? Alternatively, think of examples of issues closer to your daily experience at school: Why are you going to college? What close relationships should you form, and how will they affect your life? Which is the more important consideration in selecting a major: finding a job, or interest in the subject? How can one minimize the frustrations caused by limited campus facilities? Is it good or bad policy to go to school and work at the same time? How much educational debt should you undertake?

It is undeniable that we are constantly confronted with issues. But why do we care about them? Or, more to the point, how do we figure out *whether* or *why* we care? To a great extent, figuring out why we care about an argument involves figuring out how an argument works. How do we go from identifying a particular issue to figuring out our own feelings, our own stake, to creating a coherent argument of our own about the issue? Whatever the issue, every argument begins with what our sense of what is important to us, what *matters*. Maybe it resonates with a particular experience we have had in our personal life. Perhaps it raises questions or ideas we find intellectually engaging. For any issue, we need to begin with a very simple question: why do I care?

To answer this question, we need to dig a bit into our own personal assumptions and experiences. Take, for example, the question "should the Internet be censored?" If we wanted to better understand the stakes involved in this issue, a useful starting point would be to reflect upon our own experience with online technology. What are the particular ways I use online technologies? Do they help me communicate with people in ways that were not possible before? What new kinds of images, ideas, or information do they make available, and why is such material important? Are there, conversely, any dangers or downsides to the ways I use these technologies? Do these new forms of communication entail any threat to my personal privacy? Doing this kind of personal inventory is an essential first step in figuring out our views on the more formal questions issue present. To figure out our perspective on a given issue, we must first find the unspoken ideas and values that shape this perspective.

Whether they seem remote or close to you, all of these issues are related to larger issues that have engaged human thought for centuries. In fact, all of the really important issues—those that address life and death, the quality of life, ways and means, war and peace, the individual and society, the environment, and others like them—are discussed, debated, and negotiated everywhere in the world again and again. There are usually no simple or obvious positions to take on such important issues. Still, the positions we do take *on* them and, ultimately, the decisions and actions we take in regard *to* them can affect our lives in significant ways. In democratic societies, individuals are expected to engage in effective argument on issues of broad concern. They are also expected to make moral judgments and to evaluate the decisions and ideas that emerge from argument. Equally, they are expected to take actions based on these judgments and evaluations—to vote, to serve on a jury, to assent to or protest a policy, and so on.

The purpose of this book is to help you participate in two types of activities: the evaluation of arguments you encounter and the formulation of arguments of your own. The book is organized in parts, and each part will help you become a more effective participant in the arguments that affect your life.

3

What Is Your Current Perspective on Argument?

What do you think about when you see the word *argument?* It is best to begin the study of any new subject by thinking about what you already know. You can then use what you know to learn more, which is the way all of us acquire new knowledge. See the short list of five actual student responses describing some of their initial views about argument provided here. Check the responses that match your own, and add others if you like.

_____ 1. Argument attempts to resolve issues between two or more parties.
_____ 2. Argument is rational disagreement, but it can get emotional.
_____ 3. Argument can result in agreement or compromise.
_____ 4. Argument is angry people yelling at each other.
_____ 5. Argument is standing up for your ideas, defending them, and minimizing the opposition by being persuasive.

The responses in the list, with the exception of response 4, "angry people yelling at each other," are consistent with the approach to argument that appears in this book. We omit response 4 because no argument is effective if people stop listening, stop thinking, and engage in vocal fighting. "Yes, it is!"–"No, it isn't!" accompanied by a fist pounding on the table gets people nowhere.

What would happen if a society were to outlaw all forms of argument? In effect, under the law, all individuals are to share the same views, and there is to be no disagreement. Here are some student responses to the question. With which descriptions do you agree?

_____ 1. Everyone would think the same thing.
_____ 2. There would not be any progress.
_____ 3. There would be no new knowledge.
_____ 4. Life would be boring.

A key idea in this book is that argument is literally to be found everywhere[1] and that without it, we would have the stagnant society suggested in these student responses. You will become more aware of argument as it impacts your life if you consider the notion that argument can be found in virtually any context in which human beings interact and hold divergent views about topics that are at issue—from personal blogs to presidential debates, advertisements to newspaper op-eds, text-messages to Facebook posts. Further, argument can appear in a variety of forms: it can be written, spoken, sung, or chanted, and it can be read, heard, or observed in pictures that are either still or moving. Argument can be explicit, with a clear purpose and position, as in an advertisement for a soft drink

---

[1]I am indebted to Wayne Brockriede for this observation and for some of the other ideas in this chapter. See his article "Where Is Argument?" *Journal of the American Forensic Association* 11 (1975): 179–82.

or a brand of blue jeans; or it can be implicit, communicating a more subtle position on an issue that the audience has to think about and figure out, as in some of the photographs taken in war zones. Most issues invite a spectrum of perspectives and views for individuals to hold. Few issues are black and white, nor can most issues be viewed in pro and con terms anymore. Keep these complexities in mind as we now attempt to define argument and describe why it is important to study it and learn to argue well.

A Definition of Argument

Since the classical era, argument theorists have defined and described argument in different ways. Whatever their differences, though, these definitions all share one crucial assumption: argument always involves an attempt to reach and influence an audience. Some definitions focus on providing convincing evidence for a point of view on a controversial issue and persuading an audience to agree with it. In this argument situation, a judge or a vote sometimes declares a winner. Examples of this type of argument can be found in courts of law where lawyers argue about whether the defendant is guilty or not guilty or in legislative assemblies where legislators argue in favor of or against new legislation. Another group of definitions of argument emphasizes the importance of multiple views and perspectives, learning about them and making comparisons, and reasoning and gaining insights toward reaching an agreement or consensus on a position or point of view that is acceptable to everyone, at least for the present time. Examples of this type of argument can be found in policy meetings in which participants must agree on courses of action and in classrooms where students and professors reason together to establish viable solutions to puzzling questions and problems.

The definition of argument we shall use in this book is a broad one that includes both of these types of argument: *The goal of argument is to bring about a change in an audience's initial position on a controversial issue. Depending on the situation and audience, at times this goal is achieved by an arguer who presents a claim along with reasons and evidence to convince an audience to agree with the position taken [What is often called traditional argument]; at other times, arguers create the possibility of agreement by acknowledging different points of view and working to identify one view or a combination of views that are acceptable to most or all audience members [what is often called consensual argument].* Both types of argument are taught in this book.

The basic method that argument of both kinds employs can be described as making a claim (expressing a point of view on an issue that is communicated by the arguer) and supporting it with reasons and evidence to convince an audience to change the way they think about the issue. All forms of productive argument include these components.

Argument = **Claim** + **Support.**

Recognizing Traditional and Consensual Argument

The definition of argument presented in this chapter allows for two basic approaches to argument, the traditional and the consensual. The traditional approach to argument has been dominant in Western culture. That approach is founded in Greek classical philosophy and rhetoric. Aristotle made it clear in his book *Rhetoric,* written sometime between 360 and 334 B.C.E., that a person making an argument should find all of the available means of persuasion to convince an audience to change positions and agree with the arguer. You are familiar with this model of argument. You observe it every day when you watch news programs and political discussion shows on television, or when you read editorials and letters to the editor in magazines and newspapers. When you engage in argument, orally or in writing, you probably quite naturally either consider or turn to the traditional approach.

▶ **Examples of traditional argument.** One example of traditional argument is the ***public debate*** among candidates for public office or among other individuals who want to convince their audiences to side with them and accept their points of view. Public debates are often televised, allowing candidates to state and explain their views on many subjects; people also write about their views, explaining how their analyses or views are better than opposing positions or views. The judge or decider is the viewing public or a reader, who may or may not pick a winner. ***Courtroom argument,*** with lawyers pleading a case (opposed sets of alleged facts) before a judge and jury, is another example of traditional argument. As in debate, lawyers take opposing sides and argue to convince a judge and jury of the guilt or innocence of a defendant. The desired outcome is that one of them wins.

Another example of traditional argument, known as ***single-perspective argument,*** occurs when one person develops a perspective on an issue and argues to convince a mass audience to agree with this single view. You encounter this type of argument frequently on television and in newspapers, journals, books, and public speeches. The issue and the arguer's position are usually clear. Opposing views, if referred to at all, are refuted or otherwise dismissed. An example might be a politician who wants to convince the public that marriage should exist only between a man and a woman. This arguer provides reasons and evidence and refutes the views of another politician who favors gay marriage. It may not be clear whether anyone "wins" such an argument. Polls, letters to the editor, or a change in policy may present indications about how some members of the audience have reacted.

One-on-one, everyday argument, also a type of traditional argument, can be very different from convincing a judge or a large, unspecified audience. In the one-on-one situation, the person arguing needs to focus on and identify with the other person, think about what that person wants and values, and be conciliatory, if necessary. Each participant either wins, loses, or succeeds in part. Examples might be a salesperson who wants to sell a customer a car or a student who writes a letter to convince a professor to accept a late paper.

▶ **Examples of consensual argument.** In contrast to traditional argument with its emphasis on winning, consensual argument emphasizes agreement. You will probably encounter both of these types of argument in your college classes. In *dialectic,* one type of consensual argument, two or more people participate as equals in a dialogue to try to discover what seems to be the best position on an issue. A questioning strategy is often used to test the validity of differing views. The ancient Greek philosopher Plato used this form of argument in his *Dialogues* to examine such questions as *What is truth?* and *What is the ideal type of government?* You may have seen this type of exchange referred to as "the Socratic method" because Plato's teacher, the philosopher Socrates, asks many of the questions in the *Dialogues.*

Professors sometimes use dialectic to help students think about and finally arrive at positions that can be generally accepted by most of the class. In a philosophy class, for example, the professor may ask the question *How can one establish a personal hierarchy of values?* and then describe a situation in which an individual is faced with a conflict of values. For example, Can one remain loyal to a friend if one must break a law in the process? The professor first asks class members to describe the values that are in conflict in this situation, then to compare the relative strength and importance of these values, and finally to prioritize them in a way that is agreed to by the class. The objective is to discover, through questions and answers, a bedrock of ideas that most or all of the class can accept in common. There are no winners. There is instead a consensual discovery of a new way to look at a difficult issue. Students then may be asked to write papers in which they describe their understanding of this new consensus view.

Another type of consensual argument is *academic inquiry*. Its purpose is to discover, through reading, discussion, and writing, new views, new knowledge, and new truths about complex issues. For example, English majors engage in academic inquiry when they read, discuss, and write about their insights into the motivation of a character in a novel. Political science majors take part in academic inquiry when they find themselves contributing to a new understanding of the benefits of strong state governments. The participants in such inquiry find that there are few clear-cut pro and con positions; there is no judge; the emphasis is not on winning. Anyone can participate; there are potentially as many views as there are participants. The result of academic inquiry, ideally, is to reach well-founded consensus on academic and social issues. Consensus may take some time to emerge, and it may also be challenged later when someone proposes a completely new way of looking at a particular issue.

Negotiation and mediation are conducted in arenas where people must employ argument to reach consensus on plans of action that solve problems. The Palestinians and the Israelis, for example, cannot both claim ownership of the same land, so other solutions continue to be negotiated. Negotiation can take place between two people, one on one, or in a group meeting. A special characteristic of negotiation is that the negotiators usually represent an entire business, organization, or government, and, as a result, many people not present at the negotiating table must ultimately be as satisfied with the final agreements as the negotiators themselves. Often, negotiation involves both competition (for example, both parties claim rights to fish in the same waters) and cooperation (they have to figure out how to make that possible). For negotiation to be successful, all those involved must state their positions, including the views or claims of the groups or governments they represent, and support them with reasons and evidence both in writing and orally. Everyone must be willing to consider alternative views and reasons and to modify their original views in order to reach consensus and resolve the problem.

Mediation is becoming a frequent alternative to a court trial. A judge assigns trained mediators to help parties who are in conflict resolve a problem that would otherwise have to be solved by a judge and possibly a jury. The mediators act as go-betweens and help the individuals involved see their problems in new ways so that they can figure out how to solve them outside of the courtroom. You may be taught methods for negotiation or mediation in your business or other classes, in which case you will be able to draw on what you know about argument to help you understand and use these practices.

A final type of consensual argument you may use frequently is known as *internal argument.* Most of us argue with ourselves when we experience internal conflict because we need to increase personal motivation, make a decision, or solve a problem. New Year's resolutions, to-do lists, and time management charts are examples of internal argument and decision making. As in other forms of consensual argument, different possibilities are identified, reasons for and against are considered, and a satisfactory resolution is finally reached. Whether traditional or consensual, notice how much of argument revolves around the relationship with audience. All argument, whatever its form, is fundamentally concerned with engaging and influencing the views of others. Notice, for example, how each of these traditional arguments centers upon a particular relationship between arguer and audience. Successful arguing depends in part on the assumptions an arguer makes about her or his audience.

Recognizing Visual Argument

At the beginning of this chapter, you were advised to look at the headlines of a current newspaper or newsmagazine to identify some current issues. Did you also notice that many of the headlines and stories are accompanied by photographs and other kinds of visual images? Their purpose is often to reinforce or examine an idea in the written stories, making them more immediate, compelling, and convincing to audiences. Such images function as parallel visual arguments or as the visual extension of the ideas in the written argument. Other images may stand alone, making an argument themselves, without an accompanying story or essay. Stand-alone visual arguments of this type are usually accompanied by a few words to explain their significance as arguments.

Let us look at two examples of images that have been used to either further develop and enhance the ideas in a written argument, or to make an independent argument with only a few words of explanation to highlight the argumentative significance. As you look at these images, view them from the perspective of argument; that is, determine whether or not each image is about an issue that has not been resolved or settled and that potentially inspires two or more different perspectives or views. Describe the issue and the position the image appears to take. You will often have to infer this information because it will not always be directly stated in words either on or near the visual itself.

Figure 1.1 ▪ (on page 10) comes from a daily newspaper and reinforces the ideas developed in an accompanying article about violence in Pakistan on the day former Prime Minister Benazir Bhutto returned to that country after eight years in exile. Her return in the fall of 2007 was controversial because it was resisted by radical jihadists who also harbored negative feelings for the United States as well as by various political opponents. Suicide bombers attacked her motorcade as she made her way through Karachi, Pakistan. Later in the year, she was assassinated. The photograph in Figure 1.1 shows some of the results of the violence on individual Pakistanis the day after the first suicide bombings.

Figure 1.2 ▪ (on page 10) is a stand-alone visual argument that makes an argument about global warming. It is an illustration from a book titled *Global Warming: The Causes, The Perils, The Solutions, The Actions: What You Can Do* and published by Time Books in 2007. Notice that it is accompanied by a few words of text that explain some of its significance as argumentation. Look at these two images, read the captions, and answer the questions that accompany them to help you think about them as arguments.

You will discover that much of the same instruction that will help you read and write arguments will also help you analyze the visual argument that is present everywhere in our society. Look for visual argument on television, in newspapers and magazines, on billboards, signs, packaging and marketing materials, in movies, Web sites, video games, and books. These examples and explanations of types of traditional argument, consensual argument, and visual argument demonstrate that effective argument takes many forms, and does not take place automatically.

"Steps for Reading Visual Argument."

Step 1: Understanding Context: What background information do you need to know in order to read this image intelligibly?

Step 2: What Do You See?: What are the key details or features here that stand out? What images? What text? What supporting details?

Step 3: Identifying the Issue(s): Based on the picture it presents, what issue does this visual seem to be referencing? What debate is it part of?

Step 4: Defining the Perspective: What side in this debate is this visual taking? What perspective on this issue does this visual seem to take?

Step 5: Defining the Argument: How do we know what side of this debate the visual is taking? What specific claims about this issue does the visual seem to be making?

Step 6: Thinking in Terms of Audience: What sort of response does this visual seem to want from its viewers? What messages or lessons does it want to convey? Is it successful?

Figure 1.1 *Shroud-wrapped bodies were brought to a morgue from around Karachi, and families went there to identify the dead yesterday.*

A photograph of the aftermath of suicide bombings in Karachi, Pakistan, which took the lives of more than a hundred people. This image serves as support to reinforce the ideas in a newspaper article about these suicide bombings and the effect they had on citizens. View this image as an argument. What issue does it address? What position does it take? What effect does it have on you as a viewer of this visual argument? What makes it effective?

Figure 1.2 *This is a photograph of a polar bear trying to get its bearings in a place where most of the ice pack in its native environment has melted. This is a stand-alone visual argument that is accompanied by a few words of explanation. View it as an argument, and read the caption. What issue does it address? What position does it take? What effect does it have on you as a viewer of this visual argument? How effective is it as a visual argument?*

Like a polar bear adrift on a shrinking ice floe in the Arctic Ocean, many of us have held on to the dwindling hope that global warming is a vague concern for the future. As extreme weather patterns disrupt lives everywhere, it is clear that climate change is an immediate threat to our planet that must be addressed now.

Special conditions are necessary if argument is to be effective. Let us look at some of these conditions to expand our perspective on argument even further.

Under What Conditions Does Argument Work Best?

To work best, a productive and potentially successful argument, whether presented in writing, in speech, or in images, requires the following elements:

▶ **An issue.** An argument needs as its central focus an issue that has not yet been settled, or has become unsettled. In addition, there must be the potential for the issue to generate at least two or more views. For example, the issue of bottled water has more than two views: either in favor or against their widespread use. Between these two poles, people take a variety of positions, including the view that bottled water use may be beneficial to the environment in certain cases and detrimental in others.

▶ **An arguer.** Ideally, every argument requires a person who is motivated to initiate the argument, to take a position on the issue, to obtain and consider information, and to communicate a position to others. This person needs to develop expertise on an issue and be willing to take a risk to express his or her own ideas about it. Furthermore, the arguer should seek to go beyond the "current wisdom" about an issue and find fresh perspectives and approaches that will suggest original insights to the audience. For example, an individual arguing for tighter restrictions on bottled water needs to present fresh reasons and evidence to get people's attention and agreement. Al Gore provided such a rationale in his film about global warming, *An Inconvenient Truth*.

▶ **Audience.** An audience for an argument, whether friendly or hostile, should ideally be willing to listen to or read and consider new views or perspectives. The audience should also be capable of understanding, thinking, questioning, discussing, and answering. The arguer may be familiar with the audience's background and values or, in the case of a totally unknown audience, the arguer may have to imagine their background, motives, and values. The arguer should respect the audience and want to communicate with them. It is a compliment to draw someone into discussion on an issue, so the arguer should try to show that he or she cares about the audience, their interests and their context or state of mind. This approach will ensure an audience who reads and listens and does not shut the arguer out or otherwise try to escape. Receptive audiences are potentially willing to change their minds, a desirable outcome of argument.[2] Consider, for example, an audience member who favors the restriction of bottled water, is an

---

[2]Some of the observations in this chapter about the special conditions for argument, especially for the audience, are derived from Chaim Perelman and Lucie Olbrechts-Tyteca, *The New Rhetoric: A Treatise on Argumentation* (Notre Dame, IN: University of Notre Dame Press, 1969), pt. 1.

environmental activist, and is willing to think about an opposing view because a respectful fellow parent has written a letter to the editor describing the problem of plastic bottles inundating landfills.

▶ **Common ground.** Effective argument requires the establishment of some common ground between the audience and the arguer that is relevant to the issue. If two parties are too far apart and share no common ground, they usually do not understand one another well enough to engage in dialogue. For example, people who disagree on the abortion issue often find themselves at a standoff, they fight rather than argue, and their disagreement sometimes results in violence. At the other extreme, if two parties are already in complete agreement, there is usually no need to argue. For example, two parents who agree that their child should go to college do not argue about that part of the child's future. Common ground may be established between an arguer and an audience through the discovery of common interests—common ideas, experiences, motives, or values—or even through recognizing common friends or enemies. As soon as two parties realize they have something in common, they can more easily achieve identification, even if it is minimal, and engage in constructive argument. Imagine, once again, two parties who disagree on bottled water use. One party believes bottled water manufacture should be forbidden in order to alleviate the environmental damage such bottles cause. The other party believes people should decisions about how best to protect the environment should be left to individual consumers themselves. Both agree that harming the environment is bad, and this basic agreement provides the common ground they need to begin to engage in constructive argument about handgun ownership. Figure 1.3 ■ (on page 13) diagrams these possible situations.

▶ **A forum.**   People need forums for argument so they can feel creative and know they will be heard. Available forums include public places for argument, such as the courtroom or legislative assembly; much more widely available forums include various media, such as magazines, journals, newspapers and other print sources, television and radio programs of all sorts, motion pictures, the arts, and photographs and other graphic materials. College is a forum for argument. Professors and students argue in class, at meals, and in dorms and apartments. Outside speakers present argument. The argument class, with its discussions, papers, and other assignments, can be an excellent forum for practicing argument, particularly if both the students and the instructor work to create an environment in which all students participate and respect one another.

▶ **Audience outcomes.** Successful arguments should produce changes in the audience. At times, the arguer convinces the audience, and the members of the audience change their minds. Sometimes a successful negotiation is achieved: people find themselves in consensus, a decision is reached, and a plan of action is started. Other arguments may not have such clear-cut results. A hostile audience may be brought to a neutral point of view. A neutral audience may decide it is important to take a stand. There are times when it is a significant accomplishment just to get the audience's attention and raise the level of consciousness of those engaged. This success can lay the groundwork for a possible future change of minds.

How much can you expect to change people's thinking as you discuss and write about issues that are important to you or that you think are important to

THE ISSUE: SHOULD LIMITS BE PLACED ON HANDGUN OWNERSHIP?

Figure 1.3 *Establishing Common Ground.*

Possibility 1: *Complete agreement and no argument.*

Two individuals believe that all private citizens should be allowed to own one or more handguns to protect themselves from random shooters. They agree totally and share the same common ground. They have nothing to argue about.

Possibility 2: *Total disagreement, no common ground, and no argument.*

One individual believes private citizens should have the right to own handguns to protect themselves from random shooters, and another believes that no private citizen should own handguns for any purpose. They disagree totally, and there is no common ground. Productive argument is nearly impossible.

13

Possibility 3: *Two parties discover something in common, and there is a possibility of argument.*

The two parties discover they each hold their positions because of their fear of random shooters. One wants to own a handgun to kill a random shooter in self-defense. The other wants to banish handguns so that random shooters will have trouble obtaining them. They have an important point in common: they both want to stop random shootings. They share common ground on that point, even though they may disagree on other points. The common ground creates the possibility for productive argument about what can be done to stop random shooting, the ultimate goal.

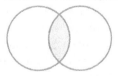

examine? For students in argument class, this can be an urgent question. They wonder whether they must convince their teachers as well as their classmates of their point of view in every paper or presentation if they are to achieve good grades. Such a demand is too great, however, since audiences and the outcomes of argument vary too much. Convincing the teacher and your fellow students that the argument paper is effective with a particular audience is a good—and probably the best possible—outcome in argument class. As one professor put it, "My ambition is to return a paper and say that I disagreed with it completely—but the writing was excellent—A!"[3]

Under What Conditions Does Argument Fail?

We have just examined the optimal conditions for argument. Now, let us look at the conditions that can cause it to flounder or fail.

▶ **No disagreement or reason to argue.** We have already seen that no argument can take place when there is no real disagreement, no uncertainty, or no possibility for two or more views. In addition, neutral people who do not have enough interest in an issue to form an opinion do not argue. Argument also cannot take place unless people perceive an issue as a subject for argument. Orientation leaders who try to persuade students to consider one major over another will not succeed with students who have already decided on their majors.

▶ **Risky or trivial issues.** Big or risky problems are difficult for some people to argue about because they can call for radical or sizable change. Finding a new career or dissolving a longtime relationship may fit into this category, and many people, wisely or not, tend to leave such difficult issues alone rather than argue about them. Religious issues or issues that threaten global disaster are also sometimes too big, too emotional, or too scary for many people to argue about them. At the other extreme, some issues may be perceived as low risk, trivial, boring, or even ridiculous. Some family arguments fall into this category, such as what to eat for dinner or who should take out the trash. One person may care, but the rest do not.

▶ **Difficulty in establishing common ground.** We have pointed out that arguments that lack common ground among participants are not effective. You may encounter difficulties when trying to establish common ground with those who have made up their minds on certain issues and who no longer want to listen or consider a change. Those individuals who hold fast to prejudiced beliefs about various groups of people, for example, may dismiss information that defies their favorite stereotypes. It is also difficult to argue with some religious people who take certain issues on faith and do not perceive them as subjects for argument. Finally, argument cannot take place when one party is not motivated to argue. "Don't bring that up again" or "I don't want to discuss that" puts an end to most arguments.

▶ **Standoffs or fights that result in negative outcomes.** When argument is not working, as in some of the situations just described, the outcomes are also negative. For example, a standoff occurs, the parties assert or retreat to their original views,

---

[3]Hilton Obenzinger, "The Israeli–Palestinian Conflict: Teaching a Theme-Based Course," *Notes in the Margins* (Winter 1994), 12.

Figure 1.4 *When Argument Fails.*

Cartoons and comic strips often make visual arguments

SOURCE: Calvin and Hobbes © 1993 Watterson. Dist. By Universal UClick. Reprinted with permission.
All rights reserved.

and then refuse to be moved. In another instance, emotions may be strong, verbal fighting breaks out, and extreme views are expressed. No one agrees with anyone else. People shake their heads and walk away, or they become hurt and upset. Some individuals may become strident, wanting to debate everyone to demonstrate that they are right.

15

One important aim of this book is to provide you with the insight and skill to manage these negative situations so that more constructive argument can take place. Students are in an excellent position to overcome much of the fear, resistance, and aversion associated with difficult issues and, by using evidence and good sense, get down to work and face some of them. Understanding audience members, especially their attitudes, needs, and values, is an important first step. Another useful idea to keep in mind is that most arguers have more success with certain audiences than with others, depending on the amount of common ground. Even in the most difficult situations, some common ground can be found among people who seem to disagree on almost everything. Recent research suggests that one vehicle for establishing common ground is through narratives, with each side relating personal experiences and stories. Even the most hostile adversaries can usually relate to one another's personal experiences and find unity in the common villains, heroes, or themes in their stories. In establishing common ground through stories, participants often find that the issues themselves change or are transformed in ways that make them easier for both parties to argue.[4]

Arguing effectively in difficult situations requires a conscious effort to avoid both stereotypical reactions and entrenched behavioral patterns. Past habits must be replaced with new strategies that work better. It is sometimes difficult to make

---

[4]Linda Putnam, in the keynote speech to the Texas Speech Communication Association Conference, Corpus Christi, TX, October 1993, reported these results from her study of negotiations between teachers and labor union leaders.

such changes because habits can be strong, but it is possible to do so, and the stakes are often high, especially when the choice is constructive argument or verbal fighting and standoffs.

Recognizing Argument in the 21st Century

What does it mean to be an arguer in the 21st century? And, more specifically, how has the rise of digital technology reshaped the way argument looks and works, the role it plays in our daily lives? To begin answering these questions, we need to start with an observation: the emergence of the Web has led to an explosion in the in sheer number and dizzying variety of arguments to which we are now exposed. As we have become users of this technology, we have found ourselves exposed to a seemingly limitless array of issues, ranging from the mundane to the momentous, the most intimately personal to the most sweepingly global. With little more than the click of a button, we can now take part in thousands of different discussions and debates. From Facebook posts to political blogs, online policy debates to web-based movie reviews, we as cultural consumers nowadays enjoy a veritable smorgasbord of argument.

Along with unprecedented increase in the volume and variety of argument, have also come profound changes in the ways we use argument to engage with each other. Social networking tools such as instant messaging and Twitter provide us with virtually instantaneous access to each other, allowing us (if we so desire) to remain in near constant conversation with counterparts throughout the world. This type of perpetual availability on a personal level is matched by the unfettered access we now enjoy to more formal sources of information and opinion. Whether it is a broadcast from the BBC, an editorial in the online version of your local paper, or an advertisement for Nike, we are constantly invited to play the role of cultural consumer. Indeed it is not going too far to suggest that this kind of exposure has become a constant, 24/7 feature of our daily lives. We can read a blog post as we are walking down the street, can respond to a text message while standing in the checkout line at the grocery store, can arbitrate a conflict between two friends on Facebook while simultaneously updating our plans for Friday night. There is literally no place in our lives where, if we choose, we cannot be part of the larger public conversation.

Yet, for all this newfound access and interactivity, the rise of the Web also presents its own set of unique challenges. While it has given us unprecedented access to a completely new universe of issues, the Web has also altered the ways we go about engaging with these issues. Along with our 24/7 exposure has come a new way of participating in argument, one that emphasizes browsing or skimming over deeper reflection. Nowadays we are more likely to engage with a given issue by darting from one link to another, traversing the surface of a discussion without necessarily delving into its underlying substance. In a world marked by perpetual distraction and interruption, where the next topic, discussion or activity is never more than an email or web link away, how do we ever develop the skill necessary to focus on and address an issue in a sustained, comprehensive way? The advantages of the Web are monumental: instantaneous access, limitless information, infinite variety and the feeling of unfettered individual choice. Nevertheless, the challenges posed by these advantages are equally numerous. The world of argument to which the Web grants us entry may well turn out to be—as the cliché goes—a mile wide and an inch deep.

In the face of such a complex situation, how do we develop a set of tools that can equip us to deal with the nature of argument in the digital age? How do we harness the enormous potential of the Web while avoiding its most problematic consequences? In the pages that follow, we will take a closer look at a framework designed to accomplish precisely this goal, that allows us to take a more sustained and deliberate look at the way argument functions online.

GETTING STARTED: QUESTIONS AND CONSIDERATIONS TO BEAR IN MIND AS YOU THINK ABOUT ONLINE ARGUMENT

Assembled below is a quick inventory of the key features and questions that define the rise of argument on the Web. As you look over this list, think about how these considerations influence the kinds of issues that are raised online, how these issues are debated, and whom these debates involve.

▶ **Volume/Variety:** As noted above, the rise of the Web has led to an explosion in both the number and types of issues to which we are exposed. As we make our way through this thicket of material, it is important that we pay attention to exactly how a given issue is being defined; what does or does not make it a valid or significant issue for public debate. In a world where issues range so widely, how do we distinguish between those that matter from those that do not?

▶ **Access:** Another feature of online argument involves the ease with which we can now join an ongoing discussion or debate of a given issue. As any number of commentators have observed, a hallmark of the Web is the degree of freedom and mobility we now enjoy. With little more than the click of a button, it is now possible for us to communicate with people from, quite literally, throughout the world, on issues that can range from the local to the global. Given this, what is the context for a given argument online? Who are the various audiences with a stake in its outcome? How do we deal with audiences who hold radically different stakes or points of view?

▶ **Relevance:** In a world where we can connect to issues and to each other so readily, argument itself could be said to occupy a far more direct, immediate and personal place in our everyday lives. Indeed the Web seems to have inaugurated a new era of what we might call *participatory argument:* a way of engaging with issues that give us a greater stake in and ownership over the issues we discuss. How does a given issue matter to me? What is my own personal stake?

▶ **Interactivity:** An additional consequence of this increased access has to do with our ability, in this new digital age, to connect and communicate more directly with our respective audience. Perhaps the single most defining feature of the Web is the degree to which it allows us the freedom to *network*: to bond with others over a shared interest in a given issue, exchange our views, to offer support or criticism, and to, quite often, do so instantaneously. How does audience feedback influence the way a given argument unfolds? How can such feedback alter or affect our own point of view?

▶ **Linked Issues:** In an environment in which everything and everyone has become so interconnected, it should come as no surprise to note how frequently an issue raised online links up with a range of other issues to which, in one way or another, it is related. Within any given argument, what is the key issue at stake? How does it differ from other related issues that the argument raises?

▶ **Multi-Modal/Multi-Media:** Another feature of online argument concerns the degree to which the discussion of issues now involves not only written text, but visual, graphic and video elements as well. How do we combine visual or graphic analysis with an analysis of written text?

▶ **Authority/Credibility:** With the exponential rise of different issues online, coupled with an equally explosive rise in the number of people arguing over these issues, it has become increasingly important to think about the basis upon which a given claim is made. In an environment in which everyone is free to express her/his opinion, how do we go about determining the validity of a given claim? On what basis—factual, logical, or emotional—do we decide a claim is legitimate?

▶ **Polarization:** As it has fostered greater engagement with and participation in various issues, the rise of the Web has in many cases, increased the intensity of feelings around them. Extreme views, it seems, occupy a more prominent place in our public debate these days. How and where do we find common ground? What assumptions can competing arguments be shown to share?

Engaging with Issues

To summarize, the most easily arguable issues are those that invite two or more views that are perceived by all parties as issues, that are interesting and motivating to all participants, and that inspire research and original thought. They also promise common ground among participants, and they do not appear too big, too risky, too trivial, too confusing, too scary, or too specialized to discuss profitably. You may, however, find yourself drawn to some of the more difficult issues that do not meet all of these criteria, and you should not necessarily shun them because they are difficult. You will need to work with your audience in creative ways and consider the entire context for argument, regardless of the nature of the issues you select. Most important at this point is that you identify several issues that are arguable and important to you and to your classroom audience. Identifying issues will help you keep a high level of motivation and receive the maximum instructional benefits from argument class. Finding arguable issues yourself is much better than accepting assigned issues as writing topics.

So, now the search begins. What will help you search out and select arguable issues? Issues exist in contexts, and the issues most engaging to you will probably emerge from the parts of your life that demand your greatest attention and energy. For example, people who are compellingly engaged with their professions think about work issues; new parents think about child-rearing issues; dedicated students think about issues raised in class; and many teenagers think about peer-group issues. To begin the search for your issues, examine those parts of your life that demand your most concentrated time and attention right now. Also, think about the special characteristics of issues in general. Here are a few of them.

▶ **Issues are compelling.** People get excited about issues, and they usually identify with a few in particular. Most people can quickly name one or more issues that are so important and so interesting to them that they think about them often, sometimes daily. If you live in the Northwest, for example, the preservation of old-growth forests may be an issue for you. If you are preparing for a career in education, an issue you may care about might be creating equal access to quality education. Can you think of particular issues that are compelling to you?

▶ **Issues often originate in dramatic life situations.** Things happen all around us—global terrorism seems out of control, people find they can download music from the Internet, but whether to pay or how to pay for it becomes an issue, the number of illegal immigrants entering the United States increases. As the issues around us change, we inevitably respond with questions: What should be done to stop global terrorism? How much is a song that is available on the Internet worth? Who should be responsible for paying for children's health care, the government or the parents of the children? Should U.S. borders be patrolled, or should immigrants be offered work permits? Pay attention to the stories that are newsworthy this week, and identify the issues associated with them. Select the ones that interest you the most.

▶ **Current issues can be linked to enduring issues that have engaged people for ages.** For example, the controversy about genetically engineering new plant and animal life is related to age-old issues associated with the preservation of life as it has evolved on this planet: Will genetic engineering help cure human disease? Or will genetic engineering be profoundly destructive to existing life forms? Affirmative action issues are linked to the enduring issue of whether or not all people are created equal: Will affirmative action contribute to racial profiling, or will it actually decrease discrimination? Look at Box 1.1 ■ for additional examples of contemporary public issues we have linked with enduring issues to demonstrate the timeless quality of many of them. See if you can add examples as you read through those in the "Current" column.

| Box 1.1 | Examples of Current and Enduring Public Issues. |

▸▸▸ What Are Some Public Issues?

CURRENT ISSUES	ENDURING ISSUES
Ways and Means Issues	
Should everyone pay taxes? In what proportion to their income?	From what sources should a government obtain money, and how should it spend it?
Should free trade be limited?	
How much business profit can be sacrificed to keep the environment clean and safe?	
Should scholarships and fellowships be taxed?	
How can we reduce our dependence on foreign oil?	
How should we finance health care?	
Is the national debt too high, and if so, what should be done about it?	
Quality of Life Issues	
Should more resources be directed to protecting the environment?	What is a minimum quality of life, and how do we achieve it?
Are inner cities or rural areas better places to live?	
How can we improve the quality of life for children and senior citizens?	
What effect will global climate change have on our lives?	
Personal Rights versus Social Rights Issues	
Should individuals, the government, or private business be responsible for the unemployed? Health care? Day care? The homeless? Senior citizens? Drug addicts? People with AIDS? Race problems? Minority problems? Dealing with criminals? Worker safety? Deciding who should buy guns?	Can individuals be responsible for their own destinies, or should social institutions be responsible? Can individuals be trusted to do what is best for society?

continued

20

Box 1.1 *continued*

CURRENT ISSUES	ENDURING ISSUES
War and Peace Issues	
How much should the government spend on the military?	Is war ever justified, and should countries stay prepared for war?
Should the United States remain prepared for a major world war?	
Should you, your friends, or your family be required to register for the draft?	
To what extent should a government pursue negotiation as an alternative to war?	
Self-Development Issues	
What opportunities for education and training should be available to everyone?	What opportunities for self-development should societies make available to individuals?
How well are job-training programs helping people get off welfare and find employment?	
Should undocumented workers be allowed the same opportunities to participate in society as citizens?	
Human Life Issues	
Should abortions be permitted?	Should human life be protected under any conditions?
Should capital punishment be permitted?	
Is mercy killing ever justifiable?	What or who will define the limits of a person's control of their own life, and what or who limits a government's interest or control?
Should stem cell research be allowed?	
Foreign Affairs Issues	
Which is wiser, to support an American economy or a global economy?	In world politics, how do we balance the rights of smaller countries and different ethnic groups against the needs of larger countries and international organizations?
How much foreign aid should we provide, and to which countries?	
Should college graduates be encouraged to participate in some type of foreign service like the Peace Corps?	
Should the United States defend foreign countries from aggressors?	

21

continued

Box 1.1 *continued*

CURRENT ISSUES	ENDURING ISSUES
Law and Order Issues	
Is the judicial system effective? Does the punishment always fit the crime? How serious a problem is racial profiling? How can global terrorism be eradicated? To what degree have we sacrificed our privacy for national security?	What is an appropriate balance between the welfare and protection of society as a whole and the rights of the individual?
Intimacy/Friendship	
Do online technologies enhance or detract from the quality of our friendships? Should there be stricter policies regulating social networking?	To what extent should our public speech or behavior be regulated?
Privacy	
What are the risks of putting so much information about ourselves online? Should people have the right to censor public information about themselves?	Is privacy a universal right?
Surveillance	
Should the government be allowed access to information about us online?	What limits should be put around government authority?
Political Activism	
Has the rise of the Web improved the quality of political campaigning?	What should be the rules governing how politicians are allowed to campaign for office?

◗ **Issues go underground and then resurface.** Public concern with particular issues is not constant. Experts may think about their issues continuously, but the public usually thinks about an issue only when something happens that brings it to public attention. How to deal with increasing population is an example of such an issue. Experts think about that issue almost daily, but the general public may note it or think about it only when new information is released. For example, the world's population is expected to reach seven billion by the end of 2011. It has more than doubled in only fifty years, a fact that prompted a considerable amount of argument in the media, particularly about future population growth and the ability of the planet to sustain it. As one commentator stated, the media often make arguments out of the news. Persistent issues are, of course, always alive in the background and always important, but we do not think about all of them all of the time. Think back. Are there some issues that used to concern you that you have neither thought about nor read about for a long time? What are they?

▶ **Issues sometimes are solved, but then new ones emerge.** Some issues command so much public attention that the people who can do something about them finally perceive them as problems and pass laws or take other measures to solve them. As soon as an issue is solved, however, other, related issues spring up in its place. For example, for many years, people argued about what to do about health care. Much of the current health care debate revolves around the fact that millions of Americans remain uninsured, and the role the government should play in remedying this situation. Are there other issues of this type that might interest you? Think of problems that now seem solved, but are probably not completely solved for all people, or for all times.

▶ **Issues seem to be getting more complex.** Issues seem to become more and more complex as the world becomes more complex. In an interview, the actress Susan Sarandon, who has always been engaged with social issues, stated that in the mid-to-late 1960s, when she was in college, the issues seemed simpler, more black and white. The issues at that time, for example, centered on civil rights and the Vietnam War. "We were blessed with clear-cut issues," she says. "We were blessed with clear-cut grievances. Things were not as gray as they are now."[5]

Because issues are now more complex, people need to learn to engage with them in more complex ways. The word *perspectives*, as used in this book, refers not only to a broader perspective on issues and argument itself, including viewing images and reading essays as though they were arguments when that is appropriate, but also to the variety of perspectives that individuals can take or must accommodate others taking on particular issues. Few issues are black and white, and not many can be viewed in pro or con terms anymore. Most invite several different ways of looking at them and require language that reflects their complexity.

As you develop your own perspectives on the complex issues that engage you, keep in mind that it takes many years to become an expert. You will want to look at what experts say and write, though you will not have the background and information to write as comprehensively as they do. When you write your argument, you will want to research and write on a limited aspect of the issue you engage, one that you can learn enough about to argue effectively. Limiting your topic will permit you to get the information and gain the perspective to be convincing. Suggestions that can help you limit your approach to a complex issue will be made in future chapters.

23

[5]Ovid Demaris, "Most of All, the Children Matter." *Parade*, March 1, 1992, 4–5.

Arguing Like a Citizen

Arguments are more than simply academic discussions. Issues have real world consequences that impact how we live, the opportunities we enjoy, the ways we interact with each other. More than an abstract or formal exercise, argument in fact is one of the most direct and vital tools we have of engaging the forces and factors that shape public life. Given this, we might well ask, what is the broader social or public significance of a given issue? How do our arguments over issues provide us with an opportunity to effect change in the world around us? How can arguing contribute to the common good?

In order to answer questions like these, we need to approach argument as more than an abstract set of skills. We need instead to understand and appreciate the ways argument is woven into the fabric of our lives, informing our assumptions and actions, our values and choices. We need, in short, to see argument as an act of citizenship.

The questions outlined below offer a framework for beginning to think about argument in terms of citizenship. For any given issue, these are questions we might consider in order to better understand the real world consequences that argument holds.

▶▶▶ Thinking Like a Citizen: Questions to Get Us Started

- Why do I care about this issue? What makes it matter to me personally? What are the factors or circumstances that determine my stake?
- Who else cares about this issue? Who are the other stakeholders? Which other individuals or groups are most likely to consider this issue important?
- What are the different perspectives on this issue others might have? How are their stakes in this issue similar to or different from my own?
- What are the factors and/or circumstances that account for these differences? How and why do people who are part of different groups or constituencies understand the significance of this issue differently?

▶▶▶ Arguing Like a Citizen: Connecting Issues to the Larger World

- How does this issue impact or affect my daily life? What difference (social, political, economic, cultural) does it make to me?
- What are the key problems or questions this issue raises for me? Are these the same problems and questions this issue raises for others?
- What are the differences among us that a discussion or debate over this issue might expose?
- How can these differences be bridged?

▶▶▶ Acting Like a Citizen: Putting Our Arguments Into Practice

- Where could I go in my community to see an example of this debate being waged?
- What concrete action could I take to change or improve the way this issue is debated?
- What sort of concrete action might help resolve this debate?

continued

Arguing Like a Citizen (*continued*)

Example: "Should states allow its citizens to cast their votes in elections online?"

▶▶▶ Thinking Like a Citizen

Why do I care about this issue? What is my stake?
I'm concerned about voter participation in elections and feel this plan would allow more voters to participate in the democratic process. My perspective is that voters should be allowed to cast votes online because it would allow more people to participate in political elections and thereby enhance the democratic process.

Who else cares about this issue? Who are the other stakeholders? Which other individuals or groups are most likely to consider this issue important?
Individuals running for public office have a clear stake in this question, as do groups or organizations whose interests might be affected by the outcome of a given vote: grass-roots activists, corporations, or "Good Government" advocates whose mission is to increase participation in the political process. Incumbent politicians who may have a vested interest in preserving the status quo might also consider this issue important.

What are the different perspectives on this issue others might have? How are their stakes in this issue similar to or different from my own?
Corporations may have a vested interest in restricting eligible or interested voters to those more likely to side with their own views. Grass roots activists, who often struggle to gain recognition or support for their initiatives, may be in favor of such a plan because of its potential to attract more supporters to their cause.

What are the factors and/or circumstances that account for these differences?
Economic factors—i.e. do I stand to gain financially with this policy? One's place in the political process: i.e. does this change give me greater influence?

▶▶▶ Arguing Like a Citizen

How does this issue impact or affect my daily life? What difference does it make to me?
As a college-age student who is only now beginning to participate in politics, this issues matters a great deal to me. As someone who uses online technology in every facet of my daily life this policy would make it much easier to care about and participate in the political process.

What are the key problems or questions this issue raises for me? Are these problems and questions the same as those this issue raises for others?
The key issues raised for me concern questions of convenience. In my view, one of the main reasons we do not have greater political participation has to do with the fact that voting requires so much effort. Democracy should make it easier for citizens to participate. Others, however, might consider the key concern to involve privacy. How do you preserve the confidentiality of the ballot box when peoples' votes are tallied online? Still others might harbor the greatest concerns over the issue of election fraud. Does online voting provide for the same degree of security when it comes to tallying up the votes themselves?

continued

25

Arguing Like a Citizen (*continued*)

What are the differences among us that a discussion or debate over this issue might expose? How might these differences be bridged?

Clearly, an issue such as this has the potential to draw distinctions between those who benefit from the current political status quo and those who do not. Citizens who feel disenfranchised by the current process, who feel their voices are not heard in public matters, are more likely to respond positively to a proposal to make voting easier and more accessible. Conversely, those with who feel the current system already provides adequate access are more likely to take an opposing view. Common ground might be found, however, if it were possible to the new policy were implemented in a way that did not replace, but rather simply supplemented, the existing voting system.

▶▶▶ Acting Like a Citizen

Where could I go in my community to see an example of this debate being waged?
League of Women Voters; college Democrats or Republicans; advocacy organizations, et al.

What concrete action could I take to change or improve the way this issue is debated? What sort of concrete action might help resolve this debate?
Take part in a "get-out-the-vote" registration drive; start a political blog designed to raise public awareness around political issues; etc.

How Should You Engage with Issues?

Remember that *issues are everywhere*. Listen for issues in lectures and look for them in your textbooks. Ask your professors to identify the major issues in their fields. Box 1.2 ■ page 27 illustrates some of the issues you are likely to encounter in your other college classes. These are examples of issues that your professors argue about, the subjects for academic inquiry. You may be expected to take positions and develop arguments yourself on these or similar issues if you take classes in some of these fields.

As you read, try to add examples from your other courses. Read newspapers and newsmagazines, look at images to get ideas (see Figure 1.5 ■ on page 28), listen to public radio, and watch television programs that hold discussions of issues. Browse through some of the newly acquired books in the library and look for issues. Listen for issues in conversations and discussions with friends and family. Identify campus issues. If you attend a house of worship or belong to organizations, listen to the issues that surface there.

As you watch for and think about the issues that might engage you, start making a list of those you particularly want to learn more about. Make a corresponding list of some of the other groups or individuals who may also be interested in these topics and jot down the views they may hold. Such lists will come in handy when it is time to select topics for your argument papers and begin analyses of your potential audiences.

Box 1.2	Examples of Academic Issues across the Disciplines.

▶▶▶ What Are Some Academic Issues?

In **Physics**—Is there a unifying force in the universe? Is there enough matter in the universe to cause it eventually to stop expanding and then to collapse? What is the nature of this matter?

In **Astronomy**—What elements can be found in interstellar gas? What is the nature of the asteroids? What criteria should be used to identify a new planet?

In **Biology**—What limits, if any, should be placed on genetic engineering?

In **Chemistry**—How can toxic wastes best be managed?

In **Sociology**—Is the cause of crime social or individual? Does television have a significant negative effect on society? What effects do computers have on their users?

In **Psychology**—Which is the better approach for understanding human behavior, nature or nurture? Can artificial intelligence ever duplicate human thought?

In **Anthropology**—Which is more reliable in dating evolutionary stages, DNA or fossils?

In **Business**—Can small, privately owned businesses still compete with giant conglomerate companies? Are chief executive officers paid too much?

In **Mathematics**—Are boys naturally better than girls are at learning math? Should the use of calculators be encouraged? Should calculators be allowed in testing situations?

In **Engineering**—How important should environmental concerns be in determining engineering processes? To what extent, if any, are engineers responsible for the social use of what they produce? How aggressive should we be in seeking and implementing alternative sources of energy? Should the government fund the development of consumer-oriented technology to the same extent that it funds military-oriented technology?

In **History**—Have historians been too restrictive in their perspective? Does history need to be retold, and if so, how? Is the course of history influenced more by unusual individuals or by socioeconomic forces?

In **Political Science**—Where should ultimate authority to govern reside: with the individual, the church, the state, or social institutions? Is power properly divided among the three branches of government in the United States?

In **Communication**—How can the best balance be struck between the needs of society and freedom of expression in the mass media? How much impact, if any, do the mass media have on the behavior of individuals in society?

In **English Literature**—Is the concept of literature too narrowly focused in English departments? If yes, what else should be considered literature?

MAKING AN ISSUE YOUR OWN

Step 1: What do I care about? What questions or problems—whether national political or personal everyday—do I find myself drawn to? Why?

Step 2: Who else cares about this, and what different kinds of views do they hold? How do these views relate to my own?

Figure 1.5 *Girls Receive Education in Bamiyan, Afghanistan.*

Step 3: Where do people talk about this? What contexts or setting?

Step 4: What point of view on this issue do I want to communicate? How?

Step 5: What is my larger goal? Why do I want to convey this viewpoint? Who is my audience, and what effect do I want to have on their views?

Review Questions

1. What did you think of when you encountered the word *argument* as you began to read this chapter? What do you think now? **(LO1)**

2. Provide three examples of your own to illustrate the statement "Argument is everywhere." One of your examples should be a visual argument. **(LO3)**

3. Describe traditional and consensual argument. Give two examples of each. **(LO2)**

4. What are some of the conditions necessary for argument to work best? **(LO4)**

5. What are some of the conditions that may cause argument to fail? **(LO4)**

6. Give two examples of an ethical argument and two examples of an unethical argument **(LO5)**

7. Identify four sources of arguable issues. **(LO6)**

Exercises and Activities

A. Class Project: Understanding Common Ground

1. *Build common ground with your classmates.* Create pairs of students, appoint one in each pair as the scribe, and have each pair take five minutes to discuss and record ideas, experiences, and so on that they have in common. Now create groups of four students by teaming two pairs, appoint a scribe for this group, and have the groups take five minutes to discuss and record what all four members have in common. The scribes then give one-minute reports about what each group has in common. As you listen to these reports, a sense of what the whole class has in common will emerge.

2. *Discover common ground about argument.* Return to your groups of four for five minutes and have the scribes record answers to these questions: (1) What do you think of when you hear the word *argument*? (2) What effect might finding common ground have on your ideas about argument? Finally, have the scribes take two minutes to report to the class on these findings.

3. *Write about common ground.* Write for five minutes about the common ground you think already exists in your classroom. What do you and your classmates have in common? How do you differ? How are your ideas about argument and common ground similar to or different from those of your classmates? What effect will common ground in your class have on the argument that takes place there? Discuss what you have written with the class.

B. Class Project: "Argument Is Everywhere"

1. Test the idea that argument can be found everywhere. Each member of the class should bring in an example of an argument and explain why it can be defined as argument. Each example should focus on an issue that people are still arguing about and on which there is no general agreement. Each student should also define a position on the issue, and the position should be supported with reasons and evidence. Look for examples in a variety of contexts: newspapers, magazines, the Internet, television, motion pictures, music, sermons, other college classes, conversations, and printed material you find at work, at school, and at home.

   Bring in actual examples of articles, images, and letters to the editor, bumper stickers, advertisements, or other easily transportable argument formats, or provide clear and complete descriptions and explanations of argument sources you cannot bring to class, such as lectures, television shows, or billboards. Students should give two- to three-minute oral reports on the example of argument they have selected, including a description of the issue and some of the reasons and evidence offered. This is most easily achieved by completing the statement "This arguer wants us to believe . . ., because. . . ." The class should decide whether all examples described in this activity are indeed examples of argument.

2. State whether you think the argument you have provided is ethical or unethical, and say why. [6]

C. Reading, Group Work, and Class Discussion: What Makes a Good Written Argument?

Read the following two argument essays. Then, in small groups, answer the questions listed below for each of them.

1. What is the issue?
2. What is the author's position on the issue?
3. What reasons and evidence are given to support the author's position?
4. What makes each of these arguments successful?
5. What are the weaknesses in the arguments, if any?

Finally, in class discussion, compile a list of the best as well as the weakest features of argumentation in each essay. Keep a copy of this list. It is a starting point. You will add to it as you learn more about what it takes to make a good argument.

Before you Read: What is the proper role parents should play with their college-age students? How closely involved should parents be?

ESSAY #1 "NO ESCAPE FROM 'HELICOPTER PARENTS'"*
Felix Carroll

Felix Carroll is a former staff writer for the *Albany Times Union*. He currently writes a regular column for the newspaper.

1 Excuse me, but you're hovering. You realize that, right?

2 The media, pediatricians, psychologists and even the college dean, they've all got you figured out—or so they say. They're calling you a helicopter parent. Get it? Because you hover?

3 You're a baby boomer, right? OK, then. Listen up, because this is what they're saying about you.

4 You're too obsessed with your children. You treat them like little princes and princesses—like they're No. 1, like they're MVPs. You've painstakingly planned their lives from their first play date to their first day of college.

5 They're your little Renaissance kids. You shuttle them from soccer practice, to clarinet lessons, to karate, and—because they will be going to a great college—to SAT prep class. Whoops! Speaking of which: You're late.

---

[6]I am indebted to Cedrick May for the basic idea for this project.

*No Escape from Helicopter Parents, by Felix Carrol, from *Albany Times Union*, January 27, 2005.

6   You inflate their egos. You give them graduation ceremonies even when it's just from preschool. You give them a trophy at the end of the season even when they lose. And by the time they get to college and are asked who their hero is, your child will say those words you long to hear: My dad. My mom.

7   Yes, helicopter parent, your intentions are good, but that rotor of yours is causing a din. Bring her down to terra firma. Let's talk.

8   A report on "60 Minutes" last fall discussed how the so-called echo boomers—the children of baby boomers, who were born between 1982 and 1995—are "over managed" and "very pressured" and treated by their parents as pieces of "Baccarat crystal or something that could somehow shatter at any point."

9   Indeed, Mel Levine, a professor of pediatrics at the University of North Carolina Medical School in Chapel Hill, says today's children "may well shatter."

10   He thinks children are being coddled and protected to a degree that threatens their ability later in life to strike off on their own and form healthy relationships and proper job skills.

11   "These parents are trying to create a really terrific statue of a child rather than a child," says Levine, author of "Ready or Not, Here Comes Life" (Simon and Schuster, 2005).

12   Beverly Low, dean of the first-year class at Colgate University, says that where before parents would drop their kids off to college and get out of the way, parents now constantly call her office intervening in a roommate dispute or questioning a professor's grading system.

13   "A lot of our students tell us, 'Hey, my mom is my best friend. My father is my best friend.' Is that a good thing? It's a different thing," she says.

14   But why is it happening? Mary Elizabeth Hughes, a sociologist at Duke University, says helicopter parenting may be an outward sign of economic anxiety, particularly when parents consider the uncertain job market that may await their children.

15   "They're very concerned that their kids do very well and excel at a lot of things as a result," she says.

16   Hughes says such parenting may reflect generational changes as well.

17   Many baby boomer parents came of age during the turbulent '60s where they could not help but experience social change and respond by creating new lifestyles including new forms of parenting.

18   Mark and Cathy Gamsjager of Greenville, N.Y., are annoyed by parents who turn their loving into hovering. But baby boomers, as a whole, may not be getting the credit they deserve, they say, particularly for some of the improvements they have brought to parenthood.

19   Mark Gamsjager, 42, fronts the rockabilly band The Lustre Kings. He skateboards and snowboards with his two boys, Austin, 13, and Thomas, 9.

20   They have a great relationship and have lots to talk about, he says.

21   But he is still their dad.

22   "I think there's got to be a line, you know?" he says. "You still have got to be the tough guy."

23   Indeed, the Gamsjagers say they try to take the best aspects of their parents—emphasizing education, independence and discipline—while improving upon their parents' shortcomings.

24   "I think parents make much more of an effort to be with their kids," says Cathy Gamsjager. "It seems to me that we've gotten away from everybody being an authoritarian. Not that we don't have authority over our kids, but there's more honesty. You spend more time actually talking to your kids about real things."

25   But being open and honest does not mean being a pushover, she says. "I'm not my kids' best friend," she says. "I'm their mom. I love being their mom, and I love being fun, but in the end, I totally get that I'm responsible for helping them make good choices. I'm responsible for where their lives head. I can enjoy them, but no, I can't be their friend."

31

For Discussion:

What are your opinions about the issue of parental involvement in the lives of their children? Is there an age-limit at which this kind of involvement becomes counterproductive? If so, when? If your parents fit the model of "helicopter parenting" outlined here, would you be pleased?

Before you Read: Are there any annoying distractions in any of your classes? What are they? What could be done to eliminate them?

ESSAY #2 **THE LAPTOP ATE MY ATTENTION SPAN***
Abby Ellin

The author lives in New York and writes a regular column, "Preludes," for the *New York Times* about starting out in business.

1   [W]hat is] the latest issue on business school campuses? It is not whether to start your own dot-com before graduation, but whether you should be allowed to use your laptop in the classroom as you please.

2   While more and more schools—especially business schools—provide Internet access in class and require students to lug their laptops with them, some are imposing rules on what their students can and cannot do with them in class.

3   But why, in the sedate hallways of graduate schools, is there need for debate on rules of discipline? It seems that some students, although smart enough to earn M.B.A.'s, have not figured out how the old, generally unwritten rules of conduct apply to the wired classroom. More and more students are sending instant messages to one another (chatting and note passing, 21st century–style), day trading (as opposed to daydreaming) and even starting their own companies, all in class.

4   The resulting commotion has annoyed many students. Jen McEnry, 28, a second-year M.B.A. student at the University of Virginia's Darden Graduate School of Business Administration, recalled that a classmate once downloaded an e-mail attachment during a finance lecture. The attachment automatically turned on the sound on the student's computer, which then delivered a booming message: "Oh my God, I'm watching porn!" Everyone roared at the practical joke, but the problem was clear.

5   "It's distracting when people are day trading, checking their e-mails or surfing the Web," Ms. McEnry said. It is even more distracting because Darden relies heavily on classroom participation.

6   At Columbia University, the business school's newspaper reported that a student-run "chat room" ended up on the overhead projector in the middle of class. University officials denied the report. By January,

cyberspace had so intruded on classroom space at Columbia that a committee of professors and students came up with a code of professional conduct. "We're trying to find ways professors and students can use technology effectively and appropriately to create leaders," said Jeff Derman, a second-year M.B.A. student who heads the panel.

7   Yet how can M.B.A. students, whose average age is about 28 nationally, not know that it is rude to click away in class? After all, they presumably know not to walk out in the middle of a lecture, however boring. The rules of etiquette should not change just because of technology.

8   Still, some business schools have gone beyond issuing rules. Two years ago, Darden officials installed a switch in each classroom; a professor can program it to shut down the students' Net-surfing at fixed times. The students, however, found that they could override the teacher's decision by sneaking over before class and flicking the switch back on. It became a kind of game, the Battle of the Button.

9   The students spent hours arguing the broader issues. Should computers be banned from class? (No, we're adults! We pay to be here!) Should networks be shut off? (Of course not! Web access is an inalienable right!) Should professors be able to turn off the systems? (That's, like, so 1984!)

10   Blood started to boil: Students got mad at professors, professors got mad at students, students got mad at each other and everyone cursed technology. Why should they have to deal with all this when all they really wanted to do was learn how to be a millionaire?

11   Ms. McEnry proposes a standard of reasonable necessity. "If I'm expecting something important, like news about a job or something, then it's O.K. to go online," she said. "There are really pressing issues in people's lives, and they need to have access."

12   She is not kidding. Ms. McEnry found out that she had been elected president of the Student Association after her friends found the news on the school's Web site and told her. In class. [. . .]

13   At the Columbia business school, Safwan Masri, Vice Dean of Students and the M.B.A. program, takes a temperate tone. "These kids have grown up with computers; they can multitask," he said, explaining why Columbia decided against a Web shutdown switch. "We don't want to act as police. They're adults. We'd like to think they can control themselves."

14   I agree. Let them control themselves. If they cannot, here is my suggestion to them: Take a computer to the Metropolitan Opera. Log on. Write e-mail. Check your portfolio. At the end of the night, you will be lucky to still have a computer.

For Discussion:

Does this article describe a problem that you have experienced in your classes or labs? What do you think instructors should do? Do you think that students ever talk on cell phones or answer their beepers at inappropriate times? Elaborate. How do you think instructors should respond to that?

D. Group Work and Class Discussion: Analyzing Visual Argument

Look at the two images reprinted in this section. They are both stand-alone visual arguments, accompanied by titles or small amounts of text. The first is a painting, and the second is a photograph. You could analyze these as works of art, but you are not being asked to do that here. Instead, you will analyze them as visual arguments. Many images are subtly and deliberately persuasive, and you can learn to recognize, analyze, and evaluate them as arguments, just as you would print materials.

Organize into small groups, read the written commentary that accompanies each image, and answer these questions.

1. What is the issue?
2. How would you state the claim (the point of view on the issue that is communicated by the arguer)?
3. What reasons and evidence are given to support the position?
4. What makes the image interesting and effective as a visual argument?

Image 1:

This painting, titled *Blessed Art Thou*, is by the artist Kate Kretz. It features the actress Angelina Jolie and three of her children floating in the heavens above the check-out counters at a Wal-Mart. It has been distributed on the Internet and has been written about in newspapers. The artist has said that even though she has made many paintings, this is the first painting that has made her famous.

For Discussion: Why were people so taken with this painting when it first appeared? What is the significance of the title of the painting? What is the final effect of depicting the actress in this way, while, at the same time, including people checking out at a Wal-Mart store in the lower part of the painting? How would you explain the meaning of this painting? Can you think of other examples of the public holding celebrities in what has seemed to be an exaggerated high regard? Describe some of the visual argument associated with these celebrities and their activities.

Image 2:

This photograph is titled *The Tide Is High*. It presents an abandoned home in Nags Head on North Carolina's Outer Banks and shows the erosion from rising sea levels surrounding it. In 2000, beach erosion in the area also forced the relocation of the nearby Cape Hatteras lighthouse approximately 2,900 feet inland from its previous ocean side location.

For Discussion: What did you first think when you looked at this photograph? How did the description of it change your perception? Do you find this photo convincing as a visual argument? What do you conclude about the alleged situation depicted here?

SOURCE: © Gary Braasch

E. Before You Write: Finding Compelling Issues for Future Argument Papers

The objective is to make a list of the issues that interest you so that you can draw possible topics from this list for future argument papers.

1. *Find "your" issues.* Most students have issues that they really care about. What are yours? Think about what has affected you in the past. Think about your pet peeves. Think about recent news items on television or in the newspaper that have raised issues for you. Make a class list of the issues that concern you and the other students in your class.

2. *Identify campus issues.* What issues on campus concern you? What could be changed at your college to improve student life and learning? Make a class list.

F. Before You Write: Applying the Twelve Tests

Before you write about an issue, apply the twelve tests of an arguable issue that appear in Box 1.3 ▪ to make certain that it is arguable. If all of your answers are yes, you will be able to work with your issue productively. If any of your answers are no, you may want to modify your issue or switch to another one.

G. Writing Assignment: Writing a Short Argument on a Campus Issue

Select the campus issue that interests you the most, apply the twelve tests in Box 1.3, and write a 250- to 300-word argument about it. Use the two short arguments on pages 30–32 and 32–33 as models. Write a title that identifies your issue. Then make a statement (a claim) that explains your position on the issue, followed by reasons and supportive evidence to convince a college official to accept your views and perhaps take action to improve the situation.

| Box 1.3 | **Twelve Tests of an Arguable Issue.** |

▶▶▶ **Do You Have an Arguable Issue?**

If you cannot answer yes to all of these questions, change or modify your issue.
Your issue (phrased as a question): _____

Yes _____ No _____ 1. Is this an issue that has not been resolved or settled?

Yes _____ No _____ 2. Does this issue potentially inspire two or more views?

Yes _____ No _____ 3. Are you willing to consider a position different from your own and, perhaps, even modify your views on this issue?

Yes _____ No _____ 4. Are you sufficiently interested and engaged with this issue to inspire your audience also to become interested?

Yes _____ No _____ 5. Do other people perceive this as an issue?

Yes _____ No _____ 6. Is this issue significant enough to be worth your time?

Yes _____ No _____ 7. Is this a safe issue for you? Not too risky? Scary? Will you be willing to express your ideas?

Yes _____ No _____ 8. Can you establish common ground with your audience on this issue—common terms, common background, and related values?

Yes _____ No _____ 9. Will you be able to get information and come up with convincing insights on this issue?

Yes _____ No _____ 10. Can you eventually get a clear and limited focus on this issue, even if it is a complicated one?

Yes _____ No _____ 11. Is it an enduring issue, or can you build perspective by linking it to an enduring issue?

Yes _____ No _____ 12. Can you predict one or more audience outcomes? (Think of your classmates as the audience. Will they be convinced? Hostile? Neutral? Attentive? Remember that any outcomes at all can be regarded as significant in argument.)

The Rhetorical Situation: Understanding Audience and Context

After studying this chapter, you will be able to:

LO1 Identify the five elements of the Rhetorical Situation, and use these elements to analyze a written argument. (p. 39)

LO2 Use these five elements to analyze a visual argument. (p. 44)

LO3 Use these five elements to analyze an online argument. (p. 46)

LO4 Use these five elements to create your own written argument. (p. 48)

LO5 Describe the different types of audience. (p. 51)

You are probably beginning to realize by now that argument does not take place in a vacuum. Instead, a situation occurs that raises questions in people's minds and motivates them to discuss and argue in an attempt to resolve the issues and problems that emerge. For example, the price per barrel of crude oil goes up and issues emerge: How can the United States become less dependent on foreign oil? What are viable alternate energy sources? How effective are hybrid cars? Professor Lloyd Bitzer calls a situation that motivates issues and argument a *rhetorical situation*, because it stimulates discussion and encourages change. Rhetorical situations existed for the Declaration of Independence in 1776 when the issue was independence and its authors declared that the North American colonies should be independent from Great Britain, and for Abraham Lincoln's Gettysburg Address that he delivered in 1863 at the site of a famous Civil War battle. The issue was national unity. The time, place, and existing circumstances of these rhetorical situations provided the motivation for the authors of these documents to write them.[1] Five

---

[1] Lloyd Bitzer, "The Rhetorical Situation," *Philosophy and Rhetoric* 1 (January 1968): 1–14.

elements, according to Bitzer, are present in every rhetorical situation, and they can be analyzed.

In this chapter, we focus on the rhetorical situation as readers, creators of visual argument, and writers employ it. Analyzing the rhetorical situation is an important critical reading strategy: it can be used as a tool for analysis throughout the reading process; it can be employed in a similar way to gain a fuller understanding of visual argument; and it is a potent critical thinking strategy that can help the writer plan and write a better argument.

Analyze the Rhetorical Situation When You Read an Argument

According to Bitzer, a rhetorical situation has five elements. We rearrange the elements in order to form the acronym TRACE, from the initial letters of these five elements, to help you remember them: the *Text,* the *Reader* or audience, the *Author,* the *Constraints,* and the *Exigence* or cause. Now look at each of them to see how they can help you read, understand, and evaluate writing that presents an argument.

Text. The text is the argument. Whether it is written, visual, or spoken, the text will have characteristics you can analyze. These include the type of text (essay, letter, book, image, debate, etc.), the content of the text, and the format, organization, argumentation strategies, language, and style that are employed by the author.

Reader. The potential reader or audience for the text ideally must care enough to read or otherwise take in the text and pay attention. An audience might change their perceptions as a result and, perhaps, will mediate change or act in a new way. A rhetorical situation invites such audience responses and outcomes. Most authors have a targeted or intended reading audience in mind. You may identify with the targeted audience, or you may not, particularly if you belong to a different culture or live in a different time. As you read, compare your reactions to the text with the reactions you imagine the targeted or intended reading audience might have had.

Author. The author writes or develops an argument to convince a particular audience. You can analyze the author's position, motives, values, and degree of expertise. If you do not have direct information about the author, you will need to infer or guess at much of this information as you consider the argument text.

Constraints. Constraints include the people, events, circumstances, and traditions that are part of the situation that constrain or limit a targeted audience and cause them to analyze and react to the situation in a particular way. Constraints also include the beliefs, attitudes, prejudices, interests, and habits that influence the audience's perceptions of the situation. The author brings another set of constraints to the situation. These include the author's character, background, available resources, and style. The limits inherent in the type of text being produced, whether written, spoken, or visual, can also provide constraints. Constraints may draw the author and audience together, or they may drive them apart. They influence the amount of common ground that will be established between an author and an audience. Look at the cartoon in Figure 2.1 ▪ for an example of constraints that are driving people apart. The constraints in this example are the basic assumptions about who governs in this family. What would you say are the father's constraints in this situation, and how do they differ from those of the rest of the family?

Here are some additional examples of constraints: (1) An audience feels constrained to mistrust the media because it thinks reporters exaggerate or lie. This constraint may cause this audience to be cynical and suspicious of an essay written by an editor that praises reporters for always writing the truth. (2) Another essay, by a famous biologist, presents the global environmental and overpopulation crisis in such catastrophic and frightening terms that a particular audience is constrained, through fear, to shut out the argument and refuse to consider it. (3) Some voters have lost their faith in political leaders. When they are mailed brochures that argue in favor of particular candidates and that ask them to support these candidates with donations, their constraints cause them to throw these materials away without looking at them.

Figure 2.1
Constraints in the Form of Basic Assumptions Driving People Apart.

SOURCE: © The New Yorker Collection 2004 Lee Lorenz from cartoonbank .com. All Rights Reserved.

"Because this family isn't ready to hold democratic elections—that's why!"

As these examples demonstrate, a constraint can include a specific attitude or assumption on the part of an author or an audience. In addition, constraints also include those external factors—from formal rules or laws to informal social norms or traditions—that play a role in shaping these attitudes and assumptions. Here are two more examples of constraints that may be closer to you: (1) You parked your car in a no-parking zone because you were late to class, and the police feel constrained by law to give you a ticket. You have different constraints, and you write to the hearings board that more and closer parking should be available to students to help them get to class on time. The hearings board has its own constraints, and will probably turn down your plea. (2) You believe everyone should share the household chores equally, and the person you live with disagrees. Both of you are constrained by your past experiences in living with other people, possibly by traditions that influence your ideas about gender roles in this type of division of labor, and also by perceptions about who has the most time to spend on the chores. Both parties may have to work hard to create the common ground necessary to resolve this issue. Notice how the constraints present on both sides in these examples influence the way the audience and the arguer react to the rhetorical situation and to the issues it generates.

> *Exigence.* Exigence is the part of the situation that signals that something controversial has occurred or is present and that a problem needs to be resolved by some response from an audience. Here are some examples of exigence for argument: people become suspicious of genetically engineered foods because of negative newspaper reports; a third-world country threatens to resume nuclear testing; a football player is badly injured in a game and the fans of the opposing team cheer in delight. In all cases, something is wrong, imperfect, defective, or in conflict. Exigence invites analysis and discussion, and sometimes a written response to encourage both individual public awareness and discourse about problematic situations.

41

Study the following set of questions. They will help you analyze the rhetorical situation and gain insight into its component parts when you are the reader.

> *Text.* What kind of text is it? What are its special qualities and features? What is it about?
> *Reader or audience.* Who is the *targeted audience?* What is the nature of this group? Can they be convinced? What are the anticipated outcomes? If you are reading a historical document—for example, the Declaration of Independence—you might ask further: How did the readers at the time the text was written differ from other readers of the time or from modern readers? Were they convinced? Did they act on their convictions?
>> Now consider how you, *as a reader,* compare with the targeted audience and ask: *Am I typical of one of the readers the writer anticipated? What is my initial position? What are my constraints? Do I share common ground with the*

author and other audience members? Am I open to change? Does this argument convince me? Am I motivated to change my mind or modify the situation? How?

Author. Who is the author? Consider background, experience, education, affiliations, and values. What is motivating the author to write?

Constraints. What special constraining circumstances will influence the reader's and the author's responses to the subject? Think about the people, events, circumstances, and traditions that are already in place along with the beliefs, attitudes, prejudices, interests, habits, and motives held by both the author and the reader that may limit or constrain their perceptions. Do the constraints create common ground, or do they drive the reader and author apart?

Exigence. What happened to cause this argument? Why is it perceived as a defect or problem? Is it new or recurring?

The student editorial from a college newspaper reprinted below addresses grading policies. Read the essay first and then read the analysis of the rhetorical situation that follows it. This analysis provides an example of how readers can use the rhetorical situation to help them understand argument.

Before You Read: What are your opinions about the grading policies in your classes?

ESSAY #1   "A" IS FOR "ABSENT"*

Chris Piper

Chris Piper was a broadcast journalism major at the University of Texas at Arlington when he wrote this essay for the student newspaper, for which he also worked as a proofreader.

1   Last semester, I enrolled in one of the most dreaded courses in any communication degree plan. Most save it until the very end of their college career, but I took it as a sophomore.

2   Remarkably, I did very well on all of the tests. Also, the professor gave me high marks on almost every project. But when final grades came out, I ended up with a "C." My absences dropped my average more than 10 points. Admittedly, I earned the grade given to me. The syllabus clearly stated what would occur if I missed more than my allotted "freebies."

3   But my refusal to attend class does not excuse policies that subvert the value of learning and education, emphasizing attendance instead.

4   Professors who implement attendance policies often argue, "If this were a job, and you failed to show up, you would be fired." There is, however, one big difference between going to work versus going to class.

5   A job pays for my service, but I pay my professors for their services. I spend plenty of money on my education, and my choice to fully take advantage of the expense is exactly that—my choice.

6   When evaluating superior standardized test scores, such as what one might make on the SAT and ACT, admissions officers don't ask whether students attended prep courses before the exam. Obviously, a high score denotes that a test taker knows the material.

7   I truly believe most professors want their students to score well, which is why they implement attendance policies. I am touched by the sentiment. But, if missing class leads to poor results by traditional grading methods—tests, quizzes, projects, etc.—then so be it. The student body could use some winnowing out.

8   I imagine a few instructors adopt attendance policies to stroke their own egos—to ensure a crowd is present when they enlighten the eager masses. But I'm arguing the validity of such rules regardless of any questionable motives. If a student can earn good grades on required work without attending class, then instructors should grade that student accordingly.

9   I encourage professors to give pop quizzes in place of attendance policies. At the very least, a quiz measures comprehension of pertinent material. Of course, such a change would mean more work for professors.

10   But that's what students are paying for.

For Discussion:

What is the issue? What is the author's position on the issue? What reasons and evidence are given to support the author's position? What is your position on this issue? How much common ground do you share with your instructors on this issue?

Here is an analysis of the rhetorical situation for "'A' Is for 'Absent.'"

▶ Example of an Analysis of a Rhetorical Situation from the Reader's Point of View

Text. This is an argumentative editorial in the student newspaper that provides reasons and personal experience to prove that professors should not have attendance policies that lower students' grades for excessive absences.

Reader or audience. The targeted readers are other students who have had or could have similar experiences. The author expects the students to identify with him and agree that such policies should be abolished. Other readers might include professors and administrators who would probably be less likely to agree with the author.

Author. The author is a sophomore majoring in communications who had good grades on tests and projects but who lost ten points and ended up with a C for missing more classes than the syllabus allowed. The author also is a proofreader for the college newspaper.

Constraints. The author is constrained by the belief that students are customers who pay professors for their services and should be able to take advantage of those services on their own terms. He is also constrained by the idea that students can learn enough material to merit good grades without going to class. He expects his readers to hold the same beliefs. Another constraint he recognizes is the right of the professors to determine grading policy.

Exigence. The student received a C grade in a course in which he thought he should have had a higher grade.

Now consider how an understanding of the rhetorical situation can help you analyze images.

Arguing like a Citizen Activity

Take another look at the issue you identified in "'A' is for 'Absent'". In order to connect the argument in this essay more directly to citizenship, answer the following questions.

▶▶▶ Thinking Like a Citizen

- Why do I care about this issue? What is my stake?
- Who else cares about this issue? Who are the other stakeholders? What other individuals or groups are most likely to consider this issue important?
- What are the different perspectives on this issue others might have? How are their stakes in this issue similar to or different from my own?
- What are the factors and/or circumstances that account for these differences?

▶▶▶ Arguing Like a Citizen

- How does this issue impact or affect my daily life? What difference does it make to me?
- What are the key problems or questions this issue raises for me? Are these problems and questions the same as those this issue raises for others?
- What are the differences among us that a discussion or debate over this issue might expose? How might these differences be bridged?

▶▶▶ Acting Like a Citizen

- Where could I go in my community to see an example of this debate being waged?
- What concrete action could I take to change or improve the way this issue is debated? What sort of concrete action might help resolve this debate?

Analyze the Rhetorical Situation When You View a Visual Argument

In our visual culture, natural disasters are the subject of extensive news coverage. The images photographers have sent back from disaster zones highlight not only the damage inflicted but the efforts to lend assistance Figure 2.2 ■. Former President Bill Clinton offering assistance to residents of Port-au-Prince, Haiti,

Bill Clinton visits Haiti
Former President Bill Clinton pledges to donate $500,000 dollars to rebuild a bridge in the earthquake-ravaged city of Port-au-Prince, Haiti.

Figure 2.2 *Photograph from the Haitian earthquake.*

This image appeared as a stand-alone image in a national United States newspaper. View this photograph as an argument. How is it different from many of the images of natural disasters you have seen on television or in newspapers? How does it affect you as a viewer?

following that country's devastating earthquake in January 2010. Look at the image, read the caption that accompanies it, and consider the questions in the margin. Then read the following analysis of the rhetorical situation of the image and notice how much more you learn about this photo and its possible effect on an audience.

▶ Example of an Analysis of the Rhetorical Situation from the Viewer's Point of View

Text. This is a photograph from the earthquake zone in Haiti. It is printed in an American newspaper. It depicts a former President Bill Clinton greeting residents of Port-au-Prince, Haiti.

Viewer or audience. The targeted viewers are people in the United States, but also in other parts of the world, who read this newspaper either online or in print. The photographer expects the audience to be interested in what is going on in Haiti in general, but also to show an interest in natural disasters of this sort. The photographer would expect a sympathetic audience who shares his humanitarian values.

Photographer or artist. This photographer works for Getty Images, a major source of digital images used by the news media.

Constraints. The artist is constrained by the idea that natural disasters often bring out the best impulses in people to lend assistance. At times, good and generous acts as well as unexpected cooperation can occur in the midst of such events. He expects viewers to accept these constraints when they view his photograph, which will result in common ground with his audience.

Exigence. A former U.S. President lends aid to suffering Haitians in the aftermath of a devastating earthquake.

Next, consider how an understanding of the rhetorical situation of written arguments also helps you as a writer.

Analyze the Rhetorical Situation When You Encounter an Argument Online

The recent BP Oil Spill in the Gulf of Mexico is considered by many to be one of the worst environmental catastrophes in American history. This spill, which released on unprecedented amount of oil into the Gulf, raised serious questions regarding our country's energy needs, our current energy consumption practices, and the effect of both on the overall health of the environment. Look at the Web site on page 47. What stands out to you about the visual images presented? What message about oil drilling, energy consumption, and the environment do they seem designed to convey? How does the written text, which accompanies these images, influence or reinforce this message? How is this message further affected by the links to other sources that this site includes? Once you have answered these questions, read the following analysis of the rhetorical situation presented by this Web site, and see whether you would add any further observations or interpretation.

Text. This is a Web site that highlights the environmental damage from the 2010 BP/Horizon oil spill in the Gulf. It is created by the British Petroleum Corporation and is part of its larger public relations campaign to deal with public criticism of the spill. It depicts an oil-covered beach, and includes text pledging the company's commitment to clean up the spill.

Viewer or audience. The targeted viewers for this text are people in the United States, and perhaps more particularly, those Americans who live in those areas affected by the oil spill. The creators of this Web site expect the audience to be aware of the spill and the extent of the damage it has caused, and also to have concerns about the degree to which BP is willing

to accept responsibility for the spill. The creators would expect a resistant or skeptical audience, but one who could be swayed by reassurances from the company.

Author. The author(s) of this Web site are the people managing the coastline response and the external communications teams who are working for BP.

Constraints. The authors are constrained by their belief that oil companies are not simply a threat to environmental safety, but can also act as legitimate and responsible corporate citizens. When presented with the opportunity, the authors believe, such companies will accept responsibility for their actions and work to preserve the quality of the environment. The audience is constrained by their own skepticism concerning the motives of such companies, a suspicion fueled in part by the media coverage of the BP/Horizon oil spill, which tended to cast BP as indifferent to public safety and environmental concerns.

Exigence. An oil rig collapses in the Gulf of Mexico, resulting in the release of millions of gallons of oil from a blown-out well. The US government attempts to work with British Petroleum to contain the spill, but these efforts fail for several months to stem the flow of oil into the Gulf, resulting in severe environmental damage to ocean life and the Gulf shoreline.

Use the Rhetorical Situation When You Write an Argument

As a writer, you can use the rhetorical situation to help you think critically and make decisions about your own writing. All five elements of the rhetorical situation are important considerations for writers. Three elements are in place before you begin to write. They are the *exigence,* the *reader or audience,* and the *constraints.* When you begin to write, the other two elements are added: you, the *author,* and the *text* that you create. Figure 2.3 ▪ provides a diagram of these five elements that depicts some of the relationships among them.

Now consider each of the five elements from the writer's point of view. Use TRACE to help you remember the elements. As a writer, however, you will think about them not in the order presented in the mnemonic but in the order suggested in the previous paragraph.

What Is the Exigence?

The exigence of a situation will provide an author with the motivation to write about an issue. Issues often emerge from real-life events that signal something is wrong. One student found a topic when a relative who had spent time in jail could not get employment after he was released. Another student from a country outside of the United States became interested in intercultural differences and decided to write about the relative value of retaining her own culture or assimilating with a new one. Yet another student discovered an exigence when she read a negative article about Barbie dolls and remembered her positive experiences with them when she was younger.

Figure 2.3 *The Five Elements of the Rhetorical Situation That the Writer Considers While Planning and Writing Argument.*

The context for argument: *exigence* and *constraints* that influence both author and audience

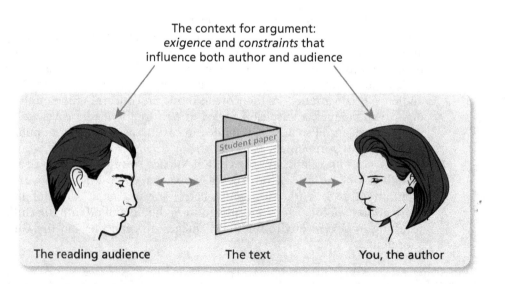

The reading audience   The text   You, the author

Such occurrences can cause the writer to ask the questions associated with exigence: *What issues, including problems or defects, are revealed? Are these new issues or recurring issues? How severe is the problem or defect?*

Who Is the Reader or Audience?

According to the definition of argument established in Chapter 1, productive argument must create common ground and achieve some definable audience outcomes. To do this, a writer needs to analyze the audience's present opinions, values, and motives, and show as often as possible that the author shares them. Both audience and author must cooperate to a certain degree for argument to achieve any outcomes at all.

To help you understand your audience, ask: *Who are my readers? Where do they stand on my issue? How can I establish common ground with them? If they disagree with me, will they be willing to change or modify their views, or not?*

What Are Some of the Constraints?

Remember that constraints influence the ways in which both you and your audience think about the issues. What background, events, experiences, traditions, values, or associations are influencing both you and them? If you decide to write to convince an audience that has no experience with criminals to hire people with criminal records, what are their constraints likely to be? How hard will it be for them to adopt your views? On the other hand, if you are an international student who is comparing your culture with the American culture to decide how much to change and adapt to American ways, and your audience is only familiar with its own culture, what will you do to help them see this problem as you see it? If you are writing for an audience that is mostly male and has no experience with or memories of Barbie dolls, what constraints would you run into if you tried to convince them that Barbie dolls are an important part of children's experience?

To help you understand the constraints held by both you and your audience, ask: *How are our training, background, affiliations, and values either in harmony or in conflict? Will constraints drive us apart or help us build common ground? If they drive us apart, what additional information can I provide to build common ground and bring us closer together? Where will my argument appear? Will it be a paper for an instructor, a letter to a supervisor, a letter to an editor, or a posting in an online chat room? Each medium has its own requirements.*

You are in a position now to think about the remaining two elements of the rhetorical situation: you, the *author*, and the *text* you will write.

Who Is the Author?

You will now need to think of yourself as an author of argument. You may have selected one or more issues to write about at this point. Before beginning your research, reflect on what you already know about your issue and what you still

49

need to learn. Draw on your own experience, if you have some that applies. For instance, one student might think about her relative's experiences in prison and imagine a better life for him, another might feel out of place in America and wonder how much he should change, and yet another student recalls her Barbie dolls and looks back with pleasure on the many hours she spent playing with them. Make brief notes on this experience to use later in your paper. If you have no direct experience to draw on, research, reading, and critical thinking will provide the material for your paper.

To better consider your role as the author, ask these questions: *Why am I interested in this issue? Why do I perceive it as a defect or problem? Is it a new or old issue for me? What is my personal background or experience with this issue? What makes me qualified to write about it? Which of my personal values are involved? How can I get more information? What is my purpose and perspective? How can I make my paper convincing?*

How Should the Text Be Developed to Fit the Situation?

Your text (paper) may be written in response to an assignment in your argument class, in which case it should meticulously follow the assignment requirements. You might also write a paper for another class, a proposal at work, or a letter to the editor of a newspaper, to name a few possibilities.

Questions such as the following will help you decide what your completed argument text might look like: *What is the assignment? What final form should this paper take? Should I use an adversarial or a consensual style? How can I build common ground? Should I state the issue and my position on it right away, or should I lead up to it? How can I make my position original and interesting? What types of support should I use? How will I conclude my argument?*

▶ Example of an Analysis of a Rhetorical Situation When You Are the Writer

Exigence: What is motivating you to write on this issue? You neglected to turn in two early assignments in a course, and you suddenly realize that the zeroes you received then will lower your final grade from a B to a C. If you get a C, you will lose your scholarship. You decide to write to your instructor to find a way to raise your grade.

Reader or Audience: Who is going to read this? Your instructor (the audience) has already announced a policy of no late work. Nothing has been said about extra-credit work, however. You will try to establish common ground with the instructor by proposing an extra-credit project that will benefit not just you, but the entire class. You will describe in detail a successful experience you had with online research on your paper topic. The class is struggling with online research, the teacher wants the students to learn it, she does not have much time to teach it, and you can help fill the gap.

Constraints: Will your values and attitudes drive you and your instructor apart, or will they help you develop common ground? The instructor will have time constraints in class and may be unwilling to give you class time for your project. To address that constraint, you decide to ask for only five minutes, and you offer to prepare handouts that describe your online research in a way that will benefit your classmates.

The instructor may also have constraints about replacing missed assignments with extra-credit work. If one student is allowed to do this, she reasons, will all the others want to also? You point out that the project you are proposing is more difficult than the early assignments you missed and probably few, if any, students will want to follow your example.

You create common ground with your instructor by showing you are serious about the course and its standards. You decide to admit to your bad judgment when you failed to complete assignments, to point out that you have done well since then, and to commit to completing the remaining assignments carefully and on time. You also explain the importance of the extra-credit work to your future as a student. Without your scholarship, you will have to drop out of school. You know that you and your teacher share a desire to keep students in school. You and your instructor have common ground on that matter as well.

Author: *What do you know? What do you need to learn?* You are the author. You have read the class policies in the syllabus and know you have to work with them. You know you have computer expertise that many others in the class lack. You need to learn how to present what you know both orally and in written handouts to help the rest of the class.

Text: *What should your argument look like?* You will write a one-page proposal to your instructor in which you describe in detail what you would like to present to the class about online research. You ask that this assignment be used to raise the zero grades you received earlier in the course. You attach a second page that shows a sample of the handouts you will prepare for the class.

The class activities and writing assignments at the end of this chapter will help you use the information about the rhetorical situation that you have learned in this chapter. For example, one of the activities instructs you to analyze the rhetorical situation for each issue you select to write about in future papers, and another asks you to conduct an audience analysis of your class members who will read the various drafts of your papers. Before you turn to the activities and writing assignments, however, you will need additional information to help you think about and analyze an audience for an argument paper.

Conducting an Audience Analysis

The purpose of argument is to bring about some change in an audience. Here are several additional considerations to help you understand your audience and plan your argument strategies to bring about change.

Determine the Audience's Initial Position and Consider How It Might Change

As part of your planning, project what you would regard as acceptable audience outcomes for your argument. Think particularly about the degree of common ground you initially share with your audience because it is then easier to plan for audience change. There are several possibilities for initial audience positions and possible changes or outcomes.

▶ *A friendly audience.* You may be writing for a friendly audience, one that is in *near or total agreement with you* from the outset. The planned outcome is to *confirm this audience's beliefs and strengthen their commitment.* You can be straightforward with such an audience, addressing them directly and openly with your claim at the beginning, supported with evidence that they can accept. Political rallies, religious sermons, and public demonstrations by special-interest groups, such as civil rights or environmental groups, all serve to make members more strongly committed to their original beliefs. When you write for a friendly audience, you will achieve the same effect.

▶ *An undecided audience.* This audience either mildly agrees with you or mildly opposes you. They *may possess no clear reasons* for their tendencies or beliefs. Possible outcomes in this case usually include (1) *final agreement* with you, (2) *a new interest* in the issue and a commitment to work out a position on it, or (3) *a tentative decision* to accept what seems to be true for now. To establish common ground with this kind of audience, get to the point quickly and use support that will establish connections.

▶ *A neutral audience.* Other audiences may be *neutral on your issue; uncommitted and uninterested in how it is resolved.* Your aim will be to *change the level of their indifference* and encourage them to take a position. You may only be able to get their attention or raise their level of consciousness. As with other audiences, you will establish common ground with a neutral audience by analyzing their needs and by appealing to those needs.

▶ *A hostile, resistant audience.* A hostile audience, which may fully disagree with you, may also be closed to the idea of change at all, at least at first. Anticipated outcomes for such audiences might include *avoiding more hostility* and *getting people to listen and consider possible alternative views.* You will learn strategies in Chapter 13 to help you appeal to such audiences. It is always possible that a hostile audience will have their minds *changed* or at least *compromise.* If all else fails, sometimes you can get a hostile audience to *agree to disagree,* which is much better than increasing their hostility.

▶ *An unfamiliar audience.* When you do not know your audience's position, it is best to *imagine them as neutral to mildly opposed* to your views and direct your argument with that in mind. Imagining an unfamiliar audience as either hostile or friendly can lead to extreme positions that may cause the argument to fail. Imagining the audience as neutral or mildly opposed ensures *an even tone* to the argument that *promotes audience interest and receptivity.*

▶ *A linked audience.* Linked audience refers to a reader not directly connected to or immediately participating in the discussion of a given issue, but who does have an interest in some issue that is related. This is often the case for arguments online, where the discussion or debate of a given issue will frequently include references or links to discussions of similar issues. What can we say about the audience to whom this linked issue is directed? What assumptions can we make about how this audience understands the issue at hand? What additional discussion or information would most help this linked audience to respond positively to the argument being made here?

Think of your relationship with your audience as if it were plotted on a sliding scale. At one end are the people who agree with you, and at the other end are those who disagree. In the middle are the neutral audience and the unknown audience. Other mildly hostile or mildly favorable audiences are positioned at various points in between. Your knowledge of human nature and argument theory will help you plan strategies of argument that will address all these audience types and perhaps cause them to change their initial position on the sliding scale.

Analyze the Audience's Discourse Community

Besides analyzing your audience's initial position and how it might change, it is also useful to identify the audience's *discourse community*. An audience's affiliations can help define the nature of the audience itself. Specialized groups who share subject matter, background, experience, values, and a common language (including specialized and technical vocabulary, jargon, or slang) are known as discourse communities.

Consider discourse communities composed of all scientists, all engineers, or all mathematicians. Their common background, training, language, and knowledge make it easier for them to connect, achieve common ground, and work toward conclusions. The discourse community itself creates some of the common ground necessary for successful academic inquiry or for other types of argument.

You are a member of the university or college discourse community where you attend classes. This community is characterized by reasonable and educated people who share common backgrounds and interests that enable them to inquire into matters that are still at issue. You are also a member of the discourse community in your argument class, which has a common vocabulary and common tasks and assignments. Outsiders visiting your class would not be members of this community in the same way that you and your classmates are. To what other discourse communities do you belong?

Compare argument in your class with argument at home, at work, or with your friends. The strategies for connecting with others, building common ground, and arguing within the context of each of your discourse communities can vary considerably. With some reflection, you will be able to think of examples of the ways you have analyzed and adapted to each of them already. You can improve your natural ability to work with audiences by learning several conscious strategies for analyzing and adapting to both familiar and unfamiliar audiences.

Analyze and Adapt to a Familiar Audience

In working with a familiar audience, ask questions such as the following to learn more about them:

▶ Who are the members of your audience and what do you have in common with them?

▶ What are some of the demographic characteristics of this audience? Consider number, age, organizational affiliations, interests, and college majors.

▶ What is the present position of audience members on your issue, and what audience outcomes can you anticipate?

▶ What experience do audience members have with your issue? Ask about their knowledge and background, including both positive and negative experiences and obstacles.

▶ What beliefs, values, motives, goals, or aims about your issue do you share?

Construct an Unfamiliar Audience

Sometimes you will not be able to gather direct information about your audience because these readers will be unfamiliar to you and unavailable for study. In this case, you will need to draw on your experience for audience analysis. To do so, imagine a particular kind of audience, a *universal audience,* and write for them when you cannot collect direct audience information.

Chaim Perelman, who has written extensively about the difficulty of identifying the qualities of audiences with certainty, developed the concept of the universal audience.[2] He suggests planning an argument for a *composite audience,* one with distinct individual differences but also important common qualities. This universal audience is educated, reasonable, normal, adult, and willing to listen. Every arguer constructs the universal audience from his or her own experiences, and consequently the concept of the universal audience varies somewhat from individual to individual and culture to culture.

The construct of the universal audience can be useful when you write papers for your other college classes. It is especially useful when the audience is largely unknown and you cannot obtain much information about them. Imagine writing for a universal audience on those occasions. Your professors and classmates as a group possess the general qualities of this audience.

---

[2]See Perelman and Olbrechts-Tyteca, *The New Rhetoric,* for additional details on the universal audience.

CONSTRUCT YOUR OWN UNIVERSAL AUDIENCE

Choose an issue and create a composite portrait of the hypothetical or universal audience you aim to address. What preexisting views on this issue does this audience hold? What constraints operate on this audience? What attitudes or assumptions influence their views? What factors influence these attitudes and assumptions? Then, based on this profile, speculate about how this audience would affect/influence your specific choices/strategies for making your argument.

When you complete the analysis of your audience, go back through the information you have gathered and consciously decide which audience characteristics to appeal to in your paper. You will then be in a position to gather materials for your paper that will be convincing to this particular audience. You will develop reasoning and support that audience members can link to their personal values, motives, beliefs, knowledge, and experience. Similarly, you need to show the same care in adapting to the needs of a universal audience. Since this audience is reasonable, educated, and adult, reasoning and support must be on their level and should also have broad applicability and acceptance. The universal audience inspires a high level of argumentation. *Careful research, intelligent reasoning, and clear writing style are requirements for this audience.*

Use your understanding of the rhetorical situation to help you read and to help you get ideas and plan your own argument writing. It can be useful at every stage when you are reading, thinking, and writing about issues. The Summary Chart of the Rhetorical Situation provides a brief version of the elements of the rhetorical situation as it applies to both reading and writing. Use it as a quick reference worksheet as you read or plan and write argument.

Review Questions

1. What are the five elements in the rhetorical situation? Use TRACE to help you remember.

2. How can a reader use the rhetorical situation to analyze an argument essay? How can a viewer use the rhetorical situation to analyze an image? How can a writer use the rhetorical situation during the planning phase of writing a paper?

3. Why is the audience important in argument? What types of positions might an audience initially hold? What possible outcomes are associated with arguments directed to each of these audiences?

4. What is a discourse community? To what discourse communities do you belong? How does a discourse community help establish common ground for its members?

5. What is the universal audience? What are the special qualities of this audience? Why is it a useful idea?

55

Exercises and Activities

A. Class Discussion: Analyzing the Rhetorical Situation for an Essay

Read the following essay by Will Harrel. Then answer the questions for discussion that follow the essay.

Before You Read: How do you understand the term "grade deflation"? In your experience, does this term describe a widespread problem within higher education? Do you see any connections between this issue and those raised by Piper regarding absence policies?

ESSAY #2   "A DEFENSE OF GRADE DEFLATION"*
Will Harrel

Will Harrel is a student at Princeton University and a contributing writer to the *Daily Princetonian*, the campus newspaper.

1   While Princeton's diverse student body rarely unifies around a single issue, nearly every student seems to have rallied against grade deflation. This forces advocates of the policy—well, the few that exist—to always be on the defensive, addressing only the apparent negatives of grade deflation without discussing the benefits. I'll begin this defense of grade deflation by once again discussing the negatives, but I will conclude by finally going on the offensive.

2   One common complaint is that grade deflation compounds students' stress. While added pressure about grades does entail added stress, this pressure encourages students to work harder and learn more. Low standards breed low results, and grade deflation is an excellent way to increase standards. If a student knows he has a guaranteed A, he has no incentive to work harder for a better grade. It's certainly nice to relax or party, but the purpose of a university is to teach, not to entertain, so Princeton's policies should focus on maximizing academics, not leisure. Rather than studying hard, if we want to breeze through college without much depth, receiving a high GPA and a diploma with honors, we could always go to Harvard. In the long run, however, knowledge and study skills are more useful than a high GPA. After a few years, achievement beyond graduation matters more than anything else.

3   Another major complaint is that grade deflation hurts our job and graduate-school prospects. While some employers and graduate schools are certainly unfamiliar with Princeton's grading system, admission rates and job placements have actually risen slightly since grade deflation was instituted, as demonstrated by statistics in the "Grading at Princeton" pamphlet. From 2004 (the last class without grade deflation) to 2009, even accounting for the economic downturn, the

percentage of seniors with full-time jobs in hand actually grew slightly, from 29.4 percent to 29.6 percent. Both medical-school and law-school acceptance rates also grew, from 92.0 percent to 93.0 percent, and 25.9 percent to 34.5 percent, respectively. Moreover, Princeton sends out a letter with every transcript explaining the grading system, and employers and graduate schools know that GPAs from different schools have different meanings. For instance, MIT has a GPA scale from 5.0 to 0.0, and nobody would compare that GPA to a 4.0 scale side-by-side. Something like MIT's scale might actually be a useful next step for Princeton to clearly differentiate its grading scheme and increase awareness about grade deflation beyond Princeton.

4   On a slightly more trivial note, I've heard complaints that grade deflation renders the A-plus obsolete. While no statistics are released, Paolo Esquivel's 2009 article, "A-pluses in a time of grade deflation," mentions many examples of people with multiple A-pluses, and I know that at least two of my friends have also received A-pluses in stereotypically difficult courses. While receiving this ultimate mark is certainly difficult, it is definitely attainable.

5   Now that I have addressed the negatives of grade deflation, I must also discuss the two major benefits. First, it differentiates students more clearly in the top of the class. When everybody receives A's, employers and graduate schools have difficulty distinguishing between the good and the excellent students. In 2001, 91 percent of Harvard seniors graduated with honors, prompting former dean and acting president of Harvard Henry Rosovksy to say, "Honors at Harvard has just lost all meaning. The bad honors is spoiling the good." This absurd "honors inflation" was certainly beneficial to the students in the 50th through 91st percentiles range, but those in the top of the class were not rewarded

for their hard work. Instead, they were clumped together with mediocre students. The bottom 9 percent of the class were essentially outcasts.

6   Princeton's goal should not be handing out diplomas with honors but rather should be educating students and rewarding exceptional students for exceptional work. We have a 4.0 scale, so why would we only use 1 or 2 points of it? Grade inflation is excellent at highlighting the worst students, because so few students get low grades. By providing rigorous grading standards, Princeton highlights the best, not just the worst. For instance, because of the transcript letter, employers know that a Princeton student with a 3.7 GPA is an excellent student, and students are still being hired at similar or better rates. While grade deflation makes a 3.7 difficult, it is certainly achievable, and those who are able to achieve it are rewarded.

7   The other major benefit of grade deflation is its consistency across classes and departments. There are still certainly many kinks to be fixed in the soft quota system, but it is an excellent step in the right direction. The beauty of the system is that departments can assign a higher proportion of A grades to more competitive courses in order to maintain consistent standards across classes and departments. This allows me to place very little weight on the difficulty of grading when choosing my courses, because I know that our grades will be based on our abilities, not the professor's arbitrary grading standards. Grade deflation discourages people from gaming the system and taking "easy" courses in which everybody gets an A. Coupled with the new pass/D/fail policy changes, these effects now encourage students to take courses that excite them, not just ones that promise A's. While the current system is not completely flawless, the harms are negligible, and the benefits are great.

B. Writing Assignment: Analyzing the Rhetorical Situation in Written Argumentation

Read one of the articles that appear in this chapter. Then write a 300- to 400-word paper in which you explain the rhetorical situation for this essay. Answer the following questions using TRACE.

1. How would you describe the text itself?

2. How would you characterize the reader or audience that the author may have had in mind while writing the essay? To what degree do you identify with this audience?

3. What do you learn about the author?

4. What are some of the possible constraints that might have influenced the author? What constraints influence you as you read this essay?

5. What is the exigence for this essay?

C. Group Work: Analyzing the Rhetorical Situation in Visual Argument

The three images reprinted here are visual arguments that memorialize historic events. They may not appear at first to be visual arguments until you learn something about the history and original rhetorical situations in which they were situated. All three are photographs, and they are accompanied by enough explanation to help you understand the rhetorical situations in which they occurred. This will allow you to evaluate their effectiveness as visual arguments, both now and when they first appeared.

Form small groups, view each image, read the written commentary and essays that provide information about the photos, and answer the "For Discussion" questions that follow them. Then answer the following questions about their rhetorical situations. Refer back to the example of the analysis of the rhetorical situation from the viewer's point of view on pages 45–46, if you need to recall its details.

1. *Image*. What type of image is it? What are its qualities and features? What is it about?

2. *Viewer or audience:* Who do you think was targeted as the most appropriate audience at the time each photo was taken? Who might still regard each of these photos as a compelling visual argument?

3. *Photographer:* What do you know about the photographer, and what may have motivated that individual to take the photo? What might have been the intended result?

4. *Constraints:* What constraints influenced the photographer? Consider the influential events, circumstances, and traditions already in place at the time each photo was taken. Consider, also, the possible beliefs, attitudes, motives, and prejudices of the photographer. How about your

constraints? Do any of your beliefs, attitudes, or prejudices seem to match those of the photographer, or are they different? Do the possible constraints you have identified create common ground between yourself and the photographer, or do they drive you apart?

5. *Exigence:* What motivated the photographer to take each of these photos? What happened? Was it perceived as a defect or problem? If yes, why? Was it new or recurring?

Image 1: This photograph was taken in 1956 early in the civil rights movement in Alabama when the issue was segregation in public facilities. Until this time, African American people were required to sit only at the back of public buses. A new national ruling gave them the right to sit wherever they wanted to sit. In the photograph, Rosa Parks, an African American civil rights activist, tests this new ruling by taking a seat in the front of the bus with a white man seated behind her. This is a famous photograph. It appears on the walls of buses in New York City and has come to symbolize change brought about by the movement for civil rights that continued into the next decades.

Rosa Parks riding a Montgomery, Ala., bus in December 1956, after the Supreme Court outlawed segregation on buses.

Image 1:
Rosa Parks Rides in the Front of the Bus.

Look at the image and read the essay that follows. It explains the history of this photograph and will provide you with the information you need to analyze the rhetorical situation.

Before You Read: What more would you like to know about the history of civil rights and racial segregation in the US? How might this historical context affect how you view the Rosa Parks photograph?

ESSAY #3   THE CIVIL RIGHTS ERA

The Library of Congress

The following excerpt is part of the project entitled "The African American Odyssey," an historical overview of African-American history created by the Library of Congress.

1   The post-war era marked a period of unprecedented energy against the second class citizenship accorded to African Americans in many parts of the nation. Resistance to racial segregation and discrimination with strategies such as civil disobedience, nonviolent resistance, marches, protests, boycotts, "freedom rides," and rallies received national attention as newspaper, radio, and television reporters and cameramen documented the struggle to end racial inequality. There were also continuing efforts to legally challenge segregation through the courts.

2   Success crowned these efforts: the Brown decision in 1954, the Civil Rights Act of 1964, and the Voting Rights Act in 1965 helped bring about the demise of the entangling web of legislation that bound blacks to second class citizenship. One hundred years after the Civil War, blacks and their white allies still pursued the battle for equal rights in every area of American life. While there is more to achieve in ending discrimination, major milestones in civil rights laws are on the books for the purpose of regulating equal access to public accommodations, equal justice before the law, and equal employment, education, and housing opportunities. African Americans have had unprecedented openings in many fields of learning and in the arts. The black struggle for civil rights also inspired other liberation and rights movements, including those of Native Americans, Latinos, and women, and African Americans have lent their support to liberation struggles in Africa.

For Discussion:

If you had no knowledge about the larger historical struggle for civil rights, how would this affect your understanding of the rhetorical situation in which the Rosa Parks photograph is situated? And how does this historical context help you better understand the rhetorical situation here? Does this context help you analyze this photo as a visual argument?

Images 2 and 3: The next two images are Holocaust photographs taken in the early 1940s during the Second World War at the Auschwitz concentration and death camp in Poland. The issues were anti-Semitism, genocide, and the desire on the part of the Nazis, who ran this camp, to create a so-called master race. More than a million Jews died in the gas chambers at Auschwitz, were the victims of deadly medical experiments, or died of other causes such as starvation. Analyze the rhetorical situation for images 2 and 3. How does this analysis help you perceive them as visual arguments? What is the effect of viewing these two photos together?

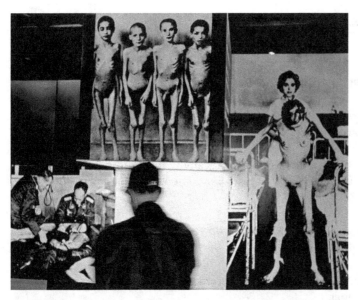

Auschwitz Exhibit at Jerusalem's Yad Vashem Holocaust Memorial

Image 2:
Auschwitz Victims of Medical Experiments.

This is a photograph of an Israeli soldier in Jerusalem, Israel, who is viewing historical photographs at the Yad Vashem Holocaust Memorial Museum of Jewish victims from Auschwitz. Photojournalist David Silverman, who works for Getty Images and has been based in Israel and the West Bank since 1991, took this photo the week before the 60th anniversary of the liberation of Auschwitz.

An SS Officer's Auschwitz Photo Album
SS officers and death camp staff at leisure near Auschwitz, one of 116 newly discovered snapshots from a Nazi officer's scrapbook donated to the Holocaust museum in Washington.

Image 3:
Camp Officials at Leisure.

This is a photograph of some of the Nazi SS who ran the Auschwitz concentration and death camp in the 1940s in Poland. Approximately 6,000 individuals worked at Auschwitz. Look at the image and analyze the rhetorical situation.

61

What conclusions can you draw about Holocaust, the Nazi death camps, the individuals imprisoned there, and the Nazi SS officers who worked there?.

D. Before You Write on Your Issue: Applying the Rhetorical Situation

The following worksheet will help you understand the rhetorical situation for any issue you have selected to write about and have already tested to see whether it is arguable (page 36). Complete the worksheet by yourself. You are working with limited information, so you may need to guess at some of the answers.

Worksheet 1	**Rhetorical Situation**

1. **Exigence**
   What is motivating you to write on this issue? What happened? Why is it compelling to you?

2. **Reader or Audience**
   Who is going to read this? Where do you think they might stand on your issue right now? What are the chances of establishing common ground? What is the best approach to change their minds?

3. **Constraints**
   How do you think your training, background, affiliations, values, and attitudes about your issue are either in harmony or in conflict with those of your audience? What constraints can you use to build common ground?

4. **Author**
   What is your position or perspective on your issue? What do you already know? What do you need to learn? How can you be convincing?

5. **Text**
   What are you writing? What should it look like? What specifications do you need to follow? Review the assignment for your paper.

E. Writing Assignment: Writing a Letter to a Specific Audience

Read the following rhetorical situation and write a letter in response to one of the four individuals in the prompts that appear immediately after it. Do not confer with other members of the class. Make sure at least some students write in response to each of the four prompts.

The Rhetorical Situation

You are enrolled in a freshman English class and your teacher allows you to be absent five times before she gives you an F for the course. If you are tardy to class three times, it counts as an absence. You have been absent five times and tardy to class twice. Your parents are angry with you for missing class so much, and they say that if you fail English you will have to get a job and start paying rent to live at home. Your teacher has explained that if you are tardy or absent from class one more time, she is going to fail you. You really want to do better; you are determined to change your ways.

On the way to class you have a blowout on the freeway. You pull over to change the tire and when you get the spare from the trunk, it is flat. This is not your fault, as you have just had your car serviced and the tires checked. A fellow motorist pulls over and helps you, but by the time you get a good tire on your car and drive to class, you are forty-five minutes late. You enter the classroom as quietly as you can. Your best friend raises her eyebrows. Your teacher gives you a stern look. You feel terrible.

The Writing Prompts

1. You are too embarrassed to talk to your teacher. Write her a letter to explain what happened and ask her for another chance.

2. Your parents are too angry to talk to you. Write them a letter to explain what happened and to ask their forgiveness.

3. You are very upset with the tire company. Write them a letter to explain what happened and ask for a reimbursement.

4. You do not have time to talk to your best friend after class. Write her a note to explain what happened and tell her what you intend to do about it.[3]

You and your classmates should now read some of these letters aloud. When you read them, do not divulge who the intended audience is. Ask the other students to guess who the intended reader of the letter is. Continue doing this until you have a sampling of all four letters and the class has guessed to whom each has been written.

Discuss the Results

What clues helped you surmise the audience for each letter? How are the letters different from each other? In your discussion, consider how each audience influenced the purpose for writing each letter, the tone of each letter, and the type and level of vocabulary used in each letter.

F. Class Discussion and Writing Assignment: Analyzing Your Class as an Audience

In Chapter 1 you began to learn about what you and other members of your class have in common (Exercise A1 on page 29). Now, learn more about your class as an audience by answering the questions listed here.

1. How many students are in your class? What are some of the qualities and features you have in common?

2. Consider some of the demographics of your class (ask for a show of hands to answer some of these): How many are traditional college-age students (18–22 years old); and how many are older, new, or returning students? Count the number of men and the number of women. How many are international students, and what countries do they represent? How would you describe the cultural diversity in the class? How many in the class agree that their heritage or native culture influences their personal life? How many are first-years and sophomores? How many are juniors and seniors? How many work part-time? How many work full-time? What are some of the types of work represented in class?

3. What college majors are represented in your class?

4. What are some of the groups class members belong to that are important to them? Consider political, religious, social, and living groups. Ask for students to volunteer this information.

5. What are some of the special interests and hobbies of class members? Make a list.

Using this class survey data, write as full of a description of your classroom audience as you can. Which of the issues that you have considered writing about would immediately interest them? Why? Which would they find less interesting? Why? What could you provide in your paper to increase their interest?

---

[3]I am indebted to Samantha Masterton for this assignment.

3

Reading, Thinking,
and Writing about Issues

After studying this chapter, you will be able to:

LO1 Describe and put into practice the steps for beginning a writing assignment. (p. 65)

LO2 Define the six types of argument purpose and apply them to written, visual and online argument. (p. 69)

LO3 Create comprehensive notes for a given reading. (p. 79)

LO4 Create a plan for revising your own written argument. (p. 82)

LO5 Write examples of summary, summary-analysis, and exploratory essays. (p. 89)

LO6 Apply the skills of summary, summary-analysis and exploration to visual argument. (p. 92)

This chapter teaches strategies to help you complete assignments that require reading, thinking, and writing about issues. Though you may now regard reading, thinking, and writing as quite separate activities, you will discover that in combining them you will produce better papers. You can practice doing so as you use the strategies taught here in writing three types of argument papers, explained later in this chapter: (1) the summary-response paper; (2) the summary-analysis-response paper; and (3) the exploratory paper. Assignments for these papers require you to interweave reading, thinking, and writing about issues.

At the outset it is useful to sharpen your awareness of how you read and write now so that you will have a solid place to start as you consider and add new strategies. Most people like their current reading and writing processes and are able to describe them. Try it. First, imagine that your professor has given you a difficult scholarly article to read. You must understand it, think about it, and remember the main ideas. How do you proceed with such an assignment? What do you typically do *before you read, while you are reading, when you encounter difficult passages,* and *after you finish reading?*

Now imagine writing a college paper on a subject that requires some research but also a considerable amount of critical thinking on your part. How would you *get started, write the first draft, break through writer's block* (if that occurs), and *rewrite and revise your paper?*

Look at the possible descriptions of the reading and writing processes as they are modified for argument in the Summary Charts. Many of the specific strategies described there will be taught in more detail below. As you read through the strategies in this chapter, notice particularly that *readers are often actively thinking and writing as they read,* and that *writers, in turn, are often reading and thinking as they write.*

Getting Started on a Writing Assignment

Before you begin work on a writing assignment for an argument paper, take some time to organize a workspace equipped with the materials you will need. Then take a few minutes to understand the assignment and schedule sufficient time to complete it. Begin by dividing the assignment into small, manageable parts: assign a sufficient amount of time for each part and set deadlines for completing each part.

IDENTIFY AN ISSUE, NARROW IT, AND TEST IT

The assignment just described directs you to identify an issue on which to write. You may start with a broad issue area such as education, technology, immigration, or the environment, but you will need to find a more narrow and specific issue to write about within this broad area. The map in Figure 3.1 ■ (on page 66) shows one technique for generating more specific issues related to a broad issue area. A group of students created this map to help them find specific issues about race. Reading about your issue can also uncover a particular aspect or interpretation that you want to explore. When you have an issue you think you can work with, write it as a question and apply the twelve tests of an arguable issue (page 36) to it. You may also take a position on the issue and write a tentative claim. Add reasons for your position on the claim, if you can at this point. Keep your audience in mind as you do so.

DO SOME INITIAL WRITING, READING, AND THINKING

Get off to a strong start by using some of these suggestions.

ISSUES RELATED TO RACE

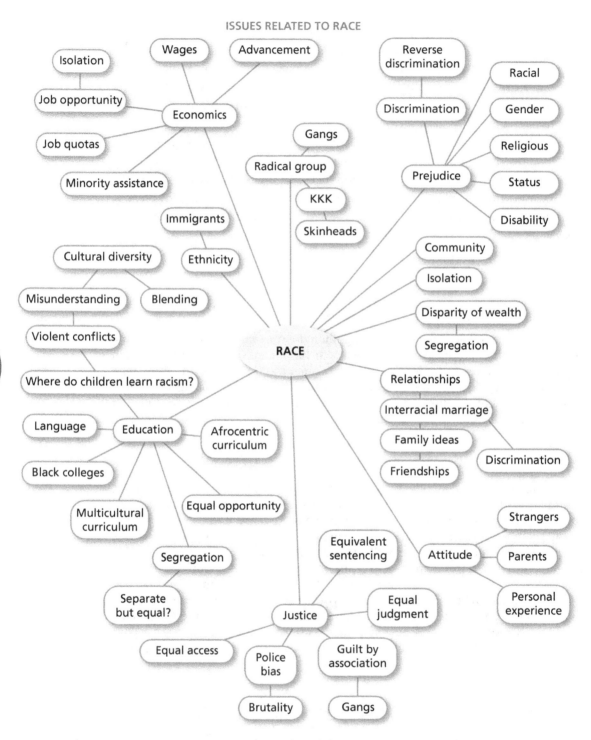

Figure 3.1 *A Map Can Help You Discover Specific Related Issues for Paper Topics.*

Write Down Everything You Now Know about Your Issue

As soon as you have an issue in mind, begin to make notes. You are often at your most creative when an idea for a paper first occurs to you, so write insights and ideas immediately to use later in your paper. This practice guarantees that some of the material in your paper will be your original ideas. Do you have an idea right now about the position you think you may take on your issue? Can you list some reasons for it? Can you think of some examples? Write out as much as possible now and enter it in your computer file or notebook.

A professional writer describes this type of writing as a tool that helps one think. This author sets out a number of suggestions that could be particularly useful for the writer of argument.

Write quickly, so you don't know what's coming next.

Turn off the censor in your head.

Write from different points of view to broaden your sympathies.

Collect quotations that inspire you and jot down a few notes on why they do.

Write with a nonjudgmental friend in mind to listen to your angry or confused thoughts.

When words won't come, draw something—anything.

Don't worry about being nice, fair, or objective. Be selfish and biased; give your side of the story from the heart.

Write even what frightens you, *especially* what frightens you. It is the thought denied that is dangerous.

Don't worry about being consistent. You are large; you contain multitudes.[1]

Read to Improve Your Background Information

Start with broad reading to find out who else is interested in your issue and what positions they take. Try the encyclopedia, books, or the Internet. Use a search engine such as *Google* or *Yahoo!* and enter a keyword in the search box that is related to your issue to begin to find basic information online. Detailed information on how to conduct more thorough and reliable online and print research appears in Chapter 13 (pages 326–355). At this point, write notes on the ideas that strike you, and write your original reactions to these ideas as they occur to you. If you find material you want to read and note further, record where you found it so that you can go back and read it more thoroughly later.

Clip or Copy Images to Add to Your File

Make your issue more vivid and memorable in your own mind by collecting some related visual materials. Do not limit yourself to photographs, prints, or drawings. Create flowcharts of ideas, include tables and graphs, or make concept maps like that shown in Figure 3.1. Fully notate the sources of these materials in case you decide later to use some of them in your paper. If you are a visual learner, this

---

[1]Marjorie Pellegrino, "Keeping a Writer's Journal," *Writer,* June 1992, 27.

practice will be especially useful in helping you understand your issue. Even if you do not use any images in your paper, your collection will help you write better descriptions of the visual aspects of your issue and that, in turn, will help the reader visualize what you are writing. It is also possible that you will decide to include an image or two in your paper to support some of your key ideas.

| Box 3.1 | Use These Prompts to Help You Think Critically about Your Issue. |

▶▶▶ Critical Thinking Prompts

What is your issue? _____
Use some, but not all, of these prompts to help you think about it.

1. **Associate it.** Consider other related issues, broader issues, or enduring issues. Also associate your issue with familiar subjects and ideas.

2. **Describe it.** Use detail. Make the description visual if you can by forming pictures in your mind or by looking at the visual materials you have collected in your file and then describing them.

3. **Compare it.** Think about items in the same or different categories. Compare your issue with topics you know or understand well. Compare what you used to think about the issue with what you think now. Give reasons for your change of mind.

4. **Apply it.** Show practical uses or applications. Show how it can be used in a specific setting.

5. **Divide it.** Illuminate your issue by dividing it into related issues or into parts of the issue.

6. **Agree and disagree with it.** Identify the extreme pro and con positions and reasons for holding them. List other approaches and perspectives. Say why each position, including your own, might be plausible and in what circumstances.

7. **Consider it as it is, right now.** Think about your issue as it exists, right now, in present time. What is its nature? What are its special, contemporary characteristics?

8. **Consider it over a period of time.** Think about your issue in the past as well as how it might present itself in the future. Does the issue change? How? Why?

9. **Decide whether it is a part of something bigger.** Put it in a larger category, and consider the insights you gain as a result.

10. **Analyze it.** Consider its parts and assess how the parts are related.

11. **Synthesize it.** Put it back together in new ways so that the new whole is different. Ask if it is clearer and better than the old whole.

12. **Evaluate it.** Decide whether it is good or bad, valuable or not valuable, moral or immoral, ethical or unethical. Give evidence to support your evaluation.

13. **Elaborate on it.** Add and continue to add explanation until you can understand the issue more easily. Give some examples to provide further elaboration.

14. **Project and predict.** Answer the question, "What would happen if . . . ?" Extend its frame outward and its meanings and possibilities forward.

15. **Ask why, and keep on asking why.** Examine every aspect of your issue by asking why.

Use Critical Thinking Prompts

Get additional insights and ideas about your issue by using some well-established lines of thought that stimulate critical thinking. The "Critical Thinking Prompts" in Box 3.1 ▪ (on previous page) will help you think about your issue in some new ways. First, write what you now think you want to prove about your issue, and then write your responses to each of the prompts. You will be pleased by the quantity of new information these questions generate for your paper. Here is an example to get you started.

▶ Example of How to Use Critical Thinking Prompts

What is your issue? My issue is old-growth forests. I want to preserve those on the western coast of the United States.

Associate it. This is an enduring environmental issue. It is associated with other environmental issues, including reducing greenhouse gases that cause global warming and saving wildlife like the spotted owl, deer, and the other animals that live in these forests. It is also associated with preserving natural beauty and the history of these areas.

Describe it. These trees are as much as 3200 years old. The giant sequoias in California, for example, are huge, majestic trees that can reach heights of 325 feet. People standing among them appear to be very small, and when they look up, they can barely see the tops. Even the sky seems farther away than usual. It is awe-inspiring to walk among these trees because of their size, their age, and their beauty.

Compare it. Saving these forests from logging is similar to preserving natural lakes, national parks and forests, and other wilderness areas from commercial interests.

These responses will give you the idea. As you work through all the prompts, you will find that some are more productive than others for a particular issue. Use as many as you can. If you do not yet know enough to respond to some prompts, add information later when you have done more reading.

Read to Develop Arguments for Your Paper

As you start reading in more detail, you will need to learn to recognize written argument.

RECOGNIZING ARGUMENTATION PURPOSE IN WRITTEN ARGUMENT

Some texts are obviously intended as argument, and others conceal their argumentation purpose, making it more difficult to recognize. You can learn to recognize argument purposes if you think of a continuum of six types of purpose,

69

ranging from obvious argument at one extreme to objective writing at the other. Each of the six types exhibits not only a different authorial intention but also a different relationship between the author and the audience. These descriptions can also help you establish your own purpose when you are the writer.

1. *Obvious argument.* The author's purpose is to take a position and to change minds or convince others. The author's point of view and purpose are clearly expressed along with reasons and supporting details that appeal to a wide audience.

2. *Extremist argument.* Authors who hold fast to prejudiced beliefs and stereotypes about various people, causes, or special projects sometimes rely on strongly expressed values and emotional language to appeal to specific audiences who may already share their views. The aim is to strengthen these views and prompt people to act. Think of an animal rights activist writing to convince others to join the cause and take action to protect animals.

3. *Hidden argument.* Some texts seem to be written to inform but, on closer reading, actually favor one position over another. Supporting material may be carefully selected to favor a particular view. Also, emotional language, vivid description, or emotional examples can be signs that the author has strong opinions and intends not only to inform but also to convince. For example, in an article about college financial aid, all of the examples are about students who failed to pay their loans, and none are about responsible students who did pay. The author has a position that manifests itself in biased reporting. The intention, even though concealed, is to convince people to question current financial aid practices.

4. *Unconscious argument.* Some authors who try to write objectively are influenced unconsciously by strong personal opinions, and the result is an unconscious intent to change people's minds. Imagine a journalist who strongly opposes war being sent to write an objective article about an active war zone. Negative perceptions creep in even as this writer presents the facts. Stacked or selected evidence, emotional language, quotations from authorities who agree with the author, or even pictures with a clear point of view may attest to an argumentative purpose though the author is unaware of it.

5. *Exploratory argument.* In exploratory essays, the author lays out and explains three or more of the major positions on a controversial issue. The reader is invited to view an issue from several perspectives and to understand all of them better. If the author has a position, it may or may not be revealed.

6. *Objective reporting.* The author may report facts and ideas that everyone can accept. The author's own point of view, opinions, or interpretations are deliberately omitted. You might find writing like this in almanacs, data lists, weather reports, some news stories, and government, business, science, and technical reports. The audience reads such material for information. Read this material carefully, however, because sometimes the author's opinion slips in even in this type of writing.

APPLYING THE SIX TYPES OF ARGUMENTATION PURPOSE TO VISUAL ARGUMENT

Even though the descriptions in the previous section apply mainly to written argument, you can easily modify them to help you analyze visual argument as well. Refer to the same six categories to help you recognize the possible intention of the person who created an image. Here are some examples. An image may take an obvious argumentation position on an issue, as in the photograph of the derelict beach house on page 34. Or images may support extremist positions that the viewers already accept. Look back at the photograph of the Israeli soldier on page 61 who is viewing the victims of the death camp experiments at Auschwitz. You can assume that the soldier sympathizes with the victims. These images may motivate him to want to continue to protect Israel. Emotional images that appear on anti-abortion, anti-war, or anti-gay marriage Web sites provide further examples. They will be persuasive to you only if you already agree with the positions they depict.

Some images at first may appear to be recording facts without creating issues or controversy, but as you look more closely, you discover unconscious or hidden bias in favor of a particular position, and you find you are looking at an argument. Take another look at the photograph on page 61 of the SS officers of the Auschwitz death camps spending leisure time. As soon as you understand the rhetorical situation for this photograph, it no longer seems merely an objective record of a few people having a good time.

Look at the photograph in Figure 3.2 ▦ (below) as another example. This photo originally appeared in a newspaper as an objective report about then-Senator

Figure 3.2 *Barack Obama Campaign Weeks Away From Election Day*

Is this photograph an example of objective reporting, or is it hidden argument?

Democratic presidential nominee Barack Obama greets people before a campaign event.

Barack Obama campaigning for president. Now, look at it again and see if you can detect some signs of hidden or unconscious argument in this picture. Take a closer look at how this figure is presented. How is he positioned in relation to the larger crowd? What do you imagine he is thinking?

Visual argument can also take the form of exploratory argument. In such cases, several images illustrate different visual perspectives on an issue in a way that is similar to an exploratory essay, which in writing identifies and explains several different perspectives on an issue. Examples of visual exploratory argument appear later in this chapter on pages 93 and 102 where, in each case, an issue is explored visually. An exercise at the end of this chapter invites you to create a visual exploratory argument yourself.

Finally, some images may be mainly objective. Tables of figures, graphs, and other presentations of numbers and additional data qualify as visual argument and may be objective in that they present information and facts everyone would accept. Scientific drawings or photos of procedures that are designed to teach fit into this category as well. Remember, however, that someone selects and presents—essentially edits out as much as includes—visual information, and even in the most ostensibly objective formats, it is always possible for bias and opinion to find its way in just as it does in written material.

APPLYING THE SIX TYPES OF ARGUMENTATION PURPOSE TO ONLINE ARGUMENT

There is a lot that online argument shares with visual argument. For one thing, web-based arguments often include visual material, and so serve as another context for visual argument. And as is the case with visual argument, we can also easily find examples of web-based material that makes obvious or extremist arguments. But as we have seen, there are also aspects of argumentation that are unique to the Web, aspects that affect the way we go about identifying and assessing the different types of purpose behind such arguments. To begin with, web-based arguments tend to be more multi-modal or multi-media in structure. More often than not, they are neither entirely written nor exclusively visual, but are rather a combination of both. When presented in this kind of hybrid form, it is possible that some of the purposes behind a given argument can remain more hidden. The same is true for unconscious argument, where an author may remain unaware of the ways her/his purpose is being shaped both by written and visual material.

Another key factor concerns the highly interactive nature of online argument. As noted in Chapter 1, audiences enjoy a much greater capacity online to speak back to arguments they encounter. An individual author may have one purpose in mind when s/he sets out to write an argument, but it is quite possible that this goal will change or evolve as different readers post their own reactions and feedback. And, given how many different audiences a particular online argument might reach, it is also possible that the purpose will change depending on the specific type of reader who responds. These effects could easily be felt in relation to an exploratory argument online, in which an author's attempt to lay out a range of differing views on a given issue could be influenced by the views reflected in the responses of different readers. Likewise for objective reporting, in which the constant interaction between author and audience online could easily complicate the question of who or what is truly objective.

ACADEMIC ARGUMENT

Much of what you read in college will be academic writing assigned by your professors and found in textbooks or scholarly journals or books. Any of the types of argumentation just described may appear in academic writing. The ideas in academic writing are often controversial, with authors taking positions on issues and presenting their ideas as either explicit or hidden argument. Academic writing may seem complex and unfamiliar, especially at the beginning of a class: it is new to you, it contains specialized vocabulary, it is dense with many new ideas and, compared with easier material, it will often contain fewer examples and transitions. Its sentences and paragraphs are often longer as well. Your purpose in reading such material is to understand it, analyze it, evaluate it, and, frequently, to take a position and write about it.

Your instructor will expect you to use academic style in your college papers. You will engage with complicated issues that invite varying perspectives that seldom take shape as simple pro and con positions. You will learn to take positions on these kinds of issues and to support your ideas with your own reasons and examples and also with paraphrased, summarized, or quoted material from other writers. Your readers will expect you to document these outside sources so that they can trace the materials you relied on to their origins. Now let's turn to some strategies–things you can do—to help you complete projects that require reading about issues.

READ WHILE CONTINUING TO THINK AND WRITE

Begin to read about the issue on which you intend to focus. Combine thinking and writing with your reading to help you gather ideas for your paper: summarize the big ideas, write your responses, and record your thoughts on paper or in an open computer file.

Reading and writing together helps with two types of thinking. First, you will think about the material you read and perhaps even rephrase or summarize it to understand it better. Second, you will think beyond the material you read to generate your own ideas. Your reading, in other words, becomes a springboard for original thoughts and ideas. The strategies offered next will help you read, think, and write about the essays in "The Reader" as well as in books and articles you locate in the library or online. These strategies will also help you create a written record of what you have read and thought so that you can use it later in your paper.

SURVEY AND SKIM TO SAVE TIME

A stack of books and a collection of articles can seem daunting if you are not sure where to start. A good way to begin is to survey and skim. Survey a book or an article before you read it for information about the type of work it is, and skim

73

parts of it to discover what the major ideas along with a few of the supporting details are. Surveying accompanied by skimming will also help you decide which parts of specific articles or books you will want to read more carefully later. This strategy saves you time and helps you confidently plan your reading. Box 3.2 ▪ (below), lists the steps for surveying books and chapters or articles.

Box 3.2	How to Survey.

▶▶▶ Steps for Surveying Books, Articles, and Chapters

Survey a book or an article before you read it to become acquainted with its structure and general qualities, and skim certain parts for the major ideas and a few of the supporting details.

Books. To survey a book (not a novel), follow these six steps in the order given.

1. Read the *title* and focus on what it tells you about the contents of the book.

2. Read the *table of contents.* Notice how the content has been divided and organized into chapters.

3. Skim the *introduction.* Look for background information about the subject and author and for any other information that will help you read the book.

4. Examine the special *features* of the book. Are there headings and subheadings in boldface type that highlight major ideas? Is there a glossary? An index? A bibliography? Are there charts? Other visuals?

5. Read the title and first paragraph of the *first* and *last chapters* to see how the book begins and ends.

6. Read the title and first paragraph of the *other chapters* to get a sense of the flow of ideas.

    This procedure should take about half an hour. It will introduce you to the main issue and approaches in a book, and your reading will then be easier and more focused.

Articles and Chapters. To survey an article or a chapter in a book, follow these six steps in this order.

1. Read the *title* and focus on the information in it.

2. Read the *introduction,* which is usually the first paragraph but can be several paragraphs long. Skim for a claim and any forecasts of what is to come.

3. Read the *last paragraph* and look for the claim.

4. Read the *headings* and *subheadings,* if there are any, to get a sense of the ideas and their sequence. If there are no headings, read the first sentence of each paragraph to accomplish the same goal.

5. Study the *visuals:* pictures, charts, graphs. Read their captions. They often illustrate major ideas or key details.

6. Identify the *key words* that represent the main concepts.

    Surveying an article or chapter takes ten to fifteen minutes. It introduces you to the issue, the claim, and some of the support.

When you finish surveying, you can begin to read the passages you have identified for closer reading. The strategies that follow will help you with close reading and creative thinking.

IDENTIFY AND READ THE INFORMATION IN THE INTRODUCTION, BODY, AND CONCLUSION

The organization of ideas in argument texts is not very different from other kinds of texts. Much of what you read, for example, follows the easily recognizable introduction, main body, and conclusion format. The introduction may provide background information about the issue and the author, inspire attention, state the main point, define important terms, or forecast some of the ideas to be developed in the main body. The text body will explain and develop the author's main point by giving reasons and support to prove it. The end or conclusion either summarizes by restating important points or concludes by emphasizing the most important point, whatever it is that the author wants you to accept, remember, or believe. Not all texts follow this pattern exactly, but enough of them do to justify your checking what you read against it.

LOOK FOR CLAIMS, SUBCLAIMS, SUPPORT, AND TRANSITIONS

All arguments have the structural components you are familiar with from other kinds of reading and writing. The main difference is their names. The thesis of an argument, which shapes the thinking of the entire text and states what the author finally expects you to accept or believe, is called the *claim*. The main ideas or *subclaims* are assertions, reasons, or supporting arguments that develop the claim. They usually require *support* in the form of facts, opinions, evidence, visual images, and examples. Support makes the claim and subclaims clear, vivid, memorable, and believable. *Transitions* lead the reader from one idea to another and sometimes state the relationships among ideas. There is a constant movement between general and specific material in all texts, including argument texts, and this movement becomes apparent when the ideas are presented in various types of outline form.

READ WITH AN OPEN MIND AND ANALYZE THE COMMON GROUND BETWEEN YOU AND THE AUTHOR

At times you will agree with an author and at other times you will disagree. Try to avoid letting your biases and opinions interfere with your comprehension of what the author is saying.

Suppose you begin to read the article on school absence policies, "'A' Is For Absent," by Chris Piper. Consider some responses that readers of argument might make at this point. If you happen to agree with this author's ideas, you are more likely to read carefully, marking the best passages and insisting on reading them aloud to someone else. However, if you believe that absence policies are genuinely necessary and beneficial to students, you may be tempted not to read the essay at all or to read it hastily and carelessly, dismissing the author as wrong-headed or mistaken. If you are neutral on this issue, with opinions on neither side, you might read with less interest and even permit your mind to wander. These responses distract you and interfere in negative ways with your understanding of the article.

Once you become aware of such unproductive responses, you can compensate for them by analyzing the common ground between you and the author. Finding common ground obligates the reader to fairness. Thus, you can use this information to help you read more receptively and nonjudgmentally. What common ground do you have with Piper? For example, could you identify with Piper's belief that students should be allowed to make up their own minds about whether or not to attend class? You may have common ground with Piper on that score. When you have established common ground, try to generate interest, read with an open mind, and suspend judgment until you have finished reading his article. Finally, reassess your original position to determine whether you now have reason to modify or change your perspective.

UNDERSTAND THE KEY WORDS

When reading material suddenly seems difficult, go back and look for words you do not understand. Always identify the key terms, those that represent major concepts. In this book so far, *rhetorical situation, survey, claim,* and *subclaim* are examples of key terms. To find the meaning of difficult words and key terms, first read the context in which you find the word or key term. A word may be defined in a sentence, a paragraph, or several paragraphs. Major concepts in argument are often defined at length, and understanding their meaning will be essential to an understanding of the entire argument. If the context does not give you enough information, then try the glossary, the dictionary, or another book on the subject. Remember that major concepts require longer explanations than a single synonym.

UNDERLINE, ANNOTATE, AND SUMMARIZE IDEAS

As you begin to read, underline with a pen or pencil and write notes in the margin to help you concentrate and understand. These notes will also help you review and find information later. The key to marking a text is to do it selectively. Do not color an entire paragraph with a highlighter. Instead, underline only the words and phrases that you can later reread and still get a sense of the whole. Use key words. Jot the major ideas in the margins, or summarize them at the ends of sections. Write the big ideas along with your personal reactions on the flyleaves of a book or at the ends of chapters or articles. If you do not own the book, write on self-stick notes and attach them to the book pages. You can also write on paper organized in a folder, or in an open computer file you are maintaining for your research.

Here is an example. This essay about polar bears and climate change has been underlined and annotated as recommended. A brief summary has been added at the end to capture the main point. Note that this material is now very easy to understand.

ESSAY #1   THE RACE FOR SURVIVAL*

Jerry Adler

Adler writes for newsmagazines and appears on television news shows.

Needed a symbol
of global warming

1   Ten years ago, when environmental lawyer Kassie Siegel went in search of an animal to save the world, the polar bear wasn't at all an obvious choice. Siegel and Brendan Cummings of the Center for Biological Diversity in Joshua Tree, Calif., were looking for a species whose habitat was disappearing due to climate change, which could serve as a symbol of the dangers of global warming. Her first candidate met the scientific criteria—it lived in ice caves in Alaska's Glacier Bay, which were melting away—but unfortunately it was a spider. You can't sell a lot of T shirts with pictures of an animal most people would happily step on.

Spider, seabird,
coral not dramatic
enough.

Polar bear is
dramatic—an iconic
species.

2   Next, Siegel turned to the Kittlitz's murrelet, a small Arctic seabird whose nesting sites in glaciers were disappearing. In 2001, she petitioned the Department of the Interior to add it to the Endangered Species list, but Interior Secretary Gale Norton turned her down. (Siegel's organization is suing to get the decision reversed.) Elkhorn and staghorn coral, which are threatened by rising water temperatures in the Caribbean, did make it onto the list, but as iconic species they fell short insofar as many people don't realize they're alive in the first place. The polar bear, by contrast, is vehemently alive and carries the undeniable charisma of a top predator. And its dependence on ice was intuitively obvious; it lives on it most of the year, lurking near breathing holes to occasionally snatch a 150-pound seal from the water with one bone-crunching bite. But it took until 2004 for researchers to demonstrate, with empirically derived climate and population models, that shrinking sea ice was a serious threat to the bears' population. On Feb. 16, 2005—the day the Kyoto Protocol to curb greenhouse-gas emissions took effect, without the participation of the United State—Siegel petitioned to list polar bears as endangered. Three years later her efforts met with equivocal success, as Interior Secretary Dirk Kempthorne—under court order to make a decision—designated the bears as "threatened," a significant concession from an administration that has stood almost alone in the world in its reluctance to acknowledge the dangers of climate change. The Endangered Species Act (ESA), whose quaint lists of snails and bladderworts sometimes seemed stuck in the age of Darwin, had been thrust into the mainstream of 21st-century environmental politics. Break out the T shirts!

Polar bear is now
on endangered
species list.

Summary:
With much time and effort, the polar bear has finally become the icon of global warming, a concern that is now central to environmental politics.

77

OUTLINES OR MAPS

If you have read, annotated, and summarized a reading selection and still feel you should understand it better, try writing an outline or a map of the key ideas in it. Both outlines and maps lay out ideas in a visual form and show how they are related to each other. Seeing the organization of ideas improves your understanding and ability to critically evaluate the selection.

Make an Outline

To make an outline, write the claim, the most general idea, at the left-hand margin; indent the subclaims under the claim; and indent the support—the specific facts, opinions, examples, illustrations, other data, and statistics—even further. You may not always need to write an outline. Sometimes you can make a simple mental outline to help you remember the claim and some of the ideas that support and develop it. Here is an outline of the essay "No Escape From Helicopter Parents" (pages 30–32).

OUTLINE OF *"No Escape From Helicopter Parents"*
  Claim: Helicopter parenting of kids in college is counterproductive.
    Subclaim: Helicopter parenting has negative effects on both parents and their college-age kids.
        This type of parenting undermines students' independence or autonomy at school.
    Support (examples): Without such parental oversight, students would take more responsibility for their work.
            They would meet their own deadlines.
            Learn to negotiate with professors themselves.
            Feel more deserving of the grades they receive.
    Subclaim: This type of parenting causes undue emotional stress for parents.
        Support: Helicopter parenting fosters greater anxiety among parents.
    Subclaim: This type of parenting undermines the relationship between parents and their college-age kids.
    Support: Kids tend to resent parents who oversee and manage their lives too closely.
  Conclusion: "Helicopter parenting is counterproductive"

Make a Map

As an alternative to summaries or outlines, make a map of the ideas in a text. For many students, maps are the preferred way to reduce and reorganize the material they read. To make a map, write the most important idea, the claim, in a circle or on a line, and then attach major subclaims and support to it. Make your map in very brief form. Figure 3.3 ▪ is a possible map of the essay "No Escape From Helicopter Parents." You can be creative with map formats. Use whatever layout will give you a quick picture of the major ideas.

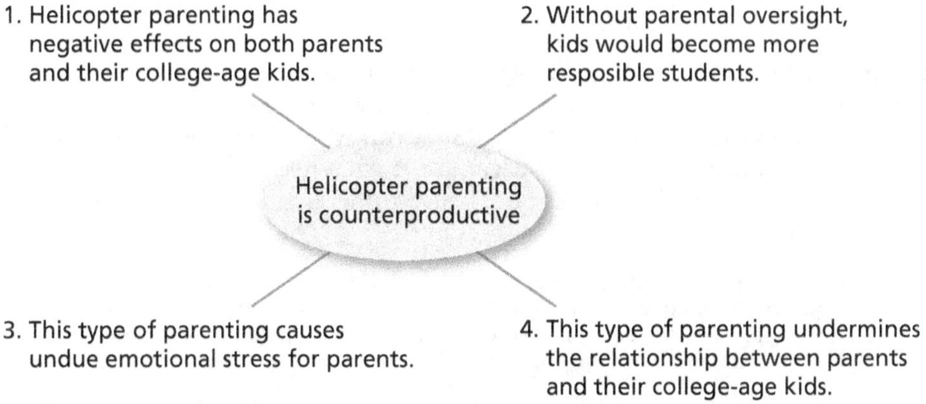

1. Helicopter parenting has negative effects on both parents and their college-age kids.

2. Without parental oversight, kids would become more resposible students.

Figure 3.3 *Map of Ideas for* "No Escape From Helicopter Parents".

Helicopter parenting is counterproductive

3. This type of parenting causes undue emotional stress for parents.

4. This type of parenting undermines the relationship between parents and their college-age kids.

Take Notes and Avoid Plagiarism

From the start, record the information from your reading that you may want to quote, paraphrase, or summarize later when you write your paper. If you have an outline or list of ideas in your computer, type in such material at appropriate spots. If you are keeping paper notes in a folder, write out the passages in full and fully identify the author and publisher information for later detailed documenting of the source. Write out or type in your own ideas as they occur to you as well.

Copy quoted material exactly as it is written and place it in quotation marks immediately, with the author's name and brief source information at the end. You must add the author's name and the location of the original material (page or paragraph number, title or site, etc.) to paraphrased or summarized material as well. Label your own ideas as "mine," or put them in square brackets [ ]. Here are examples drawn from "The Race for Survival" (page 77).

▶ Example of a Quote

"The polar bear, by contrast, is vehemently alive and carries the undeniable charisma of a top predator" (Adler, "The Race for Survival" 77).

▶ Example of a Paraphrase

Adler describes the difficulty of selecting an iconic animal that everyone would associate with global warming. ("The Race for Survival" 77).

▶ Example of a Summary

According to Jerry Adler, it took ten years to select an animal to symbolize the dangers of global warming. After rejecting less dramatic species, environmentalists selected the polar bear because it depends on ice to survive, and it is familiar. ("The Race for Survival" 77).

▶ Example of Your Idea

The polar bear is also photogenic when it appears in images that present strong visual arguments in favor of the reality of global warming.

If you follow this advice on taking notes, you will have no problem with plagiarism. Just in case you are still unclear about what plagiarism is exactly, here is a recent statement made by the Council of Writing Program Administrators that will help you.

> In an instructional setting, plagiarism occurs when a writer deliberately uses someone else's language, ideas, or other original (not common-knowledge) material without acknowledging its source. This definition applies to texts published in print or online, to manuscripts, and to the work of other student writers.[2]

Plagiarism is regarded as an extremely serious personal and academic violation because it negates the purpose of education, which is to encourage original and analytical thinking in a community in which expression of thought is both respected and protected.

Online research seems to have increased the incidence of plagiarism in student work. Some students find it tempting to copy and paste information from online articles into their own papers without using quotation marks and without documenting the source. Sometimes a student will mix their own words with the words of the quoted author and neglect to put the source's words in quotation marks. The result is a strange mix of styles and voices that creates a problem for the reader, who cannot easily sort out the student's words from those of the person being quoted. This, too, is plagiarism.

Lynne McTaggart, a professional writer whose work was plagiarized by a well-known author and commentator, explains plagiarism in this way.

> Plagiarism is the dishonorable act of passing someone else's words off as your own, whether or not the material is published. . . . Writers don't own facts. Writers don't own ideas. All that we own is the way we express our thoughts. Plagiarism pillages unique expressions, specific turns of phrase, the unusual colors a writer chooses to use from a personal literary palette. . . . In this age of clever electronic tools, writing can easily turn into a process of pressing the cut-and-paste buttons, . . . rather than the long and lonely slog of placing one word after another in a new and arresting way.[3]

McTaggart was shocked to read a book by a best-selling author that included material from her book, exactly as she had worded it, in passage after passage throughout the work, without proper acknowledgment.

Here is another example of this error. The late Stephen E. Ambrose, an author of popular history books, was accused of plagiarism when his book *The Wild Blue* was published in 2001.[4] Both professional historians and the media criticized him publicly, and he suffered considerable embarrassment. Figure 3.4 ■ (on page 81) reproduces two of several illustrations of the plagiarized

---

[2]From "Defining and Avoiding Plagiarism: The WPA Statement on Best Practices" (2003). The full statement can be accessed at www.wpacouncil.org/positions/plagiarism.html.

[3]Lynne McTaggart, "Fame Can't Excuse a Plagiarist," *New York Times*, March 16, 2002, A27.

[4]David D. Kirkpatrick, "As Historian's Fame Grows, So Do Questions on Methods," *New York Times*, January 11, 2002, A1, A19.

Excerpts

ECHOES IN PRINT

Stephen E. Ambrose, the author of historical best-sellers, appears to have reused words and phrases from other works, though passages are attributed in footnotes to original authors.

From *The Rise of American Air Power*, 1987, by Michael S. Sherry	From *The Wild Blue*, 2001, by Stephen E. Ambrose

ON JOHN STEINBECK'S WORK WRITING PROPAGANDA ABOUT AIRMEN

"Crewmen supposedly sprang from the frontier tradition of the 'Kentucky hunter and the Western Indian fighter.' . . . Like Lindbergh 15 years earlier, the airman was presented as both individualist and joiner, relic of the past and harbinger of the era, free spirit and disciplined technician, democrat and superman, 'Dan'l Boone and Henry Ford.'"	"Steinbeck wrote that the men of the AAF sprang from the frontier tradition of the 'Kentucky hunter and the Western Indian fighter.' He presented the airman as both individualist and a joiner, a relic of the past and a harbinger of a new era, a free spirit and a disciplined technician, a democrat and a superman, 'Dan'l Boone and Henry Ford.'"

ON THE DANGERS OF ANOXIA (DEPRIVATION OF OXYGEN)

"Anoxia from shortages of oxygen both compounded the perils of frostbite and posed a serious danger in and of itself."	"Anoxia from shortages of oxygen compounded the threat of frostbite and posed a serious danger in and of itself."

Figure 3.4 *Examples of Plagiarism.*
Source: David D. Kirkpatrick, "As Historian's Fame Grows, So Do Questions on Methods," *New York Times*, January 11, 2002, A19.

passages along with the original passages as they were presented in the *New York Times*. Compare the passages in the two columns until you understand why those in the right-hand column present a problem. This will help you avoid making the same mistake yourself.

Notice that Ambrose added footnotes in his book to show in general where the material came from, but he did not place quotation marks around the material that he copied directly. Kirkpatrick, the *New York Times* critic, reflects the opinions of several professional historians when he explains, "Mr. Ambrose should have marked direct quotations in the text, or at the very least noted the closeness of his paraphrase in his footnotes, historians say. College students caught employing the same practices would be in trouble."[5] When criticized, Ambrose admitted his mistake, and he was quoted as saying, "I wish I had put the quotation marks in, but I didn't."[6] He said he would do things differently in future books: "I am sure going to put quotes around anything that comes out of a secondary work, always."[7]

You can avoid plagiarism by differentiating between your ideas and those of others at all stages of the writing process. This is why you are advised to

---

[5]Ibid, A19.
[6]Ibid, A1.
[7]Ibid, A19.

enclose all direct quotations in quotation marks in your notes, to introduce paraphrases and summaries drawn from other people's works with the names of the authors in your notes, and to keep your own ideas separate from those of others by labeling them or placing them in brackets or a different font. You may safely and responsibly use other people's ideas and words in your paper, but you must always acknowledge that they are theirs.

If the passages you have drawn from outside sources are reasonably short, support your own ideas, and you clearly indicate where you found them, then you have done the right thing. If the passages are copied into your paper as though you had written them yourself, then you could receive a poor grade in the course or even be expelled from college. Understand too that you fail to link reading to thinking when you are reading to copy. It is a theft from someone else, but also from yourself. And, of course, you do not learn to improve your own writing when you copy other people's words instead of writing your own.

Write Your Paper, Read It, Think about It, and Revise It

At some point you will feel that you are ready to read through the material you have gathered and put it in some kind of order so that you can write your paper. Here are some strategies to help you accomplish that.

REFOCUS YOUR ISSUE AND RECONSIDER YOUR AUDIENCE

Read through the materials you have gathered and see if your issue has changed or shifted focus during your reading, thinking, and writing. Select the aspect of your issue that now interests you the most and that you have sufficient materials and ideas to develop. Keep in mind your time constraints and word limitations. Rewrite or refine your claim at this point to make your focus clear and convincing to your audience. You will probably want to adjust or rewrite it once again as you do your final read-through and finish your paper.

Consider whether you can strengthen your argument by doing more reading, probably in sources you have already located.

As you reconsider your audience, think about what they already know and what they still need to learn. Review your areas of agreement and disagreement and the amount of common ground you share. What will you need to include in your paper to convince them to consider your point of view. The way you organize your ideas may influence the way they receive them. For more help, review the specific kinds of audiences and how to appeal to each of them on pages 51–55.

MAKE AN EXTENDED OUTLINE TO GUIDE YOUR WRITING

A written outline helps many people see the organization of ideas before they begin to write. Other people seem to be able to make a list or even work from a mental outline. Still others "just write" and move ideas around later to create order. There is, however, an implicit outline in most good writing. The outline is often referred to metaphorically as the skeleton or bare bones of the paper because it provides the internal structure that holds the paper together. An outline can be simple—a list of words written on a piece of scrap paper—or it can be elaborate, with essentially all major ideas, supporting details, major transitions, and even some of the sections written out in full. Some outlines actually end up looking like partial, sketchy manuscripts.

If you have never made outlines, try making one. Outlining requires intensive thinking and decision making. When it is finished, however, you will be able to turn your full attention to writing, and you will never have to stop to figure out what to write about next. Your outline will tell you what to do, and it will ultimately save you time and reduce much of the difficulty and frustration you would experience without it.

WRITE THE FIRST DRAFT

The objective of writing the first draft is to get your ideas in some kind of written form so that you can see them and work with them. Include quoted, paraphrased, and summarized material in your draft as you write. Here is how a professional writer explains the drafting process.

> Writing a first draft should be easy because, in a sense, you can't get it wrong. You are bringing something completely new and strange into the world, something that did not exist before. You have nothing to prove in the first draft, nothing to defend, everything to imagine. And the first draft is yours alone, no one else sees it. You are not writing for an audience. Not yet. You write the draft in order to read what you have written and to determine what you still have to say.[8]

This author advises further that you "not even consider technical problems at this early stage." Nor should you "let your critical self sit at your desk with your creative self. The critic will stifle the writer within." The purpose, he says, is "not to get it right, but to get it written."[9]

---

[8]John Dufresne, "That Crucial First Draft," *Writer,* October 1992, 9.
[9]Ibid., 10–11.

Here is another writer, Stephen King, who advises putting aside reference books and dictionaries when concentrating on writing the first draft.

> Put away your dictionary . . . You think you might have misspelled a word? O.K., so here is your choice: either look it up in the dictionary, thereby making sure you have it right—and breaking your train of thought and the writer's trance in the bargain—or just spell it phonetically and correct it later. Why not? Did you think it was going to go somewhere? And if you need to know the largest city in Brazil and you find you don't have it in your head, why not write in Miami or Cleveland? You can check it . . . but *later*. When you sit down to write, *write*. Don't do anything else except go to the bathroom, and only do that if it absolutely cannot be put off.[10]

You will be able to follow this advice if the materials you have gathered before drafting are available to guide you and keep you on track. If you occasionally get stuck, you can write some phrases, freewrite, or even skip a section that you cannot easily put into words. You will have another chance at your draft later. Right now, work only to capture the flow of ideas, either as they are written on an outline or as they are organized in your mind. You will discover, as you write, that many of the ideas that were only half formed before you began to write will now become clear and complete as you get insight from writing.

BREAK THROUGH WRITER'S BLOCK

Most writers suffer from writer's block from time to time, and there are a number of ways to get going again if you find that you are stuck while writing your first draft.

▶ *Read what you have written so far.* Concentrate on the ideas, think about what you need to write next, and jot down a few notes to remind yourself what you want to do. Then get back to writing.

▶ *Read more about your issue.* If you do not have enough material, take notes on additional sources. Place limits by doing directed reading to meet specific needs.

▶ *Reread your outline, lists, and other idea notes.* Add new ideas that occur to you as you read, and rearrange ideas into new combinations.

▶ *Freewrite, read some more, and freewrite again.* Write fast, in phrases or sentences, on your topic without imposing any structure or order. Go through it later, crossing out what you can't use, changing phrases to sentences, adding material in places, and soon you will find that you are started again.

---

[10]Stephen King, "Everything You Need to Know about Writing Successfully—in Ten Minutes," *The Writer's Handbook*, ed. Sylvia K. Burack (Boston: Writer, 1991), 33.

▶ *Use critical thinking prompts.* Revisit Box 3.1 (page 68). These prompts will help you think in new ways about your topic and generate new ideas and information as well.

▶ *Talk about your ideas with someone else.* Either talk with someone or ask someone to read the draft as it now is and write their comments on it.

▶ *Give yourself permission to write a less than perfect first draft.* You can paralyze yourself by trying to produce a finished draft on the first try. Lower your expectations for the first draft. Remind yourself that you will need to return later and fine-tune it as well as fix any flaws or omissions.

REVISE THE DRAFT

Resist the temptation to put your paper aside when you have finished drafting and declare it finished. Now is your opportunity to become its first careful reader and to improve it in significant ways. Working with a rough draft is easier than outlining or drafting. It is, in fact, creative and fun to revise because you begin to see your work take shape and become more readable and convincing. It is worthwhile to finish your draft early enough so that you will have several hours to read and revise before you submit it in its final form to a reader.

Look at Your Draft as a Whole

When you have a draft, print it and lay it out in front of you so that you can see it as a whole. Look at organization first. How does your paper begin? Have you written an introduction that informs your audience about the subject of your paper? What are your main points? Where does each of them begin and end? Have you used enough transitional material to make your ideas stand out? Do you have enough support to make each of your main points believable to your audience? Think about your audience and decide whether you need to add information to make your paper more persuasive. How do you conclude your paper? Is your ending strong and memorable?

If you cannot answer these questions about your paper, try making a list or an outline of the most important ideas in it. Apply this test: Can you state the claim or the main point of your paper and list the parts that develop it? Take a good look at these parts, rearrange them if necessary and make them clearer and more complete.

Now, read paragraph by paragraph. Do you make links between the end of one paragraph and the beginning of another so that the ideas in them flow and appear to be clearly related to each other? Is most of each paragraph about one idea? Is that idea developed with sufficient supporting detail?

Check your sentences. Is each a complete thought? Do they all make sense? Rewrite problem sentences or sentence fragments. As a final check, read your entire paper aloud and listen for problems. Correct with pencil as you go along. You can enter corrections into the computer later.

85

Ask Revision Questions to Help You Locate Other Problems

Ask these seven questions about your draft, which direct your attention both to global revisions for improved clarity and organization and to surface revisions for errors in grammar and usage.

1. *Is it clear?* If you cannot understand your own writing, other people will not be able to either. Be critical of your own understanding as you read your draft. If you encounter confusing passages, stop and analyze why they are confusing and then rewrite them until the words represent what you mean or want to say.

2. *What should I add?* Sometimes in writing the first draft you will write such a sketchy version of an idea that it does not explain your thinking or fully state what you want to say. Add fuller explanations and examples, or do extra research to improve the skimpy or unsubstantiated parts of your paper.

3. *What should I cut?* Extra words, repeated ideas, and unnecessary material often crowd into the first draft. Every writer cuts during revision. Stephen King, who earns millions of dollars each year as a professional writer, describes how he learned to cut the extra words. His teacher was the newspaper editor John Gould, who dealt with King's first feature article, as he describes in this excerpt.

He started in on the feature piece with a large black pen and taught me all I ever needed to know about my craft. I wish I still had the piece—it deserves to be framed, editorial corrections and all—but I can remember pretty well how it looked when he had finished with it. Here is an example:

> Last night, in the ~~well-loved~~ gymnasium ~~of~~ Lisbon High School, partisans and Jay Hills fans alike were stunned by an athletic performance unequalled in school history: Bob Ransom, ~~known as "Bullet" Bob for both his size and accuracy,~~ scored thirty-seven points. He did it with grace and speed . . . and he did it with an odd courtesy as well, committing only two personal fouls in his ~~knight-like~~ quest for a record which has eluded Lisbon's ~~thinclads~~ basketball team since 1953 . . .

When Gould finished marking up my copy in the manner I have indicated above, he looked up and must have seen something on my face. I think he must have thought it was horror, but it was not: it was revelation.

"I only took out the bad parts, you know," he said. "Most of it's pretty good."

"I know," I said, meaning both things: yes, most of it was good, and yes, he had only taken out the bad parts. "I won't do it again."

"If that's true," he said, "you'll never have to work again. You can do *this* for a living." Then he threw back his head and laughed.

And he was right: I *am* doing this for a living, and as long as I can keep on, I don't expect ever to have to work again.[11]

4. ***Are the language and style consistent and appropriate throughout?*** Edit out words that create a conversational or informal tone in your paper. For example:

Change:	And as for target shooting, well go purchase a BB gun or a set of darts.[12]
To read:	For target shooting, a BB gun or a set of darts serves just as well as a handgun.

Also, edit out cheerleading, slogans, clichés, needless repetition, and exhortations. You are not writing a political speech.

In general, use a formal, rational style in an argument paper unless you have a good reason to do otherwise. Use emotional language and examples that arouse feelings only where appropriate with a particular audience to back up logical argument.

5. ***Is there enough variety?*** Use some variety in the way you write sentences by beginning some with clauses and others with a subject or a verb. Vary the length of your sentences as well. Write not only simple sentences but also compound and complex sentences. You can also vary the length of your paragraphs. The general rule is to begin a new paragraph every time you change the subject. Variety in sentences and paragraphs makes your writing more interesting to read. Do not sacrifice clarity for variety, however, by writing odd or unclear sentences.

6. ***Have I used the active voice most of the time?*** The active voice is more direct, energetic, and interesting than the passive voice. Try to use it most of the time. Here is a sentence written in the active voice; it starts with the subject.

Robotics is an exciting new technology that could enhance nearly every aspect of our lives.

Notice how it loses its directness and punch when it is written in the passive voice.

Nearly every aspect of our lives could be enhanced by robotics, an exciting new technology.

7. ***Have I avoided sexist language?*** Avoid referring to people in your paper as though they were either all male or all female. However, using such expressions as "he or she" or "himself or herself" sounds inclusive but comes across as awkward. Solve this problem by using plural nouns (*students* instead of *student*) and pronouns (*they* instead of *he or she*). Occasionally, you may need

87

---

[11]King, 30–31.

[12]From a student paper by Blake Decker: used with permission.

to rewrite a sentence in the passive voice. It is better to write, "The U.S. Constitution is often used as the guide when making new laws," than to write, "He or she often uses the U.S. Constitution as a guide when making new laws."

How to Avoid the Seven Most Common Errors Students Make

1. Write three or more similar items in a *series,* separated by commas, with the final item connected by *and* or *or.*

   Example: The National Rifle Association, firearms manufacturers, and common citizens are all interested in gun control.[13]

2. Use *parallel construction* for longer, more complicated elements that have a similar function in the sentence.

   Example: Parents who fear for their children's safety at school, passengers who ride on urban public transit systems, clerks who work at convenience stores and gas stations, and police officers who try to carry out their jobs safely are all affected by national policy on gun control.

3. Keep everything in the same *tense* throughout. Use the present tense to introduce quotations.

   Example: As Sherrill *states,* "The United States is said to be the greatest gun-toting nation in the world." Millions of guns create problems in this country.

4. Observe *sentence boundaries.* Start sentences with a capital letter, and end them with a period or question mark. Make certain they express complete thoughts. Do not punctuate a clause as a sentence. In the following sentence, the "because" clause is incorrectly punctuated as a sentence.

   Example (incorrect): Because criminals, including terrorists, can buy guns easily in this country. There should be a system for checking the background of everyone who purchases a gun.

   The clause is actually a part of the rest of the sentence. Change the period to a comma to correct this common error.

   Example (correct): Because criminals, including terrorists, can buy guns easily in this country, there should be a system for checking the background of everyone who purchases a gun.

5. Make *subjects agree* with *verbs.*

   Example: Restrictions on gun control *interfere* [not *interferes*] with people's rights.

6. Use *clear and appropriate pronoun referents.*

   Example: The *group* [one whole] is strongly in favor of gun control, and little is needed to convince *it* [not *them*] of the importance of this issue.

---

[13]The examples presented here are drawn from a student paper by Blake Decker. I have revised his sentences for the sake of illustration.

7. Use *commas* to set off long initial clauses, to separate two independent clauses, and to separate words in a series.

Example: When one realizes that the authors of the Constitution could not look into the future and imagine current events, one can see how irrational and irresponsible it is to believe that the right to bear arms should in these times still be considered a constitutional right, and according to Smith, the groups that do so "are shortsighted, mistaken, and ignorant."

Check for Final Errors, Add or Adjust the Title, and Type or Print Your Paper

Just before you submit your paper, check the spelling of every word you are not absolutely sure you know. If spelling is a problem for you, buy a small spelling dictionary that contains only words and no meanings. Also, use the spell-checker on the computer. If you use a spell-checker, you should still read your paper one last time since a computer cannot find every kind of error. At this point you should format your paper and correct all the typographical errors that remain. Add a title or adjust your existing title, if necessary. Be sure that the final title provides information that will help the reader understand what your paper is about.

Complete the revision process by reading your paper aloud one more time. Read slowly and listen. You will be surprised by the number of problems that bother your ears that were not noticeable to your eyes. Your paper should be ready now to submit for evaluation. Print out the paper so that it is easy to read.

89

Practice Your Process by Writing These Papers

You can practice reading, thinking, and writing about issues by understanding and learning to write the three types of papers that will be described next in this chapter: the summary-response paper, the summary-analysis-response paper, and the exploratory paper. These papers can help you think about and develop ideas for papers described in future chapters.

THE SUMMARY-RESPONSE PAPER

A summary-response paper is composed of two parts: (1) the summary shows that you understand what an argument says, and (2) the response shows your reaction to it, including the ideas it generates in your mind.

A summary answers these questions: *What is this about? What did the author say about it?* To write a summary, follow these steps:

a. Survey first. (See instructions on page 74.) Identify the issue, the claim, and some of subclaims, or ideas that support the claim. This will help you answer the question, *What is this about?*

b. Write a brief list of words or phrases that represent the subclaims or the main points the author makes about the claim. You may be able to do this when you finish surveying. If you cannot, go back and read section by section, or paragraph by paragraph, and make notes on what appear to be the main points. This will help you answer the question, *What did the author say about the claim?*

c. Write a summary in your own words and in complete sentences that includes the author's claim and the main points that support it. Use the words and phrases you have written to guide you.

Here is an example of a summary of "'A' Is For 'Absent'" which appears on pages 42–43.

▶ Example of a Summary

Summary of "'A' Is For 'Absent'"

The author focuses on the tendency of college professors to make classroom attendance a significant part of students' overall grade, and asserts that this practice is both unfair to students and ultimately detrimental to their overall learning. He outlines the logic professors often use to justify this practice, and then argues that different assignments and grading standards would be more beneficial. Emphasizing the role they play as "paying customers," Piper makes the case that students should be given the right to choose whether or not to attend class, and that the real job of professors is to test them on their knowledge of the course material regardless of their attendance rate.

A response answers these questions: *What are your personal reactions to this essay? How much common ground do you have with the author? What in the essay is new to you? What else does it make you think about? What do you like or dislike about it?*

▶ Example of a Response

Response to "'A' Is For 'Absent'"

I have wondered myself about the value of college attendance policies. Like the students to whom Piper refers, I have often assumed that my academic performance should be evaluated solely on my mastery of course content rather than attendance. However, I wonder about the author's description of students as "paying customers." Is this really the best way to think about the role we play as students in the classroom? Is learning in the classroom the same as shopping at the mall? Unlike the author, I think our right, as "paying customers," to choose whether or not to attend class needs to be balanced by an equivalent responsibility to actually show up.

THE SUMMARY-ANALYSIS-RESPONSE PAPER

Add an analysis to a summary-response paper* to demonstrate that you understand why a particular argument is effective. Insert the analysis between the summary and your response.

An analysis answers these questions: *How is the essay organized? What and where is the claim? What supports the claim? Is the support adequate and relevant? How does the author establish personal authority? What audience does the author assume? How does the author make the argument, including the support, effective for that audience? What overall qualities in this essay make it an effective (or ineffective) argument?*

▶ Example of an Analysis

Analysis of "'A' Is For 'Absent'"

The essay opens with the author's description of his own experiences in an especially "dreaded" college course. This description, coupled with an extended discussion of students' freedom of choice in paragraphs 4 and 5, provide the foundation for the author's major claim: that professors should use alternative activities and assignments for assessing student performacne (paragraph 9). The rest of the essay is organized around the author repeated assertion that students are "paying customers," and thus should be given the freedom to choose whether or not to attend class.

The support includes examples of different activities and assignments that could better be used to assess student performance: tests, quizzes, and class projects. These examples are helpful because they help support the author's claim that attendance is not the only legitimate way to measure student performance.

The author establishes his authority by citing these specific examples and thus demonstrates his first hand experience with and knowledge of classroom activities and assignments. He assumes an audience who is familiar with classroom life, and who perhaps has had doubts about the fairness of attendance policies. He makes his argument appeal to this audience by using language that emphasizes students' ability to make decisions for themselves. For example: "I pay my professors for their services"; "my choice to fully take advantage of the expense is exactly that—my choice." He establishes common ground with his audience throughout by presenting his critique of attendance policies from the perspective of a person who has experienced them.

This is an effective argument because the author establishes common ground not only with students who have experience with attendance policies, but also

---

*Thanks to Beth Brunk-Chavez for this assignment.

with anyone who has experienced difficulties of any kind with a professor in a classroom.

Summary-response and summary-analysis-response papers preserve ideas from your reading, including your own ideas, and often provide original material and even phrasing for future papers that you write on the same subject.

Expressing Multiple Perspectives through Visual Argument

Another way to express multiple perspectives on an issue other than an essay is through a collection of images that express different perspectives on it. An example of such an exploratory visual essay created with images as the central content appears on page 93. Most images need a few words of explanation for them to make their point. In this case, the title at the top and the five brief captions below the photographs explain the issue—walling off enemies—and various perspectives on how this has been done in four different countries. In the United States, walls are now in place on some parts of the border with Mexico, and more are being planned. Like the walls in China, Berlin, Israel, and Baghdad depicted in Images 1–4, this wall aims to separate people or keep people, such as illegal or undocumented Mexican immigrants and others who are perceived as enemies of a kind by many people, out.

Walling Off Your Enemies: The Long View

Image 1: The Chinese Perspective.

The Great Wall of China, was first built between the fifth and third centuries B.C., to protect the northern borders of China. It is about 4,000 miles long at present.

Image 2: The German Perspective.

The Berlin Wall, which separated East Berlin from West Berlin for 28 years, fell in 1989, an event that led to the reunification of Germany in 1990.

Image 3: The Israeli Perspective.

This wall separates Israelis from Palestinians in the West Bank at the present time.

Image 4: The Iraqi Perspective.

In Baghdad, Americans are putting up walls to secure neighborhoods.

These four photographs of walls provide four different perspectives on how governments have coped with perceived enemies by building walls. What do you think about the idea of building walls for protection from enemies? How effective is this solution? What other solutions can you think of that might also work or that might even work better?

Review Questions

1. Briefly describe a process for producing an argument paper that employs reading, thinking, and writing.
2. What are the advantages of outlining your ideas before you write a draft?
3. Name at least three specific suggestions for revision made in this chapter and describe in detail how you could use each of them.
4. Describe the exploratory paper along with some of the benefits for writing it. Then, describe exploring a topic visually along with some of the benefits of this form of communicating.
5. What is plagiarism, and what can you do to avoid it?

Exercises and Activities

A. Class Project: Creating Composite Lists of the Reading, Thinking, and Writing Processes of Class Members

This exercise gives you an opportunity to share with your classmates what you presently do when you read, think about, and write argument. When all class members contribute their strategies to composite class lists, the result is usually a very complete description of possible reading and writing processes. Include information, as you go along, about how you think as you read and write.

First, focus on describing what you do when you read and think about argument. Write the title "Reading Argument," and under it write the four headings "Prereading Strategies," "Reading Strategies," "Strategies for Reading Difficult Material," and "Postreading Strategies." Write five minutes to describe your current strategies in each area. Include thinking strategies in your description. Share these strategies with the class, creating master lists on the board.

Second, repeat this activity for writing argument. Write the title "Writing Argument," and under it write the four headings "Prewriting Strategies," "Drafting Strategies," "Strategies to Use When You Get Stuck," and "Postwriting Strategies." Write five minutes to describe your current strategies in each area and include thinking strategies in your description. Class members then contribute to composite lists on the board.

When you have written these lists, complete the following activities and discuss the results with the class.

1. Study the strategies for reading, thinking, and writing that your class has identified. Then,

   a. Discuss the ways in which writing is used as a part of the reading process.
   b. Discuss the ways in which reading is used as part of the writing process.
   c. Discuss how thinking is used as a part of both processes.

2. Turn to the Summary Charts and read the descriptions of possible strategies that you could employ at various stages to help you read, think about, and write argument. Discuss strategies you would consider adding to your present reading, thinking, and writing processes.

B. Class Discussion: Recognizing Written Argument

This reprinted article by Gina Kolata was published as a news article. Answer the following questions to help you figure out what type of argument is present, if any, here. Refer back to the description of six types of argumentation purpose on pages 70–72 to help you make your analysis.

1. What is the main issue in this article? It is not directly stated.

2. What are the author's attitudes toward the subject at issue?

3. What supporting material favors the author's point of view? Notice emotional language, vivid description, emotional examples, and the drawing that provide clues to the author's personal point of view.

4. What is the author's intention in this article? To explain? To convince? Or both?

5. What does the author hope you will conclude when you finish reading? Justify your answer with evidence from the article.

Before You Read: What do you know about sperm banks, and what is your present opinion of them?

ESSAY #2   PSST! ASK FOR DONOR 1913*

Gina Kolata

The author is a well-known science journalist for the *New York Times*. She has also published her work in *Science* magazine.

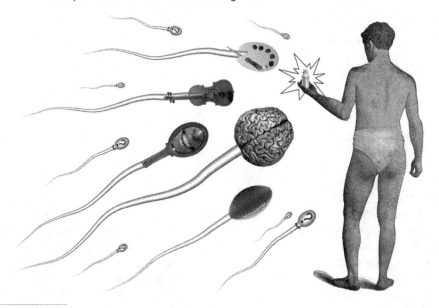

1 In the old days, nearly two decades ago, when Jeffrey Harrison was selling his sperm to California Cryobank, sperm banks did not tell clients much. Women learned that Donor 150 (Mr. Harrison, who was one of the bank's most-requested donors) was six feet tall, had blue eyes and was interested in philosophy, music and drama.

2 But they did not learn, for instance, that despite those interests, Mr. Harrison was also "sort of a free spirit," as Danielle, one of his donor-conceived daughters, said after finding him last week.

3 Mr. Harrison, 50, lives in a recreational vehicle near Los Angeles, eking out a living doing odd jobs and taking care of dogs.

4 While the women who used his sperm may be perfectly satisfied, women today seem to be looking for a more unquestionably accomplished sort of man. Handsome and brilliant. Talented and charming. Loving and kind. A match one might only dream of finding in the flesh.

5 "Many women see this as another way to give their child a head start in life," says Lori Andrews, a professor at Chicago-Kent College of Law who has studied the sperm bank industry, of the high stakes of sperm selection.

6 And increasingly, say the banks, women want proof of perfection before buying a dream donor's sperm.

7 They ask for SAT scores and personality test results. They want baby pictures, pictures of the donor as a teenager, and photos of him as an adult. They want to hear his voice on audio files and they want to read his answers to written questions.

8 As more and more is added to the profile, its compilation becomes almost a striptease as the veil of anonymity falls away, eventually revealing all but name and address.

9 The reason for offering clients previously unimaginable degrees of access to information is competition.

10 "It's kind of an arms race," explains William Jaeger, director of Fairfax Cryobank, in Fairfax, Va., which, along with California Cryobank, based in Los Angeles, is among the largest sperm banks in the country.

11 "One year someone adds a personality profile, the next year someone adds something else," Mr. Jaeger says. "If one of your competitors adds a service, you add a service."

12 Spplying donors who will be saleable is quite a burden for the banks, which say they accept only about 1 to 2 percent of donor applicants. Often a man's sperm is not good enough, reproductively, or his medical history is problematic. Others are now rejected because their looks or education or even their demeanor is wrong.

13 "We're somewhat in the position of someone who is arranging a blind date," says Dr. Charles Sims, medical director and a founder of California Cryobank.

14 So who is Mr. Right for today's woman?

15 He can't be fat.

16 "We look for a height-weight ratio that is within the norm," Dr. Sims explains.

17 Being short is negotiable.

18 "If you have a 5-foot-7 or -8 donor who is a medical student or Ph.D. scientist, that out-weighs the height issue in many situations," Dr. Sims says.

19 Education matters. California Cryobank only takes men who are in college or who graduated from a four-year college. At the Fairfax bank, "there is a preference for guys with medical and law degrees," Mr. Jaeger says.

20 Some sperm banks reveal more about their depositors than others.

21 The Fairfax bank, for example, provides adult photos if the donor agrees. The California bank does not, fearing that they could identify the donor years later and cause real problems. The Fairfax bank asks donors if their offspring can contact them when they are 18. The California bank will not do that but will try to discreetly contact a donor and ask if he wants to be identified to an adult child.

22   "We have felt we have some obligation to anticipate issues that a young man of twenty one, twenty two, or twenty three may not anticipate," Dr. Sims says. "To take an extreme example, let's say we had Bill Clinton as a donor when he was in college. Later he becomes president."

23   The Fairfax bank also includes "staff impressions" of donors in its dossiers. The staff seems to have favorable impressions of everyone, but some are more favorable than others.

24   Among the most favorable of all is a man who appears to also be the most-requested donor.

25   "Women sort of fall in love with him," says Joy Bader, director of client services.

26   The most-requested donor is of Colombian-Italian and Spanish ancestry, is "very attractive, with hazel eyes and dark hair," and, Ms. Bader adds, is "pursuing a Ph.D."

27   The bank's files have one man, Donor 1913, who fits this description.

28   Donor 1913, the staff notes in his file, is "extremely attractive," adding in a kind of clinical swoon, "He has a strong modelesque jaw line and sparking hazel eyes. When he smiles, it makes you want to smile as well."

29   Donor 1913 is an all-around nice guy, they say. "He has a shy, boyish charm,"

the staff reports, "genuine, outgoing and adventurous."

30   He also answers questions, including, "What is the funniest thing that ever happened to you?"

31   Donor 1913 relates an incident that occurred when he asked his girlfriend's mother to step on his stomach to demonstrate his strong abdominal muscles.

32   "As she stepped on top of my stomach, I passed gas," he writes,

33   Is Don Juan the gas-passer also the most popular donor at Fairfax Cryobank?

34   Mr. Jaeger, the director, says he'll never tell. He cautions that discussing the most popular donor, whoever it is, might pose a problem—there is already a waiting list for his sperm, and publicity can only make it worse.

35   "We just can't keep enough of his units on hand,"Mr. Jaeger says.

For Discussion:

Does this essay qualify as an argument? Why? Provide evidence for your answer. What does the drawing contribute? If the author had to express her opinion on the subject she writes about, what would it be? What is your opinion?

C. Writing Assignment: The Summary-Response Paper

1. Find an article related to your issue, and write a one-page summary-response paper about it.

D. Class Discussion and Writing Assignment: The Summary-Analysis-Response Paper

The following essay, "When Texting is Wrong" by Randy Cohen, is an example of the type of argument you might find in newspaper editorial or opinion column. Read, underline, and annotate the essay. Then briefly discuss answers to the following questions as a class.

1. Who is the author? What are his qualifications? What may have motivated him to write about this subject?

2. What are your own experiences with text messaging? How often do you employ this type of communication? What would you say are its advantages and disadvantages?

Arguing like a Citizen Activity

Issue: "Is sperm donation a business that should be encouraged?"

▶▶▶ Thinking Like a Citizen

- Why do I care about this issue? What is my stake?
- Who else cares about this issue? Who are the other stakeholders? Those other individuals or groups most likely to consider this issue important?
- What are the different perspectives on this issue others might have? How are their stakes in this issue similar to or different from my own?
- What are the factors and/or circumstances that account for these differences?

▶▶▶ Arguing Like a Citizen

- How does this issue impact or affect my daily life? What difference does it make to me?
- What are the key problems or questions this issue raises for me? Are these problems and questions the same as those this issue raises for others?
- What are the differences among us that a discussion or debate over this issue might expose? How might these differences be bridged?

▶▶▶ Acting Like a Citizen

- Where could I go in my community to see an example of this debate being waged?
- What concrete action could I take to change or improve the way this issue is debated? What sort of concrete action might help resolve this debate?

3. Finally, write a summary-analysis-response paper. Drawing on the notes you have taken on your reading and discussion of the essay, write a 300- to 500-word paper in which you first summarize the essay, then analyze the essay, and last, respond to the essay. Use the following prompts labeled "Summary," "Analysis," and "Response" to guide your writing.

▶ *Summary:* What is this about? What did the author say about it?

▶ *Analysis:* Describe the organization of the essay. Include a description of the claim. Describe and evaluate the support. Consider types, quantity, quality, and relevance of the support. Then answer these questions: How does the author establish his authority? What audience does the author assume? How does the author make his writing, including the support, effective for the audience? What overall qualities in this essay make it an effective (or ineffective) argument?

▶ *Response:* What are your personal reactions to this essay? How much common ground do you have with the author? What in the essay is new to you? What else does it make you think about? What do you like or dislike about it?

Before You Read: What are your own experiences with text messaging? What are the advantages and disadvantages of this particular communications technology?

ESSAY #3 WHEN TEXTING IS WRONG*

Randy Cohen

Randy Cohen writes for the *New York Times*. His column, "The Ethicist" regularly appears in the *New York Times* Magazine.

1 You're having dinner with your teenage kids, and they text throughout; you hate it; they're fine with it. At the office, managers are uncertain about texting during business meetings: many younger workers accept it; some older workers resist. Those who defend texting regard such encounters as the clash of two legitimate cultures, a conflict of manners not morals. If a community—teenagers, young workers—consents to conduct that does no harm, does that make it O.K., ethically speaking?

The Argument:

2 Seek consent and do no harm is a useful moral precept, one by which some couples, that amorous community of two, wisely govern their erotic lives, but it does not validate ubiquitous text messaging. When it comes to texting, there is no authentic consent, and there is genuine harm.

3 Neither teenagers nor young workers authorized a culture of ongoing interruption. No debate was held, no vote was taken around the junior high cafeteria or the employee lounge on the proposition: Shall we stay in constant contact, texting unceasingly? Instead, like most people, both groups

merely adapt to the culture they find themselves in, often without questioning or even being consciously aware of its norms. That's acquiescence, not agreement.

4 Few residents of Williamsburg, Va., in, say, 1740 rallied against the law that restricted voting to property-owning white men. For decades, there was little active local opposition to the sexual segregation in various Persian Gulf states. A more benign example: few of us are French by choice, but most French people act much like other French people, for good and ill. Conformity does not imply consent. It simply attests to the influence of one's neighbors.

5 So it is with incessant texting, a noxious practice that does not merely alter our in-person interactions but damages them. Even a routine conversation demands continuity and the focus of attention: it cannot, without detriment, be disrupted every few moments while someone deals with a text message. More intimate encounters suffer greater harm. In romantic comedy, when someone breaks a tender embrace to take a phone call, that's a sure sign of love gone bad. After any interruption, it takes a while to regain concentration, one reason few of us want our surgeon to text while she's

performing a delicate neurological procedure upon us. Here's a sentence you do not want to hear in the operating room or the bedroom: "Now, where was I?"

6   Various experiments have shown the deleterious effects of interruption, including this study that, unsurprisingly, demonstrates that an interrupted task takes longer to complete and seems more difficult, and that the person doing it feels increased annoyance and anxiety.

7   Mine is not a Luddite's argument, not broadly anti-technology or even anti-texting. (I'm typing this by electric light on one of those computing machines. New fangled is my favorite kind of fangled.) There are no doubt benefits and pleasures to texting, and your quietly texting while sitting on a park bench or home alone harms nobody. But what is benign in one setting can be toxic in another. (Chainsaws: useful in the forest, dubious at the dinner table. Or, as Dr. Johnson put it in a pre-chainsaw age, "A cow is a very good animal in the field; but we turn her out of a garden.")

8   Nor am I fretful that relentless texting hurts the texter herself. Critics have voiced a broad range of such concerns: too much texting damages a young person's intelligence, emotional development and thumbs. That may be so, but it is not germane here. When you injure yourself, that is unfortunate; when you injure someone else, you are unethical. (I can thus enjoy reading about a texting teen who fell into a manhole. When a man is tired of cartoon mishaps, he is tired of life. And yes, that teen is fine now.)

9   Last week, a Massachusetts grand jury indicted a Boston motorman who crashed his trolley into another, injuring 62 people: he was texting on duty. Last month, Patti LuPone berated an audience member who pulled out an electronic device during her show in Las Vegas. (Theaters forbid the audience to text during a performance, a rule routinely flouted. Perhaps stage managers could be issued tranquilizer darts and encouraged to shoot audience members who open any device during a show. At intermission, ushers can drag out the unconscious and confiscate their phones. Or we might institute something I call Patti's Law: Any two-time Tony winner would be empowered to carry a gun onstage and shoot similar offenders.)

10   These are the easy cases, of course: clearly it is unethical to text when doing so risks harming other people. And formal regulation can easily address them; a dozen states and the District of Columbia prohibit texting while driving, for example. But the problem of perpetual texting in more casual settings cannot be solved by legislation. No parent will call the cops if a son or daughter texts at table. Instead, we need new manners to be explicitly introduced at home and at work, one way social customs can evolve to restrain this emerging technology.

11   Lest casual texting seem a trivial concern, remember that some political observers trace the recent stalemate in the New York Senate to the wrath of power-broker Tom Golisano, who was offended that majority leader Malcolm Smith fiddled with his BlackBerry throughout a meeting between them. When the dust settled, the State Senate had been transformed from merely disheartening to genuinely grotesque. I wouldn't want that on my conscience.

E. Group Work: Analyzing an Argument Essay That Employs Visual Perspectives on the Issue as Support

The following essay was written at a time when some members of Congress were advocating the addition of a flag burning amendment to the United States Constitution. Read the essay, study the images, and answer the "For Discussion" questions that follow.

Before You Read: Is flag burning an issue you feel strongly about? Why or why not?

ESSAY #4   FLAG PROTECTION: A BRIEF HISTORY OF
RECENT SUPREME COURT DECISIONS*
Congressional Research Service

This excerpt, which provides an historical overview of recent US Supreme Court decisions regarding flag burning, was prepared as part of a report made to Congress in 2006.

101

1   Many Members of Congress see continued tension between "free speech" decisions of the Supreme Court, which protect flag desecration as expressive conduct under the First Amendment, and the symbolic importance of the United States flag.

2   Consequently, every Congress that has convened since those decisions were issued has considered proposals that would permit punishment of those who engage in flag desecration. The 106th Congress narrowly failed to send a constitutional amendment to allow punishment of flag desecration to the States. In the 107th and 108th Congresses, such proposals were passed by the House. This report is divided into two parts. The first gives a brief history of the flag protection issue, from the enactment of the Flag Protection Act in 1968 through current consideration of a constitutional amendment. The

second part briefly summarizes the two decisions of the United States Supreme Court, *Texas* v. *Johnson* and *United States* v. *Eichman*, that struck down the state and federal flag protection statutes as applied in the context punishing expressive conduct.

3   In 1968, Congress reacted to the numerous public flag burnings in protest of the Vietnam conflict by passing the first federal flag protection act of general applicability. For the next 20 years, the lower courts upheld the constitutionality of this statute and the Supreme Court declined to review these decisions. However, in *Texas* v. *Johnson*, the majority of the Court held that a conviction for flag desecration under a Texas statute was inconsistent with the First Amendment and affirmed a decision of the Texas Court of Criminal Appeals that barred punishment for burning the flag as part of a public demonstration.

Time, July 3, 2006, 100.

Joe Rosenthal *Marines Raising the American Flag at Iwo Jima.*

Leonard Detrick, *Anti-Vietnam War Protesters.*

Stephanie Frey, *Daughter Holding Parents' American Flag.*

4   In response to *Johnson*, Congress passed the federal Flag Protection Act of 1989. But, in reviewing this act in *United States* v. *Eichman*, the Supreme Court expressly declined the invitation to reconsider *Johnson* and its rejection of the contention that flag-burning, like obscenity or "fighting words," does not enjoy the full protection of the First Amendment as a mode of expression. The only question not addressed in *Johnson*, and therefore the only question the majority felt necessary to address, was "whether the Flag Protection Act is sufficiently distinct from the Texas statute that it may constitutionally be applied to proscribe appellees' expressive conduct." The majority of the Court held that it was not.

Congress, recognizing that *Johnson* and *Eichman* had left little hope of an anti-desecration statute being upheld, has considered in each Congress subsequent to these decisions a constitutional amendment to empower Congress to protect the physical integrity of the flag.

For Discussion:

What three perspectives on the flag of the United States are expressed in the three photographs? What three wars do they represent? What effect is created by placing photographs next to each other in this order? How does the historical overview of recent Supreme Court decisions regarding flag burning influence how you read these images?

The Core of Your Argument: Finding and Stating a Claim

At the heart of every argument is its main claim, the point you want to support, the solution to the problem that caused you to make an argument in the first place (some teachers call it your *thesis*). *Claim*, though, has two meanings: When you claim *that* something is so, you also make a claim *on* your readers' time to consider what you've written in support of it. You justify that second claim only when you offer them something in return for their reading. That's why we stress that a claim is not just a statement that you want readers to agree with, but a plausible solution to a problem that you think they should care about.

The tough part, of course, can be finding that solution. Sometimes you don't have to search far. If you believe human cloning is wrong, you know where you stand on the issue. But on other issues, you may have no ready answer: Should insurers do genetic screening for a tendency toward alcoholism? How have TV sitcoms changed our attitudes toward families in the last fifty years? We can't answer such questions for you,

> **Warrants**
>> **Acknowledgment & Response**
>>> **C**laim **R**easons **E**vidence

but we can tell you how to search for answers as experienced problem solvers and careful, critical thinkers do. We will also suggest ways to express the answers you find in a way that readers judge to be thoughtful.

Exploring Claims Without Rushing to Judgment

Whatever strategies you follow to solve your problem, you cannot wait until you have looked at all the evidence before you come up with a solution to test. Experienced problem solvers don't wait. They size up a problem quickly, then spin off a few tentative solutions that roughly fit the data they started with. Then they let those tentative solutions guide their search for more data, using those new data to test each hypothesis and, if one fits, to support it. Without those initial hypotheses, they would not know what evidence to look for or how to evaluate what they found.

But the most expert problem solvers know better than to accept their first ideas uncritically. They treat their initial hypotheses as merely "working hypotheses," *and they hold them lightly*. They do not give up their deepest convictions and beliefs easily, but neither do they embrace them so closely that they cannot step back to examine them critically, perhaps even to see past them to new, still deeper truths.

Uncritical problem solvers also jump to a quick solution, but then they cling to it, so that their first thought becomes their last. They may use that idea to guide further research, but only to confirm what they already believe. For them, research does not open up thinking but shuts it down. They don't make that mistake intentionally; it's just that all our human minds are built to make quick judgments that reflect what we want to be true, usually what we already believe. It's a habit of mind that, in the short run, helps us manage crises. But it's risky when a lot rides on making the right decision for the long run.

Think, for example, of those who propose the same solution to every problem. The next time gun-toting students shoot up a school, no matter what the facts are, some will instantly point to the too easy availability of guns, others to poor family values, still others to violent movies and video games. The business world has a maxim about such people: *To a person with a hammer, every problem is a nail.* If profits are falling, the ad manager thinks the solution is more advertising; the operations manager thinks it is to modernize the plant; the personnel manager wants to invest in recruiting and training. Each might be partly right, but when they insist on their pet solution to the exclusion of others, they risk missing the best one, because all they see is the nail that fits their particular hammer.

Admittedly, our advice to think critically about your own ideas is hard to follow, but here it is: Formulate a few tentative solutions to a problem sooner rather than later, but hold them lightly as you critically test them against the evidence. Resist what most uncritical thinkers do: Jump to a simple conclusion that they cannot give up. You cannot change human nature, but you can guard against a tendency toward hasty, superficial judgments by stepping back to think critically: Ask the toughest questions you can imagine others might ask; consider *all* the evidence you can find, especially what doesn't fit your ideas; reason through all the steps of your logic; and especially talk things over with others who disagree. In short, be as critical of your own ideas as you are about the ideas of others.

What Kind of Claim Does Your Problem Require?

Earlier, we discussed how a well-framed problem motivates readers to read. You motivate them further when you state at the end of your introduction a solution that is not self-evidently true, but seems clear, plausible, and thoughtful. As we said, we can't help you find the best claim; that requires research and testing, and every field has its own way of doing that. But we can suggest ways to evaluate, develop, and state your best claim so that your readers will at least give it a fair hearing.

IS YOUR CLAIM PRACTICAL OR CONCEPTUAL?

Above all, you need to decide early whether you can solve your problem by getting readers to understand or to act, because we make arguments about conceptual and practical problems differently. The solution to a conceptual problem asks readers only to *understand* or *believe* something, as this claim does:

> Not only do students whose first language is not English do better in class when they receive tutorial help, but in the long run they require less faculty time.

The solution to a practical problem asks readers not only to understand but to *do* something (or endorse an action). Such claims are typically built on a *should* or *must:*

> State U. should increase the budget for tutorial help for students whose first language is not English.

If you trust readers to read between the lines, you can hope they will infer your solution, as we can from this claim:

> Since students whose first language is not English require less faculty time when they also receive tutorial help, State U. could save money by increasing the budget for tutors.

Most of us, though, think readers are able to infer more than they actually do. So when in doubt, *explicitly* state what you expect of them: to understand something, with no intent that they act, or to perform (or at least support) an action.

When you can, state your claims affirmatively. For practical problems especially, a negative solution does not suggest a plan of action; a positive one does. Compare:

> The university should stop using its teaching evaluation form because it does not reveal students' feelings about learning.

> The university should develop a new teaching evaluation form that tells faculty whether their students think they are learning useful skills.

If you cannot find a plausible solution and your assignment allows it, redefine the problem: break the problem into parts, one of which you might be able to solve, or at least clarify. Suppose you start with the conceptual problem of how TV sitcom families have changed in the last fifty years, but decide that question is too large for you to answer in a short paper. You can narrow it: How have the families changed in the highest-rated sitcoms in the first year of every decade since 1950? Or, suppose Elena thinks she cannot solve the problem of the university's failure to provide international students with enough help in English. She might instead address a smaller problem: international students do not know where to find the help that is available. You can also redefine a practical problem as a conceptual one by identifying questions whose answers will eventually help solve the practical problem.

Values Claims

Claims that assert something is right or wrong, good or bad, are often called "values" claims. Some so-called values claims are covert practical claims. They imply that readers should do something to be on the side of what they say is right or good, without stating exactly what. For example, in a *Washington Times* newspaper column, restaurant owner Richard Berman complains about extremist food recommendations, such as replacing the Thanksgiving turkey with turkey-shaped tofu. His main point states values that he implies readers should act on:

> In an effort to change American eating habits to conform to their puritanical vision, groups such as the Center for Science in the Public Interest, the Vegetarian Society, and People for the Ethical Treatment of Animals are perverting the way Americans look at food.[a]

By not saying what we should do about those arguments—ignore extreme claims, cook a traditional Thanksgiving turkey, or eat in a restaurant—he relieves himself of the obligation to defend any solution.

On the other hand, a values claim is conceptual when it implies only that we should approve or disapprove, and nothing more:

> As president, John Kennedy was inspirational, but as a person, he was sexually corrupt.

That claim asks us only to disapprove of Kennedy's character. While it might imply, *Don't be like him!*, we don't have to act to solve the conceptual problem posed by the writer: *You might be wrong about what you think of John Kennedy and therefore about the role of models in political life*. That problem is solved by our negative judgment alone.

Whether you assert a values claim that is practical or conceptual, you still have to make a supporting argument with reasons, based on evidence, governed by warrants. You still have to acknowledge and respond to other views.

---

[a]*Source:* "Turkey Police, Beware," *Washington Times*, November 26, 1998, p. A19.

Values claims can be tricky, however, because they assume beliefs, definitions, and values that transcend the particular issue. We will agree that Kennedy was corrupt only if we already hold moral principles that a writer can appeal to. If not, a writer would have to state those principles, and then convince us that they are true.

HOW STRONGLY DO YOU WANT READERS TO ACCEPT YOUR CLAIM?

Some writers think that the agreement their arguments deserve is all-or-nothing, win-or-lose, agree-or-die. But that's shortsighted. You might not need readers to accept a big claim about a big problem if you can persuade them to accept a modest one about part of it. For example, Elena might think her college devotes too few resources to helping international students with their English, but she also knows it is unlikely to spend lots of money on a new language center. If, however, she can get some administrator just to consider increasing the budget for language tutors, she will achieve something valuable, even if it is only a small step toward her larger goal. Partial success is rarely total failure.

So as you formulate a claim, think how you want readers to take it. What do you want them to do?

⬤ **Respect** your reasons for making your claim and, by extension, respect you.

⬤ **Approve** of your claim and the argument supporting it.

⬤ **Publicly endorse** your claim as worth consideration.

⬤ **Believe** in your claim and in your argument supporting it.

⬤ **Act** as you propose, or support someone else's action.

Only the last two count as complete success for those who see argument as a win-or-lose proposition. But those who do must fail more often than they succeed, because few arguments completely convince anybody of anything. Your argument is a total failure only when your readers scoff not only at it, but at you, rejecting both as not worth their time, much less their respect.

Giving Readers an Alternative Solution

If you fear your readers might reject a too-costly solution, offer the solution to part of the problem that readers can implement. One good strategy is to make the too-costly solution your main claim, but mention the alternative solution in an acknowledgment and response: acknowledge the value of the lesser solution, but respond that your solution is better. As you explicitly support your preferred solution, you implicitly support the alternative:

Although more English language tutors would provide some immediate help, acknowledgement / implicitly supported alternative solution only a Center for English Language Instruction will solve the problem entirely. response / explicitly supported solution More tutors would help students with assignments and reduce faculty time spent on minor issues of grammar. But without an infrastructure to support them, international students will not improve their English enough to do well without help from tutors. support for response

Explicitly, this is an argument for building a language center; implicitly it shows the value of increasing the number of tutors.

What Counts as a Claim Worth Considering?

A claim will motivate readers to read the argument supporting it only if it seems on its face worth considering. For example, it makes little sense to make an argument supporting a claim either that the earth is round or that it's flat. Since no one questions the shape of the earth, no one would bother to read an argument for either claim. So once you have a claim you think is worth your time supporting, ask three questions to determine whether your readers will think it worth their time reading.

1. *Can Your Claim Be Contested?* Even if they have no settled beliefs about a topic, critical readers will—or should—adopt an amiably skeptical attitude: Well, that's interesting, but let's see your support. You are in trouble if instead they think, That's obvious! A claim is worth considering only if readers might contest it. You have no good reason to ask for their time to read your supporting argument if they already believe your claim or are indifferent to it. For example, how would readers respond to claims like these?

1a. Education is important to our society.
2a. We should not ridicule how people look.
3a. I will summarize current views on the disappearance of frogs.

Can you imagine a reader thinking, If that's true, I'll have to change my mind about education/ridicule/frogs? Not likely. Those claims don't need an argument, because no one would contest them.

Here's a quick way to assess whether a claim is contestable (another way of saying significant): Revise it into its negative form (or revise a negative claim into its affirmative). Then assess whether it still seems plausible or significant.

1b. Education is **not** important to our society.
2b. We **should** ridicule how people look.
3b. I will **not** summarize current views on the disappearance of frogs.

Most readers would judge claims (1b) and (2b) to be self-evidently implausible, so those claims fail the test. No one will question a claim if no one believes its opposite. The negative claim (3b), on the other hand, seems trivial. If the negative is trivial, then most readers would judge the affirmative to be trivial too. In none of these cases is the claim worth supporting, because no one would contest any of them.

We must note, however, that human thought has been revolutionized when someone has proved false a claim that at the time seemed self-evidently true:

The sun does **not** go around the earth.

We do **not** consist of solid matter.

We cannot rule out as forever false the claim that education is not important (some groups in fact believe it). You would make your reputation if you could convince us of that, but it would take a powerful argument to do so.

2. *Can Your Claim Be Proved Wrong?* At least in principle, state your claims so that they can be proved wrong (the technical term is disconfirmed). That may seem odd. Don't we make claims we can prove, not ones our readers can disprove? In fact, careful arguers make claims only when they believe that at least in principle someone might find evidence that would prove a claim right or wrong and are willing to consider that evidence.

For example, suppose a person wants to argue that ghosts exist. Imagine someone asks that person,

> What would it take to convince you that they don't?

And that person responds,

> There is no evidence that could prove they exist one way or the other, so no conceivable argument or evidence could convince me that ghosts do not exist, because I just know in my heart they do and *nothing* can prove that souls do not survive death.

Both parties might learn something about the other from an exchange of views, but there can be no rational argument if a claim is not subject to evidence. If an arguer believes that no evidence can disprove his claim, not even in principle, then he gives us no role in his argument—not only can we not participate by engaging our own views, but we cannot even be rational judges of what he says. We can simply take him at his word, or, more likely, not.

We make arguments most productively when both parties embrace an essential characteristic of a critical thinking: they can both imagine being wrong; both see the issue in question as contingent, not settled, always open to question if new evidence comes along. That means all parties in an argument should agree to a first principle in the social contract of cooperative arguments: *Both reader and writer must be able to imagine that there could be evidence that might change their minds.*

Now that principle does not disparage belief in ghosts or anything else we can't prove. We are entitled to believe whatever we please, for any reason, good or bad, or for no reason at all (we might not be thinking critically, but that would be a private matter).

But when we make *public* claims about a private belief in order to answer some significant question or solve some difficult problem that we want others to take seriously, and we ask readers to *agree* with our claim, we must open our own minds to their arguments *against* our beliefs as much as we ask them to open their minds to our arguments for them.

3. *Is Your Claim Reasonable on Its Face?* Once you have a claim that readers can contest and at least in principle disprove, you must start listening to that critical voice in the back of your mind asking questions your readers are likely to ask, questions like these:

▶ Is your solution **feasible?**

Tanya is unlikely to get a hearing from the dean if she suggests that the problem of weak teaching could be solved by shifting half the athletic budget to a Teaching Resource Center. But the dean might listen if she suggested a small tax on research grants to subsidize one.

▶ Is your solution **ethical** (or **legal, proper, fair,** etc.)?

Tanya would be instantly rejected if she proposed that the administration secretly monitor classes, but she might get a hearing if she suggested that faculty be encouraged to observe one another's teaching.

▶ Is your solution **prudent?** Might it create a problem worse than the one it solves?

Tanya would have no chance of getting the dean to cut the salary of faculty with poor teaching evaluations because they would rebel. But he might consider merit raises to reward good teaching.

What Does a Thoughtful Claim Look Like?

At some point—sooner better than later—you have to get a hypothesis out of the dark comfort of your mind into the cold light of print. Only then can you ask, *Will this claim encourage readers to judge it—and me—as thoughtful?* Sad to say, we cannot teach you how to be thoughtful. We can only describe what encourages readers to think you might be. Compare these claims:

TV makes crime seem a bigger problem than it is.

Though violent crime has declined around the country, many believe it has increased in their own neighborhoods because night after night their local TV news shows open with graphic reports of murder and mayhem, making it seem that violence happens every day just outside their front door.

The second claim seems more interesting, because its verbal complexity reflects the complex situation it describes (and indirectly the mind that made it).

Now we are *not* asserting that a wordy claim must be better than a short concise one. Too many words can obscure issues, and a few well-chosen words can focus readers on what's important. But inexperienced writers commonly make claims that are too thin rather than too thick. So in what follows we will go overboard in encouraging you to make claims as detailed as you can, even too detailed. You can always revise them later. So take what follows as an exercise in exploratory thinking, not as a plan for drafting what you will actually submit to your readers.

IS YOUR CLAIM CONCEPTUALLY RICH?

When your claims include more concepts, you give your readers and yourself more to work with. Compare these three claims:

> The **effects** of the Civil War are still **felt** today.

> The Civil War lives on in the **sunbelt axis** of the **federalist question.**

> The **ideological and social divisions** of the Civil War still **exert a historical influence** today on the **political discourse** of **North** and **South** (and the **West**), reflected in their **antithetical political theories** about the **relative scope** of **state** and **federal powers** and the **proper authority of government** over **free individuals.**

The first feels both thin and vague. It mentions unspecified *effects* that are *felt* in some general way. The second is specific, but still feels thin for readers unable to unpack the technical terms *sunbelt axis* and *federalist question.* The third expresses a richer set of concepts—in fact, too many for one claim, but remember we are exploring and developing claims, not writing final drafts yet.

A claim rich in concepts helps readers see the full implications of what you ask them to do or believe. A conceptually rich claim also helps you improve your argument in two ways:

▶ It obligates you to develop those concepts named in your argument.

▶ When readers see you return to them in the body of your argument, they are more likely to think your argument is coherent.

So when you think you have the makings of a good claim, add more concepts than you think necessary. (We show you steps for doing that in the Writing Process section below.) If you add too many, apply the Goldilocks rule to find a happy medium (not too many, not too few, but just right):

> The **ideological divisions** of the Civil War still **shape** the **political discourse of North and South** today, reflected in their **antithetical theories** about **state** and **federal powers** and the **authority of government** over **individuals.**

IS YOUR CLAIM LOGICALLY RICH?

At the core of most claims is a simple proposition like this:

> State U. should do something about rising tuition. claim

That claim borders on simplistic: What does *do something* mean? We can make its language richer:

> State U. should limit tuition increases to the rate of inflation. claim

But we can also elaborate its logic in two ways:

> 1. Add a reason-clause beginning with *because* or *if,* or a phrase beginning with *by* or *in order to.*

Compare these two claims:

> State U. should slow tuition increases to the rate of inflation. claim

> State U. could slow tuition increases to the rate of inflation claim **if it reduced its administrative costs to the level of comparable universities,** reason 1 **and its faculty taught as much as faculty do at other state schools.** reason 2

The first claim states a proposition that is logically thin. In the second, readers can see the gist of a solution in the *if*-clause and can thereby better anticipate the rest of the argument.

Note: Be aware that if the problem concerns not what is wrong but what causes it, your main claim may be in a *because*-clause. If the writer and reader agree State U should slow tuition increases, the main claim would involve the two causes for high tuition. You can avoid confusing readers by revising so that the two causes appear in a main clause:

> State U. must slow tuition increases to the rate of inflation. **Its administrative costs are significantly higher than comparable universities,** claim 1 **and its faculty teaches less than other state schools.** claim 2

2. Add a concession-clause beginning with *although, while,* or *even though* or a phrase beginning with *despite, regardless of,* or *notwithstanding.*

When you open with an *although*-clause, you acknowledge an alternative point of view. There are three common options:

▶ An alternative point of view contradicts your claim:
Although some argue that we must raise tuition to meet the rising costs of maintaining State U.'s physical plant and updating research facilities, acknowledgment of alternative conclusion State U. could slow tuition increases to the rate of inflation because its administrative costs are significantly higher than comparable universities and its faculty teaches less than professors at other state schools.

▶ There is evidence that argues against your claim:
Although State U.'s administrative costs have not risen faster than inflation and it has hired no new faculty in three years, acknowledgment of contradictory evidence State U. could slow tuition increases to the rate of inflation because its administrative costs are still significantly higher than comparable universities and its faculty teaches less than professors at other state schools.

▶ Something limits the scope of your claim:
Although college costs will always rise to reflect inflation, acknowledgment of limited scope of claim State U. could slow tuition increases to the rate of inflation because its administrative costs are significantly higher than comparable universities and its faculty teaches less than professors at other state schools.

If your claim grows too long, divide it. Put a period after the *although*-clause and delete the *although.* Then begin the main claim with *but, however, even so, nevertheless,* etc. (It is *not* a grammatical error to begin a sentence with *but* or *however.*)

The costs of maintaining State U.'s physical plant are rising, and scientific advances require it to update research facilities continually. **However,** State U. could slow tuition to the rate of inflation because its administrative costs are significantly higher than comparable universities and its faculty teaches less than professors at other state schools.

IS YOUR CLAIM APPROPRIATELY QUALIFIED?

Critical thinkers can be confident in their judgment, because they put their own ideas to the test. But even so, they know that few things in this world are 100 percent certain, unqualifiedly true. And so they rarely make claims with flat-footed certainty, and they distrust those who do. So when you state your main claim, make it judiciously modest, unlike this one:

State U. would stop tuition increases if it eliminated administrative waste and required faculty to teach more classes.

Thoughtful readers will wonder, *How can you be so sure? How can the problem be so simple?* Contrast that flat-footed certainty with this more modest, more nuanced claim:

State U. **might be able** to **slow** its rates of tuition increases, if it **could reduce** administrative costs and get **more** of its faculty to teach more classes.

(You can find vocabulary for qualifying in the Writing Process section below.)

Of course, if you overqualify, you give readers reason to doubt your confidence. It's a balancing act. Compare these claims:

1. Research proves that people with a gun at home **will** use it to kill themselves or a family member rather than to protect themselves from intruders.

2. **Some recent** research **seems** to **suggest** there **may** be a **possible risk** that **some** people with a gun at home **could** be **more prone** to use it to kill themselves or a family member rather than to protect themselves from **potential** intruders.

3. Recent research **suggests** that people with a gun at home **more often** use it to kill themselves or a family member than to protect themselves from intruders.

Most academic and professional readers would reject (1) as too absolute and (2) as wishy-washy, but find (3) closer to the confidently temperate stance they trust. Of course, it comes closest to that Goldilocks rule: not too certain, not too uncertain, maybe not just right, but closer than the first two.

Certainty in Eighteenth-Century Politics and Twentieth-Century Science

Those who think that hedging is mealymouthed might note Benjamin Franklin's account of how he deliberately created his ethos of judicious moderation by speaking

> . . . in terms of modest diffidence, never using when I advance any-
> thing that may possibly be disputed, the words *certainly, undoubtedly,*
> or any others that gave the air of positiveness to an opinion; but rather
> say, *I conceive,* or *I apprehend a Thing to be so or so It appears as to
> me,* or *I should think it so or so for such and such Reasons,* or *I imagine
> it to be so, or it is so if I am not mistaken.* This habit I believe has been
> of great advantage to me . . . To this habit (after my character of
> integrity) I think it principally owing that I had early so much weight
> with my fellow citizens when I proposed new institutions or alter-
> ations in the old, and so much influence in public councils when I
> became a member.

That advice is relevant today. Among those who make arguments for a living, scientists may distrust certainty the most because they know how fast scientific
truths can change. You see this not only in the way they test claims, but in the
language they use to make them. Here, a science journalist describes how scientists typically comment on published research:

> Notice the qualifiers on belief: "pretty much," "more or less," "don't
> particularly disbelieve." Scientists are great suspenders of belief. They
> know that their measurements often have large margins of error, their
> experimental devices are often relatively inadequate, and their own
> understanding incomplete. They know that the world is complex,
> interconnected, subtle and extremely easy to get wrong. Geologists
> once believed that the Sudbury mineral complex in Ontario, the source
> of most of the world's nickel, precipitated out of a melt formed when
> the liquid in the earth's middle rose up through the crust. But after
> finding shattered rock, microscopic mineral grains subjected to intense
> pressure, and other signs of a great impact, they now believe the
> nickel formed when a 6-mile-wide meteorite hit the Earth so hard that
> the crust melted. . . . Geologists will mostly believe that until more evi-
> dence comes along.

Source: From Ann Finkbeiner, "In Science, Seeing Is Not Believing," *USA Today,*
October 21, 1997.

Writing Process

FINDING AND STATING CLAIMS
Drafting
Use Specific Language to State Claims

When you state a claim using specific words, readers can understand it better and
then use it to help them anticipate how you will support it. Before you draft a
claim, either your main claim or major subclaims, do the following:

   1. *List additional specific terms that might fit your claim.* Concentrate on
nouns and verbs; you'll have to ask different questions about each. For example,

for the claim *The divisive effects of the Civil War are still felt today*, ask these two questions:

> ▶ For nouns, ask *What kind of?* Then ask it again for each term in your answer. Add all the terms that might apply to your list.
>
> For example, for the term *effects*, ask, *What kind of **effects?**—political rivalry, regional prejudice, economic competition, ideological differences.* Then for the term *ideological differences*, ask, *What kind of **differences?**— theories of government, states' rights, individual freedom, right to work laws, Bible belt fundamentalism.*
>
> ▶ For verbs, ask *How?* Add all the terms that might apply to your list.
>
> For example, *How are effects **felt?**—by the regions mistrusting one another, by the South voting as a political bloc, by the South seeing federal efforts toward desegregation as an imposition from the North, by old divisions influencing new attitudes, by the politicians of each region advancing different theories of government.*

Once you have a list of specific terms relevant to your claim, look for related words that might express your ideas more precisely.

> ▶ For each term, ask the question *as opposed to?* If a new term expresses your ideas better than the old one, replace the old one.
>
> For example, ***Differences*** as opposed to *divisions, disruptions, disagreements.* ***States' rights*** as opposed to *federalism, the power of the federal government, the freedom of states to govern themselves.* ***Influence*** as opposed to *determine, shape.*

    2. *Write the claim using the most appropriate words on the list.* Review your lists, picking out three or four terms that best express the key ideas of your claim (in bold). Then write a claim using those terms and any others that fit (in italics):

Relevant Kinds of Effects

ideological divisions, political rivalry, **theories of government,** *state vs. federal power, individual freedom*

Relevant Ways They Are Felt

old divisions shape new attitudes, bloc voting in the South, *politicians of each region advance different theories of government*

The **ideological divisions** of the Civil War still **shape** the *political discourse* of North and South today, reflected in their **antithetical theories** about *state and federal powers* and the *authority of government over individuals.*

Revising
Qualify Claims That Are Too Certain

Readers distrust claims (and their makers) that express arrogant, unquestioning certainty, preferring claims that show the kind of civil diffidence that communicates a critical thinker's cautious confidence: *I have tested this claim in all the ways I know, but of course we never know what new evidence might turn up.* When you review the sentences in a completed draft, check the language of your main claim and major subclaims for too much certainty.

Watch for sentences that overstate the scope of your claim by suggesting that something is *certainly* true *always* and *for everyone:*

- **Probability:** If you find *certainly, absolutely, without question,* etc., consider writing *probably, normally, likely, tend to, inclined to,* etc. If you find *impossible, inconceivable,* etc., consider writing *unlikely, improbable,* etc.
- **Frequency:** If you find *always, every time, without fail,* etc., consider writing *usually, frequently, predictably, habitually, almost always,* etc. If you find *never, not once,* etc., consider writing *seldom, rarely, infrequently, almost never,* etc.
- **Quantity:** If you find *all, every, each,* etc., consider writing *many, most, some, a majority, almost all,* etc. If you find *none, not one,* etc., consider writing *few, hardly any,* etc.

Remember that a claim may seem too certain even without any of these words. If you write the claim, "Readers distrust writers who are certain," readers may assume that you mean "*All* readers *always* distrust all writers who are certain."

At the same time, don't overqualify. You would seem wishy-washy if you wrote "Some readers are occasionally somewhat inclined to distrust writers who are certain." Usually, one qualification is enough: "Readers *are likely to* distrust. . . ," "Readers *often* distrust. . . ," "*Many* readers distrust . . ."

Even more than they distrust writers who make unqualified claims, readers distrust those who assert those claims too strongly. When you claim that your reasons or evidence support a claim, be moderate in asserting how strong your case really is:

- **Level of proof:** Unless you have the strongest possible evidence, avoid phrases like *X proves Y, X settles the question, Y is beyond question, without a doubt,* etc. If you find X *demonstrates, establishes,* or *shows* Y, consider writing X *suggests, points to, argues for, leads us to believe, indicates,* etc.

Here too, you don't want to diminish the real strength of your argument, but readers are likely to be suspicious if you exaggerate the level of your proof.

Inquiries

Reflections

1. Are those who make conceptual arguments responsible for what others do with their claims? Is a scientist who discovers something that someone uses to create new weapons responsible for their consequences? Should a geneticist get credit when his discoveries help doctors save lives? If so, should he be

blamed if those same discoveries are used in immoral ways? What about a political scientist whose ideas about limiting the power of government inspire
someone to bomb a federal building? What principle might we use to make
distinctions among these cases? Could you make a case that some claims
should never be made? What about a discovery that makes it possible for anyone to build an atomic bomb in his kitchen? What might be the unintended
consequences if researchers kept secret discoveries that they thought might be
potentially dangerous?

Tasks

2. Suppose you have been asked for suggestions about recreational facilities, in-
   tramural sports, cultural activities, or some other part of your college life.
   Make a snap judgment about what you think is a problem and offer a quick
   and easy solution. Now approach the same problem by following all three
   stages of critical thinking. Assume that quick, unreflective judgments are usually wrong. Did you identify the real problem the first time?

3. Try the negation test (pp. 109–110) on the claims in some of your old papers.
   What does it tell you about the significance of your claims?

4. What kinds of claims have you made most often in your papers, calls for action or claims that something is true? Try revising each claim that explicitly
   calls for an action into a claim that only implies one, and vice versa.

Projects

5. Suppose you are a leader in a national student organization dedicated to reducing the costs of a college education. Sketch a plan of action for asking college presidents to support a policy that will lower tuition. What role would
   negotiation or mediation have in your plan? What about propaganda (advertising, public relations, etc.)? Coercion (demonstrations, civil disobedience,
   lobbying legislators, etc.)? How would argument fit into your plans?

6. Look in your old papers for the qualities of good claims (pp. 109–111). Look
   especially for signals of cause and effect (*because, so, in order to,* etc.) and reser-
   vation (*despite, although, while,* etc.). If your claims seem thin, elaborate them
   in ways we've suggested (pp. 115–117).

Focus on Writing

1

Context. In the fairest arguments, writers present the positions of those with whom they differ in a way that their "opponents" would accept as accurate. But nothing is more common than for writers of opinion pieces in newspapers and magazines to distort the positions of those they oppose. For instance, it is likely that the three organizations named by Richard Berman in "Turkey Police, Beware" (below) would reject his characterization of their beliefs. You can find information about the organizations and their positions in the library and on the Web (www.cspinet.org; www.vegsoc.org; www.cyberveg.org; and www.peta.org).

Read Berman's "Turkey Police, Beware" before completing tasks below.

Turkey Police, Beware
Richard Berman

Food police cut more than calories by whacking feast foods. Somewhere in America, a family will eat a Thanksgiving dinner the food police would be proud of. Warm aromas of mashed tofu with fresh, creamy canola oil, baked yams with a pinch of salt-free substitute on them, boiled onions and soy-bread stuffing with low-sodium vegetable broth gravy fill the house with an air of excitement. Everyone waits for the pièce de résistance and out of it comes: A steaming, gleaming tofurky (tofu molded into a turkey), complete with fermented soy drumsticks.

In an effort to change American eating habits to conform to their puritanical vision, groups such as the Center for Science in the Public Interest, the Vegetarian Society and People for the Ethical Treatment of Animals are perverting the way Americans look at food. Nowhere is this more prevalent than in their attacks on our feast foods, those meals we eat only on special occasions. Every year the talking heads appear on the air to demonize holiday fare as unholy bastions of what CSPI calls food porn. The weeks before Thanksgiving host the now-traditional parade of health scares, tips, pranks and even outright terrorism as nanny state activists jostle for the media's attention.

Mothers against Drunk Drivers uses Thanksgiving to move almost seamlessly from its "Deadly Days of Summer" (Memorial Day to Labor Day) to its "Tie One On" (Thanksgiving to New Year's Eve) campaign. Both are intended to scare us away from even responsible drinking. As MADD's President, Karolyn Nunnallee says, "we will not tolerate drinking and driving, period." So much for any holiday cheer for those not sleeping over.

On the food front, a widely reported study—purposely released days before last Thanksgiving—claimed that just one fatty meal could induce a heart attack. (That'd sure put a damper on the giblet gravy.) Less reported was that the study surveyed only 18 men, hardly a significant medical development. That same week, other scientists released overblown warnings about malonaldehyde in turkey, arsenic in mashed potatoes, and aflatoxins in walnuts. Such arguments stretch believability. According to the American Council on Science and Health, one must eat 3.8 tons of turkey to develop cancer from malonalde-hyde. A legion of chipmunks couldn't eat enough nuts to give one of them cancer.

The science and the public interest group CSPI does its part for the holidays and its annual press conference warning us that "consumers need to treat every turkey as though it harbors a feast of bacteria." The group goes so far as to campaign against stuffing turkeys, for fear of salmonella or food poisoning. Isn't that why we cook our turkeys? Rad-ical vegetarians and PETA go further, protesting everything from barbecue to the Easter ham to (again) that icon of American food, the Thanksgiving turkey. Calling the holiday "murder on turkeys," PETA suggests we eat tofurky instead.

More sinister are the antics of the Animal Avengers, which in 1996 created a scare in Vancouver, Canada, by saying the group had laced turkeys with rat poison. Another group, the Animal Rights Militia, pulled the same trick in 1994. Such relentless attacks have done more than just cut calories from our dinner plate. Thanksgiving and the winter holidays are a time for family, reunions, friends and for literally giving thanks for what we have. Food, drink, and yes, even smoking, is often part of this experience. On an even deeper level, feast foods help define who we are as an individual, as a family and as a regional or ethnic group. "There are all kinds of signposts on people's Thanksgiving table that give away who they are," New York Times food editor Ruth Reichl said.

Author Irene Chalmers, whose book Food discusses the social, psychological and emo-tional aspects of special meals, goes further: "The construction of the meal at holidays is a way of holding hands with past and future generations." Disrupt that, she says, and the link is broken.

The incessant (and usually bogus) health scares that emasculate our beloved family recipes do just that. They scour away the joy of cooking grandmother's stuffing or Aunt Mae's yams with brown sugar and molasses. "We are a society obsessed with the harmful effects of eating," said University of Pennsylvania Professor Paul Rozin.

Such an unhealthy obsession makes that tofurky look almost palatable. At least it's safe, so the logic goes. Few of us still go over the river and through the woods for a Thanks-giving at grandma's house. But all of us have warm memories of feasts gone by. And after the meal, the hours of conversation punctuated by coffee or brandy bind the day up into a sensation that hangs with us, sometimes forever. But those memories are being replaced by anguish over naked statistics, animal rights and cancer scares. And that's not a lot to be thankful for.

Scenario 1. You have an internship with one of three organizations [choose one]: Center for Science in the Public Interest, Vegetarian Society, or PETA. Your job is to monitor the press for mentions of the organization.

Task 1(a). Berman's essay has landed on your desk. Your job is to draft a letter to the editor of the *Washington Times* correcting Berman's characterization of your organization and its position.

Task 1(b). Berman's essay has landed on your desk. Your job is to draft an opinion piece that counters Berman's essay without responding to it directly.

Scenario 2. You have an internship with the Guest Choice Network, the restaurant association founded by Berman.

Task 2(a). Berman has been notified by the *Washington Times* that it has received a response from one of the three organizations [choose one], accusing him of misrepresenting them. The paper would like to have a letter from Berman responding to their letter (nothing sells papers like controversy). Your job is to draft a letter proving that the organization is as extreme as he said it was.

Task 2(b).   Berman reads in the *Washington Times* a response from one of the three organizations [choose one], accusing him of misrepresenting them. He wants you to draft another essay, this time focusing on just the one organization, arguing that it takes extremist positions concerning food.

In a Nutshell

About Your Argument . . .

Claims are at the heart of every argument. They are your main point, the solution to your problem. Though you should try to formulate a tentative claim or hypothesis as soon as you can, you must also work hard to keep your mind open to giving it up in favor of a better one. That's why it's important to imagine a number of hypotheses and hold them all in mind as you work your way toward a best one.

Useful claims have these qualities:

 ▶ Your claim should be clearly **conceptual** or **practical.** It should assert what readers should know or what they should do.
 ▶ Your claim should be something that readers will not accept without seeing your good reasons. It should be **contestable.**
 ▶ Your claim should in principle be capable of being proved wrong, because you can imagine evidence that would make you give it up. It should be **disconfirmable.**
 ▶ Your claim should be feasible, ethical, and prudent. It should be **reasonable.**

Be clear to yourself the degree of assent you seek. What do you want your readers to do?

 ▶ **Respect** your reasons for making your claim?
 ▶ **Approve** of your claim and the argument supporting it?
 ▶ **Publicly endorse** your claim as worth serious consideration?
 ▶ **Believe** in your claim and in the argument supporting it?
 ▶ **Act** as you propose, or support someone else's action?

When you make a plan to gather evidence, think about these questions:

 ▶ What kind of evidence do readers expect you to report?
 ▶ Will the cost of searching for specific evidence be greater than the benefit of finding it?
 ▶ Where are you most likely to find the evidence you need? Libraries? The Internet? Personal interview? Observation?

When you gather evidence, follow these steps:

- ▶ Start by sampling the evidence from a source to see whether it is relevant and sufficient.
- ▶ Periodically take stock of the evidence as it mounts.
- ▶ Don't wait to get every shred of evidence before you start writing.

. . . and About Writing It

Work toward a claim that has these qualities:

- ▶ Its language is explicit and specific. It previews the central concepts that you will develop in the rest of the argument.
- ▶ It is elaborated with clauses beginning with *although, because,* and *unless.* If you think that makes the claim too long and complex, then break it into shorter sentences.
- ▶ It is hedged with appropriate qualifiers such as *many, most, often, usually, probably,* and *unlikely* instead of *all, always,* and *certainly.*

Supporting Claims: Appealing to Logos, Ethos, and Pathos

E ach type of claim, or stasis, develops in its own way with its own distinctive language. This chapter discusses how claims of all kinds are supported with reasons and evidence.

A claim by itself can be shaky and weak. Readers can reasonably ask, "How do you know?" or "Why do you think so?" Supporting claims strengthen the point by addressing the questions readers may raise. Support is like the beams and girders under a highway overpass. If there were not enough beams at the point where the highway leaves solid ground, the overpass would be shaky and no one would want to drive on it. The higher the bridge and the more traffic, the more support is needed. Similarly, the more controversial the claim and the wider the audience, the more support is needed.

The forms of support reflect the three ways we learn: from observing the world and reasoning about it (appealing to **logos** or our logical capacity), from listening to other people (**ethos** or our capacity for trust), and from consulting our senses and emotions (**pathos** or our capacity to feel). "Appeals" illustrates a few of the many ways these appeals can be made.

Appeals do not appear in any particular order and do not create delimited sections of the text. Appeals to logos, ethos, and pathos can come separately in one or several sentences each or they can be intertwined in a single sentence. The examples in this chapter will not be pure representations of a single type of appeal, but one appeal will be primary.

In public policy arguments, some varieties of appeals carry more weight than others. For example, your professors probably prefer appeals to logos over appeals to pathos, while the general public responds more to arguments with many pathos appeals. Identifying how an author supports claims is important for judging the quality of the argument: Is there enough support? Does the author rely too much on one kind of support? Is the support appropriate for the audience?

The appeals that support a claim look just like the claims that present the main points of a passage. The difference is the role of these statements in constructing the author's path. Major claims move the discussion further along the author's line of argument, moving to the next stasis or the next span. Supporting claims deepen a point instead of moving forward to a new point. Because claims and support look very similar, telling them apart is important for understanding the author's line of argument.

Appeals to Logos

As the name implies, logos appeals involve logical reasoning, what philosophers call rationality. Logos also involves observations of the world, what philosophers call empirical evidence. There are three main kinds of logos appeals: physical evidence and records; observations, testimony, and statistics; and logic, common sense, and probability.

PHYSICAL EVIDENCE AND RECORDS

You are more likely to believe a person claiming to have found a gold mine if she can produce a chunk of gold. In situations where people are arguing face to face, such as in a courtroom, actual physical objects can be produced for people to examine. For example, if a student is accused of stealing a bicycle, the bicycle can be produced in court. In both oral and written arguments, physical evidence can also be represented in graphic form, with photographs or drawings.

A **record** is a symbolic form of physical evidence. A fax machine creates a record by stamping the current date, time, and phone number on each page it sends; a cell phone records the number of every call. Everyone creates and keeps records for day-to-day activities, such as calendar entries, receipts, diaries, bills, ticket stubs, report cards, souvenirs, and paychecks. A student accused of stealing a bicycle who produces a receipt showing he or she bought it has strong support for a claim to innocence.

The **public record** is information that citizens are free to consult, such as accounts of daily events in a newspaper, official reports to a public agency, or logbooks like a police department's record of complaints.

OBSERVATIONS, TESTIMONY, AND STATISTICS

Many of our beliefs are based on our experiences, on seeing things for ourselves. We observe what is going on around us every day, we try new sports to see what they are like, and we travel to places we want to observe firsthand. In a more formal way, scientists design experiments to observe phenomena more systematically than nature allows. In public policy arguments, authors often describe what they observed as they investigated an issue or how they were personally involved in a problem. Personal experiences are an important source of evidence for Chivers, Kristof, and Shiflett in the environment topic and Brooks, Castleman, and Shapiro in the crime topic.

Most of what we know, though, concerns objects and events that we haven't actually observed. For example, you know about your neighborhood from being there and watching what happens, but you can't see everything. You learn of many events, such as break-ins or deer-sightings, by talking to neighbors or reading the newspaper. Textbooks, news reports, road maps, and Web sites are built up out of records and reports from countless individuals over years of time.

A public record of a person's direct observations is known as **testimony**. In a courtroom setting, testimony is given under oath and recorded verbatim. In public policy arguments, testimony appears in narratives and descriptions attributed to the author or another observer. The content of the testimony is an appeal to logos; the credibility of the observer is a matter of ethos, discussed in the next section.

In general, the more details in the testimony, the more convincing it is; a crime victim who is unable to provide details of an alleged attack is less likely to be believed. The more witnesses, the stronger the support; if ten people identify a suspect, the testimony is stronger than if there is only one witness.

Statistics are a form of observation because they summarize large numbers of individual reports and records. A Webmaster, for example, identifies the most popular Web sites by adding up and comparing their total hits. Simple totals can also be transformed by calculations, such as computing the average score, miles per gallon, or five-year trends in campus crimes.

While testimony and statistics seem convincing, they are surprisingly easy to challenge: Witnesses can disagree; physical evidence can be overlooked or contaminated; documents can be lost, altered or forged; data can be hard to interpret. For controversial claims, authors include even more supporting information about the procedure for collecting and analyzing the evidence. For example, in a murder investigation, the prosecutors have to trace the handling of every piece of physical evidence and the recording of every word of testimony. "Observational Logos" illustrates passages with this type of appeal.

LOGIC, COMMON SENSE, AND PROBABILITY

Another kind of logos is an appeal to logical reasoning, to what makes sense, to "what any rational adult would believe." Logical appeals grow out of physical or mathematical laws, logical principles, common sense, and probability.

Physical and Mathematical Laws

Physical laws involve concepts like gravity, velocity, and distance. Mathematical laws involve concepts like prime numbers, geometric shapes, or equations. A lawyer can appeal to physical laws to support a cause claim that a car traveling at a certain speed on a wet road could not have stopped within a certain distance. A civil engineer can appeal to principles from math and physics to estimate how

much water could be stored in a reservoir or how much energy would be produced by a hydroelectric dam.

Logical Principles

Logical principles (or propositions) look like the definition claims described in
Chapter 4 because they describe objects, features, and categories. Unlike definition claims that focus on individual cases, however, logical propositions deal with
universals. They include combination terms (or Boolean operators), such as AND,
OR, NOT, ALL, NONE, and IF . . . THEN, that you have probably seen in computer
programming classes or Internet search engines.

A logical principle called on in public policy arguments is the law of noncon-
tradiction, stating that a fact can be true or false but not both at the same time.
For example either a suspect had a gun or he didn't. Another common logical
principle in courtroom cases is the law of identity, stating that a person or object
cannot be in two places at the same time. An alibi is a claim that a suspect was
observed away from the crime scene at the moment the crime occurred. If the
alibi is true, then the claim that the suspect committed the crime must be false.
Similarly, an environmental advocate might argue that resources that are used up
today will not be around in the future.

At first glance, appealing to logical principles seems to be a clincher, the kind
of support that every reader must agree with. The drawback of logical propositions is that real-world situations never involve only logic. If problems could be
solved with logic, we wouldn't need juries or elections and we wouldn't need to
argue about public policy. Most authors, therefore, combine logical reasoning
with other kinds of support.

Common Sense

In most situations, we rely on common sense, intuitions about what is normal or
what works best, to decide what claims to believe. A lawyer is appealing to common sense if she argues that a blind client had no motive to steal binoculars.
However, common sense is not necessarily true. Nothing prevents a blind person
from wanting binoculars. Similarly, it seems absurd at first to claim that setting
fires can prevent forest fires, but many forest managers have evidence to support
this claim.

Probability

Appealing to a mathematical probability is similar to an appeal to logical principles.
For example, the statistical methods that compute the odds of buying a winning lot-
tery ticket are based on a mathematical formula relating the number of tickets
printed, the number of tickets sold, and the number of possible combinations of
"lucky numbers." In most public policy arguments, however, appeals to probability
are not based on formulas, they are more like appeals to common sense. For example, Castleman relies on probability to predict that an increase in the teen population
will increase crime; Chivers predicts that if you have eaten fish in a restaurant, it was

caught by dredging or trawling. "Common Sense Logos" illustrates this kind of support.

CERTAINTY AND ACCURACY

A common but misleading appeal to logos is a claim to absolute certainty. Beware of authors who use phrases like: "no sane person could disagree that . . . ," "you must be nuts if you think that . . . ," or "anyone who had given this a moment's thought would have to agree. . . ." An appeal to certainty often comes in place of evidence for the validity of a claim; instead of providing support, the appeal belittles the intelligence of anyone who disagrees with the author (and thus includes an emotional appeal designed to intimidate anyone who disagrees).

Authors who act as though they have "The Truth" come across as arrogant and closed-minded; they seem convincing only to readers who already agree with them and they repel those with other positions. Ironically, admitting uncertainty can strengthen an author's case, making the argument more accurate, practical, and realistic and appealing to a wider audience. In fact, in academic writing, acknowledging uncertainty is strongly preferred over claiming certainty.

"In theory, yes, Mrs. Wilkins. But also in theory, no."

Scientists like to admit uncertainty. © The New Yorker Collection 1976 Stan Hunt from cartoonbank.com. All Rights Reserved.

How could it be a good idea to admit doubts and expose the weaknesses of an argument? Aren't authors who make such concessions admitting that they are wrong? Concessions are important because certainty is rare and temporary. Many facts that now seem obvious were once controversial and even violently suppressed. Five hundred years ago, for example, when observations about the nature of the earth and heavens contradicted religious claims based on Biblical texts and authority, scientists could be punished as heretics for claiming that the earth revolves around the sun and denying that the sun rises in the east. Even today, you may feel social pressure not to question claims that others "take for granted," for example, that poor people are lazy or that criminals come from bad homes. In the readings, Meares and Kahan challenge the assumption that black inner-city residents can't protect their own civil rights; Gómez-Pompa and Kaus challenge the assumption that Western agricultural methods are better for the environment than traditional practices in underdeveloped nations.

Facts have a history; they do not exist "out there," waiting to be discovered. They are established or discredited by people using evidentiary procedures of logos, ethos, and pathos. The word "fact" itself is derived from the Latin roots *facere* and *factum,* which mean "to make" or "to do."

Certainty in a fact grows as people keep challenging its validity, testing it in different situations, in different places and times, and using different technologies. A few claims that now seem hotly contested will "stand the test of time" and start being treated as well known, unremarkable, and obvious facts. Just as important, some claims that were once considered certainties will eventually be reexamined and rejected as mistakes. This is why authors who treat all of their claims as completely certain come across as dogmatic or closed-minded.

Authors who limit the support for their claims upfront should get credit for honesty and accuracy. They are inviting you to assign the claim an appropriate degree of belief and they are arguing that even a limited degree of belief should be enough to persuade you to move forward with the line of argument.

Authors have four ways to signal their degree of certainty in a claim, presented here in order from greatest certainty to least.

Leaving a Claim Unstated vs. Asserting a Claim

A claim that is obviously true doesn't even need to be stated. Americans don't go around repeating obvious truths, such as "We are living in the United States." So when an author makes that claim explicitly, he is raising the idea that something is happening that does not fit with our knowledge of the United States. Stating a claim as a flat assertion without support signals that the author considers it to be uncontroversial general knowledge.

Identifying the Source of the Information

An author who tells you how she knows that a claim is true is admitting that the claim is not common knowledge. Even prefacing a claim with "I think" makes it seem more like an opinion than a generally held fact. So when an author appeals to ethos, citing the credibility of the witnesses or authorities, she is raising doubts.

For example, Castleman supports his claim that crime is common in his neighborhood this way: "I know because I'm a devoted reader of the police column in our monthly neighborhood newspaper, the *Noe Valley Voice*." Chivers supports his claim about the heavy use of dredging and trawling this way: "So extensive is this fishing method that it is equivalent to scouring half of the seabed between beaches and the continental shelves around the world each year, according to Elliott A. Norse, president of the Marine Conservation Biology Institute."

Limiting the Claim Through Qualifications

The author includes explicit limits on when or how often the claim will be true, such as exceptional circumstances. When Chivers says: "With a few exceptions, if you've eaten a wild oceanic product, it was probably caught by mobile gear," he admits that his claim is limited to seafood caught in the ocean and does not cover all kinds of seafood. When Castleman says: "With the exception of murder (which usually involves family or acquaintances), the vast majority of crimes are opportunistic in nature," he excludes from his claim about opportunism a large set of crimes, both murders and a few other unspecified crimes.

Using Guess Words

The author uses words that express uncertainty, labeling the claim as a "guess," "speculation," or "possibility." Chivers uses guess words here: "[T]his idea [essentially a form of ocean zoning] has gained considerable support among scientists

"A possible eureka."

Scientists like to signal uncertainty. © The New Yorker Collection 1988
James Stevenson from cartoonbank.com. All Rights Reserved.

and habitat protection advocates. . . . It also appears to meet the standards of the latest amendment to federal fishery law. . . ." Castleman supports his claim that it is normal to assume that black men are dangerous by saying, "I doubt there's an honest white liberal who acts differently."

Appeals to Ethos

As you listen or read, you are constantly making decisions about whose information to trust and how much to trust it. Partly, you are judging the information based on its contents, using logos. But a big part of your decision is also based on your judgment of the person who is providing the information. Is this the kind of person whose claims you are likely to believe? Ethos appeals give you reasons for believing a claim based on the trustworthiness and experiences of the person who is making it. Ethos appeals are about speakers and writers.

Authors appeal to ethos when they ask you to accept a claim just because of who is saying it. For example, your parents have probably asked you many times to accept their decision "because I said so." Besides parents, other people in our society who are usually trusted to speak truth are teachers, ministers, the Presi-

"1964, reaching into the cookie jar, your mother confronts you. You lie. Tell us, sir, why the jury should believe you now."

Challenging the credibility of a witness. Courtesy of
www.cartoonsStock.com

dent, and a few geniuses like Albert Einstein. At one time, a television news-caster, Walter Cronkite, was considered "the most trusted man in America." When people like these support a claim, that in itself may make it convincing to many readers, even if the content is counterintuitive.

CREDENTIALS

The most common way an author appeals to ethos is providing information about the person whose testimony or judgment is being cited: the person's credentials (from the Latin word for belief, *credere*). Credentials usually include the person's full name, job title, or experience.

Authors cite the views of many different kinds of people, such as independent experts, eyewitnesses, stakeholders, and themselves. As a reader, you must decide what kind of person is the most credible. In order to judge credibility, consider experience closely.

Independent Experts

You are probably most willing to believe testimony from an independent expert, someone who is trained to judge situations fairly and accurately and who has a great deal of experience. But how do you know that the person really is an expert? What if authors on opposing sides both appeal to experts? Which one do you believe? The more disagreement about a claim, the more credential information the author should provide about the expert, including job title, place of work, training, awards, and previous positions held.

Eyewitnesses

In some situations, the most believable person is not an expert but someone you can identify with yourself, someone you expect to react in the same way you would have if you had been there. News reporters and police investigators often seek the observations of eyewitnesses who just happened to be on the scene. To increase the credibility of the eyewitnesses, authors often describe their appearance and give some biographical information; this information makes it easier for you to identify with the witness.

Witnesses can mislead you accidentally if they don't know enough about what they are talking about. A witness may also mislead you intentionally, acting on self-interested motives. For example, a witness endorsing the effectiveness of a hair treatment may secretly be employed by the company that makes the product.

Stakeholders

The people who know most about a situation are usually the people who are directly involved. For public policy issues, the stakeholders are the officials involved in setting the policies, all the people who the policies affect, and other parties who have a special interest in the issue. For example, if a ban on fishing is proposed, the stakeholders include the hook-and-tackle fishermen, fishermen who use dredging and trawling, towns on the shore that depend on fishing and tourism, restaurants and supermarkets that want fresh fish, environmental activists, and fisheries and wildlife managers. If a neighborhood curfew is proposed, the stakeholders are local teens and their parents, other neighbors, businesses in the area, the police, and local social service agencies.

Stakeholders have personal or professional reasons for taking one side of an issue rather than the other. Having a role or interest does not make what a person says untrue. If you know what each person has at stake and if they provide other kinds of support for their claims, you can decide how much to believe each one. "Credentials" illustrates uses of these appeals.

PERSONAL IMPRESSIONS

By publishing an argument, an author is inviting you and other readers to engage in a conversation. Your willingness to join in depends on your personal impressions of the author. These impressions are influenced by the author's credentials and experiences, but are probably influenced more by subtle aspects of the writing.

You already know how to judge character by the way people behave. The same qualities come across in writing. Some authors talk down to readers or ignore other people's opinions; they seem arrogant and unapproachable. Some are careful not to exaggerate and to "do their homework" by digging into the evidence; they come across as fair. Some squander their credibility by making careless mistakes or seeming disorganized. Just about every aspect of the writing contributes to an author's ethos.

"Personal Impressions" presents examples of how authors describe themselves and their experiences. On the environment topic, Edward Abbey says explicitly why his local experiences make him qualified to speak about the dam at Glen Canyon. Yet, his use of the term "damnation" instead of "damming" indicates his strong feelings. On the crime topic, Castleman appeals to his own lawbreaking experience as a bid for credibility. Although people usually distrust what confessed criminals say, Castleman might earn points from readers for his candor and his ability to identify with young street criminals.

Authors also build credibility by their style of arguing and writing. An author who cites experts and eyewitnesses as allies comes across as responsible, giving credit to those who did the direct observational work. The more credible and well known the allies, the more "glow of association" rubs off on the author. Similarly, citing strong opponents makes an author seem ready to face any challenge.

Appeals to Pathos

It is impossible to argue without appealing in some way to emotions; we wouldn't act on a problem if we didn't care about it. Pathos appeals concern emotions, sensations, and images. The most familiar form of pathos is sympathy, derived from the Greek words for suffering and togetherness. However, authors appealing to pathos can invoke positive as well as negative emotions.

Authors writing about crime may appeal to outrage over a terrible injustice or to sympathy toward a victim; authors writing about the environment may appeal to worries about the world our children will live in or invoke the feelings of awe aroused by entering a wilderness area.

Appeals to pathos can be more powerful than appeals to logos or ethos because they add bodily reactions to abstract mental ones. The most effective pathos appeals move the reader to identify with a situation so strongly that they feel as if they are there, imagining sights, sounds, smells, textures, and tastes. The main ways to employ pathos are naming emotions, evoking physical sensations, and using visuals.

NAMING EMOTIONS

One way authors appeal to pathos is to talk directly about how to react to a claim, naming the emotions that readers should experience, such as anger, delight, horror, pity, pride, relief, shame, and wonder. Sometimes authors ask rhetorical questions, such as, "How could any patriotic American not feel a swell of pride?" or "How would you feel if this happened to you?" A less direct appeal is for the authors to describe their own feelings or those of people involved in the situation. "Emotion Names" illustrates passages with this form of appeal.

EVOKING SENSATIONS

Apart from naming specific emotions, another way to appeal to pathos is to evoke physical sensations of seeing, hearing, touching, tasting, and smelling.

When you read vivid, detailed descriptions of specific real-world events—descriptions of the people, the colors, smells, and noises in the background, the unfolding of the event over time—you imaginatively experience sensations. Your mental image of the event can seem like a memory of an actual experience. Once you imagine an event happening, you are more willing to believe that it did or could take place. If the description evokes unpleasant or painful sensations, you may attribute all kinds of negative values to the object or event, even if the author doesn't criticize it explicitly.

A subtle way of evoking physical sensations is to use writing techniques that are more commonly thought of as belonging in poetry or literature, such as rhythm and rhyme ("Don't do the crime if you can't do the time"), repetition of word patterns ("We had drive-by killings, run-by killings, sneak-up killings, gunfights and battles, car chases"), alliteration ("Ahh, the sweet smell of skunk"), metaphor ("What was a complex of sponges, shells, and other organisms was smoothed to a cobblestone street"), and colorful word choice ("Slothful vandals who are unable to haul their thick butts around without the help of an internal-combustion engine"). Language patterns can make you feel emotions, from sad to excited, just as music can. "Evoking Sensations" illustrates passages with this form of appeal.

USING GRAPHICS

Another common appeal to pathos is the inclusion of photographs, drawings, and other graphic media. Photographs appeal more strongly to emotions than drawings because they convey more realism and specificity. A photograph appeals both to logos and to pathos—logos, because the photograph is physical evidence of an observation; pathos, because the details in a photograph emphasize the uniqueness of the image and heighten its realism.

The visuals in "Photographs" convey the immediacy of a particular event. Both seal photos appeal to our human interest in furry, attractive animals with big eyes, but the photo of the trapped seal evokes feelings of pity for attractive creatures injured for no apparent purpose, while the photo of the happy seal conveys positive feelings of wonder for nature. The photos of the police present two very different perspectives. In one, the officers look menacing. In the other photo, the police officers seem protective.

Photographs

Environment

Photo evoking sympathy.   Courtesy of Ron Sunford/Photo Researchers, Inc.

Photo evoking enjoyment. Courtesy of Stephen Frink/Corbis.

Crime

Photo evoking fear. Courtesy of AP/Wide World Photos.

Photo evoking security.   *Courtesy of* Chuck Savage/Corbis.

137

USES AND MISUSES OF PATHOS

Appeals to pathos can be dangerous. At one time or another, you have probably acted impulsively in a way you later regretted. Maybe you said something rash when you were angry or excited. Maybe you believed a rumor or took a dare that you would have rejected if you were calm. Most people want to base important decisions on evidence that will seem reasonable under all conditions, not only when they are in a certain mood.

People who believe emotion is more powerful than reason are suspicious of an author who uses emotional appeals, afraid that he or she is trying to "pump up" a case that can't be supported with logos. There is reason for concern if an author appeals more to pathos than to logos. As a reader, you should pay attention to the types of appeals in an argument and their relative importance.

CLUES TO SPOTTING APPEALS

Distinguishing the types of appeals is important for judging how well an author has supported the claims and for imagining ways in which the claims might have been better supported.

When identifying an appeal, base your judgment directly on the words on the page; if you have to draw extended inferences about how a passage might be appealing to pathos or ethos, then your choice of appeal is probably off-base.

Appeals are often intertwined in the same phrases or passages. To choose the primary appeal, ask yourself, "Why should I believe this claim?" If it is mainly because of who is making the claim, the appeal is to ethos. If it is mainly because of how the passage makes you feel, it is a pathos appeal. If it is mainly because of common sense or real-world observation, it is a logos appeal.

▶ Words to Watch for: Appeals

Logos

Physical Evidence	Detailed descriptions of objects
Records	Newspapers, records, logs, journals, entries
Observations	Detailed descriptions of objects or events; noticed, saw, observed, overlooked
Testimony	Said, told, described, related, attest, vouch
Statistics	Data, numbers, percentages, amounts, trends; tables, graphs
Logic	Logic, illogic, if . . . then, either . . . or, implies, entails, valid, draw a conclusion, axiom, proposition, premise, fallacy, impossible, flawed, inconsistent
Common Sense	Sensible, reasonable, reliable, prudent, plausible, sane, intuitive, off-base, delusion, unorthodox
Probability	chance, possibility, odds, likely, long shot, toss up, expect, predict

Ethos

Credentials	Expert, authority, official; professor, doctor, officer, Senator, manager, researcher; eyewitness, by-stander, on the scene, onlooker; credentials, experience, training
Personal Impressions	Aspects of writing or references to author's life

Pathos

Naming Emotions	Love, hate, enjoy, suffer, excite, interest, cherish, anger, outrage, disgust, passion; felt, sympathized, identified with
Evoking Sensations	Saw, looked, viewed; listened, heard, sounds, ring, buzz, noise, silence; touched, felt, rough, smooth, palpable; taste, delicious, savor, bitter, sour; smell, odor, stench, whiff, aroma
Graphics	Pictures, drawings, colors

Exercises

Backtalk: What Do You Say?

What's the point of learning the names of all these types of claims and appeals? If two people are really experts, how could they disagree? Would you feel comfortable admitting uncertainty in a paper? Why?

Recognize/Evaluate

Read the passages below concerning the crime or environment topic. Identify which appeals are used (logos, pathos, ethos). Identify the subtypes of each appeal (such as naming emotions or invoking sensations for pathos). Then choose one a passage that stands out as particularly unconvincing. In one or two sentences, explain your reasons.

A. Environment

1. Dr. John Terborgh of Duke University, an expert on tropical conservation, says efforts to save nature in some parts of the world "are just doomed to fail." In his 1999 book, *Requiem for Nature* (Island Press/Shearwater), Dr. Terborgh wrote that nature "cannot long survive" a combination of inadequate nature parks, unstable societies, and faltering institutions that plagues many developing countries. "We have a long way to go before anyone can feel comfortable about the future of nature," he wrote.

2. In other instances, though, nature tends to spring back once the cause of disturbance is removed. Depleted fish populations recover once fishing stops. Forests and grasslands retake abandoned farmland, especially when given a helping hand by restorationists. . . . Rivers tend to cleanse themselves once pollutants are no longer dumped in. That is what keeps conservationists from total despair; if people can be persuaded to stop interfering with natural processes, the situation will eventually correct itself to some degree. (Stevens)

3. It may be hard to get excited about vanished sponges and overturned rocks. But for the fishing industry—like that in New England, which has lost thousands of jobs and hundreds of millions of dollars in recent years and is suffering the resultant social consequences—habitat changes caused by fishing gear are significant. (Safina)

B. Crime

1. [Marvin] Wolfgang, a liberal who has worked as a consultant to many anti-poverty programs, says: "There is no consistent correlation between poverty and crime. The studies go back 100 years, and they show only a weak correlation at best. Most poor people are law-abiding, and many rich people break the law." (Castleman)

2. As a chaplain, I visit 72 inmates in 12 cellblocks every week as they wait for trial anywhere from a year to three years. The majority of the detainees are gang members and most are black or Latino. Almost all of them live in poor neighborhoods. This experience has made me more aware that the criminal-justice system works differently for them. My white, middle-class background did not prepare me for the systematic abuses that are routine for certain members of our society. (Brooks)

3. Okay, now imagine taking a gun and pointing it at your loved one and pulling the trigger. You couldn't do it, could you? It wouldn't make any

sense. It would be illogical. It would be impossible. And that's why Jeff Henry could not have intended to kill his brother—that's why the killing had to have been an accident and the shotgun in his hands had to have just gone off. There is no other way for it to have happened, and anyone who thinks that he just murdered his brother—the prosecutor in Douglas County, Georgia, for instance—just doesn't know what it's like to be a twin and doesn't know how much Jeff and Greg Henry loved each other, how much they still love each other, how perfect that love is, and how much Jeff Henry believes in it. (Junod)

Detect

1. In an article of your choice, find a long paragraph that is interesting and persuasive. Analyze its claims and support.

2. What kind of appeals does Castleman use? Which does he rely on most? What kind of appeals does Chivers use? Which does he rely on most?

Produce

Choose one of the claims below from your topic area.

A. Environment

▶ All-terrain vehicles (ATVs) should be banned from state and national parks.

▶ Logging reduces the risk of serious forest fires.

B. Crime

▶ Watching violent video games does not lead to real-life violence.

▶ Binge drinking of alcohol is a greater danger than drug use on college campuses.

Use key words in the claim to search on the Internet for articles and sites related to this claim. Compose 3–5 statements, each of which supports the claim using a different appeal or a different subtype. Be sure to provide names and background in your statements for anyone you cite. Keep a list of any Web sites from which you quote or paraphrase.

6

The Core of Your Argument: Reasons and Evidence

T he heart of your argument is your claim; its main substance is what you offer to support that claim, reasons and evidence. Reasons and evidence work in tandem to support a claim, but they are also different, in their form, in how you find them, and in how you use them. In this chapter, we examine those differences so that you can know how best to use both reasons and evidence to support your claim.

Supporting Claims

Those who make a flat claim, expecting us to agree just because they say so, risk seeming arrogant. We expect writers to approach us as critical

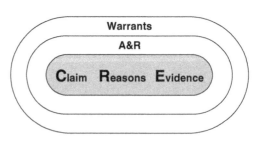

Warrants

A&R

Claim   Reasons   Evidence

thinkers who judge for ourselves, and so we look for both support for a claim and some qualification. Compare these examples:

> TV's obsession with sexuality damages the social and emotional development of our preteens. claim

> **Though the TV networks have improved children's daytime programming,** acknowledgment their prime-time obsession with sexuality **may** be damaging the social and emotional development of many preteens claim **because they model their behavior on what they see others do.** reason

The second version seems more thoughtful and respectful. It treats us as critical thinkers who want at least one good reason before we accept the claim, and it acknowledges that the issue is not cut-and-dried, but complicated enough that the claim is not unqualifiedly true.

But most critical thinkers expect more. A thoughtful reader will think that reason (children model their behavior on others) supports that claim (obsession with sexuality may be damaging) only if it is based on more than the writer's opinion, only if the writer offers *evidence* demonstrating that preteens *in fact* base their behavior on TV.

Reasons and Evidence as Forms of Support

The language we use about *having* an argument pictures it as combat. But when we describe *making* one, we sound less like combatants than builders. We *build support* for a claim by adding reasons that *rest on a firm base* of *hard* evidence. That *grounding* should create a *solid footing* so *unshakable* that critics cannot *topple* our argument by *undermining* its *foundation*. Such language visualizes an argument not as a linear sequence of elements but as a vertical structure of logical relationships something like this:

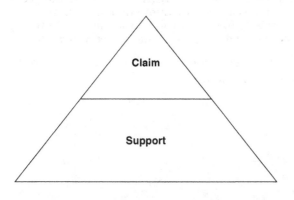

143

Those building metaphors are useful, but to understand how we actually plan and draft arguments, we need five terms with more literal meanings: *fact, data, exhibits, evidence,* and *reasons:*

- A *fact* is a statement in words or symbols that readers accept as true, or at least don't contest: *The capital of Ohio is Columbus; 2 + 2 = 4.*
- *Data* (the singular is *datum*) are sets of facts. Data can be any information you have gathered, but we often think of data as numbers. We can summarize numerical data in words: *In 1985, Abco's market share was 19.4%; by 1995, it slipped to 11.7%; but it has now grown to 22%.* But more often, we present data in tables, graphs, and charts:

Abco Market Share (%)

1985	1995	2005
19.4	11.7	22.0

- *Exhibits* are concrete examples of your object of study. They might be copies of the texts you analyze (including quotations); reproductions of paintings or other images; photographs or drawings of buildings, objects, landscapes, cloud formations, or bugs, and so on.

By themselves, however, facts data, and exhibits are just inert information. Only when you bring them into your argument do they become *evidence.*

- *Evidence* includes facts, data, and exhibits that support a reason. They become evidence when you show that they have a logical connection to the reason, when readers look at the evidence and think, *If this evidence is reliable, then this reason must be true.*
- *Reasons* are statements that generalize on the evidence to show how it backs up your claim.

Here is a brief argument with data as evidence:

Although television has improved after-school programming, its prime-time shows may be undermining the social and emotional development of many preteens claim by exposing them to sexually explicit behavior that encourages them to engage in sex play before they understand its consequences. reason In his report on the relationship between TV watching and sexual experimentation, **Kahn (1996) studied children ages 10–13 who regularly (three times in four weeks) watch sexually oriented television shows (more than five references to or images of sexual conduct). He found they are 40% more likely to engage in sexual play than those who do not watch such programs at all.** evidence

That passage presents the core of an argument in a standard form: Claim resting on Reasons resting on Evidence.

Distinguishing Reasons and Evidence

The difference between reasons and evidence seems intuitively obvious, but is more complex than it seems. We occasionally use those terms interchangeably:

> What reasons can you offer to support your claim?
>
> What evidence can you offer to support your claim?

But we also distinguish them in sentences like these:

> We need to think up *reasons* to support our request.
>
> We need to think up *evidence* to support our request.
>
> Before I accept your *reasons,* I have to see the *evidence* they rest on.
>
> Before I accept your *evidence,* I have to see the *reasons* it rests on.

Most of us find the first sentence in each pair natural, the second a bit odd.

One source of the difference is the images we associate with reasons and evidence. To describe evidence, we use metaphors like *solid* or *hard* that incline us to think that we can see evidence out in the world, "outside" our subjective experience. We feel that reasons, on the other hand, metaphorically come from "inside" our minds. We believe we could check your evidence by looking for ourselves, if you told us where to look; we don't ask where to search for your reasons.

Since we assume evidence is at least in principle *public* and *sharable,* readers ask some predictable questions about it:

> ▶ Where did you find your evidence? What are your sources? Are they reliable?
> ▶ How did you collect it? What methods and devices did you use? Could I see it for myself?
> ▶ What are its limitations? Is it reliable? What problems did you have collecting it?

We judge reasons that we think lack a foundation of evidence as "mere opinion," and mere opinion is, to continue the construction metaphor, "too flimsy" to support "sound" claims about "weighty" problems.

Distinguishing Evidence and Reports of It

You can use that construction image as a loose way to think about the core of an argument, but when you examine it closely, it turns out to be a bit misleading. In what follows, we make a distinction that may seem like academic hairsplitting, but it is crucial to understanding how arguments really work. You need to understand the distinction because what people call evidence rarely is.

DIRECT AND REPORTED EVIDENCE

As unsettling as it may seem, what we call evidence is almost always just a *report* of it, or even a report of a report. Most direct evidence cannot be "in" an argument, if we define direct evidence in the metaphorical language that we so often use for it, as that objective stuff we could find out in the world, if we just went to look for it.

- ◗ In a murder trial, the direct evidence might be a bloody glove that a prosecutor can hold up for the jury to see, but in a written argument, she can only state facts that describe the glove or show a photograph of it as an exhibit.
- ◗ An economist making an argument about unemployment could physically point to a few actual individuals with no jobs, but in a written argument, he could only refer to the millions of unemployed in words or numbers.
- ◗ In an argument about the nature of matter, a physicist can't even point to the smallest particles he investigates. He can refer to them only in mathematical terms or reproduce photographs of the traces they leave on his detectors.

What we offer as evidence is almost never direct evidence, but only a *report* that describes, pictures, represents, refers to, or enumerates actual gloves, people, and particles.

Even when you've seen "real" evidence directly with your own eyes, you can bring it into your written argument only by representing it in words, numbers, images, or sounds. For the purposes of your argument, you have to ignore a multitude of details, because it is impossible to represent them all. When you report evidence, you also smooth it out, tidy it up, make it more coherent, more regular than the "stuff out there" really is. So what you ask readers to go on is not evidence, but only your selective and reshaping report of it.

Representations as Evidence

Some students wonder about quoted words. Aren't they "the evidence itself"? Even when words are quoted correctly (which is often not the case), they are only an exhibit—selected, taken out of context, used for a new purpose, all leading us to experience them in ways that their context may contradict.

What about photographs? Even when we reproduce a photograph as exactly as possible, it is still seen on a different paper, in a different context, with a different purpose.

Try to report evidence as directly as possible, but when you read reports of it in the arguments of others, remember that just as a picture of an apple is not an apple, so a report of evidence is not the evidence.

We belabor this distinction because the word *evidence* carries so much authority and seems so weighty and objective. When someone offers what it claimed to be "hard" evidence, we are likely to be half convinced that it has an objective reality that we should not question. But evidence described in a report is neither objective nor real. What we call evidence is almost always a report of it shaped to fit an argument.

Once you grasp that distinction, you can see why critical readers want to be sure that your reports of evidence are reliable and from a good source, and why they expect you to tell them where you found the evidence or, if you rely on others' reports, who gathered and reported it. They want to know how much it's been shaped even before you found it. That's why readers look for citations to assure them that they could, if they wanted, track your reports back as close as they can get to the direct evidence "itself." Evidence is only as sound as the chain of reports leading to it, and in your argument, the last link in that chain is always you.

In a discussion among Sue, Ann, and Raj about their professors' availability during office hours, the question of evidence turned on that very issue:

Sue: Well, we pay a lot of money for our education, but we don't get near the attention customers do.

Ann: How's that?

Sue: For one thing, we can hardly see teachers outside of class. Last week I counted office hours posted on office doors on the first floor of the Arts and Sciences building. [She reads from a piece of paper.] They average less than an hour a week, most of them in the late afternoon when a lot of us work. I have the numbers right here.

Ann: Can I see?

Sue: Sure. [She hands the paper over.]

But when Ann looked at the numbers, she was still not looking directly at the evidence "itself": that was attached to doors. Ann must assume that Sue copied those hours accurately and reported them fairly. (But see also Inquiry 1 on p. 160.)

If the distinction between evidence and reports reflects how most arguments really work, then Sue's argument is not *directly* grounded on external reality, as in this diagram:

147

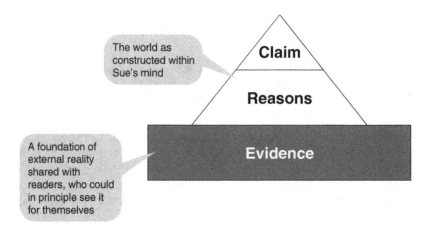

Instead, her argument—including the evidence she *refers to and describes*—is all her construction. She may rest her *report* of evidence on a ground of external, direct evidence, but that external ground cannot be a part of the argument itself:

What Sue can offer as evidence *inside* her argument is only a report that she hopes Ann and Raj accept as reliably grounded on direct evidence *outside* the argument. But Ann and Raj won't go look at the direct evidence, at the hours posted on actual doors; so from their point of view, Sue's reports of evidence are all the ground they have.

They have to trust that she got the numbers right. And that's why you must develop a reputation for reporting evidence accurately, without obviously self-interested spin, because the last person in the chain of trust is you. Betray that trust, and you lose credibility, not just for your current argument, but possibly for the next one and the ones after that.

On the Evidence of Dinosaurs

Even when it seems we can hold direct evidence in our hands, we may be holding only nature's report of it. Not long ago, paleontologists announced that they had uncovered the heart of a dinosaur, the first ever found. After examination, they decided that it had two chambers—evidence, they said, that the dinosaur it came from may have been warm-blooded. The evidence they could point to, however, was not the actual heart of that dinosaur; it was a fossil stone casting created by natural processes—nature's "report" of the evidence. Moreover, what the scientists pointed to as evidence was not even the fossil casting but a series of two-dimensional CAT scans of its internal structure that they assembled into a three-dimensional model. Their evidence that dinosaurs might have been warm-blooded is a three-dimensional model that reports on a series of two-dimensional images that report on a stone fossil that reports on an organ that no longer exists. The hard question is how much each of those reports distorts that once-beating heart (if it is in fact a heart, which some paleontologists doubt).

At this point you may have an uneasy feeling that reasons and reports of evidence are a lot alike, because both are the products of a subjective mind. They are a lot alike, but here's one way to sort them out: Think of reasons as the *outline* of an argument, its logical structure. Think of reports of evidence as what readers *accept* as true to support the points in that outline. Think of direct evidence as something a reader would have get up out of her chair to go look at.

Multiple Reasons

Even when you base a reason on reliable (reports) of evidence, readers may not accept just one reason as sufficient support for a significant claim. So you usually have to offer more reasons that relate to your claim in two ways:

- ▶ You can offer parallel reasons, each one supporting a claim directly.
- ▶ You can offer "stacked" reasons, each one resting on the one before, the first one directly supporting your claim, the last one resting on evidence (or a report of it).

REASONS IN PARALLEL

Until now, we have lumped reasons in our discussions and diagrams. But when you create an argument with parallel reasons, you need to keep them separate in your mind, on your storyboard, and in your report. That calls for a somewhat more complex picture:

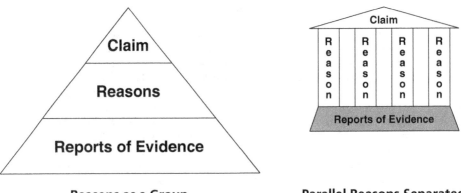

Reasons as a Group   **Parallel Reasons Separated**

With parallel reasons, each one stands independently of the others. Take one away and the claim might slump, but the other reasons might be sufficient to prop it up. Take away more, and it might collapse.

Three reasons in parallel is the standard plan for the five-paragraph essay many of us learned in high school:

¶1 There are three reasons why we should curb binge drinking. claim
¶2 First, it gives the campus a bad image. reason 1 For example, . . . report of evidence
¶3 It also creates legal liability. reason 2 Four cases have been . . . report of evidence
¶4 Finally, it causes injury and even death. reason 3 Last month, . . . report of evidence
¶5 Therefore, we can see that bingeing has become, . . . repeated claim

Some good arguments actually have only three reasons, but so many bad ones have been forced into that form that the five-paragraph, three-reason essay has an amateurish image at the college level. So avoid three if you can.

REASONS IN SEQUENCE

You can also arrange reasons not separately in parallel, but "stacked," each reason resting on another, the first directly supporting the claim, the last resting on reports of evidence:

(You can also imagine these reasons sideways, as links in chain or a series of steps.)

For example, in the following argument, the writer bases a main claim on three stacked reasons resting on a report of evidence:

> Congress should pass a law requiring colleges and universities to measure the skills that their students learn during their undergraduate careers. claim
>
> R1: We must be sure that our college graduates are learning what they will need to meet the challenge of global competition. reason 1 supporting claim
>
> R2: We know that India and China are graduating students who one day could surpass our leadership in science, technology, and business, reason 2 supporting reason 1
>
> R3: because they are graduating many more students than we are, most of whom demonstrate high levels of skills in math, science, and communication. reason 3 supporting reason 2
>
> E: The *Journal of International Education,* for example, reports that following numbers: Every year, we graduate … while China and India graduate … report of evidence supporting reason 3
>
> Only Congress can ensure that our colleges and universities are graduating students who can meet the challenges of an increasingly globalized world. claim restated

Experienced writers create arguments like these by laying deeper and deeper foundations for their claims (another of those construction metaphors), thereby thickening their arguments. The risk of such an argument is that if readers miss just one intermediate step, they lose track of the logic, and the argument collapses.

THE DEEP COMPLEXITY OF SERIOUS ARGUMENTS

When we address an issue that requires more than two or three pages of argument, we build them out of multiple reasons in parallel, each of which rests on multiple reasons in sequence, all of them based on evidence. In so doing, we create an argument of considerable complexity. Yet as complex as it might seem in writing, we create that kind of complex argument in conversation every day whenever we engage in a lot of back-and-forth about a serious issue. Your task in writing an equally complex argument is simply to plan patiently, organizing reasons in parallel and in series, all based on evidence.

Using Reasons to Help Readers Understand Evidence

If evidence anchors an argument, why bother with reasons at all? Why not just base a claim directly on reports of evidence? Sometimes we do, especially when we offer simple numbers. But reasons help readers understand and interpret complex evidence. Consider this sentence and the data that support its claim:

> Most predictions about average gasoline consumption have proved wrong. claim

151

Table 6.1	Mileage and Gasoline Consumption			
	1970	**1980**	**1990**	**2000**
Annual miles (000)	9.5	10.3	10.5	11.7
Annual consumption (gal.)	760	760	520	533 reported evidence

A diligent reader could figure out how the numbers support the claim—mileage has gone up but gas consumption has gone down. But we would understand all that more easily if the writer added a sentence explaining how the numbers relate to the claim, a more informative title, and visual help that focuses us on what to see:

> Gasoline consumption has not grown as many have predicted. claim Even though Americans drove 23 percent more miles in 2000 than in 1970, they used 30 percent less fuel. reason

Table 6.2	Per Capita Mileage and Gasoline Consumption, 1970–2000			
	1970	**1980**	**1990**	**2000**
Annual miles (000)	9.5	10.3	10.5	11.7
(% change vs. 1970)		8.4%	10.5%	23.1%
Annual consumption (gal.)	760	760	520	533
(% change vs. 1970)			(31.6%)	(29.7%)

reported evidence

Some writers fear that they insult readers when they spell out in a reason what readers can figure out for themselves. And it is true that no one wants to read the obvious. But all writers, experienced and inexperienced alike, overestimate what readers will figure out on their own. So you usually do them a service when you add a reason that points out what is important in a report of evidence, making clear how it supports your claim.

Readers need the same help when the evidence is a quotation. Here is a claim about Hamlet that rests directly on the evidence of a quotation:

> As Hamlet stands behind his stepfather Claudius while he is at prayer, he demonstrates a cool and logical mind. claim

> Now might I do it [kill him] pat, now he is praying:
> And now I'll do't; and so he goes to heaven;
> And so am I reveng'd. . . . [Hamlet pauses to think]
> [But this] villain kills my father; and for that,
> I, his sole son, do this same villain send to heaven[?]
> Why, this is hire and salary, not revenge. report of evidence

Many readers find that argument a bit hard to follow. Nothing in the quotation seems obviously to support a claim about Hamlet's cool reason. By omitting a reason, the writer forces us to figure it out on our own. Compare this version:

> As Hamlet stands behind his stepfather Claudius while he is at prayer, he demonstrates a cool and logical mind. claim **At first he impulsively wants to kill Claudius on the spot, but he pauses to reflect. If he kills Claudius while praying, he sends his soul to heaven. But Hamlet wants him damned to hell forever. So he coolly decides to kill him later:** reason
>
> Now might I do it [kill him] pat, now he is praying:
> And now I'll do't; and so . . . report of evidence

That reason tells us what to see in the quotation that relates it to the claim.

A detailed report of evidence seldom speaks for itself. Without a reason to speak for it, readers often struggle to understand what it signifies. They work less hard when you add a reason that both supports the claim and explains the evidence. Visually, it looks like this:

So when you offer evidence in the form of quotations, images, or data in tables and charts, don't just attach it to a claim. Add a reason that tells your readers what to see in the evidence.

Writing Process

REASONS AND EVIDENCE

Preparing and Planning

Be Aware What Your Reasons Imply About Your Claim (and You)

Once you assemble your reasons, consider what they imply about both you and your readers. Since every reason implies a principle of reasoning (warrant), each one tells readers something about your values and what you think of theirs. Even if a reason is true and supports your claim, it could poison your argument and your ethos if readers reject the values it rests on.

Suppose Jorge claims that plagiarism from the Internet should be curbed, offering these reasons:

> R1: Plagiarism prevents good students from standing out.
> R2: It erodes the foundations of trust that a community depends on.
> R3: If the public learns about it, it will make the university look bad.
> R4: It makes students think they can get something for nothing.

Each reason casts a different light on both Jorge and on the kind of person he imagines his reader to be. Most of us would rather be identified with preserving the social foundations of trust rather than protecting the university from bad press.

Once you have a list of reasons, test each for what it implies about your ethos and your image of your reader. If you can't tell, ask someone.

ORDERING MULTIPLE REASONS

Once you have a list of reasons, decide how to order them. Too many writers put their reasons in the order they thought of them, which is rarely the best order.

Parallel Reasons

If you have parallel reasons supporting a claim, arrange them in an order that creates the best impact and that readers will think is coherent.

Ordering Parallel Reasons by Their Substance You might find a principle of order based on the ideas or things the reasons refer to. The most obvious choice is to group them based on who or what the reasons are mostly about. For example, in these three reasons supporting the claim that even small "social" lies should be avoided, two are about liars and one is about the person lied to:

> R1: Once you get used to little lies, you tell bigger ones more easily.
> R2: The person you lie to suffers from not knowing the truth.
> R3: You eventually lose credibility.

So on the face of it, we should probably put (1) and (3) together, either before or after (2).

You can also order reasons on the basis of their relation to some preexisting order, either standard orders such as chronology and geography, or one specific to your particular claim, such as least-to-most controllable cause. For example, to explain the causes of the Holocaust someone might offer these five parallel reasons:

R1: Allied leaders did not try to stop the Holocaust for political reasons.
R2: Germany had a long history of anti-Semitism.
R3: Many societies have practiced other versions of ethnic cleansing.
R4: Hitler and those around him were uniquely evil.
R5: Jews did not resist soon enough.

It's hard to see any principle in that order. An order based on chronology would be clearer: 3 and 2 (distant and recent history), 4 (Hitler's evil), 5 (weak resistance), 1 (failure of Allies). But if you wanted to emphasize the difference between social causes and personal ones, that principle would give you this order: 3 (human culture), 2 (immediate society), 5 (collective response), 1 (lack of courage), 4 (personal evil).

Ordering Parallel Reasons by Readers' Responses   A better way to order parallel reasons is by how you want readers to respond to them. One principle of order is relative **strength.** For example, the reasons for the Holocaust might be ordered from what readers would take to be weakest to strongest, or vice versa, depending on whether we want to make a quick impact or to build toward a climax. (Of course, readers differ in which reasons they judge strong or weak.)

A second principle of order based on readers' responses is relative **acceptability.** Even when readers think a reason is strong, they may still not like hearing it. For example, it is likely that Jews, Germans, and those associated with the Allies would resist most strongly the reason that assigns responsibility to each of them. Each group would probably want to see other causes acknowledged before considering their own responsibility.

Another principle of readers' order is relative **complexity.** Readers grasp simpler reasons more easily than complex ones. (What is easier or more difficult, of course, depends on what they know.) For example, to argue that our ability to learn language is not like our ability to learn chess or algebra but is based on a genetically determined competence, we could offer three reasons:

R1: All human languages share the same complex principles of grammatical organization.
R2: Children all over the world learn to talk at about the same age.
R3: Chimpanzees can't learn the grammatical structures that two-year olds master easily.

The first reason is very difficult to grasp; the second easier; and the third easiest of all. If so, we would understand the argument better if those reasons were in reverse order, because that would allow us to build some "momentum" in understanding the argument.

Finally, reasons can be ordered by **familiarity.** (This too depends on particular readers.) Readers understand familiar reasons more readily than unfamiliar ones. For example, of the three reasons about learning language, the first is least familiar to most of us, the second most familiar for those of us who have been around children. So for them, the best order is 2–3–1.

If these principles of order conflict, the simplest principle is to put your strongest reasons last, if you are sure your reader will read to the end of your argument. If you fear your reader may not reach the end, put your strongest reason first.

Under any circumstances, choose *some* principle of order and make clear to your readers what it is.

Reasons in Series

When you offer a series of reasons, each one not supporting the claim directly, but linked to the one before and after it, you have to use different principles of order, but you have only two choices: first to last or last to first. Jumping around guarantees confusion.

Process Orders   If your reasons reflect some external process, you can order them to reflect its sequence. Begin at the beginning of the process and move to its outcome, like this:

> When buyers are satisfied with the quality of a product and the quality of service when it breaks down, step 1 they are likely to become loyal customers. step 2 Loyal customers are important, because they don't need advertising or a high-powered sales force to buy that product again. step 3 So the more loyal users a product has, the more profits a company can expect. claim

Or you can begin with the outcome and move back to its beginning, like this:

> Manufacturers increase profits and sales step 3 when they create loyal customers who buy their product once and return to buy it a second time, step 2 without the need of advertising or a high-powered sales force. Customers become loyal when they are satisfied with the quality of service they get on the product when it breaks down, but more importantly with the product's intrinsic quality. step 1 Therefore, while manufacturers should focus on both service and product quality, they should emphasize the product quality. claim

Both orders make sense. Which you choose depends on how you want readers to think about the process. The step they read last is the one they will focus on.

Reasoning Orders   You can order sequential reasons to follow not an external process but the internal process of your readers' logic. In the next example, the writer reports Thomas Jefferson's order of reasoning. The second reason depends on the logical principle stated in the first, and the third reason depends on the second (and the writer bases it all on the reported evidence of Jefferson's words):

> When Jefferson wrote "all men are created equal" with "certain inalienable rights," evidence he laid down the first principle of civil society—we all have intrinsic rights that cannot be taken away. reason 1 To protect those rights, we establish government, reason 2 but when government tries to take those rights away, we have the duty to replace it with one that will protect us. reason 3 In a democracy, we do that by the vote. But when a government is a ruthless tyranny, we have the duty to throw off its rule by force, if necessary. claim

The reverse order is possible, but harder to follow.

We can't tell you how to choose among these orders: that depends on your argument, on your situation, but most of all on your readers. So find surrogate readers on whom to try different orders. Under any circumstances, though, always question an order that you did not *choose*. Assume that the order in which you happened to write down your reasons is probably *not* the order that best helps readers grasp them.

Drafting
Quoting and Paraphrasing

When you report written evidence, you have to quote directly, paraphrase, or summarize. The difference is not one of degree:

▶ When you quote directly, you reproduce the original text word-for-word, punctuation-for-punctuation.
▶ When you paraphrase, you substitute your words for the authors' in order to make a statement clearer or to fit its context better. A paraphrase is usually shorter than the original, but it need not be. Readers should be able to say, "This sentence parallels the one on page X."
▶ When you summarize, you reword and condense the original text to less than its original length. Readers should not be able to say, "This sentence matches the one on page X."

Paraphrasing or Summarizing in Disciplines That Focus on Data
In the natural sciences and the "harder" social sciences, writers draw on sources for one or more of three reasons:

▶ to review previous work in the common ground,
▶ to acknowledge alternative positions, or
▶ to use the source's findings (main claim) or data to support their own claims and reasons.

In these cases, readers care more about results than the exact words reporting them, so writers seldom quote sources directly; instead, they paraphrase or summarize.

When you paraphrase a source, use the citation form expected in your field. Include the author's name in your paraphrase if the source is important; otherwise, put the name in a citation:

> Several processes have been suggested as causes of the associative-priming effect. For instance, in their seminal study Meyer and Schvaneveldt (1971, p. 232) suggested two, automatic (attention-free) spreading activation in long-term memory and location-shifting. Neely (1976) similarly distinguished between a process of automatic-spreading activation in memory and a process that depletes the resources of the attentional mechanism. More recently, a further associative-priming process has been studied (de Groot, 1984).

The writer thought that Meyer and Schvaneveldt as well as Neely were important enough to name in her sentences, but cited de Groot only as a minor reference.

157

Quoting in Disciplines That Focus on Words

In the humanities, writers both quote and paraphrase. Use direct quotations to

▶ cite the work of others as primary evidence
▶ focus on the specific words of a source because
  – they have been important in other arguments
  – they are especially vivid or significant
  – you want to focus on exactly how a source says something
  – you will dispute the source and want to avoid seeming to create a straw man

Paraphrase or summarize

▶ when you are more interested in the substance of reasons and evidence than in how they are expressed, and
▶ when you can say the same thing more clearly.

Don't quote just because it's easier or because you don't trust yourself to report a source fairly.

INTEGRATING QUOTATIONS INTO YOUR SENTENCES

When you offer quotations as evidence, follow the conventions in your field. They differ, but here are some common ones:

▶ Introduce a quotation with a colon or introductory phrase:

Plumber describes the accident that took Princess Diana's life in terms that reflect the cost of too little government regulation: "People like Diana believe they are immune from ordinary dangers and so don't bother with things like seat-belts. But everyone who died was not belted, and the one who survived was" (343).

▶ Weave the quotation into your own sentence (be sure grammar of the quotation fits into yours):

Plumber speaks in terms that remind us of the cost of too little government regulation when he points out that "everyone who died [in that crash] was not belted, and the one who survived was" (343).

(Note that when this writer changed the original, she used square brackets to indicate the change.)

▶ Set off quotations of three or more lines in an indented "block quote":

After Oldenberg's balloon crashed into the ocean on his fifth failed attempt to circumnavigate the globe, his wife began to suspect there was more to his obsession than the "desire to achieve." She thought she found an answer in evolutionary biology:

> The brain of the human male evolved under circumstances where caution was essential because risk was ever-present. When civilization reduced the risk, men began to feel that their natural, evolved impulse toward caution made them weak and unmanly. When men create situations of extreme risk, it's not the risk they crave but a worthy reason to exercise their caution. (Idlewild 135)

AVOIDING INADVERTENT PLAGIARISM

You know that you must cite any passages, distinctive words, or ideas that you use from a written source. But in addition to citing what you take from a source, you must also reproduce that material appropriately.

Quotations

Any time you use more than a few words from a source, you must (1) quote the words exactly as they appeared in the original, (2) indicate omissions with ellipses and changes with square brackets, and (3) show which words are quoted by putting them within quotation marks or setting them off in a block quote. You have no decision to make here: *always* set off as quotations *all* passages you take from a source. If you don't, you risk being charged with plagiarism. That's why it's so important to take good notes by copying quotations exactly and putting any quoted words in a different font or different color and surrounding them with extra-large quotation marks.

But if you use only a few words, you have a decision to make. Because you are writing on the same topic as your sources, you will inevitably use many of the same words and phrases, because they are what *anyone* might use to talk about that particular subject. Those words you should not put in quotation marks. But if you use words or phrase that are distinctive to that source, then you must indicate that they are quotations.

For example, here is a passage from a book about technology:

> Because technology begets more technology, the importance of an invention's diffusion potentially exceeds the importance of the original invention. Technology's history exemplifies what is termed an autocatalytic process: that is, one that speeds up at a rate that increases with time, because the process catalyzes itself (Diamond 1998, 301).

If you were reporting Diamond's ideas, you would not use quotation marks for a phrase like *original invention,* because those are words anyone might use. But two of his phrases are distinctive and reflect his original thought and expression: *technology begets more technology* and *autocatalytic process.* Those words you should put in quotation marks the first time you use them; after that, you can repeat them without the marks.

Paraphrase

If you paraphrase rather than reproduce the exact words of a source, you do not need quotation marks or a block quote. But you also must not paraphrase so closely that you seem to follow a source word for word. For example, the following paraphrase would plagiarize this paragraph:

> If you paraphrase, avoid language so similar to the source that your words correspond to its words, For instance, this plagiarizes what you just read.

To avoid inadvertent plagiarism, read the original; sit back and think what it means; then express it in your own words without looking back. You are too close to the original if you can run your finger along a paraphrase and recognize the same sequence of concepts (not words). The following would not be plagiarism of this paragraph:

> Williams and Colomb suggest that to keep from plagiarizing, digest the meaning of a passage, summarize it in your own words, then compare the sequence of ideas in your summary with the source (164).

Our advice applies to most fields in the humanities, but practice differs in different fields. In the law, for example, writers regularly use the exact words of a judge's ruling without quotation marks. In some social sciences, researchers closely paraphrase the main finding of an experiment. Find and follow the practice in your field.

Revising
Balance Reasons and Evidence

Beware the data dump. Readers want reliable reports of relevant evidence, not all the data you can find. If you can find the best evidence to support a reason, don't confuse the issue with less relevant evidence. If your evidence is less than best, you'll need more, but no careful reader will be convinced by tons of undigested data and quotations.

Beware as well the opinion piece. Readers want your reasons, but they expect you to back them up with evidence. If you can't find reliable evidence to support a reason, find another reason you can support. If you can't support most of your reasons with evidence, then your claim is not provable and so not suitable for argument.

To diagnose whether you have done either, highlight every quotation and statement of data:

- ▶ If you highlight more than two-thirds of your paper, you may have a data dump.
- ▶ If you highlight less than one-third, you may not have enough evidence to support your reasons.

Inquiries

Reflections

1. Sue copied the office hours from the schedules posted on professors' doors. But are the actual, physical pieces of paper listing office hours the "hard evidence" that "proves" that on average teachers are in their offices for less than an hour a week?

2. Here is something that some people might take to be a "fact" and therefore usable as evidence in favor of allowing people to carry concealed weapons:

According to an NRA press release, states that have passed laws allowing citizens to carry concealed weapons in public have experienced on average a 4.6 percent drop in daylight assaults and robbery.

How many removes from the primary evidence itself would you estimate that report of evidence is?

3. How close to the primary evidence itself are these: (a) a musical score; (b) musical recordings made from that score; (c) color reproductions of oil paintings in art history books; (d) full-size exact reproductions of etchings in art books; (e) a videotape of an automobile accident; (f) a tape recording of a meeting; (g) a transcription of that tape recording; (h) a drawing of a witness in a courtroom; (i) a photograph of a witness in a courtroom.

4. What counts as evidence for being in love? For sexual fidelity? For God directly telling someone to do something? For pain that disables someone from working?

5. Which of the following statements is closer to the truth? Does it matter?

Most of the important questions in the world are those for which we have no good evidence to decide either way.

Most of the important questions in the world are those for which we have no good reasons to decide either way.

6. When Jefferson says "We hold these truths to be self-evident," what does he base that on?

7. Consider these three statements:

   a. The comments on my history paper did not provide specific advice about improving the next paper.
   b. The comments on my history paper averaged about six words, and all of the comments expressed only approval or disapproval.
   c. The comments on my history paper were very brief and uninformative.

All might be true, but which seems closest to representing what's "out there," independent of anyone's judgment? Can you order them as a claim supported by a reason supported by evidence: "X because Y because Z"?

8. Some people refuse to judge any reason good or bad, because any reason is a good one for the person offering it. If so, then all reasons are equally good. They are in effect just opinions, and everyone's opinion is as good as anyone else's. Do you agree that all opinions are equally good? If you do, then some philosophers would claim that you have contradicted yourself. Have you?

Tasks

9. Pull out those old papers you've been working with. Select one that has the most evidence. Identify each report of evidence and grade it on a four-point scale:

   4 As close to primary evidence as anyone could get

3 Your own report of primary evidence that you directly collected or experienced

2 Your secondhand report of what is reported by the person who directly collected or experienced the primary evidence

1 Your third- or fourth-hand report of what someone else reported that someone else reported

What is your average score? Could you have raised it if you had done more research?

10. This exercise asks you to see how arguers can gain your trust by exploiting your bias to think of evidence as "out there in the world." Find a textbook that relies on complex data (experimental psychology, physics, economics). Pick out reports of evidence offered as factually true, beyond question (look for tables and graphs). Do you understand that evidence? Does it seem to you self-evident, obvious in the external world? What would you have to believe to accept this evidence as "given"? Now find the same thing in a newspaper or newsmagazine, then in a television newscast.

11. The next serious disagreement you get into, try to establish what you and the other person are willing to accept as evidence. How hard is it to do that? Is there any disagreement about what to count as evidence?

Project

12. Select one of your old papers, and imagine that you intended it for a reader who does not trust you and will question your reported evidence. What would you need to bolster each of the reports of evidence in your paper? Do some research to see whether you can get it. (You may not be able to put your hands on the evidence now, but you should be able to find out whether it is at least out there.) For quotations, imagine that your reader suspects that you quoted out of context. How could you show that you did not?

Focus on Writing

1

Context.   One good way to develop an argument is to adapt a related argument that you or your readers find convincing. For example, in literature classes students often develop arguments about a book not discussed in class by applying to it the general structure of argument and some of the evidence used to discuss a related book that was assigned for class. This is also a common practice among professionals, such as management consultants. When they investigate the case of one client, they often make arguments similar to those they have previously made for other clients. This is not plagiarism, as long as you acknowledge your source and no one is fooled into thinking that you built the argument from scratch.

Please read Paglia's "Wisdom in a Bottle" and Sullum's "Smoking and the Tyranny of Public Health" before completing the tasks below.

Wisdom in a Bottle
Camille Paglia

O Auntie Mame:
I once again find myself in the spin cycle over the latest phase of screaming campus hysterics: "Binge Drinking." Though I'm the first person to call the recent death of the Louisiana State University student at the center of this episode a real tragedy, the doting uber-mothers and fathers of Clean Campus Living are now on a new warpath—probably since date rape and heterosexual AIDS have lost their novelty as crusades. Thankfully, I'm beyond their clutches, as I graduated from my university-cum-nursery school a couple of years back. My question to you, Madam Oracle, is: Do we need any more campus babysitting for "boys" and "girls" who 20 years ago, at their age, were considered very much ADULTS? Where's the common sense in these fools? Sounds like Carry Nation wields a sledge hammer, not an ax, these days! Quick—Pass me the poppers!

Shaken, Not Stirred

Dear Shaken:
The cultural savvy of Salon readers is well-demonstrated by your raffish sobriquet alluding to one of my favorite scenes in "Auntie Mame," where Mame's schoolboy nephew perkily mixes a very professional martini for the flabbergasted banker, Mr. Babcock: "Stir never shake—it bruises the gin!"

The authoritarian Big Mommy and Daddy who run the summer camps we call colleges can't decide what a student is these days: A thinking, breathing, exploring, risk-taking adult? Or a cash cow haltered and hidebound by the thick parental checkbook? I say let the herd out of the barn, and let the hooves fall where they may! Growing up means being allowed to take a tumble in your own dung.

The absurdity of the Louisiana State University case is that alcohol was banned on campus, as if the latter were in Puritan Salem rather than Xanadu Baton Rouge, La. Thus LSU students are forced to chug-to-the-max off campus to sustain their high and then endanger their lives and others' by driving home in a sodden state.

"Binge drinking" is a Dionysian response to Apollonian overcontrol of another area of life. I have always strongly opposed the draconian raising of the legal drinking age to 21 in this country, a highly politicized and infantilizing measure that deprived the majority of young people of their freedoms in order to constrain a tiny, careless minority responsible for traffic accidents.

Camille Paglia *offers online advice for the culturally disgruntled at Ask Camille (available at http://www.salon.com).*

Alcohol, with its ancient history and its standardized, quality-controlled modern commercial production, is far preferable to drugs or pills as a tool of youthful experimentation. Manipulation of mood and alteration of consciousness are important first stages in higher education—as long as one is not destroyed by them. Identity is developed by a temporary dissolution of the mental structure imposed by parents, teachers and other adults. Creativity in the arts especially profits from that dangerous, exciting fluidity. Teetotalers may be the spine of the nation, but drinkers are its heart and balls.

European universities would never dream of meddling in their students' private lives. But American universities have reverted to "in loco parentis" (in place of the parent)—the parietal rules and repressive oversight that my 1960s generation rebelled against and smashed. Administrators are locked in Machiavellian marriage with nosy, tuition-paying parents. Even the retiring president of Bryn Mawr College (a hotbed of p.c. feminism) recently complained to the *Philadelphia Inquirer* that today's parents won't let their children grow up and that they're overinvolved with micromanaging their Bryn Mawr daughters' lives by constant e-mail and phone calls.

It's not binge drinking that's the problem—it's the banality and mediocrity of American higher education that produces students' desperate lust for gusto. I have certainly seen many talented people destroyed by alcohol and drugs. But as William Blake said, "The road of excess leads to the palace of wisdom."

My sympathies are with the orgiasts—like Oscar Wilde, who quipped, "Work is the curse of the drinking class." And like Patsy Stone of "Absolutely Fabulous," whose Ivana-blond image, with a vodka bottle plastered to her lips, is printed on one of my favorite T-shirts. In vino veritas!

Smoking and the Tyranny of Public Health
Jacob Sullum

From a public health perspective, smoking is not an activity or even a habit. It is "Public Health Enemy Number One," "the greatest community health hazard," "the single most important preventable cause of death," "a pediatric disease," "the manmade plague," "the global tobacco epidemic." It is something to be stamped out, like smallpox or yellow fever. This view of smoking is part of a public health vision that encompasses all sorts of risky behavior, including not just smoking and drinking, using illegal drugs, overeating, failing to exercise, owning a gun, speeding, riding a motorcycle without a helmet—in short, anything that can be said to increase the incidence of disease or injury.

Although this sweeping approach is a relatively recent development, we can find intimations of it in the public health rhetoric of the 19th century. In the introduction to the first major American book on public health, U.S. Army surgeon John S. Billings explained the field's concerns: "Whatever can cause, or help to cause, discomfort, pain, sickness, death, vice, or crime—and whatever has a tendency to avert, destroy, or diminish such causes—are matters of interest to the sanitarian." Despite this ambitious mandate, and despite the book's impressive length (nearly 1,500 pages in two volumes), *A Treatise on Hygiene and Public Health* had little to say about the issues that occupy today's public health pro-

Jacob Sullum *is a syndicated columnist and senior editor at* Reason *magazine. This article is adapted from* For Your Own Good: The Anti-Smoking Crusade and the Tyranny of Public Health, *published this year by the Free Press. From* Consumers Research Magazine, *July 1998.*

fessionals. There were no sections on smoking, alcoholism, drug abuse, obesity, vehicular accidents, mental illness, suicide, homicide, domestic violence, or unwanted pregnancy. Published in 1879, the book was instead concerned with things like compiling vital statistics; preventing the spread of disease; abating public nuisances; and assuring wholesome food, clean drinking water, and sanitary living conditions.

A century later, public health textbooks discuss the control of communicable diseases mainly as history. The field's present and future lies elsewhere. "The entire spectrum of 'social ailments,' such as drug abuse, venereal disease, mental illness, suicide, and accidents, includes problems appropriate to public health activity," explains *Principles of Community Health.* "The greatest potential for improving the health of the American people is to be found in what they do and don't do and for themselves. Individual decisions about diet, exercise, stress, and smoking are of critical importance." Similarly, *Introduction to Public Health* notes that the field, which once "had much narrower interests," now "includes the social and behavioral aspects of life—endangered by contemporary stresses, addictive diseases, and emotional instability."

The extent of the shift can be sensed by perusing a few issues of the American Public Health Association's journal. In 1911, when the journal was first published, typical articles included "Modern Methods of Controlling the Spread of Asiatic Cholera," "Sanitation of Bakeries and Restaurant Kitchens," "Water Purification Plant Notes," and "The Need of Exact Accounting for Still-Births." Issues published in 1995 offered articles like "Menthol vs. Nonmenthol Cigarettes: Effects on Smoking Behavior," "Compliance with the 1992 California Motorcycle Helmet Use Law," "Correlates of College Student Binge Drinking," and "The Association Between Leisure-Time Physical Activity and Dietary Fat in American Adults."

In a sense, the change in focus is understandable. After all, Americans are not dying the way they once did. The chapter on infant mortality in *A Treatise on Hygiene and Public Health* reports that during the late 1860s and early 1870s two-fifths to one-half of children in major American cities died before reaching the age of five. The major killers included measles, scarlet fever, smallpox, diphtheria, whooping cough, bronchitis, pneumonia, tuberculosis, and "diarrheal diseases." Beginning in the 1870s, the discovery that infectious diseases were caused by specific microorganisms made it possible to control them through vaccination, antibiotics, better sanitation, water purification, and elimination of carriers such as rats and mosquitoes. At the same time, improvements in nutrition and living conditions increased resistance to infection.

Americans no longer live in terror of smallpox or cholera. Despite occasional outbreaks of infectious diseases such as rabies and tuberculosis, the fear of epidemics that was once an accepted part of life is virtually unknown. The one exception is AIDS, which is not readily transmitted and remains largely confined to a few high-risk groups. For the most part, Americans are dying of things you can't catch: cancer, heart disease, trauma. Accordingly, the public health establishment is focusing on those causes and the factors underlying them. Having vanquished most true epidemics, it has turned its attention to metaphorical epidemics of unhealthy behavior.

In 1979 Surgeon General Julius Richmond released *Healthy People: The Surgeon General's Report on Health Promotion and Disease Prevention,* which broke new ground by setting specific goals for reductions in mortality. "We are killing ourselves by our own careless habits," Secretary of Health, Education, and

Welfare Joseph Califano wrote in the introduction, calling for "a second public health revolution" (the first being the triumph over infectious diseases). *Healthy People,* which estimated that "perhaps as much as half of U.S. mortality in 1976 was due to unhealthy behavior or lifestyle," advised Americans to quit smoking, drink less, exercise more, fasten their seat belts, stop driving so fast, and cut down on fat, salt, and sugar. It also recommended motorcycle helmet laws and gun control to improve public health.

Public health used to mean keeping statistics, imposing quarantines, requiring vaccination of children, providing purified water, building sewer systems, inspecting restaurants, regulating emissions from factories, and reviewing drugs of safety. Nowadays it means, among other things, banning cigarette ads, raising alcohol taxes, restricting gun ownership, forcing people to buckle their seat belts, and making illegal drug users choose between prison and "treatment." In the past, public health officials could argue that they were protecting people from external threats: carriers of contagious diseases, fumes and the local glue factory, contaminated water, food poisoning, dangerous quack remedies. By contrast, the new enemies of public health come from within; the aim is to protect people from themselves rather than each other.

Treating risky behavior like a contagious disease invites endless meddling. The same arguments that are commonly used to justify the government's efforts to discourage smoking can easily be applied to overeating, for example. If smoking is a compulsive disease, so is obesity. It carries substantial health risks, and people who are fat generally don't want to be. They find it difficult to lose weight, and when they do succeed they often relapse. When deprived of food, they suffer cravings, depression, anxiety, and other withdrawal symptoms.

Sure enough, the headline of a March 1985 article in Science announced, "Obesity Declared a Disease." The article summarized a report by a National Institutes of Health panel finding that "the obese are prone to a wide variety of diseases, including hypertension, adult onset diabetes, hypercholesterolemia, hypertriglyceridemia, heart disease, cancer, gall stones, arthritis, and gout." It quoted the panel's chairman, Jules Hirsch: "We found that there are multiple health hazards at what to me are surprisingly low levels of obesity. Obesity, therefore, is a disease."

More recently, the "epidemic of obesity" has been trumpeted repeatedly on the front page of the New York Times. The first story, which appeared in July 1994, was prompted by a study from the National Center for Health Statistics that found the share of American adults who are obese increased from a quarter to a third between 1980 and 1991. "The government is not doing enough," complained Philip R. Lee, an assistant secretary in the Department of Health and Human Services. "We don't have a coherent, across-the-board policy." The second story, published in September 1995, reported on a *New England Journal of Medicine* study that found gaining as little as 11 to 18 pounds was associated with a higher risk of heart disease—or, as the headline on the jump page put it, "Even Moderate Weight Gains Can Be Deadly." The study attributed 300,000 deaths a year to obesity, including one-third of cancer deaths and most deaths from cardiovascular disease. The lead researcher, JoAnn E. Manson, said, "It won't be long before obesity surpasses cigarette smoking as a cause of death in this country."

In his book *The Fat of the Land,* journalist Michael Fumento argues that obesity, defined as being 20% or more above one's appropriate weight, is only part of the problem. (See also "Busting the Low-Fat Dieting Myth," *Consumer Reports,* October 1997.) According to a 1996 survey, 74% of Americans exceed the weight range recommended for optimal health. "So instead of talking about a third of Americans being at risk because of being overweight," he writes, "we really should be talking about somewhere around three fourths."

If, as Philip R. Lee recommended, the government decides to do more about obesity—the second most important preventable cause of death in this country, soon to be the first—what would "a coherent, across-the-board policy" look like? As early as June 1975, in its *Forward Plan for Health,* the U.S. Public Health Service was suggesting "strong regulations to control the advertisement of food products, especially those of high sugar content or little nutritional value." But surely we can do better than that. A tax on fatty foods would help cover the cost of obesity-related illness and disability, while deterring overconsumption of ice cream and steak.

Lest you think this proposal merely facetious, it has been offered, apparently in all seriousness, by at least one economist, who wrote, in the *Orlando Sentinel:* "It is somewhat ironic that the government discourages smoking and drinking through taxation, yet when it comes to the major cause of death—heart disease—and its spiraling health-care costs, politicians let us eat with impunity . . . . It is time to rethink the extent to which we allow people to impose their negative behavior on those of us who watch our weight, exercise and try to be as healthy as possible."

Kelly Brownell, a professor of psychology at Yale University who directs the school's center for Eating and Weight Disorders, has also suggested a "junk food" tax, along with subsidies for healthy foods. "A militant attitude is warranted here," he told the *New Haven Register* last year. "We're infuriated at tobacco companies for enticing kids to smoke, so we don't want Joe Camel on billboards. Is it any different to have Ronald McDonald asking kids to eat foods that are bad for them?"

Of course, a tax on certain foods would be paid by the lean as well as the chunky. It might be more fair and efficient to tax people for every pound over their ideal weight. Such a market-based system would make the obese realize the costs they impose on society and give them an incentive to slim down.

If this idea strikes most people as ridiculous, it's not because the plan is impractical. In several states, people have to bring their cars to an approved garage for periodic emissions testing; there's no logistical reason why they could not also be required to weigh in at an approved doctor's office, say, once a year, reporting the results to the Internal Revenue Service for tax assessment. Though feasible, the fat tax is ridiculous because it's an odious intrusion by the state into matters that should remain private. Even if obesity is apt to shorten your life, most Americans would (I hope) agree, that's your business, not the government's. Yet many of the same Americans believe not only that the state should take an interest in whether people smoke but that it should apply pressure to make them stop, including fines (a.k.a. tobacco taxes), tax-supported nagging, and bans on smoking in the workplace.

In a 1977 talk show appearance, New York City lung surgeon William Cahan, a prominent critic of the tobacco industry, explained the rationale for such policies: "People who are making decisions for themselves don't always come up with the right answer." Since they believe that smoking is inherently irrational, tobacco's opponents tend to assume that smokers are stupid, ignorant, crazy, or helpless—though they rarely say so in such blunt terms. They understandably prefer to focus on the evil tobacco companies, portraying smokers as their victims.

167

Yet there is a palpable undercurrent of hostility toward smokers who refuse to get with the program. On two occasions in recent years, I was sitting at a (smoke-free) table with a group that included both a smoker and a busybody who took it upon himself to berate the smoker for his unhealthy habit. In both cases, the smoker, constrained by politeness, offered only the mildest of objections, and no one intervened on his behalf. Imagine what the reaction would have been if, instead of a smoker, the meddler had zeroed in on a chubby diner, warning him about the perils of overeating and lack of exercise. I suspect that the other diners would have been appalled, and the target, in turn would have been more likely to offer the appropriate response: Mind your own damned business. It seems we have special license to pick on smokers as a way of demonstrating our moral superiority.

The same sort of arrogance can be observed among public health specialists, but they are more consistent. Because the public health field developed in response to deadly threats that spread from person to person and place to place, its practitioners are used to dictating from on high. Writing in 1879, John S. Billings put it this way: "All admit that the state should extend special protection to those who are incapable of judging of their own best interests, or of taking care of themselves, such as the insane, persons of feeble intellect, or children; and we have seen that in sanitary matters the public at large are thus incompetent."

Billings was defending traditional public health measures aimed at preventing the spread of infectious diseases and controlling hazards such as toxic fumes. It's reasonable to expect that such measures will be welcomed by the intended beneficiaries, once they understand the aim. The same cannot be said of public health's new targets. Even after the public is informed about the relevant hazards (and assuming the information is accurate) many people will continue to smoke, drink, take illegal drugs, eat fatty foods, buy guns, speed, eschew seat belts and motorcycle helmets, and otherwise behave in ways frowned upon by the public health establishment. This is not because they misunderstood; it's because, for the sake of pleasure, utility, or convenience, they are prepared to accept the risks. When public health experts assume these decisions are wrong, they are indeed treating adults like incompetent children.

One such expert, writing in the *New England Journal of Medicine* two decades ago, declared "The real malpractice problem in this country today is not the one described on the front pages of daily newspapers but rather the malpractice that people are performing on themselves and each other . . . . It is a crime to commit suicide quickly. However, to kill oneself slowly by means of an unhealthy lifestyle is readily condoned and even encouraged."

The article prompted a response from Robert F. Meenan, a professor at the University of California School of Medicine in San Francisco, who observed: "Health professionals are trained to supply the individual with medical facts and opinions. However, they have no personal attributes, knowledge, or training that qualifies them to dictate the preferences of others. Nevertheless, doctors generally assume that the high priority that they place on health should be shared by others. They find it hard to accept that some people may opt for a brief, intense existence full of unhealthy practices. Such individuals are pejoratively labeled 'noncompliant' and pressures are applied on them to re-order their priorities."

The dangers of basing government policy on this attitude are clear, especially given the broad concerns of the public health movement. According to

John J. Hanlon's *Public Health Administration and Practice:* "Pubic health is dedicated to the common attainment of the highest levels of physical, mental, and social well-being and longevity consistent with available knowledge and resources at a given time and place." The textbook *Principles of Community Health* tells us: "The most widely accepted definition of individual health is that of the World Health Organization: 'Health is a state of complete physical, mental, and social well being and not merely the absence of disease or infirmity.'" A government empowered to maximize health is a totalitarian government.

In response to such fears, the public health establishment argues that government intervention is justified—because individual decisions about risk affect other people. "Motorcyclists often contend that helmet laws infringe on personal liberties," noted Surgeon General Julius Richmond's 1979 report Healthy People, "and opponents of mandatory [helmet] laws argue that since other people usually are not endangered, the individual motorcyclist should be allowed personal responsibility for risk. But the high cost of disabling or fatal injuries, the burden on families, and the demands on medical care resources are borne by society as a whole." This line of reasoning, which is also used to justify taxes on tobacco and alcohol, implies that all resources—including not just taxpayer-funded welfare and health care but private savings, insurance coverage, and charity—are part of a common pool owned by "society as a whole" and guarded by the government.

As Meenan noted in the *New England Journal of Medicine:* "Virtually all aspects of life-style could be said to have an effect on the health or well-being of society, and the decision (could then be) reached that personal health choices should be closely regulated." Writing 18 years later in the same journal, Faith T. Fitzgerald, a professor at the University of California, Davis, Medical Center, observed: "Both health-care providers and the commonwealth now have a vested interest in certain forms of behavior, previously considered a person's private business, if the behavior impairs a person's 'health.' Certain failures of self-care have become, in a sense, crimes against society, because society has to pay for their consequences . . . . In effect, we have said that people owe it to society to stop misbehaving, and we use illness as evidence of misbehavior."

Most public health practitioners would presumably recoil at the full implications of the argument that government should override individual decisions affecting health because such decisions have an impact on "society as a whole." Former Surgeon General C. Everett Koop, for his part, seems completely untroubled. "I think that the government has a perfect right to influence personal behavior to the best of its ability if it is for the welfare of the individual and the community as a whole," he writes. This is paternalistic tyranny in its purest form, arrogating to government the authority to judge "the welfare of the individual" and elevating "the community as a whole" above mere people. Ignoring the distinction between self-regarding behavior and behavior that threatens others, Koop compares efforts to discourage smoking and other risky behavior to mandatory vaccination of school children and laws against assault.

While Koop may simply be confused, some defenders of the public health movement explicitly recognize that its aims are fundamentally collectivist and cannot be reconciled with the American tradition of limited government. In 1975 Dan E. Beauchamp, then an assistant professor of public health at the University of North Carolina, presented a paper at the annual meeting of the American Public Health Association in which he argued that "the radical individualism inherent in the market model" is the biggest obstacle to improving public health. "The historic dream of public health that preventable death and disability ought to be minimized is a dream of social justice," Beauchamp said. "We are far from recognizing the principle that death and disability are collective problems and that all persons are entitled to health protection." He rejected "the ultimately arbitrary distinction between voluntary and involuntary hazards" and complained that "the primary duty to avert disease and injury still rests with the individual." Beauchamp called upon public health practitioners to challenge "the powerful sway market-justice holds over our imagination, granting fundamental freedom to all individuals to be left alone."

Of all the risk factors for disease and injury, it seems, freedom is the most pernicious. And you thought it was smoking.

Scenario. You work part-time in the office of the Dean of Students. Your boss, the dean, has been pressured by parents and the surrounding community to curb binge drinking among students. She has resisted because she believes that antidrinking measures infringe students' rights and hamper their growth as adults. She asked you to research the issue, and you provided her with a number of articles, including Camille Paglia's "Wisdom in a Bottle: 'Binge Drinking' and the New Campus Nannyism" and Jacob Sullum's "Smoking and the Tyranny of Public Health." The dean likes Paglia's piece and has been echoing its argument in her own statements. You have told her that you think Sullum's argument is more appropriate.

Task 1. Your boss sends you the following e-mail: "I've been thinking about your concerns about using Paglia's argument, and you may have a point. I'm going to be visiting high schools for the next few days, but I'll check my e-mail. Send me a brief summary about the problems you see in Paglia's case and why you think I should use Sullum's instead." Write an e-mail memo to send to your boss.

Task 2. Your boss wants a quick-and-dirty outline of an argument about drinking parallel to Sullum's argument about smoking. Outline Sullum's main reasons. Create a new outline by adapting, replacing, or deleting specific reasons so that the argument now applies to binge drinking.

Task 3. Your boss wants a more detailed outline that she can use as "talking points" when she speaks around campus and in the community. Add evidence to support each reason. You can borrow Sullum's evidence when it applies; when it doesn't, find evidence focused on drinking rather than smoking.

Task 4. Your boss wants you to ghostwrite an essay for the student newspaper. She will rewrite your argument to make it suit her style, but she wants a complete and polished draft from you.

Research Project

Scenario. Your proposal for a research paper has been accepted and you will be working on it for weeks. Your teacher wants to keep up with your progress by seeing your work along the way. You have two options: create a detailed outline by following steps 1, 2, and 3(a) (best for slow and careful drafters), or create a scratch outline and begin drafting by following steps 1, 2, and 3(b) (best for quick and dirty drafters).

Task. Follow these steps:

▶ **Step 1:** Determine the major sections of your paper. After selecting the most promising answer to your research question, list the major reasons in support of that claim in an order that will help your readers understand it. Try several stock orders (familiar to unfamiliar, simple to complex, less to more controversial, etc.) as well as others that come to mind. You now have a rough outline of the major sections in your paper to share with your classmates.

▶ **Step 2:** Sketch a brief introduction to each section that states what part of the main question/problem you address in that section. End it with the reason that will be the main claim/point of that section.

▶ **Step 3a** (for slow and careful drafters): Create a detailed outline for the section using the procedures in Step 1. Under each reason, indicate what evidence you offer to support it. If you already have evidence, summarize it. If not, summarize the kind of evidence you expect to collect and how you expect to get it.

▶ **Step 3b** (for quick and dirty drafters): Draft each section including evidence you have collected. Otherwise indicate the kind of evidence you will look for. If you think that you can find a particular kind of evidence, summarize it. Indicate clearly that you have not yet checked your sources. (You can start these paragraphs with a note to yourself, *Although I have not yet looked, I expect that* [SOURCE] *will show that. . . .*)

Sample Essay

The essay that follows uses evidence gathered from sources. You may not yet be writing papers as fully researched as this one, but even a shorter essay has to use its sources well. Read the essay and do the following:

Task 1. Pick out the reasons and evidence in the essay. This will be easiest if you make a copy and mark it up with different colored highlighters. Otherwise, use line numbers to identify specific sentences. (Save your marked up copies; you'll need them again.)

1. How many reasons are supported with specific evidence? How many have no evidence at all?

2. On average, how many items of evidence does the writer present in support of each of the major reasons? (You can estimate this.)

3. Estimate the following: (a) What percentage of the evidence in this paper is reported primary evidence (one step away from the evidence itself; that is, the writer observed or collected it directly)? (b) What percentage is secondary evidence (two steps away from the evidence itself; that is, the writer reports on evidence reported by someone who observed or collected it)? (c) What percentage is tertiary evidence (three or more steps away)?

Task 2. Answer the following questions, using your analysis in Task 1 as evidence for your claims.

1. In general, does the evidence in this essay support its reasons?

2. Assuming that you accept those reasons, how well do they support the claim "that guns were not popular in America until after the Civil War, and that the reasons people began to buy guns had more to do with money than with patriotism"?

3. How well do they support the claim that "People should not be duped into thinking that supporting gun control laws is unpatriotic or un-American"?

4. Does the presentation of evidence in this essay make the writer seem more or less credible? Why?

ESSAY #1 GUNS IN AMERICA

1   If you listen to the NRA, owning a gun is the ultimate symbol of American freedom and democracy. So most people believe them when they say that gun ownership has been a part of America since the Revolution and that it is a violation of basic American beliefs when the government tries to take away the people's guns. But this is just propaganda. The claim that for our forefathers owning guns was a patriotic duty is erroneous. History shows that guns were not popular in America until after the Civil War, and that the reasons people began to buy guns had more to do with money than with patriotism. People should not be duped into thinking that supporting gun control laws is unpatriotic or un-American.

2   It is true that in colonial days many Americans owned guns, but they faced many dangers, and there was no police force to protect you. The rule was, defend yourself or die. But later, when the country became more civilized, people stopped owning guns. According to historian Michael Bellesiles, "It would appear that at no time prior to 1850 did more than a tenth of the people own guns" (1966). This conclusion is based on surveys done by the states to see how many people owned guns so that they could serve in state militias. The state of Massachusetts counted all the guns owned by private citizens, and in every survey until 1840 it found that less than 11 percent of the people owned guns. "At the start of the War of 1812, the state had more spears than firearms in its arsenal" (*Economist* 1999). Also, guns were not the sort of thing people bought for a hobby, as they do today. The first magazine devoted to guns was not published until 1843.

3   One example of heroic gun owners that gun supporters talk about is the Minutemen of Massachusetts. These were farmers who, on a minute's notice, formed an army to defeat the British at Lexington and Concord, supposedly shooting the British soldiers from behind fences and hedges because they were great marksmen. But they were really a minority. Bellesiles did a study in which he checked wills and "probate inventories" (records of personal possesses when people died) between 1765 and 1790, and he found that less than 15 percent of all households had guns, and that more than half of the guns were broken (Bellesiles 1966). So by the time of the Revolution most Americans had already stopped owning guns. In 1793, less than twenty years after the Revolution, Congress passed a law to buy 7,000 muskets because it was worried that so few people owned guns that the country would not be

able to defend itself (there was still no army). But the people didn't want the guns. From 1808 to 1839, the government had a program to give a gun to every white male who belonged to a state militia, but only half the militias bothered to ask for them (*Economist* 1999). This was not because the militia members already owned guns, but because they didn't care about owning guns. In the 1830s, the general sent down by the federal government to lead the Florida militia in a war against the Seminoles, Winfield Scott, complained that the militia had almost no guns.

4   The militias are another example of heroic gun owners held up by gun supporters. But they were mostly a joke. Militia members were mostly "town paupers, idlers, vagrants, foreigners, itinerants, drunkards and the outcasts of society," according to the adjutant general of Massachusetts (*Economist* 1999). It was even more of a joke to think of them as marksmen like the Minutemen. In Pennsylvania, one militia held a shooting contest, but no one hit the target and the winner was the one who came closest. According to the newspaper, "The size of the target is known accurately, having been carefully measured. It was precisely the size and shape of a barn door" (Bellesiles 1998). Most militias stopped having shooting practice because it was embarrassing how badly they shot. In 1839, the Secretary of War complained that militias were "armed with walking canes, fowling pieces or unserviceable muskets" (*Economist* 1999).

5   If you go by the movies, everyone had a gun in the Wild West. But Robert Dykstra says that it was more peaceful in cattle towns like Tombstone, Arizona, or Dodge City, Kansas, than in the cities in the east. It is true that most cowboys carried rifles on the trail (mostly for hunting) and some of them carried pistols. But when they came to a town, they did not have to defend themselves against the dangers of the trail, so they left their guns behind because most cattle towns had strict anti-gun laws and the Sheriff would take them away. "During its most celebrated

decade as a tough cattle town, only 15 persons died violently in Dodge City, 1876–1885, for an average of just 1.5 killings per cowboy season" (Dykstra 1968). Living in these towns was more like *The Little House on the Prairie* than the *Wild Bunch*. Maybe the movies have so many guns in Westerns because gunfights are exciting and add to the action, or maybe they are just trying to support the myth that America is the land of the free and home of the brave because it is the home of the gun.

6   Why did most Americans not own a gun before the Civil War? There were two reasons. First, they didn't need them. It is a myth that violence has always been a part of American life. In the early years of the country, nine Americans out of ten did not feel that they needed a gun to protect themselves. Second, guns were expensive. A gun would cost a farmer a whole year's income (*Economist* 1999).

7   Why did more Americans own guns after the Civil War? There was one reason: money. When the war started, the Union government owned 327,000 muskets and rifles and the Confederate government owned 150,000. By the end of the war, the Union army had given out 4 million weapons to its soldiers. Of course it also trained those soldiers to shoot. The Union army had 1.5 million soldiers and the Confederate army had 1 million. When the war was over and the soldiers went home, the army let them keep their guns. Now there were many more Americans with guns they got for free (Bellesiles 1999).

8   The war also made guns less expensive. In the few years of the war, gun manufacturers made more guns to supply the war than they had made in the entire history of the country (*Economist* 1999). The gun manufacturers had to learn how to mass produce guns to supply the army with so many guns so quickly, which meant that not only did they have many more factories but that the guns were much cheaper. When the government stopped buying guns for the war, the manu-

facturers had to sell more guns or close down the new factories, but they were saved because the war had created many new customers who owned guns and had learned to shoot in the war.

9   So you can see that it is a myth that guns have always been a part of American life and that without people owning guns America would not have been able to protect its freedom. Gun supporters say people buy guns to protect themselves, but according to the statistics the only people likely to be shot by their guns are themselves or a member of their family. People say they buy guns to defend America's freedom, but who do they think they will defend it from? Those who believe in the myth of a nation of Minutemen may be sincere, but all they guard is the profits of the gun manufacturers who have blood on their hands.

Works Cited*

Bellesiles, Michael. "The Origins of Gun Culture in the United States, 1760–1865." *Journal of American History*. 83 (1966): 425–455.

Bellesiles, Michael. "Gun Laws in Early America." *Law and History Review*. 16 (1998): 567–589.

Bellesiles, Michael. *Lethal Imagination*. New York University Press: 1999.

Davidson, Osha Gray. *Under Fire*. University of Iowa Press: 1998.

Dykstra, Richard. *The Cattle Towns*. Knopf: 1968.

Economist Staff, "Guns in America." *Economist*. July 3, 1999.

National Rifle Association *NRA-ILA Research and Information Page*. The National Rifle Association Institute for Legislative Action. http://www.nraila.org/research/.

*Formatted according to earlier editions of MLA Style.

In a Nutshell

About Your Argument . . .

You rest claims on reasons and rest reasons on reports of evidence. When you report evidence that you yourself observed or that someone else has reported, report it accurately and cite your sources so that readers can check it for themselves.

Since readers usually need more than one reason before they will agree to a claim, don't be satisfied with only one.

Except for the simplest, most obvious cases, don't cite reports of evidence without also stating a reason that connects those reports to the claim. Reasons not only support claims, they also interpret evidence. The reason should tell readers what to see in the evidence that is relevant to your claim.

. . . and About Writing It

When you have multiple reasons, select an order that helps readers:

> ▶ If reasons are parallel, order them on the basis of strength, acceptability, complexity, or familiarity.
> ▶ If your reasons are linked, decide whether you want them to follow some external process or an internal process of reasoning.

Keep a balance between reasons and reports of evidence:

> ▶ Beware the argument that is made up mostly of quotations or data.
> ▶ Conversely, be certain that you have at least tried to find evidence for every reason.

CHAPTER 7

The Core of Your Argument: Reporting Evidence

In many ways, evidence is the substance of an argument: It distinguishes a well-founded claim from mere opinion or rigid dogmatism and is the largest part of most written arguments. Critical readers judge your argument and your ethos on the basis of your evidence, whether it is sufficient, of the right kind, gathered from sources they consider reliable, and reported—and cited—fully and accurately. In this chapter we show you how to find evidence, evaluate what you find, and then report it so that you readers will trust it and you.

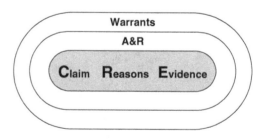

Weigh Your Burden of Evidence

In every argument, readers expect enough quality evidence to overcome their doubts. In conversation, you know you have met that burden of evidence when the other person doesn't ask for more. But when you write, you don't have readers there to tell you when they have seen enough or when they want more. You have to judge each case individually, but the following three questions will help you decide what kind of evidence you need, how much, and how good it has to be. (From here on, we use the term evidence to refer to both the *evidence* itself and your reports of it. When we have to distinguish them, we will.)

1. *What kind of evidence will your readers expect?* Readers in different academic or professional communities require different kinds of evidence. An environmental science teacher will expect you to draw toxicology data about a local lake from technical reports, not a newspaper; a history teacher will expect you to work with primary documents, not textbook accounts of them. Disciplines vary too much to give you a general rule other than this: When you write in a new community, ask an experienced member what counts as acceptable evidence in that field.

The first question to ask is whether your readers will want empirical evidence (numbers, controlled observations, etc.) or will they want "softer" forms of evidence (personal narratives, eyewitness reports, etc.). You also have to match the kind of evidence you report to the kind of problem you address. In an argument about binge drinking, for example, you would need one kind of evidence to argue that it is caused by the psychology of late adolescence, another by our culture of addiction, and another yet by a genetic predisposition to risk taking.

Each new argument presents new demands that you have to puzzle out case-by-case. Don't assume that the evidence you need is the evidence you can get most easily. Resist the temptation to rely only on what you happen to have experienced—the striking event you witnessed, the memorable person you knew, that one time you talked with a binge drinker. A "for instance" is not proof.

If your problem requires personal evidence or if that's all you can get, don't settle for anecdotes you have told and retold: Search the details of your own memory, and when you can, seek corroboration from records or other participants. Memory is a poor witness; it needs all the help you can give it.

2. *How strongly will readers resist your claim?* The more readers resist a claim, the more evidence they want. Assume your readers will want more evidence when you ask them to

- Accept a claim that contradicts what they deeply believe.
- Do something that costs them time or effort.
- Do or think something that creates new problems, such as the loss of something they like or the disapproval of others.

In these situations, their feelings matter as much as your logic. Suppose you found evidence that a famous political figure knowingly included false stories in a book that made her famous. Her political opponents will snap up any evidence against her, while her admirers will demand more and better evidence before they agree that she is a fraud, because in accepting that claim, they have to give up more than a belief. (See the case of Rigoberta Menchú in Inquiry 10 on p. 193.)

3. *How fully do you want your readers to accept your claim?* If you ask readers to accept a strong claim wholeheartedly, they will expect your best reports of the best evidence. But they may be satisfied with less if you ask less of them—for example, to approve a claim rather than act on it, or only to understand and respect your reasons for making it. If Harry asks the dean to extend library hours to accommodate students with day jobs, the dean will want more than anecdotal

177

evidence about dissatisfied students. But she may be receptive to a few good stories if Harry wants her only to have an assistant find out whether students have a reasonable complaint.

Make a Plan to Find Evidence

We risk misleading ourselves when we speak of "gathering" evidence, as if it were scattered around, waiting to be picked up. Getting evidence is closer to hunting down a specific quarry. Colomb spent five years, on and off, hunting for the address of a doctor who practiced in London at the end of the seventeenth century. You probably can't spend weeks, much less months or even years, hunting for evidence, but you'll still need to do some sleuthing to meet your burden of evidence.

Your hunting is not likely to be successful if you don't know what you're looking for or where to look. Before you fire up a search engine, invest some time to decide first what kind of evidence your readers will expect and then how you can best get it. For one plan, see the Writing Process section (pp.187–191).

The Four Maxims of Quality

Once you find evidence, you have to evaluate it as your readers are likely to. Doing that will be hard, for it is a sad but true comment on the human mind that we all tend to seize on evidence that confirms what we want to believe; and worse, we ignore, reject, or even distort evidence that contradicts it. So to meet your burden of evidence, you have to anticipate the questions readers may ask, which means seeing your evidence through their eyes.

Once you think you can meet your readers' expectations with sufficient evidence of the right kind, evaluate its quality, but again from their point of view. Readers judge evidence by four criteria: (1) accuracy, (2) precision, (3) representativeness, and (4) reliability. How severely they apply those criteria depends on their stake in your claim. For instance, for a claim that some natural herb improves Alzheimer's symptoms, FDA researchers responsible for testing such cures will demand multiple studies that meet all four criteria; family members caring for an Alzheimer's sufferer are likely to accept a lower threshold of evidence; and the producers of the herb a lower one yet. Imagine your readers asking the following questions about your evidence:

1. *Is your report of evidence accurate?* This is the prime maxim. Get one fact wrong and readers may distrust everything else you say—and you, as well.

2. *Is your report of evidence precise enough?* It is 100 percent accurate to say that the population of Ohio is between a million and a billion, but not precise enough for most purposes. What counts as precise, though, differs by both use and field. A physicist measures the life of a particle in millionths of a second; a paleontologist might be happy to date the appearance of a new species give or take half a million years. Reports of evidence can be too precise. A historian would seem foolhardy to date the collapse of the Soviet Union at "2:11 p.m. on August 18, 1991, because it was at that moment that Gorbachev...." When you write "many" or "some," critical readers will want to know how many is many and how few are some.

3. *Is the evidence you report representative?* This depends on your kind of problem. If you generalize about how people get off welfare, you need a huge sample to cover all the reasons. But if you are studying a new chemical compound, you can make big generalizations from tiny samples. Human populations vary a lot; samples of a chemical compound little or not at all. These days, representative sampling depends on statistical methods whose principles every educated person should understand.

4. *Are your reports of evidence from reliable sources?* The problem of reliable sources turns on four issues: currency, reputation, disinterestedness, and level of source.

> **Currency:**
> Is your source up-to-date? Again, this varies by field. In computer science, a year-old research report is probably out-of-date; in philosophy, ancient authorities are always relevant. In general, look for the most recent work in a field.

> **Reputation:**
> Readers are more likely to trust evidence from people with good reputations, strong credentials, important positions, and name recognition. They will be suspicious at best of data that you pull from the Web site of someone neither you nor they have ever heard of. But even expert credentials do not ensure reliability: Linus Pauling won a Nobel Prize in chemistry, but he was judged to be a flake when he moved out of his field to tout vitamin C as a cure for most ills known to medicine.
>
> Be aware that some journals have better reputations for publishing sound research than others. Find out which journals are most (and least) respected before you cite evidence from one. If you find journal articles online, be sure that whoever posted them is also reliable: You can trust one posted by the journal itself, by the author, or in your library's online databases.

> **Disinterestedness:**
> Will readers be confident that, however expert your sources, they are not tainted by self-interest? Not long ago, a government study of the safety of silicone breast implants was almost wholly discredited when it was discovered that one scientist on the panel had received research funds from a company making implants. Even if that scientist had been utterly objective, the critics were right to charge that the mere appearance of a conflict of interest was enough to undermine the image of integrity of the whole panel. The best sources of evidence are those who have something to lose in offering it. For a claim that trigger locks make guns safer, the CEO of gun manufacturer Smith and Wesson is a weightier source than Oprah.

▶ **Level of source:**

Generally, you should get as close as you can to the evidence itself. Primary sources are closest. If you are studying texts, primary sources are the original books, letters, diaries, and so on. For textual evidence, use a recent edition by a reputable publisher. If you are studying physical phenomena, primary sources are the notebooks of those who directly observed and collected the evidence "itself," along with their first-hand reports based on their notes. For physical evidence, use the original article (not just the abstract or, worse, someone's report of it).

If you can't find primary sources, look for reliable secondary sources—scholarly journals and books that report on primary sources. Tertiary sources report work found in secondary sources; they include textbooks, articles in encyclopedias, and mass publications like *Reader's Digest*. If these are the only sources available, so be it, but assume that careful readers will not accept them as authoritative. They know that a report of a report of a report is too far from the evidence itself to be trusted.

Trustworthy Reports of Evidence

We've emphasized that what you offer as evidence is more likely to be a report of it, and that a report predictably shapes evidence to suit a writer's own goals and interests. So when you gather evidence from the reports of others, be aware that your source has already shaped it, and that you will again. Even when you report your own observations of the evidence "itself," you cannot avoid giving it some "spin." To report evidence responsibly, you have to understand its different kinds, what to use each kind for, how we predictably distort it, and what are the best ways to present it.

Reports of Memories

As you read these words, you can feel the heft of this book, the texture of its pages. You can close the book and hear it snap; you can sniff it, even nibble at a page to taste it. Your nerve endings are reporting on the data from "out there," data that support your belief that this book exists. Now put the book down for a moment and look away. [_____] The instant you did that, the "self"-evidence of this book vanished, leaving you with nothing but mental traces—a lingering taste, perhaps; a visual or tactile memory. At that moment your memory was reconstructing those sense data, reporting the reports of your senses.

Memories often feel like trustworthy evidence, a record of our "direct" experience through our senses. But in fact, memory is one of the least reliable forms of evidence. When we construct a memory of an event, our minds unconsciously give it a form easy to store and recall. We shape it into a coherent story, eliminating some details, enhancing others, even inventing elements to it flesh out. And the more impressive the event, the more our memories are likely to change it.

Even if we strive to avoid consciously embellishing a memory when we report it, our mind has already reshaped it for us. So use evidence from memory cautiously and corroborate it with other evidence whenever you can.

Never Trust Eyewitnesses

In one study, people recalling a videotape of a car accident estimated the speed of the cars differently, depending on whether they were asked how fast the cars were going when they either "bumped" or "smashed" into each other. Depending on the wording of the question, the subjects even "remembered" different amounts of broken glass, though the videotape showed none at all!

Source: Elizabeth F. Loftus and John C. Palmer, "Reconstruction of Automobile Destruction: An Example of the Interaction Between Language and Memory," *Journal of Verbal Learning and Verbal Behavior* 13 (1974): 585–589.

Anecdotes

An anecdote is a report of memory designed for public consumption. Even if we try to stick only to known facts (and many of us don't), we reshape our already storylike memory into an even better story, adding and deleting still more details, reorganizing them to make the story funnier, more dramatic, more pointed to support whatever reason we had for telling the story in the first place. After we tell it a few times, we have turned that anecdote into a finely honed short story with a beginning, middle, and end—likely to have a distant relationship to the event it reports.

That's why illustrative anecdotes can be so persuasive, especially when we use one to dress up "objective" numerical data. When readers see pallid statistics enlivened by a vivid anecdote, the numbers take on the quality of evidence from "out there" because we seem to experience what they represent in our mind's eye. Compare these:

Fifty-three percent of Americans over the age of 65 have an annual income above $30,000, but 15 percent have incomes of less than $7,000 a year.

Around 9 a.m., the cabin attendant on UA flight 1643 to San Francisco asked Oliver and Sarah Peters whether they wanted the western omelet or the fruit plate for breakfast. Recently retired, they were on their way to visit their children and grandchildren in San Diego, happy to be escaping the below-zero windchill in Chicago. At about the same time, 85-year-old Amanda Wilson was sitting at her kitchen table on Chicago's south side, staring at two five-dollar bills, a quarter, and a dime, trying to figure out one more time how to get through the next two weeks on 85¢ a day. She lives on $565 a month Social Security, most of which goes for heat, light, and rent on her one-room apartment. She had a daughter once, but . . .

The anecdote is a good illustration, but bad evidence.

Some writers claim that personal experience is truer than cold, objective data. But it is not the kind of public, shared truth that readers want as a basis for a contestable claim. So be aware that if you do use a personal anecdote as evidence, readers may be too polite to question it openly, but will silently dismiss it as they think to themselves, "Anecdotal." You can anticipate that response by acknowledging the limits of personal evidence, "This is only my experience, but . . ." More importantly, look for other evidence that will corroborate it and bring it alive.

Reports from Authorities

Some students think they offer evidence when they quote an authority. But what they usually offer is only that authority's own report of evidence, or more often, just their own reason restated in someone else's more authoritative voice. For example, Mai might think she is supporting her claim with evidence in the form of a quotation, but here she only restates her reason in words more authoritative than her own:

> Teachers should be required to respond to their teaching evaluations claim because those who read them are more likely to improve their teaching than those who don't. reason According to J. Wills, for example, teachers who study their evaluations "profit from their openness to criticism" (*The Art of Teaching*, 330). reason restated

Mai may be right that the teachers are more likely to improve, but the quoted words only restate her own reason: they are evidence only that Wills has said the same thing. Mai could strengthen her claim if she reported not just Wills's claim but his evidence as well:

> Teachers should be required to respond to their teaching evaluations claim because those who read them are more likely to improve their teaching than those who don't. reason According to J. Wills, for example, teachers who study their evaluations "profit from their openness to criticism" (*The Art of Teaching*, 330). reason restated He studied 200 teachers who spent at least an hour reviewing their evaluations. The next term, they achieved 15 percent higher evaluations than those who circulated teaching evaluations but did not read them (*The Art of Teaching*, 333–335). reported evidence

When you quote authorities, you do two useful things:

- ▶ If your authority is credible, you make your own position more credible.
- ▶ If your authority gathered evidence you report, you bring readers as close as they can get, short of reading the authority itself.

Of course, you still have to show that the authority has based her reasons on sound evidence.

Why Question Others' Reports?

If you need reason to suspect the reports of evidence that you find in your sources, consider some research by Robert P. Newman and Keith R. Sanders. They studied the transcripts of a National College Debate Tournament to identify every instance where a debater cited specific testimony (quotations, numbers, etc.). They then compared each citation with its source to determine how accurately the debaters reported it. They found that more than half of the reports of reports of evidence were wrong! (Of course, we have to trust that Newman and Sanders collected their evidence accurately.)

Source: "A Study in the Integrity of Evidence," *Journal of the American Forensic Association* 2 (1965): 7–13.

Visual Reports with Photographs, Drawings, and Recordings

"Ocular proof" is compelling, because it makes us feel we can see what really happened. Like stories, visual images bring data to life by letting us experience them more directly than through words. For example, it is only when we see images of starving refugees and massacred civilians that we translate abstract claims about moral imperatives into vivid, concrete experience. And recall the power of those videos and photographs of the twin towers coming down on 9/11.

We might think that videotapes, photographs, and recordings are more reliable than memories, but as we all know, images and recordings of all kinds can be fabricated so convincingly that even experts cannot distinguish fakes from the real thing. (Always distrust images on the Web whose sources are not rock-solid reliable.) But even when they are not doctored, images and recordings reshape what they record. That's why you must tell your readers who took the pictures or made any recording you offer as evidence, and under what circumstances.

Visual Presentations of Quantitative Data

For some readers, numbers are the most compelling evidence, in fact the only acceptable evidence, partly because numbers seem most objective, partly because they are recorded by exacting types like scientists and accountants. If any evidence feels as though it is "out there" in the world, it is what we can count, and what we can count we can objectively quantify.

But just like any other report of evidence, numbers are shaped by the aims and interests of those who record them. When researchers gather data for an argument about the safety of air bags, the counters have to decide what to count—traffic fatalities, serious injuries (what counts as serious?), people brought to hospitals, those who make insurance claims, etc. They also have to decide how to organize the numbers—total fatalities, fatalities per year, fatalities per thousand, fatalities per miles driven, fatalities per trip, etc., each of which affects the impact that the numbers have on readers.

For example, imagine you are deciding whether to invest in one of two companies, Abco or Zorax. Look at the three ways shown here to represent the same "facts." Which way of representing the data helps you make the best decision?

We could also represent these data in words, but words spin the data even more than visual images do. How attractive are Zorax and Abco in these two accounts?

> Zorax improved its net profits in 1997 from 1996 by more than 50 percent despite relatively level sales. In contrast, Abco failed to increase its net profits significantly despite substantially higher sales.

> In comparison to Zorax's increased sales and profits, Abco increased its profits and significantly increased its gross 1997 income over 1996.

We might think that a table of numbers is most "objective," but that apparent objectivity is itself a rhetorical choice. While these reports offer the same factual data, we are affected by them in different ways. The right choice depends partly on the kind of evidence your readers expect, but also on how you want them to respond.

Table 7.1	Income, ABCO and Zorax			
	1996		**1997**	
	Gross Income	**Net Income**	**Gross Income**	**Net Income**
Abco	145,979,000	32,473,000	164,892,000	32,526,000
Zorax	134,670,000	25,467,000	136,798,000	39,769,000

184

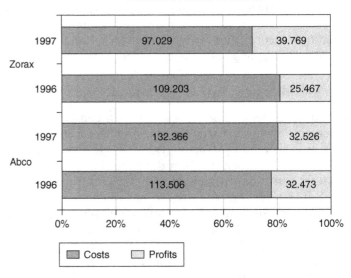

Figure 7.1 *Profit as a percentage of income, ABCO and Zorax*

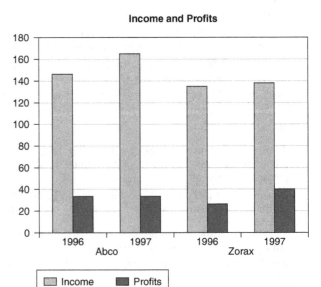

Figure 7.2 *Income and profits, ABCO and Zorax*

Our Misplaced Trust in Numbers

Numbers are useful as evidence because most readers trust them more than they should. Here are one expert's reasons why you should not put too much trust in numbers:

What do you mean when you say in your book that facts don't speak for themselves?

We all talk about facts as though they're rocks you pick up and they have an independent existence, and they don't. When you hear a statistic, someone has created that. You cannot take that number and assume that is a pure reflection of reality.

Take me through the process of how an accurate number gets transformed into an inaccurate one.

An article appears in the newsletter for the American Anorexia/Bulimia Association, and they quote a physician who says perhaps 150,000 people have anorexia, it's very serious and some people die. This was transformed, I think, first in a scholarly book, where someone said 150,000 people die from anorexia every year. You can see how this happens, maybe sloppy note-taking. Once the figure is out there, it's very hard to take back.

What's the biggest trap people fall into when hearing a number?

I think the biggest error is that we hear a number, and we automatically assume we know what is being counted. When we hear an estimate for the number of missing children, we imagine these are children abducted by strangers; we hear numbers for child abuse, and what pops into our mind is the worst possible case, and I think what people don't understand is how broadly these phenomena are being defined in order to generate these big numbers.)

Source: Interview with Joel Best, author of *Damned Lies and Statistics: Untangling Numbers from the Media, Politicians, and Activists* (2001), in the New York Times, May 26, 2001, p. A17.

Radical Skepticism

When we treat evidence and reports of evidence as matters of agreement, we seem close to giving up the metaphor of an argument resting on a solid foundation of factual evidence. And in fact, we do. Some philosophers object to that, arguing that if we base our reasoning on anything less than utterly certain, objective fact, we surrender to relativity and subvert not just the quest for truth, but the very idea that it exists. How can we be sure of anything if we define evidence merely as what we agree to?

But this definition of evidence should not threaten us if we agree to base our beliefs on the best arguments we can make, based on the best reports of the best evidence we can find. We could, for example, agree that the world is flat, and base our claim on the evidence of our senses. But to keep believing that, we would have to ignore reliable reports of other intractable, undeniably better evidence that should lead us to believe that the world is round. That makes "truth" less a matter of capricious agreement and more a matter of thoughtful inquiry and argument.

To be sure, if readers want to be difficult, they can stubbornly refuse to agree to any evidence. It is a standard trick for derailing arguments. When critics charged that New Jersey state police stopped African American drivers almost five times as often as they did whites, one participant in the debate kept questioning the data because, as he said, "everyone knows you can twist statistics to mean anything you want." In so doing, he refused to engage in a good faith argument because he denied even the possibility of reliable evidence.

So what do you say to someone who never accepts anything as uncontested but just keeps asking, What is that based on? Can you show me more? Nothing. Such a person has refused your offer to engage in a collaborative search for the truth.

Turtles All the Way Down

There is a story told by the anthropologist Clifford Geertz of an Englishman in India, who, upon being told that the world rests on the back of an elephant, asked "On what does the elephant stand?" "On the back of a turtle," he was told. "And on what does the turtle stand?" he asked. "On the back of another turtle." "And on what" the Englishman asked again, "does *that* turtle stand?" "Ah, Sahib," replied the Indian, "after that, it is turtles all the way down!"

Arguments are a bit like that. Our claim is the world that rests on the elephant of our reasons; that elephant stands on the back of a turtle of evidence. But when someone asks what that turtle rests on, we realize that our argument is potentially turtles all the way down. We can only hope that at some point readers stop asking about the next one.

In the Readings...

Trusting Authorities

In the sample essay, "Guns in America" (pp. 172–174), the writer relies heavily on the work of historian Michael Bellesiles, which is based on extensive archival research. At the time the essay was written in 2001, Bellesiles's work was highly respected, had even won awards. He had critics, but most were gun advocates who complained more about his conclusions than about his research. But by early 2002, his work was criticized by scholars who questioned his research methods. When they asked to see some of his raw data, he had to confess that some of his notes were lost when his office flooded. The criticisms concerned only a part of his archival research, but they were serious enough that historians devoted an entire issue of a journal to questioning his research and his university convened a committee to investigate charges of academic fraud. Although the committee stopped short of finding him guilty of fraud, it concluded that his documentation of his evidence was "skimpy" and "sloppy," and that he was guilty of unfairly presenting his evidence because his research was "superficial" and "thesis-driven."[a] Professor Bellesiles has since resigned.

Presumably, it was fair for the writer of "Guns in America" to rely on Bellesiles before the questions about his research became widely known. Would it be fair to rely on him now, if you knew these questions had been raised? What if the writer discovered the questions only after her paper was virtually complete and the deadline was near? Should a first-year student be responsible for checking out the reputation of apparently reliable authorities whose work she uses? Should a fourth-year student in an honors seminar be responsible for checking the reputations of sources? Does this mean you should never rely on authorities?

[a] "Report of the Investigative Committee in the matter of Professor Michael Bellesiles," July 10, 2002, http://www.news.emory.edu/Releases/Final_Report.pdf.

Writing Process

REPORTING EVIDENCE

Reading and Research

Planning Your Hunt for Evidence

Research is like diamond mining: You have to know what you are looking for and where to look; then you must process lots of dross to find a few gems; and even then your best finds need polishing. In the same way, when you address a problem that requires more than casual research, you need a systematic plan to guide your search for evidence. If you have only a topic to guide you, you may have to read widely before you find a problem worth pursuing. But as soon as you find that problem and you generate one or more hypotheses for a tentative solution, you can plan your research systematically.

Once you select a tentative claim, focus your reading or other data collecting on the evidence you'll need to test and support it. You'll waste a lot of time if you collect information randomly. Instead, invest some time to imagine the best possible evidence and use it to plan your search.

1. *Decide what kind of evidence readers expect in support of your claim.* Your reasons must be relevant to your claim, and your evidence must be relevant to your reasons. But your evidence must also be the *kind* of evidence that readers expect in support of your particular *kind* of claim. You have to step back to think critically about what you should look for—not just the kind of evidence that will convince yourself that your claim is sound, but the kind that will convince your readers. For example, what evidence would convince your particular reader that extrasensory perception exists? Striking anecdotes? Objective data generated by controlled experiments? Testimony from someone they trust? Only their own personal experience of it? Imagine that evidence, and then use what you imagine both to guide your search and to test what you find.

2. *Weigh the cost of the search against the value of the evidence.* You want the evidence that best tests and supports your claim, but second-best evidence is better than none. Decide how long it will take to find the best evidence. Is there a risk that you will find none? If the best evidence may be too hard to find, limit your risk by gathering the most readily available evidence first. For example, if Elena had only a few weeks to prepare her argument supporting a Center for English Language Studies, she could not survey every college with a center. She would have to settle for a less reliable phone survey of a few she knew about. But she would then also have to acknowledge that her evidence is less than the best (more about that in Chapter 7).

3. *Decide on the most likely source of evidence.*
You have many options:

▶ **Libraries:** A college library will provide most of the data you need. The trick is knowing how to find them. Every library has a tour, and most librarians are eager to help. An hour or two invested in learning how to find resources in different fields will pay off in time saved later.

▶ **The Internet:** The Internet is an increasingly important source of information, but it is still like an undiscriminating library without librarians. Most of the Internet has no gatekeepers to screen information for quality: some is reliable, some not. So it is a case of "browser beware." At least be sure you know who stands behind the information in a site. You can trust some sites: the site of a print journal; a peer reviewed online journal (if the site doesn't say, ask your teacher); an e-text site at a university you've heard of; the Gutenberg project; the site of a scholarly or professional organization. Otherwise, use the Net for the following purposes, cautiously:

– *To get a quick overview:* You can use Google Scholar to get a quick sense of what's been published on your question. (Just don't trust it to be as complete as a good library's online catalogue.) Also, Wikipedia and other online references can give you an overview with additional references you can check. (But go to the primary sources; don't cite any wiki as your source.)

– *To access your library's collection:* Most libraries have online catalogues and offer electronic access to articles, abstracts, and databases. If yours doesn't, try to get access to the library of a state university or go to the Library of Congress at www.loc.gov.

– *To get public materials:* Most major newspapers and magazines maintain Web sites with information on recent articles, sometimes the articles themselves. You can purchase reprints of articles in the New York Times and other major newspapers.

– *To find information too recent to be found in libraries:* Many government reports are released first on the Web, then in print.

– *To supplement information you find in libraries:* Some journals conduct Net-based discussions among readers and authors. Others use the Web to archive data not included in printed texts.

- *To find information that libraries don't collect:* For example, a student interested in steel pan music found that many steel bands have their own Web pages.

▶ **People:** You may need support beyond the written word. When you use people as sources, plan carefully to avoid wasting not just your time, but theirs.
  - Prepare questions and bring them to the interview. Use them to avoid wasting time, but don't read them like a script.
  - Record all identifying information—including the exact spelling of your source's full name. Record the date and place of the interview.
  - Tape-record the interview if you can. If you can't, try to get the exact words.
  - If you transcribe from a tape recorder, delete the *umm's* and *you know's*, but don't change anything else.

▶ **Direct observation:** Many questions can be answered only through field studies or controlled experiments conducted in ways a discipline requires. In a writing class, you're unlikely to be assigned a problem that requires such evidence, but you might construct a problem that needs it: How do instructors in different departments mark their papers? Do some bars encourage binge drinking more than others?
  - Before you start observing, record the date and place of the observations and relevant circumstantial details. If the location is relevant, take a digital photo or sketch a map.
  - If you record quantitative data, create a blank data table or chart before you start; record data precisely, right then, not later from memory.
  - In your argument, use only the data that your *records* support, not what you recall after you realize you failed to record information you should have. Be sure to tell readers how you collected the data. And if you have data that call your claim into question, you are obliged to report them as well.

▶ **"I search":** In some classes, teachers expect students to gather most of their evidence from personal reflection: not *research* but *I search*. If your assignment calls for this kind of evidence, guard against the deceptions of memory: We are all prone to remember what we think ought to have happened rather than what did. And never treat this kind of evidence as an objective "outside" source.

4. *Sample the evidence.* Don't waste time looking for evidence that a source can't provide; sample sources first to determine their value. For a survey, test your questions in a trial run or focus group. For books or articles, skim a few introductions and abstracts to see whether they look promising. For direct observation, make a quick visit to the site to see what it offers.

5. *Take stock as the evidence mounts.* Some students turn off their judgment when they start gathering evidence, reading book after book, taking endless notes before they realize that most of what they have is irrelevant to any claim they

189

might make. So from time to time, pause to consider the value of what you have collected. Avoid the common mistake of assuming that you have done your job when you have found any evidence at all. Teachers more often complain that students offer too little evidence than too much.

Taking Research Notes

When you assemble an argument based on sources, your most important preparation is taking notes. You'll need bibliographic information so that you don't have to look up a source again to cite it properly. You'll need to copy quotations accurately to avoid errors that might damage your credibility and clearly distinguish quoted words from your own so that you don't inadvertently plagiarize. When you take notes, keep several things in mind:

Notes from Written Sources
- Record all bibliographic information:
  For a book, record the full title, author, and publication date, plus the name of the publisher and city. If you photocopy the title page, write down the year of publication from the back side of the title page. Include the library call number, because you may need your source again.
  For a journal article, record the author, full title, volume number, and page numbers. Record the call number of the journal.
  For an Internet source, record the URL (uniform resource locator) and any information you can find about the author of the text and the date it was posted and last changed. For a site that changes quickly, also record the date you accessed it. If you can, save a copy of any pages you cite onto your computer.
- Summarize and paraphrase when the information is important, but its particular form of expression is not.
- Quote the exact words when they are striking or complex. If a passage or data table is long, photocopy it.

In your notes, distinguish what you quote directly from what you summarize or paraphrase, and without fail distinguish what you paraphrase from your own thinking. (Use different colored ink or cards; on a computer, different fonts.) A week later, it is easy to think that what you took as notes are your own ideas in your own words, when in fact they belong to someone else.

- Record the context. Note whether the quote is a main point, a minor aside, a concession, etc. It is unfair to your source and reader to treat what a writer says in passing as something she would stand behind.

Notes from Interviews
- Record all identifying information—including the exact spelling of your source's name. Record the date and place of the interview.
- Tape-record the interview if you can. If you can't, try to get the exact words. If you transcribe from a tape recorder, edit out the *umms* and *you knows*, but don't change anything else to make it sound better.

> Prepare your questions and bring them to the interview. Don't read them like a script, but use them to avoid wasting the time of the person you are interviewing. Before you leave, glance over your questions to see if you have missed any important ones.

Notes from Observation

> Record the date and place of the observations and any relevant circumstantial detail before you start. If the location is relevant, take a photo or sketch a map.
> Record data precisely. If you record quantitative data, create a data table or chart before you start.

Working Collaboratively
Share Plans and Resources

Of all the jobs in assembling an argument, gathering evidence is one that your teacher may be happiest to see you share. If your teacher approves, work with others to formulate a plan for gathering evidence. As you all search for evidence, you are likely to find evidence helpful to one another.

Test Each Other's Drafts

Since evidence is what readers do not question at the time, your colleagues can help you anticipate what readers will accept. Once you have a draft, try this:

> Ask two colleagues to highlight the most and least reliable reports of evidence in your paper. If they disagree, ask them to explain.
> Ask other members of the group to evaluate how well your reports of evidence meet the four maxims of quality (pp. 178–179).

When someone questions a report of evidence as not close enough to a primary or secondary source, you must accept that judgment as appropriate for that reader. If that person is responding in good faith, there is no point debating whether he or she should have questions. If several colleagues have questions, assume your readers will too.

Inquiries

Reflections

1. How many removes from "the evidence itself" are the following?

   Fourteen notices of office hours posted in Blaine Hall were as follows: 3 hours: 1; 2 hours: 2; 1 hour: 9; 30 minutes: 2.

   Faculty in Blaine Hall keep inadequate office hours.

   The average number of office hours per week that faculty in Blaine Hall keep is about one.

2. Invent three or four plausible scenarios in which others will feel you are being rude to ask them to justify a report of evidence they have just offered. What makes your question impolite?

3. In the early history of science, an experimenter invited other scientists to witness an experiment so that they could testify to the accuracy of the data gathered. Would it seem reasonable today for a scientist to insist on watching data being collected before she accepted it as sound? Why not? How then do we today get "testimony" concerning the reliability of reports of research?

4. Should reproductions count as primary evidence? How about a videotape of an event? An audiotape of a speech? A photograph? Would you trust a tape or photo more or less if you knew the person who offered it were technologically naïve? What if that person were a technological whiz? Why should that matter? Would it help to have witnesses who could testify about the circumstances in which the tape or photo was produced?

5. Are there situations in our everyday lives when we expect each other to be as hard-nosed about evidence as juries and scientists should be? Are there situations when we should not be hard-nosed about seeing the evidence for ourselves? How do you distinguish the two kinds of situations?

6. Some people think that just as there is no disputing taste, it is pointless to argue about values. Others say that we can argue about values, but that we have to use a different kind of evidence. Consider an argument about disputed values, such as whether it is morally wrong to help someone with a terminal illness commit suicide. What would count as evidence supporting reasons for or against such a position? What sources would be more authoritative than others? How do they derive their authority? Is there in fact a difference in the kind of evidence we use in arguments about values? Is there a difference in how we use it?

Task

7. Return to the old papers that we asked you to work on. Highlight in a dark color reports of evidence that you think no reader would have questioned. Then highlight in a lighter color reports of evidence that some readers might have questioned. How "weighty" is the evidence in your argument? If you have highlighted more than two-thirds of your paper, it is probably too weighty. What would you add: more reasons, warrants, acknowledgments, and responses? If, you have highlighted less than one-fourth of your paper, it is not weighty enough. How easily could you get more evidence?

Projects

8. Analyze a magazine ad as an argument. (Select one that's half a page or larger.) Assume that the main claim is an unexpressed *Therefore you should buy this product.* What does the ad offer as reasons for buying the product? What does it offer as a report of the evidence? If it is a picture, how did the ad "spin" that report?

9. Look at the advertising in four or five magazines that appeal to people with different demographic profiles. For example, a teen magazine, a techie magazine, an intellectual magazine, a sports magazine, a woman's magazine, etc. How do they differ in the ways advertisers try to get their particular readers to buy products? Do the ads in the same publication use similar kinds of reasons and evidence? Do ads for similar products use similar kinds of evidence even for different readers?

10. A book that uses stories as evidence is *I, Rigoberta Menchú*, a searing account of atrocities allegedly committed by the Guatemalan army. Written by Rigoberta Menchú Tum, the human rights activist and winner of the Nobel Peace Prize, the book became highly controversial required reading on hundreds of campuses because it sparked a debate over the "higher value" of falsehood over truth. The controversy began when prestigious schools like Stanford required the book in general education courses, in some cases replacing writers like Shakespeare. Then in 1998, David Stoll, a specialist in Mayan history, showed that Menchú had fabricated some of her most sensational stories:

   ▶ She described herself as a child working in near-slave conditions, unable to speak Spanish until adulthood, but she had actually attended Catholic boarding schools.
   ▶ She describes acts of violence as though she witnessed them; in fact, she was away at school most of the time.
   ▶ She says she watched the Guatemalan military burn her brother alive, but she wasn't there when it happened and the military probably did not do it.
   ▶ She says another brother starved to death, but she had no such brother.
   ▶ She says that her family lands were confiscated by wealthy landowners; in fact, they were lost to her father's in-laws.

Menchú at first denied that she had committed "purposeful inaccuracies," adding, "I didn't find anything in these reports that changes the fact that my people are dead. And that is my truth" (*New York Times*, January 21, 1999). Later, she admitted some inaccuracies, but has yet to recant her story.

Her critics were severe: one nominated her for the "Nobel Prize for Lying." Most of her supporters echoed her defense that she told a "larger truth." Some attacked Stoll for valuing mere fact over a "higher" truth. Others suggested that facts don't even matter: "Menchú made it clear from the outset that [she] had a political purpose, . . . to expose the atrocities committed by the Guatemalan army. This was not the fruit of some judicial investigation striving to be fair" (*Guardian*, December 16, 1998). But even before Stoll had exposed her, her admirers had argued that an oppressed person has an authenticity that lets her speak for all her people; that what matters is not truth, but personal, ethical, and economic motives that break the "silence of the oppressed."

Suppose that Menchú's critics are right: What she says she saw, she did not. In fact, some of the things she said happened never happened at all. But also suppose that in a sense she is right: things like those she described did happen to people like her and her family. Should she have described her work as a work of fiction? Would it have had the same impact? Would it have been effective to add incidents that happened to others without pretending they happened to her? List reasons for accepting or rejecting her "larger truth" defense. Which weigh more with you?

11. Given what you learned about lying in the readings, do you think Rigoberta Menchú lied? If so, was it an acceptable lie? List your reasons for saying so. What general principle (warrant) would you offer to explain why you make that judgment?

12. The Greek philosopher Aristotle argued that fiction describes events more truthfully than a history. A history, he said, has to stick to the facts, whereas fiction can describe things more plausibly—as they should have occurred, not just as they happened to. Can you think of a way to defend Menchú's book based on Aristotle's idea of truthfulness? Sketch the major steps in such an argument. Would you accept such a defense?

Focus on Writing

1

Context. It is an old belief that "factual" or "scientific" truth (the kind we establish by arguments based on evidence) is not the only truth. But in recent years, some postmodern theorists have argued that it should not be the only kind of truth we accept in fields such as law or history. It is an act of political oppression, they say, to require just the facts.

Scenario. In 1999, six Nobel Peace Prize winners gathered for a conference on the future of human rights and social justice. The event was such a success that several colleges in your state are jointly sponsoring a similar conference at the state capitol. Among the speakers will be Rigoberta Menchú, but local political groups are trying to get her removed from the conference because of the controversy over her book (see Inquiry 10). As the student representative from your school on the organizing committee, you have been appointed to the subcommittee assigned to respond to those who oppose Menchú's participation.

Task 1. Your subcommittee has asked you to write a brief summary of the controversy. (You can find a list of articles, including abstracts, in the newspaper databases available in most libraries.) Be sure not to represent the controversy as a simple for-or-against debate.

Task 2. The subcommittee has decided to respond to what it sees as an unfairly one-sided presentation of the issue by the opponents. Your assignment is to draft an essay describing the controversy, which will be published in the student newspapers of all participating colleges. Above all, the committee wants you to represent the different positions fairly, including the support for the claims.

Task 3. The subcommittee wants to make the entire Menchú episode a learning experience for those who attend the conference. It will include in the conference program a collection of essays on the issue of factual evidence versus larger truths. Your assignment is to write an essay taking a stand on the issue. Since the subcommittee wants these essays to be models of fair argument, be sure that your argument acknowledges the strengths of the other positions.

RESEARCH PROJECT

Scenario. Your teacher has made it clear that he will focus on the quality of the evidence in your research paper.

Task. For each report of evidence, summarize why you think it is (1) accurate, (2) precise, (3) representative, and (4) reliable.

SAMPLE ESSAY

Task 1. Return to your marked-up pages evaluating the evidence in "Guns in America" (pp. 172–174). Select the four most important items of evidence. Evaluate each in terms of the four maxims of quality (pp. 178–179).

Task 2. Compare the evidence offered in support of the first major reason, "guns were not popular in America until after the Civil War," with the evidence offered in support of the second, "the reasons people began to buy guns had more to do with money than with patriotism." Which evidence is stronger? Why? Should the writer have downplayed the reason with the weaker evidence? Why or why not? What other options might the writer have for acknowledging this disparity in the evidence?

Task 3. Here again is the introduction to "Guns in America." Identify its elements by picking out the common ground, destabilizing condition, cost or consequences, and solution or promise of solution.

Guns in America

If you listen to the NRA, owning a gun is the ultimate symbol of American freedom and democracy. So most people believe them when they say that gun ownership has been a part of America since the Revolution and that it is a violation of basic American beliefs when the government tries to take away the people's guns. But this is just propaganda. The claim that for our forefathers owning guns was a patriotic duty is erroneous. History shows that guns were not popular in America until after the Civil War, and that the reasons people began to buy guns had more to do with money than with patriotism. People should not be duped into thinking that supporting gun control laws is unpatriotic or un-American.

Now read this revised introduction with the new title, "The Minuteman Myth: The True Story of Guns in America." Identify its elements by picking out the common ground, destabilizing condition, cost or consequences, and solution or promise of solution.

The Minuteman Myth: The True Story of Guns in America

1   When the English colonists sailed to America, they brought to this continent many ideas that made America what it is today: religious freedom, dedication to liberty, and the belief that people should govern themselves. Did they also bring over the American love of guns? One of the first laws passed in Jamestown, Vir-
5   ginia, required every man to own a gun for defending the settlement. By the Revolution, most of the colonies had laws requiring citizens to own guns (Davidson, 1998), and after the Revolution, since the federal government had no army, local governments were required to have a militia made up of gun-owning citizens (*Economist*, 1999). Also, the Bill of Rights included the idea that the safety
10 of the country depended on people owning guns: "A well-regulated militia being necessary to the security of a free State, the right of the people to keep and bear Arms shall not be infringed."

Today the government passes laws, not to require citizens to own guns, but to restrict them from owning guns the government thinks are dangerous, such
15 as assault rifles. Supporters of gun control say we need laws because of all the crazies and criminals who get their hands on guns: Lee Harvey Oswald, John Hinkley, the Columbine killers, drug pushers, and many others. Opponents of gun control like the NRA try to offset this by talking about gun-owning American heroes from history, such as the Minutemen of the Revolution and Daniel
20 Boone (NRA, 1999). They say that even if bad people get guns, good people need them too for the same reason that the colonists and the other historical heroes needed them—namely, to defend themselves and their families. Besides, owning a gun is presented as the ultimate symbol of American freedom and democracy. So most people believe them when they say that gun ownership has
25 been a part of America since the Revolution and that it is a violation of basic American beliefs when the government tries to take away the people's guns.

But this is just propaganda. People should not be duped into thinking that supporting gun control laws is unpatriotic or un-American. The gun control opponents' claim about Americans always owning guns because we believed
30 that owning guns was a patriotic duty is erroneous. History shows that guns were not popular in America until after the Civil War, and that the reasons people began to buy guns had more to do with money than with patriotism.

1. Which introduction makes the writer seem more knowledgeable? More even-handed?

2. How does the inclusion of evidence affect your response to the "Minuteman" introduction?

3. How does the new title better prepare readers for the rest of the essay?

4. How does the expanded common ground better prepare readers?

5. How do the new title and expanded common ground change your perception of the writer's ethos?

In a Nutshell

About Your Argument . . .

No skill is more useful than distinguishing reasons, evidence, and reports of evidence from your readers' point of view. You need more and better evidence when you want readers to change important beliefs, to do something costly or difficult, or to accept a solution that may create new problems. Your biggest challenge will be to find enough evidence to satisfy your readers, because we all tend to be satisfied with less evidence than our readers want.

Once you think you have enough evidence, evaluate it: Is it accurate, precise, representative, and authoritative? Use each kind of evidence only in the ways it is most reliable:

◗ Memories are always unreliable, because our minds shape them into a storylike structure influenced by what we believe or want to be true. Always try to find corroborating evidence.

◗ Anecdotes are even less reliable, because we impose on them an even more shapely story structure. Anecdotes can be good illustrations, but they are never the best evidence.

◗ Reports from authorities may be evidence only of what they believe. Distinguish what they offer as reasons from the evidence they report.

◗ Photographs and recordings are never objective. Even when they haven't been doctored, they depict just a slice of what they seem to represent.

◗ Quantitative data can be represented in different ways, and each gives it a "spin."

Remember that you ask readers to accept reports of evidence in lieu of the evidence itself, so they must be confident that you report it accurately. Along with warrants, evidence is one of the two anchors that readers must agree on before you can even make an argument.

. . . and About Writing It

When you report what a written source says, ask whether your readers expect the exact words or a paraphrase. In general, those in the humanities are more likely to expect the exact words; those in other fields will accept close paraphrases.

When you copy notes into your argument, be aware of how easy it is to forget that what you copy is not your own words, but those of your sources. You can avoid that by scrupulously distinguishing in your notes your own words and those from a source. If you take notes on a computer, use a distinctive font; if you write them out, use colored ink or cards—whatever will help you distinguish your own words from those of your sources. You can afford to be wrong; you cannot afford to be accused of plagiarism.

Your Reader's Role in Your Argument: Acknowledgments and Responses

ou can build the core of an argument by answering just three of argument's five questions:

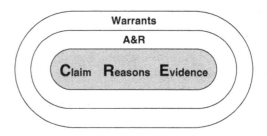

What are you **claiming?**

What are your **reasons** on which you base your claim?

What is your **evidence** on which you base your reasons?

Occasionally, that alone will convince a reader. But just the core of an argument is rarely enough when your readers are thoughtful and critical or you address complex and contested issues. In that case, if you fail to bring your readers' views into your argument, you can seem ignorant of them or, worse, arrogantly indifferent; or worst of all, you can seem to be a dogmatic, narrow thinker who sees things only one way and expects everyone else to do the same. None of that adds to your credibility.

You will seem more cooperative, more open to discussion and debate when you add to the core of your argument another layer, one that acknowledges and responds to the differences between you and your readers. When you do that, you show readers that you arrived at your claim not by jumping to a conclusion but by carefully considering all relevant factors, including their beliefs. In short, you demonstrate that you are a reliable critical thinker. But that kind of critical thinking also requires an act of critical imagination. To acknowledge readers' views, you must first be able to imagine the questions critical readers are likely to ask:

▶ But what about these alternatives, reservations, and objections?

▶ How would you respond to someone who said. . . ?

Imagining and answering the questions of others can be hard if you don't like to acknowledge that you might be less than entirely right. Faced with such questions, some of us go into a combative stance, counterattacking any objections. But when you can imagine and then amiably answer such questions, not just once but throughout your argument, you do more than improve your thinking and deepen and broaden your argument. You also project the ethos of a judicious, careful thinker, someone willing to scrutinize your own ideas as rigorously as you do those of others. Over time, that attitude creates an ethos that becomes your reputation.

The Importance of Other Viewpoints

When we say, ***There are two sides to every question,*** we underestimate how complex most issues are—the sides are more often three or four, and they differ not just over claims but what counts as reasons, evidence, warrants, even the existence of a problem at all. How many sides are there on the question of whether Congress should apologize for slavery? How many ways do different people judge the quality of American education?

In conversation, those who offer endless alternatives and objections seem willfully obstructive—and sometimes they are. But in arguments about serious issues, you serve others badly if, to avoid seeming obstructive, you offer only mindless agreement or, worse, silent dissent. All parties to an argument have a duty to air alternatives and raise objections in a spirit not of contention but collaboration, to create the soundest and most thoughtful argument possible.

But even those who speak up to question others' arguments often struggle to think as critically about their own. Most of us find it hard to engage alternatives and objections for four reasons. Two have to do with the limits of our knowledge and critical imagination:

▶ We are ignorant of others' contrary views because we overlook them or never seek them out.

▶ We can't imagine that there could be other views to consider.

But two have to do with our fear of losing:

> ▶ Even when we know or can imagine other views, we feel defensive about acknowledging that we might be wrong, or at least not entirely right.

> ▶ Some of us fear that we undermine our own argument when we acknowledge any uncertainty in it or any strength in the arguments of others.

But in most cases, the truth is the opposite: We should fear losing less than we fear seeming ignorant or arrogant. Thoughtful readers who take a cooperative stance tend to distrust those who lack the knowledge—or confidence—to acknowledge that others might think differently.

Regardless of age, education, intelligence, and even experience, we all have to resist the most common flaw in human thinking: We hold tight to our own beliefs, seeking only evidence that supports them, ignoring contradictory evidence, or twisting what we do find until it supports our position. We don't do it knowingly. It's just what we are all are inclined to do.

You can compensate for that bias if you actively seek out views that contradict your own and study them until you understand why someone could believe them. If you are making an argument about an issue without well-known contradictory views, imagine a skeptical but helpful friend questioning two aspects of your argument, its intrinsic quality and its failure to consider all factors:

> ▶ If she challenges the intrinsic soundness of your argument, she will object that your claims, reasons, evidence, or warrants are wrong or unjustified, that you have too little evidence or too few reasons.

> ▶ If she acknowledges that your argument is not intrinsically flawed but thinks it incomplete, she will offer alternatives that complicate or qualify it: other claims, reasons, evidence, or warrants or other interpretations of your evidence and warrants.

To help you imagine that friend raising objections or alternatives, we offer a checklist of questions in the next sections.

Questions About Your Problem and Its Solution

At the most general level, readers may question how you frame your problem and solution, even whether there is a problem at all. If Sue, a student who believes that students are customers and should be treated as such, raised the issue of a lack of convenient office hours with her dean, the dean might ask some blunt questions (most questioners would be more tactful):

1. *What makes you think there is a problem?* How many students in fact can't see their instructors when they have to?

2. *Why have you posed the problem that way?* *Could the problem be not office hours but the willingness of students to make an effort to see teachers?*

3. *Exactly what kind of solution are you asking me to accept?* *How should we treat you like customers? What exactly should we do?*

4. *Have you considered limits on your claim?* *Are you saying that every instructor in every department should treat you as a client? Most? Some?*

5. *Why do you think your solution is better than the alternatives?* *What's wrong with the student as client model?*

Most important, though, are two objections that every solution to a pragmatic problem must overcome:

6. *How do you know your solution won't cost more to implement than the problem costs?* *To treat you like customers, we'll have to retrain everyone, which will take resources from current programs.*

7. *How do you know your solution won't make things worse by creating a bigger problem?* *If we treat you like customers, we will erode the teacher-student relationship that a sound education depends on.*

Questions About Your Support

After your readers question your problem and solution, they are likely to question its support. They will probably start by questioning whether you have enough evidence. Imagine the dean responding to Sue's charges:

1. *Your evidence is not sufficient.* *You gathered office hours from a single floor in one building. That can't be more than twenty offices. I need more evidence to take your claims seriously.*

Next are challenges to the quality of her (reports of) evidence:

2. *Your evidence is not accurate.* *I looked at those offices, and you counted three faculty who are on leave.*

3. *Your evidence is not precise.* *You said faculty average "about" an office hour a week. What's the exact figure?*

4. *Your evidence is not current.* *Are those hours from this semester or the last one?*

5. *Your evidence is not representative.* *You looked at offices from the same department. What about other departments? Are they all about the same or do most faculty keep more with only a few keeping much less?*

6. *Your evidence is not authoritative.* *How do you know the posted hours are the only times teachers see students? Have you asked the teachers?*

Finally, there are possible objections concerning warrants (see Chapter 9):

7. *Your warrant is not true.* *You say someone who pays money for something is a customer. Why should I believe that?*

8. *Your warrant is too sweeping.* *You say that anyone who pays money for something is a customer, but that's too broad. Employers pay employees.*

9. *Your warrant does not apply.* *What students pay for is nothing like what a customer buys. An education is not a stove, so paying tuition is not like buying appliances.*

10. *Your warrant is inappropriate.* *The idea of applying the principle of buying and selling in higher education is simply unacceptable.*

We have phrased these responses bluntly, not to make Sue's dean seem antagonistic, but to encourage you to be honest with yourself. Face-to-face, most people would raise their objections more amiably: ***I wonder whether these office hours represent all office hours. Do you suppose that there might be cases where people pay money for something but aren't customers?*** But readers are likely to ask their questions and make their objections very directly in the privacy of their minds. In whatever spirit they ask them, though, they are meeting a responsibility we must all accept: the duty to engage actively to find the best solution to a problem, and that always means asking questions that most of us don't much like answering.

Questions About Your Consistency

Readers will look for one other weakness in your argument—that you contradict yourself or have failed to consider obvious counterexamples.

> Senator, how can you condemn me for accepting contributions from the National Rifle Association when you accept contributions from the Ban Handguns Alliance?
>
> How can you say that children's moral growth is harmed by sexually explicit movies when you also say that it is not harmed by violence on TV?

Readers will think you contradict yourself when you seem to apply a warrant selectively, using it when it suits your purposes and ignoring it when it does not. For example, if you claim that children are harmed by sex in the movies, readers will infer that the claim is based on a general principle of reasoning something like this:

> Whenever children experience vivid representations of glorified behavior, they are more likely to approve of and imitate it.

But that warrant does not distinguish between sex in the movies and violence on TV. If we believe one is harmful, then we must believe that the other is as well, unless you can show that a more narrow warrant applies—perhaps that older children are more influenced by representations of sex than of violence because their awakening sexuality makes them respond to sexual images more intensely. But, of course, you would have to state that narrow warrant explicitly and, since it is not obvious, support it.

If a critic can show that a claim in one case contradicts a claim in another or that you have ignored an obvious counterexample, you will seem to be guilty of intellectual inconsistency—a charge profoundly damaging to your ethos, especially when the inconsistency seems self-interested:

▶ In a practical argument about what to do, you will seem unfair if you expect others to follow a principle that you ignore.

▶ In a conceptual argument about what to believe, you will seem *intellectually dishonest* (or at least careless) if you apply a principle selectively to get an answer you want.

So in planning your argument, ask whether your readers can apply the principle behind the case at hand to all similar cases. If not, you have to formulate a more narrow principle that distinguishes your case from the others.

Example
How to Use a Response to Restate Your Argument

The excerpt below is from an argument claiming that undergraduate majors should be abolished because students do not benefit from specialized studies and need more general education. The writer acknowledges and responds to possible objections while simultaneously restating both the gist of his main claim and its support. Here, in outline, are the steps he follows:

1. He imagines that those who raise the objection already accept part of his claim, *Students need more general education*, thus reinforcing it.
2. He states the objection as an alternative solution, but one that partially agrees with his proposed action: *Majors should be, not abolished, but reduced.*
3. In response to that alternative, he indirectly restates the remaining part of his claim: *Specialization does not benefit students.*
4. Then, to support that response/claim, he restates his three reasons why specialization is not a benefit.
5. Finally, he acknowledges a qualification to his claim, Some students might benefit from specialization, but then restates his claim again. Other students should not be forced to specialize.

Here's the passage:

Another objection I anticipate [to my argument that majors should be abolished] is from people who would agree that the basic liberal arts learning students get today is inadequate, and who would buy into the idea of an expanded general education program restatement of part of main claim . . . [but who would still argue for] a minimally sized major. Students could have the best of both worlds: the advantages of specialism along with the advantages of generalism. alternative solution

Certainly a curriculum like this would be preferable to what we have now; more, it would be a great improvement. benefits of alternative solution But there is still a difficulty. It is still assumed that having a specialization, regardless of its size, is truly an advantage for students. And that is precisely what I am throwing into question. response / restatement of part of main claim I have suggested that there is no more rigor in forcing the mind toward the greater depth of a major than there is in forcing it toward the lesser but significant depths of several different fields. restatement of reason 1 supporting response / main claim And I have suggested that the way in which a major fine-tunes the mind may end up as a limitation more than an asset—inclining a student to see things from the narrows of one perspective alone. restatement of reason 2 Add to this the fact that many students' interests aren't strongly enough defined to make a commitment to a major, and the fact that many others don't need one for the vocational preparation they desire since they will be getting that in graduate school. restatement of reason 3 These are all telling reasons for questioning the practice of requiring students to have a major, and together they form a powerful and sensible rationale.

All of this isn't to say that no student should have a major. acknowledgment of limitation But it is to say that we should not require it of all students. restatement of main claim Those in fields like engineering and architecture, those who have an obvious and strong inclinations in other fields, should take majors . . . [But] for other students, there is no good reason for forcing them to specialize.

> *Source:* Reprinted by permission of Transaction Publishers, "Do College Students Need a Major?" by William Casement, *Academic Questions,*
> Summer 1998. Copyright © 1998 by Transaction; all rights reserved.

◆◆◆

Responding with Subordinate Arguments

When you explicitly acknowledge views different from your own, you signal readers that you welcome and respect their views. But you show readers you are even more thoughtful and respectful when you respond to their views not with bald restatements of your own but with additional reasons and evidence that show why you respond as you do.

For example, here is part of an argument claiming that a university should invest more resources in course evaluations beyond simple in-class surveys:

> . . . Faculty can continue to improve if they get as much information as we can give them about our responses to their teaching.
>
> Some students may ask "If faculty aren't interested enough to improve their teaching on their own, why would they respond to our criticisms?" acknowledgment of objection We think that view is cynical and that most teachers do care about our education. partial rebuttal of objection But even if they have a point, partial concession to objection the new information we propose to gather will include more than just student gripes. Once the information is part of the record, teachers will not ignore it. response / claim This happens in many professions. When doctors, airlines, or car manufacturers learn about problems with their products or services, they try to improve. reason For example, when data about the quality of the university hospital were made public, hospital officials tried to do better because they were concerned about loss of business. Now the hospital advertises its standings in surveys on TV. report of evidence When the shortcomings of a profession become public, they take action to improve. warrant

This writer imagines and acknowledges a possible objection from colleagues, conceding they might be partly right. But she then responds to that objection with reasons, evidence, and a warrant to show why it would not apply in this case.

The writer might anticipate, however, that her readers will in turn question her response. For example, she might imagine that her most demanding readers would reject the comparison between teachers and airlines:

> But teachers are not like airlines; they have tenure and can't be fired, and colleges are not out to make money, so your analogy doesn't hold.

If she imagines that objection, she must respond to it with yet another argument:

Of course, tenured professors differ from doctors and airlines because they don't need the approval of customers to stay in business. acknowledgment of limitation But most professors are responsible professionals who understand that colleges have to attract students. response / claim Even state universities depend on tuition, especially higher out-of-state tuition. reason Last year, out-of-state students saved us from a deficit that threatened faculty raises. report of evidence Students have many choices and can shop around. reason When they research schools, they consider the quality of teaching in deciding where to go. warrant

We can imagine someone criticizing that response too, but at some point enough is enough. Life and papers are too short to answer every objection. But you don't have to answer every one to show that you have been thoughtful enough to consider some.

What if you can't answer a question? Our recommendation may seem naïve, but it is realistic: If you believe your argument has flaws but none so serious as to defeat it, concede them. Then assert that the balance of your argument compensates for its imperfections:

> We must admit that not every teacher will take these evaluations seriously. But even so, if we can get a substantial number to . . .

Conceding what cannot be denied is how thoughtful arguers respond to legitimate uncertainty.

Nothing reveals more clearly the kind of mind you have, indeed the kind of **person** you are, than your ability to imagine and then respond calmly to alternatives, objections, and reservations. You cannot be a true critical thinker without that kind of critical imagination.

To be sure, few of us consistently do it well. But when you exercise your own critical imagination even occasionally, not only will your argument gain credibility, so will you, particularly when you acknowledge objections and reservations that are not simply wrong, but not well thought out—and then respond by presenting readers your more thoughtful account.

Writing Process

ACKNOWLEDGMENT AND RESPONSES
Reading and Research
Use Others' Acknowledgments to Understand Context

When you read an argument in a new field, you may not see what is at stake in every part of it. But you can infer some of that from the common ground, especially if the writer reviews research leading up to her question. You can find more context in the objections and alternatives that she acknowledges and responds to. She defines the limits of debate in her field in what she acknowledges or dismisses and defines what she thinks is relevant to her position in what she concedes or responds to at length.

Collect Alternatives as You Read

When it is hard to imagine alternatives, start by making a list of pros and cons and add to it as you prepare your argument, especially cons. But if you have to do research to gather evidence, you'll find lots of alternatives you might acknowledge in your sources.

▶ Take notes on positions your sources respond to. If you disagree with the source, those objections may support your own position and suggest further reading. If you agree with it, you can acknowledge and respond to some of those alternatives and objections (after you look at them for yourself, of course).

▶ Don't record only claims that support your position; also record those that contradict it, along with the reasons and evidence offered in support. If you decide to acknowledge and respond to it, you will need a full argument to respond well.

▶ When you collect evidence to support your reasons, keep track of what might limit or contradict them. You may decide not to acknowledge those reservations, but they might help you imagine others.

Preparing and Planning
Add Acknowledgments After You Draft

When you sketch an outline or create a storyboard, don't focus on the alternatives or objections you intend to acknowledge, but on your own core argument. When you draft, focus on imagining all the possible forms of support for your position, not every possible objection. That invites writer's block. Then *after* you draft your core argument, work through it point by point, imagining questions readers might ask.

You might even include objections that you can imagine but that readers might not. They don't want to follow you down every blind alley, but they benefit when you share alternatives you pursued but ultimately rejected. They will also respect your candor. We know this advice seems disingenuous—being candid about failure as a rhetorical strategy to ensure success. Nevertheless, readers judge your ethos by how open you are to alternatives, and they will know that only if you show them which ones you considered.

Locate Acknowledgments and Responses Where Readers Are Likely to Think of Them

Once you identify alternatives to acknowledge, think of a response, outline it, and decide where to put it. Acknowledge alternatives early if they are well established and relate to your whole argument:

▶ If your whole argument directly counters another, acknowledge that other argument in the common ground of your introduction and again early in the body of your argument.

▶ If your whole argument relates to another but you want to drop the other one quickly, acknowledge it only in the common ground:

Many teachers believe that the most important skill they can teach is the ability to solve problems. acknowledgment / common ground But as important as that skill is, it is less important than the ability to discover, then articulate a problem clearly. As Einstein said, "A problem well put is half solved." response / destabilizing condition

▶ If your whole argument relates to another that will occur to readers once they see your problem and solution, acknowledge it right after your introduction, as background:

. . . The most valuable skill for students is the ability to discover and then articulate problems clearly. claim

The issue of problem formulation, however, has received little attention from teachers. Their traditional focus has been on teaching students to analyze problems in order to . . . acknowledgment

▶ Respond to incidental alternatives as they become relevant:

There is a Web site that rates colleges based on students' reports of their experience. That may not be a reliable source, acknowledgment but it is one that students check. response / claim For example, . . .

Building a Whole Argument Around Alternatives

If you know that readers will think of more than one alternative to your solution, you can organize your argument by sequentially eliminating those alternatives, leaving your solution as the last one standing.

How then should we respond to global warming? It has been suggested that we just ignore it. [explanation] But that won't work because . . .

It has also been suggested that we exploit it by adapting our lives and agriculture to warmer conditions. [explanation] But that won't work either because . . .

At the other extreme, some argue that we should end all atmosphere emissions immediately. [explanation] But that idea is impractical because . . .

None of these responses addresses the problem in a responsible way. The only reasonable way to deal with global warming is . . .

Drafting

The Vocabulary of Acknowledgment and Response

Writers fail to acknowledge and respond to alternatives usually for three reasons. First, they don't know and cannot imagine any. Second, they think that by acknowledging them, they weaken their argument. But a third reason is more mundane and more easily solved: They simply don't know the expressions experienced writers use to introduce alternatives and responses.

We offer here that lexicon of words and phrases. To be sure (there is one of them right there), your first efforts may feel clumsy (*may* is common in acknowledgments), acknowledgment but (a response usually begins with *but* or *however*) as you use them, they will come to seem more natural. response / claim

Acknowledging

When you respond to an anticipated question or objection, give it the weight that readers do. You can mention and dismiss it, or address it at length. We order these expressions roughly in that order, from most dismissive to most respectful.

1. You can downplay an objection or alternative by summarizing it briefly in a short phrase introduced with ***despite, regardless of,*** or ***notwithstanding:***

   Despite Congress' claims that it wants to cut taxes, acknowledgment the public believes that . . . response

   Regardless of problems in Hong Kong, acknowledgment Southeast Asia remains a strong . . . response

   Notwithstanding declining crime rates, acknowledgment there is still a need for vigorous enforcement of . . . response

   You can use ***although,*** and ***while,*** and ***even though*** in the same way:

   Although Congress claims it wants to cut taxes, acknowledgment the public believes that . . . response

   While there are problems in Hong Kong, acknowledgment Southeast Asia remains a strong . . . response

   Even though crime has declined, acknowledgment there is still a need for vigorous enforcement of . . . response

2. You can indirectly signal an objection or alternative with seem or appear, or with a qualifying adverb, such as ***plausibly, justifiably, reasonably, accurately, understandably, surprisingly, foolishly,*** or even ***certainly.***

   In his letters, Lincoln expresses what ***seems*** to be depression. acknowledgment But those who observed him . . . response

   Smith's data appear to ***support*** these claims. acknowledgment However, on closer examination . . . response

   This proposal ***may*** have some merit, acknowledgment but we . . . response

   Liberals have made a ***plausible*** case that the arts ought to be supported by taxes. acknowledgment But they ignore the moral objections of . . . response

3. You can acknowledge alternatives by attributing them to unnamed sources or to no source at all. This kind of acknowledgment gives a little weight to the objection. In these examples, brackets and slashes indicate choices:

   It is easy to [***think / imagine / say / claim / argue***] that taxes should . . .

   There is [***another / alternative / possible / standard***] [***explanation / line of argument / account / possibility***] . . .

   Some evidence [***might / may / can / could / would / does***] [***suggest / indicate / point to / lead some to think***] that we should . . .

4. You can acknowledge an alternative by attributing it to a more or less specific source. This construction gives more weight to the position you acknowledge:

   There are some [***many / few***] who [***might / may / could / would***] [***say / think / argue / claim / charge / object***] that Cuba is not . . .

208

[*Most / Many / Some / A few*] knowledgeable college administrators [*say / think / argue / claim / charge / object*] that researchers . . .

One advocate of collaboration, Ken Bruffee, [*says / thinks / argues / claims / charges / objects*] that students . . .

5. You can acknowledge an alternative in your own voice or with a passive verb or concessive adverb such as ***admittedly, granted, to be sure,*** and so on. You concede the alternative has some validity, but by changing the words, you can qualify how much validity you acknowledge.

I [*understand / know / realize / appreciate*] that liberals believe in . . .

It is [*true / possible / likely / certain*] that no good evidence proves that coffee causes cancer . . .

It [*must / should / can*] be [*admitted / acknowledged / noted / conceded*] that no good evidence proves that coffee causes cancer . . .

[*Granted / admittedly / true / to be sure / certainly / of course*], Adams stated . . .

We [*could / can / might / may / would*] [*say / argue / claim / think*] that spending on the arts supports pornographic . . .

We have to [*consider / raise*] the [*question / possibility / probability*] that further study [*could / might / will*] show crime has not . . .

We cannot [*overlook/ ignore / dismiss / reject*] the fact that Cuba was . . .

What X [*says / states / writes / claims / asserts / argues / suggests / shows*] may [*be true / have merit / make sense / be a good point*]: Perhaps Lincoln did suffer . . .

Responding

You signal a response with *but, however,* or *on the other hand.* Remember that after you state your response, readers may expect reasons and evidence supporting it, because they will take that response to be a claim needing its own support. You can respond in ways that range from tactfully indirect to blunt:

1. You can state that you don't entirely understand:

    But I do not quite understand . . . / I find it difficult to see how . . . / It is not clear to me that . . .

2. You can state that there are unsettled issues:

    But there are other issues . . . / There remains the problem of . . .

3. You can respond more bluntly by claiming the acknowledged position is irrelevant or unreliable:

    But as insightful as that point may be, it [*ignores / is irrelevant to / does not bear on / was formulated for other situations than*] the issue at hand.

    But the evidence is [*unreliable / shaky / thin / not the best available*].

    But the argument is [*untenable / wrong / weak / confused / simplistic*].

    But that view [*overlooks / ignores / misses*] key factors . . .

    But that position is based on [*unreliable / faulty / weak / confused*] [*reasoning / thinking / evidence*].

Addressing Logical Error

When you differ with a reader because you are reasonably sure the reader has not thought through the issues as carefully as you, you need a few phrases to introduce your point of view civilly. Here are a few:

> That evidence is certainly important, but we have to look at all the evidence available.
>
> That explains some of the problem, but it is so complex that no single explanation is enough.
>
> That principle does hold in many cases, but we must also consider exceptions.

You get the idea: Acknowledge the value of a particular view, but suggest that there is more to consider.

Working Collaboratively
Ask Tough Questions

It is hard to imagine alternatives on your own, but you can help one another do that by asking tough questions. For each argument you review, find enough weak points and strong alternatives to make the argument seem questionable. Of course, your real aim is to identify just the two or three key alternatives or objections that each writer should acknowledge. Try this in a spirit of goodwill (someone should record what follows):

▶ Ask the writer of the argument to raise the most severe objections.

▶ Have each person in turn add objections.

▶ When the group runs out of ideas, rank the objections from most to least serious and alternatives from most to least viable.

From these two ranked lists, each writer can decide what to acknowledge.

If the group has trouble getting into the spirit of this game, run down the following list of comments and questions. Remember to smile when you offer them.

Problem

1. This is not a problem. Everyone knows that . . .
2. The real problem is not this, but the fact that . . .

Solution

1. I can think of three exceptions to your claim: First . . . , second . . . , and third, . . .
2. I can think of two better solutions/answers: First . . . , and second. . . .
3. This solution will cost too much. It will cost . . .
4. This solution will create several new and bigger problems: First, it will . . .

Reasons

1. I can think of two reasons not to accept your claim: First . . .
2. I can think of three exceptions to your reason: First . . .
3. Why haven't you included this other reason?

Evidence

1. There is better evidence. Why didn't you include it?
2. That evidence is from an untrustworthy source. Why do you believe it?
3. That evidence is not entirely representative. Why should we trust it?
4. That evidence is vague/imprecise. What makes it good enough for the purpose?
5. I doubt your evidence is accurate. How do you know it is?

Warrants

1. You seem to assume that when X is true we can infer Y, but I think that when X is true we must infer Z.
2. That reason/claim does not seem to be a good example of the reason/claim side of the warrant.
3. I can think of three exceptions to that warrant: First . . .

Inquiries

Reflections

1. In most academic and professional situations, we make arguments stronger by acknowledging their limitations. But different standards apply in some professional situations—a lawyer defending a client in court, for example. Can you think of other circumstances in which you should not acknowledge any weakness in your argument? How do those circumstances differ from those that you normally find in academic and professional arguments?

2. Suppose that just before you turn in a paper for a class, you discover an objection to your argument that substantially weakens it. You cannot think how to counter the objection. In fact, you now think your argument is wrong. What should you do? This question is both ethical and practical. Are you ethically obligated to reveal this objection? Why or why not? Practically speaking, would it be wise to tell your teacher that you recognized the objection, but it was too late to do anything about it? Or should you just keep quiet and hope your teacher doesn't notice? Which response do you think will project the best ethos?

Tasks

3. In Chapter 7 we asked you to highlight the evidence in some old papers. Return to those marked-up copies and question the evidence in as many ways as seem appropriate. Do you see weaknesses in your argument now that you did not see then? How would you acknowledge and respond to them?

4. Look at the editorial and op-ed pages of your local newspaper. Identify all the acknowledgments and responses. Which pieces use them best? Do these acknowledgments make the arguments persuasive? Do the same with some TV talk shows. Do the participants acknowledge and respond to other points of view as often? If not, why not?

Projects

5. Spend an hour or so with the editorial and op-ed page of your local newspaper. Identify the parts of argument in each, and then formulate reasonable questions that raise objections or alternatives for each. Finally, sketch how you would answer those questions if you were the author.

6. Return to the old papers you used for Task 3. Add more acknowledgments and responses than you really need, then eliminate those that don't make your argument more presuasive. How far short of this optimum did your original paper fall?

Research Project

Scenario. Your teacher has asked the class to review each other's drafts before presenting them.

Task. Find one or two people who will review your draft not to make editorial suggestions but to share their responses: *Where are they confused? Where do they want more evidence? More reliable evidence? Where do they have objections or want to add important qualifications?* If they are confused about your logic, add warrants. If they want more or better evidence, add it. If you can't, acknowledge the problem and respond as best you can. If they raise objections or qualifications, acknowledge and respond to them. Using those responses, produce a final draft. Be sure, as a last step, to revise your prose in accord with the procedures in Writing Processes 12 and 13.

In a Nutshell

About Your Argument . . .

You communicate the quality of your critical thinking by how candidly you acknowledge and respond to views different from your own. Admittedly, nothing is harder than finding those views, so you need a list of questions to ask yourself on behalf of your readers. Anticipate questions and objections about two aspects of your argument:

- Readers question the quality of your claims, reasons, evidence, or warrants. They assert that you are just wrong.
- They find nothing wrong with your argument per se, but think of alternative claims, reasons, and evidence, even ways to frame the issue.

Readers may also question how you frame the problem:

1. Why do you think your problem is a serious one?
2. Why did you pose the problem this way rather than that?
3. Exactly what claim are you asking me to accept?
4. Have you considered these exceptions to your claim?
5. Why do you think your solution is better than an alternative one?
6. How do you know your solution won't cost more than the problem?
7. How do you know your solution won't create a new problems?

Readers also question evidence: They question whether it is sufficient, current, accurate, precise, representative, and authoritative. They might also question whether your warrants are true, too broad, inapplicable to your reasons and claims, or inappropriate for your readers.

. . . And About Writing It

When you acknowledge and respond to an imagined objection or question, you can follow a well-established formula:

- Begin with a phrase such as *to be sure, admittedly, some have claimed,* etc. Then state the acknowledgment.
- Follow with *but, however, on the other hand,* etc. Then state your response.

When you respond to these kinds of objections and alternatives, you have an opportunity to thicken your argument by supporting your response with reasons, evidence, warrants, and yet more acknowledgments and responses to your response.

The Logic of Your Argument: Warranting Claims and Reasons

Y ou create your most effective arguments when you answer your readers' questions before they are asked. Readers first want to know what you think: what you are claiming, why you believe it, and the evidence on which you base your reasoning. You enter into a more critical dialogue with readers when you imagine them asking more questions about what *they* think, questions that reflect their disagreements, objections, and different points of view. Indeed, by asking those questions *on your readers' behalf*, you draw them into your argument, joining their voices with yours. You may find such questions and objections vexing, but you can also use them as opportunities not just to connect with your readers but to test your own thinking and create a more compelling argument.

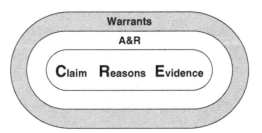

Warrants

A&R

Claim Reasons Evidence

There is, however, one kind of critical question that is especially difficult to ask and answer because it questions not the substance of your argument but the quality of your thinking. The problem is that we are usually so unaware of our own processes of reasoning that we are surprised when someone questions them. But if readers cannot tell how we reach a conclusion even after they understand our reasons, evidence, and responses to their views, then we have failed to establish the most important relationship our readers need from us: a sense of shared logic and assumptions.

For example, recall Sue's argument about tuition and services:

Sue: We think the university should stop treating us only as students and start treating us like customers. . . . We pay a lot of money for our education, but we don't get near the attention customers do.

Raj agreed with Sue on a lot of points, but he asked one question indicating that on that matter he couldn't follow Sue's logic, her line of reasoning.

Raj: . . . I don't see how tuition makes us customers. What's the connection?

That kind of question goes to the heart of Sue's thinking, but she was able to answer it:

Sue: Well, when you pay for a service, you buy it, right? And when you buy something you're a customer. We pay tuition for our education, so that means we're customers and should be treated like one.

Sue answered Raj's question by offering him an explicit statement of the general logical principle that governs her line of reasoning. With that general statement, she explains how her specific reason (*we pay tuition*) connects to her specific claim (*we are therefore customers*). We call that kind of explicit statement of a general logical principle by many terms: a *premise,* an *assumption,* a *general principle.* Those who study arguments have a technical term for it. They call it a *warrant.*

Now imagine that Sue were writing her argument and that Raj had not been there to ask that question. Sue probably would have thought that everyone could see the connection between tuition and customers. But if her readers were like Raj, then at least one of them would have thought, "Wait a minute. I don't see the connection. I don't follow that thinking." And when that happens, an argument fails.

Your arguments can succeed only if your readers can follow you from evidence to a reason to a claim. To do that, they must see—or hear from you—the logical principles that make those connections.

The Reasoning Behind Reasons

Here is an example of public argument that actually failed because the public could not see the logical connection between a reason and a claim. When diet sodas first became popular in the 1960s, some scientists warned that the sweetener in them, cyclamate, increased the risk of cancer:

> We believe that people who drink diet sodas sweetened with cyclamate increase their risk of cancer claim because laboratory rats fed large doses of cyclamate show an increased rate of cancer. reason That relationship is based on these data. . . . evidence

Most diet soda drinkers did not believe that claim. No one disputed the fact that rats got more cancer when they consumed cyclamates, but most people did not see any logical connection between the rats' health and their own. What does one have to do with the other?

The scientists responded by stating a general principle to connect their reason (*rats getting cancer*) with their claim (*diet soda drinkers more likely to get cancer*), a principle that most people in their field accepted (boldfaced):

> Based on many studies, we know this: **When large doses of a substance cause cancer in laboratory rats, we can conclude that small doses of that substance will cause some cancer in humans.**

Today, almost everyone accepts this principle: when scientists show us that something is bad for animals, we believe it is also bad for us. At that time, however, few people believed that principle and the scientists did not explain it well enough, so the public thought the argument made no sense, rejected its claim, and drank more diet soda than ever.

Those scientists were not being *illogical*: their argument made good sense to experts who already believed the general principle. Their problem was that, like most of us, they did not think anyone else would question their reasoning. They assumed that everyone would think as they did, so that the public would share even their unspoken assumptions. It is a problem that we all have to guard against.

You cannot assume that you and your readers think alike. You always have to consider the possibility that readers might look at your reasons and think, as did Raj and those who heard about the dangers of cyclamates, "Your reason may be factually true, but I don't see how it supports your claim. How do the two connect?"

If you can imagine that your readers might ask that question, you have to give them a general principle stated as a warrant that makes the connection explicit. And if, as in the case of the cyclamate warnings, they do not understand or believe the general principle that the warrant states, then you also have to make an argument to explain the principle or show them that your warrant is true.

This chapter will show you how warrants work, how to know when you need one, and how to construct one your readers will accept—not because you need one in every argument, but because your arguments will fail when you do need a warrant but you don't know how one works.

What Warrants Look Like

Warrants come in all shapes and sizes, but they always have or imply two parts. One part names a general circumstance:

> Winter roads are slippery. part 1: a general condition

The second part states a general conclusion that we can infer from that circumstance:

> You need four-wheel drive. part 2: a general consequence

Put together, the two parts explicitly state a general principle of reasoning that a certain general condition leads to a certain general consequence:

> When winter roads are slippery, general condition you need four-wheel drive. general consequence

We can also state that warrant in ways that only imply the connection between the parts:

> Winter roads condition require a four-wheel drive. consequence

We can also reverse the order

> You need a four-wheel drive consequence on winter roads. condition

There is no one right way to state a warrant, but for our purposes we will state them in the same way every time, not because that's how you should too, but because it is the clearest way for us to explain how they work. We will follow this formula:

> Whenever X, condition Y. consequence

Sometimes, we might choose other introductory words: *if, when, if and only if.* But *whenever* is useful because it encourages you to consider how widely you can apply a warrant. *Whenever* implies that a warrant is true under all circumstances, something that is rarely the case. So the *whenever* form will help you think of limits or qualifications to your warrants.

Warrants are most familiar to us as proverbs:

> When the cat's away, the mice will play.

Schematically, we can represent that warrant like this:

The authority is absent—[so we infer] those under that authority will slack off.

If you believe that *general* principle, then you can link a *specific* instance of authority being absent to a *specific* instance of those under that authority slacking off. Schematically, the link looks like this:

217

	WARRANT	
General Circumstance	*predictably allows*	General Conclusion
When the cat's away		the mice will play.
✔		✔
Coach can't supervise practice ₍reason₎	*therefore*	the team will probably goof off. ₍claim₎
Specific Circumstance	*lets us infer*	Specific Conclusion
	CORE OF ARGUMENT	

The check marks indicate that we think the specific circumstance qualifies as a valid instance of the general circumstance in the warrant, and the specific conclusion qualifies as a valid instance of the warrant's general conclusion. (Later, we'll see cases where they don't.) In most cases, readers connect claims and reasons on their own, but when you think they may not, warrants show them how.

How Warrants Work

Suppose Leah is telling Tariq about the new place she rented:

> Leah: I'm so lucky. I found a place to rent on Carter's Mountain that feels like it's miles away from civilization. I've always wanted to live deep in the woods.
>
> Tariq: Good for you, but you'll have to trade in your car for something with four-wheel drive. claim In winter the roads are too steep and slippery for a car. reason
>
> Leah: That makes sense. Thanks for the good advice.

Any time we make or accept a claim based on a reason, we connect that claim and reason by a general principle of reasoning. In this case, the principle is based on our experience of the world: *when you live on a bad road, you need a vehicle that can handle it,* a principle that Leah believes. Since she also believes that Tariq's reason is true, she thinks his claim follows from his reason. As she says, the connection "makes sense."

But sometimes, we don't see the connection, and the claim doesn't make sense. In that case, we ask a question: *Why does that specific reason lead to that specific claim?*

> Tariq: If you're going to live alone in the woods, reason you should also buy a gun. claim
>
> Leah: I don't like guns. Why does living alone mean I should buy one?

This time Leah does not see how living in the woods is a reason for owning a gun. To show her, Tariq has to offer a general principle that explains it:

Tariq: When you live alone in an isolated place, you need protection. warrant

Before Leah accepts Tariq's claim that she should own gun, she has to accept two more claims: that the general principle is true and that it applies to her circumstances.

Here's how that works in detail. (*Warning:* What follows may sound like Logic 101.) First Leah must believe that the warrant is true: That is, if you live alone in an isolated place, then it is true that you need protection. But it is not enough that Leah believe the principle. She must also believe that it *applies* to Tariq's specific reason and specific claim:

> ▶ The specific reason (*you live all alone in the woods*) must be for her a valid instance of the general condition (*you live alone in an isolated place*). Since she lives alone and the woods is an isolated place, that connection between the general condition and the specific instance seems evident enough.
> ▶ The specific claim (*you should buy a gun*) must be for her a valid instance of the general condition (*you need protection*). Since a gun is a form of protection, that connection between the general and specific also seems plausible.

If Leah accepts the principle and believes it applies to her situation, then Tariq has shown her why his claim follows from his reason. We can diagram that outcome like this:

WARRANT		
General Circumstance	*predictably allows*	General Conclusion
When someone lives in an isolated place		that person needs protection.
✔		✔
You will live alone in the woods_{claim}	*therefore*	you should buy a gun. _{reason}
Specific Circumstance	*lets us infer*	Specific Conclusion
CORE OF ARGUMENT		

But what if Leah thinks that a gun is not an *acceptable* form of protection? Then she would object:

Leah: Maybe I need some form of protection. But for me a gun is not good protection. A gun is more likely to harm its owner than anyone else. Besides, I could never shoot a gun.

In other words, for Leah Tariq's claim is not a valid instance of the general conclusion because even though a gun may be a form of protection for someone else, it is not suitable protection for her. We can diagram that outcome like this:

WARRANT		
General Circumstance	*predictably allows*	General Conclusion
When someone lives in an isolated place		that person needs protection.
✔		✔
You will live alone in the woods._{claim}	*therefore*	you should buy a gun._{reason}
Specific Circumstance	*lets us infer*	Specific Conclusion
CORE OF ARGUMENT		

Now Tariq has two choices. He can offer Leah an alternative that she *will* see as a valid instance of protection:

Tariq: If you won't get a gun, at least have an alarm installed.

Or he can defend his principle by making an argument that a gun is the best form of protection, even if Leah doesn't like them. And in doing so, he'll have to make two more arguments: one against Leah's counterprinciple that guns are dangerous for their owners and another against her claim that she could never use one. Now we begin to see why it is so hard to reach agreement on vitally contested issues.

Knowing When to Use Warrants in a Written Argument

We use warrants less often than other elements of an argument because readers usually accept the connection between a claim and its reason without even thinking that they need a principle to connect them. And we would bore or even insult readers if we explained the obvious. So to use warrants successfully, we have to identify those few occasions when readers need them.

That's seldom a problem in conversation, because others usually tell us when they need a warrant: They object, ask questions (as Leah did), frown, or in some way show that they don't see the connection between a reason and a claim. But when we write, we have to anticipate those occasions on our own.

The problem is that you cannot know when readers will need a warrant just by reading your draft, because nothing seems more obvious to you than your own way of thinking. Sometimes you can find out when you need a warrant from surrogate readers (such as a writing group), who will read your argument and tell you when connections between reasons and claims are a problem. But usually, you'll have to *imagine* readers asking a question—an exercise more challenging for warrants than for any other element of an argument.

THE MOST COMMON USES FOR WARRANTS

You can anticipate that readers will need warrants when your experience and knowledge are very different from theirs. One common case is when specialists write for nonspecialist readers (as in the cyclamate example). All specialized fields rely on principles of reasoning not widely shared outside the field—that's part of what makes a field hard for outsiders to understand. So a specialized argument is likely to fail with ordinary readers unless its writer uses warrants to explain those principles.

For example, here is an argument that may puzzle you:

The words *pork* and *beef* refer to meat that we eat at table, reason so we can assume that they were borrowed from French into the English language after 1066. claim The words *swine* and *cow* refer to the animals that pork and beef come from, reason so we can assume they are probably native English words. claim

Linguists see that argument as perfectly logical because they know the principle of reasoning behind it, which they could, if asked, state like this:

When an English word names a kind of meat that has been prepared for eating, condition that word was probably borrowed from the French after 1066. consequence When a word names the animal the meat comes from, condition that word is probably a native English word. consequence

That principle is familiar to anyone who knows the history of the English language: After the Norman conquest in 1066, English servants used French names for food they prepared for their French masters, while field hands kept using their native words. Specialists are unlikely to realize that ordinary readers would need them to explain that principle in a warrant: It is so deeply embedded in their thinking that for them it goes without saying—unless they are forced to say it because of a reader's question or the useful habit of imagining such questions on their reader's behalf.

Another occasion that commonly calls for warrants is when you write for readers with different backgrounds, values, or cultures. Most principles of reasoning are based on experiences so much a part of our way of life that they feel not learned but natural. So when we write for people who do not share our experiences, what seems natural to us may seem foreign, alien, inexplicable, even abhorrent to them.

For example, in our culture most of us immediately see the connection between this reason and claim:

The editor of the school newspaper believes that the university has ignored racial tensions on campus, reason so he has the right to express that concern in an editorial. claim

We take for granted the principle that connects the reason to the claim, a principle that we could express in a warrant like this:

When an editor of a newspaper has an opinion, he or she has the right to print it.

In other parts of the world, however, that argument would be considered ridiculous and the warrant dangerous.

221

You may have to state and defend many warrants for readers who don't share your experience, values, or culture. But don't defend your principles by arguing that theirs are wrong—you will not convince them to change deeply held values and beliefs. Instead, state your principle, explain how it works, and acknowledge that others might see things differently. You probably won't convince anyone to change their way of thinking, but you can convince them to respect your specific principles and to consider the conclusions you draw from them.

Warrants as Expressions of Cultural Codes

Warrants help us understand why people of different cultures struggle to make good arguments together. We all reason alike, but different cultures start from different assumptions. Those assumptions are not just static beliefs, but dynamic principles that tell us how to reason about specific facts. We often express them in proverbs that reveal much about how we think and what we value. For example, suppose we say of a child *She really stands out from the crowd because she thinks for herself and says what she thinks.* We might then conclude, *When she grows up, she'll get her way,* because we have a cultural assumption reflected in a familiar proverb:

The squeaky wheel gets the grease.

But the Japanese have a proverb that warns people not to stand out:

The nail that sticks up gets hammered down.

In other words, when someone stands out from the crowd, that person will be—rightly—forced to conform. So we agree on the same fact, a child standing out from the rest, but our different communities justify different conclusions from it because they reason from different assumptions. Such differences cause many cultural conflicts. Expressing them clearly as warrants is difficult, but it lets us, if not always resolve, at least understand the source of our differences.

TWO SPECIAL USES FOR WARRANTS

We normally state warrants when we think readers will not readily connect our reason and our claim, because they do not know or do not accept our principle of reasoning. But we use warrants in two other ways, both of which are easier to manage because we do not have to know or imagine what our readers might be thinking. We also use warrants to emphasize a key point or to build consensus for a controversial one.

Using Warrants for Emphasis

Readers generally dislike explanations for obvious connections. But you can state an obvious principle for emphasis *after* presenting the reason and evidence it covers. Recall, for example the argument that tries to prove that a college is committed to undergraduate education:

We have tried to make our commitment to undergraduate education second to none claim by asking our best researchers to teach first-year students. reason For example, Professor Kinahan, a recent Nobel Prize winner in physics, is now teaching physics 101. evidence To be sure, not every researcher teaches well, acknowledgment but recent teaching evaluations show that teachers such as Kinahan are highly respected by our students. response Of the last twenty recipients of the college teaching award, sixteen have been full professors with distinguished records of research. further evidence

The writer assumes that her readers can recognize the principle that connects that claim and reason:

When an educational institution commits its best faculty to an activity, it shows that it gives that activity its highest priority. warrant

If the writer imagined that her readers might not know or accept that principle, she would state it as a warrant, usually before presenting the claim and reason. To use that principle for emphasis, she would state the warrant in abbreviated form at the end of this mini-argument:

We have tried to make our commitment to undergraduate education second to none claim by. . . . Of the last twenty recipients of the college teaching award, sixteen have been full professors with distinguished records of research. further evidence **Given this record, it's clear that we back up our commitment to teaching with our resources.** warrant

Warrants used for emphasis are more common in public, business, or informal contexts than in academic ones, where some readers consider them too obvious.

Using Warrants to Build Consensus

When you ask readers to accept a difficult or unwelcome claim, they sometimes feel that you are being pushy because you are encouraging—forcing—them to consider evidence and reasons that lead to a result they do not like. You can both soften the blow and increase the chance that readers will follow your argument, if you start out with warrants that remind readers that they do in fact believe in your principles, even if they don't like where they lead.

Perhaps the most famous example of this strategy is that part of the Declaration of Independence that so many of us have memorized:

We hold these truths to be self-evident . . . when a long train of abuses and usurpations, pursuing invariably the same Object evinces a design to reduce them under absolute Despotism, general condition side of the warrant it is their right, it is their duty, to throw off such Government, and to provide new Guards for their future security. general consequence side of the warrant Such has been the patient sufferance of these Colonies [i.e., a long train of abuses in this specific case]; specific condition / reason and such is now the necessity which constrains them to alter their former Systems of government [i.e., the duty to throw off such government in this specific case]. specific consequence / claim

Here's how the same strategy would work in the example about teaching:

As Dean, I am proud of the education we offer our students. But I am also keenly aware of how much students and their families sacrifice to afford that education. And I cannot deny that, in order to keep costs down, we have increased the size of the student body, which has led to more large lecture classes and fewer small classes with more students in them. problem But we all know that the most valuable resource of any school is its faculty. And while smaller classes are desirable, it is the quality of teaching that is most responsible for a quality learning experience. **There is no better way for any institution to ensure the quality of its undergraduate education than to see that students learn from its very best minds.** warrant We continue to make our commitment to undergraduate education second to none claim by asking our best researchers to teach first-year students. reason For example, Professor Kinahan. . . .

How to Test a Warrant

Since you will use at most a few warrants in any argument, you have time to test each one to make sure that you need it and correctly state it. To decide whether a warrant is necessary, ask yourself this question:

Will readers question whether that reason clearly and unequivocally supports your claim?

Most cases fall somewhere between, leaving you to decide case-by-case which principles to state and which not. To do that, you have to anticipate when readers either cannot imagine any principle for connecting your reason and claim or might imagine one different from yours. Consider this little argument:

Our school needs more writing tutors claim because we are unsure our education is worth our rising tuition costs. reason 1 Tuition has gone up faster than inflation. reason 2 In 1997, inflation was 2.4%, but tuition rose 5.1%; in 1998, inflation was 2.1%, but tuition rose 6.7%. evidence

The dean might respond:

True, tuition has gone up faster than inflation. You may even be right that we need more writing tutors. But why do you think we need them *because* you are not sure you are getting your money's worth? Why does your reason—you're not sure you're getting your money's worth—*have anything to do with* your claim—that we need more tutors? I don't see the connection.

That is a hard question. The dean is not saying that she rejects either the reason or the claim, but that she cannot imagine any principle that would make the claim follow from the reason.

WARRANT		
General Circumstance	*predictably allows*	General Conclusion
?????????????????? **?**		?????????????????. **?**
Not sure getting money's worth_{reason}	*therefore*	need writing tutors._{claim}
Specific Circumstance	*lets us infer*	Specific Conclusion
	CORE OF ARGUMENT	

If you cannot think of a principle connecting a reason to your main claim, your readers probably cannot either. In that case, you need to state one explicitly. Here is a way to do that.

1. Replace the specific terms in your reason and claim with general ones:

   We are not sure we are getting our **money's worth** from our **tuition,** so we need more writing tutors.

money's worth —> value equal to our cost   writing tutors —> services

   We are not sure we are getting a **value equal to our cost,** so we are entitled to more **services.**

2. Rephrase the general version with a *whenever:*

   Whenever we are uncertain that we are getting value equal to our cost, we are entitled to more services.

You can know whether your readers will accept a warrant only after you state it for yourself. But that one seems dubious: Why should uncertainty about value for cost entitle a person to demand more? If you offer a warrant, you must therefore ask yourself three more questions:

▶ Will readers think your warrant is true?

▶ Will they think that it applies to the reason and claim?

▶ Will they think it is appropriate to their community?

1. Is Your Warrant True?

A warrant fails when readers reject it as false. Here is an argument about gangsta rap:

The lyrics of gangsta rap are so vulgar toward women reason that the FCC should ban them from the radio. claim Whenever language is degrading to any group of people, we should not allow it to circulate over public airwaves. warrant

We can rephrase that warrant into our standard form, *Whenever X, Y:*

WARRANT		
General Circumstance	*predictably allows*	General Conclusion
Whenever language is degrading, to any group of people,		we should not allow it to circulate over public airwaves.
✔		✔
Gangsta rap lyrics are vulgar toward women reason	*therefore*	the FCC sould ban them from radio. claim
Specific Circumstance	*lets us infer*	Specific Conclusion
CORE OF ARGUMENT		

If we accept the warrant and reason, then the claim follows. But a reader might believe that the principle is not true because another warrant trumps it:

> I can't agree. Whenever we express our ideas, the Constitution bars the government from interfering with that right. competing warrant According to the Supreme Court, the First Amendment protects sexually explicit movies that are degrading to women. So even though you may not like the degrading language in gangsta rap, it has the same constitutional protection as those movies or any other free expression of ideas.

If the counterargument is relevant, it contradicts the original warrant and replaces it with another one.

Schematically, the counterargument looks like this:

WARRANT		
General Circumstance	*predictably allows*	General Conclusion
Whenever people express their ideas,		the Constitution bars the government from interfering with them.
✔		✔
Rap lyrics express ideas *reason*	*therefore*	the FCC cannot ban them from radio. *claim*
Specific Circumstance	*lets us infer*	Specific Conclusion
CORE OF ARGUMENT		

Now the question of banning such lyrics turns into a question of which warrant is more important in our system of beliefs. To settle that, the person making that argument would have to make another argument treating those dueling warrants as claims needing their own reasons, evidence, and yet more warrants. At this point, we can understand why some arguments never get settled: The participants cannot agree on first principles.

Overreaching Warrants

We might accept some warrants as true in general but not when people try to use them to justify extreme cases. What about the following argument?

> I helped you wash your car two years ago, reason so you should help me paint my house. claim After all, one good turn deserves another. warrant

If your friend did help you wash your car, you might feel you owed him something, but not as much as he asks:

> You did help me wash my car, and in general one good turn deserves another, but only when the magnitude of the returned favor is proportional to the original one.

In other words, the warrant is generally true, but it has limits. And once you think of one limit, you can think of more:

> . . . and so long as I am capable of doing it, and so long as the favor is requested reasonably close in time to the first good turn, and so long as . . .

When we state a warrant like *One good turn deserves another,* we rarely, if ever, add the obvious limitations: *Of course you can do only what you are able to; of course you expect that a returned favor won't be asked for thirty years later.* All that goes without saying, so we don't say it. What's tricky about using warrants is not just that we usually take them for granted; even when we do state them, we take for granted their default limitations, as well.

2. Will Readers Think Your Warrant Applies to the Reason and Claim?

This next problem with warrants is the most difficult to grasp. Consider this argument:

> I helped you wash your car, reason so you should help me cheat on my test. claim
> After all, one good turn deserves another. warrant

Represented graphically, it looks like this:

WARRANT		
General Circumstance	*predictably allows*	General Conclusion
When someone does you a good turn,		you should do one in return.
✔		?
I helped you wash your car reason	*therefore*	you should help me cheat. claim
Specific Circumstance	*lets us infer*	Specific Conclusion
CORE OF ARGUMENT		

The warrant is true, and helping you wash your car is a valid instance of doing a good turn. So if your friend did help you wash your car, how could you refuse to help him cheat? You might say,

> True, one good turn deserves another, but in this case, helping you cheat on a test does not count as a legitimate example of "a good turn." In fact, it would be a bad turn. So your reason is not relevant to your claim.

The warrant does not apply to the claim, because the claim is not a valid instance of the conclusion part of the warrant.

3. Will Readers Think Your Warrant Is Appropriate to Their Community?

Warrants can fail in one more way, having less to do with truth or reasoning, than with their appropriateness. Some warrants are shared by most of us:

> When people tell many lies, we eventually distrust what they say.

Other warrants reflect the beliefs of different historical times. A change between these two warrants marked a change from one period in European history to another:

> When evidence contradicts traditional beliefs and authorities, ignore the evidence.
> When evidence contradicts traditional authority, question the authority.

The second characterizes what some call the modern skeptical mind.

There are also beliefs shared by most of us in the United States, but not by all societies:

> When an action is protected by a Constitution, government may not interfere with it.

As communities become smaller, they share increasingly specialized warrants. For example, first-year law students often have a hard time "thinking like a lawyer." Like most of us, they start law school holding beliefs based on common sense. We can state one of those common sense beliefs as a warrant:

> When someone does another an injustice, courts should correct it.

Seems reasonable. But part of the painful education of law students is learning that common sense warrants do not always apply in the law, because other warrants may trump them. For example,

> When people fail to meet legal obligations, even inadvertently, they must suffer the consequences.

More specifically,

> When old people forget to pay real estate taxes, others can buy their house for back taxes and evict them.

That warrant justifies common sense injustice, but if buyers obey the law, they can argue that the house is theirs. Against their most decent instincts, law students have to learn that justice is not what most of us think it should be, but what courts say the rule of law must be.

When you write as one member of a community to others, you have to be sure not only that your warrant is true and applicable, but that it also seems appropriate to that community. On the other hand, when you write as a member of a community to outsiders, you not only have to state the warrants that are unique to your community but also to explain how and why they apply as they do.

But when you are a newcomer trying to sound like a member, you have the hardest task of all. You want to be able to write the way those you read do, but professionals writing to professionals leave only glimpses of their assumptions, enough for other experts, but not for newcomers. None of us can avoid moments in our education when we feel baffled because those at home in a community we are just entering do not feel obligated to justify their reasoning to newcomers. We learn those unstated ways of reasoning only from experience.

Distinguishing Reasons and Warrants

At first glance a warrant seems a lot like a reason, and so it's easy to confuse them. Consider this argument:

> Though Franklin Roosevelt would not appear in public in his wheelchair or be photographed in it, his federal monument should depict him in his chair. claim He overcame a great disability to become a great leader, statement of support 1 and a great

leader should be remembered as much for the challenges he overcame as for his achievements. statement of support 2

Those two supporting statements both feel like reasons. In fact, in ordinary conversation, that is what we might call them both:

The Federal monument dedicated to Franklin Roosevelt should depict him in his wheelchair. claim The first reason is that he overcame a great disability to become a great leader. statement of support 1 The second reason is that any great leader should be remembered as much for the challenges he overcame as for his achievements. statement of support 2

But those two statements support the claim in such different ways that to understand how arguments work we have to use different terms to name them.

▶ The first statement refers specifically to Roosevelt and to Roosevelt alone. It is a *specific* reason to support the *specific* claim that a monument should depict Roosevelt in his wheelchair.

▶ The second statement has nothing specifically to do with Roosevelt or his monument. It is a *general* principle stating that we should remember *any* great leader for overcoming a challenge *of any kind*. If we believe that Roosevelt was a great leader who overcame great obstacles, then he is covered by that generalization we call a warrant.

Warrants Versus Reasons

In ordinary talk, it does no harm to call a warrant a reason. Warrants are, after all, reasons for connecting a reason and a claim. One of our students called warrants extended reasons. And in fact, that captures a bit of what a warrant does: it "extends" over a specific reason and claim, holding them together. Other students have asked us, *Doesn't a warrant just say the same thing as the reason and claim, but in a different way?* Not quite. A warrant covers a conceptual territory similar to the reason and claim, but a much broader one that includes an indefinite number of other reasons and claims, involving not only leaders and challenges we know of, but countless others we don't, even those still to be born.

Review: A Test Case

Warrants are easier to understand in practice than in an abstract analysis, so here is one more example that can serve as a review. (If you think you understand warrants, skip to p. 232.)

Phil: A lot of people condemn gangsta rap, but I think it should be accepted as legitimate artistic expression claim because it reflects the experience of many who listen to it. reason

Mary: It may reflect the experience of many who listen to it. But why does that count as a reason for accepting it as legitimate artistic expression? I don't get it.

Mary can't see how Phil's reason is relevant to his claim, so she asks him to explain his reasoning. He might offer this warrant:

> When an artistic work reflects the experiences of those who enjoy it, it should not be censored or condemned.

Now that Mary knows the warrant, she might ask three more questions.

1. Is your warrant true?

Mary might reject Phil's warrant entirely: *That's just not so.* Or she can acknowledge that the warrant is sometimes true, but deny that it applies to all artistic expression, no matter how vile:

> You say that when an artistic work reflects the experiences of those who enjoy it, it should not be censored or condemned. But would you say that about lyrics that described sexually abusing and killing children? Some people might enjoy that because the lyrics reflect their evil behavior, but would you really allow music like that?

Or she can offer a warrant that contradicts Phil's original one:

> Any music should be censored and condemned if it degrades human dignity. When art degrades human dignity, it should be kept out of public circulation. counterwarrant That is more important than complete freedom of expression.

Phil has three options: (1) He can limit the scope of his original warrant to make it more acceptable; (2) he can find an entirely new warrant; or (3) he can make an argument to convince Mary that his original warrant is true.

2. Is your specific reason a valid instance of the first part of your warrant?

Will a reader think that the specific circumstance counts as a good example of the general circumstance side of the warrant? That is, does the warrant "cover" the reason?

WARRANT		
General Circumstance	*predictably allows*	General Conclusion
When a work of artistic expression reflects the experience of those who enjoy it,		it should not be condemned or censored.
?		
Gangsta rap reflects the real experience of those who enjoy it*reason*		
Specific Circumstance	*lets us infer*	Specific Conclusion
	CORE OF ARGUMENT	

Mary might accept Phil's warrant as true—we should not ban artistic expression that reflects the experiences of those who enjoy it, even when it degrades others. But she might still think that gangsta rap *does not qualify* as an example of "artistic expression," and therefore Phil's warrant does not cover his reason.

If so, Phil has two options. He can make an argument to convince Mary that gangsta rap is a form of artistic expression. Or, if Phil decides he cannot make that argument to Mary's satisfaction, he could revise his warrant to accommodate his reason:

WARRANT		
General Circumstance	*predictably allows*	General Conclusion
When a work of artistic expression reflects the experience of those who enjoy it,		it should not be condemned or censored.
?		
Gangsta rap reflects the real experience of those who enjoy it*reason*		
Specific Circumstance	*lets us infer*	Specific Conclusion
CORE OF ARGUMENT		

Now the warrant fits the reason (but only if we believe gangsta rap is a popular form of expression). But is this warrant still true for Mary? She might defend serious artistic expression from censorship but not what she considers to be merely popular drivel.

3. Is your specific claim a valid instance of the second part of your warrant?

Assume that Mary accepts Phil's warrant and reason. She still might reject his argument if she thinks his claim does not match the conclusion side of his warrant:

WARRANT		
General Circumstance	*predictably allows*	General Conclusion
When a **popular** form of expression reflects the experience of those who enjoy it,		it should not be condemned or censored.
?		**?**
Gangsta rap reflects the real experience of those who enjoy it*reason*	*therefore*	it should be accepted as legitimate artistic expression.*claim*
Specific Circumstance	*lets us infer*	Specific Conclusion
CORE OF ARGUMENT		

She might argue that the claim *accepting lyrics as legitimate artistic expression* is not a valid instance of *not censoring or condemning* them because the warrant requires only that we *tolerate* such music, not *embrace* it as in Phil's claim.

If so, Phil has three options: (1) He can change his warrant to make it stronger: *popular expression should be accepted as art;* (2) he can weaken his claim: *gangsta rap should be tolerated;* (3) he can make an argument to convince Mary that not to condemn offensive art is to accept it as legitimate.

Information Overload?

If you are reacting as have many students using this book, you may be feeling overwhelmed with detail. We've given you a lot to think about and, what's harder, to put into practice. So don't be discouraged if you are feeling like the student who e-mailed us this question:

> Why do I feel less in control of making arguments as I read more about them? I feel like I'm writing worse, not better.

What we told him may encourage you: Several years ago some researchers tested new medical students to learn how well they could read X-rays for lung cancer. They found something odd. New med students quickly learned to do it pretty well, but as they gained more experience, they got worse. Then they got better at it again. The researchers concluded that at first, medical students saw exactly what they were told to see. But as they learned more about lungs, chests, and everything else that casts an X-ray shadow, they got confused: The more they learned, the less able they were to sort it out. But once they did learn to sort it out, they could see what was relevant and got better at reading X-rays again.

That's probably what's making you feel less in control of making arguments. You have more to think about than you did a few weeks ago. But it's not just that: you are probably demanding more of yourself, because you see more clearly what you must do. So as paradoxical as it may seem, your temporary confusion is a sign of progress. Or as the saying goes, if you're not confused, you haven't been paying attention.

Warranting Evidence

Readers expect evidence to connect to reasons in the same way that they expect reasons to connect to claims. And for the most part, you warrant that connection in the same way:

> People condemn gangsta rap but I think it should be accepted as legitimate artistic expression. claim because it reflects the experience of many who listen to it. reason Every teen-ager I know has at some time felt anger and rage against authorities. report of evidence When a lot of people share an emotion, then whatever expresses that emotion reflects their experience. warrant

What gets tricky is warranting a body of evidence consisting of numerical data, quotations, pictures, and drawings as relevant to some reason. For example,

> As Hamlet stands behind his stepfather Claudius while he is at prayer, he demonstrates a cool and rational mind. claim He impulsively wants to kill Claudius on the spot, but he pauses to reflect. If he kills Claudius while praying, he sends his soul to heaven. But Hamlet wants him damned to hell forever. So he coolly decides to kill him later: reason
>
> Now might I do it [kill him] pat, now he is praying:
> And now I'll do't; and so he goes to heaven;
> And so am I reveng'd....[Hamlet pauses to think]
> [But this] villain kills my father; and for that,
> I, his sole son, do this same villain send to heaven[?]
> Why, this is hire and salary, not revenge. report of evidence

Someone might question the relevance of that report of evidence to the reason:

> I don't see how those words show that Hamlet coolly decides to kill his father later.

If so, we'd have to describe the quotation in words that make its evidence match the evidence side of the warrant:

> Here, Hamlet carefully considers the consequences of killing Claudius step-by-step. That is a sign of a man who has put aside passion, at least temporarily, in favor of cool reason warrant.

The same is true with tables, charts, graphs, pictures, musical scores, and so on: Describe what you see in the evidence that matches the evidence side of your warrant.

EXAMPLE

The History of a Warrant

In this passage, Suzanna Sherry explains the history of a cherished, but contested warrant: our constitutional guarantee of free speech. She shows how the Supreme Court expanded that warrant by narrowing one of its exceptions: The warrant now covers more kinds of supposedly dangerous speech because the court changed the "dangerous speech exception" to cover fewer instances.

Legislatures have . . . frequently attempted to restrict speech because they believed it to be dangerous. Just before the Civil War, many southern states put abolitionists in prison for publishing their views. During World War I, the government jailed bolshevist sympathizers . . . because they urged men to resist the draft. The McCarthy era saw nationwide crackdowns on anyone with leftist beliefs. . . . And during the war in Vietnam, the government tried to prevent publication of the infamous Pentagon Papers.

The justification for these limits on speech is always the same: Especially in times of crisis, we cannot allow speech that will incite lawlessness or endanger lives. It was not until the 1960s that the courts began to reject that justification [that is, warrant]. Recognizing that all speech is an incitement designed to persuade the listener to action, the Supreme Court, in 1969, specified very narrow circumstances under which a speaker can be liable for the harm that results from his speech: only when the speech is intended to produce, and is likely to produce, imminent lawless action. In other words, we can blame the speaker for the actions of others only when "the evil apprehended is so imminent that it may befall before there is an opportunity for full discussion." Why? Because to do otherwise is to forge a link between speech and action—a link that might be found in any unpleasant speech.

Source: Suzanna Sherry, "I Hate What They Say, but I Won't Stop Them," *Washington Post*, February 14, 1999.

◆◆◆

Arguing by Evidence Versus Arguing by Warrants

We make most arguments in one of two ways: We support reasons with evidence or we derive claims from warrants. Most academics and professionals base their arguments on evidence, which puts a premium on fact; some civic and many personal arguments rest on warrants, which puts a premium on principle.

For example, suppose a sociologist opposed a needle-exchange program by making this argument based on evidence:

> We should abolish the Southport needle-exchange program. claim It has made the drug problem worse reason 1 because it encourages people to use more drugs. reason 2 A study of those who have participated in it shows that 70% have increased their use of drugs; the average rate has grown from 5.7 to 9.2 injections per week. evidence

Someone who disagreed might question the source or soundness of the evidence, but she would not question its connection to the reason because it seems obvious: *of course* we should abolish a program that increases drug use.

But suppose a politician made this argument opposing the same program:

> We all know that when you make risky behavior safer, you encourage more people to engage in it. warrant Since the Southport needle-exchange program makes drug use safer, reason 1 it encourages people to use more drugs. reason 2 We should therefore abolish the program. claim

That is an argument whose claim is derived from a *principle expressed as a warrant.* When we make that kind of argument, we feel no need to offer any evidence at all if we can show that our general principle applies to the specific case. In fact, this one is an all-purpose argument that could be used against any program intended to reduce the cost of *any form of risky behavior,* from automobile seat belts and antilock brakes to the distribution of condoms in schools.

Most thoughtful readers are skeptical of arguments from principle because they ask us to accept a claim based only on doctrinal or ideological truths rather than on the facts of the matter. The danger in making such claims is that your entire argument falls if readers either reject the principle or deny that it applies.

Writing Process

WARRANTS

Preparing and Planning
Identify Your Key Assumptions

When you plan an argument, don't focus only on your key points; you also have to understand the assumptions that you can't imagine questioning, but that your reader might: *What do I believe that my readers must also believe (but may not) before they will think that my reasons are relevant to my claims?*

Suppose you want to argue that the drinking age should be lowered to eighteen because eighteen-year-olds are subject to the draft: What general principle must your readers *already* believe before they will accept that argument?

> When you're old enough to vote, marry, or die for your country, you're old enough to drink.

But is that true? If so, it is perhaps because you believe a more general warrant:

> When a person is old enough to assume basic civic responsibilities, then that person is old enough to engage in all adult activities.

But is that true? Why do you think so?

Before they agree that eighteen-year-olds should be allowed to drink, some readers would also have to hold other beliefs unconnected to drinking in particular but still relevant to the issue:

> When we determine maturity of judgment, we cannot decide on the basis of age alone.
>
> When we want to prevent bad consequences of overindulging in an activity, we should not ban the activity but try to prevent excess.
>
> When we criminalize behavior that many people approve of, we do not prevent that behavior, we just make it more attractive.

None of those beliefs directly concerns drinking, but if you are against drinking by eighteen-year-olds based on those assumptions, you have to hope that your readers would not reject them out of hand. Or if you think they would, then you have to make an argument supporting them. You must also think about their limits: Are those principles true under any and all circumstances? You might finally decide not to state any of these principles as warrants in your argument, but you benefit from the discipline of trying to figure out what they are.

Locate Warrants Where They Do the Most Good

Finding the best place for warrants is tricky, but here are two generally reliable principles:

1. Lay out important warrants before you offer specific claims and reasons. If you think readers might reject them, make an argument supporting them.

For example, suppose you want to argue that schools should teach not facts but skills. Rather than jumping straight into the reasons and evidence, you might lay down some general principles that you intend to argue from:

> **When we educate young people in a democracy, our first job is to help them become productive citizens who can make the good decisions necessary for living in a dynamic democratic system.** warrant [Add reasons and evidence supporting this assertion.] Given that responsibility, reason our schools should focus on more than transmitting facts; they should develop children's ability to analyze those facts critically. claim

2. State warrants that readers are unlikely to contest as a logical flourish after you've offered a specific claim and supporting reasons, like a punch line that leaves readers with a sense that the conclusion was inevitable.

235

We can no longer be objective about Senator Z's private behavior. claim There are too many reports of unsavory incidents to think that he's innocent of everything he's been charged with. reason **After all, where there's smoke, there's fire.** warrant

Use Analogies as Surrogate Warrants

You can imply a warrant using analogies. The following claim is based on a warrant:

Don't worry if you begin to feel less in control of making arguments as this book goes on. claim **When people learn a difficult skill requiring complex knowledge, they almost always perform worse when they first learn that knowledge but improve as they gain experience using it.** warrant So you'll have a period of confusion before you master the craft of argument. reason

We can base the same claim on an analogy:

Don't worry if you begin to feel less in control of making arguments as this book goes on. Just as medical students predictably get worse at reading X-rays before they became experts, so you'll have a period of confusion before you master the craft of argument. analogy

The analogy implies that an unstated warrant covers both cases and connects a claim known to be true (the *just* as part) to a claim in question (the *so* part).

And, of course, you can combine them:

Don't worry if you begin to feel less in control of making arguments as this book goes on. claim When people learn a difficult skill requiring complex knowledge, they almost always perform worse when they first learn that knowledge but improve as they gain experience using it. warrant Just as medical students predictably get worse at reading X-rays before they became experts, so you'll have a period of confusion before you fully master the craft of argument. analogy

Readers judge analogies as they do warrants. They must first believe that your point of comparison (the *just* as part) is true—med students do in fact read X-rays worse as they first gain experience but then get better. Then they must believe that your analogy matches the claim and reason you are trying to connect—that *getting worse at reading X-rays* matches *being confused about arguments* and that *becoming expert at reading X-rays* matches *mastering the craft of argument.*

Use analogies

▶ when you think readers will respond better to a vivid concrete example than to a general statement of a principle

▶ when you can't think of a way to state the warrant convincingly

▶ when you have stated several warrants and don't want to overdo it

Avoid analogies

▶ when readers might question your comparison

▶ when they might not see how the comparison applies to the reason and claim

▶ when they might infer a warrant different from yours

EXAMPLE

Analogy

In this passage, the movie critic Michael Medved uses analogy to defend a proposal to require age identification before young people can see movies rated PG-13 and R.

Skeptics raise substantive objections to nearly all the current reform proposals. In today's multiplexes, a resourceful kid might easily buy a ticket to "Tarzan," but then quietly slip into the theater that's showing "The Matrix." Serious new policies might also give rise to a flourishing new market for fake ID's. Meanwhile, the "forbidden fruit" effect may well kick in. By making adult material more difficult to see, we may succeed only in making it seem more alluring and desirable.

Such arguments might also be deployed, however, against long-standing age-based restrictions on the purchase of tobacco and alcohol. Yet no one doubts that these restrictions reduce the levels of youthful indulgence. We don't let twelve-year-olds legally buy cigarettes even though some of them are wily enough to circumvent the rules.

Source: Michael Medved, "Hollywood Murdered Innocence,"
Wall Street Journal, June 16, 1999.

Working Collaboratively

Most of the people we know share most of our beliefs and values, so we seldom think about warrants at all. That's why even experienced writers have to work hard to figure out which warrants their readers need to see. This is another instance where a group can help by offering an outside point of view. As you read one another's drafts, look for places where the logic seems a bit off:

- You can't think of anything in particular to disagree with, but you just don't like the argument. It doesn't seem to "hang together."

- You don't agree with the claim, but you can't put your finger on anything in the argument that explains why. The reasons offered just don't seem like good ones.

These are often signs that you want the writer to state an explicit warrant.

If the group is tough-minded about pursuing such points of uncertainty, it will force you to explain your logic by stating your warrants.

Inquiries

Reflections

1. Any warrant can be made broader or narrower. Here is a fairly broad one:

   When a form of expression encourages brutality, it must be rejected as a legitimate form of artistic expression.

You can broaden this warrant by replacing "form of expression" with the more general "symbolic behavior" or narrow it with "song lyrics." When you change its range, do you change the conditions under which it is true?

2. Suppose you offered this objection to the claim that gangsta rap should be accepted as legitimate art:

Ordinarily we should accept legitimate artistic expression enjoyed by those who create it, but not when it encourages brutal behavior. In other words, when a form of expression encourages brutality, it should be condemned under any and all circumstances.

Someone responds,

What about "Onward Christian Soldiers, onward as to war"? Do you condemn that hymn?

Where do you go from there?

3. Is it possible for two people to agree that some reason supports some claim, even though they are relying on completely different warrants? For example, here's a reason and claim that two people might agree on:

Grades should be assigned on a curve claim because then we would know who are the most deserving students. reason

But here are two different warrants that would "cover" that claim and reason:

When society wants to identify its future elite, it should do so in a way that makes sharp distinctions in quality of performance.

Whenever you want to make teachers objectively identify the hardest-working students, you should force them to rely on the statistically sound assignment of grades.

Imagine two people who accepted the claim, but each on the basis of a different warrant. Would they stop agreeing if they learned about the other's warrant? In other words, are some agreements too shallow to survive shared knowledge?

4. Suppose two people agree to the following:

Whenever you want to make teachers objectively identify the hardest-working students, you should force them to rely on statistically sound assignment of grades. warrant Grades should therefore be assigned on a curve. claim

Can we conclude that the two people have deeper agreement because they agree on a shared warrant? Suppose they had these two reasons:

We need to prevent teachers from judging students on superficial matters of personality, reason so grades should be assigned on a curve. claim

We need to make sure teachers identify students who do not work hard, reason so grades should be assigned on a curve. claim

Both reasons would count as valid instances of the reason side of the warrant. But do these two people really agree? Would they feel that they agreed? Maybe when we agree, we do not agree as much as we think. Are there times when we should be satisfied with superficial agreement? Are there times when we should not?

5. We have discussed principles of reasoning as if they were always in our minds even when they are not stated as warrants and we do not think about them. But when you connect a reason to a claim but do not state a warrant, must there always be a principle "in the back of your mind"? In other words, when people connect reasons to claims, do they always have a principle available to justify the connection? Or do they just connect a reason to a claim because nothing seems to contradict it? How would we find out?

Tasks

6. Here is a middle-sized warrant that many people believe:

   When a tourist encounters a local custom characteristic of the country she visits, she should participate in that custom.

   That warrant might remind you of the proverb, *When in Rome, do as the Romans do.* Is the proverb broader or narrower than its explicit statement as a warrant? Select two more proverbs that express principles you believe. Restate them as middle-sized warrants like the one above. Then make each broader and narrower. Do you still accept the principle after you broadened it? If not, why not? If so, broaden it again. Do you accept it now?

7. The warrant about good turns is one that we might describe as signaling obligation: "When X is the case, we should do Y." Here are some popular proverbs. Turn them into "When, then" warrants, then decide what kind of relationship they signal. Is it cause-effect, effect-cause, appearance-reality, etc.?

   Where there's smoke there's fire.

   One rotten apple spoils the barrel.

   You can't tell a book by its cover.

   Look before you leap.

   If you've seen one, you've seen them all.

   What sorts of limitations apply to these?

Project

8. From a dictionary of proverbs, select a dozen or so that you find odd, puzzling, untrue. For each one, try to construct a little story in which someone follows the proverb. For example,

   Alana wanted to go dancing on Saturday with her friend Tanya, who already had a date. So Tanya tells Alana, "There's a guy in my chem lab this afternoon who would love to go with you. Want me to talk to him?" "Maybe," says Alana, "but first I want to come by the lab." "Why?" asks Tanya. Replies Alana, "Look before you leap."

   Do you find it hard to invent stories in which people would follow a puzzling or untrue proverb? What does that tell you about your ability to understand the warrants of others? Can you imagine yourself acting in the way the characters in your stories do? What does that tell you about your ability to accept the warrants of others?

Focus on Writing

1

Context. Proverbs offer insights into different cultures. For example, here is a Japanese saying we mentioned earlier:

> The nail that sticks up gets hammered down.

This means that if you are different from everyone else, you will be forced into conformity, and (according to Japanese thinking) that is a good thing. Here is another Japanese proverb:

> If you love your child, send him on a journey.

That means that if you want your child to become part of the larger community, send him out on his own where he will be cared for by strangers and learn the ways of the community. Are there corresponding proverbs in English? If not, what does that mean?

Task. This project will require collaborative activity. It will lead, not to a paper but to more informal writing. Spend some time with students from other cultures, asking them for proverbs in their culture. Distinguish those that have parallels in English from those that do not. Then read some proverbs in English to those foreign students and ask if they have any parallels. The group should then share its findings. Once you see the similarities and differences, try to imagine some situations where we and someone from another culture would reason about a circumstance differently.

Here are some English proverbs you might read to people from other cultures. Notice that all of these have to do with different attitudes toward being cautious versus being bold.

> The early bird gets the worm.
> Nothing ventured nothing gained.
> A rolling stone gathers no moss.
> Look before you leap.
> Don't count your chickens before they're hatched.
> Strike while the iron is hot.
> Once burned, twice shy.
> Better safe than sorry.
> He who hesitates is lost.
> No guts, no glory.
> A bird in the hand is worth two in the bush.

Do *not* assume that there are no differences between cultures if every proverb you hear corresponds to one in English and if every proverb you offer corresponds to one in that other language. It probably means that you haven't found unique ones yet.

Research Project

Scenario.   You have worked on this project so long that you fear you cannot see your draft from your reader's point of view.

Task.   Complete your first draft. For each major reason in each major section, list the warrants that connect it to the main claim. Also list the warrants that connect it to its own reasons and evidence. State them using the formula, *Whenever X,* then *Y.* Use the following list to test your draft:

▶ Are the warrants true? Do they apply? Do they need to be qualified?

▶ Will readers need you actually to state them in your text?

▶ Will readers accept them, or must you include an argument to support them?

In a Nutshell

About Your Argument . . .

A warrant is a general statement that explicitly or implicitly relates a set of general conditions to a set of general consequences. We've expressed warrants in this regular way:

> When children behave in violent ways, it is because they have been influenced by violent movies, TV, and computer games.

But they can be expressed in a less explicit way:

> Violent movies, TV, and computer games cause violent children.

However we express a warrant, it serves to link a reason to a claim:

> More children are playing Mortal Kombat than ever before. reason Since violent movies, TV, and computer games cause violent children, warrant we will see more children attacking other children. claim

> If we believe the warrant and the reason, we have to believe the claim.

. . . and About Writing It

You might have problems with warrants in five ways:

▶ Readers do not see your warrant.

▶ They think it is not true.

▶ They think that it is true, but needs to be limited.

▶ They think the warrant does not "cover" the reason or the claim.

▶ They think the warrant is not be appropriate to your audience.

When you address highly contested issues, step back and ask yourself what you think your readers must believe *in general* about your issue *before* they will accept your specific reasons as relevant to your specific claims. If you think that your readers do not share those warrants, then you have to make them the center of their own argument, treating the warrants as claims that need their own reasons, evidence, and warrants.

Visual Argument

After studying this chapter, you will be able to:

LO1 Describe the features particular to visual argument.

LO2 Use the Toulmin model and the list of fallacies to critique visual argument.

LO3 Create written arguments that incorporate visual elements.

LO4 Create stand-alone visual arguments.

I n a world where we are so inundated with visual material–from magazine covers to movies, billboards to YouTube videos—you may very well feel that you spend more time *viewing* argument than you do reading and writing it. Even though it relies far more on pictures, graphics, and images than words to convey its message, visual material does nonetheless express its own perspective on argument.

When viewed from the perspective of argument, in fact, images frequently take on additional meaning. An image can often be perceived as a visual argument in that it makes a claim about an issue and supports it, just as written argument does. The idea introduced in Chapter 1 that argument is everywhere takes on expanded meaning when you apply it to visual as well as to written argument.

Visual argument, however, also has certain special characteristics that make it unique. Those characteristics are the subject of this chapter, which teaches you not only to analyze visual argument but also to create it yourself. Instruction and examples appear in the "Exercises and Activities" section at the end of the chapter.

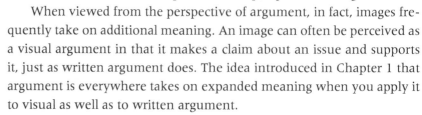

Recognizing Visual Argument

You will need to discover, first, whether you are looking at an argument. You discover this by asking, *Is the visual about an issue that has not been resolved or settled?* and *Does this issue potentially inspire two or more different views?* If your answer to both of these questions is yes, then attempt to describe the issue and the perspective being developed. Next, use two types of information for further analysis. First, analyze the special features of visual argument that are explained later in this chapter to get a sense of how the argument works and how powerful it is. Second, apply argument theory to understand the material better as an argument.

Review the section "Apply the Six Types of Argumentation Purpose to Visual Argument" on pages 70–72 to help you recognize and classify types of visual argument. Just like written argument, visual argument can be straightforward, with an obvious purpose and claim; covert, with a hidden claim that you may need to infer; or even unconscious, with the artist advocating a point of view without being fully aware of it. Furthermore, argument expressed through pictures and speech can represent either commonly held or extreme points of view and can present one or several different views on an issue.

You will encounter visual argument both online and in print in a variety of forms, including advertisements, photographs, drawings, illustrations, paintings, sculptures, cartoons, diagrams, flowcharts, various types of graphs, visual demonstrations, tables of numbers, or even maps. Marketers use visual argument on billboards, on signs, and in packaging and other marketing materials such as brochures or various other types of promotional materials. All this visual material can be (and increasingly is) employed to further an argument and convince you of a particular point of view.

Notice how many of these venues for visual argument are a part of the modern media, a particularly potent context for visual argument. A recent study by the Kaiser Family Foundation found that young people ages 8–18 now spend up to six and a half hours a day listening, watching, reading, or interacting with materials that they access through modern media formats. Reflect on the amount of time you spend each day taking in or sending information via new media, and you may be surprised how much your life is impacted. Whenever you encounter visual argument in the media or anywhere else, make a point of identifying its purpose because it always has one.

Now let us look at some of the special features of visual argument that make it particularly effective for advancing arguments.

Why Visual Argument Is Convincing: Eight Special Features

The following special features of visual argument will demonstrate how it works and why it is convincing. However, not all visual argument demonstrates all of the special features described in this list, and sometimes these features combine or overlap with one another. They are separated and described here for purposes of instruction. Becoming aware of them will help you look at visuals as potential argument and also understand how images achieve their persuasive effect with an audience. The examples of visual argument in this chapter include classic photographs that illustrate issues associated with dramatic periods in U.S. history, such as World War II, the civil rights movement, and the Vietnam War. Others illustrate contemporary issues.

1. *Visual argument is immediate and tangible and pulls you into the picture.* Visual argument works on a different level of perception than written argument. To use a new media word, it has velocity. It communicates fast and evokes a rich, dense, and immediate response from a viewer. For example, if you are watching a moving picture, you may have the experience of either sharing or even taking part in the action yourself. At the least, you will react in some immediate way to what you are seeing. If the picture is still, you may experience its immediacy and timelessness. A moment has been captured and preserved forever on film. Look at the photograph in Figure 10.1 ▪. It has been characterized as the most famous picture from the Vietnam War.

2. *Visual argument often establishes common ground and invites viewer identification through shared values and points of view.* You learned in Chapter 1 that common ground is a necessary ingredient of productive argument. Visual argument usually establishes common ground, including a sense of personal identification and shared values with the characters, the action, or the scene, and it does so more quickly than words in print. All viewers, however,

Figure 10.1 *Visual argument is immediate and tangible and pulls you into the picture.*

In this photograph an officer in the South Vietnamese army is shooting a suspected member of the Vietcong, an armed rebel force supported by North Vietnam, and the photographer has captured the moment when the bullet enters this man's head and kills him. This picture provoked strong antiwar arguments in its time, and it continues to invite responses to issues associated with war. What pulls you into this picture? What issue does it raise for you? What position do you take on the issue?

Street Execution of a Vietcong Prisoner, 1968.

may not experience the same degree of common ground or the same type of identification.

Look at the photograph in Figure 10.2 ▪ taken by American Douglas Martin. This is a picture of Dorothy Counts, an African American girl who enrolled in a newly desegregated high school in Charlotte, North Carolina, during the civil rights movement. Escorted by the individuals on either side of her, she makes her way to her first day of school. Dorothy is being taunted by white students in the background who wanted to keep their school segregated.

Dorothy Counts, now Dot Counts Scoggins, still lives in Charlotte, North Carolina. In 2007 the Charlotte-Mecklenburg Schools community celebrated both the 40th anniversary of the desegregation of the school system and the 50th anniversary of the difficult days that the young Dorothy Counts (she was 15 in 1957) spent in Harding High School in an effort to help desegregate public schools. The school district also invited a couple of the students who were screaming at her and making faces in this picture to the ceremony. They were present, and they apologized, after all these years.[1]

Dorothy Counts Entering a Newly Desegregated School, 1957.

Figure 10.2 *Visual argument often establishes common ground and invites viewer identification through shared values and points of view.*

This photograph won The Associated Press, World Press Photo of the Year Award in 1957 and remains one of the most famous pictures from the civil rights era. With whom do you identify and experience the greatest amount of common ground in this picture? Do you identify with Dorothy as she moves toward her first experiences in her new school? Do you identify with either of the individuals escorting her? Do you have anything in common with the white students in the background? What values are embedded in this image? What issue does the picture raise for you, and what position would you take on it?

247

---

[1]From information supplied by Professor Andy Brown and student Kristina Wolfe, of the University of North Carolina at Charlotte, and Dave Morris, long-time resident of Charlotte, NC.

Attitudes and values have changed radically in the years since this photograph was taken. The picture demonstrates the potential power and influence of visual argument. It memorializes an event that has now become a part of history and that vividly depicts the changed views on school segregation that are recognized now throughout the United States.

3. *Visual argument often evokes an emotional response.* Visual argument operates more directly on the emotions than written argument because images communicate more immediately than words. Because of this, visual images often invite a different, sometimes more powerful, form of critical attention. Look, for example, at the picture presented in Figure 10.3 ■. This image, which appeared in October 2010, was one of many news stories detailing the devastation wrought by the floods in Pakistan. Notice how powerfully this picture conveys the effects of this natural disaster, eliciting a far more emotionally charged response than would a written statistical report.

4. *Visual argument often relies on the juxtaposition of materials from very different categories, inviting the viewer to make new links and associations.* In placing objects, people, or actions that are not usually associated with each

Figure 10.3 *Visual argument often evokes an emotional response.*

A Pakistani flood survivor is pictured in a flood-affected area of southern Pakistan. The floods have devastated this woman's village, and she now waits for aid to be delivered to her community. Would you characterize your response to this picture as primarily rational or emotional? What in this image prompts your response? Describe your response.

A Vietnam War Protester offering flowers to troops during an Antiwar Demonstration, 1967.

Figure 10.4 *Visual argument often relies on the juxtaposition of materials from very different categories, inviting the viewer to make new links and associations.*

The juxtaposition of flowers and soldiers in the context of an antiwar demonstration invites the viewer to respond directly to how these different things appear together. What associations do you have with flowers and soldiers? Think of them separately and then together. How would you state the claim in this picture? Would you accept or argue against this claim?

249

other in a common context, a photographer invites the viewer to establish new associations and to reach new conclusions. Figure 10.4 ▪ is a well-known photograph of an anti–Vietnam War demonstrator at a march in 1967. She is offering flowers that symbolize peace to troops that have been called in to protect the area.

5. *Visual argument often employs icons to prompt an immediate response from a viewer.* Icons are images that people have seen so often that they respond to them immediately and in predictable ways—or at least, it is on this that people who include iconic references in visual argument rely. The American eagle, for example, is more than a bird to most U.S. citizens. It symbolizes the nation and the values associated with a democratic form of government. Icons appear on computer screens and on the cash registers at McDonald's to prompt quicker responses than the words or numbers they replace. The photograph on the next page (see Figure 10.5 ▪) of Marines raising the U.S. flag on Iwo Jima toward the end of World War II has been printed so many times, including on postage stamps, that it has become a national icon. It has also inspired a famous statue in Arlington Cemetery in Washington D.C.

In the twenty-first century, the polar bear stranded on a small chunk of ice in a larger ocean of floating ice chunks has become the iconic visual argument for the movement to reduce global warming. See page 10 for one version of it.

Figure 10.5 *Visual argument often employs icons to prompt an immediate response from a viewer.*

What does this photograph, taken toward the end of World War II, communicate to you? What is its purpose? What is the effect of not seeing the faces of the men? Describe the composition, including the focal point of the picture and the arrangement of the different parts. What feelings does it evoke? Why has it become a national icon? Do you think the polar bear image (see page 10) will be as lasting or become as influential an icon (in this case, for global warming) as have these Marines raising the flag in commemoration of victory in World War II? Why or why not?

Marines Raising the Flag on Iwo Jima, 1945.

6. *Visual argument often employs symbols.* You have seen how icons invite viewers to respond with the commonly held, established meanings and feelings, or even to add to those that are usually associated with them. Icons are symbolic since most people look beyond their literal meaning and add the extra meanings they have come to represent. However, of the many symbols used in argument, few are so familiar that they can be classified as icons. Look at the color photograph of the split tree in Figure 10.6 ▪ (on page 251). This photograph appears in *The Border: Life on the Line* by Douglas Kent Hall. The caption under the picture is "Near El Paso, Texas." El Paso is located on the Texas-Mexico border. This particular tree is a symbol, but not an icon.

7. *Visual argument is selective.* Whenever you look at a visual argument, it is important to think not only about what is included in the picture but also about what is omitted from it. If you could stand back and see more of the entire scene, of which the picture itself is only a small part, your perception of the picture might change a great deal. In any such framed image, you are allowed to see only what the photographer sees or wants you to see. You can infer or imagine what else is there or what else is going on outside the frame of the picture. The power of images often resides in this "edited" quality, but it is also a limit that the viewer must keep in mind.

Figure 10.6 *Visual argument often employs symbols.*

This quotation by Graham Greene can be found in the front of the book in which this picture appears: "How can life on the border be other than reckless? You are pulled by different ties of love and hate." Consider the location of this tree and that it was included in a book describing life on the United States–Mexico border. What symbolic meaning would you assign to it in this border context? How would you describe this meaning? What claim do you infer from looking at this picture? How might someone refute that claim? What type of proof is the tree in this context?

Tree Located on the Texas-Mexico Border.

Look at the photographs in Figure 10.7 ▪ of different people participating in the recent debate around health care reform. Notice that each picture provides emotional proof (pathos).

8. *Visual argument invites* [varied] *interpretations from viewers.* Usually no two people looking at a visual argument will interpret it in exactly the same way

Figure 10.7 *Visual argument is selective.*

Each of these images presents viewers with an example of the recent town hall meetings regarding health care reform. How do the two images compare? In what ways do they encourage viewers to form opposing views about the health care reform initiative? In the first, President Obama greets Minnie Small, 84, of Silver Spring, MD, after a national teleconference town hall meeting at the Holiday Park Multipurpose Senior Center. The second shows Senator Arlen Specter's town hall being greeted by tea party protesters and other local conservatives. How would the first picture be different had the photographer decided to photograph the entire scene in this room, with everyone in the room receiving equal attention? What is the effect of moving in on one individual to the exclusion of everyone else? How does this compare to the group shot that the second picture presents? What claim does each of these images seem to be making?

since individual viewers bring information and associations from their own past experience and use it to fill in some of the meaning suggested by the picture. Readers do that too, of course, particularly when they infer a claim or supply the warrants in a written argument. When viewers, like readers, draw on their backgrounds to fill out the meaning of a visual argument, they become vested in its message since some of the meaning now belongs to them. As a result, these viewers are more likely to accept the argument.

Look, for example, at two images on page 269. Image 1 shows a detail from Michelangelo's scenes of the Creation, which appear on the ceiling of the Sistine Chapel in Rome. Here God is passing life to human beings by stretching out His life-giving finger to the lifeless, limp finger of Adam. Now look at the close-up of the hands in Image 2 below Image 1. In this postcard picture, God is passing a baseball along with the first impulses of human life. One viewer, looking at this picture, says the artist is claiming, "We have had baseball from the beginning of time." Another puts the claim this way: "God is giving baseball to the entire universe." A third viewer has a different idea: "God is playing games with human beings." How would you interpret the meaning of this picture? How would you argue in favor of your interpretation? Your answer, at least in part, will probably depend on your views about baseball.

Now look at Figure 10.8 ■, which is a visual argument that invites individual interpretations. This is a photograph of two animal rights activists in Germany who have created a tableau with the girl sitting in the cage and the person dressed like a chicken sitting outside of the cage. Both are holding signs, written in German, that state, when translated into English: "Free the hens. Get rid of all cages by 2012!" It is aimed at companies that keep chickens confined and crowded in small wire cages where they lay eggs and are fattened for the market.

Figure 10.8 *Visual argument invites unique interpretations from viewers.*

The claim of this argument is clear from the writing on these activists' signs. Translated, the signs demand, "Free the hens. Get rid of all cages by 2012!" What is not clear, and therefore open to interpretation, is the significance of the support for the claim. Why do you think these individuals chose to stage their protest in this way? Why is the girl nearly nude, and why is she confined in a wire cage similar to a chicken's? Why is the individual outside of the cage in a chicken suit? What is the meaning of this support? What warrants are you expected to supply that will link this support to the claim? You are expected to make some inferences to understand this argument, and not everyone may make the same inferences.

Animal Rights Activist: Free Hens from Cage!

A nude animal rights activist holds a billboard on which is written, "Free the hens. Get rid of all cages by 2012!" The activists protested raising hens in the cage, in Berlin, Jan. 16, 2008.

Many American students are also activists in the free-the-chickens movement, and, in some colleges and universities, they have persuaded their administrations to purchase only cage-free eggs for the student cafeterias. There is no correct interpretation of how the argument in Figure 10.8 is supposed to persuade a viewer to agree with the activists. Your guess may turn out to be as good as the next person's.

RECOGNIZING THE VISUAL IN ONLINE ARGUMENT

As mentioned previously, the emergence of web-based technologies has dramatically expanded both the volume and variety of visual material to which we are exposed. Indeed not only has the rise of the Web increased the amount of visual material in our world, it has also given rise to a different way of engaging and responding to it. Included below is a checklist of the key considerations that are most relevant to visual argument online. As you look over this list, think about the ways these considerations influence how we read and analyze this particular form of visual argument.

▶ *Volume/Variety:* The rise of the Web has led to an explosion in the number and type of images we encounter. This means we need to be especially attentive to the range of different issues online visuals can raise. Choose a Web site with which you are familiar. How do the different visuals included there compare? Do they raise issues that seem related or unrelated? What larger point are the creators of this Web site trying to make by placing these issues together?

▶ *Interactivity:* Another defining feature of the Web is the degree to which it allows us the freedom to interact with each other: to exchange ideas, share impressions, convey ideas. Choose a Web site that includes a "comments section," allowing viewers to post their responses. How many different reactions or interpretations do these comments reflect? Which of these responses most closely approximates your own? Do you find your own reaction influenced or altered by reading through the comments offered by other viewers?

▶ *Linked Issues:* Through things like weblinks and hypertext, it is becoming increasingly easy to connect the images depicted in one Web site to images depicted in others. When assessing such links, ask yourself the following questions: what visuals do other, linked sites present? What issues do these images raise? Are these images and issues related to those presented in the initial Web site?

▶ *Multi-Modal/Multi-Media:* Another defining feature of the Web concerns the extent to which it brings together different types of text: written, visual, graphic, video, etc. When you come across a Web site that combines different elements, think about the ways these elements help reinforce the argument these visuals seem to be making.

Let us turn now to a review of the argument theory you have learned in preceding chapters and consider how it can be used to analyze and critique visual argument.

253

Using Argument Theory to Critique Visual Argument

Consider the rhetorical situation to gain insight into the context for the argument, including the type of visual argument you are examining, the intended viewers, the artist's background and motivation, the possible constraints of all parties, and the exigence or outside motivation for the argument. Apply the Toulmin model to discover the claim, support, warrants, backing for the warrants, and the presence of a rebuttal or a qualifier.

Learn more about the claim and purpose for the argument by asking the claim questions. Establish which type of claim tends to predominate: a fact claim establishes what happened; a definition claim defines and clarifies what it is; a cause claim looks for causes and sometimes shows effects; a value claim looks at whether it is good or bad; and a policy claim establishes what we should do about it.

Then analyze the proofs. Which are present, *logos, ethos,* and/or *pathos,* and which type of proof predominates in the argument? What is the effect of the proofs? Then look at specific types of proof, including signs, induction, cause, deduction, analogies, definition, statistics, values, authority, and motives. How do those that are present further the argument? Refer to the tests of validity for each of the proofs you identify to judge their effectiveness.

Also, look for fallacies and consider the effect they have on the overall argument. Look for visual fallacies in particular. For example, ask if the image may have been selected or changed to represent a particular point of view. Ask whether a photo or film clip represents a unique or an exaggerated way of viewing a subject, or whether it is an accurate picture of what really exists or happened. Consider the photographs taken of disasters, such as major floods or volcanic eruptions: they usually depict the worst, most extreme results of the disaster. You can at least wonder how representative these pictures are of what actually has happened.

Remember, too, that computers can be used to augment or change images. Tabloid newspapers sometimes create humorous composite images by placing one person's head on another person's body. Examine whether there is any evidence that a visual has been changed, doctored, or recreated in any way so that what you see as present in the image is a consequence of manipulation rather than insightful framing. Take time to look at visuals carefully. This helps you understand what is really going on in them and make some judgments about their accuracy and value.

Bias in Visual Argument

You will encounter bias in visual argument just as you do in written argument. All argument, by definition, shows bias for a particular point of view or a particular position. When you spot a visual argument that strikes you as biased, identify the source and type of bias being expressed. Here are examples of two images, each of which provides a biased take on the role that the Internet is

Figure 10.9

This photo depicts a Facebook privacy setting. How do you interpret this visual icon? What argument does it seem to be making about privacy and identity online?

playing in our lives. Figure 10.9 ■ is an icon that raises fears about the risks to privacy posed by online technologies. Figure 10.10 ■ offers a different portrait of these technologies, showcasing their role in facilitating our work.

Watching for fallacies, visual distortions, exaggerations, Photoshop changes in original images that have been applied to make them more persuasive, and outright or even less obvious bias in visual argument will help you make fair and objective critiques. In addition, ask these questions to make ethical evaluations

Figure 10.10

How would you describe the biased point of view in this picture?

of images: Does the arguer understand the issue and its consequences? Is the position proposed in the best interests of the audience? Is the arguer honest and fair-minded?

Sample Analysis of a Visual Argument

The following analysis of the political cartoon in Figure 10.11 ▪ draws on both the special features of visual argument and argument theory.

Special Features of Visual Argument Employed in the Cartoon

Visual argument pulls the viewer in, creates common ground, evokes an emotional response, uses juxtaposition, employs icons, uses symbols, is selective, and invites a unique interpretation from the viewer.

1. I am pulled into this picture by the striking image of police officers surrounding a seemingly innocent diner at a restaurant. Furthermore, common ground is established through the presence of such recognizable, everyday items as a tablecloth, utensils, and wine glasses.

Figure 10.11 *A political cartoon making a visual argument.*

SOURCE: © Tribune Media Services, Inc. All Rights Reserved. Reprinted with permission.

2. The juxtaposition of an ordinary eating scene and police raid causes me to associate restaurant dining with the issue of crime, and thereby invites me to begin thinking about whether there are rules around how and what we eat that we are not supposed to break.

3. The diner with a napkin tucked in his shirt, the table set with utensils and tablecloth have been depicted so often in ads and other media that they can be considered icons. Thus, they communicate quickly and forcefully.

4. The cartoonist, Larry Wright, has selected what he wants to feature in this picture: the stereotypical depiction of a fancy restaurant, the circle of police officers with guns drawn, and the key phrase "trans fat." As a result, the focus is on conventional dining habits, and the prevailing rules about what we are and are not supposed to eat.

5. I interpret this picture by remembering all the different occasions when I have eaten out at restaurants, and I wonder about whether I should possibly rethink whether I should curtail eating so much of this food in order to preserve my health. On the other hand, I also interpret this picture by wondering whether the current warnings about the unhealthy effects of food are perhaps overblown, as suggested by the overreaction of the police in this picture.

Argument Theory Used for Analysis of the Cartoon

257

Useful theory includes applying the rhetorical situation (TRACE), the Toulmin model, the claim questions, and the types of proof, including *logos, ethos,* and *pathos;* identifying fallacies; bias; and determining whether or not the argument is convincing and ethical.

Rhetorical Situation:

Text: Political cartoon with an argumentation intent.

Reader/viewer: People who eat out at restaurants or who consume food high in trans fats.

Author/artist: Larry Wright, a cartoonist for Wright/Cagle cartoons.

Constraints: Some viewers may be suspicious of public warnings about food health because such warnings seem to change so routinely; the artist seems to share this attitude by suggesting that our current concerns about trans fat might be overblown.

Exigence: The FDA's recent issuing of warnings about the dangers of trans fat.

Types of Proof (logos, ethos, pathos):

Cause: Excessive worrying about food health can lead to an infringement of individual choice.

Analogies: The choice of where to eat is analogous to other individual rights.

Value: We value individual freedom of choice.

Motivation: Everyone should enjoy the same prerogative to choose what they eat, free from government interference or coercion.

Fallacies: We could test the validity of the analogy between eating at a restaurant and the broader issue of freedom of choice by wondering whether there are other rights in which it might be appropriate to set limits or boundaries.

Bias: It is biased in favor of individual freedom of choices.

Ethical Evaluation:

Best interests of society? Yes, because preserving individual freedoms benefits every member of society.

Ethical? Perhaps. It depends on whether we think individual freedom of choice is a more important consideration than public health.

We have described visual argument, explained why it is convincing, and illustrated how you can analyze it by examining its special features and applying argument theory. Let us change the focus now to present some ideas that will help you create visual arguments of your own. Visual argument can be used to provide support for a written argument, or it can stand alone as an independent argument. We will examine both possibilities.

Add Visual Argument to Support Written Argument

You may, at times, decide to add pictures, photographs, drawings, flowcharts, graphs, or other images to your papers as support for your claim. You can see from studying the images presented so far in this chapter that visual argument, when compared to written argument, is immediate and concrete, can appeal powerfully to the emotions, and can enhance an argument's message by making it convincing in ways that words alone cannot do. When an image is used as support, be certain that it functions as support for the specific claim or subclaim you are presenting. You will want your words and your visuals to work together to make your point, just as they do in Figure 10.7 on page 251.

Include images in your argument writing by adding clip art from the Internet or by using various types of printed visual material drawn from books, magazines, and newspapers. Downloaded images from the Internet can be pasted into your paper electronically. You can also use Photoshop to juxtapose or combine images that will invite your viewer to think about your claim in a new way. Printed images or drawings can be photocopied and pasted into your paper. Of course, if you prefer to, draw your own diagrams, flowcharts, or sketches to add visual support for the claim. Also, decide whether or not to add a line or two of explanation under each visual to explain its relationship to the written text. You will need to do that if the relationship between the ideas in the text and the visual support is not immediately clear to the reader. Document all visual sources to show where you obtained them.

When you have quantities of numerical data, experimental results, or complex plans that are too cumbersome to describe in the written body of your paper, present it visually. Graphs, charts, tables, and flowcharts are valuable for condensing such material, often making it more easily accessible to the audience.

There are many different types of graphs, but the most commonly used are line, bar, and circle (or pie) graphs. These three kinds of graphs can be generated through common word processing packages such as Microsoft Word or WordPerfect for insertion in a paper. The examples that follow present graphs of data from *The World Almanac and Book of Facts*, an excellent source for up-to-date statistics on many subjects.

Bar graphs in particular are used when you want to compare measurements of some kind. The numbers used in the measurements are often large, and the bar graph offers a picture that makes the numbers easily understandable in relation to one another. Figure 10.12 ■ provides an example of a bar graph that shows the most current number of AIDS cases reported in Africa as compared with other parts of the world. There are 24,500,000 cases in Africa compared with

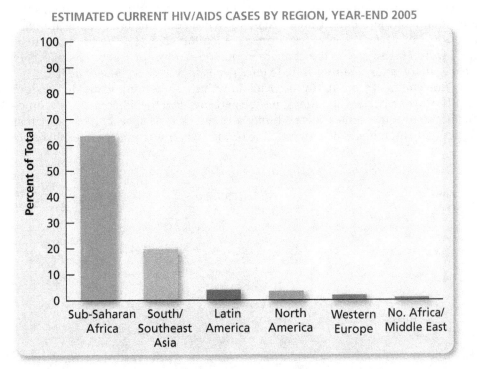

ESTIMATED CURRENT HIV/AIDS CASES BY REGION, YEAR-END 2005

Figure 10.12 *Bar Graph Comparing Large Numbers.*

Figure 10.13 *Line Graph Showing Change Over Time.*

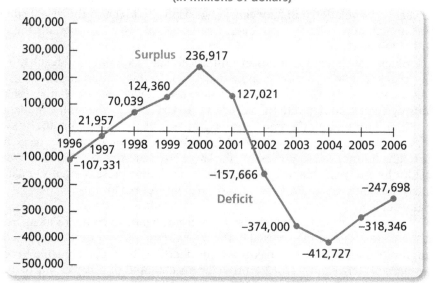

SUMMARY OF SURPLUSES AND DEFICITS
IN U.S. BUDGET, 1996–2006
(in millions of dollars)

38,600,000 in the world. The graph reports percentages. This graph appears in a paper that argues that AIDS education in Africa has been ineffective.

Line graphs are most often used to show a change in a measurement over time. Some of the different measurements associated with line graphs are temperature, height and weight, test scores, population changes, and profits or deficits. Figure 10.13 ▪ shows the changes in the U.S. budget over time. It appears in a paper that argues that the United States needs to reduce its budget deficit.

Circle graphs are ordinarily used to show how something is divided. Figure 10.14 ▪ shows a circle graph that sums the percentage of the different sizes of automobiles sold in the United States during a recent year. It appears in a paper that argues that automobiles help deplete the ozone layer in the upper atmosphere.

Figure 10.14 *Circle Graph Showing How a Population or Market Is Divided into Sectors.*

SALES OF U.S. CARS BY SIZE (2005)

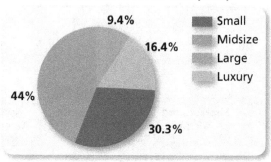

Population Projections for Selected Countries and World: 2006, 2025, and 2050

COUNTRY	2006	2025	2050
Bangladesh	147,365,352	204,538,715	279,955,405
Brazil	188,078,227	217,825,222	228,426,737
China	1,313,973,713	1,453,123,817	1,424,161,948
India	1,111,713,910	1,448,821,234	1,807,878,574
Iraq	26,783,383	40,418,381	56,360,779
Japan	127,463,611	120,001,048	99,886,568
Mexico	107,449,525	130,198,692	147,907,650
Nigeria	131,859,731	206,165,946	356,523,597
Russia	142,069,494	128,180,396	109,187,353
United States of America	298,444,215	349,666,199	420,080,587
World	6,528,089,562	7,963,750,137	n.a.

Figure 10.15 *Table Presenting Comparison Data.*

Whatever kind of graph you use, you must be sure that it is correctly and clearly titled and labeled, that the units of measurement are noted, and that you report the source of the statistical information used in the graph.

When you find that the statistical information you want to include in a paper is too detailed and lengthy for a graph, a chart or a table is usually recommended. For example, Figure 10.15 ■ provides the projected figures for population growth for ten major countries as well as for the world as a whole. It appears in a paper that argues in favor of zero population growth.

Create Visual Arguments That Stand Alone

We have suggested ways to use visual materials as illustrations that support ideas in written arguments. Many visual arguments are, however, quite independent of written text and stand alone as persuasive arguments themselves without the benefit of accompanying verbal explanations. Creating visual arguments of this type requires imagination, creativity, and critical thought. Like other types of argument, you will find visual arguments that stand alone all around you. Look at book covers, bulletin boards and displays, posters, tee shirts, and even your fellow students. Some of your classmates may dress and arrange their hair so that they are walking visual arguments. Figure 10.16 ■ (on page 262) provides two examples.

You can use the same types of images and equipment for all visual argument. These include single or composite images, moving images, photographs,

 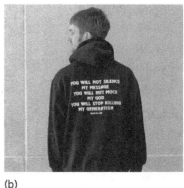

(a)   (b)

Figure 10.16 *Clothing Can Make an Argument. (a) Singer, songwriter, and activist Bono, member of the rock group U2, makes a statement with his jacket. (b) Student Daniel Goergen and his message.*

drawings, paintings, or even three-dimensional installations with objects placed in juxtaposition to make a claim. For example, a stack of books and a light bulb could make the claim that reading helps people think and get ideas. Experiment with stock photography from the Internet, Photoshop or Paint Shop Pro, cameras and camcorders, poster board and markers, scissors and paste.

For visual argument, as with other types of argument, you will need to make a claim about an issue that generates more than one perspective. Select an issue that is important to you and that you can make important to your audience. Reflect on all of the elements in the rhetorical situation as you would in creating a verbal argument. These include the materials and methods you will use; the characteristics and interests of your viewers; your own resources and interests; the constraints, including values, that either pull you and your viewers together or push you apart; and your exigence or motivation for working with this issue in the first place. Consider also how you can use *logos, ethos,* and *pathos* to create a persuasive and convincing argument.

Think through the eight special features of visual argument and how you will employ some of them to make your argument more convincing. You will want to create images that:

▶ Communicate quickly and have immediate and tangible effects on viewers.

▶ Invite viewer identification and establish common ground through shared values.

▶ Engage the emotions of the viewers.

▶ Juxtapose materials from different categories so that the viewer will make new links and associations.

▶ Employ familiar icons that prompt immediate responses from viewers.

▶ Present visual symbols that viewers can easily interpret.

▶ Include only materials that viewers should focus on and omit everything else.

▶ Invite unique interpretations from viewers through visual subtleties that do not mean the same things to all people.

Consider adding a few words to your visual argument to enhance or extend its meaning. Pete Rearden, an artist who created the visual argument in Figure 10.17 ▪, suggests limiting word art, if it is used at all, to no more than two or three short sentences. Use minimum punctuation and make the words as immediate and concrete as possible.

In his visual argument, Rearden has photographed an area that a homeless person has established as an outdoor camp. Rearden is deeply concerned with homeless people and the fact that more than half of them are also mentally ill. These individuals have often told him that they are only camping out and will soon be returning to their homes. This rhetorical situation prompted Rearden to create the visual argument reproduced here. Notice that the words superimposed on the photograph add a dimension of meaning to the picture. They do not serve as a photoline that describes the picture. Instead, they create common ground by reminding viewers of going to camp without their parents. They juxtapose Dear Mom (with its immediate links to ideas of home) and the mess of the camp (which is less immediately readable) to invite associations; and they add emotional appeal with the words *mom, camp,* and *fun,* and the question, "Why don't you write me any more?" By adding these words, Rearden invites a more complex and personal interpretation from a viewer than the picture alone could provide. Notice, finally, what is left out of this picture. Consider that for many people, the homeless are the invisible members of society. Not all people would state the claim this picture makes in exactly the same way. How would you state it?

263

Figure 10.17 *Visual Argument That Uses Words to Extend Its Meaning.*

Arguing Like a Citizen

Answer the following questions to connect Rearden's visual argument to the issue of citizenship.

▶▶▶ **Thinking Like a Citizen**

- Why do I personally care about the issue of homelessness? How and why does this issue make a difference to me? What makes me a stakeholder in this debate?

- Who else cares about this issue? How are their concerns about and stake in this debate different from my own?

▶▶▶ **Arguing Like a Citizen**

- What are the social questions the issue of homelessness raises for me? What are the key social questions this issue raises for others?

- What responses or solutions to these questions might I propose?

▶▶▶ **Acting Like a Citizen**

- Where in my community is the impact of homelessness felt? Among whom is this issue most often debated?

- What concrete action could I take to help resolve this issue?

Practice applying the theory explained in this chapter by analyzing and creating visual arguments in the "Exercises and Activities" that follow.

Review Questions

1. Where are you likely to encounter visual argument? How do you recognize it?

2. What are the eight special features of visual argument that make it convincing?

3. What information about argument theory from earlier chapters in this book might you employ to help you analyze visual argument?

4. Describe some ways that you might use visual argument as support for a written argument.

5. What ideas from this chapter might help you create an effective visual argument that stands alone?

Exercises and Activities

A. Group Work and Class Discussion: Analyzing Visual Argument

In small groups, view the five photographs on the following pages from the perspective of argument, analyze them, and discuss them as a class. Here are some general questions to guide your discussion. Additional "For Discussion" questions accompany each image.

1. Is this a visual argument? Why do you think so?

2. What was occurring and in what context that prompted the photographer to take the photograph?

3. What is it about? What is the claim? What are the implied values or point of view?

4. Does it engage your emotions? What is your emotional reaction?

5. Does it establish common ground? Do you identify with anyone or anything in it?

6. What other special features of visual argument make it effective?

   ▶ Is it immediate and tangible? How does it pull you into the picture?
   ▶ What is included? Left out? Changed? Distorted? Exaggerated?

Image 1:

West Bank Barrier.

This photograph appeared over the caption "Father and daughter waving a Palestinian flag stand near the Israeli separation barrier being constructed in the West Bank. This barrier, projected to be 436 miles long when completed, has been controversial since 2002 when the Israeli government decided to build a wall to protect its citizens from Palestinian suicide bombers.

265

Image 2:

Crossing Over.

These two photos appeared together in *Newsweek* magazine, April 3, 2006, accompanied by the following caption: "Crossing Over: Mexicans traverse the U.S. border, protesters rally in D.C."

For Discussion: Each photo makes a different claim. Describe them along with the support provided for each. What warrants are implicit in each photo? What backing, in the form of pervasive cultural values in the United States and Mexico, enhance the persuasive strength of these photos? Compare the fence in this photo with the West Bank barrier (Image 1). Some people in the United States advocate building a strong barrier along the U.S.–Mexican border to keep Mexican workers and others from crossing over illegally; other people reject this idea. State your position on this issue along with your reasons for holding it.

Image 3:

Coming Home to a Destroyed Neighborhood.

This photo is captioned, "Affluent Lebanese drive down the street to look at a destroyed neighborhood, August 15, 2006, in southern Beirut, Lebanon." During the summer of 2006, Hezbollah in Lebanon fired rockets into northern Israel, and Israel retaliated by bombing Hezbollah headquarters, airports, and major highways in Beirut, Lebanon. This photograph was taken the first day of the ceasefire. It shows four young women who have borrowed a car and a driver to return to their neighborhood. It is a candid shot, and the photographer, Spencer Platt, won the World Press Photo Award in 2007 for it.[2]

For Discussion: According to the photographer, many people look at this picture and ask if it is actually taken in the Middle East. What about it invites that reaction? Compare it with war zone photographs that you have seen of Iraq. What special characteristics of visual argument are present in this photo? Which predominate? State the claim. How would others in your class state the claim?

267

Image 4:

LeBron James.

This photograph comes from the collection of the best sports photographs of 2007, compiled by *Sports Illustrated* magazine. LeBron James is the key figure in the photograph. He plays for the Miami Heat. The photograph was taken on February 18, 2007.

For Discussion: What pulls you into this picture? When viewed from the perspective of argument, what claim does this photograph make? Photographers sometimes say that they have to capture a particular moment to get a good picture. How does that observation apply to this picture? What other special features of visual argument are apparent here?

[2]Miki Johnson, "Spencer Platt Wins World Press Photo Award, PopPhoto.com, February 9, 2007, http://www.popphoto.com/photographynewswire/3794/spencer-platt-wins-world-press-photo-award.html.

Image 5:

At Home Outdoors.

The individuals in this picture are aboriginal people of Balgo in the Great Sandy Desert of northwest Australia. Otherwise known as indigenous Australians, they are descended from the first known inhabitants of Australia. Traditionally, they spend their time outdoors. The house in this photograph is provided by the government, presumably to improve their lives, and it is used mostly for storage. This picture first appeared in *National Geographic* magazine in 1991.

For Discussion: What are the people in this photograph doing? Describe the cultural values shown in this photograph. Are there any conflicts in values? What does the photograph suggest about attempts by governments or organizations to impose new cultural customs or values on groups of people? How would you state the claim made by this picture? Comment on the use of juxtaposition here. What, if any, added content is related to the time of day indicated in the photograph?

   ▶ Does it rely on juxtaposition? How? To what effect?
   ▶ Does it use icons? To what effect?
   ▶ Does it use symbols? To what effect?
   ▶ Would everyone interpret it in the same way? What is your interpretation?

7. What do you conclude about the purpose, meaning, and effectiveness of this image?

B. Group Work, Class Discussion, and Writing Assignment: Analyzing Multiple Perspectives on an Issue Expressed through a Collection of Visual Arguments

1. Review "Expressing Multiple Perspectives through Visual Argument" along with the images on pages 93 and 102.

2. Look at the three images on pages 269 and 270, understand the context for each of them, and answer the questions for discussion on page 271 that accompany them.

3. Write a title for the images that communicates what they have in common and what issue they address when viewed as a group of images that makes an argument.

4. Write an essay in which you describe the four different perspectives on the issue expressed by the photographs; write in detail about how each is related to and contributes to the development of the idea in your title. Draw a conclusion about this set of images that expresses your final assessment of them.

Image 1:
Adam and God.

This image is a reproduction of a work of art. It was painted on the ceiling of the Sistine Chapel in Rome by Michelangelo in 1511, where it can be viewed today; it depicts the creation of Adam.

Image 2:
Play Ball.

This is a postcard collage, titled *Play Ball,* which adds a baseball to the hand of God reaching toward Adam.

Image 3:

Robot with a Grappler.

This photo ran in the *New York Times* in 2002 over the caption, "A robot with a grappler holding a wounded Palestinian yesterday on a highway in Megiddo, Israel, 12 miles southeast of Haifa. Israeli Radio said the man was a suicide bomber whose explosives detonated prematurely."

For Discussion:

Compare the hands in each of the four photographs. How are they similar? How are they different? Discuss how juxtaposition is used in each of these photographs. What is the effect? What additional associations form in your mind as you look at each of these four photographs? What is your personal interpretation of each of them? That is, what does each communicate to you? How effective are each of these images as arguments? How effective are they as a collection of images that makes an argument?

C. Individual Work and Class Discussion: Analyzing a Cartoon

To help you with this exercise, follow the model for the analysis of a cartoon provided on pages 256–258 of this chapter, which employs both the special features of visual argument and argument theory as tools for analysis. Look at the cartoon, answer the questions that follow it on the next page, and discuss your answers with the class.

Questions about the Special Features of Visual Argument

1. What pulls you into this cartoon? What do you notice first? What can you say about the composition that draws you into it?

2. Do you experience common ground with anyone in the image? Are any values expressed that you share?

3. Does this cartoon arouse your emotions? What is your emotional reaction?

4. Does the cartoon rely on juxtaposition? What is placed in juxtaposition, and what is the effect?

5. Do any icons appear in this cartoon? If yes, describe them. What do they contribute?

6. Do any symbols appear in this cartoon? If yes, describe them and consider what they contribute.

7. Is the image selective? That is, what is included, what is left out, and what is the effect?

8. How would you interpret this cartoon? What do you think the photographer's purpose is, what is the final effect, and what do you conclude about it?

D. Individual Work: Locating a Visual Argument and Analyzing It in Class

Find a visual argument. Look online or in printed magazines, newspapers, or books, and bring it to class. Why do you think the item you have selected is a visual argument? Identify the issue. Point out the special features of visual argument that make it convincing. State your interpretation of the claim, even if you have to infer it. Point out the support and the warrants and describe the backing. State why you do or do not find the argument convincing.

E. Creating a Stand-Alone Visual Argument and Writing an Analysis of It

This assignment requires you to create a visual argument, to write a paper in which you analyze it, and then to present and explain it to the class.

a. Identify an issue that you can make an argument about by using visual material. You may choose an issue either from one of the argument papers you have written or from one of the essays or visual arguments that appear in this book, or you may select a new issue.

b. Make a claim about the issue.

c. Create a visual argument. Draw on the suggestions made in this chapter (pages 261–264).

d. Include just enough writing on your visual argument to help viewers understand your claim.

e. Write a paper, about 250–350 words long, that explains and interprets your visual argument. Consider the following to include in your analysis or add other information. Your goal is to describe what you have expressed in your visual argument and explain to your viewers just how you created it to accomplish this goal.

1. Explain the rhetorical situation: What is the context for your issue and your visual argument?

2. Write a Toulmin analysis of your visual argument. Here is an example of a possible Toulmin analysis of the student-made collage on page 274 about artworks:

Issue: Has art become too expensive?

Claim: Art is too expensive.

Support: The examples of art pasted on the dollar sign are expensive.

Warrant: I cannot afford those artworks.

Backing: Most people viewing this collage know how expensive these famous artworks are.

Inferred rebuttal: I have money to buy less expensive artworks, and I think they are just as enjoyable to own.

3. Identify the type of claim, and describe how you have used *logos, ethos,* and *pathos.*

4. Describe your own interpretation of your argument. Why did you put it together as you did?

f. Share your visual argument with the class. Include the ideas in your written analysis. Ask for other interpretations from class members.

g. *Examples:* Three student-made visual arguments appear on pages 274 and 276–277. The first is a collage, the second is a sculpture, and the third is a graphic novel written for children that makes an argument through images and text. The second and third examples are accompanied by short analyses that explain what the students accomplished from their points of view.

STUDENT VISUAL
ARGUMENT 1

Untitled.

Elisabeth Elsberg, a student in a first-year writing class, created this collage from print images that were cut and pasted on to a painted background.

For Discussion: To work with audiences, icons must be immediately recognizable to most people. What parts of this artwork would you classify as iconic? Are they clearly iconic? How does this student use juxtaposition? Comment on the use of selectivity in this piece. What has been selected? What has been left out? How do you interpret this visual argument? How would you state its claim?

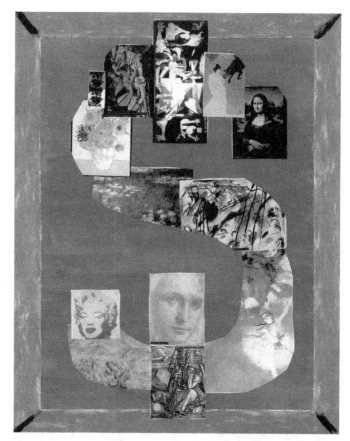

STUDENT VISUAL
ARGUMENT 2

Never Again.

Karen Hernandez, the student who made this visual argument, created the figures out of clay. She then installed the clay figures on a platform that displays photographs from the Holocaust, with a title that expresses the claim: "Never Again".

ANALYTICAL ESSAY OF STUDENT VISUAL ARGUMENT 2

NEVER AGAIN
Karen Hernandez

The artist was a student attending the University of Texas at Arlington when she made the sculpture and wrote this essay about it. The graphic novel *Maus* by Art Spiegelman provided the inspiration for this argument. *Maus* had been a reading assignment in her writing class. It tells the story of Spiegelman's parents' experiences during the Holocaust.

1   In 1938 Hitler and the Nazi government began a reign of terror and death that would leave over ten million people dead through pogroms and in prison camps. The book *Maus* tells one survivor's story, and I have tried to speak with this work of art of the horror that these people endured, just as the author of the book does. The skeletal figures of my piece are made of clay because it creates the closest appearance to human bones, and the figures are skeletal because this is the way many of the survivors looked when they were rescued from the camps. I have also left them in various sizes and shapes just as real people are; however, my figures are left incomplete (no hands or feet) because this is how the Germans viewed them, as less than human beings.

2   Even though the figures are skeletal, they have taken on an almost lifelike quality of expression in the way some heads are bowed, while others are held up. Some of the figures lean as if in pain or fatigue, and others seem to look at those standing nearby or into space. The longer I look at them, the more human they become to me, and I hope I have been able to impart this to the viewer as well.

3   I have also included, on the box below, pictures of victims and survivors of the Holocaust so that the observer will know that this work is more than just the artist's imagination, and that these horrors really did occur. I also chose to place the title across the front of the piece so that, like the group who first used it in the Holocaust museum, I might impart to the viewer the reminder that those who died during this terrible time of death and horror will not have done so in vain, and they will be remembered. Something like this will happen NEVER AGAIN.

For Discussion:

What do you find most striking about this visual argument? What pulls you in as you look at this photograph of it? How is juxtaposition used, and what is the effect? Are the words written on the front of the visual argument sufficient to suggest the claim it is making? How does the analytical essay help you further understand this visual argument?

275

FARM TOWN NEWS
Debbie Bryan

Debbie Bryan, the student who made this visual argument, describes it as a graphic novel. She created it for a children's audience. The artist explains how she made it: "The artwork is completely my own and is totally drawn and colored in the creative art program Adobe Photoshop CS3. After the graphic novel was completed frame by frame, I transferred the files to Adobe InDesign CS3. There I added the storyline text to each page of the novel. This program also enabled me to line up and link the pages for viewing ease."

As Torny and Bonter left the newspaper stand, Torny said, "Have you read today's issue of *Big Town News* yet, Bonter? This article is ridiculous!"

"According to Reverend Jason Jokestone, cows and horses are mortal enemies. He says historically cows have caused every problem that horses have today. Horses have to work and herd cows, while the cows just graze all day. There are even reports that cows are getting out of their pastures just to get horses in trouble."

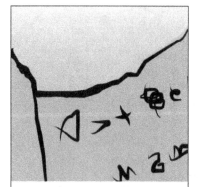

"Jokestone warns horses not to trust any cows in their town. 'Cows are really prejudiced against horses,' he says. 'Don't turn your back on them or they might gore you,' he warns. He says that cows and horses are being involved in race riots all over the country."

"That is so silly! Just look at Grumdo and Fark. They have been best friends since they were born."

"*Big Town News* just doesn't have a grasp on the truth in our town. *Farm Town News* is much more accurate."

"They live here and see how it really is between horses and cows. They are really great companions."

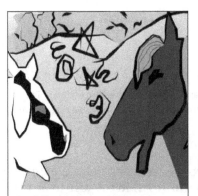

The following month peace in Farm Town would come to an end. Grumdo and Fark began to constantly argue.

"Torny," said Bonter, "just look at Grumdo and Fark! It is so upsetting to see them fighting like that! What could have happened to make them hate each other in such a short time?"

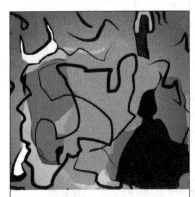

"I don't understand it," Torny replied. "Seeing them act that way just makes me want to cry. Look! They are hitting each other, and all over a silly patch of fresh grass! There is plenty for both of them here. If they keep this up, I don't know how they can ever be friends again!"

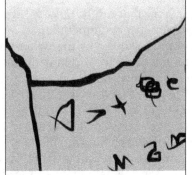

"Torny, you know that the *Farm Town News* has been reporting that pressure is building between horses and cows in Farm Town for two weeks now. An article in yesterday's paper read that cows are hogging all the fresh grass. But Grumdo and Fark never fought like this before."

"Now *both* newspapers are printing the same information. Since they both say the same thing, I guess it *has* to be true. See, the headlines read . . . Wait! Look at the small print under the title *Farm Town News!* It reads, 'now a member of the Big Town News Corporation.'"

277

FARM TOWN NEWS
Debbie Bryan

Debbie Bryan was a student at the University of Texas at Arlington when she created her graphic novel *Farm Town News*. Ideas and discussions from her writing class inspired her to create this visual argument.

1   The news media has an obligation to tell the truth from an unbiased point of view. However, in the race to be first with sensational stories, sometimes the truth becomes less important than the breaking story. Some news media show disregard for the injuries to innocent individuals by hastily reported stories.

2   The general public has an unquestioning trust of newspapers and television news programs, but this trust should not be given so lightly. As portrayed in *Farm Town News,* damage is done through the unethical telling of a story. In my graphic novel, a friendship was lost because Fark and Grumdo believed information reported by two newspapers that were, in fact, owned by the same corporation and were, therefore, printing the story from the same point of view.

3   Any major story that can be reported will vary from station to station or newspaper to newspaper. Sometimes, in the case of covering politicians, these stories can be skewed by the writer's or the newspaper owner's political views. In a time when a few multimedia information companies own a vast portion of the news networks and newspapers, this is detrimental for the public. The trust that the viewing public puts in the media affects their choices for political leaders. Without the opportunity to hear, see, and gauge for themselves the issues and characters of the potential political leaders, blind and uninformed choices are made.

4   Until the news media reclaims the ethics of telling only the proven facts and not just the sensational tidbits, bad leadership choices will be made. Worse yet, people will have their lives changed in negative ways.

For Discussion:

What is your understanding of the claim made in this graphic novel? Is the graphic novel format an effective way to make such a claim? Elaborate on your answer. Can you provide an example of unethical reporting or advertising through the media that misled an audience from your own experience? Describe it. Besides the collage, the sculpture, and the graphic novel that are used as examples of student-made visual argument, how else might you and your fellow students create visual arguments? What materials would you use? What would these arguments finally look like? What do you need to present it to the class?

Worksheet 3   Visual Argument Development

1. Write an issue question to focus your issue (example: *How can the unemployed be put back to work?*)

2. Write a claim that answers your issue question (example: *The government should create green-collar jobs to help the unemployed and the environment.*) Refer to the "Claim Development Worksheet" on page 349 to help you get ideas to develop your claim.

3. Check the type of visual argument you will create (check more than one, if necessary):

   _____ stand-alone argument   _____ photograph

   _____ support for my essay   _____ drawing

   _____ composite image   _____ painting

   _____ single image   _____ collage of images

   _____ still image   _____ graphic story (comics)

   _____ moving image   _____ 3-dimensional installation

   _____ all original   _____ PowerPoint

   _____ images from print sources   _____ sculpture

   _____ images from Internet   _____ video

4. Check the materials you will need:

   _____ computer   _____ video camera

   _____ Paint Shop Pro   _____ poster board

   _____ Photoshop   _____ colored markers

   _____ PowerPoint   _____ scissors and paste

   _____ magazines   _____ paints

   _____ newspapers   _____ other art supplies

   _____ still camera   _____ objects for installation

5. Which of the eight special features of visual argument will be evident in my work?

6. What words should I add to make it clear to my audience?

CHAPTER 11

Rogerian Argument and Common Ground

After studying this chapter, you will be able to:

LO1 Define the purpose and key aspects of Rogerian argument.

LO2 Create your own examples of Rogerian argument.

LO3 Apply the principles of Rogerian argument to academic writing.

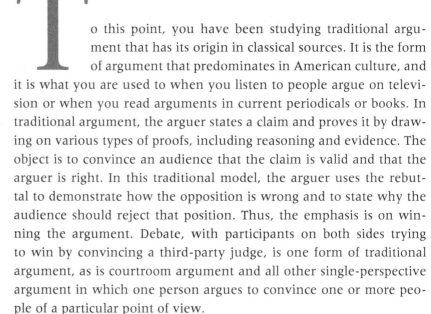

To this point, you have been studying traditional argument that has its origin in classical sources. It is the form of argument that predominates in American culture, and it is what you are used to when you listen to people argue on television or when you read arguments in current periodicals or books. In traditional argument, the arguer states a claim and proves it by drawing on various types of proofs, including reasoning and evidence. The object is to convince an audience that the claim is valid and that the arguer is right. In this traditional model, the arguer uses the rebuttal to demonstrate how the opposition is wrong and to state why the audience should reject that position. Thus, the emphasis is on winning the argument. Debate, with participants on both sides trying to win by convincing a third-party judge, is one form of traditional argument, as is courtroom argument and all other single-perspective argument in which one person argues to convince one or more people of a particular point of view.

As you know from your own experience and from reading about argument in this book, traditional argument does not always achieve its aims with the audience. Indeed, in certain situations when strongly held opinions or entire value systems are challenged, traditional argument may not be effective at all. The audience might simply stop listening or walk away. When that happens, it is useful to have another argumentation strategy to turn to, one that might work better in cases in which there seems to be a standoff or a lack of common ground among the arguing parties.

Rogerian argument, so called because it evolved from techniques originally applied by psychotherapist Carl Rogers, is a technique that is particularly useful for reducing conflict and establishing common ground between people who hold divergent positions and who may at times express hostility toward each other. Common ground often seems impossible to achieve in such situations, but two opposing parties can almost always find something to agree on if they try hard enough.

While establishing common ground in Rogerian argument uncovers what two parties have in common, Rogerian argument also involves more than that. Rogerian argument employs rebuttal differently. Instead of using rebuttal to show how the opposition is wrong, as in traditional argument, Rogerian argument requires that the arguer spend at least some time at the beginning of the argument not only explaining how the opposition's position is right but also identifying situations in which it might be valid. The arguer cannot do this very successfully without finding some common ground with the opposition. It is almost impossible to show how any part of another individual's opposing position is valid if you disagree with it totally.

Look back at the example in Chapter 1 (page 13) about the two individuals who are seeking common ground on methods for stopping random shooters. One of these individuals advocates that private citizens arm themselves with handguns as a deterrent to shooters. Another believes that the availability of handguns is the problem and advocates that private gun ownership be abolished. Common ground exists between the two parties because of their common concern for personal safety. To use Rogerian argument in this situation, the anti-handgun party would restate the pro-handgun party's position and would emphasize the common concern they both have for protecting their safety, before they search together for a solution on which they can agree.[1]

You may find Rogerian argument frustrating at first, especially if you favor contention and agonistic debate in situations in which your ideas and values seem to be under threat. Because Rogerian argument emphasizes making connections with the opposition and reducing hostility in such situations, you will need to curb your instincts to launch your argument by letting the opposition know how wrong you think they are. You can learn to use Rogerian argument, even if it is not your preferred or most natural style of arguing, in situations where traditional argument is no longer effective. It is a useful strategy when other strategies are failing. Let us look at a couple of examples.

---

[1] I am indebted to Jenny Edbauer for this example.

Achieving Common Ground
in Rogerian Argument

In 2005, Cal Thomas, a politically conservative newspaper columnist, and Bob Beckel, a liberal political analyst and consultant, began co-authoring their popular column "Common Ground" that appears in the newspaper *USA Today*. In 2007, they published *Common Ground: How to Stop the Partisan War That Is Destroying America,* and in it Cal Thomas describes their collaboration.

> We're a good example of how common ground can work. Before we knew each other, we only knew "about" each other. I saw you [Beckel] as a liberal Democrat with "evil" ideas and positions conservatives associate with that label. You saw me as a conservative Republican with similar "evil" ideas and suspect friends. When we got to know each other and talked about politics, as well as personal and family challenges, we stopped seeing each other in stereotype and came first to respect and then (shock, shock) even to admire each other. The politics became less important than the relationship. And, most surprising of all, we found ourselves in agreement about quite a number of things, though we occasionally still differ on the best ways to achieve our common goals.[2]

Their purpose in writing the book, they make clear, is to encourage U.S. politicians to follow their example and make it a rule to seek common ground as part of the political process for resolving difficult and divisive issues. Indeed, Thomas and Beckel claim they are presenting "a plan that makes polarization the issue and common ground the solution." They "believe the time is right to challenge polarization and for common ground to become the next dominant strategic force in national politics."[3] To support this idea, they argue that the public prefers this approach: "Surveys conducted over several years have found that Americans believe even the most partisan issues—from abortion to the Iraq war—can be resolved with an honest commitment by elected leaders in Washington to finding consensus."[4]

Rogerian argument, with its emphasis on finding common ground and reaching consensus, can sometimes help people who differ strongly in their views find a bedrock of values and ideas that they can all hold in common. As a result, divided individuals are often able to resolve at least some of their differences. The process of seeking political common ground that Thomas and Beckel believe is beginning to occur in political discussions, and that they hope will occur more often, includes listening, understanding, and accepting points of view different from one's own, recognizing that both positions have some merit, and finally finding a way to resolve some of the differences. This process is at the heart of Rogerian argument strategy.

Let us look at another real-life example of building common ground between disagreeing parties with each side demonstrating an understanding of the other's

---

[2]Cal Thomas and Bob Beckel, *Common Ground: How to Stop the Partisan War That Is Destroying America* (New York: Harper-Collins, 2007), 257.
[3]Thomas and Beckel, 12.
[4]Thomas and Beckel, 10.

point of view. Environmentalists, who typically want to protect the environment at all costs, often find themselves in opposition to individuals who make their living by exploiting the environment. Loggers, ranchers, mill owners, and other industrialists, for example, can fall into this second category. Individuals from both groups, stereotyped as "nature haters" and "eco-freaks" by the press, met in Idaho to discuss efforts for protecting endangered wildlife in the area. The environmentalists went to the meeting with some trepidation, but "as they joked and sparred over steak and beer, they discovered that neither side lived up to its stereotype. 'We found that we didn't hate each other,' said Alex Irby, a manager at the Konkolville sawmill. 'Turns out, we all like to do a lot of the same things. We love the outdoors.'" Timothy Egan, who wrote about the details of the meeting, makes this comment: "Loggers in the back country sitting down with environmentalists is an astonishing change."[5] One can infer that the common ground established in this meeting was brought about by each side describing to the other the value they placed on the environment and on outdoor activity in general. In such an exchange, both parties perceived that they had been heard, and further dialogue was then possible.

As you can see from both of these examples, understanding the rhetorical situation in general and the audience in particular by analyzing the thoughts and values of the parties involved is of critical importance in Rogerian argument. In Chapter 2 you learned how to analyze an audience as part of the planning process for writing argument papers. As you read the rest of this chapter, including the examples of Rogerian arguments written by students at the end of the chapter, pay particular attention to how Rogerian arguers analyze their audiences' dissenting opinions and values and then respond to them as part of their overall strategy.

Rogerian Argument as Strategy

Carl Rogers was a psychotherapist who was well known for the empathetic listening techniques he used in psychological counseling. Here is how he describes the importance of listening:

> I like to be heard. A number of times in my life I have felt myself bursting with insoluble problems, or going round and round in tormented circles, or during one period, overcome by feelings of worthlessness and despair. I think I have been more fortunate than most in finding at these times individuals who have been able to hear me and thus to rescue me from the chaos of my feelings. I have been able to find individuals who have been able to hear my meanings a little more deeply than I have known them. These individuals have heard me without judging me, diagnosing me, appraising me, evaluating me. They have just listened and clarified and responded to me at all levels at which I was communicating. I can testify that when you are in psychological distress and someone really hears you without passing judgment on you, without trying to take responsibility for you, without trying to mold you, it feels damn good.

[5]Timothy Egan, "Look Who's Hugging Trees Now," *New York Times Magazine,* July 7, 1996, 28.

At these times it has released the tension in me. It has permitted me to bring out the frightening feeling, the guilt, the despair, and the confusions that have been a part of my experience. When I have been listened to and when I have been heard, I am able to reperceive my world in a new way and to go on. It is astonishing how elements which seem insoluble become soluble when someone listens, how confusions which seem irremediable turn into relatively clear flowing streams when one is heard. I have deeply appreciated the times that I have experienced this sensitive, empathic, concentrated listening.[6]

Rogers later became interested in how listening techniques could be used to improve communication in other difficult, emotionally charged situations. Richard Young and his colleagues Alton Becker and Kenneth Pike built on Rogers's ideas to formulate Rogerian argument, a method for helping people in difficult situations make connections, create common ground, and understand one another. The object was to avoid undue conflict or, even worse, a mutual standoff.[7]

According to Young, Becker, and Pike, written Rogerian argument reduces the reader's sense of threat and conflict with the writer so that alternatives can be considered. Four goals are met with this strategy.

Goal 1. Writers let readers know they have been understood. To accomplish this purpose, the writer restates the opponent's position in summary form by using dispassionate, neutral language. The writer demonstrates that the reader has been heard and that the writer understands the issue exactly as the reader does. The loggers and the environmentalists listened and understood one another in the example cited earlier.

Goal 2. Writers show how readers' positions are valid in certain contexts and under certain conditions. The writer demonstrates to the reader that at least part of the reader's position is both valid and acceptable and thereby makes it easier for the reader to reciprocate and accept part of the writer's position. Both the loggers and the environmentalists discovered validity in each other's positions since neither group wanted to destroy wildlife.

Goal 3. Writers help readers understand that both of them share the same values, types of experience, attitudes, and perceptions and are thus similar in significant ways. The loggers and environmentalists made it clear to each other that they shared a love of the outdoors, held some of the same values, and enjoyed the same types of experience.

Goal 4. Writers propose solutions made up of elements from both sides that can be agreed to by both parties. At this point, environmentalists discovered that loggers were quite willing to pursue ways to preserve wildlife.

The most important feature of Rogerian argument is listening empathetically and nonjudgmentally. Rogers perceived that people usually listen judgmentally

---

[6]Carl R. Rogers, *A Way of Being,* Boston: Houghton Mifflin, 1980, 12–13. I thank Barbara Ciarello for calling this to my attention.

[7]Richard Young, Alton Becker, and Kenneth Pike, *Rhetoric: Discovery and Change* (New York: Harcourt, Brace, and World, 1970), 7–8, 274–90.

and evaluatively. They are eager to jump in, point out what is right or wrong, and make corrections or refutations, whereas Rogerian listening requires that insight into the other's position precede evaluation. Thus, a writer of Rogerian argument takes the reader's place, and this is achieved by requiring that the writer provide neutral summaries of the reader's position that show sympathetic understanding of it and its context. In doing this, the writer encourages a continued and open exchange of ideas with the reader. In Rogers's words, the writer "listens with" as opposed to "evaluating about."

In real life, Rogerian argument is used frequently, particularly in business and perhaps increasingly in politics, where agreement is indispensable. Some people in business claim they could not get anything done if they did not use Rogerian strategies on a daily basis. William L. Ury, one of the founders of the Program on Negotiation at Harvard Law School, claims that in business now, the best way to compete is to be able to cooperate. Cooperation is necessary because of the numerous mergers and cooperative ventures between companies. Many companies now work with the same markets and the same customers, and they cannot compete, as in former times, without weakening themselves as much as their competitors.[8]

Box 11.1 ■ contrasts Rogerian argument, as explained by Young, Becker, and Pike, with the traditional model of argument.

ROGERIAN ARGUMENT ONLINE

While the emergence of the Web has fostered greater public engagement with issues, it has, in many cases, also led to a greater polarization. Extreme viewpoints, those that evince no interest in hearing, let alone accepting, the views of the other side, are found throughout writing online. Choose an example of an online argument that, in your view, is especially polarizing. What does this debate look like? What views does it pit against each other? Moreover, what is it about these views that makes this debate so polarizing? Then, using the goals of Rogerian argument outlined above, write an explanation of how these differences might bridged. How and where, within this debate, is it possible to find common ground? What values, views and goals could these opposing sides actually be said to share?

---

[8]William L. Ury, "Getting Past No . . . to Yes! The Art of Negotiation." Workshop, Dallas, October 12, 1999.

Box 11.1	Traditional and Rogerian Argument Compared.

▶▶▶ **What Is Rogerian Argument?**

	TRADITIONAL ARGUMENT	**ROGERIAN ARGUMENT**
Basic strategy	Writer states the claim and gives reasons to prove it. Writer refutes the opponent by showing what is wrong or invalid.	The writer states opponent's claim to demonstrate understanding and shows how it is valid.
Ethos	Writer establishes own character by demonstrating fair-mindedness, competence, and goodwill.	Writer builds opponent's *ethos* and enhances own character through empathy.
Logos	Writer appeals to reason to establish a claim and refute the opponent's claim.	Writer proceeds in an explanatory fashion to analyze the conditions under which the position of either side is valid.
Pathos	Writer arouses emotions with evocative language to strengthen the claim.	Writer uses descriptive, dispassionate language to cool emotions on both sides.
Goal	Writer seeks to change opponent's mind and thereby win the argument.	The writer creates cooperation, the possibility that both sides might change, and a mutually advantageous outcome.
Use of argument techniques	Writer draws on conventional structures and techniques.	Writer throws out conventional structures and techniques because they may be threatening and focuses instead on connecting empathetically.

Writing Rogerian Argument

To write Rogerian argument, according to Young, Becker, and Pike, the writer proceeds in phases rather than following set organizational patterns or argumentation strategies. These phases are as follows:

1. The writer introduces the issue and shows that the opponent's position is understood by restating it.

2. The writer shows in which contexts and under what conditions the opponent's position may be valid. Note that the opponent is never made to feel completely wrong.

3. The writer then states his or her own position, including the contexts in which it is valid.

4. The writer states how the opponent's position would benefit if the opponent were to adopt elements of the writer's position. An attempt is finally made to

show that the two positions complement each other and that each supplies what the other lacks.

Rogerian Argument in Academic Writing

Rogerian argument as described by Young, Becker, and Pike is rarely, if ever, written exactly according to their format. You can learn more about Rogerian argument, however, by using their format as practice. The "Exercises and Activities" section of this chapter provides four examples of Rogerian argument papers written by students who followed Young, Becker, and Pike's formulations. You also will be invited to write a Rogerian argument paper using this format.

As you read professionally written argument, however, you are much more likely to find elements or variations of Rogerian argument rather than arguments that include all of the parts of the Young, Becker, and Pike model. Here are some variations of Rogerian argument that you may encounter in your academic reading.

1. *Report on past research at the beginning of an academic argument.* Authors of academic argument, as a matter of convention, often begin with a review of what previous writers have contributed to the subject. They identify the writers by name and summarize their contributions before identifying and developing their own contribution to the subject. Thus an ongoing chain of conversation is established that acknowledges what has gone before the new material that is the actual subject of the article.

2. *Research proposal.* Research proposals that request funds and resources from granting agencies typically begin with a positive summary of the contributions of past researchers. Only after this former work has been acknowledged does the researcher explain how the new proposed research will build on what has gone before.[9]

3. *Rogerian response paper.* This paper is written in response to an essay written by another person with whom the author disagrees. The author of a response paper typically rejects the position that the author of the other essay presents but hopes to create common ground and understanding with that person to keep a dialogue on the issue going. The goal is to make a connection with the author of the other essay and thus create a context of understanding so that both authors can continue exploring the issue. Such papers usually begin with a restatement of the other author's position along with an acknowledgment of what is valuable about that position before the author goes on to present a different view of the matter. You will be invited to try writing a Rogerian response paper yourself in Exercise B.

As you read arguments written by other authors, look for elements of Rogerian argument. The three examples just cited by no means exhaust the possibilities.

---

[9]I am indebted to Mary Stanley for alerting me to this use of Rogerian argument.

Using Rogerian Principles to Argue Like a Citizen

One criticism sometimes leveled at Rogerian argument when it is first encountered, is that it can be perceived to be manipulative. Though it can be used in this way, it is not inherent to this form of argumentation. People who use Rogerian argument in unethical ways to manipulate other people may exhibit a condescending attitude or fake sincerity. They may also use some of the same tactics that unethical arguers use in traditional argument: for example, hiding the real purpose of the argument by misrepresenting the issue; using inappropriate emotional appeals, including emotionally loaded language; manufacturing evidence; or the use of inaccurate evidence, exaggerations, or lies.

Individuals who practice ethical Rogerian argument, on the other hand, make a genuine attempt to understand an issue and its consequences from a range of different perspectives. Participants in Rogerian argument have to sincerely believe that the position they propose is in the best interests of both parties and, possibly, the larger society as well. They need to be able to answer the questions, *Who are benefited by what I want?* and *Who are burdened or hurt?* and to scrupulously consider the consequences of their answers to those questions. They need to listen and hear nonjudgmentally; they need to seek genuine agreement with at least part of the opponent's position; and they need to develop some unconditional positive regard for the individuals with whom they are engaged and show that regard in all that they say. In other words, participants in Rogerian argument need to think, argue, and act like a citizen.

In order to test out this premise, return for a moment to the online issue you analyzed above. Now that you have explained how Rogerian argument can help overcome the polarization we so often see in online debates, build upon this work by exploring how this same framework can help us connect argument to citizenship. To do this, answer the following questions: Where in my community is this particular issue of greatest importance? Who are the participants with the greatest stake in this debate? What concrete action could be taken with this community to achieve the common ground revealed by Rogerian argument? What action, decision or policy would most likely enable a Rogerian solution to this debate?

Review Questions

1. What are the four goals of Rogerian argument, and how do they differ from those of traditional argument?

2. What are some of the advantages and disadvantages of Rogerian argument?

3. In what type of argumentation situation do you think you might find Rogerian argument more productive than traditional argument? Describe an issue, along with the rhetorical situation, which might prompt you to resort to Rogerian argument.

4. In what type of argumentation situation do you think you might find traditional argument more productive than Rogerian argument? Describe an

issue, along with the rhetorical situation, which might prompt you to use traditional argument instead of Rogerian argument.

5. What difficulties, if any, do you personally contemplate in using Rogerian argument? How do you feel about using this strategy?

Exercises and Activities

A. Class Discussion: Understanding Rogerian Argument as a Strategy

The excerpt below is taken from Edward O. Wilson's book *The Future of Life*. Read the passage, analyze the Rogerian strategy, and answer the questions at the end.

Before you Read: What is your present attitude about preserving the environment? Do you know of anyone who holds a different view? What is it?

ESSAY #1   THE FUTURE OF LIFE*

Edward O. Wilson

Wilson, a well-known scientist and Harvard professor, has been called the father of the modern environmental movement. His book *The Future of Life* provides plans for conserving earth's biodiversity.

1 Everyone has some kind of environmental ethic, even if it somehow makes a virtue of cutting the last ancient forests and damming the last wild rivers. Done, it is said, to grow the economy and save jobs. Done because we are running short of space and fuel. *Hey, listen, people come first!*—and most certainly before beach mice and louseworts. I recall vividly the conversation I had with a cab driver in Key West in 1968 when we touched on the Everglades burning to the north. Too bad, he said. The Everglades are a wonderful place. But wilderness always gives way to civilization, doesn't it? That is progress and the way of the world, and we can't do much about it.

2 Everyone is also an avowed environmentalist. No one says flatly, "To hell with nature." On the other hand, no one says, "Let's give it all back to nature." Rather, when invoking the social contract by which we all live, the typical people-first ethicist thinks about the environment short-term and the typical environmental ethicist thinks about it long-term. Both are sincere and have something true and important to say. The people-first thinker says we need to take a little cut here and there: the environmentalist says nature is dying the death of a thousands cuts. So how do we combine the best of short-term and long-term goals? Perhaps, despite decades of bitter philosophical dispute, an optimum mix

of the goals might result in a consensus more satisfactory than either side thought possible from total victory alone. Down deep, I believe, no one wants a total victory. The people-firster likes parks, and the environmentalist rides petroleum-powered vehicles to get there.

For Discussion:

What is the issue in this passage? What two groups of people are identified? Why might they feel hostile? What are their differences? How does Wilson create common ground between the two groups? How does Wilson use Rogerian strategy? Summarize the two positions and describe the Rogerian elements in the passage. Why do you think Wilson uses Rogerian strategy in this part of his book? How do you think Wilson might describe his audience for this passage?

B. Writing Assignment: Write a Rogerian Response

Read the following essay that appeared in another chapter: "'A' Is for 'Absent'" (pages 42–43). As an option, find a letter to the editor in a newspaper that you disagree with and write a Rogerian response to it. Use either essay or personal letter format. Your paper should be from 300 to 500 words long.

Prewriting

Write a brief summary of the position taken by the author of the essay you have selected. Then write a brief summary of your position. Make certain you understand both positions clearly.

Writing

Do all of the following in your paper:

1. State the opposition's position as presented in the article (or letter) and describe in what instances this position might work or be acceptable. As you write, imagine that the individual who wrote the article or letter will be reading your response. Write so that that person will feel "heard."

2. Write a clear transition to your position on the issue.

3. State how your position would also work or be acceptable.

4. Try to reconcile the two positions.

C. Class Discussion: Creating Images for Visual Rogerian Argument

Creating images to support visual arguments, or creating stand-alone Rogerian visual arguments, can be challenging because not one, but two positions need to be portrayed as equal and potentially correct. Further, the idea of consensual agreement needs to be part of the picture as well. Images 1, 2, and 3 can be used as images to represent Rogerian argument. No detailed captions appear with these images. They speak for themselves. Look at each of them, and then answer the "For Discussion" questions.

Image 1:
Hands across the World.

Image 2:
Bridging the Gap.

Image 3:
Bipartisanship and What It Can Achieve.

For Discussion: What do these three images have in common? In what argumentation contexts and for what types of issues would each be appropriate? To answer this question, study the icons used in each visual. What do they communicate about the broader context of each argument? The book jacket for *Common Ground: How to Stop the Partisan War That Is Destroying America,* quoted earlier in this chapter (page 282), shows the two authors in four small photos frowning, angry, and aggressively pointing their fingers at each other as they argue, and then, in a larger photo, they are standing with their arms on each other's shoulders while smiling at the camera. Do you have any ideas for visual argument that communicate the methods and goals of Rogerian argument? Use your imagination, and describe your ideas for the class.

291

D. Group Activity: Creating Your Own Rogerian Web site

First, choose an issue that seems especially controversial or polarizing. What does the debate around this issue typically look like? What are the different views that are expressed, and how are they different? Next, use the principles of Rogerian argument to create a hypothetical Web site in which these differences might be resolved. How would this Web site present the issue at hand? How would it speak to the stakeholders in this debate with such differing or opposing views? What specific features would most effectively help achieve this goal?

E. Writing Assignment: Rogerian Argument

You are now going to write a Rogerian argument of around 1,000 words on an issue of your choice. There are several ways to set up this assignment.

Read through the following options, select one that appeals to you, and proceed with the rest of the instructions for the assignment. The basic instructions in option 1 apply to all four options. Examples for options 1, 2, and 3 are provided at the end of this exercise.

Option 1. If you wrote an exploratory paper, write a Rogerian argument in response to the position you discovered that is most unlike the position you favor. You may have already articulated this opposing position in your exploratory paper. Move this position to the beginning of your Rogerian argument paper, and rewrite it until you believe you have fairly and dispassionately represented that other point of view. People who hold that view need to be able to agree that you have heard and understood them.

Look for common ground with that other view. Use that common ground to describe contexts and conditions in which the opponent's position might be valid. Do not show what is wrong with this other position.

Now write a transition that changes the subject to your position. Describe your position, and show the contexts in which is it valid.

Finally, reconcile the two positions. Show how they can complement each other, how one supplies what the other lacks, and how everyone would benefit if elements of both were finally accepted. (See Example 1.)

Option 2. Select any issue that you understand from at least two opposing points of view. You should feel strongly about your point of view, and you should have strong negative feelings about opposing viewpoints. Write a Rogerian argument in response to an opposing viewpoint. (See Example 2.)

Option 3. Recall the last time you were in an argument in which there was a stalemate and no one seemed to win. Write a letter to the individual with whom you were arguing. Use Rogerian strategy. (See Example 3.)

Option 4. Team up with a classmate who disagrees with you on a specific issue. Take turns articulating your partner's position until that person feels "heard" and understood. Then write a Rogerian argument in response to that position.

Prewriting

Write a one-paragraph summary of the opposing position and a one-paragraph summary of your position. Refer to these summaries when you write your paper.

Writing

Write your paper, making sure you do all of the following:

1. Introduce the issue and restate the opposing position to show you understand it.

2. Show in which contexts and under what conditions the opposing position may be valid. State it so that it is acceptable to the opposition.

3. Write a clear transition that moves the reader from the position you have just explained to the position that you favor and will now defend.

4. State your own position and describe the context in which it is valid.

5. Show how the opposing position would be strengthened by adding elements of your position. Then try to reconcile the two positions.

Examples

Here are three examples of Rogerian argument written by students.

Example 1 *(Option 1).* "Human Cloning: Is It a Viable Option?" was written by a student in an argument class who had also written an exploratory paper on this subject. In writing this paper, the student began with the position she had researched that was most unlike her own and rewrote it until she thought it would satisfy the individuals who hold that position. Notice that she was able to use the research for her other paper to add support for this paper as well. The marginal annotations make it easier for you to distinguish the parts of her paper.

Following the student's paper is a Rogerian argument evaluation sheet that has been filled out to show how her argument conforms to the recommended parts of a Rogerian argument. The requirements for the Rogerian argument paper are described in the left column, and the right column shows how well this paper met those requirements. When you have finished reading the papers in Examples 2 and 3, see if you can identify and describe the parts of those papers well enough to complete evaluation sheets like the sample. These analyses will help you understand how to write your own Rogerian argument.*

293

STUDENT PAPER #1   Angela A. Boatwright
Professor Thorne
English 1302
30 April 2011

Human Cloning: Is It a Viable Option?

Introduction to issue and summary of rhetorical situation.

1   Well, hello Dolly! Although research in animal or human cloning is not new, the technology has never had as much potential as it does today. Interest in what is and is not considered ethical in cloning research has surfaced since the historic announcement in Scotland of the existence of a cloned sheep named Dolly. Scientists were able to create a cloned sheep by taking the genes from a six-year-old sheep and putting them into an enucleated egg from another sheep. This egg was then implanted in the womb of yet another sheep, resulting in the birth of an identical twin that is six years younger than its sister (Bailey). This is the first known asexual reproduction of a mammal.

---

*For all the student papers in Chapter 11, see Appendix 1 for the actual MLA format guidelines.

It seems a reasonable assumption that a human clone is the next logical step down this technological pathway.

Explanation of opposing position to create common ground.

2   Those who support unregulated human cloning experimentation justify their position by citing the medical gains and potential benefits the technology has to offer. They believe that the possible benefits of this technology far outweigh the risks and, furthermore, that it is an ethical practice because of its potential benefits. Some of these benefits include the generation of skin grafts for burn victims and bone marrow for patients undergoing cancer chemotherapy (Butler and Wadman 8). Cloning also shows promise for treating infertility and could become an option either for infertile couples or for people who have genetic defects and fear passing these defects on to their offspring.

3   Supporters of cloning believe that the arguments against cloning are vague and speculative and that they simply do not justify a ban. It is not the technology that frightens people so much as it is a lack of understanding. When people picture the result of an attempt at human cloning, they see images of Frankenstein or an army of Hitlers. Researchers believe that given time to digest the information, the public will one day regard cloning with the same openness and sense of normalcy that it now regards blood transfusions and organ transplants. They also reason that a ban on cloning could drive the technology underground, leading to a greater potential for unsafe, unregulated, and exploitative misuse.

Description of context in which opposing position is valid

4   Everyone would probably agree that technological advances have changed our lives in positive ways, and cloning research is not likely to be an exception. The fear held by cloning supporters, that the sensationalism created by this issue has clouded the judgment of the public and lawmakers who support a ban on cloning, is certainly a valid concern. Although it is not clear that human cloning will offer any great benefits to humanity, no one has yet made a persuasive case that it would do any real harm either (Macklin 64). It would be an injustice to completely abandon the possibilities that could enhance the lives of so many people based solely on hypothetical applications of a technology that may never be realized. Each disease we are able to eradicate is another huge step for humankind.

Transition to author's view

Explanation of author's view.

5   I agree that we should do everything in our power to improve the longevity and quality of life of all people, but I do not believe it should be at the expense of the dignity of human life. Many people who oppose cloning view it as an "invasion of personality." Even Dr. Ian Wilmut and his colleagues, the creators of Dolly, hold the position that cloning of humans would be unethical (64). He points out that it took 277 attempts to produce one live lamb. Of the 277 "reconstructed" embryos, 29 were implanted into recipient ewes, and 3 out of 5 lambs showed developmental abnormalities and died soon after birth. He believes similar tests with humans would not be acceptable.

6   Those of us who advocate anticloning measures believe that the potential abuse of such power could have disastrous consequences. The fear of the creation of human clones for the sole purpose of harvesting them for "spare parts" is too great to ignore. Another concern is that cloning will lead to

efforts to breed individuals with perceived exceptional genetic qualities, eliminating the diversity that makes the human race what it is. There is a widespread belief that parents might create unrealistic expectations for cloned children, believing they no longer have the potential limitations of their genetic ancestors (Pence 135). Cloning is really a major step toward regarding our children as acceptable only if they conform to the choices of our will (Carey).

7   Many of us are also bound by the religious ideas we have been brought up with, telling us that only God has the right to create life. It is sinful to think of removing that sovereign right from an omnipotent God and placing it in the hands of mere mortals. Like the majority of Americans, I believe that human cloning experimentation should be banned before it can become an out-of-control reality.

Personal example to introduce idea of reconciliation of the two opposing positions.

8   I am fortunate to be the mother of a wonderful and beautiful baby girl. If I had been given the opportunity to choose her characteristics, would I have elected to change my child? I absolutely would not. I would not trade any of her personal traits for something "better." I love her just as God gave her to me. Yet with absolute certainty, I can admit that if she developed a life-threatening ailment, I would not hesitate for a second to utilize any cloning technology available to cure her. This is not to say I would sacrifice another life for hers, only that I would employ any and all resources available short of that alternative.

Reconciliation of positions

9   If we can agree that human life should always be held in the highest esteem, we have the basis for reconciling our positions. Cloning should not be used to pick and choose the type of people who are allowed to exist, but we should explore the potential medical benefits of cloning technology research. Many of the medical procedures we take for granted every day were once as controversial as cloning is at this very moment. Most of these procedures became successful at the cost of testing on live beings, but with their consent. We must never allow human beings to be the subjects of experimentation without their knowledge or permission. We may not impose conditions on human beings that they might not have consented to if allowed to make the decision for themselves.

10   A moratorium might be a better solution than an outright ban. A moratorium would authorize a temporary delay of human cloning research and allow us the time to sort out the details and ensure that an educated decision is made. It is easier to make an intelligent decision when there is not a feeling of impending doom hanging over our heads. "In a democratic society we don't usually pass laws outlawing something before there is actual or probable evidence of harm" (Macklin 64). This statement can serve as a guide for future policy on human cloning.

Works Cited

Bailey, Ronald. "The Twin Paradox: What Exactly Is Wrong with Cloning People?" *Reason* May 1997. *Reasononline.* Web. 12 Mar. 2008.

Butler, Declan, and Meredith Wadman. "Calls for Cloning Ban Sell Science Short." *Nature* 6 Mar. 1997: 8–9. Print.

Carey, John. "Human Clones: It's Decision Time." *Business Week* 10 Aug. 1998: 32. Print.

Macklin, Ruth. "Human Cloning? Don't Just Say No." *U.S. News & World Report* 10 Mar. 1997: 64+. Print.

Pence, Gregory E. *Who's Afraid of Human Cloning?* Lanham: Rowman, 1998. Print.

Wilmut, Ian. "Roslin Institute Experiments: Creation of Dolly the Sheep." *Congressional Digest* Feb. 1998: 41+. Print.

For Discussion:

Describe a rhetorical situation in which it would be better to write this paper about cloning in this form, using Rogerian strategy, than it would be to write it as a position paper, using traditional argument. Describe the readers, constraints, and, in particular, the exigence as you imagine the rhetorical situation for this paper.

Evaluation Sheet for Rogerian Argument Paper

REQUIREMENTS OF ROGERIAN ARGUMENT	WHAT THE AUTHOR DID
1. Introduce the issue and state the opposing position to show that you understand it.	1. Introduced the issue in paragraph 1 and presented the opposing view accompanied by good reasons in paragraphs 2 and 3.
2. Show how the opposition might be right.	2. Showed the contexts in which the other position might be valid in paragraph 4.
3. Write a clear transition from the opposing position to your position.	3. Wrote a transition in the first sentence of paragraph 5 to move from opposing to own position.
4. Give your position and show how you might be right.	4. Presented own position in paragraphs 5, 6, and 7.
5. Reconcile the two positions.	5. Reconciled the two views in paragraphs 8, 9, and 10.

Example 2 *(Option 2)*. "Let Those Who Ride Decide!" was written by a student who depends on his motorcycle for all of his transportation. When you have finished reading this paper, see if you can identify and describe its parts and complete an evaluation sheet like the sample above. This analysis will help you understand how to write your own Rogerian argument.

STUDENT PAPER #2   Eric Hartman
Professor Wood
English 1302
30 April 2011

Let Those Who Ride Decide!

1   Should the law mandate that motorcyclists wear a helmet? Texas law presently does not require that a helmet be worn by those over twenty-one who have taken a motorcycle safety course or who have at least $10,000 in health insurance coverage for injuries sustained while operating a motorcycle. In the past, Texas has had a helmet law that was universal, and many neighboring states still do. There are many in Texas who would like to see the old law reinstated so that all motorcyclists, regardless of their age, would be required to wear a helmet at all times.

2   Proponents of helmet laws are concerned with motorcyclists' safety. Their argument, that one is more likely either to survive a motorcycle wreck or to minimize physical damage if wearing a helmet, is very strong. Thus the value put on safety clearly is significant, especially for those who have lost a loved one in a motorcycle fatality. Similarly, because damage is less likely for helmet wearers, a motorcyclist in an accident is perceived as less likely to become disabled and require monetary support from the government (i.e., the taxpayers). The argument here is that a motorcyclist is potentially not only hurting him or herself but also those who might have to financially support these unfortunate motorcyclists.

3   It is not too difficult to see why one would be a proponent of mandatory helmet laws. Indeed, it would be unfortunate and unfair for anyone to have to support financially an incapacitated individual who might not be in such a condition had he or she been wearing a helmet. It is also almost inconceivable to argue that one is safer on a motorcycle without a helmet. Certainly the arguments in favor of mandatory helmet laws are so strong that it is difficult to imagine any alternative position.

4   However, there is another position, and one that is held just as passionately by some people as the one just described. As unlikely as it seems, there is a debate about the effectiveness of helmets. I agree with many people who ride motorcycles who believe helmet laws should be completely abolished. If that cannot be accomplished, the mandatory age should at least be lowered from twenty-one to eighteen. Individuals who hold this point of view cite studies that suggest helmets have the potential to severely damage the spinal cord and/or vertebrae in an accident, causing varying degrees of paralysis and death. Full-face helmets are criticized for obstructing a rider's hearing and vision, especially peripheral vision. Helmets, furthermore, prevent the body's natural process of cooling through the head and can contribute to heat exhaustion or heat stroke, as riders in Texas are aware (Quigley).

5   Even the notion that is often termed the "social burden" theory is questionable. The famous Harborview Medical Center study showed that injured motorcyclists relied on public funds 63.4 percent of the time, which is

significant. But it was later determined that 67 percent of the general population relied on public funding for hospital bills over the same period of time. Statistically, there does not seem to be any significant distinction between the reliance of motorcyclists and the general public on public funding. Thus the social burden theory seems primarily to be just that, a theory. It sounds good, but it seems to lack statistical validation ("Critics").

6   Even though I can see the validity of some of the arguments made by the proponents of helmet laws, I think there is ultimately some question regarding the strength of their arguments, and even some question of whether their arguments address the real issue that is built on a different value altogether, namely freedom. We have certain inalienable rights, rights to life, liberty, and the pursuit of happiness. It seems to me that mandatory helmet laws are in violation of such rights. Governments have a responsibility to protect their inhabitants from being harmed by each other in reasonable situations. It is not necessarily the responsibility of the government to try to prevent people from ever encountering danger. One could die on a plane, in a car, or in an electrical fire in one's house, but the government would not think to outlaw airplanes, automobiles, or electricity. The fact that one incurs danger without a helmet is not a sufficient reason to mandate use of a helmet.

7   There is understandably a tension between safety and freedom, and these two values are often in conflict. In many instances people may not be in a position to make an educated decision with regard to their safety, and we understand such decisions being made for them. For example, children are not seen as capable of making certain decisions concerning the use of seat belts in automobiles or watching certain movies. Making those decisions for them seems reasonable as does requiring those under eighteen to wear a helmet. Yet, for those of sound mind who are deemed responsible, it seems unreasonable to strip away their freedom to choose by requiring them to wear a helmet.

8   I appreciate the care and concern of those proponents of helmet laws and understand their passion, and I am not unilaterally against helmets. When I ride on the highways, I tend to use mine. You might say that I am pro-choice when it comes to helmets. I believe in the rider's right to choose whether or not he or she wants to wear a helmet. I am in no way opposed to educating and informing riders about helmets as part of the licensing process. Then riders are more likely to make the best decision with the best information at their disposal. I just want the riders to decide whether or not to wear a helmet instead of someone else making that decision for them as if they were children. In short, I echo many of my fellow motorcyclists who say, "Let those who ride decide."

Works Cited

"Critics Falsely Claim That Bikers Are a Burden on Society." *Bikers Rights Online!* N.p., 2001. Web. 27 Apr. 2008. <http://www.bikersrights.com/ama/ABCWNTBurden .html>.

Quigley, Richard. "NHTSA's Safety Standards Are Shown to Be Anything but Safe." *Helmet Law Defense League Report.* 3rd ed. N.p., Mar. 1994. Web. 27 Apr. 2008. <http://usff.com/hldl/report/3rdEditiona.html\#R302>.

For Discussion:

Describe a rhetorical situation in which you think it would be better to write this paper about helmets in this form, using Rogerian strategy, than it would be to write it as a position paper, using traditional strategy. Describe the readers, constraints, and, in particular, the exigence as you imagine the rhetorical situation that might have prompted this paper.

Example 3 *(Option 3)*. "Dear Boss" was written by a student who worked part-time while going to college and needed to change her working hours and some of her responsibilities. She had already spoken to her boss about making some changes but ended up with more responsibility instead of less. She was worried that her boss might think she was selfish and unconcerned about the welfare of the company. She was also worried that working too many hours would endanger her scholarship. It was very important to her that she reach a resolution to her problem. She decided to use Rogerian strategy to come to a better resolution of her dilemma with her boss. (After reading "Dear Boss," complete on evaluation using the sheet on page 296.)

STUDENT PAPER #3   Elizabeth Nabhan
Professor Wood
English 1302
30 April 2011

Dear Boss

1 Dear Boss,

I am writing to you in response to our recent conversation regarding my responsibilities as an employee of Smith and Smith. You indicated to me that you felt I had a surplus of free time at work and suggested that I was obviously capable of handling a greater workload. Shortly thereafter, you delegated to me several new tasks that are to be performed on a regular basis. I understand that you believe I should pick up the additional workload to ensure that I am performing at a maximum level of output on a day-to-day basis. Also, you think I would complete the tasks more effectively than the individuals previously assigned to them.

2   I understand your reasoning that I should maintain a high level of output on a daily basis. As an employee of the company, it is my obligation to be productive for the duration of my workday. Not producing enough work results in idle time that, in turn, results in a loss to the company. It is intrinsic to the very nature of my role as a corporate auditor to ensure that the company does not engage in wasteful expenditures. If I worked nonstop every workday I would maximize my rate of efficiency and save the company the cost of hiring an additional employee. Furthermore, I accept your opinion that I am the employee who could most efficiently handle the new tasks you would like me to take on. My knowledge and experience with the required tasks puts me at an advantage over the employees previously delegated this

work. Because of this, I would be able to complete the tasks much more quickly than other employees who would likely require more research time. Your perspective is fundamentally valid. However, I would like to introduce several factors that I believe may also bear consideration. In doing so, I believe it will be possible to reach a satisfactory conclusion regarding the issue of my workload and responsibilities.

3   According to the terms of my employment, I am required to complete a minimum of twenty hours per week. It was mutually agreed that any time I am not enrolled in school, I am free to work up to forty hours per week. The period during which I had an unusually ample amount of "down time" occurred during the summer months when I was not enrolled in school. As a result, I did briefly have an increased number of work hours. During this interim period I could have easily increased my workload, but I was not assigned any new tasks. In fact, additional duties were not assigned to me until after I commenced the fall semester. My hours are now reduced by nearly one-half, and, as a result, my idle time has diminished significantly. An increased workload now will limit the time I spend on each project and could result in a decrease in the quality of the work I complete.

4   I do not think there is any great concern as to whether the employees originally assigned to my newest tasks are able to complete them satisfactorily. These employees were hired based on their skills for completing the tasks at hand, and none of these tasks could be considered as falling outside of the scope of their regular duties. Furthermore, I believe it would be counterproductive to reassign their tasks to me, as it would essentially undermine these other employees' expertise. This type of situation can often lead to a decrease in morale, which would in turn affect each employee's total output. Finally, I would like to reconsider the belief that idle time on my part results in decreased productivity. During my free time I am in a position to assist other staff members as necessary. I also utilize this time to observe subordinate employees, which is consistent with my role as the corporate auditor.

5   Our individual points of view share the common purpose of doing what is best for the company as a whole. Therefore, I believe it is possible to accomplish this goal via compromise. According to your perspective, I should take on additional responsibilities to fill gaps in my productivity while relieving less-qualified employees. From my point of view, I feel that my time is already effectively spent. I suggest the following steps be taken in order to ensure that each of our needs are met: First, my reduced hours must be taken into consideration when assigning me work. When I am in a position to take on additional duties, I feel I should be assigned those most compatible with my job description. More general tasks should be delegated to other employees. To alleviate your hesitation regarding their ability to perform these, I accept the responsibility of overseer and will offer them any help they may need. In doing so, I will apply my own expertise to more specific tasks without overburdening myself in such a way as to reduce my overall efficiency. Additionally, this will allow other employees the opportunity to sharpen their skills, while remaining under my observation. I propose this delegation

of duties be put into effect under a probationary period, during which time we can observe the success of the program, and, if needed, redelegate tasks. Thank you for your consideration.

Sincerely,
Elizabeth Nabhan

For Discussion:

What is the issue? What is the boss's position? What is the student's position? If you were the boss, how would you respond to this letter?

F. Class Project: Combining Strategies in a Class Debate with Attempts to Reconcile the Opposing Positions

This activity provides the opportunity to combine elements of traditional and Rogerian argument theory that you have learned in Chapters 10–11.

Debate is a traditional forum for argument, and a common model for debate is to have two people on each side of the issue present their views and a judge who declares a winner. Your class can set up a debate in which everyone participates. For this class debate, however, we will use a somewhat different strategy that involves not only stating the opposing viewpoints but also working to find some common ground between the two opposing positions to achieve more productive argument and to avoid a standoff with no agreement and no resolution of the issue.

We draw on *social judgment theory* to help organize the debate. Social judgment theorists, who study the positions that individuals take on issues, plot positions on a continuum that ranges from extremely positive to extremely negative. They then describe these positions in terms of latitudes of acceptance. Individuals at the extremes of the continuum have narrow latitudes of acceptance and can usually tolerate only positions that are very close to their own. Somewhere in the middle is a latitude of noncommitment. People in this area, who are not strongly involved with the issue, have comparatively wide latitudes of acceptance and can tolerate a wide range of positions. The object of this debate is to increase everyone's latitudes of acceptance so that productive argument can take place.

Preparing for the Debates

1. *Select an Issue*

The class can either nominate possible issues from the following list of topics and articles in this book or make recommendations of their own. They can then vote on which one of them is to be the topic for debate. The issue should be written in statement form, as in the list, so that individuals can either agree or disagree with it.

Resolved: Traditional families are best, with the mother taking care of the children and the father working to support the family. See the article by Pederson.

Resolved: Dating services in America and arranged marriages in other countries are the best ways of finding a suitable husband or wife. See the articles by Jain and Hassler.

301

Resolved: Relying on egg donors and sperm banks can be the best way to conceive brilliant and successful children. See the articles by Kolata and Orenstein.

Resolved: The grading system conventionally use in elementary and high school should be abolished. See the articles by Gatto, Jaschik.

Resolved: The United States should build a fence along the United States–Mexico border to control illegal immigration. See the articles by Goldberg and Aaronovitch.

Resolved: Wars are inevitable. See the articles by James and Mead.

Or: Brainstorm campus or current events issues and then vote on which one to debate.

2. *Create Three Groups*

The class will divide into three groups. Two groups are encouraged to take strong affirmative and negative positions and to argue from those points of view, presenting pro and con arguments, with presumably narrow latitudes of acceptance. A third group with a wider latitude of acceptance will take the middle-ground positions and present suggestions for resolving some of the conflict. This group will look for common ground in the extreme positions, try to resolve conflict, and work to achieve better understanding and perhaps even a change of views in the opposing groups.

Group 1 is the affirmative group that is in favor of the subject for debate. Group 2 is the negative group that is against it. Group 3 is the moderate group that will attempt to resolve the conflict. The groups should be equal in size. To achieve this equality, some students may have to argue for positions that they do not in fact actually hold.

3. *Do Background Reading and Writing*

All three groups should do some background reading on the subject for debate. The negative and affirmative teams will read to get ideas for their arguments and to develop ideas for refutation. The moderates should read to understand the opposing positions. Students in groups 1 and 2 will write 250-word papers outside of class that present some arguments to support their positions. After they have listened to the debate, the moderates will write 250-word papers that make an effort to resolve the conflict.

Conducting the Debate

Day One

1. *Begin with the opening papers* (10 minutes). Two students from the affirmative group and two from the negative group agree to start the debate by reading their papers. The first affirmative, first negative, second affirmative, and second negative read papers in that order.

2. *Others join in* (20 minutes). Students may now raise their hands to be recognized by the instructor to give additional arguments from their papers. Each person should stand to speak. The speakers should represent each side in turn. The class should decide whether everyone should first be

allowed to speak before anyone is permitted to speak a second time. The instructor should cut off speakers who are going on too long.

3. *Caucus and closing remarks* (15 minutes). The affirmative and negative groups caucus for 5 minutes to prepare their closing arguments. Each group selects a spokesperson who then presents the group's final, strongest arguments in a 2-minute closing presentation.

4. *Moderates prepare responses.* The moderates write 250-word responses outside of class that answer the following question: Now that you have heard both sides, how would you resolve the conflict?

Day Two

1. *Moderates read* (20 minutes). All moderates read their papers. Each paper should take about 2 minutes to read.

2. *Analyze outcomes* (30 minutes). The class should now discuss the outcomes of the debate by addressing the following questions:

   a. What, in general, were some of the outcomes?
   b. Who changed their opinions? Which opinions? Why?
   c. Who did not change? Why?
   d. What are some of the outcomes of the attempts to reduce conflict and establish common ground?
   e. What strategies have you learned from participating in this debate that can help you in real-life arguments?
   f. Did you detect any fallacies that weakened the arguments?

CHAPTER 12

Review and Synthesis of the Strategies for Reading, Writing, and Viewing Argument

After studying this chapter, you will be able to:

LO1 Summarize the key points about argument and argument theory contained in Chapters 1–11.

LO2 Use these points to analyze two specific texts. (p. 307, 310, and 311)

LO3 Use these points to create your own argument analysis essay. (p. 325)

T he purpose of this chapter is to provide you with the opportunity to review and synthesize what you have learned about reading, writing, and viewing argument in the first eleven chapters of this book. Your task here is to apply argument theory as you read and analyze two letters. The first, "A Call for Unity: A Letter from Eight White Clergymen" was published in a Birmingham, Alabama, newspaper in April 1963. The second, "A Letter from Birmingham Jail," was written shortly thereafter by Martin Luther King Jr. in response to the clergymen's letter.

As you read the two letters, assess the rhetorical situation from visual as well as textual material, notice the positions both parties take on the issue, and identify the claims, support, warrants, and backing for the warrants in each letter. Look for and analyze fallacies and refutation. As part of a final evaluation, decide whether each letter is primarily ethical or unethical. Consider that you must formulate reasons and evidence for your final evaluation. Plan to make some notes on these matters as you read.

Then, in the "Exercises and Activities" section that follows these example arguments, you are asked to apply your understanding to write an argument analysis paper. In this paper, you will explain the results of your reading and analysis. You will not be criticizing or showing what is wrong with the letters; you will not be arguing with the ideas or attempting to refute them. Instead, your purpose will be to explain the argumentation methods that these authors use to make their arguments. You will rely on information about argument theory that you have learned in earlier chapters in this book to help you make your evaluations and write a thorough analysis paper. A side benefit of this assignment is that you will learn to write a type of paper that is sometimes required in other classes.

Reading for the Argument Analysis Paper

Use the following information to help you read and analyze the letters:

1. The rhetorical situation for the letters is detailed on pages 307–308. Read this section first to help you situate these letters in their historical context.

2. Focus topics that identify relevant argument theory are listed along with directed questions on pages 308–310. Page numbers for each topic are provided, if you need to review. When you finish reading the two letters, you should be able to answer the questions that accompany each of the topics. A group work and discussion exercise to help you understand and work with these topics is provided on page 325.

3. Questions appear in the margins of the letters that will direct your attention to various argumentation techniques and methods that the clergymen and King are employing. Answer these questions as you read. Your answers will help you understand the letters, respond to the questions that accompany the topics, and gather the information you will need to write your paper. Underline the information in the letters that answers the questions in the margins. Write your own insights and thoughts in the margins. These activities will help you generate plenty of material for your paper.

Writing the Argument Analysis Paper

The complete assignment for the argument analysis paper appears at the end of this chapter on page 325. You may want to read it now so that you will know what you will finally be asked to do. Here are some ideas to help you write this paper.

1. Create a structure for your essay, even if it is little more than a list of your main points. Or, if you prefer, make an outline. Place your ideas in an order that makes sense to you. Since you will be comparing and contrasting the two letters in this paper, you may want to write first about the clergymen's letter and then about King's letter and draw conclusions about both of them last. Or, as an alternative, set up topics, such as *emotional proof* or *writing style,* and then describe how each author, in turn, employs each technique in their letters.

2. You will be asked to explain the rhetorical situation. Be sure to place each letter in historical context and to describe the audiences each one addresses. Then explain the issue from both points of view and summarize the authors' positions. An example of a summary appears on pages 89–91. Your summaries should be no longer than this example. You may be able to make them shorter, but plan to include enough detail to help your reader understand the ideas in each letter and how each is organized. Make a brief outline of each letter to guide your summary writing.

3. You will be asked to state the claims and describe the support in both letters.

4. Include summarized, paraphrased, or quoted material from the letters to provide evidence to support your main points.

Place page numbers in parentheses at the end of each summarized, paraphrased, or quoted passage to show where you found it in this textbook, as in the example above.

5. Write a conclusion in which you evaluate these letters. Are they ethical or unethical? Is one more effective and convincing than the other? Why? Write a final evaluative claim about the letters that is based on the ideas and evidence in your paper. At this point, decide whether you want to leave your claim at the end of your paper or to move it to an earlier position in your paper. Where would it be most effective?

6. Read your draft, revise it, and submit it.

Rhetorical Situation for "A Call to Unity: A Letter from Eight White Clergymen" and "Letter from Birmingham Jail"

Birmingham, Alabama, was a very strange place in 1963. Black people were allowed to sit only in certain parts of buses and restaurants, they were required to drink from separate water fountains, and they were not allowed in white churches, schools, or various other public places. The Reverend Martin Luther King Jr. was a well-known minister in the black Baptist church and a leader in the civil rights movement at that time. The purpose of the movement was to end segregation and discrimination and to obtain equal rights and access for African Americans in the United States, but especially in the South.

Dr. Martin Luther King Jr. was jailed more than once during the civil rights movement. In this 1960 photo, police in Atlanta, Georgia, are taking him to court in handcuffs for participating in a sit-in at a segregated lunch counter in a department store. He was sentenced in this instance to four months of hard labor and was released on bail pending appeal only after Bobby Kennedy[1] phoned the judge.

For Discussion: What special features of visual argument are apparent in this photograph? (Review pages 245–253)

307

---

[1]Bobby Kennedy, brother of President John F. Kennedy, was the U.S. Attorney General at this time.

Dr. King and others carefully prepared for demonstrations that would take place in Birmingham in the spring of 1963. The demonstrators began by "sitting in" at lunch counters that had never served blacks before and by picketing stores. Twenty people were arrested the first day on charges of trespassing. The civil rights leaders then applied for permits to picket and hold parades against the injustices of discrimination and segregation. They were refused permission, but they demonstrated and picketed anyway. Dr. King was served with an injunction granted by a circuit judge. It said civil rights leaders could not protest, demonstrate, boycott, or sit in at any facilities. King and other leaders decided that this was an unfair and unjust application of the law, and they decided to break the law by ignoring the injunction.

King himself decided to march on Good Friday, and he expected to go to jail. (As the photograph and caption document, Dr. King had long been aware that nonviolent civil disobedience required acceptance of any consequent punishments so as to create the tension of protest.) Indeed, before he had walked half a mile, he was arrested and jailed, along with fifty other people. King stayed in jail for eight days. During that time, he wrote his famous letter. It was written in response to a letter signed by eight white clergymen that had been published in a local newspaper.

After King left jail, there were further protests and some violence. Thousands of people demonstrated, and thousands were jailed. Finally, black and white leaders began to negotiate, and some final terms were announced on May 10, 1963. All lunch counters, restrooms, fitting rooms, and drinking fountains in downtown stores were to be desegregated within ninety days; blacks were to be hired in clerical and sales jobs in stores within sixty days. The many people arrested during the demonstrations were to be released on low bail, and permanent lines of communication were to be established between black and white leaders. The demonstrations ended then, and the city settled down and began to implement the agreements.[2]

Focus Topics to Help You Analyze the Letters

Answer the questions that accompany the eight focus topics listed. Use the questions in the margins of the letters to help you locate the information you need to address the questions as well as suggestions posted under each topic.

1. *Rhetorical situation (pages 39–42).* Consider each of these points.

   a. What is the *exigence* for these two letters? What caused the authors to write them? What was the problem? Was it a new or recurring problem?

---

[2]This account is drawn from Lee E. Bains Jr., "Birmingham, 1963: Confrontation over Civil Rights," in *Birmingham, Alabama, 1956–1963: The Black Struggle for Civil Rights*, ed. David J. Garrow (Brooklyn: Carlson, 1989), 175–83.

b. Who is the *audience* for the clergymen's letter? For King's letter? What is the nature of these audiences? Can they be convinced? What are the expected outcomes?

c. What are the *constraints?* Speculate about the beliefs, attitudes, habits, and traditions that were in place that limited or constrained both the white clergymen and King. How did these constraining circumstances influence the audience for both letters at that time?

d. Think about the *authors* of both letters. Who are they? Speculate about their backgrounds, experience, affiliations, and values. What motivated them to write?

e. What kind of *text* is each letter? What effect do its special qualities and features have on the audience?

f. Think about *yourself as the reader.* What is your position on the issue? Do you experience constraints as you read? Do you perceive common ground with either the clergymen or King, or both? Describe it. Are you influenced by these letters? How?

2. *Organization and claims.* Divide each letter into its main parts. What is the subject of each part? Why have the parts been placed in this particular order? What is the relationship between them? What is the main claim in each letter? What types of claims are they? What are some of the subclaims? What types of claims are they?

3. *Logical proofs and style.* Analyze the use of logical proof in each of the letters. Provide examples. Describe their effect on the audience. Provide an example of the language of rational style in one of the letters.

4. *Emotional proofs and style.* Analyze the use of emotional proof in each of the letters. Provide examples. Describe their effect on the audience. Provide an example of the language of emotional style in one of the letters.

5. *Proofs and style that establish ethos.* Analyze the use of proofs that establish *ethos* or credibility in the letters. Provide examples. Describe their effect on the audience. Provide an example of language that establishes *ethos* in one of the letters.

6. *Warrants and Backing.* Identify the warrants (both logical and contextual) in each of the letters. What appeals to community values provide backing for the warrants? How much common ground do you think exists between the authors of the letters? How much common ground do you share with the authors? As a result, which letter do you find more convincing? Why?

7. *Fallacious thinking and rebuttals.* Provide examples of reasoning that is considered fallacious or wrongheaded by the opposing parties in each of the letters. What rebuttals are made in response to these? How effective are they?

8. *Ethical or Unethical.* Do the clergymen and King both make an adequate effort to understand the issue and its consequences? Does each also understand the position held by the other? How just and fair-minded is each party? Is their support fair, accurate, and/or convincing? Can you, as the reader, accept their warrants? Can you accept the references to community values that serve as backing for these warrants? Should the claims be qualified, if they are not

already? Do the clergymen and King sincerely believe their positions are in the best interests of the people in Birmingham as well as of the larger society? Do you agree with them? Who is benefited, and who is burdened by their positions? Do you find evidence that either the clergymen or King are trying to manipulate the audience by hiding their real purpose, using inappropriate emotional appeals, manufacturing evidence, using inaccurate evidence, or telling lies? Do either of the arguers change the usual definitions of words to cloud perceptions, or do they minimize issues to trivialize them? What do you conclude about the ethical and unethical qualities of the letters?

ESSAY #1   A CALL FOR UNITY: A LETTER
FROM EIGHT WHITE CLERGYMEN*

The eight white Alabama clergymen who wrote this letter to the editor of a Birmingham, Alabama, newspaper represent various religious denominations.

April 12, 1963

What is the issue?

What is the clergymen's position?

What is the claim?

What type of claim is it?

What are the rebuttals?

How do the authors build *ethos*?

1   We the undersigned clergymen are among those who, in January, issued "An Appeal for Law and Order and Common Sense," in dealing with racial problems in Alabama. We expressed understanding that honest convictions in racial matters could properly be pursued in the courts, but urged that decisions of those courts should in the meantime be peacefully obeyed.

2   Since that time there had been some evidence of increased forebearance and a willingness to face facts. Responsible citizens have undertaken to work on various problems which cause racial friction and unrest. In Birmingham, recent public events have given indication that we all have opportunity for a new constructive and realistic approach to racial problems.

3   However, we are now confronted by a series of demonstrations by some of our Negro citizens, directed and led in part by outsiders. We recognize the natural impatience of people who feel that their hopes are slow in being realized. But we are convinced that these demonstrations are unwise and untimely.

4   We agree rather with certain local Negro leadership which has called for honest and open negotiation of racial issues in our area. And we believe this kind of facing of issues can best be accomplished by citizens of our own metropolitan area, white and Negro, meeting with their knowledge and experience of the local situation. All of us need to face that responsibility and find proper channels for its accomplishment.

How do they appeal to logic?

5   Just as we formerly pointed out that "hatred and violence have no sanction in our religious and political traditions," we also point out that such actions as incite to hatred and violence, however technically peaceful those actions may be, have not contributed to the resolution of our local problems. We do not believe that these days of new hope are days when extreme measures are justified in Birmingham.

How do they appeal to emotion?

6   We commend the community as a whole, and the local news media and law enforcement officials in particular, on the calm manner in which these demonstrations have been handled. We urge the public to continue to show restraint should the demonstrations continue, and the law enforcement officials to remain calm and continue to protect our city from violence.

What are the warrants?

7   We further strongly urge our own Negro community to withdraw support from these demonstrations, and to unite locally in working peacefully for a better Birmingham. When rights are consistently denied, a cause should be pressed in the courts and in negotiations among local leaders, and not in the streets. We appeal to both our white and Negro citizenry to observe the principles of law and order and common sense.

Describe the predominant style.

(Signed)
C.C.J. Carpenter, D.D., L.L.D., Bishop of Alabama; Joseph A. Durick, D.D., Auxiliary Bishop, Diocese of Mobile-Birmingham; Rabbi Milton L. Grafman, Temple Emanu-El, Birmingham, Alabama; Bishop Paul Hardin, Bishop of the Alabama–West Florida Conference of the Methodist Church; Bishop Nolan B. Harmon, Bishop of the North Alabama Conference of the Methodist Church; George M. Murray, D.D., L.L.D., Bishop Coadjutor, Episcopal Diocese of Alabama; Edward V. Ramage, Moderator, Synod of the Alabama Presbyterian Church in the United States; Earl Stallings, Pastor, First Baptist Church, Birmingham

311

ESSAY #2   LETTER FROM BIRMINGHAM JAIL*

Martin Luther King Jr.

Martin Luther King Jr. was a Baptist minister who preached nonviolence and equal justice. He was a pivotal leader in the civil rights movement of the 1960s.

April 16, 1963

My Dear Fellow Clergymen:

What is the issue? What is King's position?

1   While confined here in the Birmingham city jail, I came across your recent statement calling my present activities "unwise and

*Letter from a Birmingham Jail, by Dr. Martin Luther King, Jr. Copyright © 1963 by Dr. Martin Luther King, Jr., copyright renewed 1991 by Coretta Scott King. Reprinted by arrangement with The Heirs to the Estate of Martin Luther King, Jr., c/o Writers House as agent for the proprietor, New York, NY.

Identify and describe the Rogerian elements and efforts to establish common ground throughout this letter.

untimely." Seldom do I pause to answer criticism of my work and ideas. If I sought to answer all the criticisms that cross my desk, my secretaries would have little time for anything other than such correspondence in the course of the day, and I would have no time for constructive work. But since I feel that you are men of genuine good will and that your criticisms are sincerely set forth, I want to try to answer your statement in what I hope will be patient and reasonable terms.

2   I think I should indicate why I am here in Birmingham, since you have been influenced by the view which argues against "outsiders coming in." I have the honor of serving as president of the Southern Christian Leadership Conference, an organization operating in every southern state, with headquarters in Atlanta, Georgia. We have some eighty-five affiliated organizations across the South, and one of them is the Alabama Christian Movement for Human Rights. Frequently we share staff, educational and financial resources with our affiliates. Several months ago, the affiliate here in Birmingham asked us to be on call to engage in a nonviolent direct-action program if such were deemed necessary. We readily consented, and when the hour came we lived up to our promise. So I, along with several members of my staff, am here because I was invited here. I am here because I have organizational ties here.

How does King build *ethos*?

3   But more basically, I am in Birmingham because injustice is here. Just as the prophets of the eighth century B.C. left their villages and carried their "thus saith the Lord" far beyond the boundaries of their home towns, and just as the Apostle Paul left his village of Tarsus and carried the gospel of Jesus Christ to the far corners of the Greco-Roman world, so am I compelled to carry the gospel of freedom beyond my own home town. Like Paul, I must constantly respond to the Macedonian call for aid.

What is the effect of the comparison with Paul?

Draw a line at the end of the introduction.

Draw a line at the end of each of the other major sections of material. Label the subject of each section in the margin.

4   Moreover, I am cognizant of the interrelatedness of all communities and states. I cannot sit idly by in Atlanta and not be concerned about what happens in Birmingham. Injustice anywhere is a threat to justice everywhere. We are caught in an inescapable network of mutuality, tied in a single garment of destiny. Whatever affects one directly, affects all indirectly. Never again can we afford to live with the narrow, provincial "outside agitator" idea. Anyone who lives inside the United States can never be considered an outsider anywhere within its bounds.

What is the subject of this first section?

What is the claim?

What type of claim is it?

Is it qualified?

5   You deplore the demonstrations taking place in Birmingham. But your statement, I am sorry to say, fails to express a similar concern for the conditions that brought about the demonstrations. I am sure that none of you would want to rest content with the superficial kind of social analysis that deals merely with effects and does not grapple with underlying causes. It is unfortunate that demonstrations are taking place in Birmingham, but it is even more unfortunate that the city's white power structure left the Negro community with no alternative.

Identify and analyze the effect of the emotional appeals.

6   In any nonviolent campaign there are four basic steps: collection of the facts to determine whether injustices exist; negotiation; self-purification; and direct action. We have gone through all these steps in Birmingham. There can be no gain-saying the fact that racial injustice engulfs this community. Birmingham is probably the most thoroughly segregated city in the United States. Its ugly record of brutality is widely known. Negroes have experienced grossly unjust treatment in the courts. There have been more unsolved bombings of Negro homes and churches in Birmingham than in any other city in the nation. These are the hard, brutal facts of the case. On the basis of these conditions, Negro leaders sought to negotiate with the city fathers. But the latter consistently refused to engage in good-faith negotiation.

7   Then, last September, came the opportunity to talk with leaders of Birmingham's economic community. In the course of the negotiations, certain promises were made by the merchants—for example, to remove the stores' humiliating racial signs. On the basis of these promises, the Reverend Fred Shuttlesworth and the leaders of the Alabama Christian Movement for Human Rights agreed to a moratorium on all demonstrations. As the weeks and months went by, we realized that we were the victims of a broken promise. A few signs, briefly removed, returned; the others remained.

313

What are some of the values expressed in this argument?

8   As in so many past experiences, our hopes had been blasted, and the shadow of deep disappointment settled upon us. We had no alternative except to prepare for direct action, whereby we would present our very bodies as a means of laying our case before the conscience of the local and the national community. Mindful of the difficulties involved, we decided to undertake a process of self-purification. We began a series of workshops on nonviolence, and we repeatedly asked ourselves: "Are you able to accept blows without retaliating?" "Are you able to endure the ordeal of jail?" We decided to schedule our direct-action program for the Easter season, realizing that except for Christmas, this is the main shopping period of the year. Knowing that a strong economic-withdrawal program would be the by-product of direct action, we felt that this would be the best time to bring pressure to bear on the merchants for the needed change.

Identify and describe the rebuttals.

9   Then it occurred to us that Birmingham's mayoral election was coming up in March, and we speedily decided to postpone action until after election day. When we discovered that the Commissioner of Public Safety, Eugene "Bull" Connor, had piled up enough votes to be in the runoff, we decided again to postpone action until the day after the runoff so that the demonstrations could not be used to cloud the issues. Like many others, we waited to see Mr. Connor defeated, and to this end we endured postponement after postponement. Having aided in this community need, we felt that our direct-action program could be delayed no longer.

What is the effect of the comparison with Socrates?

What is King's planned argumentation strategy?

Why does King refer to history?

Why does he refer to Niebuhr?

Identify and analyze the emotional proof.

To what human motives and values does King appeal?

10   You may well ask: "Why direct action? Why sit-ins, marches and so forth? Isn't negotiation a better path?" You are quite right in calling for negotiation. Indeed, this is the very purpose of direct action. Nonviolent direct action seeks to create such a crisis and foster such a tension that a community which has constantly refused to negotiate is forced to confront the issue. It seeks so to dramatize the issue that it can no longer be ignored. My citing the creation of tension as part of the work of the nonviolent-resister may sound rather shocking. But I must confess that I am not afraid of the word "tension." I have earnestly opposed violent tension, but there is a type of constructive, nonviolent tension which is necessary for growth. Just as Socrates felt that it was necessary to create a tension in the mind so that individuals could rise from the bondage of myths and half-truths to the unfettered realm of creative analysis and objective appraisal, so must we see the need for nonviolent gadflies to create the kind of tension in society that will help men rise from the dark depths of prejudice and racism to the majestic heights of understanding and brotherhood.

11   The purpose of our direct-action program is to create a situation so crisis-packed that it will inevitably open the door to negotiation. I therefore concur with you in your call for negotiation. Too long has our beloved Southland been bogged down in a tragic effort to live in monologue rather than dialogue.

12   One of the basic points in your statement is that the action that I and my associates have taken in Birmingham is untimely. Some have asked: "Why didn't you give the new city administration time to act?" The only answer that I can give to this query is that the new Birmingham administration must be prodded about as much as the outgoing one, before it will act. We are sadly mistaken if we feel that the election of Albert Boutwell as mayor will bring the millennium to Birmingham. While Mr. Boutwell is a much more gentle person than Mr. Connor, they are both segregationists, dedicated to the maintenance of the status quo. I have hope that Mr. Boutwell will be reasonable enough to see the futility of massive resistance to desegregation. But he will not see this without pressure from devotees of civil rights. My friends, I must say to you that we have not made a single gain in civil rights without determined legal and nonviolent pressure. Lamentably, it is a historical fact that privileged groups seldom give up their privileges voluntarily. Individuals may see the moral light and voluntarily give up their unjust posture; but, as Reinhold Niebuhr has reminded us, groups tend to be more immoral than individuals.

13   We know through painful experience that freedom is never voluntarily given up by the oppressor; it must be demanded by the oppressed. Frankly, I have yet to engage in a direct-action campaign that was "well-timed" in the view of those who have not suffered unduly from the disease of segregation. For years now I have heard the word "Wait!" It rings in the ear of every Negro with piercing familiarity. This "Wait" has almost always meant "Never." We must

come to see, with one of our distinguished jurists, that "justice too long delayed is justice denied."

Identify emotional language, examples, and vivid description.

14   We have waited for more than 340 years for our constitutional and God-given rights. The nations of Asia and Africa are moving with jetlike speed toward gaining political independence, but we still creep at horse-and-buggy pace toward gaining a cup of coffee at a lunch counter. Perhaps it is easy for those who have never felt the stinging darts of segregation to say, "Wait." But when you have seen vicious mobs lynch your mothers and fathers at will and drown your sisters and brothers at whim; when you have seen hate-filled policemen curse, kick and even kill your black brothers and sisters; when you see the vast majority of your twenty million Negro brothers smothering in an airtight cage of poverty in the midst of an affluent society; when you suddenly find your tongue twisted and your speech stammering as you seek to explain to your six-year-old daughter why she can't go to the public amusement park that has just been advertised on television, and see tears welling up in her eyes when she is told that Fun-town is closed to colored children, and see ominous clouds of inferiority beginning to form in her little mental sky, and see her beginning to distort her personality by developing an unconscious bitterness toward white people; when you have to concoct an answer for a five-year-old son who is asking, "Daddy, why do white people treat colored people so mean?"; when you take a cross-country drive and find it necessary to sleep night after night in the uncomfortable corners of your automobile because no motel will accept you; when you are humiliated day in and day out by nagging signs reading "white" and "colored"; when your first name becomes "nigger," your middle name becomes "boy" (however old you are) and your last name becomes "John," and your wife and mother are never given the respected title "Mrs."; when you are harried by day and haunted by night by the fact that you are a Negro, living constantly at tiptoe stance, never quite knowing what to expect next, and are plagued with inner fears and outer resentments; when you are forever fighting a degenerating sense of "nobodiness"—then you will understand why we find it difficult to wait. There comes a time when the cup of endurance runs over, and men are no longer willing to be plunged into the abyss of despair. I hope, sirs, you can understand our legitimate and unavoidable impatience.

What is the effect of the emotional proof?

315

What is the predominant type of proof in the first section of the letter?

Draw a line where the subject changes. What is the subject of the second section?

15   You express a great deal of anxiety over our willingness to break laws. This is certainly a legitimate concern. Since we so diligently urge people to obey the Supreme Court's decision of 1954 outlawing segregation in the public schools, at first glance it may seem rather paradoxical for us consciously to break laws. One may well ask: "How can you advocate breaking some laws and obeying others?" The answer lies in the fact that there are two types of laws: just and unjust. I would be the first to advocate obeying just laws. Conversely,

one has a moral responsibility to disobey unjust laws. I would agree with St. Augustine that "an unjust law is no law at all."

How and why does King use definition?

16   Now, what is the difference between the two? How does one determine whether a law is just or unjust? A just law is a man-made code that squares with the moral law or the law of God. An unjust law is a code that is out of harmony with the moral law. To put it in the terms of St. Thomas Aquinas: An unjust law is a human law that is not rooted in eternal law and natural law. Any law that uplifts human personality is just. Any law that degrades human personality is unjust.

How does he support the definition?

All segregation statutes are unjust because segregation distorts the soul and damages the personality. It gives the segregator a false sense of superiority and the segregated a false sense of inferiority. Segregation, to use the terminology of the Jewish philosopher Martin Buber, substitutes an "I-it" relationship for an "I-thou" relationship and ends up relegating persons to the status of things. Hence segregation is not only politically, economically, and sociologically unsound, it is morally wrong and sinful. Paul Tillich has said that sin is separation. Is not seg-

What is the effect of the support?

regation an existential expression of man's tragic separation, his awful estrangement, his terrible sinfulness? Thus it is that I can urge men to obey the 1954 decision of the Supreme Court, for it is morally right; and I can urge them to disobey segregation ordinances, for they are morally wrong.

Explain the example of just and unjust laws.

17   Let us consider a more concrete example of just and unjust laws. An unjust law is a code that a numerical or power majority group compels a minority group to obey but does not make binding on itself. This is *difference* made legal. By the same token, a just law is a code that a majority compels a minority to follow and that it is willing to follow itself. This is *sameness* made legal.

18   Let me give another explanation. A law is unjust if it is inflicted on a minority that, as a result of being denied the right to vote, had no part in enacting or devising the law. Who can say that the legislature of Alabama which set up the state's segregation laws was democratically elected? Throughout Alabama all sorts of devious methods are used to prevent Negroes from becoming registered voters, and there are some counties in which, even though Negroes constitute a majority of the population, not a single Negro is registered. Can any law enactment under such circumstances be considered democratically structured?

How does King further elaborate on this idea?

19   Sometimes a law is just on its face and unjust in its application. For instance, I have been arrested on a charge of parading without a permit. Now, there is nothing wrong in having an ordinance which requires a permit for a parade. But such an ordinance becomes unjust when it is used to maintain segregation and to deny citizens the First-Amendment privilege of peaceful assembly and protest.

Analyze the deductive reasoning in this paragraph.

20   I hope you are able to see the distinction I am trying to point out. In no sense do I advocate evading or defying the law, as would the rabid segregationist. That would lead to anarchy. One who breaks an unjust law must do so openly, lovingly, and with a willingness to accept the

penalty. I submit that an individual who breaks a law that conscience tells him is unjust, and who willingly accepts the penalty of imprisonment in order to arouse the conscience of the community over its injustice, is in reality expressing the highest respect for law.

Identify and describe the effect of the historical analogies.

21   Of course, there is nothing new about this kind of civil disobedience. It was evidenced sublimely in the refusal of Shadrach, Meshach and Abednego to obey the laws of Nebuchadnezzar, on the ground that a higher moral law was at stake. It was practiced superbly by the early Christians, who were willing to face hungry lions and the excruciating pain of chopping blocks rather than submit to certain unjust laws of the Roman Empire. To a degree, academic freedom is a reality today because Socrates practiced civil disobedience. In our own nation, the Boston Tea Party represented a massive act of civil disobedience.

What type of proof predominates in the second part of the letter?

Draw a line where the subject changes. What is the subject of the third section?

22   We should never forget that everything Adolf Hitler did in Germany was "legal" and everything the Hungarian freedom fighters did in Hungary was "illegal." It was "illegal" to aid and comfort a Jew in Hitler's Germany. Even so, I am sure that, had I lived in Germany at the time, I would have aided and comforted my Jewish brothers. If today I lived in a Communist country where certain principles dear to the Christian faith are suppressed, I would openly advocate disobeying that country's antireligious laws.

23   I must make two honest confessions to you, my Christian and Jewish brothers. First, I must confess that over the past few years I have been gravely disappointed with the white moderate. I have almost reached the regrettable conclusion that the Negro's great stumbling block in his stride toward freedom is not the White Citizen's Councilor or the Ku Klux Klanner, but the white moderate, who is more devoted to "order" than to justice; who prefers a negative peace which is the absence of tension to a positive peace which is the presence of justice; who constantly says: "I agree with you in the goal you seek, but I cannot agree with your methods of direct action"; who paternalistically believes he can set the timetable for another man's freedom; who lives by a mythical concept of time and who constantly advises the Negro to wait for a "more convenient season." Shallow understanding from people of good will is more frustrating than absolute misunderstanding from people of ill will. Lukewarm acceptance is much more bewildering than outright rejection.

What are King's warrants in this passage?

How do King's warrants differ from the clergymen's?

24   I had hoped that the white moderate would understand that law and order exist for the purpose of establishing justice and that when they fail in this purpose they become the dangerously structured dams that block the flow of social progress. I had hoped that the white moderate would understand that the present tension in the South is a necessary phase of the transition from an obnoxious negative peace, in which the Negro passively accepted his unjust plight, to a substantive and positive peace, in which all men will respect the dignity and worth of human personality. Actually, we who engage in nonviolent direct action are not the creators of tension. We merely bring to the surface the hidden

How and why does King use definition here?

tension that is already alive. We bring it out in the open, where it can be seen and dealt with. Like a boil that can never be cured so long as it is covered up but must be opened with all its ugliness to the natural medicines of air and light, injustice must be exposed, with all the tension its exposure creates, to the light of human conscience and the air of national opinion before it can be cured.

25   In your statements you assert that our actions, even though peaceful, must be condemned because they precipitate violence. But is this a logical assertion? Isn't this like condemning a robbed man because his possession of money precipitated the evil act of robbery? Isn't this like condemning Socrates because his unswerving commitment to truth and his philosophical inquiries precipitated the act by the misguided populace in which they made him drink hemlock? Isn't this like condemning Jesus because his unique God-consciousness and never-ceasing devotion to God's will precipitated the evil act of crucifixion? We must come to see that, as the federal courts have consistently affirmed, it is wrong to urge an individual to cease his efforts to gain his basic constitutional rights because the quest may precipitate violence. Society must protect the robbed and punish the robber.

26   I had also hoped that the white moderate would reject the myth concerning time in relation to the struggle for freedom. I have just received a letter from a white brother in Texas. He writes: "All Christians know that the colored people will receive equal rights eventually, but it is possible that you are in too great a religious hurry. It has taken Christianity almost two thousand years to accomplish what it has. The teachings of Christ take time to come to earth." Such an attitude stems from a tragic misconception of time, from the strangely irrational notion that there is something in the very flow of time that will inevitably cure all ills. Actually, time itself is neutral; it can be used either destructively or constructively. More and more I feel that the people of ill will have used time much more effectively than have the people of good will. We will have to repent in this generation not merely for the hateful words and actions of the bad people but for the appalling silence of the good people. Human progress never rolls in on wheels of inevitability; it comes through the tireless efforts of men willing to be coworkers with God, and without this hard work, time itself becomes an ally of the forces of social stagnation. We must use time creatively, in the knowledge that the time is always right to do right. Now is the time to make real the promise of democracy and transform our pending national elegy into a creative psalm of brotherhood. Now is the time to lift our national policy from the quicksand of racial injustice to the solid rock of human dignity.

27   You speak of our activity in Birmingham as extreme. At first I was rather disappointed that fellow clergymen would see my nonviolent efforts as those of an extremist. I began thinking about the fact that I stand in the middle of two opposing forces in the Negro community. One is a force of complacency, made up in part of Negroes who, as a

Identify and describe the effects of the analogies in these paragraphs.

What is the fallacious thinking King complains of here?

Summarize King's reasoning about time.

318

Describe the two opposing forces.

result of long years of oppression, are so drained of self-respect and a sense of "somebodiness" that they have adjusted to segregation; and in part of a few middle-class Negroes who, because of a degree of academic and economic security and because in some ways they profit by segregation, have become insensitive to the problems of the masses. The other force is one of bitterness and hatred, and it comes perilously close to advocating violence. It is expressed in the various black nationalist groups that are springing up across the nation, the largest and best-known being Elijah Muhammad's Muslim movement. Nourished by the Negro's frustration over the continued existence of racial discrimination, this movement is made up of people who have lost faith in America, who have absolutely repudiated Christianity, and who have concluded that the white man is an incorrigible "devil."

How and why does King attempt to reconcile the opposing forces?

28   I have tried to stand between these two forces, saying that we need emulate neither the "do-nothingism" of the complacent nor the hatred and despair of the black nationalist. For there is the more excellent way of love and nonviolent protest. I am grateful to God that, through the influence of the Negro church, the way of nonviolence became an integral part of our struggle.

Identify and describe the causal proof.

29   If this philosophy had not emerged, by now many streets of the South would, I am convinced, be flowing with blood. And I am further convinced that if our white brothers dismiss as "rabble-rousers" and "outside agitators" those of us who employ nonviolent direct action, and if they refuse to support our nonviolent efforts, millions of Negroes will, out of frustration and despair, seek solace and security in black-nationalist ideologies—a development that would inevitably lead to a frightening racial nightmare.

319

Summarize King's reasoning about the effects of oppression.

30   Oppressed people cannot remain oppressed forever. The yearning for freedom eventually manifests itself, and that is what has happened to the American Negro. Something within has reminded him of his birthright of freedom, and something without has reminded him that it can be gained. Consciously or unconsciously, he has been caught up by the *Zeitgeist*, and with his black brothers of Africa and his brown and yellow brothers of Asia, South America and the Caribbean, the United States Negro is moving with a sense of great urgency toward the promised land of racial justice. If one recognizes this vital urge that has engulfed the Negro community, one should readily understand why public demonstrations are taking place. The Negro has many pent-up resentments and latent frustrations, and he must release them. So let him march; let him make prayer pilgrimages to the city hall; let him go on freedom rides—and try to understand why he must do so. If his repressed emotions are not released in nonviolent ways, they will seek expression through violence; this is not a threat but a fact of history. So I have not said to my people: "Get rid of your discontent." Rather, I have tried to say that this normal and healthy discontent can be channeled into the creative outlet of nonviolent direct action. And now this approach is being termed extremist.

What is the effect of these comparisons?

31   But though I was initially disappointed at being categorized as an extremist, as I continued to think about the matter I gradually gained a measure of satisfaction from the label. Was not Jesus an extremist for love: "Love your enemies, bless them that curse you, do good to them that hate you, and pray for them which despitefully use you, and prosecute you." Was not Amos an extremist for justice: "Let justice roll down like waters and righteousness like an everflowing stream." Was not Paul an extremist for the Christian gospel: "I bear in my body the marks of the Lord Jesus." Was not Martin Luther an extremist: "Here I stand; I cannot do otherwise, so help me God." And John Bunyan: "I will stay in jail to the end of my days before I make a butchery of my conscience." And Abraham Lincoln: "This nation cannot survive half slave and half free." And Thomas Jefferson: "We hold these truths to be self-evident, that all men are created equal . . . ." So the question is not whether we will be extremists, but what kind of extremists we will be. Will we be extremists for hate or for love? Will we be extremists for the preservation of injustice or for the extension of justice? In that dramatic scene on Calvary's hill three men were crucified. We must never forget that all three were crucified for the same crime—the crime of extremism. Two were extremists for immorality, and thus fell below their environment. The other, Jesus Christ, was an extremist for love, truth and goodness, and thereby rose above his environment. Perhaps the South, the nation and the world are in dire need of creative extremists.

Summarize King's description of the oppressor race.

What types of proof are used in this third section?

32   I had hoped that the white moderate would see this need. Perhaps I was too optimistic; perhaps I expected too much. I suppose I should have realized that few members of the oppressor race can understand the deep groans and passionate yearnings of the oppressed race, and still fewer have the vision to see that injustice must be rooted out by strong, persistent and determined action. I am thankful, however, that some of our white brothers in the South have grasped the meaning of this social revolution and committed themselves to it. They are still all too few in quantity, but they are big in quality. Some—such as Ralph McGill, Lillian Smith, Harry Golden, James McBride Dabbs, Ann Braden and Sarah Patton Boyle—have written about our struggle in eloquent and prophetic terms. Others have marched with us down nameless streets of the South. They have languished in filthy, roach-infested jails, suffering the abuse and brutality of policemen who view them as "dirty nigger-lovers." Unlike so many of their moderate brothers and sisters, they have recognized the urgency of the moment and ·sensed the need for powerful "action" antidotes to combat the disease of segregation.

Draw a line where the subject changes. What is the subject of the fourth section?

Reconsider the rhetorical situations: What went before? What will come later?

33   Let me take note of my other major disappointment. I have been so greatly disappointed with the white church and its leadership. Of course, there are some notable exceptions. I am not unmindful of the fact that each of you has taken some significant stands on this issue. I commend you, Reverend Stallings, for your Christian stand on this past Sunday, in welcoming Negroes to your worship service on a

non-segregated basis. I commend the Catholic leaders of this state for integrating Spring Hill College several years ago.

34   But despite these notable exceptions, I must honestly reiterate that I have been disappointed with the church. I do not say this as one of those negative critics who can always find something wrong with the church. I say this as a minister of the gospel, who loves the church; who was nurtured in its bosom; who has been sustained by its spiritual blessings and who will remain true to it as long as the cord of life shall lengthen.

How does King build *ethos* in this fourth section?

35   When I was suddenly catapulted into the leadership of the bus protest in Montgomery, Alabama, a few years ago, I felt we would be supported by the white church. I felt that the white ministers, priests and rabbis of the South would be among our strongest allies. Instead, some have been outright opponents, refusing to understand the freedom movement and misrepresenting its leaders; all too many others have been more cautious than courageous and have remained silent behind the anesthetizing security of stained-glass windows.

What common ground did King hope would be clear? How was he disappointed?

36   In spite of my shattered dreams, I came to Birmingham with the hope that the white religious leadership of this community would see the justice of our cause and, with deep moral concern, would serve as the channel through which our just grievances could reach the power structure. I had hoped that each of you would understand. But again I have been disappointed.

321

37   I have heard numerous southern religious leaders admonish their worshipers to comply with a desegregation decision because it is the law, but I have longed to hear white ministers declare: "Follow this decree because integration is morally right and because the Negro

How and why does King use vivid description?

is your brother." In the midst of blatant injustices inflicted upon the Negro, I have watched white churchmen stand on the sideline and mouth pious irrelevancies and sanctimonious trivialities. In the midst of a mighty struggle to rid our nation of racial and economic injustice, I have heard many ministers say: "Those are social issues, with which the gospel has no real concern." And I have watched many churches commit themselves to a completely other-worldly religion which makes a strange, unBiblical distinction between body and soul, between the sacred and the secular.

38   I have traveled the length and breadth of Alabama, Mississippi and all the other southern states. On sweltering summer days and crisp autumn mornings I have looked at the South's beautiful churches with their lofty spires pointing heavenward. I have beheld the impressive outlines of her massive religious-education buildings. Over and over I have found myself asking: "What kind of people worship here? Who is their God? Where were their voices when the lips of Governor Barnett dripped with words of interposition and nullification? Where were they when Governor Wallace gave a clarion call for defiance and hatred? Where were their voices of support when bruised and weary Negro

men and women decided to rise from the dark dungeons of complacency to the bright hills of creative protest?"

39   Yes, these questions are still in my mind. In deep disappointment I
have wept over the laxity of the church. But be assured that my tears
have been tears of love. There can be no deep disappointment where
there is not deep love. Yes, I love the church. How could I do otherwise? I am in the rather unique position of being the son, the grand-
son and the great-grandson of preachers. Yes, I see the church as the
body of Christ. But, oh! How we have blemished and scarred that body
through social neglect and through fear of being nonconformists.

40   There was a time when the church was very powerful—in the time
when the early Christians rejoiced at being deemed worthy to suffer for
what they believed. In those days the church was not merely a ther-
mometer that recorded the ideas and principles of popular opinion; it
was a thermostat that transformed the mores of society. Whenever the
early Christians entered a town, the people in power became disturbed
and immediately sought to convict the Christians for being "disturbers
of the peace" and "outside agitators." But the Christians pressed on, in
the conviction that they were "a colony of heaven," called to obey God
rather than man. Small in number, they were big in commitment. They
were too God-intoxicated to be "astronomically intimidated." By their
effort and example they brought an end to such ancient evils as infanti-
cide and gladiatorial contests.

41   Things are different now. So often the contemporary church is a
weak, ineffectual voice with an uncertain sound. So often it is an arch-
defender of the status quo. Far from being disturbed by the presence of
the church, the power structure of the average community is consoled
by the church's silent—and often even vocal—sanction of things as
they are.

42   But the judgment of God is upon the church as never before. If
today's church does not recapture the sacrificial spirit of the early
church, it will lose its authenticity, forfeit the loyalty of millions, and
be dismissed as an irrelevant social club with no meaning for the twen-
tieth century. Every day I meet young people whose disappointment
with the church has turned into outright disgust.

43   Perhaps I have once again been too optimistic. Is organized religion too inextricably bound to the status quo to save our nation and
the world? Perhaps I must turn my faith to the inner spiritual church,
the church within the church, as the true *ekklesia* and the hope of the
world. But again I am thankful to God that some noble souls from
the ranks of organized religion have broken loose from the paralyzing
chains of conformity and joined us as active partners in the struggle
for freedom. They have left their secure congregations and walked the
streets of Albany, Georgia, with us. They have gone down the highways
of the South on tortuous rides for freedom. Yes, they have gone to jail
with us. Some have been dismissed from their churches, have lost the

What is the effect of the historical analogy?

How does King contrast
organized religion and the
inner church? What is the
effect?

support of their bishops and fellow ministers. But they have acted in the faith that right defeated is stronger than evil triumphant. Their witness has been the spiritual salt that has preserved the true meaning of the gospel in these troubled times. They have carved a tunnel of hope through the dark mountain of disappointment.

44   I hope the church as a whole will meet the challenge of this decisive hour. But even if the church does not come to the aid of justice, I have no despair about the future. I have no fear about the outcome of our struggle in Birmingham, even if our motives are at present misunderstood. We will reach the goal of freedom in Birmingham and all over the nation, because the goal of America is freedom. Abused and scorned though we may be, our destiny is tied up with America's destiny. Before the pilgrims landed at Plymouth, we were here. Before the pen of Jefferson etched the majestic words of the Declaration of Independence across the pages of history, we were here. For more than two centuries our forebears labored in this country without wages; they made cotton king; they built the homes of their masters while suffering gross injustice and shameful humiliation—and yet out of a bottomless vitality they continued to thrive and develop. If the inexpressible cruelties of slavery could not stop us, the opposition we now face will surely fail. We will win our freedom because the sacred heritage of our nation and the eternal will of God are embodied in our echoing demands.

45   Before closing I feel impelled to mention one other point in your statement that has troubled me profoundly. You warmly commended the Birmingham police force for keeping "order" and "preventing violence." I doubt that you would have so warmly commended the police force if you had seen its dogs sinking their teeth into unarmed, nonviolent Negroes. I doubt that you would so quickly commend the policemen if you were to observe their ugly and inhumane treatment of Negroes here in the city jail; if you were to watch them push and curse old Negro women and young Negro girls; if you were to see them slap and kick old Negro men and young boys; if you were to observe them, as they did on two occasions, refuse to give us food because we wanted to sing our grace together. I cannot join you in your praise of the Birmingham police department.

46   It is true that the police have exercised a degree of discipline in handling the demonstrators. In this sense they have conducted themselves rather "nonviolently" in public. But for what purpose? To preserve the evil system of segregation. Over the past few years I have consistently preached that nonviolence demands that the means we use must be as pure as the ends we seek. I have tried to make clear that it is wrong to use immoral means to attain moral ends. But now I must affirm that it is just as wrong, or perhaps even more so, to use moral means to preserve immoral ends. Perhaps Mr. Connor and his policemen have been rather nonviolent in public, as was Chief Pritchett in Albany, Georgia, but they have used the moral means of nonviolence to maintain the immoral end of racial

Why does King use historical analogies here?

What types of proof are used in the fourth section?

Draw a line where the subject changes. What is the subject of the fifth section?

323

What is the predominant type of proof in this fifth section?

Provide some examples.

Describe the effect.

injustice. As T. S. Eliot has said: "The last temptation is the greatest treason: To do the right deed for the wrong reason."

47   I wish you had commended the Negro sit-inners and the demonstrators of Birmingham for their sublime courage, their willingness to suffer and their amazing discipline in the midst of great provocation. One day the South will recognize its real heroes. They will be the James Merediths, with the noble sense of purpose that enables them to face jeering and hostile mobs, and with the agonizing loneliness that characterizes the life of the pioneer. They will be old, oppressed, battered Negro women, symbolized in a seventy-two-year-old woman in Montgomery, Alabama, who rose up with a sense of dignity and with her people decided not to ride segregated buses, and who responded with ungrammatical profundity to one who inquired about her weariness: "My feets is tired, but my soul is at rest." They will be the young high school and college students, the young ministers of the gospel and a host of their elders, courageously and nonviolently sitting in at lunch counters and willingly going to jail for conscience's sake. One day the South will know that when these disinherited children of God sat down at lunch counters, they were in reality standing up for what is best in the American dream and for the most sacred values in our Judaeo-Christian heritage, thereby bringing our nation back to those great wells of democracy which were dug deep by the founding fathers in their formulation of the Constitution and the Declaration of Independence.

48   Never before have I written so long a letter. I'm afraid it is much too long to take your precious time. I can assure you that it would have been much shorter if I had been writing from a comfortable desk, but what else can one do when he is alone in a narrow jail cell, other than write long letters, think long thoughts and pray long prayers?

49   If I have said anything in this letter that overstates the truth and indicates an unreasonable impatience, I beg you to forgive me. If I have said anything that understates the truth and indicates my having a patience that allows me to settle for anything less than brotherhood, I beg God to forgive me.

50   I hope this letter finds you strong in the faith. I also hope that circumstances will soon make it possible for me to meet each of you, not as an integrationist or a civil-rights leader but as a fellow clergyman and a Christian brother. Let us all hope that the dark clouds of racial prejudice will soon pass away and the deep fog of misunderstanding will be lifted from our fear-drenched communities, and in some not too distant tomorrow the radiant stars of love and brotherhood will shine over our great nation with all their scintillating beauty.

Yours for the cause of Peace and Brotherhood,
Martin Luther King, Jr.

Draw a line to set off the conclusion. What is the concluding idea?

What is King's purpose in this conclusion?

Do you find the two letters convincing? Why or why not?

Are the clergymen's and King's arguments moral or immoral according to your values and standards?

Review Questions

1. Describe the argument analysis paper.
2. What is the purpose of this paper?
3. What do you need to avoid doing in this paper that might be a part of other types of argument papers?
4. Describe the rhetorical situation for the letters by the eight white clergymen and Dr. Martin Luther King Jr.
5. What are the focus topics? Provide three examples of them.

Exercises and Activities

A. Group Work and Discussion: Understanding the Focus Topics

Divide the class into eight groups, and assign each group one of the eight focus topics listed on pages 308–310. Here are the topics: rhetorical situation; organization and claims; logical proofs and style; emotional proofs and style; proofs and style that establish *ethos;* warrants and backing; fallacious thinking and rebuttals; and ethical or unethical qualities. Utilize the questions that accompany each focus item on the list. To prepare for the group work, all students will read the two letters outside of class and make notes individually on the focus topic assigned to their group. The brief questions in the margins of the letters will facilitate this reading and note taking. In class, the groups will meet briefly to consolidate their views on their topic. Each of the groups will then make a brief oral report on their topic, and other class members will discuss the results and take some notes. These notes will be used as prewriting materials for the argument analysis paper.

B. Writing Assignment: An Argument Analysis Paper

Write a four-page double-spaced argument analysis paper of at least 1,000 words in which you analyze the two letters by the clergymen and King. Put the letters in historical context by describing the rhetorical situation, with particular emphasis on the exigence, the audiences, and the constraints. Explain the issue from both points of view. Summarize the positions taken on the issue in both letters. State the claims in both letters. Describe and evaluate the support, warrants, and backing in both. Identify any fallacies and describe how the authors use rebuttal. Finally, evaluate the ethical or unethical qualities that appear in these letters and write a conclusion in which you make a claim about the relative effectiveness of the two letters. Which letter is more effective? Why? Have your own views been modified or changed? How?

The Research Paper: Planning, Research, and Invention

After studying this chapter, you will be able to:

LO1 Analyze a research assignment.

LO2 Write a clear research claim.

LO3 Create a coherent research plan.

LO4 Describe the role audience plays in the research process.

LO5 Create a plan for gathering and evaluating sources.

LO6 Organize and present sources in accepted bibliographic form.

LO7 Take and organize effective notes.

LO8 Apply these research skills to two rhetorical invention strategies.

T his chapter and the one that follows form a self-contained unit. You may think of them as one long assignment. They present the information you will need to help you plan, research, and write a researched position paper. Some of the procedures for the researched position paper, however, are more elaborate than those you have encountered before in this book because a research paper is more complicated than the other papers you have written. As you read, you can expect to encounter some familiar information along with some new material and ideas. All of this information, including the assignments in the "Exercises and Activities" at the end of each chapter, is included for one purpose: to help you plan and write a successful and well-researched argument paper. Stay on top of these assignments, and you will be pleased with the final results.

The definition of argument presented in Chapter 1 will help you focus on your final objective in writing this paper: you will try to persuade your reading audience to agree, at least to some extent, with your claim and the ideas you use to support it.

Understanding the Assignment and Getting Started

You may want to review the Researched Position Paper Assignment from the Preface (P66-P69) and turn to pages 365–366 to read about preparing the final copy of the RPP so that you will know from the outset what this paper should finally look like. Then, to get you started on your paper, consider following some of the suggestions made in earlier chapters. They will ease you into this assignment, help you think, and make you feel knowledgeable and confident.

1. *Decide on an issue and write an issue proposal.* An issue may be assigned by the instructor, or it can be left entirely up to you. You may have made lists of issues as subjects for future papers when you finished reading Chapter 1. Look back at them now. If your concerns have shifted, think instead about the unresolved issues in your other classes or in current Web sites, newspapers, and television newscasts. Work to find an issue that captures your attention and interest. Submit it to the twelve tests of an arguable issue in Box 1.3 (page 36). These tests will help you ascertain whether or not your issue is potentially arguable. If it is, write an issue proposal to focus the issue and help you think about what more you need to learn. Follow the assignment and model on pages 35–36.

2. *Do some initial reading.* If you are not familiar enough with your issue, locate one or more sources about it and begin to do some background reading. Read enough material to form an idea of the various positions that people are likely to take on this issue. If you need advice about locating sources, read pages 336–339.

Writing a Claim and Clarifying Your Purpose

Whether you write an issue proposal and an exploratory paper or not, you will want to write your claim for your position paper as early in the process as possible. Your claim is important because it provides purpose, control, and direction for everything else that you include in your paper. Mapping your issue or freewriting about it (Chapter 3) can help you narrow and focus an issue and write a claim.

Some Preliminary Questions to Help You Narrow and Develop Your Claim

Ask the following questions to clarify and develop your claim. Some tentative answers to these questions now can help you stay on track and avoid problems with the development of your paper later.

Is the Claim Narrow and Focused?

You may have started with a broad issue area, such as technology or education, that suggests many specific related issues. If you participated in mapping sessions in class, you discovered a number of the specific related issues in your issue area. This work likely helped you narrow your issue. However, you may now need to narrow your issue even further by focusing on one prong or aspect of it. Here is an example:

> *Issue area:* The environment
>
> > *Specific related issue:*
> > What problems are associated with nuclear energy?
> >
> > *Aspects of that issue:*
> > What should be done with nuclear waste?
> > How hazardous is nuclear energy, and how can we control the hazards?
> > What are the alternatives to nuclear energy?

In selecting a narrowed issue to write about, you may want to focus on only one of the three aspects of the nuclear energy problem. You might, for instance, decide to make this claim: *Solar power is better than nuclear energy.* Later, as you write, you may need to narrow this topic even further and revise your claim: *Solar power is better than nuclear energy for certain specified purposes.* Any topic can turn out to be too broad or complicated when you begin to write about it.

You could also change your focus or perspective to narrow your claim. You may, for example, begin to research the claim you have made in response to your issue but discover along the way that the real issue is something else. As a result, you decide to change your claim. For example, suppose you decide to write a policy paper about freedom of speech. Your claim is, *Freedom of speech should be protected in all situations.* As you read and research, however, you discover that an issue for many people is a narrower one related to freedom of speech, specifically as it relates to violence on television and children's behavior. In fact, you encounter an article that claims that television violence should be censored even if doing so violates free speech rights. You decide to refocus your paper and write a value paper that claims, *Television violence is harmful and not subject to the protection of free-speech rights.*

Which Controversial Words in Your Claim Will You Need to Define?

Identify the words in your claim that may need to be defined. In the example just used, you would need to be clear about what you mean by *television violence, censorship,* and *free-speech rights.*

Can You Learn Enough to Cover the Claim Fully?

If the information for an effective paper is unavailable or too complicated, write another claim, one that you know more about and can research more success-fully. You could also decide to narrow the claim further to an aspect that you understand and can develop.

What Are the Various Perspectives on Your Issue?

Make certain that the issue you have selected invites two or more perspectives. If you have written an exploratory paper on this issue, you already know what several views are. If you have not written such a paper, explore your issue by writing several claims that represent a number of points of view, and then select the one you want to prove. For example:

Solar power is better than nuclear energy.
Solar power is worse than nuclear energy.
Solar power has some advantages and some disadvantages when compared
    with nuclear energy.
Solar power is better than nuclear energy for certain specified purposes.

As you identify the perspectives on the issue, you can also begin to plan some refutation that will not alienate your audience. An angry or insulted audience is not likely to change.

How Can You Make Your Claim both Interesting and Compelling to Yourself and Your Audience?

Develop a fresh perspective on your issue when writing your claim. Suppose you are writing a policy paper that claims public education should be changed. How-ever, you get bored with it. You keep running into old reasons that everyone already knows. Then you discover new aspects of the issue that you could cover with more original ideas and material. You learn that some people think parents should be able to choose their children's school, and you learn that competition among schools might lead to improvement. You also learn that contractors can take over schools and manage them in order to improve them. You refocus your issue and your perspective. Your new fact claim is, *Competition among schools, like competition in business, leads to improvement.* The issue and your claim now have new interest for you and your audience because you are looking at them in a whole new way.

At What Point Are You and the Audience Entering the Conversation on the Issue?

Consider your audience's background and initial views on the issue to decide how to write a claim about it. If both you and your audience are new to the issue, you may decide to stick with claims of fact and definition. If your audience understands the issue to some extent but needs more analysis, you may decide on claims of cause or value. If both you and your audience have adequate background on the issue, you may want to write a policy claim and try to solve the problems associated with it. Keep in mind also that issues and audiences are dynamic. As soon as audiences engage with issues, both begin to change. Therefore, you need to be constantly aware of the current status of the issue and the audience's current stand on it.

What Secondary Purpose Do You Want to Address in Your Paper?

Even though you establish your predominant purpose as fact, for example, you may still want to answer the other claim questions, particularly if you think your audience needs that information. You may think it is important to speculate about cause and provide definitions for the key words. You might also choose to address value questions to engage your audience's motives and values. Finally, you may think it is important to suggest policy even though your paper has another predominant purpose.

Developing a Research Plan

A research plan will guide your future thinking and research and help you maintain the focus and direction you have already established. Even though you may not know very much about your issue or your claim at this point, writing out what you do know and what you want to learn can be valuable. Add some ideas to the plan for beginning research and getting started on a first draft. Box 13.1 ■ provides an example.

Box 13.1   A Research Plan Helps You Get Started.

▶▶▶ A Research Plan

Value Claim Plus Reasons.
Television violence is harmful and should not be subject to the protection of free speech rights because:

Violence on television and violence in life seem to be related.

Children do not always differentiate between television and reality.

Parents do not supervise their children's television viewing.

Even though free speech is a constitutional right, it should not be invoked to protect what is harmful to society.

Research Needs.
I need to find out how free speech is usually defined. Does it include all freedom of expression, including forms of violence on television? Also, I will need to find the latest studies on television violence and violent behavior, particularly in children. Will I find that there is a cause–effect relationship? Even though I want to focus mainly on value and show that violent television is bad, I will also need to include definition and cause in this paper.

Plan for First Draft.
I will define television violence and free speech. I need to do some background reading on censorship and freedom of speech and summarize some of this information for my readers. My strongest material will probably be on the relationship between violence on television and violence in real life. I think now I will begin with that and end with the idea that the Constitution should not be invoked to protect harmful elements like television violence. I am going to write for an audience that either has children or values children. I will use examples from an article I clipped about how children imitate what they see on television.

You now have the beginning of an argument paper: a claim, some reasons, and some ideas to explore further. Your claim may change, and your reasons will probably change as you think, read, and do research. Before going further, however, you need to think more about the audience. The nature of your audience can have a major influence on how you will finally write the argument paper.

Understanding the Audience

Why is it important to understand your audience? Why not just argue for what you think is important? Some definitions and descriptions of effective argument emphasize the techniques of argument rather than the outcomes. They encourage the arguer to focus on what he or she thinks is important. For example, an argument with a clear claim, clear logic and reasoning, and good evidence will be described by some theorists as a good argument. The position in this book, however, has been different. If the argument does not reach the audience and create some common ground in order to convince or change their views in some way, the argument, no matter how skillfully crafted, is not productive. Productive argument, according to the definitions we used in Chapter 1, must create common ground and achieve some definable audience outcomes.

In order for the writer of argument to reach the audience, create common ground, and bring about change, two essential requirements need to be met. First, the audience must be willing to listen and perhaps be willing to also change. Second, the author must be willing to study, understand, and appeal to the audience. Such analysis will enable the author to relate to the audience's present opinions, values, and motives and to show as often as possible that the author shares them in ways that reveal or highlight the common ground essential for effective argument. Thus, both audience and author need to cooperate to a certain degree for argument to achieve any outcomes at all.

Four strategies will help you begin the process of understanding and appealing to your audience:

1. ***Assess the Audience's Size and Familiarity.*** Audiences come in all sizes and may or may not include people you know. Audiences often include specific, known groups such as family members, classmates, work associates, or members of an organization to which you belong. You may also, at times, write for a large, unfamiliar audience composed of local, national, or international members. Of course, some audiences are mixed, with people you know and people you do not know. Your techniques will vary for building common ground with large and small, familiar and unfamiliar audiences, but the aim of your argumentation will not change.

2. ***Determine What You and the Audience Have in Common.*** You may or may not consider yourself a member of your audience, depending on how closely you identify with them and share their views. For example, if you are a member of a union, you probably identify and agree with its official positions, particularly on work-related issues. If you work with management, you likely hold other views about work-related issues. The methods you use to achieve common ground with each of these audiences will be somewhat different, depending on whether you consider yourself a member of the group or not.

3. ***Determine the Audience's Initial Position and How It Might Change.*** Remember that there are several possible initial audience positions and several ways in which they might change. For example, a friendly audience might read your argument, confirm their original belief, and strengthen their commitment. An audience that mildly agrees or mildly opposes your position may finally agree with you, become interested in the issue for the first time, or tentatively accept your views, at least for now. A neutral audience may become less neutral and may even decide to accept your position, and a

hostile audience might be willing to consider some of your views, or agree to compromise, agree to disagree, or actually change and agree with you. It is possible that you have fellow students in your class who represent all of these potential initial positions.

Your task will be to create some changes in the starting or initial positions of your audience. You probably will be assigned to a small group of students who will read various drafts and versions of your paper. In your first meeting with this group, ask them for their initial positions on your issue. When you complete your project, you can then ask how their initial ideas have changed.

4. ***Analyze the Discourse Community in Your Class.*** As a member of a college class in argumentation, your discourse community will be quite well defined, and as a result, you will have already developed a significant amount of common ground with your audience because of your common background, assignments, and course goals. Your instructor is also a member of your discourse community, and by now you should have some good ideas about the quality of writing that is expected of you. Keep these individuals and what you have in common with them in mind when you write your paper.

Analyzing Your Class as Your Audience

At an early stage in the writing process, you need to answer certain key questions about your audience. To get this information, you can simply ask members of your audience some questions. Asking questions is not always possible or advisable, however. More often, you will have to obtain your own answers by studying the audience and doing research.

The following list presents thirteen questions to ask about a familiar audience. You do not have to answer every question about every audience. You may need to add a question or two, depending on your audience. Answer questions that are suggested by the particular rhetorical situation for your argument. For example, the age range of the audience might be a factor to consider if you are writing about how to live a successful life; the diversity of the class might be important if you are writing about racial issues; or class member interests, particularly outdoor interests, might be useful to know if you are writing about the environment.

Exercise F in Chapter 2 (page 63) directed you to ask some general information questions about your class as an audience. Therefore, if you completed this assignment, you already have answers to the first four questions on this list. Compare your answers with the examples below, and then ask the rest of the questions to learn what your audience thinks now about your issue.

As you read through the audience analysis questions, imagine that you are continuing to work on the argument paper on the topic of jury trials. Recall that your claim is, *Juries need pretrial training in order to make competent judgments.* The information that you uncover about your audience follows each question.

1. Describe the audience in general. Who are its members? What do you have in common with them?
2. What are some of the demographics of the group? Consider size, age, gender, nationality, education, and professional status.
3. What are some of their organizational affiliations? Consider political parties, religion, social and living groups, and economic status.
4. What are their interests? Include outside interests, reading material, and perhaps majors.
5. What is their present position on your issue? What audience outcomes can you anticipate?
6. Will they interpret the issue in the same way you have?
7. How significant is your issue to the audience? Will it touch their lives or remain theoretical for them?
8. Are there any obstacles that will prevent your audience from accepting your claim as soon as you state it?
9. How involved are audience members in the ongoing conversation about the issue? Will they require background and definitions? Are they knowledgeable enough to contemplate policy change?
10. What is the attitude of your audience toward you?
11. What beliefs and values do you and your audience share?
12. What motivates your audience? What are the members' goals and aims?
13. What argument style will work best with your audience?

Go through these questions, and try to answer them for your potential audience at an early stage of the writing process. To help you answer questions 11 and 12 about values and motives, refer to Box 3.1 (page 68).

Constructing an Unfamiliar Audience

When the information about your audience elicited by these questions is not available, you will have to construct the audience you will be addressing by imagining what they might be like. As a student writing college papers, you can safely imagine an educated audience with a broad range of interests. Any time you construct an unknown audience, remember that it is best to assume that this group is either neutral or mildly opposed to what you will write. If you assume that your audience is either friendly or hostile, you may cause them to take unexpected and extreme positions.

Using Information about Your Audience

When you complete the analysis of your audience, examine all the information you have gathered and consciously decide which audience characteristics to appeal to in your paper. Look at the cartoon on the next page. In this humorous

Image 1:

The Results of a Careful Audience Analysis.

"I'll tell you what this election is about. It's about homework, and pitiful allowances, and having to clean your room. It's also about candy, and ice cream, and staying up late."

For Discussion: Describe the appeals this speaker makes to this audience. Why might they be effective?

example, the speaker thinks he has assessed what concerns motivate his audience. Suppose that you are the student who is planning to write a paper about the value of providing jury training in order for jurors to make competent judgments. Your audience is your argument class. You decide that the general questions about the makeup of the group suggest that you have a fairly typical college audience. Its members are varied enough in their background and experience so that you know they will not all share common opinions on all matters. They do have in common, however, their status as college students. Furthermore, all of you belong to the same group, so you can assume some common values and goals. All of them, you assume, want to be successful, to graduate, and to improve themselves and society; you can appeal to these common motives. All or most of them read local newspapers or watch local news programs, so they will have common background on the rhetorical situation for your issue. You have asked about their present views on jury training, and you know that many are neutral. Your strategy will be to break through this neutrality and provoke commitment for change.

You decide, furthermore, that you may have to focus the issue for them because they are not likely to see it your way without help. They should also, you decide, know enough to contemplate policy change. You can appeal to their potential common experience as jurors and their need for physical safety, fairness, and good judgment in dealing with criminals. You can further assume that your audience values competence, expertise, and reasonableness, all important outcomes of the training system you intend to advocate. Your argument style will work with the group members because you have already analyzed styles, and yours is familiar to them. They either share your style or are flexible enough to adapt to it.

With this audience in mind, you can now gather materials for your paper that audience members can link to their personal values, motives, beliefs, knowledge, and experience. Odd or extreme perspectives or support will usually not be acceptable to this audience. An example is the electric light causing brainless babies in "Green Guilt and Ecological Overload." This example does not have universal appeal. Your classmates are reasonable and well educated, and they should inspire a high level of argumentation. Careful research, intelligent reasoning, and clear writing style are requirements for your audience of fellow students.

Get Organized for Research

You can prepare for your research by implementing some of the initial ideas about reading, thinking, and writing described in Chapter 3 to help you get off to a strong start (pages 69–73). As recommended there, begin by writing what you already know and think about your issue, and by reading broadly to both expand your background information and refine your research. You may also want to use the critical thinking prompts to help you generate ideas (Box 3.1, page 68). Most of your effort, however, will be guided by the research plan you completed. The following suggestions will aid you in reading efficiently to meet these prerequisites for your paper.

▶ **Link your research to your research plan.** As you read, expand on the brief outline you wrote using the research plan worksheet. You do not need to make the plan elaborate, but you will need some kind of list or outline to help you decide on tentative content and a possible order for your ideas. Chapter 14 provides some standard patterns of organization to consider in developing this outline.

Each piece of research material that you gather and each creative idea should be related to an item on your list or outline. Change the outline when necessary. Once you begin research, you may find you need to narrow your topic and write on only one aspect of it, add additional reasons as support, or even change the pattern of organization. Stay flexible and adjust your outline or list as you go along so that it continues to focus and guide your research.

▶ **Think about your audience.** Write out what your audience needs as background. Also, consider what reasons and evidence they might find particularly convincing.

▶ **Think of some search keywords.** Make a list of keywords associated with your issue that will help you locate sources on library and online search engines. For example, if you are writing about college entrance tests, you could enter terms such as *testing, standardized testing, college entrance tests, standardized college entrance tests,* or *tests and college admission.* To focus your search more specifically, enter a less broad term such as *new SAT.* Keyword searches will help you find both relevant and irrelevant information. Refine and narrow sources by trying different combinations of keywords and, as you proceed, by using terms that are less broad.

▶ **List the types of research materials you will seek.** Jot down where you can find them as well. Books and articles will be high on your list, but you may also want to use other sources, such as personal interviews, speeches, television programs, radio programs, advertisements, song lyrics, graphs, photographs, drawings or paintings, maps, letters, or any other types of material that would help you write an argument that is convincing to your audience.

Locating Sources for Research

Begin your research by becoming acquainted with the general layout of your library. Locate the library's online catalog, which indexes all its holdings; find out where the books, magazines, and journals are located; and then find the microforms, the government documents, the reference books, and the media section that houses video and audio materials. In addition, learn where the copy center or copy machines are located. Then find the reference desk and the reference librarians who will help you whenever you are stuck or need advice.

Use the Library's Online Catalog

Most libraries store information about all of their holdings, including all books and periodicals (magazines, journals, and newspapers), in an online index. Note that the periodicals are indexed in the online catalog and not the articles themselves.

Any computer with access to the Internet will allow you to search your library's online catalog. Search for a book by entering the author's name, the title, or the subject, and look for a particular magazine or journal by entering the title or the subject. Online catalogs also permit you to search by keyword. The keyword search is a powerful and effective research tool that can help you find mainly books but also other materials relevant to your topic, such as reference books, government documents, and various magazines and newspapers that have been reduced in size and preserved on microfilm.

Start with a keyword that represents your topic, such as *clear-cutting*, and the computer will display all titles of the books and other holdings in the library that contain that word. Read the titles as they appear on the screen and identify those that might be useful. When you have found a title that looks promising, move to the screen that shows a more complete description of that book. There you will find all of the other subject headings under which that book is listed in the index. Use those subject headings, or keywords extracted from them, to expand your search. For instance, you might move from your first keyword, *clear-cutting*, to a new keyword, *erosion*, in order to access more varied material. Online catalogs are user-friendly and will tell you on the screen how to use them. Follow the directions exactly, and ask for help if you get frustrated.

Find a Library Book

To locate the actual books or other research materials you think you want to use, copy the *call number* listed with the title in the online catalog. Copy it exactly; find out where the source is located by consulting a directory. If you cannot find it, look at the other books and resources in the area. They will often be on the same or a similar subject. Some libraries allow you to click on the call number of a book in the online catalog to find a list of the volumes that are shelved in close proximity. Books often contain bibliographies, or lists of related books and articles, which can lead you to additional sources.

Use Library Subscription Services to Find Articles

Most libraries subscribe to huge licensed online databases that allow you, with a single command, to search through articles from a large number of different print periodicals for information on your topic. All of these databases provide full publishing information about the articles they index, including the author, title, and date and place of publication. Some databases also provide either abstracts or full-text versions of the articles themselves. Many students now conduct at least some of their research on their home computers, printing copies of the material at home. Also, most of these databases allow the user to forward either article information or an entire article to one's e-mail account to be read later.

Verify which database services your library subscribes to before you begin. Here are a few of the most common ones:

Academic Search Complete describes itself as the "world's largest scholarly, multi-discipline, full text database," with peer-reviewed articles from more than four thousand periodical titles;

CQResearcher provides full-text articles on topics of current interest that include a wide range of issues;

LexisNexis Academic indexes six thousand international titles, including national and international newspapers, provides full text, and is updated hourly; and

EBSCO *host* allows you to search multiple databases at the same time.

Some databases specialize in particular areas of research and list journals, magazines, newspapers, books, and other media related to that area. Check each database you use to see how far back in time it goes. Some cover only the last twenty to twenty-five years, while others go back one hundred years or more.

Use databases by typing in subjects or keywords and executing a search. A list of associated articles in periodicals and scholarly journals will be displayed on the screen, with the most current appearing first. Read the title and, if there is one, the brief annotation of what the article is about to help you decide which articles to locate and read.

Find a Printed Journal or Magazine Article

If the database does not provide you with the full text of an article, you will have to find it in the printed periodical in which it first appeared. Look up the name of the periodical, including the volume number, issue number or month, and year, in the online catalog and copy the call number. Then look for it in the same way you would a book. You can learn additional information about the magazine or journal itself, including who publishes it and why, the types of material it publishes, and its overall quality by visiting its Web site and reading about it. Scholarly journals, for example, are often described as "refereed," which means the articles in them are read by several expert reviewers before they are accepted for publication and appear in print. As a general rule, such articles are very reliable sources.

Find Newspaper Articles

The databases we have just described will lead you to newspaper articles as well as journal and magazine articles, and many of them are full text. When they are not, you may be able to find the newspaper in which the article appeared in the microfilm section of the library. When you encounter the abbreviations *mic, mf, cm,* or *mfc* as part of the catalog information for a book or magazine, you will need to find these sources in the microfilm section of the library.

Find Reference Materials and Government Documents

Two other areas of the library can be useful for research. The reference area contains a variety of volumes that provide factual, historical, and biographical information. Government documents contain data and other forms of information that are useful for argument. Indexes, such as the *Public Affairs Information Bulletin,* which your library may have online, show you the types of factual information you can expect to find in documents printed by the government. Your librarian will help you locate the actual documents themselves.

339

Make Appropriate Use of the World Wide Web

Since the World Wide Web, unlike library databases, is free and available to everyone, not all of the materials on the Web are quality sources. Unlike the sources indexed in library databases that have also appeared in print, not all of the material you find on the World Wide Web goes through a publisher or editor. In fact, anyone familiar with computers can set up a Web site and put articles or other documents on it. To maintain your own credibility with your audience, a good rule of thumb is that no source from the Internet or in print should be used unless it has gone through a submission process and has been selected for publication by an editor of a reputable publication. While finding sources from well-known magazines and journals or professional organizations is generally safe, selecting sources from second-rate publications or from individuals lacking credentials reflects negatively on your credibility. Consequently, it is wise to use online articles and information sparingly, unless directed otherwise by your instructor. Your paper will benefit from your use of a variety of sources.

Use Web Browsers and Search Engines

Use a browser such as Safari, Firefox, Netscape Navigator, or Microsoft Internet Explorer to gain access to the World Wide Web. You can then surf the Internet to find information for your paper by using search engines like *Google* at www.google.com,

Yahoo! at www.yahoo.com, or *Firefox* at www.firefox.com. These search engines take the search terms (keywords) that you enter, comb the Net, and give you a search report, which is a list of titles and descriptions along with hypertext links that take you directly to the documents. The results that the engine measures most relevant (often based on frequency of visits) will be at the top of the list.

Vary Keyword Searches

Some engines allow you to use operators like *and, or,* and *not* to combine your search terms in a more focused way so that the results can be more relevant. By using specific keywords and their grammatical variations and synonyms along with these operators, you can find more particular information. Some of the search engines take you directly to your subject, and others first present a directory of categories that are generated by the authors of the Web sites. They include subject guides (lists of categories like *science* and *education*) that can lead you to good general information about your issue as well as sites that serve as good starting points by offering lots of links.

Use *Wikipedia*, Blogs, E-mail, and Chat Rooms With Caution

Wikipedia, the free, online encyclopedia that is open to anyone who has information to contribute, can be a good source of background information when you begin to think about your topic. Some of the entries, for example, are accompanied by useful bibliographies that can lead you to additional sources. Be cautious, however, about quoting *Wikipedia* in your paper. Some schools have policies that discourage the use of *Wikipedia* as a source for a scholarly paper because the entries have not been refereed by panels of experts and because anyone can write or edit material on this site at any time. Ask about the policy at your school. If you do use *Wikipedia* as a source, use it in a limited way just as you would any encyclopedia, to provide a few basic facts or definitions. Do cite it as a source for any information you use from it that is not general knowledge. It should not be the only source you cite for that information, however.

Blogs are virtual journals that may be written by anyone who wants to do this type of writing on the Internet. Blogs are personal, opinionated, and idiosyncratic. Explain exactly why you are quoting a blog. For example, you might quote a sampling of opinions on an issue from a few blogs. If you do, make your sources of information clear, explain how they contribute to your paper, and say why you have used them. Follow this same general advice for material you quote from e-mail, chat rooms, or personal networking sites like Facebook.

Evaluating Sources

As you locate the sources you think you will use for your paper, take a few minutes to evaluate each of them, and discard those that do not meet your standards. Good, reliable sources add to your credibility as an author, making your argument more convincing. In the same way, bad sources reflect poorly on your judgment and detract from your credibility. It is essential that you evaluate every source you use in your paper, whether it is a print or an online source. Print sources that are also to be found online, such as those you access through the library's databases, should be evaluated as published print sources.

Analyze the Author's Purpose

Look back at the continuum of the different purposes for writing argument, ranging from obvious argument at one extreme to objective reporting at the other and including extremist, hidden, unconscious, and exploratory argument (see Chapter 3, pages 69–70). Getting an idea of how the author's argumentation purpose is presented in each of your sources will help you both understand the argument better and analyze the rhetorical situation.

Analyze Web Address Extensions to Determine the Purpose of Web sites

Web sites have a variety of purposes. A site may be created to sell a product, persuade the reader to vote for a political candidate, provide entertainment, or offer educational information. Understanding how to read a Web site address can provide valuable clues to help you determine the purpose of a site. The following examples demonstrate common Web site extensions that provide information about the general category of a Web site and an indication of its basic purpose:

341

- The *.gov* extension means the Web site was created by a government agency. An example is *irs.gov.*
- The *.edu* extension means an educational institution produced the Web site. An example is *stanford.edu.*
- The *.mil* extension means the site is produced by the military. An example is *army.mil.*
- The *.com* extension means the Web site has a commercial purpose. An example is *honda.com.* The most common Web extension on the Internet is *.com.*
- The *.org* extension means the Web site was produced by a nonprofit organization. An example is *npr.org.*
- The *.net* extension stands for network. An example is *asp.net.*
- The *.int* extension stands for international. An example is *who.int,* the address of the World Health Organization.

It is difficult to generalize about the reliability of the different types of sites. Consider, however, that *.gov, .edu,* and *.mil* sites are created by established institutions with stated public purposes, and *.com, .net,* and *.org* can be set up by any person or group with a particular self-interest. Knowing you are on a commercial or special interest site can be useful when you are trying to access reliable information for a research paper.

Analyze the Rhetorical Situation of Your Sources

This will help you gain even more insight into them. Remember TRACE. Consider the *text:* analyze its point of view on the issue, compare it with other sources on the same subject, analyze the values implicit in it, look at the types of support it contains, and examine its conclusions. Ask, Who is the intended *reader?* Notice where (in what city or nation or which institution) the publication is from and when (the date of publication). Is the source intended for a particular category of readers or a universal audience? Would you classify yourself as one of the intended readers?

Learn more about the *author.* Read the preface of a book or the beginning or end of an article for author information (if there is any). Use the Internet for additional information by accessing *Google* and entering the author's name. Many authors have individual Web sites where you can learn more about their interests and other publications. You can also type in an author's name at www.amazon .com and see what other books he or she has written or edited.

Imagine each source in a context, and think about the *constraints* that may have influenced the author to write about an issue in a certain way. Also, think about the constraints that might influence you as you read it. Try to understand the author's motivation or *exigence* for writing on the issue.

Evaluate the Credibility of Your Sources

To help you determine the credibility of all sources, but particularly online sources, ask the following questions.

1. *Is the source associated with an organization that is recognized in the field?* For example, an American Civil Liberties Union Web site on capital punishment is credible because the ACLU is a nationally known organization that deals with issues of civil rights.

2. *Is the source listed under a reputable domain?* Look at what comes after "www" in the URL. For example, information found at www.stanford.edu has some credibility because it is associated with a university. Universities are considered reliable sources of information. Of course, any Stanford student, faculty member, or staff member with authorized access to the domain can publish material online. The material would not automatically be credible, so you still must review it carefully.

3. *Is the source published in a print or online journal that is peer-reviewed?* Check the journal's Web site or look at a print copy. The journal will usually advertise this on its front page. For example, *Modern Language Notes*, published by Johns Hopkins University Press, is credible because everything written in it has been reviewed by a panel of experts to ensure that the work meets a high standard of scholarship. Articles in such sources also meet the standards for academic writing, which makes them valuable potential sources for your research.

4. *Is the online source duplicated in print?* For example, material appearing on www.nytimes.com is credible because the *New York Times*, a nationally respected edited newspaper, sponsors it.

5. *Is the source accessed by a large number of people?* For example, a daily updated news site, www.cnn.com, is read and talked about across the country.

6. ***Is the source directed mainly to extremists?*** You will recognize such sources by their emotional language, extreme examples, and implicit value systems associated with extremist rather than mainstream groups. Learn what you can about such groups and try to determine whether or not they have a wide appeal. Your goal should be to find information with sufficiently wide appeal so that it might be acceptable to a universal audience.

7. ***Is the evidence in the source stacked to represent one point of view?*** Again, an unusual amount of emotional language, carefully selected or stacked evidence, and quotations from biased sources and authorities characterize this material. You can attack the obvious bias in this material, if you want to refute it.

8. ***Is the source current?*** Check to see when a Web site was published and last updated. Many topics are time sensitive. A Web site that discusses foreign policy in the Middle East, but is dated before 2001 (especially before 9/11), might have limited value unless you are examining the history of American foreign policy in this area. If you are looking for the latest ideas about global warming or immigration, check the date of the Web site, which is sometimes at the bottom of the document or on the home page.

9. ***Is the source sloppily edited, undocumented, or unreasonable?*** Material that is poorly edited, infrequently updated, or old may be untrustworthy. Other red flags are inflammatory language and no identified author. Sweeping generalizations made without evidence, undocumented statistics, or unreasonable arguments indicate questionable sources for research.

10. ***Is the source moral, immoral, ethical, or unethical, according to your values?*** This is the bottom-line question that will help you differentiate credible from non-credible sources for research.

Create a Bibliography

The bibliography is the alphabetically arranged (by author's last name) list of evaluated sources you have decided are credible, related to your issue, and potentially valuable to your research. You will begin by reading them. You may not use all of them, and some of them may lead you to other sources that you will add later. You will either enter these items directly into a computer, or write them on note cards to be typed later.

Copy and paste bibliographical information for each of your sources into a computer file or use 3 by 5 note cards. Use the journalist's questions to help you get the basic information you will need: *who* is the author, *what* is the title, *where* was the source published, *when* was it published, *which* medium of publication is it,[1] and *why* would I use it? For each source, add a note to suggest why you might use it in your paper. You will need this information later when you assemble the bibliography or list of works cited in your paper, so write or type all of it out accurately. You will not want to have to find a source again later. Here are some examples in MLA style.

---

[1]Theodore Roszak, "Green Guilt and Ecological Overload," *New York Times*, June 9, 1992, A27.

In examples 1 and 3, a search by author and title on a search engine such as *Google* or a database such as *JSTOR* locates the source, and no URL is necessary.[2]

▶ ***Bibliographical information for a book*** must include the author, the title italicized (underlined in handwritten notes),[3] the place of publication, publisher, date of publication, and medium of publication. To help you, add the call number so that you can find it later in the library.

Example:
Stock, Gregory. Redesigning Humans: Our Inevitable Genetic Future. Boston: Houghton, 2002. Print.
[Call number in stacks, QH438.7 S764]

▶ ***Bibliographical information for a printed article*** must include the author's name (if there is one), title of the article (in quotation marks), name of the publication (italicized), volume. Issue numbers (for scholarly journals), date of publication, page numbers, and medium of publication. Add the call number or a location.

Example:
Sandel, Michael J. "The Case Against Perfection: What's Wrong with Designer Children, Bionic Athletes, and Genetic Engineering." *Atlantic Monthly,* Apr. 2004: 51–62. Print.
[photocopied article; in research file folder]

▶ ***Bibliographical information for online material accessed on the Web or a database*** must include as many of the following elements as are available or needed for the type of source: author's (editor's, etc.) name; title of article (in quotation marks); title of the journal or book (italicized); volume. Issue numbers (for a scholarly journal) and date of publication (or last update); page or paragraph numbers (if numbered, N. pag. when unpaged) for articles; name of the Web site or database (italicized); sponsor, owner, or publisher of the site (or N.p. if not available), date of sponsorship, publication, or update (use n.d. when unavailable); medium; access or use date; and the address (URL, within angle brackets for MLA) of the service or site when an author-title search does not locate the source. A URL follows the access date.

Example:
Hayden, Thomas. "The Irrelevant Man." *US News & World Report* 3 May 2004. *Academic Search Complete.* Web. 15 May 2008.

ADD ANNOTATIONS TO YOUR BIBLIOGRAPHY

Your instructor may ask you to create an annotated bibliography to help you organize the research for your paper. Even when not required, it is important to the quality of your research that you hone your critical and evaluative skills with this

---

[2]This is a new MLA documentation standard, published in 2008. See the third example in this list as well. For more complete information, see Appendix 1, pages 377–396.

[3]Italicize the titles of books and journals in your bibliography when following both MLA style and APA style. Underlining in written notes is understood to mean "place in italics." See additional MLA and APA information and examples in Appendix 1, pages 369–419.

practice. The annotation is a critical or explanatory note. An annotated bibliography is an alphabetical listing of all of the sources you might use in your paper, with notes or annotations that explain, describe, or critically evaluate the material. That is, your written assessment accompanies each listing. These can include a summary of the argument and authority of the source; a description of the contents and a brief, critical evaluation; and an interpretation of how you could use the material in your paper.

Taking and Organizing Your Notes

You may want to open a file in your computer where you will enter your own ideas and as well as the various types of reading notes you want to record, including material you *quote* word for word, the material you *paraphrase* or rephrase in your own words, and the material you *summarize*. On the other hand, you may prefer to keep such materials in a research notebook, in a paper folder, or on note cards. A combination of these possibilities may work best for you. The cardinal principle in whatever note taking system you use is to clearly indicate on every note which ideas and language belong to other authors and which of them are your own. Add the author's name and the page number to all quoted, paraphrased, or summarized material; place direct quotations in quotation marks; and set off your own ideas and comments in square brackets [ ], place them in a different font or color in your computer files, or label them "mine."

Use your research plan both to guide your research and to help you organize your notes and ideas. Arrange your notes as you go along and enter them under appropriate headings in a computer file or on the list or outline that you have prepared to guide your research, or on note cards. Add additional headings to this plan when you need them. One way to accomplish this on a computer is to open two windows or document pages side by side. One window displays the headings from your research plan that may become major sections in your paper, and the other window displays an online article you are reading and noting. Copy and paste quoted material from the article and drop it into your outline. Get in the habit of *always* enclosing such material in quotation marks, and then add the name of the author at the end. Add the page number as well, if you can. Many online sources do not have page (or paragraph) numbers. You do not need at this point to add the title, place, or date of publication of each source since that information is available in your bibliography by author name. If you are using more than one book by the same author, write both the author's name and a short version of the title at the end of the citation.

When you are taking notes, you can omit words in a direct quotation to make it shorter and more to the point; indicate where words have been omitted with three spaced periods, known as an *ellipsis*. If the omitted material occurs at the end of a sentence, add a period immediately after the last quoted word, followed by the three spaced periods. Add the page number after the closing quotation mark.

If your research leads you to a new source and you want to use it, add full information about it to your bibliography. Every source you quote should be represented in your bibliography. Conversely, you should not have any items in your eventual Works Cited list that you do not quote, paraphrase, or summarize in your paper.

Clearly distinguish paraphrased and summarized material from your own ideas, just as you would quoted material. Introduce each paraphrase or summary that you enter into your document with a phrase that attributes it to its original author. "According to Scott . . ." or "Jones points out . . ." will make it clear who is responsible for the material that follows, even if it has been reworded and does not appear in quotation marks. Add a page number at the end, if it is from a paged source.

Two Invention Strategies to Help You Think Creatively about Your Research and Expand Your Own Ideas

When you have completed or nearly completed your research, try using one or both of the following invention strategies to help you gain a more comprehensive idea of what you want to do in your paper and to help you develop specific lines of argument in your paper.

USE BURKE'S PENTAD TO GET THE BIG PICTURE AND ESTABLISH CAUSE

Asking *why* will help you establish cause for controversial incidents and human motives. So too will a systematic application of Kenneth Burke's pentad, as he describes it in his book *A Grammar of Motives*.[4] In his first sentence, Burke poses the question, "What is involved, when we say what people are doing and why they are doing it?" Burke identified five terms and associated questions that can be used to examine possible causes for human action and events. Since establishing cause is an important part of many arguments, and especially of fact, cause, and policy arguments, the pentad is potentially very useful to the writer of argument.

Here are Burke's terms and questions. Apply Burke's questions to your own issue to help you think about possible ways to describe its cause. The questions force a close analysis of an issue, and they will help you gain additional insight into the controversy associated with your issue. Burke's pentad, by the way, is similar to the journalist's questions *who, what, where, when, why,* and *how,* except that it yields even more information than they do.

1. *Act: What was done?* What took place in thought or deed?
2. *Scene: When or where was it done?* What is the background or scene in which it occurred?
3. *Agent: Who did it?* What person or kind of person performed the act?

---

[4]Kenneth Burke, *A Grammar of Motives* (New York: Prentice Hall, 1945), xv. James Wood pointed out to me the value of Burke's pentad in attributing cause in argument.

4. *Agency: How was it done?* What means or instruments were used?

5. *Purpose: Why did it happen?* What was the main motivation?

Notice that you can focus on a part of an answer to any one of the five questions and argue that it is the main cause of the controversy. Notice also that each of the five questions provides a different perspective on the cause. Furthermore, the answers to these questions stir controversy. As Burke puts it, "Men may violently disagree about the purposes behind a given act, or about the character of the person who did it, or how he did it, or in what kind of situation he acted; or they may even insist upon totally different words to name the act itself."[5] Still, he goes on to say, one can begin with some kinds of answers to these questions, which then provide a starting point for inquiry and argument. Apply Burke's pentad to every issue you write about to provide you with a deeper perspective on it, including the causes or motives behind it.

USE CHAINS OF REASONS TO DEVELOP LINES OF ARGUMENT

Another method of developing a claim or subclaim in your paper is to use chains of reasons to help you get a line of thinking going. You use this method quite naturally in verbal argument when you make a claim: someone asks you questions like *why* or *what for,* and you give additional reasons and evidence as support. For example:

You claim:	The university should be more student-friendly.
Someone asks:	Why do you think so? I think it's okay.
You answer:	Because students are its customers, and without us, it would not exist.
Someone asks:	Why wouldn't it?
You answer:	Because we pay the money to keep it going.
Someone asks:	Why do students keep it going? There are other sources of income.
You answer:	Because our tuition is much more income than all of the other sources of funding combined.

You get the idea. Imagining that you are in a dialogue with another person who keeps asking *why* enables you to create quantities of additional support and detailed development for your claim. Also, by laying out your argument in this way, you can see where you need more support. In the preceding example, you need to provide support to show what portion of the operating budget is funded by student tuition. You might also give examples of insensitive treatment of students and explain what students have in common with customers.

---

[5]Ibid., xv.

To chain an argument, repeat the *why . . . because* sequence three or four times, both for your main claim and for each of your subclaims. Add evidence in all the places where your argument is sketchy. You will end up with a detailed analysis and support for your claim that will make it much less vulnerable to attack. You are now ready to think about how to organize all of this material and write your paper, which is the subject of the next chapter.

Review Questions

1. What are the claim questions, and how can they be used to establish major and minor purposes in your position paper?
2. What is the purpose of the research plan? What three main types of information are included on it?
3. What are a few items described in this chapter that you consider particularly important in conducting an audience analysis?
4. What is a bibliography? What is an annotated bibliography? How might writing an annotated bibliography help you research and write your paper?
5. Name some of the characteristics of a credible source.
6. Why would you create a research plan to guide your research?
7. Why would you use Burke's pentad and chains of reasons as part of the process of gathering material for a research paper?

Exercises and Activities

A. The Researched Position Paper: Creating Peer Writing Groups

Do an analysis of the small group of four or five individuals in your class who will serve as readers and critics of your paper from now until you hand it in. Your aim is to get an idea of how your audience regards your issue before you write, and to help your audience become interested in your paper. Do this as a group project, with each group member in turn interviewing the others and jotting down answers to the questions in Worksheet 4 below.

Worksheet 4	Audience Analysis

1. Describe your issue. What is your audience's present position on this issue? Describe some other perspectives on your issue, and ask for reactions to those ideas. State your claim and ask if there is anyone who cannot accept it as stated. If there is, ask why.
2. How significant is your issue to the audience? If it is not considered significant, describe why it is significant to you. Talk about ways you can make it more significant to the audience.

Worksheet 4   *continued*

3. How involved are audience members in the ongoing conversation about the issue? What do they already know about it?

4. How will you build common ground? What beliefs and values do you and your audience share about your issue? What motivates audience members in regard to your issue?

5. What argument style will work best with them? A direct adversarial style? Or a consensual style? Why?

6. Write what you have learned from this analysis to help you plan your appeal to this audience. Include values and motives in your discussion.

B. The Researched Position Paper: Writing a Claim and Clarifying Your Purpose

Complete Worksheet 5 by writing answers to the questions. The questions will help you focus on your claim and on ways to develop it. Discuss your answers with the members in your peer writing group, or discuss some of your answers with the whole class.

Worksheet 5   Claim Development

1. Write an issue question to focus your issue.

2. Freewrite in response to the claim questions. They are as follows:

   Fact: Did it happen? Does it exist?

   Definition: What is it? How can I define it?

   Cause: What caused it? What are the effects?

   Value: Is it good or bad? What criteria will help us decide?

   Policy: What should we do about it? What should be our future course of action?

3. Read what you have written and decide on a purpose. Write your claim as a complete sentence.

4. Which will be your predominant argumentation purpose in developing the claim: fact, definition, cause, value, or policy?

5. What is your original slant on the issue, and is it evident in the claim?

6. Is the claim too broad, too narrow, or manageable for now? Elaborate.

7. How will you define the controversial words in your claim?

8. Do you predict at this point that you may have to qualify your claim to make it acceptable to the audience? How?

C. Pairs of Students: Becoming Familiar with the Library

Visit the library with a classmate or with your entire class and learn how to access the online catalog, the subscription databases of periodical articles, and the World Wide Web. Find out how to print full-text articles in the library or send them to your e-mail address at home. Arrange for passwords, if those are required. Then learn to locate the following: books and bound periodicals in the stacks; current periodicals; microfilm or microfiche, including how to use the viewers; and the government documents. Finally, locate the reference desk and the reference librarians, who are always willing to help you with a research project.

D. The Researched Position Paper: Conducting Research

Follow the steps delineated in the research worksheet below.

E. The Researched Position Paper: Evaluating Your Research

Look back over your bibliography and the other research and ideas you have gathered and complete the worksheet on the next page. Make certain all of the information you want to use is complete and that you have the information you need to cite all sources. Add, correct, or eliminate any material that might weaken your argument.

F. The Researched Position Paper: Using Burke's Pentad to Develop an Expanded Perspective on Your Issue

Use Burke's pentad to analyze the whole context and, in particular, the cause for your issue. Write out your issue so that you will focus on it, and then answer the following questions.

1. *Act:* What was done?
2. *Scene:* When or where was it done?
3. *Agent:* Who did it?
4. *Agency:* How was it done?
5. *Purpose:* Why did it happen?

Indicate how you can use the information generated by these questions in your paper.

G. Pairs of Students: Using Chains of Reasons to Develop Lines of Argument for the Researched Position Paper

1. Write a 100-word synthesis of your thinking and research on your issue to this point.
2. Exchange your synthesis with a classmate. Read each other's syntheses, and write a thought-provoking question that asks for additional information or clarification about the topic or about the author's point of view. Return the paper to its author. Each author should read the question and write a reasoned response of two or three sentences. Exchange papers again, read the responses, and ask another question. Continue this questioning and answering until time is called.

3. When the time is up, read over the questions and answers you have developed for your issue. What surprises you? What do you need to research more? Where do you think your answers were the strongest? Once you have examined this material closely, add to your outline or draft plan to indicate how this additional information might apply when you write your paper.

H. The Researched Position Paper: Inventing Ideas

Read through the list of invention strategies on Worksheet 8, which follows on this page and the next. The list is a composite of the approaches described in this and earlier chapters. Some of them will be "hot spots" for you. That is, they will immediately suggest profitable activity for developing your paper. Check those that you want to use at this point and complete them. There may be only two or three. You should include the Toulmin model, nevertheless. It is one of the best invention activities for argument.

I. The Researched Position Paper: Adding Proofs

If either your evaluation of your research or your answer to item 12 on the invention worksheet about adding proofs indicate that you need more proof in your paper, use Worksheet 9 to help you plan additional proofs. Proofs are powerful. They help make your paper convincing to your audience.

Worksheet 6	**Research**

1. Get organized for research: gather cards, pencils, money for the copy machine, paper, and a big envelope or folder.
2. Locate a variety of sources on your issue and make evaluative judgments about each of them.
3. Gather ten to twelve of your most reliable sources. Include books, print and online articles, and other potential sources. Create a bibliography. Add annotations.
4. Survey and skim for specific information. Take notes.
5. Read critically to understand, and read creatively for original ideas. Take notes.

Worksheet 7	**Research Evaluation**

Examine the research you have done so far.

a. Do I have enough information to be convincing? What can I add?
b. Is my information reliable and convincing? How can I make it more so?
c. Is anything exaggerated or oversimplified? How can I be more accurate?
d. Do I rely too much on my own authority ("This is true because I say it is") instead of giving support? Can I add opinions of other authorities to be more convincing?
e. Am I weakening this argument with too much emotional material? Should any of it be eliminated?

Worksheet 8   Invention

Your claim: _____

Begin to develop your claim by using some of the following invention strategies. If you cannot generate information and ideas, do some background reading and then return to these strategies.

1. Freewrite for five minutes.

2. Brainstorm additional ideas and details in brief phrases for another five minutes.

3. Make a list or map that shows the parts of your paper.

4. Explain to someone in your class or group what you expect to accomplish in your paper, or talk into a tape recorder about it.

5. Write your insights in a computer file, a journal, or on sheets of paper filed in a folder.

6. Mentally visualize and write a description of a scene related to your claim.

7. Make a research plan. Write your claim plus three to five reasons. Add ideas for research and a draft plan.

8. Think about possible organizational patterns to shape your paper. What might work best—a claim with reasons, problem–solution, cause and effect, compare and contrast, chronology or narrative, or a combination of two or more patterns?

9. Think through the rhetorical situation. Remember TRACE: text, reader, author, constraints, exigence.

10. Ask the claim questions: Did it happen? What is it? What caused it? Is it good or bad? What should we do about it?

11. Decide on proofs that are suited for your type of claim.

12. Utilize critical thinking prompts. Start with your claim, but then make these recursive; that is, apply them at any point and more than once during the process.

Associate it.	Think about it as it is now.	Evaluate it.
Describe it.	Think about it over time.	Elaborate on it.
Compare it.	Decide what it is a part of.	Project and predict.
Apply it.	Analyze its parts.	Ask why.
Divide it.	Synthesize it.	

13. Use Burke's pentad to establish cause: act, scene, agent, agency, purpose.

14. Use chains of reasons to develop your ideas through five repetitions of *claim* (or *subclaim*)-*why*-*because*. Describe where you need to add evidence.

15. Make a more complete outline, set of notes, or list to guide your writing.

16. Write chunks or bits of your paper as they begin to form in your mind.

Worksheet 9	Proofs and Language Development

Write your claim: _____

a. *Signs:* What symptoms or signs will demonstrate that this might be true?

b. *Induction:* What examples can I use? What conclusions can I draw from the examples? Can my readers make the "inductive leap" from the examples to an acceptance of the conclusion?

c. *Cause:* What is the main cause of the controversy? What are the effects?

d. *Deduction:* What conclusions will I draw? On what general principles, warrants, and examples are they based?

e. *Analogies:* What comparisons can I make? Can I show that what happened in the past might happen again or that what happened in one case might happen in another? Can I use a figurative analogy to compare items from different categories?

f. *Definition:* What words or concepts will I need to define?

g. *Statistics:* What statistics can I use? How should I present them? Would they be more convincing in graph form? (If yes, see examples of graphs in Chapter 10, pages 258–261.)

h. *Values:* What values can I appeal to? Should I spell them out, or is it best to leave them unstated? What emotional narratives, examples, descriptions, and emotional language would make my appeals to values stronger?

i. *Authority:* Whom should I quote? What background information should I supply both for myself and for those I quote to establish our expertise? How can I use language to create common ground and establish *ethos?*

j. *Motives:* What do my readers need and want in regard to my issue? How can I appeal to those needs? What emotional material might help?

k. *Language:* What type of language do I want to predominate in my paper: the language of reason? emotional language? language that establishes *ethos?* a mix of styles? Make a few notes to help you plan language.

CHAPTER 14

The Research Paper: Using Sources, Writing, and Revising

After studying this chapter, you will be able to:

LO1 Incorporate research into your first draft.

LO2 Revise and prepare your final research draft.

LO3 Present your research orally to your class.

I n this chapter, you will learn to write a research paper in which you take a position on your issue organize your research material and notes, and write a research paper that is convincing to your audience of readers. Instruction in this chapter includes organizing and outlining the paper, incorporating research into your first draft, and revising and preparing the final copy.

How to Match Patterns and Support to Claims

Some of the organizational patterns are particularly appropriate for specific types of claims. Table 14.1 (page 357) suggests patterns you might want to consider as promising for particular argumentation purposes. You could, of course, combine more than one pattern to develop a paper. For example, you may begin with a narrative of what happened, then describe its causes and effects, and finally propose a solution for dealing with the problems created by the effects.

When you use organizational patterns to help you think, these same patterns can function to organize your ideas into a complete argument. However, the patterns may be too constraining if you start with one and try to fill it in with your material. If you prefer to work with ideas first, without the conscious constraints of a pattern to guide you,

Table 14.1   **Appropriate Patterns for Developing Types of Claims—in Descending Order of Suitability.**

CLAIMS OF FACT	CLAIMS OF DEFINITION	CLAIMS OF CAUSE	CLAIMS OF VALUE	CLAIMS OF POLICY
Claim with reasons	Deduction	Cause and effect	Applied criteria	Problem–solution
Induction	Claim with reasons	Claim with reasons	Cause and effect	Applied criteria
Chronology or narrative	Compare and contrast	Rogerian argument	Claim with reasons	Cause and effect
Cause and effect	Rogerian argument	Deduction	Chronology or narrative	Claim with reasons
Rogerian argument	Exploration	Exploration	Rogerian argument	Rogerian argument
Exploration	Induction		Induction	Exploration
			Deduction	
			Compare and contrast	
			Exploration	

though, at some point, patterns of argumentation must be considered. When you are finished, or nearly finished, organizing your research and ideas, move out of the creative mode and into the critical mode to analyze what you have done. You may find that you have arranged your ideas according to one or more of the patterns without being consciously aware of it. This is a common discovery. Now use what you know about the patterns to improve and sharpen the divisions among your ideas and to clarify these ideas with transitions. You will ultimately improve the readability of your paper by making it conform more closely to one or more specific patterns of organization.

Some proofs and support work better than others to establish different types of claims.[1] Table 14.2 (page 358) offers suggestions, not rules, for you to consider. Remember that a variety of types of proof and a generous amount of specific support create the best, most convincing argument papers.

---

[1] I am indebted to Wayne E. Brockriede and Douglas Ehninger for some of the suggestions in Table 12.2. They identify some types of proof as appropriate for different sorts of claims in their article "Toulmin on Argument: An Interpretation and Application," *Quarterly Journal of Speech* 46 (1960): 44–53.

Table 14.2 Proofs and Support That Are Particularly Appropriate for Developing Specific Types of Claims.

CLAIMS OF FACT	CLAIMS OF DEFINITION	CLAIMS OF CAUSE	CLAIMS OF VALUE	CLAIMS OF POLICY
Facts	Reliable authorities	Facts	Value proofs	Facts
Statistics	Accepted sources	Statistics	Motivational proofs	Motivational proofs
Real examples	Analogies with the familiar	Historical analogies	Literal analogies	Value proofs
Quotations from reliable authorities	Examples (real or made up)	Literal analogies	Figurative analogies	Literal analogies
Induction	Signs	Signs	Quotations from reliable authorities	Reliable authorities
Literal and historical analogies		Induction	Induction	Deduction
Signs		Deduction	Signs	Definition
Informed opinion		Quotations from reliable authorities	Definition	Statistics
			Cause	Cause

Outline Your Paper and Cross-Reference Your Notes

You have already been provided with a rationale and some ideas for outlining in Chapters 3 and 13. Some people find they can draft simple papers that require little or no research without an outline or list. They can later rearrange material on the computer until it is in a logical order. Most people, however, need some sort of outline or list to guide their writing when they are working with their own ideas, or with material from outside sources.

If you have not already, try making an outline or list for your research paper, and make one that works best for you. Think of your outline as a guide that will help you write later. At the very least, indicate on your outline the major ideas, in the order you intend to write about them, and add the ideas and research you will use for support and development. Read your original ideas and research notes, and check to make certain that all are cross-referenced in some way to the outline. Identify the places where you need more information and research. If you have stored research material in computer files, reread each item, check to make certain you have placed quotation marks around quoted material, and make certain you have recorded the original source for every quoted, para-phrased, or summarized item. Arrange the items under headings on your outline in the order you think you are likely to use them. If you have photocopied or printed material from online, use numbers to cross-reference to your outline the highlighted passages you intend to quote. If you have gathered research mate-rial on cards, paperclip the cards to the places on the outline where you will use them later. Work with your outline until it flows logically and makes sense. Pay attention to the parts, the order of the parts, and the relationships among the parts.

If you have the opportunity, discuss your outline or plan with your instruc-tor, a peer editing group, or a friend. Someone else can often tell you whether the organization is clear and logical, whether you have sufficient support or will need more support and evidence, and whether the warrants will be generally acceptable.

The following sample outline is an outline of the student-written researched position paper that appears in the Appendix. This outline would be complete enough to guide writing for some people. Other people might want to add more detail to it before attempting the first draft. It is the sort of outline one might take to a peer editing group to discuss and receive suggestions for the actual writing of the paper.

359

Sample Outline | Working Title: "The Big Barbie Controversy"

▶▶▶ Strategy for Paper:

Summarize positions in mapping paper in introductory paragraphs and describe personal interest in Barbie to create my own *ethos;* establish and apply criteria for judging Barbie doll as both good as a role model for building girls' self-esteem and bad for that purpose; conclude by stating that Barbie is neither good nor bad and should not be the focus of this issue; instead, parents and community are responsible for helping children build self-esteem. Value claim at the end.

▶▶▶ Introduction (Summary of Positions in Mapping Paper and Background History):

- ▶ My childhood interest in Barbie—loved her. My sister's disinterest.
- ▶ Feminism—how changed my view: new respect for sister.
- ▶ New commonsense view: Barbie just a doll with marketable appeal.
- ▶ History of Barbie doll: new concept in 1959; offers choices to girls; evidence of success.

continued

Sample Outline *continued*

▷▷▷ Is Barbie Good for Building Girls' Confidence and Self-Esteem?

▷ A powerful icon; evidence of doll's popularity.
▷ Criteria for showing Barbie is good for girls: Barbie is everywhere; people all over the world play with these dolls; it is fun to play with Barbie; Barbie stimulates imagination and is a good role model because she can take on many roles.

▷▷▷ Is Barbie Bad for Harming Girls' Confidence and Self-Esteem?

▷ Criteria for showing Barbie is bad for girls: she creates a poor body image; encourages eating disorders; encourages stereotypes; is a negative role model.

▷▷▷ Refutation: Does Barbie Have to Be Either Good or Bad?

▷ Refute those who say all bad: anorexia older than Barbie; cannot protect children from everything that might be a negative influence.
▷ Refute those who say all good: people who played with Barbie still self-critical and have limited insight into themselves.

▷▷▷ Conclusion:

It is not Barbie's responsibility to create a self-image in children.

▷▷▷ Claim:

Adults and society are responsible for children's self-images. Barbie is being used as a scapegoat.

Note that this outline is worked out in detail in some areas but not in others. The ideas in it so far, however, belong to the author. The peer group that critiques it at this stage would be able to help the author decide whether she has gathered enough source material to write a credible paper or whether she needs to read and take more notes. When your own research seems to be complete, and the notes you intend to include in the paper are either copied in a computer file, on cards, or highlighted on photocopies, they can now be cross-referenced to your outline and stacked in the order in which you will use them in the paper. You are ready to write the draft next. Most of the material in the paper will be your own insights, observations, ideas, and examples. The researched material will be incorporated into the paper to add information, interest, clarity, and credibility.

Incorporating Research into Your First Draft

Use common sense in working your research materials into your draft. Your objective is to create a smooth document that can be read easily while, at the same time, demonstrating to your readers exactly which materials are yours and which are drawn from outside sources. Here are some suggestions to help you accomplish this.

1. *Use quoted material sparingly.* You want to have the controlling voice in your paper. No more than 20 percent of your paper should be made up of direct quotations of other people's words. When you do quote, select material that is interesting, vivid, and best stated in the quoted words.

2. *Paraphrase or summarize when you do not know enough to use your own explanations.* Use your own words to rephrase or summarize other people's explanations and ideas so that yours is the dominant voice in your paper.

3. *Begin and end your paper with your own words instead of a quotation, paraphrase, or summary of other people's ideas.* The beginning and end are emphatic places in a paper. Put *your* best ideas there, not someone else's.

4. *Whenever you can, introduce each quotation, paraphrase, or summary in your paper so that your readers will know who wrote the original material.* Make it clear where your words and ideas leave off and where someone else's begin. Introduce each quotation, paraphrase, or summary with the name of the person you are quoting or otherwise citing. Consider adding a description of that person's credentials to establish his or her *ethos* and authority.

5. *Integrate every quotation into your paper so that it flows with the rest of the text and makes sense to the reader.* Work in the quotations so that they make sense in context.

6. *If your author quotes someone else and you want to use that quote in your own paper, introduce the quotation by indicating who originated it.* Make clear you are quoting someone your source quoted.

7. *Cite the source of the quotation, paraphrase, or summary in parentheses at the end of it.* Further instructions for writing in-text parenthetical citations are given in the Appendix.

Write all quotations, paraphrases, and summaries into your first draft so that your entire paper will be in place for smooth reading.

CLEARLY IDENTIFY WORDS AND IDEAS
FROM ALL SOURCES TO AVOID PLAGIARISM

Whenever you use quoted, paraphrased, and summarized material from other sources in your paper, you must indicate where your words leave off and someone else's begin, and you must identify the original source for all borrowed material.

Sometimes students mix their words in with the words of the author they are quoting and, as a result, the reader cannot easily sort out the students' words from those of the person being quoted. This is a form of plagiarism.

DOCUMENT YOUR SOURCES

Some of the main features of source acknowledgment are explained in the Appendix. Use this section as a reference guide when you are working borrowed material into your paper and when you are preparing the final list of the works you have used. These methods will inform your reader about exactly what material in your paper is yours, what belongs to other people, and where you found the material in your research.

As you incorporate borrowed material from other sources, you will need to follow a system and a set of conventions that has been prescribed for this purpose. Two such systems are described in the later in the chapter: MLA style, which is recommended by the Modern Language Association for papers written in the humanities, is explained first. MLA documentation style provides advice on how to acknowledge the work of other individuals in your paper itself and how to give full information about these sources in a list of "Works Cited" at the end of your paper. Following the discussion of MLA style is a researched position paper in MLA style format. It was written by a student, and you can use it as an example when you write your own paper. Study the annotations in the margins of this paper. They demonstrate how quoted and summarized material can be incorporated into papers and acknowledged according to MLA style. Answer the questions that accompany this paper to further develop your expertise in using MLA style.

Make Revisions and Prepare
the Final Copy

Review Chapter 3 for additional information to help you write and revise your paper. It may take several tries, but you will eventually get a version of your paper that you are content to show to other readers. Seek the help of your peer editing group, a tutor, your instructor, or other readers once again, when you have improved your paper as much as possible on your own. When you arrive at this point, you will think your paper is pretty good. However, a new reader will always find ways to improve your paper. This is the time, then, to put aside pride and let others take a final look at what you have written. A fresh set of eyes (and ears) usually adds to the careful refining you are trying to accomplish.

1. Find your claim. Is it clear? Is it well-positioned?
2. Check the quantity and quality of your support. Is there enough? Is it relevant? Is it authoritative and accurate?
3. Check your warrants. Are they likely to be acceptable to your audience?
4. Think about backing for your warrants. Should you explain backing for your warrants to make them stronger and more acceptable to your audience?
5. Focus on your rebuttal, if you have one. Does it effectively address the opposing arguments?
6. Consider a qualifier. Ask yourself: Would a qualified claim make your argument stronger?

As you go through your paper these final times, make all the remaining changes, large and small. If you have not done so, write a meaningful title that reflects the content of your paper; rewrite parts by using more evocative words; cut out anything that does not contribute to the meaning and add text where necessary; rearrange sentences or parts if you have a good reason to do so; read your paper aloud to catch additional problems; and make all final corrections. You will reach a point where you are finally satisfied. Now it is time to prepare the final copy.

Type your paper on standard 8½ by 11 inch paper and double-space all of it, including the "Works Cited" or "References" pages. If you are following MLA style, leave 1-inch margins all around. Type your last name and the page number 1/2 inch from the top of the right-hand corner. Repeat this on all subsequent pages, including the Works Cited list. One inch from the top of the first page, by the left-hand margin, type and double-space your name, your instructor's name, the course name and number, and the date. Double-space again, and type the title, centered. Double-space once more, and begin typing your paper. Attach the list of "Works Cited" at the end, beginning on a new page.

Spell-check your paper if you are using a computer, and proofread it one last time. Correct all of the errors that you can find. Errors in a research paper damage your *ethos* with your readers. Careless errors communicate that you do not really value your own work or your audience. When your paper is as error-free as you can make it, it is ready for submission.

Present Your Paper Orally to the Class

Your instructor may ask you and your classmates to present the results of your research to the class in the form of oral argument. Like written and visual argument, oral argument possesses special features that make it uniquely effective for presenting arguments. Oral argument has been around much longer than written argument. In earlier chapters, you read about Aristotle's *Rhetoric,* which was written twenty-five hundred years ago to train public speakers to be convincing to audiences. Then, as now, people recognized that speakers have certain advantages over writers in presenting effective argument. Listed below are a few of these advantages.

1. *Oral argument is immediate.* When the speaker and the audience are together in the same physical location, face to face, the potential for effective argument is greatly enhanced. This is true of all forms of oral argument, whether spoken, chanted, or sung. The physical presence of an effective speaker intensifies what is said, and the audience is thus more likely to pay attention and be influenced. Furthermore, a good speaker is always aware of the audience and can adapt both words and delivery to keep listeners' attention and influence them in desired ways. Oral argument delivered through the media, such as television, the Internet, print, radio, or film, usually lacks some of the sense of immediacy and consequent power that the actual presence of the speaker provides, but it can still be very effective.

2. *Oral argument employs physical as well as verbal strategies.* Speakers are able to influence perception in ways that writers cannot. For example, speakers can use physical gestures, vocal inflections, facial expressions, eye contact, physical setting, dress, and physical appearance in effective and dramatic ways to strengthen delivery and make their words more powerfully convincing. Combine these physical attributes with a strong message and a sincere motivation to persuade the audience through direct speech, and the potential for successful and productive argument is usually stronger than in a written essay.

3. *Oral argument is a continuous stream of fleeting content that is sometimes difficult to monitor and evaluate.* A reader of written argument can always stop to reread or turn back to find a previous passage that could illuminate a confusing passage. Listeners do not have this advantage. They have only one chance to understand the speaker. Sometimes, of course, listeners have the opportunity to interrupt and ask the speaker to repeat or clarify what has just been said. This is often not the case, however. As a result, the listener does not have the same opportunity the reader has to accomplish a close evaluation of the speaker's content. Instead, a listener is usually left with a powerful impression of the main argument that the speaker wants to communicate, along with some of the ideas and examples that support that argument. This fact can be an advantage to a speaker who wants to overwhelm and convince the audience. The listener, always hearing the next words, has a diminished opportunity to consciously monitor and critique everything that is said during the speech. Think of evangelists and politicians you have heard who rely on physical setting, their voice, gestures, and appearance, and a stream of content that often includes emotionally loaded language and examples that are crafted to convince you. In many cases, such speakers can be more powerfully convincing than writers can.

4. *Oral argument usually employs a less formal style than written argument and can be easier to respond to and understand.* When compared with written argument, oral argument usually has fewer main points, more support of all kinds, and more obvious transitions to help the listener move from one idea to another. Oral argument is usually also more repetitious, contains more personal pronouns (*I, you, we, us*), includes direct questions that engage the audience, and contains less perfect sentence structure than written argument. Such informality results in an enhanced rapport and the establishment of more common ground between the speaker and the audience. The informality of spoken argument, when compared with written argument, is often more inviting to an audience and makes it easier for listeners to pay attention, believe the speaker, and become convinced.

Analyze oral argument just as you would written or visual argument. That is, when listening to oral argument, you can recognize and understand the rhetorical situation; analyze the use of *logos, ethos,* and *pathos;* identify and expose fallacies; apply the Toulmin model; and make ethical judgments, just as you would when reading an essay or viewing a visual argument. Apply these methods of analysis when you create oral argument. Exercise B on pages 366–367 explains how to prepare your researched position paper for oral presentation in a class symposium.

Review Questions

1. What steps can you take to avoid plagiarism when you are incorporating research materials into your draft and when you are preparing the final copy?
2. What is the purpose of the "Works Cited" page (MLA)?
3. What are some of the special features of oral argument?

Exercises and Activities

A. Writing Assignment: The Researched Position Paper

1. *Write a list, outline, or partial manuscript that will serve as a plan for your paper, and bring it to class.* In peer editing groups of three or four students, explain to the group what your paper is about, and how you plan to organize and develop it. Suggestions from the others can help with ideas and organization, as well as adding research. Decide whether or not to add visual images as support.

2. *Create a class peer critique sheet.* The peer critique sheet provides a guide for critiques and revision. Make a list of all of the special requirements for a researched position paper: a title, a clear claim, adequate support, clear organization, accurate documentation, and so on. Select five to ten items from this list that you believe are essential elements to consider during revision. Organize them on a peer critique sheet. Use these sheets in your peer editing group to critique individual student papers and make good recommendations for revision.

3. *Write a draft of your paper, revise it, and bring it to class.* At this point, it is useful to have one or more people read your paper and give you ideas

for improving it. Your readers may use the peer critique sheets created in Exercise A2 above, either writing their comments on them or on the papers. This can be accomplished in one of the following ways:

a. Groups in class: The members of your peer group should first read all of the papers written by your group and make a few notes about each of them on the peer critique sheets or on the papers. As an alternative, the authors can read their papers aloud, with each paper discussed in turn. Members of the group should offer observations and recommendations for improvement to each author, and as the discussion progresses, they may continue to add suggestions to the peer critique sheets, which should be given to the authors at the end of the session.

b. Individuals outside of class: Exchange papers with a classmate and critique each other's work outside of class. Before the next class period, read the paper you have been assigned carefully and make as many useful suggestions as you can on the paper itself and on the peer critique sheet. When you return to class, talk through your suggestions with the author. Then listen to that individual's ideas for improving your paper.

4. *Make final revisions, and then prepare the final copy.* Your researched position paper should be a length specified by your instructor. It should be double-spaced and should use a specified number of outside sources. Use MLA format throughout. The student paper demonstrates general format, in-text citations, and "Works Cited" requirements for MLA style.

5. *Write a submission letter to your instructor.* Submit a letter to your instructor with your final paper, and in it describe what you like about your paper and what still dissatisfies you. Identify problems or passages on which you would like some feedback.

B. Class Project: Conducting a Class Symposium and Presenting Your Research

Adapt your researched position paper to create a five-minute oral presentation of the research you have completed. Follow these instructions:

1. Work with your written manuscript to change it into an oral report. Underline and number the most important ideas. Since oral argument usually has fewer main ideas than written argument, limit yourself to three to five main ideas so that you can explain them in the time you have.

2. Think about your audience. How much background information about your topic will you have to present or possibly add at the beginning of your speech to help your audience understand it?

3. Remember, also, that your listeners have only one chance to understand the main ideas. Add some obvious transitions to clarify your main ideas and make them stand out. These might include, for example, explaining your main points in your introduction, numbering them as you explain them, and restating and summarizing them at the end of your speech.

4. You will not read your speech, but you will probably want some speaking notes to refer to as you speak. Accomplish this by writing a 250-word abstract of your researched position paper. State the claim, the main points made about it, some of the evidence, and your conclusion. Now go back and underline the points in the abstract that you want to talk about and number these in the margin. While you are speaking, you might need to glance at your abstract from time to time to remind yourself of the next point, and, if you find that you are stuck, you can read a sentence or two. Writing the abstract in sentences will also help you get the phrasing right so that you will speak more fluently.

5. Organize members of your class in groups around the same or related topics. The best group size is five to seven students with a moderator. The moderator will call on the students in your group to present your abstracts of your research papers.

6. Practice your speech and time it. If anything in the speech seems to be unclear or awkward, make revisions. Work with the speech until it fits within the time frame of five minutes.

7. Add a visual to your presentation to make it more forceful and memorable. Copy or create single or composite pictures, graphs, or other visuals than can be used to make your claim more convincing. Or, you may want to include visuals in a PowerPoint presentation. Here are the rules for using visuals during an oral presentation: (a) make it large enough for your audience to read easily, and (b) do not put it in front of your audience until you are ready to discuss it.

8. Practice the speech several times until you can give it fluently.

9. When you give your speech, use eye contact and experiment with some gestures. Above all, concentrate on communicating with your audience.

10. Answer questions from the class. Participate in a brief class discussion of the ideas presented by your group.

How to Document Sources

Using
MLA Style

How to Document Sources Using MLA Style

The following material will demonstrate, first, how to use in-text citations to show your readers exactly what material you have included in your paper from outside sources; and, second, how to prepare a final list of sources with publication details at the end of your paper. This list is called either Works Cited, if you are following MLA style, or References, if you are following APA style. In-text citations are structured to make clear to the reader who is to be credited with the words or ideas and where in the Works Cited or References list to find the full documentation of that source. You will have noted that this book utilizes the footnote style preferred by the University of Chicago Press and described in the *Chicago Manual of Style* (15th ed., 2003) to make the same information clear to the reader.

The first section of this appendix discusses MLA documentation. For additional detail on how to use MLA style, consult the *MLA Style Manual and Guide to Scholarly Publishing* (3rd ed., 2008) or the *MLA Handbook for Writers of Research Papers* (due to publish in a 7th ed., 2009),* both published by the Modern Language Association.

The MLA portion of this appendix is itself divided into two sections, as described above: (1) how to cite sources in the body of the text, and (2) how to cite sources in the Works Cited list. If you need information only on how to format sources for the Works Cited page, turn to page 377.

---

*The Modern Language Association has determined to alter some of the standard formats published in 2003. The 2008 changes have been included in this text.

MLA: How to Cite Sources in the Body of the Text

The MLA system of documentation is very simple to learn and understand. The system asks that you show where you originally found a direct quotation or the information for a paraphrase or a summary by inserting a brief parenthetical citation at the end of the borrowed material in your written text. The typical in-text parenthetical citation contains the author's last name and the page number: (Jones 5). However, if you include the author's name in the text, then you do not need to include it in the citation. If you include a book or journal title because no author is available, place the title in italics (for a book) or quotation marks (for an article).

To help you quickly find what you need, use the following list.

1. A direct quotation with the author mentioned in the text—page 372
2. A direct quotation with the author not mentioned in the text—page 372
3. A paraphrase or summary with the author mentioned in the text—page 372
4. A paraphrase or summary with the author not mentioned in the text—page 373
5. Two or more authors—page 373
6. Two books by the same author—page 373
7. A corporate or group author—page 373
8. An unknown author—page 373
9. A work reprinted in a book or journal—pages 373–374
10. Short quotations versus block quotations—page 374
11. Ellipsis points and quoted material—pages 374–375
12. Tables—page 375
13. Graphs, artwork, photographs, and other illustrations—page 375
14. Poetry and song lyrics—page 376
15. Electronic sources—page 376

1. *A direct quotation with the author mentioned in the text* If you introduce the author's name in the body of the text before you quote directly, then there is no need to include the name in the parenthetical citation.

> Although various critics have accused Arnold Schoenberg's musical compositions of being "atonal," Alex Ross points out that the composer was "simply offering a tonality of a less familiar kind" (176).

2. *A direct quotation with the author not mentioned in the text*

> Although various critics have accused Arnold Schoenberg's musical compositions of being "atonal," others argue that the composer was "simply offering a tonality of a less familiar kind" (Ross 176).

3. *A paraphrase or summary with the author mentioned in the text*

> According to Calvin Tomkins, the rebuilding and expansion of the New York Museum of Modern Art proves that modern art has not reached its end (72).

4. *A paraphrase or summary with the author not mentioned in the text*

If the rebuilding and expansion of the New York Museum of Modern Art is any indication, claims that modern art has reached its end may soon be proven wrong (Tomkins 72).

5. *Two or more authors* If two or three authors have written the material you have borrowed, include all of their last names in either the introductory wording or the citation.

Pimentel and Teixeira remind us, "Virtual reality is all about illusion" (7).

"Virtual reality is all about illusion" (Pimentel and Teixeira 7).

For more than three authors, use only the first author's last name and add *et al.* to the citation. (*Et al.* is an abbreviation of the Latin *et alii,* meaning "and others." It is not italicized in your paper.)

"Television is not primarily a medium of entertainment in all societies" (Comstock et al. 25).

6. *Two books by the same author* To indicate which book you are citing, either include the name of the book in the introductory material or add a shortened title to the parenthetical information to differentiate between the books. For example, if you are using *The Second Self: Computers and the Human Spirit* (1984) and *Life on the Screen: Identity in the Age of the Internet* (1995), both by Sherry Turkle, document as follows:

Sherry Turkle says the computer is like a mirror that has a strong psychological hold over her (*Second Self* 306). She explains further that "the computer tantalizes me with its holding power" (*Life* 30).

If the author is not mentioned in the text, include the author's name followed by a comma before the shortened title of the work: **(Turkle,** *Life* **30).**

7. *A corporate or group author* Sometimes written materials are attributed to a corporate or group author (e.g., a corporation, company, association, or organization) rather than to an individual author. In this case, use the name of the corporation or group, preferably in the wording that precedes the quotation.

The RAND Corporation observes that "when the No Child Left Behind Act was passed into law in January 2002, it heralded the beginning of one of the most expansive efforts to reform public education" (7).

If the corporate author is not mentioned in the text, include the corporate author's name as part of the citation before the page number.

(RAND Corporation 7)

8. *An unknown author* When no author is listed for either a book or an article, use the title or the first words of an abbreviated title in your citation.

Article: ("Creativity and Television" 14)

Book: (*World Almanac* 397)

9. *A work reprinted in a book or journal* If you quote an article, poem, story, or any other work that is reprinted not in its original but in another compilation, cite the author you are quoting in the text and the page number. The author or editor of the compilation is not cited in the parenthetical citation, but is fully cited in the Works Cited. Thus a quotation that includes words from both pages of the essay by Edward O. Wilson on pages 289–290 of this book by Nancy V. Wood would be cited in the text as **(Wilson 289-90)**.* (See page 381, Works Cited example 18.)

10. *Short quotations versus block quotations* Short quotations do not exceed four lines of text. For short quotations, place quotation marks around the quoted material, insert the citation information in parentheses, and place the period outside it.

> According to Nate Stulman, many college students in his dormitory "routinely stay awake all night chatting with dormmates online. Why walk 10 feet down the hall to have a conversation when you can chat on the computer—even if it takes three times as long?" (268).

Quotations that exceed four lines of text should be blocked. To block a quotation, you should eliminate the quotation marks and indent each line 1 inch (or ten spaces) from the left margin, including the first line if you quote all or part of a single paragraph (that is, do not set a paragraph indent). If you quote two or more full paragraphs, indent the first line of each paragraph an additional ¼ inch (or three spaces), as in the example below. Place the period at the end of the text, followed by the parenthetical citation. Use double-spacing, as you do throughout your paper. It is good writing style to provide a brief introduction to a long quote and to finish the quote with a concluding thought.

> Nate Stulman describes some of the uses of computers by the students at his school that he has observed:
>
> > Several people who live in my hall routinely stay awake all night chatting with dormmates online. Why walk 10 feet down the hall to have a conversation when you can chat on the computer—even if it takes three times as long?
> > You might expect that personal computers in dorm rooms would be used for nonacademic purposes, but the problem is not confined to residence halls. The other day I walked into the library's reference department, and five or six students were grouped around a computer—not conducting research, but playing Tetris. Every time I walk past the library's so-called research computers, it seems that at least half are being used to play games, chat, or surf the Internet aimlessly. (268)
>
> These experiences may be typical of students' computer use at other colleges as well.

11. *Ellipsis points and quoted material* Occasionally, you will want to delete material from the original source either to make your document shorter or to make the writing that includes the quote more readable. If you do so, indicate by inserting ellipsis points to signal that you have removed words. The following example shows how to use ellipsis points to indicate you have omitted words in the middle of a sentence. (Other information on ellipsis points can be found in Chapter 13, pages 345–346).

> "If there were a wider appreciation for motherhood in society, women might . . . hold their heads high when going to the boss and asking for a reduced hour work schedule" (Hewlett 308).

When deleting the ending of a sentence in a short quotation, indicate that deletion by using three spaced points and a fourth after the parenthetical citation. The fourth point serves as the period to the sentence.

> "A weakness of mass entertainment is its impersonality . . ." (Jones 226).

---

*Note that inclusive page ranges in MLA style ellide the hundred- or thousand-place numeral for the closing page in the range, as long as it is clear which pages are being cited. For example, 199–203 would not be ellided.

When there is no parenthetical citation (for example, within a large block quotation), then the sentence is completed by placing the period before the ellipsis.

12. *Tables* Place tables as close as possible to the text they explain or illustrate. At the top, place with the word *Table* and assign an Arabic numeral. On a new line, give it a caption capitalized headline style. Provide source information immediately below the table. Notes, if any, follow, numbered with lowercase letters (*a, b, c,* etc.). Double-space throughout (for a small table) and align as shown. Indent the second or more lines in the caption and source line two spaces; indent the first line of notes five spaces.

Table 1

Travel and Entertainment Cost Savings Using Electrovision

Source of Savings	Amount Saved per Year[a]
Switching from first-class to coach airfare	$2,300,000
Negotiating preferred hotel rates	940,000
Negotiating preferred rental car rates	460,000
Systematically searching for lower airfares	375,000
Reducing interdivisional travel	675,000
Reducing seminar and conference attendance	1,250,000
Total Potential Savings	$6,000,000

Source: Courtland L. Bovee and John V. Thill, *Business Communication Today,* 6th ed. (Upper Saddle River: Prentice, 2000) 539. Print.
[a]In U.S. dollars.

13. *Graphs, artwork, photographs, and other illustrations* Graphs, artwork, photographs, and other illustrations are labeled Fig., the abbreviation for *Figure,* followed by an Arabic numeral; the caption (see format below) is followed on the same line by any source material. This is an example created in a word processing program.

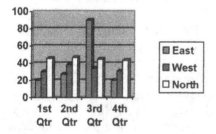

Fig. 1. Quarterly earnings according to region.

14. *Poetry and song lyrics* Quote three lines or less of poetry in your text by using quotation marks and a slash with spaces on each side [/] to separate the lines. The parenthetical citation should contain the line numbers.

> As "Gacela of the Dead Child" shows, Lorca's goal was to express the character of *duende:* "The dead wear mossy wings. / The cloudy wind and the clear wind / are two pheasants in flight through the towers," (5-7).

For more than three lines, indent the quotation 1 inch (or ten spaces) from the left margin.

> In fact, *duende* invades much of Lorca's work:
>
> > Death goes in
> > and death goes out
> > of the tavern
> > Black horses
> > and sinister people
> > roam the hidden trails
> > of the guitar. (1-7)

15. *Electronic sources* Cite electronic sources in the text just as you would print sources. Introduce the quotation with the author's name, or cite the author's last name (or a short title, if there is no author) with a page or paragraph number in parentheses at the end. If the source has no page or paragraph numbers, or if you are citing or quoting from the whole source as a single document, place only the author's name in the parentheses. Here is an example of a quotation from an online journal that numbers paragraphs.

> "Rose represents the unnamed multitude of women who were placed in the same circumstances but whose stories were never told" (Mason, par. 8).

If you use the author's name in the body of the text introducing the quotation, then place only the paragraph number in the citation.

> According to Mason, "Rose represents the unnamed multitude of women who were placed in the same circumstances but whose stories were never told" (par. 8).

Some online sources do not provide page or paragraph numbers. There are two ways to cite such sources. If you place the author's name in the text, there is no parenthetical citation at the end.

> Carlos Oliveira phrases the question about media and reality this way: "Take, for instance, the alteration of our reality through the mass media. Do the media create reality? Or do they alter or destroy it?"

If you do not mention the author in the text, place only the author's name in the citation.

> "Take, for instance, the alteration of our reality through the mass media. Do the media create reality? Or do they alter or destroy it?" (Oliveira).

Also, some online sources are a single page, which may or may not be numbered. When your source is a single page, include any page number in the Works Cited entry but use the no-page-number model in your text. For example, look at the quotation from Rachel Sa in paragraph 15 of the MLA student research paper titled "The Big Barbie Controversy" on page 393. No page number is included in the text since this is a single-page source. Now turn to page 395 and look at the Works Cited entry for Sa. Notice that the page number is included here.

MLA: How to Cite Sources in the Works Cited Page

Attach to the draft a list of all the works you have quoted, paraphrased, or summarized in your paper along with full publication information for each source. This list is titled Works Cited, and it begins on a new page, which is numbered consecutively. It is alphabetized according to the last names of the authors or, if no author is listed, by the title of the works, ignoring any initial *A, An,* or *The.* Note: *All the information on the list should be double-spaced, just like the rest of your final paper.*

Look at the Works Cited page at the end of the MLA-style student paper appearing on pages 394–395. Include on any works cited list only those works actually cited or borrowed from in your paper. The easiest way to prepare this list for your paper is to alphabetize your bibliography cards or notes, in the manner just explained. If you have prepared an annotated bibliography, simply eliminate the annotations to create the Works Cited list. Start each citation at the left margin and indent each successive line ½ inch (or five spaces; this is called a hanging indent). Note: Use day, month (abbreviated), year order for dates.

The Internet has increased not only personal access to printed source material, but also proliferated the number and type of published forms or mediums available as credible source material. A writer's ethical responsibility in documenting sources requires that the audience be able to locate and examine the cited sources readily. Accordingly, the Modern Language Association now requires that the medium of publication be clearly documented in all citations in MLA style. That is, all mediums, vehicles, or forms of publication will be identified as a standard element of citation. Here is a list of mediums, which will usually appear at the end of an entry, followed by a period.

Print.	Web.	CD.
CD-ROM.	DVD.	DVD-ROM.
Radio.	Television.	Performance.
Audiocassette.	LP.	Film.
Videocassette.	Laser disc.	Address.
MS.	E-mail.	Microform.
Microsoft Word file.	MP3 file.	Digital file.

Examine the basic formats provided next, and then locate and use the many specific examples for documenting sources in specific mediums that follow in this section on MLA style.

Basic Format for Books, Articles, and Electronic Sources

Books

Author. *Title of Book.* City: Publisher Name in Shortened Form, year of publication. Medium of publication.

Articles in newspapers

Author. "Title of Article." *Name of Newspaper* date of publication, edition, if relevant: page numbers. Medium.

Articles in magazines

Author. "Title of Article." *Name of Magazine* date of publication: page numbers. Medium.

Articles in scholarly journals

Author. "Title of Article." *Name of Journal* volume number.issue number, if available (year of publication): page numbers. Medium.

Documents from the Internet that can be located by author and title search

Author. "Title."/*Title.* Print publication information. *Site.* Web. Access date.

or

Author. "Title."/*Title Database/Site.* Sponsor/Owner/Publisher, Publication date or latest update. Web. Access date.

Documents from the Internet that require a URL to be located

Author. "Title"/*Title Database.* Print publication date. *Site.* Sponsor, publication date or latest update. Web. Access date.*

Note: If you can find an Internet site easily by entering the author and title into a search engine, like *Google* or *Firefox,* omit the Web address or URL (for uniform resource locator). Add the URL when a site or document would be difficult to locate without it.

Documents from online scholarly articles located through library subscription services

Author. "Title of Article." [Follow the basic model for either a Newspaper, Magazine, or Journal article]. *Database Name.* Medium. Access date.

Note that in book titles, article titles, names of periodicals, names of Web sites, and other titles of works or publications, MLA capitalizes all important words, headline style. Also note that article, short story, and poem titles are placed within quotation marks, whereas titles of books, newspapers, journals, magazines, Web sites, databases, software, and so forth are italicized. For electronic sources, print publication information (when it exists) is listed first, followed by the electronic publication information, medium of publication, date of access, and uniform resource locator (URL) in angle brackets (included only when it is needed to access that specific source). A period ends the entry. Eliminate the volume number, issue number, and parentheses around the date when citing newspaper or magazine articles.

Examples of many of the types of sources most commonly cited for argument papers are provided on the next several pages. Consult the following list to quickly find the formats you need.

How to List Print Books

1. A book by one author—page 380
2. A book by two or three authors—page 380
3. A book by more than three authors—page 380
4. Two or more books by the same author—page 380

5. A book by a corporate or group author—page 380

6. A book with no author named—page 380

7. A republished book—page 380

8. A translation—page 381

9. A second or subsequent edition—page 381

10. Proceedings from a conference or symposium—page 381

11. An introduction, preface, foreword, or afterword—page 381

12. A government document—page 381

How to List Print Articles

13. An article from a magazine—page 381

14. An article from a newspaper—page 381

15. An article in a periodical with no author listed—page 381

16. An article in a journal—page 381

17. An edited collection of articles or an anthology—page 381

18. An article in an edited collection or an anthology—page 381

19. A cross-reference to an edited collection or an anthology—pages 381–382

20. A reprinted article in an edited volume or collection—page 382

21. A signed article in a reference work—page 382

22. An unsigned article in a reference work—page 382

23. A review—page 382

24. A letter to the editor—page 382

25. An editorial—page 382

26. A published interview—page 382

27. A personal interview—page 382

28. A lecture, speech, or address—page 382

How to List Electronic Sources

29. A document from an Internet site—page 383

30. A digital file—page 383

31. An entire Internet site—page 383

32. A home page for a course—page 383

33. A personal home page—page 383

34. An online book—pages 383–384

35. A part of an online book—page 384

36. An article in an online newspaper—page 384

37. An article in an online magazine—page 384

38. An article in an online scholarly journal—page 384

39. A review—page 384

40. A publication on a CD-ROM or DVD-ROM—page 384

41. A work from a library subscription service—page 384

42. A television or radio program—page 384

43. An advertisement—pages 384–385

44. A cartoon or comic strip—page 385

How to List Other Nonprint Sources

45. An audio recording—page 385

46. A film or video recording—page 385

47. A videotape or DVD—page 385

48. A painting, sculpture, or photograph—page 385

49. A map or chart—page 385

50. An e-mail—page 385

How to List Print Books

1. *A book by one author*

Melvern, Linda. *Conspiracy to Murder: The Rwandan Genocide*. London: Verso, 2004. Print.

2. *A book by two or three authors*

Chayes, Antonia H., and Martha Minow. *Imagine Coexistence: Restoring Humanity after Violent Ethnic Conflict*. San Francisco: Jossey, 2003. Print.

3. *A book by more than three authors*

Stewart, Charles J., et al. *Persuasion and Social Movements*. 3rd ed. Prospect Heights: Waveland, 1994. Print.

4. *Two or more books by the same author* As demonstrated in the first entry of this example, an initial *The* (or *A* or *An*) is disregarded in the alphabetized titles. Replace the author's name after the first entry with three hyphens followed by a period. Shorten the words *University* and *Press* as U and P in the publisher information; note other standard abbreviations in various entries.

Shaviro, Steven. *The Cinematic Body*. Minneapolis: U of Minnesota P, 1993. Print.

---. *Connected, Or, What It Means to Live in the Networked Society*. Minneapolis: U of Minnesota P, 2003. Print.

5. *A book by a corporate or group author*

Harvard Business School Press. *The Results-Driven Manager: Winning Negotiations That Preserve Relationships: A Time-Saving Guide*. Boston: Harvard Business School P, 2004. Print.

6. *A book with no author named*

The World Almanac and Book of Facts. New York: World Almanac, 2007. Print.

7. *A republished book*

Locke, John. *An Essay Concerning Human Understanding*. 1690. New York: Dover, 1959. Print.

8. *A translation*

Virilio, Paul. *Ground Zero*. Trans. Chris Turner. London: Verso, 2002. Print.

9. *A second or subsequent edition*

Wood, Nancy V. *Perspectives on Argument*. 6th ed. Upper Saddle River: Prentice, 2009. Print.

10. *Proceedings from a conference or symposium*

Medhurst, Martin J., and H. W. Brands, eds. *Presidential Rhetoric: Critical Reflections on the Cold War Linking Rhetoric and History*. Texas A&M Conf. on Presidential Rhetoric, 5–8 Mar. 1998. College Station: Texas A&M UP, 2000. Print.

11. *An introduction, preface, foreword, or afterword*

Rajchman, John. Introduction. *Pure Immanence*. By Gilles Deleuze. Trans. Anne Boyman. New York: Zone, 2001. 7–23. Print.

12. *A government document*

United States. FBI. Dept. of Justice. *National Instant Criminal Background Check System*. Washington: GPO, 2004. Print.

How to List Print Articles

Include all the page numbers of the article. Use a plus sign when the pages are not consecutive; otherwise, cite the range of inclusive pages. Elide the first digit of the ending page above 99 (e.g., *122–25*), but only when elliding a digit will not cause confusion (see examples 20 and 40).

13. *An article from a magazine*

Tomkins, Calvin. "The Modernist." *New Yorker* 5 Nov. 2001: 72-83. Print.

14. *An article from a newspaper*

Rutenberg, Jim, and Micheline Maynard. "TV News That Looks Local, Even If It's Not." *New York Times* 2 June 2003: C1+. Print.

15. *An article in a periodical with no author listed*

"Metamorphosis." *New Yorker* 5 Nov. 2001: 10. Print.

16. *An article in a journal*

Mountford, Roxanne. "The Rhetoric of Disaster and the Imperative of Writing." *Rhetoric Society Quarterly* 31.1 (2001): 41-48. Print.

17. *An edited collection of articles or an anthology*

Handa, Carolyn, ed. *Visual Rhetoric in a Digital World*. Boston: Bedford, 2004. Print.

18. *An article in an edited collection or an anthology*

Stroupe, Craig. "Visualizing English: Recognizing the Hybrid Literacy of Visual and Verbal Authorship on the Web." *Visual Rhetoric in a Digital World*. Ed. Carolyn Handa. Boston: Bedford, 2004. 13-37. Print.

19. *A cross-reference to an edited collection or an anthology* To avoid duplicating information when citing more than one source from a collection or anthology, set up a cross-reference in the Works Cited list. Cite the whole anthology or collection as you would any source. For the entire collection, the editor is the author.

Handa, Carolyn, ed. *Visual Rhetoric in a Digital World*. Boston: Bedford, 2004. Print.

Cite each article from the anthology that you have used but instead of duplicating the anthology's full publication information, include the last name of the editor of the collection and pertinent page numbers only. Alphabetize each entry in this case by the cited article author's last name.

> Stroupe, Craig. "Visualizing English: Recognizing the Hybrid Literacy of Visual and Verbal Authorship on the Web." Handa 13-37.

20. *A reprinted article in an edited volume or collection* The following shows a chapter from Gunther Kress's book *Literacy in the New Media Age* reprinted in the collection by Handa.

> Kress, Gunther. "Multimodality, Multimedia, and Genre." *Literacy in the New Media Age.* London: Routledge, 2003.106–21. Rpt. in *Visual Rhetoric in a Digital World.* Ed. Carolyn Handa. Boston: Bedford, 2004. 38-54. Print.

21. *A signed article in a reference work* Omit page numbers for reference works that arrange entries alphabetically.

> Davidson, W. S., II. "Crime." *Encyclopedia of Psychology.* Ed. Raymond J. Corsini. 4 vols. New York: Wiley, 1984. Print.

22. *An unsigned article in a reference work*

> "Quindlen, Anna." *Current Biography Yearbook.* Ed. Judith Graham. New York: Wilson, 1993. Print.

23. *A review*

> Ottenhoff, John. "It's Complicated." Rev. of *The Moment of Complexity: Emerging Network Culture,* by Mark C. Taylor. *Christian Century* 119.21(2002): 56-59. Print.

24. *A letter to the editor*

> Cooper, Martin. Letter. *Business Week* 17 May 2004: 18. Print.

25. *An editorial*

> "Consider Cloning Source of Organs." Editorial. *USA Today* 22 Oct. 2003: 19A. Print.

26. *A published interview*

> Rice, Condoleeza. Interview by Nathan Gardels. *New Perspectives Quarterly* 18.1 (2001): 35-38. Print.

27. *A personal interview*

> Wick, Audrey. Personal interview. 27 Dec. 2008.

28. *A lecture, speech, or address*

> King, Martin Luther, Jr. "I Have a Dream." March on Washington. Lincoln Memorial, Washington, DC. 28 Aug. 1963. Address.

How to List Electronic Sources

A helpful rule for electronic sources is to use Web sites that are as unchanging as possible so the reader will be able to access the information at a later date. Sites that are refereed, authoritative, or based on historical texts or that have print counterparts should prove to be stable, at least in the immediate future. Entries for Internet sources consist of six basic divisions: the author's name, title of the document, print publication information (where applicable), electronic publication information, medium, date of access, and URL (required only when it is necessary to lead a reader to the source directly).

29. *A document from an Internet site* List print publication information, if any, first. If none is available, list only the electronic publication information: author's name, document title or short selection (in quotes), Internet site name or title (italicized), sponsor or host (if applicable), date of electronic publication or last update (if available), medium (Web.), and date of access, ended by a period. Add a URL (in angle brackets) if a Google search does not lead to the article, as in this example. This is an online source with no print version. The journal is archived, and this specific article can be located by using the Search box on the journal's home page, as shown here, or the URL for the document page, as in example 43. (In MLA style, break a URL *only* after a slash.)

> McPhaul, Kathleen M., and Jane A. Lipscomb. "Workplace Violence in Health Care: Recognized but Not Regulated." *Online Journal of Issues in Nursing* 9.3 (2004). American Nurses Association, 2008. Web. 20 June 2008. <http://www.nursingworld.org/MainMenuCategories/ANAMarketplace/ANAPeriodicals/ OJIN.aspx>. Search path: McPhaul and Lipscomb.

30. *A digital file* A digital file is a document created electronically, either on a computer using a software program or on some other digital producer—a camera, sound equipment, and so on. Digital files can be uploaded to the Internet, where they can be researched on a search engine, or they can exist and be exchanged and utilized independently from it. To cite such a document, identify its form or type (a book, recorded music, a manuscript, etc.) and follow the citation model for that kind of document. The file format, for example, *PDF, XML, MP3,* or *JPEG,* is the medium of publication. When the format is not known, use *Digital file.* (The file format or medium is not italicized unless a software name is part of its name, as in *Microsoft Word.*) If the file has versions, name the version or identify the one cited as shown in the example.

> Norman. Don. "Attractive Things Work Better." *Emotional Design,* Ch. 1. File last modified 24 Feb. 2003. PDF file. 22 Aug. 2008.

31. *An entire Internet site* Include the site name (its title) italicized, name of the editor (if available), name of any sponsoring organization, date of electronic publication, and date of access.

> *CNN.com.* Cable News Network, 2008. Web. 24 May 2008.

32. *A home page for a course* Include the instructor's name, the course title, the label *Course home page,* dates or semester of the course, names of the department and the institution, date of access, and the URL.

> Stern, David. Heidegger. Course home page. Fall 2000. Dept. of Philosophy, U of Iowa. Web. 15 June 2008. <http://www.uiowa.edu/ c026036/>.

33. *A personal home page* Include the owner's name, title of the site (if available), the label *Home page,* date of the last update (if available), and an access date. Add the URL only if a name search does not lead directly to the page.

> Blakesley, David. Home page. 18 Sept. 2003. Web. 22 Nov. 2008.

34. *An online book* Include the author, title of the book (italicized), print publication information (if available), title of the Web site (italicized), date of electronic publication, medium of publication, and date of access. The following is an example of an online book that is out of print.

Mussey, R. D. *An Essay on the Influence of Tobacco Upon Life and Health.* Boston: Perkins and Marvin, 1836. *Project Gutenberg.* Project Gutenberg Online Book Catalog, 2006. Web. 31 Mar. 2008.

35. *A part of an online book*

Mussey, R. D. "Cases Illustrative of the Effects of Tobacco." *An Essay on the Influence of Tobacco Upon Life and Health.* Boston: Perkins and Marvin, 1836. *Project Gutenberg.* Project Gutenberg Online Book Catalog, 2006. Web. 31 Mar. 2008.

36. *An article in an online newspaper* Include the author, title of the article, name of the newspaper, date of publication, page or paragraph numbers (if available), medium of publication, and date of access.

Webb, Cynthia L. "The Penguin That Ate Microsoft." *Washington Post.* Washington Post, 27 May 2004. Web. 28 May 2008.

37. *An article in an online magazine*

Reiss, Spencer. "The Wired 40." *Wired* July 2006. Conde'Net, 2008. Web. 6 Aug. 2008.

38. *An article in an online scholarly journal* If the article is included within a database, state the name of the database (italicized) after the print publication information.

Wishart, Jocelyn. "Academic Orientation and Parental Involvement in Education during High School." *Sociology of Education* 74.3 (2001): 210–30. *JSTOR.* Web. 27 Oct. 2008.

39. *A review*

Gray, Donna. Rev. of *Psychic Navigator,* by John Holland. *BookReview.com.* 18 Oct. 2004. Web. 20 Oct. 2008.

40. *A publication on a CD-ROM or DVD-ROM* Cite as you would a book or a work in a book, and add the label *CD-ROM* or *DVD-ROM* after the publication information. The CD-ROM is the medium of publication.

Leston, Robert. "Drops of Cruelty: Controlling the Mechanisms of Rhetorical History." *Proceedings of the Southwest/Texas Popular and American Culture Associations: Years 2000–2003.* Ed. Leslie Fife. Emporia: SW/TX PCA/ACA P, 2003. 681–91. CD-ROM.

41. *A work from a library subscription service* In addition to the print information, you should include the name of the database (italicized), the name of the service, medium, and the date of access. Omit the URL assigned by the service to the article itself.

Goldwasser, Joan. "Watch Your Balance." *Kiplinger's Personal Finance* 58.3 (2004): 96. *LexisNexis Academic.* LexisNexis. Web. 22 June 2008.

42. *A television or radio program* If you are citing the transcript of a program instead of the program itself, at the end of the entry write *Print. Transcript.* (not italicized).

Rehm, Diane. *The Diane Rehm Show. With E. L. Doctorow.* American University Radio, 24 May 2004. Web. 12 June 2008.

43. *An advertisement* Cite the product's name or company name, followed by the label *Advertisement.*

Lanvin. Advertisement. *Haut Fashion.* Web. 17 June 2008. <http://www.hautfashion .com/fashion-ads/lanvin-spring-summer-2008-ad-campaign>.

For advertisements found in a print source, include the print publication information and eliminate the electronic publication information.

44. *A cartoon or comic strip* Include the creator's name and the title, followed by the label *Comic strip* and the publication and/or electronic access information.

> Adams, Scott. "Dilbert." Comic strip. *Dilbert.com.* United Feature Syn., 27 Sept. 2004. Web. 20 Oct. 2008. <http://www.dilbert.com/> Search path: 27 Sept. 2004.

For cartoons or comic strips found in a print source, include the print publication information and eliminate the electronic publication information. (Typically, a print archive is a more secure resource.)

How to List Other Nonprint Sources

If the sources in this section are accessed online, add the medium of publication, date of access, and the URL to the entry, if needed. See model 30 for a digital file.

45. *An audio recording* Include the name of the performer (or conductor or composer), the title of the recording, the manufacturer, and the date. Song titles appear in quotation marks; album titles are italicized.

> James, Bob. *Dancing on the Water.* Warner Bros., 2001. Audiocassette.

46. *A film or video recording* Begin with the title, then list the director, distributor, and year of release. However, if you are citing a particular individual contributor, first begin with the person's name, followed by their title or functions: Capra, Frank, dir. or Chaplin, Charles, perf.

> *Rabbit-Proof Fence.* Dir. Phillip Noyce. Miramax, 2002. Film.

47. *A videotape or DVD* Insert the type of publication medium at the end of the entry.

> *Composition.* Prod. ABC/Prentice Hall Video Library. Prentice, 1993. Videocassette.

48. *A painting, sculpture, or photograph* Cite the artist's name, the title of the work, the date of creation (optional), and the name and city of either the institution that houses the work or the individual who owns it.

> Klee, Paul. *Red Balloon.* 1922. Guggenheim Museum, New York. Visual artwork.

49. *A map or chart* Include the title of the map or chart, the label *Map* or *Chart,* and the publication information.

> *Oregon.* Map. Chicago: Rand, 2000. Print.

For an online map or chart, include the title (in quotation marks), the label *Map* or *Chart,* name of the reference source (italicized), sponsoring organization, date of publication or update, medium, date of access, and the URL, if needed.

> "New York City Transit." Map. *Mta.info.* Metropolitan Transportation Authority. Web. 3 July 2007.

50. *An e-mail message* Here the medium of publication is *E-mail.* The title is the subject line enclosed in quotation marks.

> Harris, Omar. "Re: Artist Statement." Message to [Your Name]. 25 Apr. 2008. E-mail.

AUTHOR'S LAST NAME ⟶ Virasin 1

1/2 INCH

1 INCH

PAGE NUMBER

DOUBLE-SPACE

Prisna Virasin

Professor Wood

English 1302

19 April 2011

The Big Barbie Controversy

DOUBLE-SPACE

1   As a twenty-something female who grew up in America, I am very
interested in the Barbie debate. I played with Barbie dolls almost
obsessively from first to third grade. I designed clothes for them out
of handkerchiefs and tissues and dreamed about becoming a fashion
designer. I remember envying the girls who had Barbie Ferraris and dream
houses. I looked on in horror as my little sister cut her Barbie's hair short
and colored it hot pink with a marker.

Author establishes ethos *in first three paragraphs*

1 INCH

1 INCH

2   I would later learn, as a first-year student in a small, liberal arts
college, that by turning Barbie into a punk rocker, my sister was actually
"queering Barbie" or using the doll in a way unintended by Mattel (the
makers of Barbie). I was proud of my sister for this creative venture
because this was around the time I was introduced to feminism. Through
the lens of feminism, the horror I felt by watching my sister destroy
Barbie transformed into a reverence for my little sister. At the age of
five, she acted on her instinct to deconstruct Barbie, and I could not see
her political defiance for what it was until I was nearly twenty. In my
women's studies classes, I tried to deny any past connection to Barbie.
I was ashamed to have ever associated with this figure. I felt duped by
Barbie. I thought that she had tricked me into wanting to be seven feet
tall with long blond hair and a body that wouldn't quit. I felt sorry for the

Summaries of positions in exploratory paper in paragraphs 2 and 3

Personal narrative

1 INCH

(continued)

Virasin 2

girls who looked like walking Barbie dolls, always worried about looking perfect. It was obvious that they were still under "the Barbie spell."

3   Now, as a returning student, with a few years of working "in the real world" behind me, I'm not sure whether my feminist instinct to hate Barbie is lying dormant or whether it has been replaced by common sense. I have seen little girls playing with Barbies, and I do not have the urge to snatch the dolls out of their hands. However, I still feel a twinge of guilt because a part of my mind continues to wonder if Barbie or the image of Barbie is doing irreparable damage to the self-image of children everywhere.

4   There are many people who say that Barbie is "just a doll." These people believe that the Barbie debate is a "FemiNazi" creation to breed fear in the hearts of parents. These skeptics in the Barbie debate view Barbie as a toy, stating that she does not have power or influence over little girls or grown women. If Barbie is just a doll, then the Barbie debate is indeed without foundation. In reviewing Barbie's history, I found that she was created to make a difference in girls' lives and has succeeded in becoming a very marketable product.

5   The Barbie doll was created in 1959 by Ruth Handler, the cofounder of Mattel. Handler created the doll after seeing her daughter, whose nickname was Barbie, and her daughter's friends play with their paper dolls. According to Gaby Wood and Frances Stonor Saunders, Handler realized that little girls wanted a doll "they could aspire to be like, not aspire to look after" (38). This was a revolutionary idea because before the creation of Barbie, the toy store doll selection mainly consisted

Margin annotations:

Focus on issue

Transition to Barbie's history

Quotation: authors identified in text

387

(continued)

1 INCH

1/2 INCH

of baby dolls, which encouraged little girls to pretend to be mothers.

Ruth Handler states that Barbie "has always represented the fact that

a woman has choices" (39). In 1959, Mattel sold 350,000 Barbie dolls. In

2004, according to the "Barbie Dolls" discussion on the History Channel

Web site, "ninety percent of all American girls in the last forty years have

owned at least one Barbie." This Web site provides additional evidence

of Barbie's continued popularity: "If every Barbie doll ever manufactured

were laid end-to-end, they would circle the earth three-and-one-half

times." The Barbie doll and other Barbie products average sales of

1.9 billion dollars a year.

6   Barbie is also marketed internationally, in more than 140 countries.

Stephanie Deutsch, who has written a book about collecting Barbie

dolls and who is a collector herself, says, "It is fascinating to see how

Barbie dolls from other countries reflect the ideals of foreign societies,"

and she goes on to describe the "wild and sexy" dolls of Brazil, and

the Barbie dolls strapped to candles for little girls in Greece to carry in

religious processions (5). In 1968, Barbie dolls were first provided with the

mechanism to talk. Besides English, some Barbie dolls spoke Spanish, and

others spoke French, German, or Japanese. One of Barbie's friends spoke

with a British accent (34).

7   I believe that Barbie's influence lies in her pervasiveness. She is

everywhere, and therefore she is on the minds of many people. I

don't think that Barbie is "just a doll." With the overarching product

placement, marketing force, and popularity of the Barbie doll, she is

undeniably a powerful icon of American society.

1 INCH

Online source mentioned in text; no page number available

1 INCH

1 INCH

Transition to why Barbie's good

388

(continued)

Virasin 4

8   Avid Barbie fans span many different age groups. There are three-
to six-year-olds who play with Barbie dolls, wear Barbie brand clothes,
and sleep on Barbie brand beds with matching sheet sets. Barbie doll
collectors have met for over twenty years to celebrate all things Barbie.
Special collection Barbies are auctioned for thousands of dollars.

Criteria for goodness — Supporters of Barbie state that, apart from being a national icon, Barbie
is just a fun part of growing up. They refer to the simple fun of playing
with Barbie dolls. They believe that Barbie is a tool in building girls'

imaginations. They also maintain that Barbie
is a positive role model because she is able to

Appeals to motives and values — do almost anything. Barbie was an astronaut
before the first woman went into space. Barbie
is a veterinarian, a doctor, a businesswoman,
and to top it all off, a presidential candidate.
Figure 1 shows the Barbie that was dressed to

Fig. 1 *A President 2000 Barbie.*
Source: Carlos Osorio/ AP Wide World Photos. Web.

run for President of the United States in 2000.
Included in the package are a blue campaign
suit, a red ball gown, campaign material, and
an Internet Web site. In her article about growing up with Barbie, Patricia
reminisces:

Quote longer than four lines —
> What always fascinated me about Barbie was that she could be—
> and was—anything I wanted her to be. By extension, I felt the same
> was true for me. That's the real magic of Barbie. Deciding which
> career she ought to pursue on any given day fired my imagination
> far more than pushing a baby-size doll around in a carriage ever did.

389

(continued)

Virasin 5

9   Handler's creation of Barbie as a challenge to the idea that the proper

Transition to why Barbie's bad

role for a woman was that of a mother has become ironic in light of feminist

protests against the Barbie doll. Barbie protesters have stated that Barbie is

responsible for the development of poor body image in girls. They believe

that Barbie's proportions create impossible images of beauty toward which

Criteria for badness

girls will strive. If Barbie were human, she would be seven feet tall with a

thirty-nine-inch chest measurement, twenty-two inch waist measurement,

and thirty-three inch hip measurement ("History of Toys"). The Barbie

protesters also believe that the poor body image resulting from playing with

Barbie could lead to eating disorders such as anorexia and bulimia.

10   In addition to protests of Barbie's physical appearance, there is also the

issue of Barbie's intellectual image. Barbie detractors have criticized the

Barbie lifestyle, which seems to center around clothes, cars, dream homes,

and other material possessions. According to Jacqueline Reid-Walsh and

Two authors quoting another author

Claudia Mitchell, the feminist leader Betty Friedan believed that "Barbie

was a product of consumerism who spent all her time shopping, a model

for women who are defined by their relationships with men rather than

their accomplishments as people" (184). Protests followed the release of

the talking Barbie, which was enabled with such expressions as "Math

is hard" and "Let's go shopping." Parents feared that the first sentence

would reinforce the stereotype that girls were less skilled at math than

boys. The second sentence seemed to reinforce the importance of clothes,

physical appearance, and material goods. Writing for the Barbieology

Appeals to values

Web site, Ophira Edut criticizes educational materials based on Barbie for

the image they reinforce. Edut states that the Barbie computer is bundled

(continued)

Virasin 6

with typing tutor software, while the boy's Hot Wheels (a kind of tricycle) computer is bundled with adventure games. Also, the Barbie Rapunzel CD-ROM is touted by Mattel to expose girls to fine art and creativity, when the only creative function of the program is the option of changing Barbie's clothes and hairstyle interactively on the computer screen.

11   Some people have questioned whether or not Barbie is a suitable American icon. They challenge Barbie's ability to represent the all-American woman positively. In 2004, Mattel announced the release of a new California Barbie doll that would more accurately reflect the times ("It's Splittsville"). This Barbie has broken up with Ken, who is now "just a friend," and has taken up with Blaine, an Australian surfer. California Barbie uses modern "instant messaging to stay connected to her game. Her ears can be pierced. Her car has a working CD player" (Verdon 18A).

Summary of an article

Fig. 2 *Jenna Debryn shows off her Razanne doll, a modest Muslim alternative to Barbie.*
Source: Reed Saxon/ AP Wide World Photos. Web.

12   Still, a television advertisement following the release of the Cali Girl Barbie shows she has not changed that much from the old Barbie. In this ad, Barbie says she is "born to shop," and she can "never have too much stuff" or "too many friends."

According to Seth M. Siegel, the government of Iran has banned Barbie, and police officers are confiscating Barbie dolls from toy stores all over that country. The Iranian government believes that Barbie is "un-Islamic" because of the way she represents Western immorality. She dresses provocatively and has a close relationship with a man who is not her

391

(continued)

husband. For many Iranians, Barbie has become a symbol of American women in a very negative sense (22–24). As an alternative, little Muslim girls are encouraged to play with the Razanne doll that better reflects Muslim culture and values. Figure 2 provides a picture of a Muslim girl, who lives in the United States, and her Razanne doll.

13   Does the Barbie debate boil down to whether Barbie is good or bad? I believe that if she has the power to convey all of the positivity that Barbie fans believe she embodies, then the same power can be used to contaminate the world with all of the negativity that the Barbie protesters warn us against. She is a pervasive image in American society, but that does not necessarily mean that we have to label her as either good or bad. As a feminist, I am willing to concede that women are neither all good nor all bad. As a female image, Barbie plays the dual role quite well. We can make Barbie into whatever we want. She can be an astronaut or a punk rocker or a punk-rock astronaut. I believe that Barbie supporters have made her into a goddess, while Barbie protesters have turned her into a demon. In both cases, I believe she has become a scapegoat.

14   In addressing the issue that Barbie causes poor body image that could lead to eating disorders, the obvious statement that I can make is that eating disorders were around long before Barbie was created. Also, because of Barbie's immense popularity, if the doll truly caused eating disorders, eating disorders would have reached epidemic proportions. In actuality, only about five percent of women suffer from eating disorders. Barbie supporters also ask why male action dolls are not protested against when they have similar unattainable proportions.

Transition to refutation

Refutation of those who say Barbie's all bad

(continued)

15   By banning Barbie, we will not be solving the problem of poor body

image. Also, Barbie's image is so pervasive that it would be almost

No need to cite a
page number for a
one-page source

impossible to shelter children from her. In a satirical editorial by Rachel

Sa, she muses on the absurdity of sheltering children from all things

Barbie: "Maybe the safest thing is to just keep your little girls in their

bedrooms. Yes! Just keep them shut away until all of that icky stuff

disappears or until they grow up—surely by then they will have figured

out how to deal with it all on their own."

16   If one were to believe the argument made by Barbie supporters that

Barbie creates positive self-image in girls, and combine this belief with

Refutation of
those who say
Barbie's all good

the fact that Barbie is very pervasive in the United States, it should follow

that American females who have played with Barbie would have nearly

eradicated any thoughts of negative self-image. Theoretically then, at

least ninety percent of American women would have conquered self-

critical thoughts about their physical or intellectual state as a result of

their contact with Barbie. However, women know that these self-critical

thoughts are a part of many women's daily lives, and even the most

ardent Barbie fanatic has "bad hair days" or "fat days."

17   It is not the responsibility of the Barbie doll to create positive or

The real issue

negative self-images in children. The ability to influence children falls

mainly on the shoulders of all adults in the communities in which these

children live. This includes the global community in which we now

find ourselves living. The issue of self-image should be addressed by all

cultures early on and continuously in children's lives. Only by positively

reinforcing unconditional acceptance of children's physical appearance

(continued)

393

Virasin 9

are we going to be able to curb the problem of negative body image. We, as an entire culture, need to look at our ideologies on beauty and what we are teaching children about themselves.

18   The Barbie controversy is so called because the Barbie sometimes becomes the focus of how we view ourselves as women. I realize now that I cannot blame thoughts of being fat, short, or out of style on a doll or girls that look like dolls. The Barbie debate between "Barbie good" and "Barbie bad" has actually masked the true issue. Instead, we need to address how we value beauty, how we value ourselves, and how we act upon these beliefs in the larger context of our community. As a first step, we need to take the doll off of the pedestal and stop blaming Barbie.

Value claim

Virasin 10

Works Cited

"History of Toys: Barbie Dolls." *History.com.* A&E Television Networks, 2008. Web. 15 Apr. 2008.

California Barbie. Advertisement. The WB Network, 18 Mar. 2004. Television.

Deutsch, Stephanie. *Barbie: The First Thirty Years.* 2nd ed. Paducah: Collector, 2003. Print.

Edut, Ophira. "Giga-What? Barbie Gets Her Own Computer." *AdiosBarbie .com,* n.d. Web. 3 Apr. 2008. <http://www.adiosbarbie.com/bology/ bology_computer_html>.

The Works Cited follows the text, but always on a new page, numbered consecutively. Center the title, double-space, and use a hanging indent, as shown.

5 SPACES

In MLA style, divide a URL only after a slash; never add a hyphen or other mark.

394

(continued)

"It's Splitsville for Barbie and Ken." *CNN.com.* Cable News Network, 12 Feb. 2004. Web. 15 Apr. 2008.

O'Connell, Patricia. "To Ruth Handler: A 21 Barbie Salute." *BusinessWeek Online* 1 May 2002. *Academic Search Complete.* Web. 11 Apr. 2008.

Reid-Walsh, Jacqueline, and Claudia Mitchell. "Just a Doll? Liberating Accounts of Barbie-Play." *Review of Education/Pedagogy/Cultural Studies* 22.2 Aug. 2000: 175-90. *Academic Search Complete.* Web. 3 Apr. 2008.

Sa, Rachel. "Blame It on Barbie: How Was I Supposed to Know She Was Warping Our Minds?" *Toronto Sun* 4 May 2002: 15. *LexisNexis.* Web. 3 Apr. 2008.

Seigel, Seth M. "Sell the West as a Brand." *Brandweek* 10 June 2002: 22-24. *Academic Search Complete.* Web. 3 Apr. 2008.

Verdon, Joan. "Barbie Says, Bye-Bye Doll." *Fort Worth Star-Telegram* 13 Feb. 2004: 1A+. Print.

Wood, Gaby, and Frances Stonor Saunders. "Dream Doll." *New Statesman* 15 Apr. 2002: 38-40. *Academic Search Complete.* Web. 3 Apr. 2008.

Cognitive Biases and Fallacies

Cognitive Biases and Fallacies

Throughout this book we have discussed both how good critical thinking can improve your argument and, no less important, how your argument can improve your critical thinking. We have shown you how to use the elements of an argument to guard against common mistakes in reasoning that can lead your thinking astray in ways that most of us do not even notice. Here we explain two common strategies for avoiding the most common errors.

Cognitive Biases

Perhaps the most serious challenge to sound critical thinking is a set of deep-seated cognitive biases that all of us share. Many of them have been uncovered by cognitive scientists in an attempt to understand why our reasoning is so often so unreliable. Here is a list of those biases and mistakes with references to where we have discussed ways to guard against them:

GENERAL BIASES AND MISTAKES IN REASONING

1. You believe that something is true, so you distort evidence, ignore the lack of evidence, or place too much weight on the evidence you have.
2. You are too confident in your judgment, leading you to believe that you must be right.
3. You want something to be true, so you believe that it is.
4. You seize on the first answer that occurs to you, causing you to anchor your thinking on that answer.
5. You reason from ideological principles rather than from evidence.
6. You oversimplify an issue, thinking that there is One True Explanation for your problem.

LINGUISTIC BIASES AND MISTAKES

7. You think that the meaning of a word is naturally connected to the referent of the word, so that the meaning is all you need to know about the referent.
8. You fail to respect the difference between common meanings and definitions and authorized meanings and definitions.
9. You engage in a conceptual argument about the meaning or definition of a word but fail to recognize that your question is only a surrogate for a practical problem.
10. You use emotional or polarizing language that distorts your thinking or that of your readers.
11. You manipulate the subject of verbs to make it seem that an instrument or abstraction is the source of an action performed by an identifiable individual or entity.
12. You create misleading metaphorical scenarios.

CAUSAL BIASES AND MISTAKES

13. You focus on causes that are easier to notice and ignore less obvious ones.
    - You notice causes that are immediate, present, and vivid rather than ones that are remote, absent, and obscure.
    - You notice causes that are surprising rather than ones that are routine or expected.
14. You focus on a single cause rather than multiple ones.
15. You focus on causes that match effects in kind and magnitude.
16. You confuse correlation with causation.
17. You fail to investigate whether two events that are closely correlated might be not cause and effect, but both effects of some third cause.

18. In human actions, you overemphasize personal motives and intentions and undervalue circumstances, or vice-versa.

Fallacies

There is, however, another tradition in studying flawed thinking that is almost 2,500 years old. It focuses on errors in reasoning called *fallacies*. A fallacy is not a false belief, like thinking the earth is flat. Rather, it is a bias or logical misstep in reasoning your way to a sound conclusion. In fact, you can reason validly and conclude that the earth is flat or fallaciously and conclude that it is round. There is some overlap between this classical tradition and modern studies of flawed thinking, but the classical tradition has such a long history that anyone interested in critical thinking should know about it.

Over the centuries, logicians have identified scores of fallacies and given them formidable Latin names such as *post hoc ergo propter hoc, ad verecundiam, non sequitur*. We will discuss here only the most common ones. Some of them always undermine your reasoning, while others do so only in certain circumstances. So we group them into two categories: those fallacies that you should always avoid and those that you should avoid when the circumstances require it.

FUNDAMENTAL ERRORS IN REASONING

These fallacies are outright errors in getting from a reason to a claim. We'll introduce each of these fallacies as if you're being charged with it, and then add the technical explanation.

1. **"But what you said doesn't follow!" (Your reason is irrelevant to your claim.)**

    Cyberspace will eventually make government irrelevant ₘₐᵢₙ ₒₗₐᵢₘ by making all data instantly available. ᵣₑₐₛₒₙ ₁ Once we can be in instant contact with everyone else, ᵣₑₐₛₒₙ ₂ artificial national borders will wither away ₒₗₐᵢₘ / ᵣₑₐₛₒₙ ₃ and government will have nothing to do. ₒₗₐᵢₘ / ᵣₑₐₛₒₙ ₄
    You might be right, but I don't see why making information available faster makes government irrelevant. Second, I don't see how being in contact with everyone will make national borders disappear. And third, I don't see why the lack of borders leaves government nothing to do. I can see some connection between governments having nothing to do and their being irrelevant, but the steps between are too much of a stretch.

When we cannot see the logical connection between a reason and its claim, we call the claim a *non sequitur*, pronounced "nahn SE-kwi-toor," which means literally *It doesn't follow*. If your readers think you have committed a *non sequitur*, you have to think about the warrant that connects the reason to the claim: Do readers share your underlying assumptions, and have you failed to state warrants you should have?

2. **"You're arguing in a circle and begging the question!"** (Your reasons just restate your claim.)

> To ensure our safety, we should be free to carry concealed guns _{claim 1} because we should have the right to carry a weapon to protect ourselves. _{reason 1} When criminals know that we might have a gun and would use it, _{reason 2} they'll realize that we are ready to defend ourselves. _{claim 2} Only when criminals worry about their own safety _{reason 3} will we be able to stop worrying about our own. _{claim 3}
>
> *You are reasoning in a circle. You keep saying the same thing—we should be free to do something because we have the right to do it. That makes a kind of sense, but it's no argument. Then you say that when criminals know something they know something. That may be true, but it doesn't support the claim either.*

You argue in a circle when your claim and reason mean the same thing. You can test for a circular argument by switching the claim and reason. If the sentence means the same after the switch, you are arguing in a circle:

> To ensure our safety, we should be free to carry concealed guns _{claim} because we need the right to carry one to protect ourselves. _{reason}

> We need the right to carry a weapon to protect ourselves _{claim} because we should be free to carry concealed guns to ensure our safety. _{reason}

If you cannot switch the reason and claim, your argument is not circular. Compare the last sentence in the example, which does not reason in a circle:

> Only when criminals worry about their own safety _{reason} will we be able to stop worrying about our own. _{claim}

> Only when we are able to stop worrying about our own safety _{reason} will criminals worry about theirs. _{claim}

3. **"You're assuming a fact that we haven't settled!"** (Your reason is not supported with evidence or an argument.)

> We should reject the mere opinion _{implied claim} of a known liar like Smith. _{reason}
>
> *Who says that what Smith says is "mere opinion," and who says he is a "known liar"?*

This is cousin to begging the question. It's like *When did you stop beating your dog?* You commit this fallacy when you assume a judgment or fact that readers do not accept because it has not been proven, then use that judgment or fact as a reason for your claim.

4. **"But you can't use the lack of evidence to prove an affirmative claim!"** (You rely on a false warrant: When a claim has not been proven false, we should accept it as true.)

> People who say they have been kidnapped by aliens from outer space should be taken seriously, _{claim} because no one has proved their stories are false. _{reason}
>
> *Hold on! No one has proved that I don't have an oilfield under my back yard, but that doesn't mean that I'm going to start drilling. You can't expect me to believe something is true because I don't know for sure that it's not.*

The technical term for this fallacy is *ad ignorantiam,* pronounced "add ignore-AHN-tee-em." If you make a claim, you have to offer *affirmative* reasons for believing it. It is not up to the other person to disprove it. A claim is not true simply because no one can think of a good alternative.

A somewhat weaker strategy is to say, *Well, it* could *be true*. In a sense, anything could be true, even alien abductions. We can leave room for the chance that a claim could be true, but we should file such claims in a corner of our minds reserved for unsubstantiated possibilities.

5. **"You can't prove something by claiming that the consequences of not accepting it are intolerable!" (You rely on a false warrant: When it would hurt us to believe something, we should not believe it—or vice versa.)**

The Constitution protects our right to privacy, _{claim} because if it did not, then states could regulate our most intimate behavior, including our sexual lives. _{reason} That would be intolerable. _{reason}

You're right; it's intolerable that states should be able to interfere in our private lives. But that's irrelevant to what the Constitution does or doesn't say. As bad as it may seem, the Constitution gives states the power to snoop in our bedrooms.

This fallacy is called *ad baculum*, pronounced "add BACK-yu-lum." It means "with force." Those who argue like this imply that if we do not agree, something bad will happen to us.

INAPPROPRIATE RHETORICAL APPEALS

Unlike fundamental errors in reasoning, which are always logical blunders, these next steps may or may not be errors, depending on the circumstances of the case. The problem is relying on a warrant that applies in some cases, but not all. The trick is to know when your readers will accept these appeals and when they will not.

Inappropriate Appeals to Intellectual Consistency

6. **"But what you say now contradicts what you said before!"**

Students should evaluate teachers every semester, because only then will they know whether they are helping students achieve their goals.

But last month, you argued that teachers should not evaluate students because their tests do not fairly represent your strengths and abilities. How can you say that you should evaluate us when you reject our evaluations of you?

This fallacy is called *tu quoque* (pronounced "too kwo-kway"), literally "You too." It is a charge of inconsistency, at worst of dishonesty.

But this charge is tricky: It is legitimate to point out inconsistency—we distrust those who are. But what someone said in the past may have nothing to do with the merits of the case at hand: So what if someone contradicts herself? Regardless of what a person said before, we have to judge the issue before us on its own merits.

Yet so strongly do we dislike those who contradict themselves that we reject even a good argument when made by hypocrites. If readers might think that you contradict yourself, you should consider acknowledging that what you said before is not consistent with what you are saying now and show why the inconsistency is not fatal.

7. "If you take this one step you will go all the way!"

We can't legalize marijuana for medical purposes $_{claim}$ because if physicians prescribe it for dying patients, they'll prescribe it for people only in pain, then for people who just claim to be in pain. $_{reason}$

You insult the intelligence of physicians, implying that they don't know the difference between taking this one step and going all the way. It's like claiming that if you drive one mile over the speed limit, you will end up driving 100 miles an hour.

This fallacy is called the *slippery slope*. It's a claim that one step must inevitably lead to the next, and the next, and the next. But we know that this is not always true.

A particular kind of slippery slope is called *reductio ad absurdum*—reduction to absurdity, pronounced "ruh-DUK-tee-o ahd ab-ZERD-um." Instead of claiming that a claim would begin a slippery slope, someone asserts that it has hit bottom.

You want students to evaluate their teachers? I suppose you also want the criminally insane to evaluate their psychologists or criminals to evaluate their judges or children to evaluate their parents.

When a critic reduces an argument to an absurd version and then attacks it, we say the critic has built a straw man.

Appeals to Inappropriate Perspectives

8. "You offer a false choice between only two alternatives. There are more!"

This fallacy is related to the issue of polarizing language (p. 308).

It's time to end the debate between "whole word" reading and phonics. The failure of "whole word" pedagogy $_{reason}$ demands that we return to the time-tested phonics method. $_{claim}$

But most good teachers use some of both and a few other ways of teaching.

It's misleading to insist on either-or choices when the facts of the matter allow both more-or-less or some-of-both. As you plan your argument and find yourself arguing for a choice between two exclusive alternatives, stop and think: Could you choose both, or at least some combination? Are there third, fourth, or even fifth choices? (In some cases, however, the choice really is between two and only two mutually exclusive alternatives, such as capital punishment or no capital punishment.)

9. "That's just a metaphor! You can't act as though it's literally true."

Sick ideas such as gay marriage can infect those too weak to resist them $_{reason}$ so we must isolate people who would spread their sick ideas. $_{claim}$

You may be right that the idea may spread, but ideas are not diseases. You can't stop ideas from spreading the way you stop TB.

Metaphors may mislead us, but the fact is, we cannot communicate without them: The problem is not the metaphoric language itself; it's how it's used. So think hard about whether you are pushing the metaphors too far.

Inappropriate Appeals to Social Solidarity

10. "You're just appealing to the crowd! Why should we go along with everyone else?"

When parents pay for the education of their children, they have the right to decide what should be taught. ₍warrant₎ Most people think intelligent design should be taught alongside evolution, ₍reason₎ so that's what school systems should teach. ₍claim₎

That caters to popular ignorance. Suppose most parents thought that the earth was flat? Should that be taught?

This fallacy is called *ad populum,* pronounced "add PAH-poo-lum." It means the arguer puts more weight on what most people believe than on the truth. The basis of an *ad populum* argument is probably our inherited human bias to conform with the thinking of the tribe.

But an appeal to popular will is not always a fallacy:

The city council must reject the plan to build a new stadium, ₍claim₎ because the people don't want to pay for it. ₍reason₎ This is a democracy. ₍warrant₎

If readers might think your appeal to popular opinion is inappropriate, acknowledge and respond to the objection:

The city council must reject the plan to build a new stadium, ₍claim₎ because the people don't want to pay for it. ₍reason₎ In matters of public spending, the people and not the Chamber of Commerce decides. ₍response₎ This is a democracy. ₍warrant₎

Your argument will legitimately appeal to the popular will when you can legitimately use this warrant:

When most people believe / decide X, we should accept X.

11. "We don't have to accept your claim just because X says so!"

According to Senator Wise, the predicted rise in atmospheric carbon dioxide will help plant growth, ₍reason₎ because plants take in carbon dioxide and give off oxygen. ₍report of evidence₎ He was born on a farm, ₍reason₎ and he knows plants. ₍claimed authority₎ So we ought not fear greenhouse gases. ₍claim₎

Senator Wise may be an admirable person, but being born on a farm doesn't make him an expert on atmospheric chemistry.

This fallacy is called *ad verecundiam,* pronounced "add vare-uh-COON-dee-ahm." It literally means the "modesty" we should exhibit before authority. The psychological basis for this appeal is probably the deference we feel to power and prestige. An appeal to authority goes wrong when the authority has no reason to deserve our trust. The fact that Wise was born on a farm is irrelevant to his authority to make predictions about greenhouse gases.

But the problem is that some people are real authorities whose expertise we should respect. So when you want to use an authority, you have to weigh three questions: Is this a case where expertise matters? Is your authority truly an expert in this field? Will your readers be willing to defer ("be modest") in this case?

If readers might question an authority, anticipate their questions. You address the first two by telling them why they should accept your authority as an expert in this case and the third by reporting not just what the authority claims but the reason for claiming it.

> According to Dr. Studious, we would be prudent to stockpile medication in antici-pation of a new outbreak of bird flu. _{claim} As Director of Epidemiology at the Na-tional Institutes of Health, he was responsible for our being ready for the epidemic of 1987. _{basis of authority} In his research on that and twenty other epidemics, _{basis of authority} he found that the lag between the first cases and an epidemic is about two months. _{reason} Now that the first cases have begun to appear, we know that we have about two months to prepare. _{reason}

12. "You are just engaging in mud-slinging! Unfair personal attacks have nothing to do with the issues."

> Senator Boomer avoided the draft during the Vietnam War, _{reason} so he is disqual-ified from judging the use of military power in Iraq. _{claim} No one who shirks his duty can say anything about the service he scorned. _{warrant}
>
> *Stick to the issue instead of making a personal attack! His actions as a 20-year old are irrel-evant to his current analysis of the facts of the matter.*

This fallacy is called *ad hominem*, pronounced "add HA-mi-nim." It literally means "against the person." It is the corollary of a fallacious appeal to authority: Just as we err when we accept an argument because we admire the person mak-ing it, so can we err when we reject an argument by someone we dislike. At times, however, we should question an argument on the basis of who makes it, if that person is regularly dishonest, unreliable, or careless.

A version of this appeal is "guilt by association," which is sometimes fair and sometimes not.

> Professor Hack claims that crime drops when citizens carry concealed weapons. But his research is funded by gun manufacturers, _{reason} and he serves on a commit-tee for the National Rifle Association. _{reason 2} He might be right, but we should look at his research skeptically. _{claim}

If readers might think you are unfairly attacking the person who makes an argument, then you have to acknowledge and respond to their objection:

> . . . We should look at his research skeptically. _{claim} That doesn't mean his research is necessarily biased, _{acknowledgment} but the source of his support gives us reason to look at his methodology carefully. _{response} Even a cautious researcher can be influ-enced by the interests of those who support his or her work. _{warrant}

13. "Don't give me that sob story. You're just appealing to my pity!"

> Teachers here at State U. are so anxious over rumors about eliminating depart-ments _{reason} that adding a new teaching evaluation form will make them insecure and fearful. _{claim}

> *Our job is to improve teaching. If that makes teachers unhappy, too bad. It's irrelevant to creating a sound undergraduate education.*

This technical term for this fallacy is *ad misericordiam,* pronounced "add miz-AIR-uh-CORE-dee-um." It asks us to put our sympathies ahead of reasons and evidence. The foundation of such an appeal is our sound intuition that we should respond sympathetically to the suffering of others and mitigate it when we can.

Although we can be wrong to put sympathies ahead of our reasons, we can also be right to do so:

> States have released people from institutions for the mentally ill, pushing them onto the streets, where they are homeless and helpless. It's inhuman _{claim} to abandon those who cannot care for themselves. _{reason}

If readers might reject an argument based on sympathy, you have to give them reasons that go beyond it:

> . . . care for themselves. _{reason} We must never put politics and economics above basic human dignity. _{warrant} That's not being a bleeding-heart. _{acknowledgment} If we knowingly refuse to help the helpless, _{reason} we become a morally callous people who will lose all sensitivity to injustice. _{claim}

There are many other so-called "fallacies," but these are the most common ones. Be alert to these fallacies in what you read, but their real value is that they help you reflect on your own thinking.

APPENDIX 3

Charts

TRACE

THE RHETORICAL SITUATION

FOR YOU AS THE READER

Text. What kind of text is it? What are its special qualities and features? What is it about?

Reader. Are you one of the readers the writer anticipated? Do you share common ground with the author and other audience members? Are you open to change?

Author. Who is the author? How is the author influenced by background, experience, education, affiliations, or values? What is the author's motivation to write?

Constraints.* What beliefs, attitudes, habits, affiliations, or traditions will influence the way you and the author view the argument?

Exigence. What caused the argument, and do you perceive it as a defect or problem?

FOR THE TARGETED READER AT THE TIME THE TEXT WAS WRITTEN

Text. What kind of text is it? Is it unique to its time?

Reader. Who were the targeted readers? What qualities did they have as the original audience? Were they convinced? How are they different from other or modern readers?

Author. Who is the author? What influenced the author? Why was the author motivated to write?

Constraints.* What beliefs, attitudes, habits, affiliations, or traditions influenced the author's and the readers' views in this argument?

Exigence. What happened to cause the argument? Why was it a problem? Has it recurred?

FOR YOU AS THE WRITER

Text. What is the assignment? What should your completed paper look like?

Reader. Who are your readers? Where do they stand on the issue? How can you establish common ground? Can they change?

Author. What is your argumentation strategy? What is your purpose and your perspective? How will you make your paper convincing?

Constraints.* How are your training, background, affiliations, and values either in harmony or in conflict with your audience? Will they drive you apart or help build common ground?

Exigence. What happened? What is motivating you to write on this issue? Why is it compelling to you?

*Do not confuse constraints with warrants. Constraints are a broader concept.

The Process

Be selective and flexible in using the strategies, and remember that there is no best order. You will backtrack and repeat.

WHEN YOU ARE THE READER

Prereading Strategies

▶ **Read the title and first paragraph; consult your background.** Identify the issue. Free-associate and write words and phrases that the issue brings to mind.

▶ **Evaluate and improve your background.** Do you know enough? If not, read or discuss to get background. Look up a key word or two.

▶ **Survey the material.** Locate the claim (the main assertion) and some of the subclaims (the ideas that support it); notice how they are organized. Do not slow down and read.

▶ **Write out your present position on the issue.**

▶ **Make some predictions, and write one big question.** Jot down two or three ideas that you think the author may discuss, and write one question you would like to have answered.

Reading Strategies

▶ **Pick up a pencil, underline, and annotate** the ideas that seem important. Write a brief summary.

▶ **Identify** and **read** the information in the **introduction, body,** and **conclusion.**

▶ **Look for the claim, subclaims, and support.** Box the **transitions** to highlight relationships between ideas and changes of subject.

▶ **Find the key words** that represent major concepts, and jot down meanings as needed.

▶ **Analyze the rhetorical situation.** Remember TRACE: Text, Reader, Author, Constraints, Exigence.

▶ **Analyze argument strategies.**

▶ **Read with an open mind, and analyze the common ground** between you and the author.

Strategies for Reading Difficult Material

▶ **Read all the way through once** without stopping.

▶ **Write a list** of what you understand and what you do not understand.

▶ **Identify words and concepts** you do not understand, look them up, and analyze how they are used in context.

WHEN YOU ARE THE WRITER

Prewriting Strategies

▶ **Get organized to write.** Set up a place with materials. Be motivated.

▶ **Understand the writing assignment,** and **schedule time.** Break a complicated writing task into manageable parts, and set aside time to write.

▶ **Identify an issue, and do some initial reading.** Use the twelve tests to make certain you have an arguable issue (Box 1.3).

▶ **Analyze the rhetorical situation,** particularly the exigence, the audience, and the constraints.

▶ **Focus** on your issue and **freewrite.**

▶ **Brainstorm, make lists, and map ideas.**

▶ **Talk it through** with a friend, your instructor, or members of a peer editing group.

▶ **Keep a journal, notebook, or folder of ideas.**

▶ **Mentally visualize** the major concepts.

▶ Do some directed **reading and thinking.**

▶ **Use argument strategies.**

▶ **Use reading strategies.**

▶ **Use critical thinking prompts.**

▶ Plan and conduct **library research.**

▶ Make an **expanded list or outline** to guide your writing.

▶ **Talk it through again.**

Drafting Strategies

▶ **Write the first draft.** Put your ideas on paper so that you can work with them. Use your outline and notes to help you. Either write and rewrite as you go or write the draft quickly with the knowledge that you can reread and rewrite later.

Strategies to Use When You Get Stuck

▶ **Read more** and **take more notes.**

▶ **Read your outline, rearrange parts, and add information to it.**

▶ **Freewrite** on the issue, **read some more,** and then **freewrite** some more.

(continued)

411

The Process *(continued)*

WHEN YOU ARE THE READER

▶ **Reread the material,** and add to your list of what you can and cannot understand.

▶ **Reread again** if you need to do so.

▶ **Discuss the material** with someone who has also read the material for further clarification and understanding.

Postreading Strategies

▶ **Monitor your comprehension.** Insist on understanding. Check the accuracy of your **predictions,** and answer your **question.**

▶ **Analyze the organization,** and write a **simplified outline,** a **map,** or a **summary** to help you understand and remember.

▶ **Write a response** to help you think.

▶ **Compare your present position** with your position before you began to read.

▶ **Evaluate the argument.** Decide whether it is ethical or unethical and convincing or not convincing.

WHEN YOU ARE THE WRITER

▶ **Talk about your ideas** with someone else.

▶ **Lower your expectations for your first draft.** At this point, the writing does not have to be perfect.

Postwriting Strategies

▶ **Read your draft critically** and also **have someone else read it.** Put it aside for 24 hours, if you can, to develop a better perspective for reading and improving.

▶ **Rewrite and revise.** Make changes and additions until you think the paper is ready for others to read. Move sections, cross out material, add other material, and rephrase for clarity, as necessary.

▶ **Check your paper** for final mechanical and spelling errors, **write the final title,** and **type or print the paper.**

Types of Claims

CLAIMS OF FACT

What happened? Is it true? Does it exist? Is it a fact?

Examples:

Increasing population threatens the environment.
Television content promotes violence.
Women are not as effective as men in combat.

READERS

▶ Look for claims that state facts.

▶ Look for facts, statistics, real examples, and quotations from reliable authorities.

▶ Anticipate induction, analogies, and signs.

▶ Look for chronological or topical organization or a claim plus reasons.

WRITERS

▶ State the claim as a fact, even though it is controversial.

▶ Use factual evidence and expert opinion.

▶ Use induction, historical and literal analogies, and signs.

▶ Consider arranging your material as a claim with reasons.

CLAIMS OF DEFINITION

What is it? What is it like? How should it be classified? How should it be interpreted? How does its usual meaning change in a particular context?

Examples:

We need to define what constitutes a family before we discuss family values.
A definition will demonstrate that the riots were an instance of civil disobedience.
Waterboarding can be defined as a form of torture.

READERS

▶ Look for a claim that contains or is followed by a definition.

▶ Look for reliable authorities and sources for definitions.

▶ Look for comparisons and examples.

▶ Look for compare-and-contrast, topical, or deductive organization.

WRITERS

▶ State your claim, and define the key terms.

▶ Quote authorities, or go to dictionaries, encyclopedias, or other reliable sources for definitions.

▶ If you are comparing to help define, use compare-and-contrast organization.

▶ Use vivid description and narrative.

▶ Use deductive organization.

CLAIMS OF CAUSE

What caused it? Where did it come from? Why did it happen? What are the effects? What probably will be the results on both a short-term and a long-term basis?

Examples:

Clear-cutting is the main cause of the destruction of ancient forests.
Censorship can result in limits on freedom of speech.
The American people's current mood has been caused by the state of the economy.

READERS

▶ Look for a claim that states or implies cause or effect.

WRITERS

▶ Make a claim that states or implies cause or effect.

▶ Use facts and statistics.

(continued)

413

Types of Claims *(continued)*

▶ Look for facts and statistics, comparisons such as historical analogies, signs, induction, deduction, and causal arguments.

▶ Look for cause-and-effect or effect-and-cause organization.

▶ Apply Burke's pentad to focus the main cause.

▶ Use historical analogies, signs, induction, and deduction.

▶ Consider using cause-and-effect or effect-and-cause organization.

CLAIMS OF VALUE

Is it good or bad? How good? How bad? Of what worth is it? Is it moral or immoral? Who thinks so? What do those people value? What values or criteria should I use to determine its goodness or badness? Are my values different from other people's or the author's?

Examples:

Computers are a valuable addition to modern education.
School prayer has a moral function in the public schools.
Animal rights are as important as human rights.

READERS

▶ Look for claims that make a value statement.

▶ Look for value proofs, motivational proofs, literal and figurative analogies, quotations from authorities, signs, and definitions.

▶ Expect emotional language.

▶ Look for applied criteria, topical, and narrative patterns of organization.

WRITERS

▶ State your claim as a judgment or value statement.

▶ Analyze your audience's needs and values, and appeal to them.

▶ Use literal and figurative analogies, quotations from authorities, signs, and definitions.

▶ Use emotional language appropriately.

▶ Consider the applied criteria, claim with reasons, or narrative organizational patterns.

CLAIMS OF POLICY

What should we do? How should we act? What should future policy be? How can we solve this problem? What course of action should we pursue?

Examples:

The criminal should be sent to prison rather than to a mental hospital.
Sex education should be part of the public school curriculum.
Battered women who take revenge should not be placed in jail.

READERS

▶ **Look for claims** that state that something **should be done.**

▶ Look for statistical data, motivational appeals, literal analogies, and argument from authority.

▶ Anticipate the problem–solution pattern of organization.

WRITERS

▶ **State the claim as something that should be done.**

▶ Use statistical data, motivational appeals, analogies, and authorities as proof.

▶ Use emotional language appropriately.

▶ Consider the problem–solution pattern of organization.

Types of Proof and Tests of Validity

LOGICAL PROOFS

Do not confuse proofs with support. A proof represents a complete line of argument that includes a claim, support, and warrant. A proof demonstrates a particular way of thinking about and developing the main claim of the argument. The logical proofs have been arranged according to the mnemonic SICDADS: Sign, Induction, Cause, Deduction, Analogies, Definition, Statistics.

WHEN YOU ARE THE READER		WHEN YOU ARE THE WRITER 📖
	Sign	
Look for clues, symptoms, and occurrences that are explained as signs or symptoms that something is so.	Pointing out the symptoms or signs that something is so. *Example:* *Claim:* The child has chickenpox. *Support:* The child has spots. *Warrant:* Those spots are a sign of chickenpox. **Test of Validity:** Ask whether this is really a sign of what the author claims, or is there another explanation.	Think of symptoms or signs that you can use to demonstrate that something is so.
	Induction	
Look for a conclusion or claim based on examples or cases.	Drawing a conclusion (claim) from a number of representative cases or examples. *Example:* *Claim:* Everyone liked that movie. *Support:* I know three people who liked it. *Warrant:* Three examples are enough. **Tests of Validity:** Ask whether there are enough examples, or is this a "hasty" conclusion or claim. Try to think of an exception that would change the conclusion or claim. See if you can make the "inductive leap" from the examples to the conclusion or claim and accept it as probably true.	Give some examples and draw a conclusion/claim based on them; *or* make the claim and back it up with a series of examples.

(continued)

415

Types of Proof and Tests of Validity *(continued)*

LOGICAL PROOFS

WHEN YOU ARE THE READER	WHEN YOU ARE THE WRITER
Cause	
Look for examples, trends, people, or events that are cited as causes for the claim. Look for effects of the claim.	Placing the claim in a cause-and-effect relationship to show that it is either the cause of an effect or an effect of a cause.	Make a claim, and ask what caused it. Apply Burke's pentad to focus the main cause.
	Example: *Warrant:* Depression in a group of people has increased. *Support:* This group of people has also increased its use of the Internet. *Claim/conclusion:* The Internet may be causing depression.	What was done? Where was it done? Who did it? How was it done? Why did it happen?
	Tests of Validity: Ask whether these causes alone are sufficient to create these effects, or is it that these effects result from other causes. Try to think of exceptions to the cause-and-effect outcome.	
Deduction	
Locate or infer the general principle (warrant). Apply it to the example or case. Draw a conclusion or claim.	Applying a general principle (warrant) to an example or a case and drawing a conclusion.	Make a general statement. Apply it to an example or a case. Draw a conclusion. Decide whether to make the general statement (warrant) explicit or implicit.
	Example: *Warrant:* Most uneven footprints are left by people who limp. *Support:* These footprints are uneven. *Claim:* The person who left these footprints walks with a limp.	
	Test of Validity: Ask whether the general principle (warrant) and the support are probably true, because then the claim is also probably true.	

(continued)

416

Types of Proof and Tests of Validity *(continued)*

LOGICAL PROOFS

WHEN YOU ARE THE READER	WHEN YOU ARE THE WRITER

Analogies: Literal, Historical, and Figurative

Interpreting what we do not understand by comparing it with something we do. Literal and historical analogies compare similar items, and figurative analogies compare items from radically different categories.

WHEN YOU ARE THE READER

Literal and historical analogy:
Look for items, events, people, or periods of time that are being compared.

Figurative analogy:
Look for extended metaphors or items being compared that are from totally different categories.

Example of historical analogy:
Claim: Many people will die of AIDS.
Support: Many people died of the Black Death.
Warrant: AIDS and the Black Death are similar.

Example of literal analogy:
Claim: The state should spend more money on education.
Support: Another state spent more money with good results.
Warrant: The two states are similar, and the results of one will be the results of the other.

Example of figurative analogy:
Claim: Reading a difficult book should take time.
Support: Digesting a large meal takes time.
Warrant: Reading and eating are sufficiently alike that they can be compared.

Tests for Validity: For literal analogies, ask whether the cases are so similar that the results of one will be the results of the other. For historical analogies, ask whether history will repeat itself. For figurative analogies, ask whether the qualities of the items being compared are real enough to provide logical support or are they so dissimilar that they do not prove anything.

WHEN YOU ARE THE WRITER

Literal and historical analogy:
Think of items in the same category that can be compared. Show that what happened in one case will also happen in the other. Or, demonstrate that history repeats itself.

Figurative analogy:
Think of comparisons with items from other categories. Try to compare items that have similar qualities, characteristics, or outcomes.

(continued)

417

Types of Proof and Tests of Validity *(continued)*

LOGICAL PROOFS

WHEN YOU ARE THE READER	WHEN YOU ARE THE WRITER
Definition	
Look for definitions of key words or concepts.	Define the key terms and concepts in your claim.
Describing the fundamental properties and qualities of a term or placing an item in a category and proving it "by definition."	Define all other terms that you and your reader must agree on for the argument to work.
Definitions can be short (a word or sentence) or long (several paragraphs or an entire essay).	Place some ideas or items in established categories and argue that they are so "by definition."
Example:	
Warrant: Family values characterize the good citizen.	
Notice whether the reader is supposed to accept the claim "by definition" because it has been placed in an established category.	*Support:* Radical feminists lack family values.
	Claim: Radical feminists are not good citizens.
Tests of Validity: Ask whether the definition is accurate and reliable, or are there exceptions or other definitions that would make it less reliable. Ask whether the item belongs in the category in which it has been placed.	
Statistics	
Look for numbers, data, and tables of figures along with interpretations of them.	Find data, statistics, and tables of figures to use as evidence to back up your claim.
Using figures or data to prove a claim.	Make clear where you find the statistics, and add your interpretations and those of experts.
Example:	
Claim: We should end draft registration.	
Support: It costs $27.5 million per year.	
Warrant: This is too much; it proves we should end it.	
Tests of Validity: Ask where the statistics came from, to what dates they apply, and whether they are fair and accurate. Ask whether they have been exaggerated or skewed. Ask whether they prove what they are supposed to prove.	

(continued)

Types of Proof and Tests of Validity *(continued)*

LOGICAL PROOFS

PROOF TO ESTABLISH *ETHOS*

Authority

Quoting established authorities or experts or establishing one's own authority and credibility.

Example:
Claim: California will have an earthquake.
Support: Professors and scientists say so.
Warrant: These experts are reliable.

Tests of Validity: Ask whether the experts, including both outside authorities and the author, are really experts. Remember that argument from authority is only as good as the authorities themselves.

Look for references to the author's credentials, background, and training. Look for credential statements about quoted authorities.

Refer to your own experience and background to establish expertise. Quote the best and most reliable authorities.

Establish common ground and respect by using appropriate language and tone.

EMOTIONAL PROOFS

Motives

Appealing to what all audiences are supposed to need, such as food, drink, warmth, shelter, sex, security, belonging, self-esteem, creativity, and self-expression. Urging audiences to take steps to meet their needs.

Example:
Claim: You should support this candidate.
Support: The candidate can help you get job security and safe neighborhoods.
Warrant: You want job security and safe neighborhoods.

Tests of Validity: Ask whether you really need what the author assumes you need. Ask whether doing what is recommended will satisfy the need as described.

Look for references to items or qualities you might need or want and advice on how to get them.

Look for emotional language, description, and tone.

Think about what the members of your audience need, and show how your ideas will help them meet these needs.

Use emotional language and tone where appropriate.

419

(continued)

Types of Proof and Tests of Validity *(continued)*

LOGICAL PROOFS

WHEN YOU ARE THE READER

Values

Look for examples or narratives that display values.

Infer values (warrants) that are not explicitly stated.

Look for emotional language and tone.

Appealing to what all audiences are supposed to value, such as reliability, honesty, loyalty, industry, patriotism, courage, conviction, faithfulness, dependability, creativity, integrity, freedom, equality, devotion to duty, and acceptance by others.

Example:
Claim: The curriculum should be multicultural.
Support: A multicultural curriculum will contribute to equality and acceptance.
Warrant: You value equality and acceptance.

Tests of Validity: Ask whether you share the author's values. Ask about the effect that differences in values will have on the argument.

WHEN YOU ARE THE WRITER

Appeal to your audience's values through warrants, explicit value statements, and narratives that illustrate values.

Use emotional language and tone where appropriate.

420

Credits

423

International Herald-Tribune (June 2, 2007). Reprinted by permission.

Daniel R. Weinberger, "A Brain Too Young for Good Judgment," *The New York Times* (March 10, 2001). Copyright © 2001 by The New York Times Company. Reprinted with permission. All rights reserved.

Alan Feuer, "Out of Jail, Into Temptation," *New York Times* (February 28, 2002). Copyright © 2002 by The New York Times Company. Reprinted with permission. All rights reserved.

"Revenge Begins to Seem Less Sweet." From http://www.economist.com/ displaystory.cfm?story_id = 9719806. *The Economist*, August 30, 2007. Reprinted by permission.

Claudia Wallis, "Too Young to Die." *Time* (March 14, 2005, p. 40). © 2005 Time Inc. Reprinted by permission.

Robert Tanner, "Studies Say Execution Does Deter Crime." *Fort Worth Star-Telegram* (June 11, 2007, p. 4A). Reprinted by permission.

Richard Rodriguez, "Surnames Reflect the Changing Face of America." *NewsHour*, PBS, January 25, 2008. Reprinted by permission.

Emma Daly, "DNA Test Gives Students Ethnic Shocks," *New York Times* (April 13, 2005, p. A18). Copyright © 2005 by The New York Times Company. Reprinted with permission. All rights reserved.

"Go Back to Black," by K.A. Dilday. From http://www.nytimes.com/2008/02/27/opinion/27dilday.html. *The New York Times* (February 27, 2008). Copyright © 2008 by The New York Times Company. Reprinted with permission. All rights reserved.

Yahling Chang, "Asian Identity Crisis," *Newsweek* (June 22, 1998). © 1998 Newsweek, Inc. All rights reserved. Used by permission and protected by the Copyright Laws of the United States.

Katie Halper, "My Life as a Secular Jew." *jbooks* (April 10, 2006). Reprinted by permission.

Richard Dyer, "The Matter of Whiteness," *White.* © 1997 Routledge. Reprinted by permission of Taylor & Francis.

Dorrine K. Kondo, "On Being a Conceptual Anomaly," from *Crafting Selves: Power, Gender and Discourses of Identity in a Japanese Workplace.* Chicago: University of Chicago Press, 1990, pp. 11–17. Reprinted by permission.

"I Have a Dream," © 1963 Martin Luther King, Jr., copyright renewed 1991 by Coretta Scott King. Reprinted by arrangement with the Estate of Martin Luther King, Jr., c/o Writers House as agent for the proprietor, New York, NY.

Brian Clark, "The Butterfly Effect and the Environment: How Tiny Actions Can Save the World," from http://www.copyblogger.com/butterfly-effect-environment. Reprinted by permission of Brian Clark.

Al Gore, from *Introduction* to *An Inconvenient Truth: The Planetary Emergency of Global Warming and What We Can Do About It.* New York: Rodale Books, 2006, pp. 1–2. Reprinted by permission.

Erik Reece, "Moving Mountains: The Battle for Justice Comes to the Coal Fields of Appalachia," *Orion* Magazine (January/February, 2006). Reprinted by permission.

Brian Wingfield, "For Job Market, Green Means Growth." Forbes.com, July 3, 2007. Reprinted by permission of FORBES.com. © 2008 Forbes.com

Gregg Easterbrook, "Some Convenient Truths." *The Atlantic Monthly* (September 2006, pp. 29–30). Reprinted by permission.

Stuart Price, "Carving Up the Congo." *New African* (October 1, 2007, pp. 46–47). Reprinted by permission.

Claire Andre, Manuel Velasquez, "Ethics and the Spotted Owl Controversy." *Issues in Ethics*, 4.1 (Spring 1991). Reprinted by permission.

George Will, "An Inconvenient Price." *Newsweek* (October 22, 2007, p. 68). Reprinted by permission.

Tom Harris, "Al Gore, Global Warming: Inconvenient Truth: Scientists Respond to Gore's Warnings of Climate Catastrophe," *Canada Free Press* (June 12, 2006). Reprinted by permission.

Lynn Ahrens, "The Great American Melting Pot." © 1977 American Broadcasting Music, Inc. Reprinted by permission.

Editorial, "Signs of the Times." *America: The National Catholic Weekly* (January 7, 2008, p. 6). © 2008 America Press Inc. All Rights reserved. Reprinted by permission.

Jae Ran Kim., "The Great American Melting Pot?" *Antiracist Parent* (March 5th, 2007). Reprinted by permission.

Miguel Bustillo, "A Town Against the Wall." *Los Angeles Times* (December 17, 2007). Reprinted by permission.

Marc Cooper, "Exodus." *The Atlantic Monthly* (May 2006). Reprinted by permission.

James Montague, "They Just Won't Mix." *New Statesman* (January 3, 2008). Reprinted by permission.

Peter Wilby, "The Right to Sell Labor." *New Statesman* (November 15, 2007). Reprinted by permission.

Daniel Altman, "Shattering Stereotypes about Immigrant Workers." *The New York Times* (June 3, 2007, p. 4). Copyright © 2007 by The New York Times Company. Reprinted with permission. All rights reserved.

Arian Campo-Flores, "America's Divide." From *Newsweek* (October 15, 2007).

© 2007 Newsweek, Inc. All rights reserved. Used by permission and protected by the Copyright Laws of the United States.

"Town's Residents Say They Support Solution." *Fort Worth Star-Telegram* (October 22, 2007, p. A2). Reprinted by permission.

Jonah Goldberg, "To Wall or Not to Wall." *National Review Online* (August 25, 2005). Reprinted by permission.

Kevin G. Hall, "Low-Tech Fence Cuts Down on Problems." *Fort Worth Star-Telegram* (October 22, 2007, p. A2). Reprinted by permission.

William James, "The Moral Equivalent of War." First published by the Association for International Concilliation in 1910 and McClure's 1910. From *The Best American Essays of the Century*, Joyce Carol Oates, ed. and Robert Atwan, coed. New York: Houghton Mifflin, 2000, pp. 45–49, 52–55.

Gerard F. Powers, "Our Moral Duty in Iraq." *America: The Weekly Catholic Magazine* (February 18, 2008, pp. 13–16).

Richard Rhodes, "Living with the Bomb." *National Geographic* (August 2005, pp. 98–113).

Haim Watzman, "When You Have to Shoot First." *The New York Times* (July 28, 2005).

Susan Neiman, "To Resist Hilter and Survive." *The New York Times* (February 3, 2008). © 2008 The New York Times Company. Reprinted by permission. All rights reserved.

Chris Hedges, "War Is a Force That Gives Us Meaning." From 2005, pp. 2–14. Reprinted by permission of Public Affairs, a member of Perseus Books Group.

William J. Bennett, "Why We Fight," from *Why We Fight: Moral Clarity and the War on Terrorism* by William J. Bennett. Used by permission of Doubleday, a division of Random House, Inc.

Robert Hirschfield, "Battle Stories Bring Former Enemies Together." *National Catholic Reporter* (February 2, 2007, p. 8).

Joan Ryan, "Army's War Game Recruits Kids." *San Francisco Chronicle* (September 23, 2004, B1).

Hamza Hendawi, "Iraqi Kids Play Make-Believe War Games." *Washington Post* (February 24, 2007). Reprinted by permission.

Michael Walzer, "The Politics of Rescue," in *Arguing about War* (New Haven and London: Yale University Press, 2004), pp. 67–81.

Margaret Mead, "Warfare: An Invention: Not a Biological Necessity", *Asia* 40.8. (August 1940: pp. 402–405).

Photo Credits

Chapter Openers, Image 1: Lizette Potgieter/Shutterstock; **Image 2:** Todd Davidson/Illustration Works/Corbis; **Image 3:** Jan Martin Will/Shutterstock; **Image 4:** Paula Bronstein/Getty Images; **Image 5:** Kate Kretz; **Figure 1.1:** Paula Bronstein/Getty Images; **Figure 1.2:** Jan Martin Will/Shutterstock; **Figure 1.4:** Calvin and Hobbes © 1993 Watterson. Dist. By Universal UClick. Reprinted with permission. All rights reserved; **Figure 1.5:** Lizette Potgieter/Shutterstock; **Page 34, Image 1:** Kate Kretz; **Page 34, Image 2:** Gary Braasch; **Figure 2.1:** Lee Lorenzo/The New Yorker, Collection/www.cartoonbank.com; **Figure 2.2:** Thony Belizaire/AFP/GettyImages/Newscom; **Page 47:** Maurice Savage/Alamy; **Page 59, Image 1:** Library of Congress, Prints & Photographs Division, NYWT&S Collection [LC-USZ62-111235]; **Page 61, Image 2:** David Silverman/Getty Images News; **Page 61, Image 3:** United States Holocaust Memorial Museum; **Figure 3.2:** AP Images/M. Spencer Green; **Page 93, Image 1:** Flashon Studio/Shutterstock;

Page 93, Image 2: Mike Abrahams/Alamy; **Page 93, Image 3:** Steve Whyte/Alamy; **Page 93, Image 4:** Megapress/Alamy; **Page 93:** Lou Beach; **Page 102 (left):** Joe Rosenthal/Library of Congress Prints and Photographs Division [LC-USZC4-4835]; **Page 102 (center):** Leonard Detrick/New York Daily News; **Page 102 (right):** Stephanie Frey/Shutterstock; **Figure 10.1:** AP Images/-Eddie Adams; **Figure 10.2:** Bettmann/CORBIS; **Figure 10.3:** Rizwan Tabassum/AFP/Getty Images; **Figure 10.4:** National Archives [594360]; **Figure 10.5:** Joe Rosenthal/Library of Congress Prints and Photographs Division [LC-USZC4-4835]; **Figure 10.6:** Douglas Kent Hall; **Figure 10.7 (left):** Fabiano/SIPA/Black Star/Newscom; **Figure 10.7 (right):** Douglas Graham/Roll Call Photos/Newscom; **Figure 10.8:** John Macdougall/AFP/Getty Images; **Figure 10.9:** digitallife/Alamy; **Figure 10.10:** Andrew Stawicki/Zuma Press/Newscom; **Figure 10.11:** Larry Wright/Cagle Cartoons; **Figure 10.16 (left):** Patrick Schneider/Newscom; **Figure 10.16 (right):** David Scull; **Figure 10.17:** Peter K. Rearden; **Page 265, Image 1:** Ryan

Rodrick Beiler/Alamy; **Page 266, Image 2 (top):** Yannis Kontos/Polaris Images; **Page 266, Image 2 (bottom):** Shawn Thew/EPA/Corbis; **Page 267, Image 3:** Spencer Platt/Getty Images; **Page 267, Image 4:** Phil Masturzo/MCT/Newscom; **Page 268, Image 5:** Sam Abell/National Geographic/Getty Images; **Page 269, Image 1:** SuperStock/SuperStock; **Page 269, Image 2:** Michael Langenstein, "Play Ball" 1982, Photographer Robert Rubic; **Page 270, Image 3:** AFP Photo/Yariv Katz/Newscom; **Page 271:** Frederick Deligne/Cagle Cartoons; **Page 274, Argument 1:** Nancy V. Wood; **Page 274, Argument 2:** Karen Hernandez; **Page 276:** Debbie Bryan; **Page 277:** Debbie Bryan; **Page 291, Image 1:** Douglas Pulsipher/Alamy; **Page 291, Image 2:** Chuck Carlton/Photolibrary; **Page 291, Image 3:** James Steidl/Shutterstock; **Page 307:** Donald Uhrbrock/Time Life Pictures/Getty Images; **Page 335, Image 1:** Robert Weber/The New Yorker, Collection/www.cartoonbank.com; **Page 351, Image 1:** Berton Chang, shot for Wired magazine, May 2007.

425

Index

TOPIC

Academic argument, 73
Academic inquiry, 7–8
Academic issues, 27
Academic Search Complete, 338
Academic writing, 212
  accuracy, in appeals to logos,
    130–132
  Rogerian argument in, 287–288
  values of, 114, 177
Access, online argument and, 17
Acknowledgment and response,
    108, 198–213
  as alternative solution, 108
  collecting alternatives, 206
  in common ground, 206
  dialogue, 222
  language of, 208–210
  locating, 202–207
  in previous research, 206
  restating main argument,
    203–204
  as subordinate argument,
    204–206
Active voice, 87
Analogy, causation, warrant,
    236–237
Anecdotes, as evidence, 182, 187,
    192
Annotated bibliography
  adding annotations to,
    344–345
Annotations, bibliography
  definition of, 124
  distinguishing among, 144
  to *ethos*, 133–136
  to *logos*, 125–132
  to *pathos*, 126–141
  spotting, 141–142
  vs. claims, 125
  vs. spans, 125
  vs. stases, 125
Anthropology, issues in, 27
Arguers, 11

Argument, about causes, [five]
    questions of
  academic, 143, 145, 185
  based on alternatives, 207–208
  based on warrants, 234
  conceptual, 106–108, 117, 203
  as construction, 143–145, 151
  conversation, 199–200
  core, 206–207
  discourse community, 154–155,
    177, 211, 213
  hostile, 199–200
  questioning stance, 176, 187
  questions about, 200–202
  questions as basis of, 198–202
  questions of others, 198–202
  thickening, 151, 204–205
  values, 107–108
  as war, 155, 201–202, 211, 222
Argument. *See also* Visual
    argument; Written
    argument
  arguable issues, 18–28
  consensual, 7
  definition of, 5
  online, key features and questions
    rising from, 17–18
  perspective on, 2–36
  purpose (*See* Purpose, types of)
  in rhetorical situation, 38–63
  Rogerian, 280–303
  successful, 11–14
  traditional, 6
  in 21st century, recognizing,
    16–17
  unsuccessful, 14–16
  visual, 244–279
Argument analysis paper
  focus topics for, 308–310
  reading for, 305
  rhetorical situation for,
    307–324
  writing, 305–306

Argumentation purpose. *See also*
    Purpose, types of
  in online argument, 72–73
  in visual argument, 70–72
  in written argument, 69–70
Argument theory
  key points in
    argument analysis essay
      created with, 305–306
    summary of, 306
    texts analyzed with, 307–308,
      310–324
  in visual argument
    critique of, 254
    sample analysis of, 257–258
Aristotle, 194
Arrangement
  arrogance, certainty and,
    130
Articles in journals, magazines,
    and newspapers
  bibliography for, 344
  library access to, 338–339
  refereed, 339
Assumption(s), *See* Warrant(s)
Astronomy, issues in, 27
Audience
  composite, 54
  constructing, 54–55
  familiar, 54
  friendly, 52
  hostile, 52
  linked, 53
  neutral, 52
  outcomes, 12
  reconsidering, in written
    assignment, 82
  resistant, 52
  role of, in successful arguments,
    11
  undecided, 52
  unfamiliar, 52
  universal, 55

Audience analysis
    conducting, 51–55
    of discourse community, 53–54
    of familiar audience, 54
Audience in research paper
    analysis worksheet, 348–349
    class as, 333–334
    information about, using,
        334–336
    understanding, 331–333
    unfamiliar, 334
Authority. *See also* Quotes
    online argument and, 18
Authority, as evidence, 179,
        182–183, 192, 197

Background information in
        writing assignment,
        65–68
Bar graphs, 259–260
Bellesiles, Michael, 174, 186
Berman, Richard, 117
Best, Joel, 185
Bias
    in visual argument, 254–256,
        257, 258
    in writing assignment, 75
Bias, about language
    cognitive, 105–106, 200
    guarding against, 200
Bibliography, 343–345. *See also*
        Annotated bibliography
    for book, 344
    creating, 343–344
    for online material, 344
    for printed article, 344
Biology, issues in, 27
Blogs, 340
Books
    bibliography for, 344
    in library, finding, 338
Browsers, 339–340
Burke's pentad, 346–347
Business, issues in, 27

Casement, William, 204
Cause
    in visual argument, 258
Cause-and-effect
    absolute, 130
    in appeals to logos, 130–132
Chains of reasons, 347–348
Character fallacies *(ethos)*
    in traditional *vs.* Rogerian
        argument, 286

in visual argument, 254, 257,
        258, 262
Charts
    flowcharts in visual argument,
        245, 258, 259
    in visual argument, 259
Chat rooms, 340
Chemistry, issues in, 27
Circle graphs, 260
Citation, forms, 157
Claim *(See* Main)
    articulating, 149–151
    colored by reasons, 154
    conceptual richness, 113–114
    contestable, 109–110, 121, 181
    degree of acceptance, 108–109,
        177–178
    disconfirmable, 110–111
    hypothesis, 105–106, 187
    logical richness, 112–113
    negation test, 109–110, 118
    qualifying, 114–115, 117, 121
    questions about, 200–201,
        212–213
    reasonable, 110, 121
    testing, 109–111, 178
    values, 107–108
Claims
    definition of, 5
    in research paper
        development worksheet, 349
        questions to help narrow and
            develop, 328–330
        writing, 327, 349
    in visual argument, 257,
        258–259
    in writing assignment, 75
Class as audience, 333–334
Coercion vs argument, 118
Collaborative writing, language
        of criticism, questions in,
        211
.com extension, 341
Commas, 89
Common ground
    establishing, 12
    in Rogerian argument, 282–283
    for successful arguments, 13
    for unsuccessful arguments, 15
    in visual argument, 246–248
Common ground, as alternative
        view, 207
    in appeals to *logos*, 129
Communication, issues in, 27
Composite audience, 54

Conceptual problem, 106–108,
        117
    importance of, 130
Conclusion format, in writing
        assignment, 75
Consensual argument, 7
    academic inquiry, 7
    dialectic, 7
    internal argument, 8
    mediation, 8
    negotiation, 7–8
Conversation, as argument,
        199–200
Courtroom argument, 6
CQResearcher, 338
Creative reading
    credentials, in appeals to *ethos,*
        133–135
Credibility
    in online argument, 17–18
    of research sources, evaluating,
        342–343
Critical thinking, 143, 174,
        200
    barriers to, 105–106
    critical imagination, 205, 207,
        213, 214–216
    as evidence, 143–144, 157–159,
        183
Critical thinking prompts,
        68–69
Cultural diversity, 221–222
Current issues, 19–22

Data, 105, 161, 175, 204–207,
        208
    numerical, 179, 182–185,
        232–233
    questions, 176, 187, 198, 212,
        214, 215
    stages, 118
    testing ideas, 105–106,
        113–114, 199, 214–215
    value of others' views,
        198–202
    visual presentation, 184–186
Diagrams in visual argument,
        245, 259
Dialectic, 7
Discourse community,
        audience's, 53–54
Discourse community, evidence,
        157–159, 177, 182
Discourse community, specialists,
        222–223

Document structure, coherence, ten steps, locating acknowledgment and response
locating warrant, 207
plan, 235
Draft
ask revision questions, 86–88
errors made in, 88–89
first, 83–84
language and style in, 87
look at draft as whole, 85
revising, 85–89
Dramatic life situations, issues in, 19

EBSCO *host*, 338
.edu extension, 341
Ellipsis, 345
E-mail
as research source, 340
Emotion, 177
Emotional fallacies *(pathos)*
in traditional *vs.* Rogerian argument, 286
in visual argument, 254, 257, 258, 262
Emotional response from visual argument, 248
Emotions
naming of, in appeals to *pathos*, 137
Engineering, issues in, 27
English literature, issues in, 27
Ethics, 114, 176, 202
Ethics in visual argument, 258
Ethos, 114, 177, 211
Ethos. See Credibility
credentials in, 133–135
definition of, 124, 133
ethos, appeals to, 133–136
experts in, 134
eyewitnesses in, 134
implied by reasons, 154
personal impressions in, 135–136
readers' trust, 116–117, 180–184, 194, 196, 200, 206
stakeholders in, 134
Everyday argument, 7
Evidence. *See also* Support
accuracy of, 181, 197, 201, 202
anecdotes as, 180, 181, 197
authority, 147, 182, 183

balancing with reasons, 160, 175
burden of, 176–178
currency, 179, 213
direct, 147–149, 180
discourse community, 177–187
documenting, 157, 174, 190–191
drawings as, 183–185, 232–233
explained by reason, 151–153, 232–233
as foundation, 148–149
interviews, 190–193
kind readers expect, 177, 187
memories as, 177, 180, 183, 197
metaphor for, 143, 145, 185
notes, 159, 190–191, 205–206
numerical data as, 143–144, 179, 182–183, 232–233
photographs as, 146, 183–184, 197, 228
plan for finding, 178, 187–188
precision of, 178–179, 197, 213
quality of, 178–179
questions about, 145, 178, 200, 201, 212
recordings as, 183–184, 197
reliability of, 178–179, 192
reports of, 145–150, 176–197
representative, 179–180, 195, 197, 213
searching, 178, 187–188
skepticism, 185
testimonial, 182, 187, 192
vs. reasons, 145–146
vs. reports of, 146–149
visual image as, 146, 183–184, 197, 228
Exhibit, as evidence, 145–148
experts, in appeals to *ethos*, 134
Exploratory argument, 70
Exploratory paper, eyewitnesses, in appeals to *ethos*, 134
Extremist argument, 70

Fact, 143–144
fact, vs. opinion, 131
Fallacies
in traditional *vs.* Rogerian argument, 286
in visual argument, 254, 257, 258
Familiar audience, 54
Fights, 14

Finkbeiner, Ann, 114
Flowcharts in visual argument, 245, 258, 259
Foreign affairs issues, 21
Forums, 12
Franklin, Benjamin, 114
Friendly audience, 52
Friendship issues, 22

Geertz, Clifford, 186
Google, 339, 342, 344
Google Scholar, 188
graphics, in appeals to pathos, 139–141
.gov extension, 341
Graphs in visual argument, 245, 258, 259, 260–261
bar graphs, 259–260
circle graphs, 260
line graphs, 260
Grounds. *See* Common ground; Support guess words, 132

Hidden argument, 70
History, issues in, 27
Hostile audience, 52
Human life issues, 21
Hypothesis, 105–106, 187

Icons in visual argument, 249–250
Ideas in writing assignment
annotating, 77
summarizing, 77
underlining, 77
Images
in rhetorical situation, analyzing, 44
Interactivity
in online argument, 18
in online visual argument, 253
Internal argument, 8
Internet, as source of topics, evidence from, 188, 190
.int extension, 341
Intimacy issues, 22
Introduction, 106–112, 206
Introduction in writing assignment, 75
Invention strategies for research paper, 346–348
Burke's pentad, 346–347
chains of reasons, 347–348
worksheet, 354

Issues
  academic, 27
  common ground on, 12, 13, 14
  compelling, 19
  complexity of, 23
  current, 19–22
  definition of, 2
  in dramatic life situations, 19
  emerging from solved
    issues, 23
  enduring, 19–22
  foreign affairs, 21
  friendship, 22
  human life, 21
  intimacy, 22
  law and order, 22
  making your own, 27–28
  personal rights vs. social rights,
    20
  political activism, 22
  privacy, 22
  quality of life, 20
  resurfacing, 22–23
  risky, 14
  self-development, 21
  successful arguments based on,
    11–14
  surveillance, 22
  trivial, 14
  unsuccessful arguments based
    on, 14–16
  war and peace, 21
  ways and means, 20
  in writing assignment, 65–67

Jefferson, Thomas, 156, 161
JSTOR, 344

Kennedy, John F., 107–108
Key words
  in Internet searches, 340
  in writing assignment, 76

Language
  development in research paper
    (worksheet), 355
Language and style
  active voice in, 87
  appropriate, 87
  appropriate and consistent, in
    writing, 232
  commas used in, 89
  consistent, 87
  errors made in, 88–89
  parallel construction and, 88

pronoun referents, clear and
    appropriate, 88
  sentence boundaries and, 88
  sexist, 87
  subjects agreeing with verbs, 88
  tense and, 88
  variety in, 87
Language, abstract vs. concrete,
    metaphor for argument,
    143
  of acknowledgement and
    response, 208–210
  metaphor for evidence, 143,
    145, 185
Law and order issues, 22
LexisNexis Academic, 338
Library, 337–338
  articles in journals or
    magazines and, 338–339
  becoming familiar with, 350
  finding books in, 338
  library subscription services
    and, 338
  newspaper articles and, 339
  online catalog and, 337
  reference materials and, 339
  World Wide Web and, 339
Library, evidence from, 188
Line graphs, 260
Linked audience, 53
Linked issues, in online
    argument, 18, 253
Listening, Rogerian, 283–285
  empathetic, 283, 284–285
  goals of, 284
  judgmental, 284–285
  use of, in daily life, 285
Loftus, Elizabeth F., 181
Logic, 106, 151, 156, 210,
    214–243. See Fallacies
  addressing errors in, 210
  common sense in, 129
  concessions in, 130
  definition of, 124, 125
  logic, in appeals to logos,
    126–129
  logic in, 128–129
  observations in, 126–127
  probability in, 129
  qualifications in, 132
  source identification in,
    131–132
  statistics in, 126–127
  testimony in, 126–127
  types of, 125

Logical fallacies (logos)
  in traditional vs. Rogerian
    argument, 286
  in visual argument, 254, 257,
    258, 262

Main body in writing assignment,
    75
Main claim, 104–106, 192–193
Main point, 104, 121
Maps
  in writing assignment, 78–79
Mathematics, issues in, 27
Mediation, 8
Medved, Michael, 237
Memories, as evidence, 180, 183,
    197
Metaphor, fallacy
  for argument, 144
  for evidence, 143, 145, 185
.mil extension, 341
Motivation in visual argument,
    258
Multi-modal/multi-media, in
    visual argument, 18, 253

Negotiation, 7–8, 114
.net extension, 341
Networking, 18
Neutral audience, 52
Newspaper articles, 339
Notes
  in research paper, 345–346
  in writing assignment, 67,
    79–82
Notes, taking, 159–160, 190–191,
    197, 204
  in appeals to logos, 126

Obvious argument, 70
One-on-one argument, 6
One True Principle, personal
    investment, 177
Online argument
  argumentation purpose in,
    72–73
  features and questions rising
    from, 17–18
    access, 17
    authority/credibility, 18
    interactivity, 17–18
    linked issues, 18
    multi-modal/multi-media, 18
    polarization, 18
    relevance, 17

Online argument *(Continued)*
  volume/variety, 17
  plagiarism in writing assignment
    research, 80
  rhetorical situation, analyzing,
    46–47
  visual in, 253
Online catalog, 337
Online databases, 338
Online material, bibliography for,
    344
Online research. *See* Library and
    online research
  vs. fact, 131
Opinions
  in writing assignment, 75
.org extension, 341
Others' views, 105–106,
    199–200, 213, 215, 233
  imagining, 202–203, 206, 210,
    224–225
  from reading, 206
  respect for, 199
  from surrogate readers, 157,
    220
Outline(s), 206. *See* Plan
Outlines in writing assignment,
    78–79
  to develop arguments for, 78–79
  extended, to guide writing, 83

Palmer, John C., 181
Parallel construction, 88
Paraphrase, 157–158, 159, 190
  discourse community, 152, 159
Paraphrase in writing assignment
  example of, 79
  in first draft, 83
  notes and, 345, 346
  plagiarism and, 79–82
Paraphrasing
  pathos, appeals to, 136–141
  definition of, 124, 136–137
  graphics in, 139–141
  misuse of, 141
  naming emotions in, 137
  poetics in, 138
  power of, 137
Participatory argument, 17
pathos, appeals to, 136–141
  definition of, 124, 136–137
  graphics in, 139–141
  misuse of, 141
  naming emotions in, 137
  poetics in, 138
  power of, 137

Personal rights *vs.* social rights,
    20
Perspectives, 23
Photographs, as evidence,
    183–184, 197
  physical evidence, in appeals to
    logos, 126
Physics, issues in, 27
Plagiarism, 158, 197
  avoiding, 159, 190–191
  documenting sources, 157, 174,
    190–191
Plagiarism in researched position
    paper, 362
Plagiarism in writing assignment
  avoiding, 79–82
  examples of, 79–82
  online research and, 80
  paraphrase and, 79–82
  quotes and, 79–82
  summarized material and,
    79
Plan, for argument about
    personal responsibility,
    for finding evidence, 178,
    187–188
  poetics, in appeals to *pathos*,
    138
Polarization, online argument
    and, 18
Political activism, 22
Political science, issues in, 27
Practical problem, 106–108
Preliminary plans. *See* Outlines
Premise. *See* Warrant
Premises. *See* Support probability,
    in appeals to *logos*, 139
Privacy issues, 22
Problem, 104–106, 121, 187,
    200–201, 207
  conceptual, 106–107, 117
  practical, 106–107
  questions about, 200–201, 210
  solving, 105–106
Pronoun referents, 88
Proof
  in research paper, 355
  in visual argument, 257, 258
Propaganda, 118
Proverb, as warrant, 217,
    239–242
Pseudoproof. *See* Fallacies
Psychology, issues in, 27
Public Affairs Information Bulletin,
    339
Public debate, 6

Public debates, in appeals to *logos*,
    126
Purpose, types of, 69–70.
    See also Argumentation
    purpose
  exploratory argument, 70
  extremist argument, 70
  hidden argument, 70
  objective reporting, 70
  obvious argument, 70
  unconscious argument, 70

Qualification, 114
  of claim, 114–115, 117
  qualification, in appeals to *logos*,
    132
  of warrant, 217–218, 230
Quality of life issues, 20
Question, about argument,
    200–204
  about claim/solution, 200–201,
    210, 212–213
  about consistency, 202–203
  about evidence, 145–149,
    176–178, 212
  about logic, 224
  about problem, 200–201, 210
  about reasons, 212
  about warrant, 201–202, 210,
    233–237
  critical thinking, 198–202
  imagining on behalf of readers,
    198–202, 202–203, 205
Questioning stance, 176, 187
Quotation, 157–158
  discourse community, 158
  as evidence, 152–153, 182, 190,
    232– 233
  integrating, 159, 190–191, 206
Quotes
  in research paper, 340, 345–346
  in writing assignment
    example of and, 79
    in first draft, 83
    plagiarism and, 79–82

Rationality, subject to evidence,
    110–111
Read to develop arguments for
    writing assignment,
    69–79. *See also*
    Argumentation purpose
  academic argument, 73
  biases and, 75
  claims and, 75
  conclusion format, 75

ideas and, annotating, 77
introduction in, 75
key words and, 76
main body in, 75
maps and, 78–79
opinions and, 75
outlines and, 78–79
subclaims and, 75
summarize ideas, 77
support and, 75
survey and skim to save time, 73–74
thinking and writing combined with, 73
transitions and, 75, 83
underline ideas, 77
Reader, dialogue with, 198–213
anticipating questions of, 198–203, 221, 224–225
motivating, 106
surrogate, 157, 220
Reading, for other views, 206
Reasons, 187, 216, 228–229
vs. warrant, 222
Recordings, as evidence, 183–184, 197
See Bias
records, in appeals to *logos*, 126
Reference materials, 339
Relevance, online argument and, 17
Reporting, objective, 70
Research, 187
See also Library and online research
academic, 114, 223
balancing with evidence, 159, 175
coloring claim, 154
consequences of, 117
explaining evidence, 151–153, 232–233
influence on *ethos*, 154
language of, 115, 223
multiple, 149–151
notes, 159, 190–191, 197, 206
as outline of argument, 146
in parallel, 149–151
previous, 159, 190–191, 205–206
questions about, 213
in series, 156–157
Researched position paper, 326–355
assignment, analyzing, 327

audience in, 331–333, 348–349
claims in, 327–330, 349
final draft, 362–363
first draft, 361
document sources, 362
plagiarism, 362
invention strategies for, 346–348, 354
language development worksheet, 355
notes, 345–346
oral presentation of, 363–365
organization, 336–337
outlining and cross-referencing notes, 358–360
patterns and support matched to claims, 356–358
peer writing groups, creating, 348
plan, developing, 330–333
proofs added to, 355
purpose, clarifying, 327, 349
research evaluation worksheet, 352
research worksheet, 350
Research in Rogerian argument, 287
Research proposal, in Rogerian argument, 287
Research sources. See also Bibliography; Library; World Wide Web
author's purpose, analyzing, 341
credibility of, evaluating, 342–343
evaluating, 340–343, 352
library, 337–338, 350
locating, 337–340
rhetorical situation of, analyzing, 342
Resistant audience, 52
Revising written assignment, plan created for, 82–89
audience and, reconsidering, 82
extended outline to guide writing, 83
issue and, refocusing, 82
revise draft, 85–89
write first draft, 83–84
writer's block, 84
Rhetorical situation, 38–63
analyzing
audience, 51–55

images, 44
online argument, 46–47
when reading an argument, 39–44
when viewing a visual argument, 44–46
for argument analysis paper, 307–324
definition of, 38
elements of (See TRACE acronym)
for an essay, 56–63
for reading an argument, 42–44
in visual argument, 254, 257, 262, 263
to write an argument, 48–51
constraints in, 49
example of, 50–52
identify reader (or audience), 49
identify the author, 49–51
text developed to fit the situation, 50
Rogerian argument, 280–303
common ground in, achieving, 282–283
formulation of, 284
listening in, 283–285
online, 285
purpose of, 282–283
response paper for, 287
as strategy, 283–285
vs. traditional argument, 286
writing, 286–288
academic, 287–288
phases in, 286–287

Sanders, Keith R., 182
Search engines, 339–340
Self-development issues, 21
Sentence boundaries, 88
Sexist language, 87
Sherry, Suzanna, 233
Single-perspective argument, 6
Skepticism, radical, 185
See Questioning stance
Skimming in writing assignment, 73–74
Social networking tools, 16
Sociology, issues in, 27
Socratic method, 7
Solution, 104–106, 121, 187, 200–201, 207
hypothesis, 105–106

Solution *(Continued)*
 questions about, 200–201, 210,
  212–213
 See Claim
Source, primary, 180, 190
 secondary, 180
 tertiary, 180
Sources, documenting
 in appeals to *ethos*, 134
 sources. *See also* Support
Standoffs, 14
 vs. appeals, 125
Statistics, in appeals to *logos*,
  126–127
Storyboard, 149, 206
Subclaims
 in writing assignment, 75
Sullum, Jacob, 164, 170
Summarized material
 in research paper, 345, 346
 in writing assignment
  example of, 79
  in first draft, 83
  plagiarism and, 79
Summary, 194
Summary-analysis-response
  paper, 91–92
Summary-response paper,
  89–91
 example of a response, 90–91
 example of a summary, 90
Support
 in writing assignment, 75
Support, for claims
 support, *See also* sources,
  124–142
Surveillance issues, 22
Surveying and skimming
  materials for reading and
  writing, 155, 156
Surveying in writing assignment,
  73–74
Symbols, use of testimony, in
  appeals to *logos*, 126–127
Symbols in visual argument, 250,
  251

Tables
 in visual argument, 245, 259
Tense, 88
Themes (key concepts), 113–114
Thesis, 104
Thinking in writing assignment,
  73
Topic, 187

Toulmin model of argument
 in visual argument, 254, 257,
  262
TRACE acronym. *See also*
  Rhetorical situation
 Text, in analyzing rhetorical
  situation
  definition of, 39
  from online argument, 46
  questions to ask to gain
   insight, 41
  from reader's point of view,
   43
  from viewer's point of view,
   46
  in writing an argument, 50,
   51
 Reader (or audience), in
  analyzing rhetorical
  situation
  definition of, 39
  from online argument,
   46–47
  questions to ask to gain
   insight, 41–42
  from reader's point of view,
   43
  from viewer's point of view,
   45
  in writing an argument, 49,
   50
 Author, in analyzing rhetorical
  situation
  definition of, 39
  from online argument,
   47
  questions to ask to gain
   insight, 42
  from reader's point of view,
   43
  from viewer's point of view,
   46
  in writing an argument, 49,
   51
 Constraints, in analyzing
  rhetorical situation
  definition of, 39–40
  examples of, 40–41
  from online argument, 47
  questions to ask to gain
   insight, 42
  from reader's point of view,
   43
  from viewer's point of view,
   46

 in writing an argument, 49,
  50–51
 Exigence, in analyzing
  rhetorical situation
  definition of, 41
  from online argument, 47
  questions to ask to gain
   insight, 42
  from reader's point of view,
   43
  from viewer's point of view,
   46
  in writing an argument,
   48–49, 50
Traditional argument, 6
 courtroom argument, 6
 one-on-one (or everyday
  argument), 6
 public debate, 6
 single-perspective argument,
  6
Transitions in writing assignment
 definition of, 75
 in outline, 83
Truth, 185
Tum, Rigoberta Menchú, 177,
  193–194

Unconscious argument, 70
Undecided audience, 52
Universal audience, 55

Value
 in visual argument, 258
Values, 154–155, 210, 221–222
 claim, 107–108
Variety in online argument, 17,
  253
Verbs, subjects agreeing with, 88
Visual argument, 244–279
 analogies in, 258
 analysis of, sample, 256–258
  argument theory used for
   analysis, 257–258
  features of visual argument
   used in, 256–257
 argument theory used to
  critique, 254
 bias in, 254–256, 257, 258
 cause in, 258
 claim in, 257, 258–259
 common ground in, 246–248
 emotional response evoked
  from, 248
 ethical evaluation in, 258

fallacies in, 254, 257, 258, 262
features of, 245–253, 262–263
interpretation from viewers, varied, 251–253
juxtaposition of materials, 248–249
motivation in, 258
proofs in, 257, 258
reading, steps for, 9
recognizing, 8–11, 245, 253
response evoked from
    icons used to prompt, 249–250
    immediate and tangible, 246
rhetorical situation in, 254, 257, 262, 263
selective nature of, 250–251
stand-alone, 261–264
symbols employed in, 250, 251
Toulmin model in, 254, 257, 262
value in, 258
written argument supported by, 258–261
Visual Image, as evidence, 146, 183–186
Visual materials in writing assignment, 67
Vividness, 181
    evidence, 181
Volume in online argument, 17, 253

War and peace issues, 21
Warrant, 214–243
    analogy, 236–237
    applicable, 213, 225–226, 228
    appropriate, 213, 227–228
    assumption, 214
    connection of claim and reason, 216–219
    for consensus, 222–223
    culture, 221–222, 232
    discourse community, 221–223, 240
    for emphasis, 222–223
    evidence, 232–233
    failure of, 221–222, 225–228
    limitations on, 217–218, 230, 239, 241
    locating, 236
    matrix, 237

premise, 215
    as principle of reasoning, 213–216, 225, 227–228, 242
    questions about, 201–202, 210, 212–213, 224–227
    specialists, 221–223
    testing, 224–228
    TRUE, 217, 225–228, 230
    vs. reason, 222
    when to use, 221–225
Ways and means issues, 20
Web site extensions, analyzing, 341
Web sites, as sources, 188
    taking notes from, 179
Wikipedia, 340
World Wide Web
    bibliographical information for online material accessed on, 344
    blogs and, 340
    browsers and, 339–340
    chat rooms and, 340
    credible sources on, 342
    e-mail and, 340
    keyword searches and, 340
    library access to, 339
    search engines and, 339–340
    URL and, 342, 344
    Web site extensions, analyzing, 341
    Wikipedia and, 340
Writer's block, 84
Writing assignment
    beginning, steps for, 65–69
        background information, reading for, 67
        critical thinking prompts, using, 68–69
        issue on which to write, identifying, 65, 66
        notes created for, 67
        visual materials, collecting related, 67–68
    note taking in, 79–82
    papers used in, types of, 89–92
        summary-analysis-response paper, 91–92
        summary-response paper, 89–91
    paraphrase in

example of, 79
    in first draft, 83
    plagiarism and, 79–82
plagiarism in, 79–82
quotes in
    example of and, 79
    in first draft, 83
    plagiarism and, 79–82
read to develop arguments for, 69–79 (*See also* Argumentation purpose)
    academic argument, 73
    biases and, 75
    claims and, 75
    conclusion format, 75
    ideas and, annotating, 77
    introduction in, 75
    key words and, 76
    main body in, 75
    maps and, 78
    opinions and, 75
    outlines and, 78
    subclaims and, 75
    summarize ideas, 77
    support and, 75
    survey and skim to save time, 73–74
    thinking and writing combined with, 75
    transitions and, 75, 83
    underline ideas, 77
revising, plan created for, 82–89
    audience and, reconsidering, 82
    extended outline to guide writing, 83
    issue and, refocusing, 82
    revise draft, 85–89
    write first draft, 83–84
    writer's block, 84
summarized material in
    example of, 79
    in first draft, 83
    plagiarism and, 79
Written argument
argumentation purpose in, 69–70
to support visual argument, 258–261

Yahoo!, 340

AUTHOR-TITLE

Adler, Jerry, "The Race for Survival," 77, 79

"'A' Is for 'Absent'" (Piper), 42–43, 75, 91–92, 287

Alexander, Sean Hamilton, "Artifacts from the Future," 351

Ambrose, Stephen E., *The Wild Blue*, 80, 81

"A-pluses in a time of grade deflation" (Esquivel), 57

Aristotle
 Rhetoric, 6

"Artifacts from the Future" (Alexander), 351

"As Historian's Fame Grows, So Do Questions on Methods" (Kirkpatrick), 80, 81

Bailey, Ronald "The Twin Paradox: What Exactly Is Wrong with Cloning People?", 295

Bains, Lee J., Jr., "Birmingham, 1963: Confrontation over Civil Rights," 308

"Barbie Controversy, The" (Virasin, student), 394

Beckel, Bob, *Common Ground: How to Stop the Partisan War That Is Destroying America*, 282

Becker, Alton, *Rhetoric: Discovery and Change*, 284, 285–287

"Birmingham, 1963: Confrontation over Civil Rights" (Bains), 308

Bitzer, Lloyd, "The Rhetorical Situation," 38–39

Boatwright, Angela A. (student) "Human Cloning: Is It a Viable Option?", 293–296

Bono, 262

Brockriede, Wayne "Where Is Argument?", 5

Brunk-Chavez, Beth, 91

Bryan, Debbie, *Farm Town News*, 276–278

Burke, Kenneth, *A Grammar of Motives*, 346, 347

Butler, Declan, "Calls for Cloning Ban Sell Science Short," 295

"Call for Unity: A Letter from Eight White Clergymen, A," 310–311

"Calling Blue: And On That Farm He Had a Cellphone" (Heffernan), 290

"Calls for Cloning Ban Sell Science Short" (Butler and Wadman), 295

Carey, John, "Human Clones: It's Decision Time," 296

Carroll, Felix, "No Escape From 'Helicopter Parents'", 30–32, 78

Ciarello, Barbara, 284

Cohen, Randy, "When Texting is Wrong," 97, 99–101

Common Ground: How to Stop the Partisan War That Is Destroying America (Thomas and Beckel), 282, 291

"Dear Boss" (Nabhan, student), 299–301

Decker, Blake (student), 87, 88

"Defense of Grade Deflation, A" (Harrel), 56–57

Demaris, Ovid "Most of All, the Children Matter," 23

Derman, Jeff, 33

Deutsch, Stephanie, *Barbie: The First Thirty Years*, 394

Dialogues (Plato), 7

"Dream Doll" (Wood and Saunders), 395

Dufresne, John, "That Crucial First Draft," 83

Edbauer, Jenny, 281

Edut, Ophira, "Giga-What? Barbie Gets Her Own Computer," 394

Egan, Timothy, "Look Who's Hugging Trees Now," 283

Ehninger, Douglas, 357

Ellin, Abby, "The Laptop Ate My Attention Span," 32–33

Elsberg, Elisabeth (student), 274

Esquivel, Paolo, "A-pluses in a time of grade deflation," 57

"Everything You Need to Know about Writing Successfully-in Ten Minutes" (King), 84

"Fame Can't Excuse a Plagiarist" (McTaggart), 80

Farm Town News, (Bryan), 276–278

Frost, Robert
 "The Mending Wall," 265

Future of Life, The (Wilson), 289–290

Gamsjager, Cathy, 31

Gamsjager, Mark, 31

"Getting Past No . . . to Yes! The Art of Negotiation" (Ury), 285

"Giga-What? Barbie Gets Her Own Computer" (Edut), 394

Global Warming: The Causes, The Perils, The Solutions, The Actions: What You Can Do, 9

Goergen, Daniel (student), 262

Gore, Al
 An Inconvenient Truth, 11

Gould, John, 86–87

Grammar of Motives, A (Burke), 346, 347

Greene, Graham, 251

"Green Guilt and Ecological Overload" (Roszak), 343

Harrel, Will, "Defense of Grade Deflation, A," 56–57

Hartman, Eric (student), "Let Those Who Ride Decide!", 297–299

Hernandez, Karen (student), "Never Again," 274, 275

Hughes, Mary Elizabeth, 31
"Human Clones: It's Decision
    Time" (Carey), 296
"Human Cloning? Don't Just Say
    No" (Macklin), 296
"Human Cloning: Is It a Viable
    Option?" (Boatwright,
    student), 293–296

Inconvenient Truth, An (Gore), 11
"Israeli–Palestinian Conflict:
    Teaching a Theme-
    Based Course, The"
    (Obenzinger), 14

Johnson, Miki, 264
"Just a Doll? Liberating Accounts
    of Barbie-Play" (Reid-
    Walsh and Mitchell), 395

"Keeping a Writer's Journal"
    (Pellegrino), 67
King, Martin Luther, Jr., 307–
    308
    "Letter from Birmingham Jail,"
    307, 311–324
King, Stephen, 86
    "Everything You Need to
    Know about Writing
    Successfully-in Ten
    Minutes," 84
Kirkpatrick, David D., "As
    Historian's Fame Grows,
    So Do Questions on
    Methods," 80, 81
Kolata, Gina, "Psst! Ask for
    Donor 1913," 95–97

"Laptop Ate My Attention Span,
    The" (Ellin), 32–33
"Letter from Birmingham Jail"
    (King, Jr.), 307, 311–324
"Let Those Who Ride Decide!"
    (Hartman, student),
    297–299
Levine, Mel, "Ready or Not, Here
    Comes Life," 31
"Look Who's Hugging Trees
    Now" (Egan), 283
Low, Beverly, 31

Macklin, Ruth, "Human Cloning?
    Don't Just Say No," 296
Masri, Safwan, 33
Masterton, Samantha, 63

Maus: A Survivor's Tale, excerpts
    (Spiegelman), 275
McEnry, Jen, 32, 33
McTaggart, Lynne, "Fame Can't
    Excuse a Plagiarist," 80
"Most of All, the Children
    Matter" (Demaris), 23

Nabhan, Elizabeth (student),
    "Dear Boss," 299–301
"Never Again" (Hernandez,
    student), 274, 275
*New Rhetoric: A Treatise on
    Argumentation, The*
    (Perelman and Olbrechts-
    Tyteca), 11, 54
"NHTSA's Safety Standards Are
    Shown to Be Anything but
    Safe" (Quigley), 297, 298
"No Escape From 'Helicopter
    Parents'" (Carroll), 30–32,
    78

Obenzinger, Hilton "The Israeli–
    Palestinian Conflict:
    Teaching a Theme-Based
    Course," 14
Olbrechts-Tyteca, Lucie, *The
    New Rhetoric: A Treatise on
    Argumentation,* 11, 54

Pellegrino, Marjorie, "Keeping a
    Writer's Journal," 67
Pence, Gregory E., *Who's Afraid of
    Human Cloning?,* 295,
    296
Perelman, Chaim, *The New
    Rhetoric: A Treatise on
    Argumentation,* 11, 54
Pike, Kenneth, *Rhetoric: Discovery
    and Change,* 284, 285–287
Piper, Chris, "'A' is for 'Absent'",
    42–43, 75, 91–92
Plato, *Dialogues,* 7
"Psst! Ask for Donor 1913"
    (Kolata), 95–97
Putnam, Linda, 15

Quigley, Richard, "NHTSA's
    Safety Standards Are
    Shown to Be Anything but
    Safe," 297, 298
Quindlen, Anna,
    "Undocumented,
    Indispensable," 306

Race for Survival, The (Adler),
    77, 79
"Ready or Not, Here Comes Life"
    (Levine), 31
Rearden, Pete, 263
Reid-Walsh, Jacqueline, "Just a
    Doll? Liberating Accounts
    of Barbie-Play," 395
Rhetoric (Aristotle), 6
"Rhetorical Situation, The"
    (Bitzer), 38–39
Rhetoric: Discovery and Change
    (Young, Becker, and Pike),
    284, 285–287
Rise of American Air Power, The
    (Sherry), 81
Rogers, Carl R., 281, 284–285
    Way of Being, A, 283–284
"Roslin Institute Experiments:
    Creation of Dolly the
    Sheep" (Wilmut), 294,
    296
Roszak, Theodore, "Green Guilt
    and Ecological Overload,"
    343

Sherry, Michael S., *Rise of
    American Air Power, The,*
    81
Socrates, 7
Spiegelman, Art, *Maus: A
    Survivor's Tale,* Excerpts,
    275
Stanley, Mary, 287

"That Crucial First Draft"
    (Dufresne), 83
Thomas, Cal, *Common Ground:
    How to Stop the Partisan
    War That Is Destroying
    America,* 282
"Twin Paradox: What Exactly
    Is Wrong with Cloning
    People, The?" (Bailey),
    295

"Undocumented, Indispensable"
    (Quindlen), 306
Ury, William L., "Getting Past
    No . . . to Yes! The Art of
    Negotiation," 285

Virasin, Prisna, (student),
    "The Barbie Controversy,"
    394

Wadman, Meredith, "Calls for
    Cloning Ban Sell Science
    Short," 295
Way of Being, A (Rogers),
    283–284
"Where Is Argument?"
    (Brockriede), 4

Who's Afraid of Human Cloning?
    (Pence), 295, 296
Wild Blue, The (Ambrose), 80, 81
Wilmut, Ian, "Roslin Institute
    Experiments: Creation of
    Dolly the Sheep," 294,
    296

Wilson, Edward O.
    Future of Life, The, 289–290
Wright, Larry, 257

Young, Richard, *Rhetoric:
    Discovery and Change,* 284,
    285–287